WORD
BIBLICAL
COMMENTARY

Editorial Board

Volumes

1   Genesis 1–15 .... Gordon J. Wenham
2   Genesis 16–50 .... Gordon J. Wenham
3   Exodus................. John I. Durham
4   Leviticus ....John E. Hartley
5   Numbers .... Philip J. Budd
6a   Deuteronomy 1:1–21:9, 2nd ed... Duane L. Christensen
6b   Deuteronomy 21:10–34:12 ...... Duane L. Christensen
7a   Joshua 1-12, 2nd ed........ Trent C. Butler
7b   Joshua 13-24, 2nd ed...... Trent C. Butler
8   Judges .... Trent C. Butler
9   Ruth–Esther........... Frederic W. Bush
10   1 Samuel, 2nd ed.......... Ralph W. Klein
11   2 Samuel .... A. A. Anderson
12   1 Kings, 2nd ed. .... Simon J. Devries
13   2 Kings..................... T. R. Hobbs
14   1 Chronicles ....Roddy Braun
15   2 Chronicles .... Raymond B. Dillard
16   Ezra, Nehemiah ......H. G. M. Williamson
17   Job 1–20 .... David J. A. Clines
18a Job 21–37 .... David J. A. Clines
18b Job 38–42 .... David J. A. Clines
19   Psalms 1–50, 2nd ed...... Peter C. Craigie, Marvin E. Tate
20   Psalms 51–100 .... Marvin E. Tate
21   Psalms 101–150, rev. ed. ....Leslie C. Allen
22   Proverbs.............. Roland E. Murphy
23a Ecclesiastes .... Roland E. Murphy
23b Song of Songs/Lamentations ....Duane H. Garrett, Paul R. House
24   Isaiah 1–33, rev. ed......John D. W. Watts
25   Isaiah 34–66, rev. ed..... John D. W. Watts
26   Jeremiah 1–25 .... Peter C. Craigie, Page H. Kelley, Joel F. Drinkard Jr.
27   Jeremiah 26–52 .... Gerald L. Keown, Pamela J. Scalise, Thomas G. Smothers
28   Ezekiel 1–19.............Leslie C. Allen
29   Ezekiel 20–48............Leslie C. Allen
30   Daniel .... John E. Goldingay
31   Hosea–Jonah** .... Douglas Stuart
32   Micah–Malachi**........ Ralph L. Smith
33a Matthew 1–13......... Donald A. Hagner
33b Matthew 14–28........ Donald A. Hagner
34a Mark 1–8:26** ....Robert A. Guelich
34b Mark 8:27–16:20 ....Craig A. Evans
35a Luke 1–9:20 .... John Nolland
35b Luke 9:21–18:34.......... John Nolland
35c Luke 18:35–24:53......... John Nolland
36   John, 2nd ed. ... George R. Beasley-Murray
37a Acts 1–14* ....Stephen J. Walton
37b Acts 15–28* ....Stephen J. Walton
38a Romans 1–8 ....James D. G. Dunn
38b Romans 9–16 ....James D. G. Dunn
39   1 Corinthians* ....Andrew D. Clarke
40   2 Corinthians, rev. ed. .....Ralph P. Martin
41   Galatians .... Richard N. Longenecker
42   Ephesians .... Andrew T. Lincoln
43   Philippians, rev. ed. ...Gerald F. Hawthorne, rev. by Ralph P. Martin
44   Colossians, Philemon** ... Peter T. O'Brien
45   1 & 2 Thessalonians** .... F. F. Bruce
46   Pastoral Epistles ...... William D. Mounce
47a Hebrews 1–8............ William L. Lane
47b Hebrews 9–13........... William L. Lane
48   James ....Ralph P. Martin
49   1 Peter................J. Ramsey Michaels
50   Jude, 2 Peter** ...... Richard J. Bauckham
51   1, 2, 3, John, rev. ed.....Stephen S. Smalley
52a Revelation 1–5 ....David E. Aune
52b Revelation 6–16 ....David E. Aune
52c Revelation 17–22 ....David E. Aune

*forthcoming as of 2014
**in revision as of 2014

14 WORD BIBLICAL COMMENTARY

1 Chronicles

RODDY BRAUN

General Editors: David A. Hubbard, Glenn W. Barker
Old Testament Editor: John D. W. Watts
New Testament Editor: Ralph P. Martin

ZONDERVAN

1 Chronicles, Volume 14
Copyright © 1986 by Thomas Nelson, Inc.

Previously published as *1 Chronicles*.

Formerly published by Thomas Nelson. Now published by Zondervan, a division of HarperCollins*Christian Publishing*.

Requests for information should be addressed to:

Zondervan, 3900 *Sparks Dr. SE, Grand Rapids, Michigan 49546*

This edition: ISBN 978-0-310-52218-8

The Library of Congress has cataloged the original edition as follows:

Library of Congress Control Number: 2005295211

Printed in the United States of America

Contents

Author's Preface   ix
Editorial Preface   x
Abbreviations   xi

INTRODUCTION AND BIBLIOGRAPHY   xvii
  Commentaries on 1 Chronicles   xvii
  Name and Place in the Canon   xviii
  Authenticity, Integrity, and Scope   xix
  Text   xxi
  The Chronicler and His Sources   xxiii
  Literary Forms in Chronicles   xxiii
  Speech, Sermon, and Prayer in Chronicles   xxiv
  Purpose and Date   xxv
  Theological Themes:
    The Temple   xxix
    Priests and Levites   xxxi
    David and Solomon   xxxii
    All Israel   xxxv
    Retribution   xxxvii
    Repentance   xxxix
    The Disposition of the Heart   xl
  Outline of 1 and 2 Chronicles   xli
  Additional Bibliography   xli

TEXT AND COMMENTARY   1
The Genealogical Prologue (chaps. 1–9)   1
  From Adam to Israel (1:1–54)   13
    From Adam to Noah and His Sons (1:1–23)   14
    From Shem to Abraham and His Sons (1:24–54)   18
  Descendants of Israel and Judah (2:1–4:23)   25
    Sons of Israel and Judah (2:1–8)   29
    From Hezron to David (2:9–17)   32
    Descendants of Caleb (Chelubai) and Jerahmeel
      (2:18–55; 4:1–7)   35
    Descendants of David (3:1–24)   47
    Additional Judahites (4:8–23)   55
  Summary: The Descendants of Judah (2:1–4:23)   61
  Descendants of Simeon (4:24–43)   63
  The Transjordanian Tribes: Reuben, Gad, East Manasseh
    (5:1–26)   69

Sons of Levi (5:27–41; 6:1–66 [6:1–81])   80
  The Sons of Levi: the High Priests (5:27–41 [6:1–15])   82
  The Levites (6:1–15 [16–30])   86
  Additional Levites and Priests (6:16–38 [31–53])   89
  The Levitical Cities (6:39–66 [54–81])   95
Descendants of Issachar (7:1–15)   103
The Descendants of Benjamin, Dan (?) and Naphtali
    (7:6–13)   106
Descendants of Manasseh (7:14–19)   110
The Descendants of Ephraim (and Manasseh) (7:20–29)   113
Descendants of Asher (7:30–40)   117
Additional Descendants of Benjamin (8:1–40)   120
Inhabitants of Jerusalem (9:1–44)   129
David and Solomon (chaps. 10–29)   145
  The Death of Saul (10:1–14)   147
  The Rise of David (chaps. 11–12)   153
    The Beginning of the Rise of David (11:1–9)   153
    David and His Mighty Men (11:10–47)   156
    David at Ziklag and the Stronghold (12:1–23)   163
    The Rise of David, Concluded (12:24–41 [23–40])   167
  David, the Ark, and the Cult (chaps. 13–17)   172
    David, the Ark, and the Cult (a) (13:1–14)   172
    David, the Ark, and the Cult (b) (14:1–17)   176
    The Transfer of the Ark to Jerusalem (chaps. 15–16)   180
    The Promise to David (17:1–27)   195
  David's Wars (chaps. 18–20)   201
    David's Wars (a) (18:1–17)   202
    David's Wars (b) (19:1–19)   205
    David's Wars (c) (20:1–8)   208
  David's Census (21:1–22:1)   212
Transitional Unit (chaps. 22–29)   219
  David's First Speech (22:2–19)   219
  David's Organization of the Levites (chaps. 23–27)   228
    Genealogy and Duties of the Levites (23:1–32)   228
    Divisions of the Priests (24:1–31)   236
    The Musicians (25:1–31)   241
    Doorkeepers and Other Levites (26:1–32)   247
    Other Officials of David (27:1–34)   255
  David's Second Speech (28:1–21)   265
  David's Third Speech (29:1–9)   277
  David's Blessing (29:10–19)   281
  Solomon's Enthronement (29:20–30)   287

Indexes   295

Author's Preface

My study of Chronicles began in the late '60s when working on a doctoral dissertation at Concordia Seminary, St. Louis. Beginning with a study of David in the non-synoptic portions of the work, that study later narrowed itself to 1 Chronicles 22, 28, and 29, chapters which I felt then (and continue to feel) were of fundamental importance for understanding the work of the Chronicler. In the years following I have attempted to expand that study into all portions of Chronicles and post-exilic literature and history in general.

It was therefore with considerable enthusiasm that I accepted the invitation of Word Books to prepare a commentary on 1 Chronicles. Although I will not deny that that enthusiasm sometimes wavered in the midst of, e.g., the genealogies of chaps. 1–9 or multitudinous other lists, the writing of such a commentary has been both rewarding and educational. My indebtedness to scholars of the past and the present, above all to W. Rudolph, E. Curtis, and more recently, H. G. M. Williamson, will be readily apparent. The study of any biblical book is never complete, and I am painfully aware of many of the limitations of this one. There remains a limitless number of aspects of problems and points of view to be pursued. At the same time, it is my hope that, if no new ground is broken here, at least a beginning, or a further step, may be taken in understanding Chronicles sympathetically and on its own terms, and a greater appreciation gained of the theological viewpoint of the writer and of the thoroughness, determination, and skill with which he pursued that point.

Special thanks is due to Dr. John D. W. Watts, whose help was always generous and patient, and to my wife, Doretta, who not only encouraged and supported me in the several years of this project, but who also typed the final manuscript from often illegible notes.

RODDY L. BRAUN

Our Savior Lutheran Church
Arlington, Virginia

Editorial Preface

The launching of the *Word Biblical Commentary* brings to fulfillment an enterprise of several years' planning. The publishers and the members of the editorial board met in 1977 to explore the possibility of a new commentary on the books of the Bible that would incorporate several distinctive features. Prospective readers of these volumes are entitled to know what such features were intended to be; whether the aims of the commentary have been fully achieved time alone will tell.

First, we have tried to cast a wide net to include as contributors a number of scholars from around the world who not only share our aims, but are in the main engaged in the ministry of teaching in university, college and seminary. They represent a rich diversity of denominational allegiance. The broad stance of our contributors can rightly be called evangelical, and this term is to be understood in its positive, historic sense of a commitment to scripture as divine revelation, and to the truth and power of the Christian gospel.

Then, the commentaries in our series are all commissioned and written for the purpose of inclusion in the *Word Biblical Commentary.* Unlike several of our distinguished counterparts in the field of commentary writing, there are no translated works, originally written in a non-English language. Also, our commentators were asked to prepare their own rendering of the original biblical text and to use those languages as the basis of their own comments and exegesis. What may be claimed as distinctive with this series is that it is based on the biblical languages, yet it seeks to make the technical and scholarly approach to a theological understanding of scripture understandable by—and useful to—the fledgling student, the working minister as well as to colleagues in the guild of professional scholars and teachers.

Finally, a word must be said about the format of the series. The layout in clearly defined sections has been consciously devised to assist readers at different levels. Those wishing to learn about the textual witnesses on which the translation is offered are invited to consult the section headed "Notes." If the readers' concern is with the state of modern scholarship on any given portion of scripture, then they should turn to the sections on "Bibliography" and "Form/Structure/Setting." For a clear exposition of the passage's meaning and its relevance to the ongoing biblical revelation, the "Comment" and concluding "Explanation" are designed expressly to meet that need. There is therefore something for everyone who may pick up and use these volumes.

If these aims come anywhere near realization, the intention of the editors will have been met, and the labor of our team of contributors rewarded.

General Editors: *David A. Hubbard*
Glenn W. Barker†
Old Testament: *John D. W. Watts*
New Testament: *Ralph P. Martin*

Abbreviations

PERIODICALS, REFERENCE WORKS, AND SERIALS

AJSL	American Journal of Semitic Languages and Literature
ANET	Ancient Near Eastern Texts, J. B. Pritchard, ed.
Ang	Angelicum
ASTI	Annual of the Swedish Theological Institute
ATD	Das Alte Testament Deutsch
BA	Biblical Archaeologist
BAR	Biblical Archaeologist Reader
BASOR	Bulletin of the American Schools of Oriental Research
BDB	F. Brown, S. R. Driver and C. A. Briggs, Hebrew and English Lexicon of the Old Testament
BHK (BH³)	Biblia hebraica, R. Kittel, ed.
BHS	Biblia hebraica stuttgartensia
Bib	Biblica
BJRL	Bulletin of the John Rylands University Library of Manchester
BKAT	Biblische Kommentar: Altes Testament
BL	Book List
BSac	Bibliotheca Sacra
BWANT	Beiträge zur Wissenschaft vom Alten und Nuen Testament
BZ	Biblische Zeitschrift
BZAW	Beihefte zur ZAW
CAT	Commentaire de l'Ancien Testament
CBC	Cambridge Bible Commentary
CBQ	Catholic Biblical Quarterly
CBSC	Cambridge Bible for Schools and Colleges
CJT	Canadian Journal of Theology
ConB	Coniectanea Biblica
CBOTS	Coniectanea Biblica Old Testament Series
CQR	Church Quarterly Review
CTM	Concordia Theological Monthly
DBSup	Dictionnaire de la Bible, Supplement, eds. L. Pirot, et al., Paris: Librarie Letouzey et Ané, 1960
EB	Encyclopaedia Biblica, ed. T. K. Cheyne (New York: Macmillan and Co., 1902)
EI	Eretz Israel
EncJud	Encyclopaedia judaica (1971)
ETL	Ephemerides theologicae lovanienses (EThL)
EvT	Evangelische Theologie (EvTh)
ExpTim	Expository Times
GKC	Gesenius' Hebrew Grammar, ed. E. Kautzsch, tr. A. E. Cowley
GTT	Gereformeerd Theologisch Tijdschrift
HAT	Handbuch zum Alten Testament
HKAT	Handkommentar zum Alten Testament

HR	*History of Religions*
HSM	Harvard Semitic Monographs
HTR	*Harvard Theological Review*
HTS	Harvard Theological Studies
HUCA	*Hebrew Union College Annual*
IB	*Interpreter's Bible* (Nashville: Abingdon Press, 1951–57)
ICC	International Critical Commentary
IDB	G. A. Buttrick (ed.), *Interpreter's Dictionary of the Bible* (Nashville: Abingdon Press, 1962)
IDBSup	Supplementary Volume to *IDB* (Nashville: Abingdon Press, 1976)
IEJ	*Israel Exploration Journal*
Int	*Interpretation*
JAOS	*Journal of the American Oriental Society*
JBC	*The Jerome Biblical Commentary*, R. E. Brown, et al., eds.
JBL	*Journal of Biblical Literature*
JBR	*Journal of Bible and Religion*
JETS	*Journal of the Evangelical Theological Society*
JNES	*Journal of Near Eastern Studies*
JPOS	*Journal of the Palestinian Oriental Society*
JQR	*Jewish Quarterly Review*
JSOT	*Journal for the Study of the Old Testament*
JSS	*Journal of Semitic Studies*
JTS	*Journal of Theological Studies*
KAI	H. Donner and W. Röllig, *Kanaanäische und aramäische Inschriften*
KAT	Kommentar zum Alten Testament, E. Sellin, ed.
KB	L. Koehler and W. Baumgartner, *Lexicon in Veteris Testamenti libros*
KD	*Kerygma und Dogma*
KHAT	Kurzer Handkommentar zum Alten Testament
LCL	Loeb Classical Library
NCBC	*New Century Bible Commentary*
OLP	Orientalia lovaniensia periodica
OTM	Old Testament Message
OTS	*Oudtestamentische Studien*
PCB	*Peake's Commentary on the Bible*, M. Black and H. H. Rowley, eds.
PEQ	*Palestine Exploration Quarterly*
PJ	*Palästina-Jahrbuch*
RAC	*Reallexikon für Antike und Christentum*
RB	*Revue biblique*
RGG	*Religion in Geschichte und Gegenwart*
RTP	*Revue de Theologie et de Philosophie*
SBLMS	SBL Monograph Series
SBT	*Studia Biblica et Theologica*
SBT	Studies in Biblical Theology
SJT	*Scottish Journal of Theology*
SNTSMS	Society for New Testament Studies Monograph Series

ST	*Studia theologica* (*StTh*)
TBC	Torch Bible Commentary
TDOT	*Theological Dictionary of the OT*
TLZ	*Theologische Literaturzeitung*
TQ	*Theologische Quartalschrift* (*ThQ*)
TS	*Theological Studies*
TSK	*Theologische Studien und Kritiken* (*ThStK*)
TWAT	G. J. Botterweck and H. Ringgren (eds.), *Theologisches Worterbuch zum Alten Testament* (*ThWAT*)
TynBul	*Tyndale Bulletin*
TZ	*Theologische Zeitschrift* (*ThZ*)
Ü.S.	M. Noth, *Überlieferungsgeschichtliche Studien* (see Bibliography)
VT	*Vetus Testamentum*
VTSup	Vetus Testamentum, Supplements (Leiden: E. J. Brill)
WMANT	Wissenschaftliche Monographien zum Alten und Neuen Testament
WTJ	*Westminster Theological Journal*
ZAW	*Zeitschrift für die alttestamentliche Wissenschaft*
ZDPV	*Zeitschrift des deutschen Palästina-Vereins*
ZTK	*Zeitschrift für Theologie und Kirche* (*ZThK*)

MODERN TRANSLATIONS

AB	Anchor Bible
AV	Authorized Version
GNB	Good News Bible
JB	Jerusalem Bible
KJV	King James Version
NAB	New American Bible
NEB	New English Bible
NIV	New International Version
RSV	Revised Standard Version
RV	Revised Version

TEXTS, VERSIONS, AND ANCIENT WORKS

G	Septuagint
G^A	G MS, Codex Alexandrinus
G^B	G MS, Codex Vaticanus
G^L	G MSS, Lucianic recension consisting of boc_2e_2
G^{-L}	Septuagint, excluding Lucianic MSS
G^*	Septuagint, uncorrected
MT	Masoretic text
OG	Old Greek
OL	Old Latin
Seb	Sebir, the usual form of the word noted in the margin
SamPent	Samaritan Pentateuch
Syr	Syriac
Tg	Targum

Theod.	Theodotion
Vg	Vulgate
α′	Aquila

This commentary is based on the printed Hebrew text of the *Biblia Hebraica Stuttgartensia* (Stuttgart: Deutsche Bibelstiftung, 1967–77). Chapter and verse enumeration throughout are those of the Hebrew Bible. Where these differ from the standard English versions, references to the latter have been given in brackets following the Hebrew number. The LXX text cited is that of A. Rahlfs, *Septuaginta* (Stuttgart: Württembergische Bibelanstalt, 1935).

BIBLICAL AND APOCRYPHAL BOOKS

Gen	Genesis	Mic	Micah
Exod	Exodus	Nah	Nahum
Lev	Leviticus	Hab	Habakkuk
Num	Numbers	Zeph	Zephaniah
Deut	Deuteronomy	Hag	Haggai
Josh	Joshua	Zech	Zechariah
Judg	Judges	Mal	Malachi
Ruth	Ruth	1–2 Esdr	1–2 Esdras
1–2 Sam	1–2 Samuel	1–2 Macc	1–2 Maccabees
1–2 Kgs	1–2 Kings	Matt	Matthew
1–2 Chr	1–2 Chronicles	Mark	Mark
Ezra	Ezra	Luke	Luke
Neh	Nehemiah	John	John
Esth	Esther	Acts	Acts
Job	Job	Rom	Romans
Ps(s)	Psalm(s)	1–2 Cor	1–2 Corinthians
Prov	Proverbs	Gal	Galatians
Eccl	Ecclesiastes	Eph	Ephesians
Cant	Canticles, Song of Solomon	Phil	Philippians
		Col	Colossians
Isa	Isaiah	1–2 Thess	1–2 Thessalonians
Jer	Jeremiah	1–2 Tim	1–2 Timothy
Lam	Lamentations	Titus	Titus
Ezek	Ezekiel	Phlm	Philemon
Dan	Daniel	Heb	Hebrews
Hos	Hosea	Jas	James
Joel	Joel	1–2 Pet	1–2 Peter
Amos	Amos	1–2–3 John	1–2–3 John
Obad	Obadiah	Jude	Jude
Jon	Jonah	Rev	Revelation

GRAMMATICAL AND OTHER ABBREVIATIONS

abs	absolute
accus	accusative

chap(s).	chapter(s)
constr	construct
Chr	Chronicles, the Chronicler
dittogr	dittography
Dtr	the Deuteronomic writer
DSS	Dead Sea Scrolls
E	the Elohistic source
ed(s).	editor(s), edited by
Ev(v)	English verse(s)
fem	feminine
haplogr	haplography
Heb.	consonantal Hebrew
hiph	hiphil
hithp	hithpael
homoiotel	homoioteleuton
hoph	hophal
impf	imperfect
impv	imperative
inf	infinitive
J	the Yahwistic source
juss	jussive
K	Kethib, "written"
LXX	the Septuagint
LXX^{min}	later Greek MSS in small letters
LXX^{Sam}	the first Greek MS of Samuel from Qumran Cave IV
M	the Masora
masc, m	masculine
MS(S)	manuscript(s)
niph	niphal
nom	nominative
n.s.	new series
NT	New Testament
OT	Old Testament
P	the Priestly source
pf	perfect
pl	plural
PN	personal name
ptcp	participle
Q	Qere, to be "read"
sg	singular
(Vg), (Syr)	supported by the Vulgate, Syriac, etc.
>	is lacking in
=	equals
+	adds

Introduction

COMMENTARIES ON 1 CHRONICLES

One might well ask at the beginning what the occasion is for another commentary on Chronicles. Other comprehensive commentaries are indeed available, including above all the valuable treatments by **E. L. Curtis** and **A. A. Madsen** (*A Critical and Exegetical Commentary on the Books of Chronicles,* ICC [Edinburgh: T. & T. Clark, 1910]), **J. Rothstein** and **J. Hänel** (*Das erste Buch der Chronik,* KAT [Leipzig: A. Diechertsche, 1927]), and more recently **W. Rudolph** (*Chronikbücher,* HAT [Tubingen: Mohr, 1955]). The general reader has also been well cared for in briefer and more popular commentaries such as those by **P. R. Ackroyd** (*I & II Chronicles, Ezra, Nehemiah,* TBC [London: SCM, 1973]), **Jacob Myers** (*I Chronicles,* AB [Garden City, NJ: Doubleday, 1965]), **R. J. Coggins** (*The First and Second Books of the Chronicles,* CBC [Cambridge: University Press, 1976]), and **H. G. M. Williamson** (*1 and 2 Chronicles,* NCBC [London: Marshall, Morgan & Scott, 1982]), as well as in the one-volume Bible commentaries such as **R. North** (*JBC,* 402–14) and **A. S. Herbert** (*PCB,* 357–69). Many of these, while suffering from limitations of space, are especially sensitive and well done, such as the treatments by Coggins and Williamson, or contain a wealth of data not otherwise readily available, such as the archaeological references in Myers.

In addition to commentaries, standard studies including those of **C. C. Torrey** (*Ezra Studies,* 1910, reprinted with a new prolegomena by **W. F. Stinespring** [New York: Ktav, 1970]), **A. Welch** (*The Work of the Chronicler, Its Purpose and Date* [London: Oxford University Press, 1939]) and **G. von Rad** (*Das Geschichtsbild des Chronistischen Werkes* [Stuttgart: Kohlhammer, 1930]), have after a lengthy hiatus now been joined by a comparative avalanche of more extensive studies by **T. Willi** (*Die Chronik als Auslegung* [Göttingen: Vandenhoeck und Ruprecht, 1972]), **P. Welten** (*Geschichte und Geschichtsdarstellung in den Chronikbüchern,* WMANT 42 [Neukirchen: Neukirchener Verlag, 1973]), **R. Mosis** (*Untersuchungen zur Theologie des Chronistischen Geschichtswerkes,* Freiburger theologische Studien 92 [Freiburg: Herder, 1973]), **D. L. Peterson** (*Late Israelite Prophecy,* SBLMS 23 [Missoula, MT: Scholar's Press, 1977]), **R. M. Polzin** (*Late Biblical Hebrew* [Missoula, MT: Scholar's Press, 1976]), and **H. G. M. Williamson** (*Israel in the Books of Chronicles* [New York: Cambridge University Press, 1977]). These have been supplemented by a host of articles on Chronicles *per se* by **S. Japhet, H. G. M. Williamson, J. Newsome, David Pedersen,** the author, and others, and on related areas such as textual criticism and Samaritan studies by such men as Frank Cross, David Freedman, Werner Lemke, R. J. Coggins, and others. The cumulative effect of these newer studies has been to reopen for discussion significant elements of the understanding of Chronicles which have for many years been considered as established facts. These include:

(1) the supposed common authorship of Chronicles and Ezra-Nehemiah;
(2) the date of Chronicles;

(3) the purpose of the Chronicles;
(4) the role of the priests and Levites in Chronicles;
(5) the relationship between Chronicles and Samuel–Kings;
(6) the text of Chronicles;
(7) the role of David in Chronicles;
(8) eschatology in Chronicles.

With questions of such importance again open for discussion, a new study of Chronicles needs to reconsider the text in its own right, apart from the presuppositions which have often accompanied its study in the past, and hopefully to begin movement towards a new and more complete understanding of the message of Chronicles. If this commentary is able to contribute in any small way toward that understanding, it will have achieved its purpose. Other commentaries on Chronicles include:

Barnes, W. E. *The Books of Chronicles.* CBSC 14. Cambridge: University Press, 1899. **Bennett, W. W.** *The Books of Chronicles.* Expositor's Bible 12. London: Hodder and Stoughton, 1894. **Benzinger, I.** *Die Bücher der Chronik.* KHAT 20. Tübingen: Mohr, 1901. **Bertheau, E.** *Commentary on the Books of Chronicles.* Trans. J. Martin. Edinburgh: T. & T. Clark, 1857. **Bückers, H.** *Die Bücher der Chronik; oder, Paralipomenon.* Herder's Bibelkommentar 4/1. Freiburg: Herder, 1952. **Cazelles, H.** *Les Livres des Chroniques.* 2d ed. Paris: Les Éditions du Cerf, 1961. **Ellison, H. L.** "1 and 2 Chronicles." *New Bible Commentary Revised.* Ed. D. Guthrie et al. London: 1970, 369–94. **Elmslie, W. A. L.** *The Books of Chronicles.* CBSC 14. 2nd ed. Cambridge: Cambridge Press, 1916. ———. "Introduction and Exegesis to 1–2 Chronicles." *IB* 3. Nashville: Abingdon Press, 1954. 339–548. **Galling, K.** *Die Bücher der Chronik, Esra, und Nehemia.* ATD 12. Göttingen: Vandenhoeck und Ruprecht, 1954. **Goettsberger, J.** *Die Bücher der Chronik; oder, Paralipomenon.* Die Heilige Schrift des Alten Testaments 4/1. Bonn: Hanstein, 1939. **Harvey-Jellie, W. R.** *Chronicles.* CB 7, 8. London: Caxton, 1906. **Keil, C. F.** *The Books of the Chronicles.* Commentary on the Old Testament 3. Grand Rapids: Eerdmans, 1978 (1872). **Kittel, R.,** and **Siegfried, D. C.** *Die Bücher der Chronik und Esra, Nehemiah, und Esther.* HKAT. Göttingen: Vandenhoeck und Ruprecht, 1902. **Mangan, C.** *1–2 Chronicles, Ezra, Nehemiah.* OTM 13. Wilmington, DE: Glazier, 1982. **Michaeli, F.** *Les Livres des Chroniques, d'Esdras et de Néhémie.* CAT. Neuchatel: Delachaux & Niestlé, 1967. **Rehm, M.** *Die Bücher der Chronik.* Wüuzburg: Echter Verlag, 1949. **Slotki, I. W.** *Chronicles.* Soncino Books of the Bible 14. London: Soncino Press, 1952.

NAME AND PLACE IN THE CANON

Bibliography

Albright, W. F. "The Date and Personality of the Chronicler." *JBL* 40 (1921) 104–24. **Bea, A.** "Neue Arbeiten zum Problem der Biblischen Chronikbücher." *Bib* 22 (1941) 46–58. **Braun, R. L.** *Chronicles, Ezra, and Nehemiah: Theology and Literary History.* VTSup 30. Leiden: E. J. Brill (1979) 52–64. **Cross, F. M., Jr.** "A Reconstruction of the Judean Restoration." *JBL* 94 (1975) 4–18. **Freedman, D. N.** "The Chronicler's Purpose." *CBQ* 23 (1961) 436–42. **Japhet, S.** "The Supposed Common Authorship of Chronicles and Ezra-Nehemiah Investigated Anew." *VT* 18 (1968) 330–71. **Newsome, J. D.** "Toward a New Understanding of the Chronicler and His Purposes."

JBL 94 (1975) 210–17. **North, R.** "Does Archaeology Prove Chronicles Sources?" *Light Unto My Path: Old Testament Studies in Honor of J. M. Myers.* Ed. H. N. Bream, et al. Philadelphia: Temple University Press, 1974, 375–401. **Plöger, O.** "Reden und Gebete im deuteronomistischen und chronistischen Geschichtswerk." *Festschrift für Günther Dehn.* Ed. W. Schneemelcher. Neukirchen: Kreis Moers, 1957. 35–49.

The name given 1 and 2 Chronicles in the Hebrew Bible is דברי הימים, "the words (or events) of the days." These two books are counted as one in the Hebrew canon, where they normally stand at the end (although a few manuscripts place them at the head) of the Writings, the third major portion of the canon, preceded somewhat anomalously by Ezra-Nehemiah, commonly considered their sequel. The division into two books in our English Bible, as well as their position with the "historical" books, can be attributed to the influence of LXX, which named the books Παραλειπομενῶν (*Paralipomenon*), i.e., "the things left over," and placed them after Kings. Unfortunately this somewhat derogatory and nontheological view of Chronicles has often been shared by later readers, who have tended to see it in large measure as a repetition of Samuel-Kings, supplemented by a collection of priestly trivia, and hence have ignored its unique contents and message.

The phrase דברי הימים, preceded by "book," is quite common in the OT (cf. 1 Kgs 14:19, 29; 15:7, etc.), but always with a following qualifying phrase, such as "the words of the days of King David" (1 Chr 27:24), except in Esth 2:23; 6:1; Neh 12:23. In its present form, Chronicles stretches from Adam (1:1) to the Persian king Cyrus (2 Chr 36:22–23), justifying Jerome's statement that we might call it "the chronicle of the whole of sacred history." From that statement is derived our name "Chronicles." While the books have sometimes been viewed suspiciously, their canonicity has not been seriously questioned. The remark of Jesus recorded in Matt 23:35, referring to the death of the priest Zechariah, would indicate that at his time these books were considered Scripture and stood at or near the end of that collection (cf. 2 Chr 24:20–22).

AUTHENTICITY, INTEGRITY, AND SCOPE

Bibliography

Brunet, A. M. "Paralipomenes." *DB Sup* 6. Ed. L. Pirot, et al. Paris: Library Letouzey et Ané, 1960. Cols. 1220–61. **Japhet, S.** "Chronicles, Book of." *EncJud.* Vol. 5. Cols. 517–34. **Mangenot, E.** "Paralipomenes." *DB* 4. Ed. F. Vigouroux. Paris: Library Letouzey et Ané, 1908. Cols. 2128–51.

With the vast majority of OT scholarship, we have assumed that the greater part of 1 and 2 Chronicles is the work of one author, whom we may for the sake of convenience call the Chronicler. Major additions and revisions to his work occur principally in the genealogies of 1 Chr 1–9 and 1 Chr 23–27, and lesser ones chiefly in connection with expansion of lists and genealogical data. However, there are two trends that have combined to shift the focus of our attention. First, the common authorship of Chronicles and Ezra–Nehemiah, accepted since the time of Zunz as scholarly orthodoxy and buttressed by the support of men of the stature of W. F. Albright (*JBL* 40 [1921] 104–24), has been seriously questioned, initially by Sara Japhet (*VT* 18 [1968] 330–71).

Japhet noted five phenomena held as evidence of a common authorship (the presence of the first verses of Ezra at the end of Chronicles, the fact that 1 Esdras begins with 2 Chr 35–36 and continues through Ezra, common vocabulary, style and syntax, and uniformity of theological conceptions) and concluded on the basis of vocabulary and syntax and style that the two works could not have been by the same author. Others have arrived at the same conclusion, due both to the work of Japhet and their own research (cf. D. N. Freedman, *CBQ* 23 [1961] 436–42; H. G. M. Williamson, *Israel in the Books of Chronicles*; J. Newsome, *JBL* 94 [1975] 210–17; and the author). While admitting that many themes and much common vocabulary and style and syntax are common to Chronicles and Ezra-Nehemiah, there are also sizeable divergencies. In particular, the differences in such significant theological themes as retribution and the author's appraisal of such a prominent figure as Solomon make it seem most unlikely that Ezra–Nehemiah in its present form could have come from the same hand as Chronicles (cf. Braun, VTSup 30 [1979] 52–64).

Second, studies of the text of Chronicles (and Samuel-Kings) have also had a significant impact upon the view of the integrity of the book. In conjunction with his studies of the "local text" traditions, F. Cross (*JBL* 95 [1975] 4–18) concluded that the books of Chronicles passed through at least three different editions. The first edition ended with the account of the laying of the temple's foundation (Ezra 3:13 = 1 Esdr 5:65). The second edition added the Ezra narrative, essentially in its 1 Esdras format, with Ezra 5:1–6:19 as its introduction. A third edition added the genealogies of 1 Chr 1–9 and the Nehemiah Memoirs, disrupting the order of the Ezra material in the process while suppressing elements of earlier traditions exalting Zerubbabel as well.

One cannot be dogmatic about the question of the end of the Chronicler's history. Newsome (*JBL* 94 [1975] 215) has argued that the Chronicler's work did not include the rebuilding of the temple. Such a position, however, is difficult to defend in view of the domination of the temple motif throughout Chronicles. Thus, Freedman concluded that the Chronicler's account originally included the rebuilding and dedication of the temple, but that the original ending has been disturbed by the intrusion of Ezra 4:6–6:18. Some such theory of the end of the Chronicler's work, while leaving much unsaid, appears to be necessary. More radically, it may be suggested that the Chronicler's conclusion is included in his description of the Persian king Cyrus (2 Chr 36:23; Ezra 1:2–3). The Chronicler boldly states that it is Yahweh who has given all the kingdoms of the earth into Cyrus's hands and who has charged him to build the temple at Jerusalem. Is it possible that the Chronicler, like Isa 45:1; 55:3, has reinterpreted the "everlasting covenant" with David and now views the Persian king Cyrus as the founder of the rebuilt temple and the guarantor of Israel's existence in Palestine? (Cf. Braun, VTSup 30 [1979] 62.)

At the same time, there is a continuity between Chronicles and Ezra-Nehemiah that cannot be denied, a development which at times extends to the use of a specific vocabulary and suggests immediate dependence upon the earlier work. In an earlier study we noted that Ezra 1–3 and 6:14–18 lay closest to the thought world of the Chronicler, and that both Ezra 4 and 6 show signs of redactional activity. Ezra 7–8 and Neh 8 approximate Chronicles in tone, although there is here additional emphasis upon the centrality of the law. The prayer of Ezra 9 and at least the framework of the prayer of Neh 9 show a note of hostility toward the peoples of the land that is continued in Ezra 10 and Neh 10 and 13. By way of concepts, we note the centrality of the temple in the initial chapters of Ezra and the manner in which its restoration is described. Similarly, the author or redactor of the prayers in Ezra 9 and Neh 9 has used elements of the Chronicler's retribution and remnant vocabulary, although adapting them to a new situation. Plöger believes that the writer of Ezra-Nehemiah has in fact made a conscious effort to parallel the activities of Ezra and Nehemiah, as the Chronicler had done in the case of David and Solomon (*Festschrift für Günther Dehn,* 35–49). Such parallels strongly suggest that the conclusion of the Chronicler's work has been overlaid with one or more layers of later tradition, and that the literary program of such an author(s) is responsible for the chaos of Ezra–Nehemiah analyzed from a chronological point of view.

TEXT

Bibliography

Allen, L. C. *The Greek Chronicles. The Relation of the Septuagint of I and II Chronicles to the Masoretic Text.* Part I: The Translator's Craft. VTSup 25. Leiden: E. J. Brill, 1974. ———. *The Greek Chronicles. The Relation of the Septuagint of I and II Chronicles to the Masoretic Text.* Part II: Textual Criticism. VTSup 27. Leiden: E. J. Brill, 1974. **Botterweck, G. J.** "Zur Eigenant der Chronistischen Davidgeschichte." *TQ* 136 (1956) 402–35. **Brunet, A. M.** "Le Chroniste et ses sources." *RB* 60 (1953) 481–508; *RB* 61 (1954) 349–86. **Cross, F. M. Jr.** "The Contributions of the Qumran Discoveries." *IEJ* 16 (1966) 81–95. ———. "The History of the Biblical Text in the Light of the Discoveries in the Judean Desert." *HTR* 57 (1964) 281–99. **Gerleman, G.** *Studies in the Septuagint II: Chronicles.* London: C. W. K. Gleerup, 1947. ———. *Synoptic Studies in the Old Testament.* London: C. W. K. Gleerup, 1948. **Greenberg, M.** "The Stabilization of the Text of the Hebrew Bible." *JAOS* 76 (1956) 161–63. **Jellicoe, S.** "Septuagint Studies in the Current Century." *JBL* 8 (1969) 191–99. ———. "Some Reflections on the καιγε Rescension." *VT* 23 (1973) 15–24. **Lemke, W. E.** "The Synoptic Problem in the Chronicler's History." *HTR* 58 (1965) 349–63. ———. "Synoptic Studies in the Chronicler's History." Diss.: Harvard University, 1965. **Montgomery, J. A.** "A Study in Comparison of the Texts of Kings and Chronicles." *JBL* 50 (1931) 115–16. **Orlinsky, H. M.** "The Septuagint, Its Use in Textual Criticism." *BA* 9 (1946) 22–34. ———. "The Textual Criticism of the Old Testament." *The Bible and the Ancient Near East.* Ed. G. E. Wright. Garden City, NY: Doubleday, 1961. **Rehm, M.** *Textkritische Untersuchungen zu den Parallelstellen der Samuel-Königsbücher und der Chronik.* Münster: Aschendorff, 1937. **Roberts, B. J.** *The Old Testament Text and Versions.* Cardiff: University of Wales Press, 1951. **Shenkel, J. D.** *Chronology and Rescensional Development in the Greek Text of Kings.* HSM. Cambridge, MA: Harvard University Press, 1968. ———. "A Comparative Study of the Synoptic Parallels in I Paralipomena and I–II Reigns." *HTR* 62 (1969) 63–85. **Thackeray, H. St. John.** "The Greek Translators of the Four Books of Kings." *JTS* 8 (1907) 262–78. **Torrey, C. C.** "The Apparatus of the Textual Criticism of Chronicles–Ezra–Nehemiah." *Old Testament and Semitic Studies in Memory of William Rainey Harper.* Vol. 2. Ed. R. F. Harper, et al. Chicago: University of Chicago Press, 1908. 55–111. ————. "The Chronicler as Editor and as Independent Narrator." *AJSL* 25 (1908/09) 157–73, 188–217. ————. *The Chronicler's History of Israel; Chronicles–Ezra– Nehemiah Restored to Its Original Form.* New Haven: Yale University Press, 1954. **Vannu- telli, P.** *Libri Synoptici Veteris Testamenti seu Librorum Regum et Chronicorum loci paralleli.* 2 vols. Rome: Pontifical Biblical Institute, 1931–34.

Most studies of Chronicles in the past have concentrated upon the so-
called synoptic portions of Chronicles, i.e., those portions of the book with
parallel sections in Samuel-Kings, and specifically upon the historical problems
resulting when the texts of the two works differ. Whenever Chronicles differed
from its supposed *Vorlage* in Samuel or Kings, an attempt was made to explain
the difference in terms of the supposed theological viewpoint of the Chronicler
(cf. A. M. Brunet, *RB* 60 [1953] 483–508; *RB* 61 [1954] 349–86; G. J. Botterweck, *TQ* 136 [1956] 402–35). While this approach is justified to a point
(and will be pursued in this commentary also), the result has often been a
certain artificiality and forced exegesis. Moreover, it has led to an ignoring
of significant portions of the Chronicler's work, the so-called non-synoptic
sections.

Recent discoveries have made this approach even more untenable. The
study of fragments of ancient Hebrew texts found near the Dead Sea conducted by scholars such as F. M. Cross, has shown that not every variant is
to be attributed to the intention of the writer, but that in at least a number
of cases the variations are due to the fact that the writer had before him a
text of Samuel-Kings differing from the Masoretic text found in our Hebrew
Bibles. (Cf. especially F. M. Cross, Jr., *HTR* 57 [1964] 281–99; *IEJ* 16 [1966]
81–95.) In fact, the text available to the Chronicler appears to have contained
readings similar to some previously known to us only in the Lucianic recension
of the LXX, represented in the MSS boc_2e_2 in the LXX editions. Cross's
study suggests that a separate manuscript tradition had arisen in Palestine,
represented now in the Lucianic LXX, Chronicles, fragments from the Dead
Sea Scrolls, and readings from Josephus, separate from other manuscript
traditions developing in Babylonia and Egypt.

In a dissertation written under Cross at Harvard, Werner Lemke has investigated the relationship of Chronicles to Samuel-Kings in the light of these
ancient fragments and the LXX, and he has pointed out cases in which the
new textual evidence suggests we revise our theories of the Chronicler's supposed *Tendenz* (cf. W. E. Lemke, "Synoptic Studies," *HTR* 58 [1965] 349–
63). As a result of his studies, Lemke suggests that future research should
reverse the customary methodology and begin rather with the study of the
material peculiar to Chronicles, the non-synoptic sections. It was in agreement
with this suggestion that I wrote my own dissertation ("The Significance of
1 Chronicles 22, 28, and 29 for the structure and Theology of the Work of
the Chronicler" [Diss.: Concordia Seminary, St. Louis, 1973]) which had as
its primary objective the ascertainment of the theological *Tendenz* of the writer

on the basis of the nonsynoptic sections of Chronicles commonly acknowledged to be from the hand of the Chronicler, so that this information might then be related to the understanding of the synoptic sections. This commentary may then be viewed as in part a completion of the task previously begun, with the nonsynoptic portions utilized to illuminate the synoptic. At the same time, it should be stated that, in my opinion, these textual divergencies have not altered appreciably our understanding of the major emphases of Chronicles.

THE CHRONICLER AND HIS SOURCES

Bibliography

Brunet, A. M. "Le Chroniste et ses sources." *RB* 60 (1953) 481–508. ———. "Le Chroniste et ses sources." *RB* 61 (1954) 349–86.

It is commonly agreed that the Chronicler used as his primary source the books of Samuel-Kings although they may well have been in a form somewhat divergent from that found in our Hebrew Bibles or major LXX manuscripts. While a few textual differences may be due to varying text types, and while in some cases no satisfactory explanation has been found (cf. 1 Chr 21 and 2 Sam 24), the great majority of variations is easily seen to have their origin in the Chronicler himself, either as a part of his theological *Tendenz* or otherwise. Concerning other source materials utilized by the author, we are in the dark. Most likely, this author, or a later one, did have before him certain materials, of which genealogical lists, especially those related to the priests and Levites, are most prominent. A second type of material may have sprung from military/census type lists, such as we find incorporated in 1 Chr 11–12. Apart from this, it is probably fanciful to ascribe knowledge of additional sources to the writer. Basing himself broadly upon a host of OT traditions, the writer has with considerable literary skill drafted his history, building upon Samuel-Kings and interpreting, supplementing, and deleting as he felt compelled by his theological standards. Thus seen, the speeches of David in 1 Chr 22, 28 and 29, the speech of Abijah in 2 Chr 13, and the account of Uzziah's prosperity and punishment in 2 Chr 26, for example, all reflect a common point of view which we may identify with the Chronicler's own. The attempt to establish or protect the reputation of the writer through tests of historical accuracy and the like are in that sense to be considered misguided.

LITERARY FORMS IN CHRONICLES

The major part of 1 Chronicles is composed of four literary forms: (1) genealogies, such as, above all, chaps. 1–8 (see especially pp. 1–12 below); (2) Lists, such as 1 Chr 9:3–23; 11:10–47; 12; and much of chs. 22, 28, and

29; (3) Speeches, sermons, and prayers such as those of chaps. 22, 28, and 29 (see below); (4) An unnamed genre reflected in such chapters as 1 Chr 10–11, 13–14, 16, 17–21, consisting in the main of extracts from Samuel-Kings (and, in chapter 16, Psalms), often related verbatim, but also with alterations, additions, and deletions. While some of these variations may be due to a different text-type utilized by the author (see above), it seems likely that most reflect the mind of the author of Chronicles himself, who has used this means to convey Israel's past in such a way as to make it more ideologically appropriate to his concerns for the present.

One may ask what form of literature this is which draws so heavily upon a Scriptural source but feels free to alter details, to omit, and to expand as seems desirable. In large measure, the ostensible form of this literature is that which it exhibited in its earlier setting; however, that form has become largely insignificant in its new setting, and its earlier purpose has been adapted to a new one. Some have in this connection draw a comparison with later Jewish midrashic literature, which for the sake of entertainment and edification may elaborate upon a chosen text. Many of the variations found in 1 Chronicles, however, really do not fit that mold. For the sake of convenience, therefore, in this commentary the material taken by Chronicles from its source is simply called "the narrative" or "story." The Chronicler's own contribution then might best be viewed as history in the pregnant sense of the term (facts plus interpretation) or as an early example of theological interpretation or the writing of a biblical commentary.

SPEECH, SERMON AND PRAYER IN CHRONICLES

Bibliography

Ap-Thomas, D. R. "Some Notes on Old Testament Attitude Toward Prayer." *SJT* 9 (1956) 422–29. **Blank, S. H.** "Some Observations Concerning Biblical Prayer." *HUCA* 32 (961) 75–90. **Boecker, H.** "Anklagereden und Verteidignungsreden im Alten Testament." *EvT* 20 (1960) 398–412. **Bratsiotis, N.** "Der Monolog im Alten Testament." *ZAW* 72 (1961) 30–70. **Braun, R. L.** "The Significance of I Chronicles 22, 28, and 29 for the Structure and Theology of the Work of the Chronicler." Diss.: Concordia Seminary, St. Louis, 1971. **Hornig, B.** "Das Prosagebet der nachexilischen Literatur." *TLZ* 83 (1958) 644–46. **Rad, G. von.** "The Levitical Sermon in I and II Chronicles." *The Problem of the Hexateuch and Other Essays.* Tr. E. W. T. Dicken. New York: McGraw-Hill, 1966. 267–80.

The question of the role played by the various speeches, sermons, and prayers in Chronicles has surprisingly not been studied thoroughly, the most extensive treatments being those of von Rad (*The Problem of the Hexateuch*) and Plöger (*Festschrift für Günther Dehn*, 35–49). In general I would conclude that von Rad's form-critical study leaves much to be desired, and has been accepted too readily by scholars (see Braun, 242–49). The more general study by Plöger, pointing out the significance of the speeches and their position within the total work of Chronicles (and in this case Ezra–Nehemiah), is also incomplete, but has not received the attention it deserves.

It is difficult to avoid the conclusion that von Rad's analysis of the Levitical sermon has been unduly influenced by his negative appraisal of the Chronicler's literary ability and viewpoint and his opinion of the Levites. Nevertheless, it does seem probable that the Chronicler was familiar with a type of religious exhortation that we may with some reservations call a sermon. Our studies have led us to conclude that the Chronicler was a person of much greater literary skill than is usually attributed to him. He has shown considerable freedom in his use of the sermon, vividly exhibited by the various situations into which he inserts them, the variety of speakers to whom they are assigned, the subjects with which they deal, and not least their great variety in both style and length, reflecting greater and lesser degrees of amplification, summarization, and alteration of the writer's supposed model.

It is also clear that the writer was obviously familiar with the prophetic judgment oracle and has to a limited degree distinguished his prophetic forms from the sermon. This is evident first of all in that, despite other similarities, he has not applied prophetic inspiration nor titles to any of his kings, nor do their speeches contain any reminiscences of prophetic formulae otherwise so common. While it is true that the Chronicler has diverged quite drastically from the older form of the judgment oracle, it is equally true that signs of an immediate connection remain. That the Chronicler has used these prophetic forms to express his own judgment upon the events to which he refers does not alter this fact, but rather points to its significance for the writer. On the other hand, it cannot be denied that the prophetic oracle and the homiletical interpretation are increasingly flowing into each other.

The Chronicler repeatedly includes emphases, concerns, and interpretations within sermons and prayers found in other parts of Chronicles. His interest in the cult and the Levites is well known, yet astonishingly, this concern finds expression only in the edicts and speeches of the king and never of the prophet. The doctrine of retribution forms the major message of the prophets introduced by the Chronicler (and of King Solomon in 1 Chr 28:9) and is the primary concern according to which he has ordered his post–Solomonic history. Obviously, if he used sources for such material, he was in complete agreement with those sources. On the other hand, the simplest explanation is that the Chronicler himself is completely responsible for the contents of these speeches, edicts, and prayers, and has used them to give prophetic, royal, and ultimately divine authority to institutions and conceptions dear to his own heart.

PURPOSE AND DATE

Bibliography

Botterweck, G. J. "Zur Eigenart der chronistischen Davidgeschichte." *TQ* 136 (1956) 402–35. **Braun, R. L.** "A Reconsideration of the Chronicler's Attitude Toward the North." *JBL* 96 (1977) 59–62. **Coggins, R. J.** *Samaritans and Jews: The Origins of Samaritanism Reconsidered.* Atlanta: John Knox, 1975. **Eissfeldt, O.** *The Old Testament, An Introduction.* Tr. P. Ackroyd. New York: Harper and Row, 1965. **Freedman, D. N.** "The

Chronicler's Purpose." *CBQ* 23 (1961) 436–42. **Newsome, J. D.** "Toward a New Under-standing of the Chronicler and His Purposes." *JBL* 94 (1975) 210–17. **Noordtzij, A.** "Les Intentions du Chroniste." *RB* 39 (1940) 161–68. **Noth, M.** *Überlieferungsge-schichtliche Studien. Die sammelnden und bearbeitenden Geschichtswerke im Alten Testament.* Tü-bingen: Niemeyer, 1943. **Payne, D. F.** "The Purpose and Methods of the Chronicler." *Faith and Thought* 93 (1963) 64–73. **Stinespring, W. F.** "Eschatology in Chronicles." *JBL* 80 (1961) 209–19. **Waltke, B. K.** "The Samaritan Pentateuch and the Text of the Old Testament." *New Perspectives on the Old Testament.* Ed. J. B. Payne. London: Word Books, 1970. 212–39. **Welten, P.** *Geschichte und Geschichtsdarstellung in den Chronik-büchern.* WMANT 42. Neukirchen: Neukirchener Verlag, 1973. **Wilda, G.** *Das Königsbild des chronistischen Geschichtswerkes.* Bonn: Rheinische Friedrich-Wilhelms-Universität, 1959. **Williamson, H. G. M.** "Eschatology in Chronicles." *TynBul* 28 (1977) 115–54.

During the reigns of David and Solomon, the author has spoken repeatedly of the immediate and unanimous assent given by all Israel to the reigns of these kings and to their efforts on behalf of the cult. Following the dissolution of the monarchy, we have seen that the Chronicler does not cease to be concerned with the north, but admonishes them for rejecting the Jerusalem temple, exhorts them to return to it in repentance, and invites them to partici-pate in its ceremonies. With the possible exception of 2 Chr 13, the writer is not at all negative in his appraisal of the north and does not hesitate to report the favorable response of a portion of the northern tribes. It is probably significant that it was in the reign of Hezekiah, the first pious king of Judah after the fall of the north, that the most extensive consideration of the question of the north is presented. Even in the face of the writer's generally favorable reaction to the north, he insisted that recognition of and return to the Jerusa-lem temple was essential (2 Chr 13:5–11, 30:8).

With such a view of the importance of the Jerusalem temple, the reason for the emphasis upon David and Solomon and the erection of the temple becomes apparent. It is these two kings who ruled over the united kingdom of Israel and Judah, and who commanded the allegiance—as the Chronicler has repeatedly reminded us—of both north and south. The temple at Jerusa-lem is the common sanctuary of a united Israel, constructed by its anointed kings with the concurrence of all Israel and dedicated and frequented by both north and south. The connection between Israel's political and religious unity may also explain the emphasis placed upon Hezekiah's invitation to the north to return to the legitimate temple—an invitation following only shortly the end of the north as a political entity—and the elaborate descriptions of the festivities surrounding the rededication of the temple and the participa-tion of all Israel in the passover which followed. Israel was once again a unity, as it had been in the days of David and Solomon.

However, it was not sufficient for the Chronicler to demonstrate that the Jerusalem temple had been the original sanctuary of both north and south. He is at pains also to show that its unique position was the result not merely of political alliances but of the divine decree, and each phase of the temple construction—from the choice of the temple site through the temple builder, the plans, the transfer of the ark and the final ceremonies of dedication—was marked by the divine choice and/or approval. This emphasis probably provides the major reason for the great emphasis upon Solomon's election as temple builder. It may be assumed that when turmoil arose between north and south over the claims of the Jerusalem temple, Solomon's participation in the venture would be a major source of embarrassment to those advocating its supremacy. Upon what authority did he build, and how was the Jerusalem location determined? Was it not this same Solomon who had himself built other cult sites, and had not Solomon been rejected by Yahweh himself and been made to bear the brunt of the responsibility for the divisions within Israel? The Chronicler, however, has effectively removed these objections both by pointing to Solomon's divine choice and by remaining judiciously silent concerning his later apostasy.

Therefore the added emphasis upon Solomon serves both as a means of emphasizing the unity of Israel and as a guard against placing the unique role of the Jerusalem temple in jeopardy. But to say this means that undue emphasis should not be placed on David, Solomon, or the Davidic dynasty apart from their role in the construction of the temple. The emphasis upon the dynasty is minimal throughout the work, and the concluding chapters of Chronicles give us little if any reason to assume that the author looked forward to the reestablishment of that dynasty in any sense. If the original work of the Chronicler ended with 2 Chr 36:21, there is even less reason to suppose that he expected the restoration of the dynasty than is the case at the end of 2 Kings. If his original account included the account of Zerubbabel's rebuilding of the temple, as assumed by Freedman, it is still remarkable that no emphasis is placed upon Zerubbabel's Davidic lineage (cf. 1 Chr 3:17–19). If all of Ezra and Nehemiah be from the hand of the same writer as Chronicles, the situation becomes still more problematic, since the activities of Ezra and Nehemiah leave little room for a Davidic hope of any kind.

David, Solomon, and all Israel had built a temple where the name of Yahweh might dwell (1 Chr 22:7) and to which Israel might pray (2 Chr 6:20). But beyond that the temple was for the Chronicler a "house of rest for the ark of the covenant of Yahweh" (1 Chr 28:2; 2 Chr 6:41) and a house of sacrifice (2 Chr 2:3 [4]; 7:12), and most of all it was the place where all Israel performed its joyous ministry to Yahweh (2 Chr 5:12–13; 7:6; 8:14). By the time of the author, the Davidic dynasty appears to have disappeared from the scene. However, the other great institution of Israel, the temple, remained and in it the work of the Davidic dynasty was embodied. As the Sinaitic covenant needed to be reinterpreted to provide a place for the Davidic covenant, so the Davidic covenant was now to be understood in terms of the temple which it had left as a legacy for all Israel. While it is unprofitable to argue whether this should or should not be considered an eschatological hope, it amounted to a reinterpretation of the David-Jerusalem tradition in theological rather than political terms, as correctly seen by Welch, Rudolph, and Ackroyd, among others. Attempts to find a full-blown messianic eschatology in Chronicles, seen in such scholars as von Rad, Noordtzij, Stinespring, and Mosis, cannot in my opinion be sustained.

The Chronicler's emphasis upon retribution and the need for joy and generosity in the service of Yahweh provides us with little additional information concerning the precise period in which he wrote, but it may illuminate somewhat the audience to which he spoke. The Chronicler shows no hesitation in accepting the general applicability of the doctrine. It would appear that the Chronicler would have denied the allegation that wickedness may befall the righteous, although conversely he may believe that through God's grace the wicked are not always punished to the degree justified. It is impossible to determine, however, whether the concern for theodicy, so prominent in the later wisdom writings, was written in protest to views such as those expressed by the Chronicler, or whether the Chronicler himself might not be entering into a frontal attack upon some who did not see God's hand working so immediately in history.

A similar ambiguity exists in regard to the joy and generosity which the Chronicler seeks from his readers. The constant and recurring emphasis upon the joy accompanying the cultic celebrations and the emphasis upon the generosity which is necessary in support of the cult pictures an age in which religious enthusiasm was at a low point. While we are immediately tempted to think of the situation reflected in such prophets as Haggai and Malachi, our meager knowledge of the following three centuries suggests that there were probably few periods when the exhortation would have been less relevant.

We may conclude then that the author was interested above all in presenting the Jerusalem temple as the only legitimate temple of Yahweh. While it is impossible to date his message with precision, it may, contrary to current consensus, best be placed *prior to* the time when tensions between Judah and her neighbors, especially the Samaritans, became severe and hardened into intransigence. This statement, however, becomes less than helpful for determining the date of the work, since it has become apparent that this happened much later than assumed before (cf. Waltke, *New Perspectives on the OT*, 219–39; Coggins, *Samaritans and Jews*; Braun, *JBL* 96 [1977] 59–62). Chronicles is concerned to present the temple as the common property of both north and south. At the same time that the north is invited to return to it, the south is urged to commit itself wholeheartedly to participation in its cult, to the support of its services, and to experience the joy resulting from it. These exhortations are reinforced with countless examples from Judah's past and supported with the promise of rewards for faithfully seeking Yahweh and the threat of punishment for forsaking him.

Arguments for dating Chronicles have thus far been inconclusive, varying widely from the early Persian period to as late as the Maccabees. Williamson has argued that the daric was a Persian coin first minted at the earliest in 515 B.C. (*TynBul* 28 [1977] 123–26), and fragments of Chronicles have been said to have been found among the Qumran manuscripts, (cf. Myers, lxxxvii) thus establishing the extremes within which the work is to be dated.

Welten (*Geschichte*) has supported a date about 300–250 B.C., but his major argument probably results from a misreading of 2 Chr 26:15. Polzin's study (*Late Biblical Hebrew*) of linguistic data concludes that Chronicles and the Ezra Memoir are linguistically similar, which would appear to favor a date shortly before 400 B.C., but his methodology and conclusions are insufficiently critical when dealing with the data of Chronicles. Most recently Williamson (15–16) has opted for a date of about 350 B.C., but accepted the authenticity of many passages more commonly considered later additions.

In general, it may be said that while any date from about 515–250 B.C. is possible, the separation of Chronicles from Ezra–Nehemiah at a minimum permits an earlier dating for Chronicles than would otherwise be the case. While certainty is impossible, it is at least interesting to consider a date nearer the rebuilding of the temple as the occasion for the initial stratum of Chronicles, i.e., about 515 B.C. This initial edition would then have been expanded and updated somewhat in the manner proposed by Cross, reaching its final form about 350–300 B.C.

THEOLOGICAL THEMES

THE TEMPLE

Bibliography

Ackroyd, P. R. "The Theology of the Chronicles." *Lexington Theological Quarterly* 8 (1973) 101–16. **Braun, R. L.** "Solomon, the Chosen Temple Builder: The Significance of I Chronicles 22, 28, and 29 for the Theology of Chronicles." *JBL* 95 (1976) 581–90. ————. "The Message of Chronicles: Rally 'Round the Temple.'" *CTM* 42 (1971) 502–14. **Clements, R. E.** *God and Temple.* Oxford: Blackwell, 1965. **Davies, G. H.** "Ark of the Covenant." *IDB* 1:222–26. ————. "Tabernacle." *IDB* 4:498–506. **Galling, K.** "Könige und nichtkönige Stifter beim Tempel von Jerusalem." *Beiträge zur Biblischen Landes und Altertumskunde* 68 (1951) 134. **Haran, M.** *Temples and Temple Service in Ancient Israel.* Oxford: Clarendon Press, 1978. **Herbert, A. S.** *Worship in Ancient Israel.* Richmond: John Knox, 1959. **North, R.** "Theology of the Chronicler." *JBL* 82 (1963) 519–24. **Rad, G. von.** "The Tent and the Ark." *The Problem of the Hexateuch and Other Essays.* Tr. E. W. T. Dicken. New York: McGraw-Hill, 1966. 103–24. **Rowley, H. H.** "From the Exodus to the Founding of the Temple." *Worship in Ancient Israel.* Philadelphia: Fortress, 1967. 37–70. ————. "The Temple and Its Place in Worship." *Worship in Ancient Israel.* Philadelphia: Fortress, 1967. 71–100. **Weiser, A.** "Die Tempelbaukrise unter David." *ZAW* 72 (1965) 153–68. **Wright, G. E.** "Cult and History." *Int* 16 (1962) 3–20.

The position of the temple is central in 1 Chronicles (as well as 2 Chronicles and Ezra-Nehemiah). Leaving aside 1 Chr 1–9 as a probable later addition to the work, the relationship of each unit of 1 Chronicles to the temple is clear, except for chaps. 10–12, 18–20, where it may be reasonably argued that David's rise is told in prospect of his relationship to the ark and temple. The first event narrated after David's anointing in Hebron (1 Chr 11:1–3) is the capture of Jerusalem, which is destined to be the site of the temple. Then David's supporters (chaps. 11–12) are immediately assembled to bring the ark to Jerusalem (chap. 13). After chap. 14, which points to David's prosperity, the theme of the ark is resumed in chaps. 15–16. (Later additions in these chapters related chiefly to the priests and Levites really serve only to emphasize the point.) With chap. 17, the emphasis upon the temple and the role of David and Solomon in its construction is even more central. Chaps. 18–20 form something of an interlude, but even here the account of David's wars, borrowed largely from 1–2 Samuel, is related to the construction of the temple (cf. 1 Chr 18:8). The account of David's census, resulting in the purchase of the site of the temple (1 Chr 21), is included because it underlies the site of the temple (cf. 22:1). The totality of chaps. 22, 28, and 29 narrates David's preparations and prayers for the building of the temple and the delegation of the final task to Solomon.

In the account of Solomon's reign, the Chronicler has moved immediately to the subject of the temple (cf. 2 Chr 1:18 [2:1]) and has devoted no less than seven chapters to that subject, revising his *Vorlage* extensively to concentrate more clearly upon it. While the focus admittedly changes in 2 Chr 10–36, here too the temple remains central. The programmatic speech in 2 Chr 13 of Abijah (he and Solomon are the only kings whose evaluation is radically altered by the Chronicler) emphasizes the revolt of the north against the Davidic dynasty but retains the central position of the temple and its cult (cf. 2 Chr 13:8–12). Otherwise the writer retains in general the methods and evaluations of his Kings *Vorlage,* which is itself based on the relationship of the various kings to the temple. But the Chronicler has typically carried through with greater thoroughness the pattern adopted from his source. While the writer of Kings gave limited approval to Asa, Jehoshaphat, and Joash but reserved removal of the high places for Hezekiah and Josiah alone, the Chronicler has attributed cultic reforms to all of these, including in his narrative some indications of their favorable attitude toward the cult. This concern for the temple and its cult reaches its climax in his account of Hezekiah, where the Chronicler has greatly expanded his Kings *Vorlage.* Chronicles dedicates three chapters to the cultic concerns of Hezekiah, which must mark the high point of his narrative of the post-Solomonic kings. Included here too, it should be noted, is an important statement concerning the role of the temple in determining Judah's prosperity (2 Chr 29:3–11), the cleansing of the temple and the ceremony following it (29:12–36), the great Passover with its invitation to the north to "come to Yahweh's sanctuary which he has sanctified for ever" (30:8) and the reforms arising from it (31:1); and the reordering of the Levites and the contributions of the people in their behalf (31:2–19). The celebration of the passover is concluded with the significant statement that "since the time of Solomon the son of David, king of Israel, there had been nothing like this in Israel" (30:26), a statement obviously recalling the fourteen-day celebration which concluded the dedication of the temple according to the Chronicler's alteration in 7:9. The conclusion of Hezekiah's reign is likewise marked with a statement significant not only for the many aspects of the Chronicler's thought which it reveals, but also for the specific reference to the temple: "And every work that he undertook in the service of the house of God and in accordance with the law and the commandments, seeking his God, he did with all his heart, and prospered" (2 Chr 31:21, RSV).

In passing, it should be noted that the temple and its cult are frequently mentioned with those kings whom the Chronicler evaluates as wicked (cf. 2 Chr 21:11; 25:24; 26:16; 28:24). Concern for the temple also dominates the final chapter of 2 Chronicles. Upon each of Nebuchadnezzar's three invasions of the land, note is taken of the disposition of the temple vessels. The final verses concerning the destruction of Jerusalem mention again both the burning of the temple and the destruction of its vessels (2 Chr 36:19), the latter being considered the final result of the people's disobedience to the prophetic voice. The proclamation of Cyrus (2 Chr 36:22–23 = Ezra 1:1–3), whether original with the Chronicler or appended here by another, correctly sustains this emphasis: above all, it is God's charge to this Persian king to build him a temple in Jerusalem that lies at the heart of his decision to permit the people to return to their land. Despite numerous difficulties, the text of Ezra 1–6 concludes with the dedication of the rebuilt temple (Ezra 6:15–18), told in terms highly reminiscent of the great cultic ceremonies in Chronicles.

PRIESTS AND LEVITES

Bibliography

Bartlett, J. R. "Zadok and His Successors at Jerusalem." *JTS* 19 (1968) 1–18. **Begrich, J.** "Das Priesterliche Heilsorakel." *Gesammelte Studien zum Alten Testament.* Munich: Chr. Kaiser Verlag, 1964. **Cross, F. M. Jr.** "The Priestly Tabernacle." *BAR* I. Chicago: Quadrangle Books, 1961. **Emerton, J. A.** "Priests and Levites in Deuteronomy." *VT* 12 (1962) 129–38. **Gese, H.** "Zur Geschichte der Kultsänger am zweiten Tempel." *Abraham unser Vater. Festschrift Otto Michel.* Ed. O. Betz, et al. Leiden: E. J. Brill, 1963. **Haran, M.** "Shiloh and Jerusalem: The Origin of the Priestly Tradition in the Pentateuch." *JBL* 81 (1962) 14–24. ———. *Temples and Temple Service in Ancient Israel.* Oxford: Clarendon Press, 1978. **Mohlenbrink, K.** "Die levitischen Überlieferungen des Alten Testaments." *ZAW* 52 (1931) 115–16. **Rad, G. von.** *Die Priesterschrift im Hexateuch.* Stuttgart: W. Kohlhammer, 1934. **Vink, J. G.** "The Date and Origin of the Priestly Code in the Old Testament." *Oudtestamentische Studien.* Vol. 5. Ed. P. A. H. DeBoer. Leiden: E. J. Brill, 1969. **Zeron, A.** "Priestly Messianism in the Old Testament." *Angelicum* 42 (1965) 318–41.

It is common to point to the material in 1 and 2 Chronicles concerning the priests, and especially the Levites and the Levitical choir, as indications of the Chronicler's great concern, and to place the author of Chronicles among the Levitical choristers. Such an emphasis, however, appears overstated. The studies of Noth and Rudolph have concluded that large portions of the materials included here are to be attributed to a later revisor (chiefly 1 Chr 1–9, 23–27, and larger parts of 1 Chr 15–16). Despite the reservations and contrary conclusions of Williamson, their suggestions seem well founded. Within these chapters differing strata reflecting different ages are apparent.

In his comprehensive study, H. Gese (*Abraham unser Vater*) has pointed to several stages in the evolution of the Levites. (1) After the return from exile, the singers are simply called "sons of Asaph" and are not yet reckoned as Levites. (Cf. Ezra 2:41 = Neh 7:44.) (2) At Nehemiah's time, the singers are reckoned as Levites and divided into two groups, the sons of Asaph and the sons of Jeduthun. (Cf. Neh 11:3–19; 1 Chr 9:1–18.) (3a) The Levitical singers are in three groups, Asaph, Heman, and Jeduthun. (Cf. 1 Chr 16:37–42; 2 Chr 5:12; 29:13–14; 35:15.) (3b) Three groups remain, but Jeduthun has been replaced by Ethan and Heman has become more prominent than Asaph. (Cf. 1 Chr 6:31–48; 15:16–21.)

While there has been general acceptance of these stages, there is no agreement upon the dates of groups 3a and 3b. Gese himself assigned stage 3a to the Chronicler (hence dating him post-Nehemiah), and 3b to a subsequent stage. Williamson, seeking to preserve a greater part of the text for the Chronicler, argues that the Chronicler stood at stage 3b and incorporated older strata into his work. Again, certainty is impossible, although my inclination is that additions to the text in this regard are more rather than less numerous. In addition, as Williamson himself notes, the hand of a "priestly revisor" is frequently detectable, interested in preserving priestly genealogies and prerogatives against intrusion by the Levites. Such additions in the case of both the Levites and priests, it should be noted, normally affect only the volume of the text, expanding themes and emphases already present. As such it is almost always difficult to state categorically whether they stem from the hand of the original writer, who may have had at his disposal a variety of sources, or were added by a later one.

DAVID AND SOLOMON

Bibliography

Amsler, S. *David, Roi et Messie. La Tradition davidique dans l'AT.* Neuchatel: Delachaux, 1963. **Bach, R.** "David." *RGG* 2. Ed. K. Galling. 3rd ed. Tübingen: Mohr, 1958. 47–48. **Barnes, W. E.** "David of the Book of Samuel and the David of the Book of Chronicles." *Expositor* 37 (1909) 49–59. **Blenkinsopp, J.** *The Promise to David: Where We Stand.* Glen Rock, NJ: Paulist Press, 1964. **Botterweck, G. J.** "Zur Eigenart der Chronistischen Davidsgeschichte." *TQ* 136 (1956) 402–35. **Braun, R. L.** "The Significance of I Chronicles 22, 28, and 29 for the Structure and Theology of the Chronicler." Diss.: Concordia Seminary, St. Louis, 1971. ———. "Solomonic Apologetic in Chronicles." *JBL* 92 (1973) 503–16. **Brueggemann, W.** "David and His Theologian." *CBQ* 30 (1968) 156–81. **Carlson, R. A.** *David, the Chosen King. A Traditio-historical Approach to the Second Book of Samuel.* Tr. E. J. Sharpe and S. Rudman. Stockholm: Almquist & Wiksell, 1964. **Clements, R. E.** *Abraham and David. Genesis 15 and Its Meaning for Israelite Tradition.* SBT 2/5. Naperville, IL: A. R. Allenson, 1967. **Danielou, J.** "David." *RAC* 3. Ed. T. Klauser. Stuttgart: Anton Hiersemann, 1957. **Delekat, L.** "Tendenz und Theologie der David-Salomo Erzälung." *Festschrift L. Rost.* Ed. F. Maass. Berlin: Topelmann, 1967. **Dillard, R. B.** "The Chronicler's Solomon." *WTJ* 43 (1980) 289–300. ———. "The Literary Structure of the Chronicler's Solomon Narrative." *JSOT* 30 (1984) 85–93. **Elliger, L.** "Die dreissig Helden Davids." *PJ* 31 (1935) 29–75. **Grintz, J. M.** "The Life of David in Samuel and Chronicles." *BMik* 1 (1956) 69–75 (Heb.). **Kapelrud, A. S.** "König David and die Söhne des Saul." *ZAW* 67 (1955) 198–205. **Leach, E.** "The Legitimacy of Solomon. Some Structural Aspects of Old Testament Theology." *Archives européen de Sociologie* 7 (1966). **Liver, J.** "Book of the Acts of Solomon (I Kings 11)." *Bib* 48 (1967) 75–101. **Mazar, B.** "Daniel's Reign in Hebron and the Conquest of Jerusalem." *In the Time of Harvest. Essays in Honor of Abba Hillel Silver on the Occasion of His 70th Birthday.* New York: Macmillan, 1963. 235–44. ———. "The Military Elite of King David." *VT* 13 (1963) 310–20. **O'Ceallaigh, G. C.** "And So David Did to All the Cities of Ammon (2 Sam. 12:31)." *VT* 12 (1962) 179–89. **Phillips, A.** "David's Linen Ephod." *VT* 19 (1969) 485–87. **Porten, B.** "The Structure and Theme of the Solomonic Narrative." *HUCA* 38 (1967) 93–128. **Rad, G. von.** *Das Geschichtsbild des Chronistischen Werkes.* Stuttgart: Kohlhammer, 1930. **Rost,**

L. *Die Überlieferung von der Thronnachfolge Davids.* Stuttgart: Kohlhammer, 1926. **Thornton, T. C. G.** "Solomonic Apologetic in Samuel and Kings." *CQR* 169 (1968) 159–66. **Weiser, A.** "Die Legitimation des Königs David; zur Eigenart und Entstehung der sogenannten Geschichte von Davids Aufstieg." *VT* 16 (1966) 325–54. **Williamson, H. G. M.** "The Accession of Solomon in the Books of Chronicles." *VT* 26 (1976) 351–61. ———. " 'We are yours, O David': the Setting and Purpose of I Chronicles xii 1–23." *OTS* 21 (1981) 164–76. **Zeron, A.** "Tag für Tag, kam Mann zu David, um ihm zu helfen." *TZ* 30 (1974) 257–61.

The Chronicler's concentration upon David has long been recognized, and hardly needs to be restated here. Von Rad's classic monograph, *Das Geschichtsbild des Chronistischen Werkes,* is arranged under the themes of David and the ark, David and the cult personnel, David and the temple, David and the cult, and David and Israel.

There is no denying that an unusually large proportion of the Chronicler's work seems to concern itself with David. The Chronicler has viewed David as the originator of the musical instruments of the cult, a contributor to the lyrics of some of the chants and the one responsible for those Levitical groups concerned with music in the temple. It is probable that the Chronicler has also viewed David as responsible for the remaining Levitical divisions, although the precise nature of his activity here is more difficult to evaluate. Moreover, significant passages from Samuel-Kings which might be considered unfavorable to David, such as the details of his outlaw days, his adultery with Bathsheba and the ensuing murder of Uriah, and the physical weakness of his latter days, are absent in Chronicles, resulting in an idealized account which appears to be further enhanced by the writer in various ways (cf. 1 Chr 12:39–41 [38–40]). As a result, David's role has often been highlighted to the virtual exclusion of all other kings of Judah, and his role in considering the goal of the Chronicler's history and Israel's eschatological hopes has been strongly emphasized.

While there is some truth to this picture, it should be noted that the Chronicler does not present to us a blameless David. His responsibility for the abortive census, for example, is magnified in Chronicles (1 Chr 21). Above all, his rejection as the temple builder is specifically charged to the fact that he has shed much blood (1 Chr 22:8) and is a man of war (28:3).

In the picture of Solomon, however, the Chronicler diverges to an even greater extent from his Deuteronomistic *Vorlage.* In Samuel-Kings, Solomon is apparently viewed as the chosen successor of David (cf. 1 Kgs 5), but his rise to power is nevertheless viewed as the result of power plays, court intrigue, and Bathsheba's personal influence upon David (1 Kgs 1). In Kings, the major part of Solomon's activity is centered upon the construction of the temple (1 Kgs 6–8). However, the final evaluation of Solomon's reign is not based on this relationship to the temple, but on his syncretistic worship practices. While Solomon's frequenting of the high places prior to the erection of the temple seems to be largely condoned by the writer (1 Kgs 3:2), the same cannot be said for the report of 1 Kgs 11. There Solomon's marriage with foreign women is explicitly condemned; twice it is stated that his heart was not wholly true to the Lord (vv 4, 6); and the high places built for his foreign wives are clearly considered idolatrous (v 8). Moreover, there is common agreement that the present wording of Deut 17:16–17 has particular reference to Solomon (cf. 1 Kgs 10:23–29), so that Solomon has in fact become the primary example of the evil of kingship. Consequently, Yahweh is angry with Solomon (1 Kgs 11:9), and the result is the division of the kingdom. Whereas earlier portions of the book mention only items reflecting Solomon's prosperity, the remainder of the chapter now speaks of "adversaries" whom God raised up against Solomon (vv 14–25). The customary notice of Solomon's death is given in 1 Kgs 11:41–43, and nothing favorable is reported concerning him in the remainder of Kings. Particular attention is given to the fact that Josiah, whose reforming activity is the center of the Deuteronomic history, broke down the high places that Solomon had made, thus finally abolishing the practice instituted by Solomon centuries before.

Chronicles presents Solomon's rise to the throne in a completely different light. Here the divine designation of Solomon as *the* son to whom the promises of 2 Sam 7 had reference stands in vivid contrast to 1 Kgs 1 and 2 (cf. 1 Chr 22:9–10; 28:6, 7, 10). Moreover, Israel's acceptance of Solomon as her legitimate king is represented by 1 Chr 29:22–25 as instantaneous and unanimous. In contrast to the palace intrigue of 1 Kgs 1 and 2, *all Israel* was immediately obedient to him—the princes, the warriors, and even the king's sons. Even before Solomon's reign began, Chronicles reported: "he (Solomon) prospered . . . Yahweh made him great . . . and gave to him royal honor such as no king had had before him" (1 Chr 29:23, 25). A view of Solomon's rise more divergent from that of Kings can hardly be imagined!

The Chronicler's concern for Solomon's role in the construction of the temple is apparent in numerous ways that cannot be detailed here. Suffice it to say that, in contrast to his usual method of dealing with his *Vorlage*, his account of Solomon's reign amounts to a virtual rewriting of that history (cf. Braun, "Significance," 131–36). For him, the account of Sheba's visit becomes the final account of Solomon's prosperous career, which he has climaxed with the statement previously omitted from 1 Kgs 10:1: "he (Solomon) ruled over all the kings from the Euphrates to the land of the Philistines and to the border of Egypt" (2 Chr 9:26).

The final evaluation of Solomon given in Chronicles is consistent with this favorable picture. No indication is given that any part of Solomon's reign was characterized by anything other than complete obedience and service to Yahweh. The condescending tone of 1 Kgs 3:2–3 is completely lacking in 2 Chr 1:3–6, which instead pictures Solomon as the enthusiastic leader of all Israel engaged in proper worship before the legitimate tent and altar at Gibeon. But most significantly, the entire thrust of 1 Kgs 11, which condemned Solomon for the high places built for his wives, declared that "his heart was not wholly true to the Lord as was the heart of David his father" (1 Kgs 11:4), and therefore pronounced the impending disruption of the kingdom and the consequent retention of only a single tribe for David's house, has disappeared. The end of Solomon's reign, like its beginning, is marked with prosperity and world-wide recognition of his wisdom (2 Chr 9). Like David, he completes a full reign of forty years (2 Chr 9:30 = 1 Kgs 11:42). (See further Braun, *JBL* 92 [1973] 503–16; Williamson, *VT* 26 [1976] 351–61.)

We are led to conclude that the Chronicler has dealt in a very similar fashion with David and Solomon, and has in fact pictured their reigns in an essentially parallel and complementary way. Both kings occupy the throne by divine choice, and in both cases this rule receives the immediate and unanimous support of its subjects. Both kings immediately express their concern for temple and cult, and through their combined activities the temple is erected and dedicated. Both kings end lengthy reigns of forty years as they had begun them, in complete loyalty and devotion to Yahweh.

Numerous examples of this paralleling of David and Solomon may be found (cf. 1 Chr 22:12 and 2 Chr 1:10; 1 Chr 29:12 and 2 Chr 1:11–12; 1 Chr 22:3–4 and 2 Chr 2:1–2, etc.; see further Braun, "Significance," 139–42). In three cases, the Chronicler has stated this parallel explicitly. First, 1 Kgs 8:66 marks the departure of the worshipers following the dedication of the temple with the phrase that they returned to their homes "joyful and glad of heart for all the goodness that the Lord had shown to David his servant and to Israel his people." The Chronicler has altered the passage to read "for the goodness that the Lord had shown to David *and to Solomon* and to Israel his people" (2 Chr 7:10). In the second case, the first part of the reign of Rehoboam is summarized by the Chronicler as an age of faithfulness, in which Judah "walked for three years in the way of David and Solomon" (2 Chr 11:17). This viewpoint would have been inconceivable from the point of view of the Deuteronomistic writer. Finally, the Chronicler also views Solomon's activity as parallel to that of David in relationship to the Levites. Josiah instructs the Levites in connection with his passover to prepare themselves "following the directions of David king of Israel and the directions of Solomon his son" (2 Chr 35:4, cf. Neh 12:45). In view of such passages, it is difficult to assume that the writer of Neh 13:26, which faults Solomon for his marriage to foreign wives, is to be identified with the Chronicler.

It will be noted in our outline of 1 Chronicles that, in line with the above analysis of the roles of David and Solomon, chaps. 22 (23–27), 28, 29 have been considered, as a transitional unit further uniting the reigns of David and Solomon. While these chapters have normally been included within the "Davidic History" portion of the work, they deal equally with Solomon and have been used by the author to join the reigns of the two most prominent figures in his work, David and Solomon, into a unity centered in the construction of the temple. Nowhere else in the OT, it may be noted, have the final words of a father to a son or a ruler to his successor been recounted in such detail.

ALL ISRAEL

Bibliography

Braun, R. L. "A Reconsideration of the Chronicler's Attitude Toward the North." *JBL* 96 (1977) 59–62. **Mettinger, T.** *Solomonic State Officials. A Study of the Civil Government Officials of the Israelite Monarchy.* ConB. OT Series 5. Lund: Gleerup, 1971. **Schofield, J. N.** " 'All Israel' in the Deuteronomic Writers." *Essays and Studies Presented to Stanley Arthur Cook.* Ed. D. W. Thomas. London: Foreign Press, 1950. 25–34. **Vriezen,**

T. C. *The Religion of Ancient Israel*. Philadelphia: Westminster Press, 1967. **Williamson, H. G. M.** *Israel in the Books of Chronicles*. New York: Cambridge University Press, 1977.

The Chronicler is at great pains to demonstrate the enthusiastic and unanimous participation of "all Israel" in the activities surrounding the kingship of both David and Solomon, as well as in significant cultic events such as the transfer of the ark and the construction of the temple. Building once again upon his Deuteronomistic source, the Chronicler depicts David's assembling of all Israel in Hebron (1 Chr 11:1 = 2 Sam 5:1). Then David and all Israel proceed to Jerusalem to take the city (1 Chr 11:4 = 2 Sam 5:6; cf. 1 Chr 13:5–6 = 2 Sam 6:1–2). But Chronicles has once again pursued this theme to much greater lengths than has the writer's *Vorlage*. (Cf. 1 Chr 13:5–6 with 2 Sam 6:1–2.) The all-Israel theme quite probably lies at the base of the various lists of chaps. 11–12, cf. 11:10 and again 12:39–41 [38–40], where the participation of all Israel is joyously affirmed. All Israel is also involved in the various stages of the transferal of the ark to Jerusalem (cf. 13:1–4, 5–6; 15:3; 16:3). All of Israel's officials are present for David's speech to Solomon (1 Chr 28), and once again the presence of "all Israel" and their unanimous support of the kingship of Solomon is the explicit theme of 1 Chr 29:22–26. The Chronicler has fittingly noted the presence of all Israel at the dedication of Solomon's temple in 2 Chr 7:8, as had Kings before him (1 Kgs 8:55).

This same emphasis is carried through with necessary modification also in the Chronicler's description of the post-Solomonic period. Like the Deuteronomistic historian, the Chronicler has Rehoboam appear before all Israel at Shechem to be made king (2 Chr 10:1 = 1 Kgs 12:1). After the disruption, there is considerable divergence in the use of the term *Israel*, with "all Israel" used both for the northern tribes (cf. 2 Chr 13:4, 5, 15, 18) and at least portions of the south (2 Chr 24:5–6). A full discussion of this problem lies beyond the scope of this commentary (see most recently Williamson, *Israel in the Books of Chronicles*). Here it must suffice to note that throughout 1 Chr 10–2 Chr 36, the Chronicler pictures various southern kings as active in the north, both in warfare and in religious activities (2 Chr 13:19; 15:8; 17:2; 31:1; 34:6). Also, the participation of Israelites from the north in the worship at Jerusalem is noted (2 Chr 11:16; 15:9–10; 30:11, 18, 21, 25 [where the common translation "only a few came . . ." is erroneous, and should be "however, some men . . . repented"]).

The conclusion of this Passover narrative indicates the programmatic significance of the event for the Chronicler's theology. Israel and Judah were again reunited in a common worship, as they had been in the days of David and Solomon (2 Chr 30:25–26). The phrase "all Israel who was present" (31:1) alludes to the purification of Judah, Benjamin, Ephraim, and Manasseh, i.e., both north and south, from the pollution of idolatrous cults. Similarly, people from both north and south participate in the Passover of Josiah through their offerings (2 Chr 34:9), and the king's request to Hilkiah in Chronicles adds Israel to Judah to those for whom Hilkiah is to inquire of the Lord (2 Chr 34:21; cf. 2 Kgs 22:13). Such passages indicate that the writer has certainly not excluded the north from his purview, but has instead taken pains to show their regular participation in the Jerusalem cult. (See further Braun, *JBL* 96 [1977] 59–62.) In three particular passages the Chronicler deals more extensively with the problem of the north and the south, dynasty and temple. 2 Chr 13 affirms Yahweh's selection of the Davidic dynasty and the Jerusalem temple, which however the north had rejected. 2 Chr 28:8–15 recognizes both the presence of true prophets of Yahweh in the north and pictures a faithful and generous response by some "good Samaritans" in returning their Judahite brothers to their relatives in Jericho. Finally, the letter of Hezekiah in 2 Chr 30:6–9 recognizes that Yahweh's grace is available also to those of the north who will repent and turn to him, although again it is apparent that this "repentance" included a recognition of and return to the Jerusalem temple.

In this sense then, it is incorrect to say that the Chronicler was not interested in the north following its fall, or that the separation between north and south was viewed as either desirable or permanent. Rather the repeated thrust is that north and south, "all Israel," ought to be one, but their unity was to be based on their common worship of Yahweh centered in the Jerusalem temple.

RETRIBUTION

Bibliography

Dillard, R. B. "Reward and Punishment in Chronicles: The Theology of Immediate Retribution." *WTJ* 46 (1984) 164–72. ———. "The Reign of Asa (2 Chr 14–16): An Example of the Chronicler's Theological Method." *JETS* 23 (1980) 207–18.

The dogma of retribution is enunciated clearly for the first time in 1 Chr 28:9, "if you (Solomon) seek him (God), he will be found by you; but if you forsake him, he will cast you off forever," so that it might be argued that the concept is of little importance to the Chronicler. Of special note, however, is that the doctrine as applied by the Chronicler has little relevance to the reigns of David and Solomon, so that its introduction here in any sense is very surprising. Moreover, while it is given expression here for the first time, it has been latent in such passages as 1 Chr 10:13–14; 13:14; 15:13. The centrality of retribution is evident in that in three additional cases he has repeated it in almost identical terms (2 Chr 12:5; 15:2; 24:20). While the full implications of this theme of retribution lie outside the scope of this commentary, it needs to be stated that retribution is the major, if not the sole, yardstick used in writing the history of the post-Solomonic kings.

Several examples of the Chronicler's historiography illustrate the function of retribution as a standard. The Chronicler's evaluation of Asa as a king who did that which was good and right in Yahweh's eyes is taken with only slight alteration from 1 Kgs 15:11, and both accounts relate his reforming zeal in some detail. For the Chronicler such loyalty is rewarded with a ten-year period of rest (2 Chr 13:23 [14:1]), as well as by other signs of prosperity (2 Chr 14:5–7 [6–8]). An invasion by Zerah the Ethiopian with no less than a million soldiers is easily repelled during this period by a force of only half that size, since Asa demonstrated the necessary faith in Yahweh (2 Chr 14:8–14 [9–15]). By way of explanation, the Chronicler has the prophet Azariah appear, who reiterates the principles of retribution (2 Chr 15:1–7), after which still other reforming activities of Asa are listed culminating in a covenant to "seek" (שׁרד) Yahweh in the fifteenth year of Asa's reign (2 Chr 15:8–15). However, Kings includes an account of Asa's alliance with Ben-Hadad of Syria against Baasha of Israel, although the alliance is undated and reported in a matter-of-fact way (1 Kgs 15:16–21). The Chronicler never permits such an alliance, which for him exhibits a lack of faith in and reliance upon Yahweh, to pass without condemnation. The Chronicler has the prophet Hanani appear to condemn Asa's alliance, which he dates in the thirty-sixth year of Asa's reign, predicting continuous wars for Asa as the result of this "faithlessness." The account of Asa's diseased feet (2 Chr 16:12 = 1 Kgs 15:23) in his thirty-ninth year follows, with the added statement that even when his disease was severe Asa did not "seek" Yahweh.

Three aspects of the Chronicler's handling of the Asa material are characteristic of his general methodology. (1) He has accepted the evaluation of the Deuteronomistic historian as the basis for his own, as is true in every case except Solomon and Abijah. (2) The Chronicler frequently divides the reign of a given king into two or more distinct periods depending upon his theological assessment of the data available to him from Kings. Thus the doctrine of retribution is then made applicable not only to the reign of the king as a whole, but to each detail within the reign, with the Chronicler providing whatever information is necessary to make the scheme complete. (3) In cases such as that of Asa, to whom the Chronicler is quite favorably disposed, religious zeal is normally demonstrated very early and for a prolonged period of his reign, so that the period of the king's apostasy is relegated to the final few years of his reign (cf. also Jehoshaphat, 2 Chr 17:3; Hezekiah, 2 Chr 29:3; 32:4; and Josiah, 2 Chr 34:3 [contrast 2 Kgs 22:3]).

Hence to the statement that Uzziah "did what was right in the eyes of the Lord" (2 Chr 26:4 = 2 Kgs 15:3), Chronicles adds a section which relates in some detail his initial prosperity and its cause (2 Chr 26:5–15). But in view of the statement of 2 Kings that Uzziah was smitten with leprosy, the Chronicler has included in vv 16–21 an account of Uzziah's attempt to usurp priestly prerogatives, which is then given as the cause of the disease. Examples could be multiplied from the reign of almost every one of Judah's kings. Perhaps the most striking concerns the evil Manasseh, whose reign in 2 Kgs 21:10–15 is pictured as so wicked that it called forth the destruction of Judah, a judgment which even the work of the pious Josiah could not reverse (2 Kgs 23:26). In view, apparently, of Manasseh's unprecedented reign of fifty-five years (2 Kgs 21:1), Chronicles includes an account of his repentance (2 Chr 33:12–14) and ensuing prosperity (although note the evaluation of him in v 22 is unchanged!). It is this "repentance" that becomes the source of the apocryphal Prayer of Manasseh. On the other hand, the death of the good king Josiah at the hands of Necho must be provided with a cause, as it is in 2 Chr 35:21–23, where disobedience to Necho's words are interpreted as disobedience to God himself!

There can be little doubt that the Chronicler has adopted the dogma of retribution, personal and immediate, as the framework into which the lives of the various kings are fitted, and has added, either from sources otherwise unknown to us or more probably from his own theological judgment, whatever details were necessary to make each individual fit into his scheme.

The manner in which this obedience and disobedience is portrayed and the pictures of punishment and prosperity painted to exemplify the resulting wealth or woe are most instructive for the study of 2 Chronicles but they lie beyond the scope of this commentary (cf. Braun, "The Significance," 172–81; and Welten, *Geschichte und Geschichtsdarstellung in den Chronikbüchern,* who isolates a number of the themes associated with prosperity in 2 Chronicles.) However, of the concepts introduced in 1 Chronicles, it may be noted that the theme of prosperity, denoted by the Hebrew צלח introduced in 1 Chr 22:11, 13 and attached to Solomon in 29:23, is found in 2 Chronicles without parallel in the writer's *Vorlage* for each of the kings to whom he is most favorably disposed (Solomon, 2 Chr 7:11; Asa, 14:5; Jehoshaphat, 2 Chr 20:20; Uzziah, 2 Chr 26:5; and Hezekiah, 2 Chr 31:21; 32:30). Such a selection can hardly be accidental. Similarly, the theme of rest (נוח) is applied to later periods in Judah's history to point to the peace attending a God-pleasing reign. This is most apparent in the reign of Asa, where three occurrences of נוח are clustered with one of מנוחה ("resting place") (2 Chr 14:4–7; 15:15). See also 2 Chr 20:30 (Jehoshaphat) and 2 Chr 32:22, where the writer adds to a narrative generally taken over from Kings: "Yahweh gave them rest on every side."

REPENTANCE

Lest the Chronicler's theology be denigrated, it must be noted that he too knows of a grace of God which surpasses the strict requirements of retribution and which is found through repentance. While the Chronicler's language here is often general in nature, instances such as that in 2 Chr 12:6–12 are clear in their intent. When Shishak's forces approach Jerusalem, Rehoboam and his people humble themselves, or repent (כנע, niphal, with this meaning common in Chronicles), and Yahweh announces through his prophet Shemaiah that they will not be destroyed (cf. also v 12). Instances of past repentance are cited for the people's example (2 Chr 15:4), and even the rebellious north is assured that the grace and mercy of God will not permit him to ignore those who return to him (2 Chr 30:6–9). Hezekiah's repentance prevents God's wrath from coming upon him during his lifetime (2 Chr 32:26), and even the villainous Manasseh is forgiven when he repents (2 Chr 33:12–14).

The ultimate affront to Yahweh's mercy, however, is the rejection of the message of the prophets who appear periodically to instruct and warn Israel as to the proper action to take. While this voice is sometimes obeyed, resulting in prosperity (cf. 2 Chr 12:5–6; 20:15–17; 25:7–13), it is more often rejected. In such cases Chronicles emphasizes strongly the resulting punishment, which appears impossible to avoid in these circumstances (cf. 2 Chr 16:10–12; 24:20–27; 25:15–16; 26:18–19; 36:15–16). The full results of the rejection of the prophetic message is apparent in the fall of Jerusalem, where Zedekiah is condemned for his failure to repent at the words of Jeremiah, and where the Chronicler concludes, much in the style of Jeremiah: "The Lord, the God of their fathers, sent persistently to them by his messengers, because he had compassion on his people and on his dwelling place; but they kept mocking the messengers of God, despising his words, and scoffing at his prophets, till the wrath of the Lord arose against his people, till there was no forgiveness [sic]. Therefore he brought up against them the king of the Chaldeans. . ." (2 Chr 36:15–16).

THE DISPOSITION OF THE HEART

For Chronicles it is not sufficient that Israel observe the letter of the law, i.e., bringing contributions to the temple and being present for its ceremonies. What is required is obedience with a perfect heart (1 Chr 28:9; 29:9, 17), contributions willingly given (29:1–9, 14, 17), and participation with joy (29:9, 17, 22).

These themes, found somewhat sparsely in 1 Chronicles because of the subject matter, are prominent throughout 2 Chronicles. While it is surprising that the Chronicler does not explicitly say that David or Solomon were perfect in Yahweh's service, such a statement is made of the remainder of the kings with whom the Chronicler was particularly pleased. In fact, the Chronicler uses the phrase "with a perfect heart" or "with all the heart" twenty-one times, of which only three have parallels in the Deuteronomistic history. (See 2 Chr 15:17 = 1 Kgs 15:14 [Asa]; 2 Chr 22 [Jehoshaphat]; 2 Chr 31:21 [Hezekiah]; and 2 Chr 34:31 = 2 Kgs 23:3 [Josiah].) While it is probable here that the Chronicler has been influenced by his *Vorlage*, the consistency with which he carries out his plan is characteristic.

A second feature pointing to the disposition of the people in rendering their service is found in the note of joy regularly attending her celebrations. First found in 1 Chr 12:39–41 [38–40], this note is especially present in 1 Chr 29:9, 22, where it characterizes the mood of the people in making their contributions to the temple and at the feast accompanying Solomon's coronation. Such joy is a common theme both in Deuteronomy and the Deuteronomistic history, but Chronicles employs it more constantly, using the root שׂמח ("be glad, rejoice") some fifteen times, without parallel in the Deuteronomistic history. While some of the usages reflect the mood of the Levites and singers in the temple services (1 Chr 15:16; 2 Chr 23:18; 29:30), a greater number concern the mood of other lay participants in various kinds of cultic activity (cf. 2 Chr 7:10 = 1 Kgs 8:66; 2 Chr 15:15; 24:10; 29:36; 30:21, 23, 25; see also Ezra 3:13; 6:22; Neh 8:12, 17; 12:27). Rarely does the Chronicler fail to note such joyful participation in the ceremonies of which he was apparently so fond.

A closely related emphasis is that of the generosity of the people and its leaders in supporting the monarchy and cult. This element is first found in conjunction with what might be called David's coronation (1 Chr 12:39–41 [38–40]), and is expounded at length in 1 Chr 29, probably in partial dependence upon the Tabernacle pericope. The same feature is again most characteristically present in the account of Hezekiah's reform, 2 Chr 31. The large numbers of sacrificial animals regularly given by kings and princes for major feasts and reform movements present a different side of the same emphasis, cf. 2 Chr 29:20–24, 31–35; 30:24–25; 31:4–10; 35:7–9. That such contributions are patterned somewhat after the model of Solomon as recorded in 2 Chr 7:5 (=1 Kgs 8:63) appears likely.

OUTLINE OF 1 AND 2 CHRONICLES

The following outline reflects the conclusion that the reigns of David and Solomon are presented as complementary, representing a single unit with its focus upon the temple:

I. Genealogical Prologue, chaps. 1–9
II. The United Monarchy, chaps. 10–29
  A. The David history, chaps. 10–21
    1. The death of Saul, chap. 10
    2. The rise of David, chaps. 11–12
    3. David, the Ark, and the cult, chaps. 13–17
    4. David's wars, chaps. 18–21
  B. Transitional Unit, chaps. 22–29
    1. David's first speech, chap. 22
    2. Secondary arrangements, chaps. 23–27
    3. David's speeches, blessing, and death, chaps. 28–29
  C. The Solomon history, 2 Chr 1–9
III. The Divided Monarchy, 2 Chr 10–36

ADDITIONAL BIBLIOGRAPHY
(Books and Articles Not Cited in the Introduction)

For a general bibliography on priests and Levites, see at 5:27. For a general bibliography on genealogies, see at chap. 1.

Ackroyd, P. R. "History and Theology in the Writings of the Chronicler." *CTM* 38 (1967) 501–15. ———. "The Interpretation of Exile and Restoration." *CJT* 14 (1968) 3–12. ———. *Israel under Babylon and Persia.* New Clarendon Bible 4. Oxford: Oxford Press, 1970. **Ahlström, G.** "Der Prophet Nathan und der Tempelbau." *VT* 11 (1961) 113–27. ———. "Solomon the Chosen One." *HR* 8 (1968) 93–110. **Albright, W. F.** *Archaeology and the Religion of Israel.* 5th ed. Baltimore: Johns Hopkins Press, 1968. ———. *From the Stone Age to Christianity.* Garden City: Doubleday Anchor Books, 1957. ———. "New Light on the Early Recensions of the Hebrew Bible." *BASOR* 140 (1955) 27–33. **Allrik, H. L.** "I Esdras according to Codex B and Codex A as appearing in Zerubbabel's List in I Esdras 5:8–23." *ZAW* 66 (1954) 272–90. **Amit, Y.** "The Role of Prophecy and the Prophets in the Teaching of Chronicles." *BMik* 28 (1982/83) 113–33. (Heb.) **Asmussen, Peter.** "Priesterkodex und Chronik in ihren Verhältnis zueinander." *TSK* 79 (1906) 165–79. **Baltzer, Klaus.** *Das Bundesformular.* Neukirchen: Kreis Moers, 1960. ———. "Das Ende des Staates Juda und die Messiasfrage." *Studien* zur Theologie der alttestamentlichen Überlieferungen. Ed. R. Rendtorff und K. Koch. Neukirchen: Neukirchener Verlag, 1961. 33–43. **Barag, D.** "The Effects of the Tenant's Rebellion on Palestine." *BASOR* 183 (1966) 6–12. **Barnes, W. E.** "The Religious Standpoint of the Chronicler." *AJSL* 13 (1896/97) 14–20. **Bickerman, E. J.** "The Edict of Cyrus in Ezra 1." *JBL* 65 (1946) 249–75. ———. "The Historical Foundations of Postbiblical Judaism." *From Ezra to the Last of the Maccabees.* New York: Schocken, 1962. **Bin-Nun, S. P.** "Formulas from Royal Records of Israel and Judah." *VT* 18 (1968) 414–32. **Blank, S. H.** "Some Observations Concerning Biblical Prayer." *HUCA* 32 (1961) 75–90. **Bright, John.** *A History of Israel.* 3d ed. Philadelphia: Westminster, 1981. **Brongers, H. A.** "Bemerkungen zum Gebrauch des Adverbialen W^e^{c}attāh im Alten Testament." *VT* 15 (1965) 289–99. **Brueggemann, W.** Isaiah 55 and Deuteronomic Theology." *ZAW* 80 (1968) 191–203. ———. "The Kerygma of the Deuteronomistic Historian." *Int* 22 (1968) 387–402. **Brunet, A. M.** "La Theologie du Chroniste. Theocratie et messianisme." *Sacra Pagina* 1 (1959) 384–97. **Busche, H. van den.** "Le teste de la prophétie de Nathan sur la dynastie davidique (II Samuel VII-1 Chronicles XVII)." *ETL* 24 (1948) 354–94. **Calderone, P. J.** *Dynastic Oracle and Suzerainty Treaty, 2 Samuel 7, 8–16.* Manila: Loyola House of Studies, 1966. **Caquot, A.** "Peut-on parler de messianisme dans l'oeuvre du Chroniste?" *RTP* 99 (1966) 110–120. **Cazelles, H.** "La Mission d'Esdras." *VT* 4 (1954) 113–40. **Clements, R. E.** "Deuteronomy and the Jerusalem Cult Tradition. *VT* 15 (1965) 300–12. ———. *Prophecy and Covenant.* SBT 1/43. London: SCM, 1965. **Coggins, R. J.** "The Old Testament and Samaritan Origins." *ASTI* 6 (1968) 35–48. **Cooke, G.** "The Israelite King as Son of God." *ZAW* 73 (1961) 202–25. **Cross, F. M., Jr.** *Canaanite Myth and Hebrew Epic: Essays in the History of the Religion of Israel.* Cambridge: Harvard University Press, 1973. ———. "The Earliest Manuscripts from Qumran." *JBL* 74 (1955) 147–72. ———. "A New Qumran Fragment Related to the Hebrew Underlying the Septuagint." *BASOR* 31 (1953) 15–26. **Delcor, M.** "Hinweise auf das Samaritanische Schism im Alten Testament." *ZAW* 74 (1962) 281–91. **Dion, P-E.** "The 'Fear Not' Formula and Holy War." *CBQ* 32 (1970) 565–70. ———. "The Patriarchal Traditions and the Literary Form of the 'Oracle of Salvation.'" *CBQ* 29 (1967) 198–206. **Donner, H., and Röllig, W.** *Kanaanäische und Aramäische Inschriften.* 3 vols. Wiesbaden: Harrassowitz, 1962. **Elmslie, W. A. L.** "Prophetic Influences in the Sixth Century B.C." *Essays and Studies Presented to Stanley Arthur Cook.* Ed. D. W. Thomas. London: Taylor's Foreign Press, 1950. 15–24. **Fuente, O. G. de la.** "'Buscar' en el vocabulario de Isaias 1–39." *Augustinianum* 7 (1967) 486–501. **Gerleman, G.** *Studies in the Septuagint II: Chronicles.* Lund: C. W. K. Gleerup, 1947. **Gooding, D. W.** "Jeroboam's Rise to Power: A Rejoinder." *JBL* 91 (1972) 529–33. ———. "The Septuagint's Version of Solomon's Misconduct." *VT* 15 (1965) 325–35. **Gordis, R.** "Democratic Origins in Ancient Israel—the Biblical "edāh.'" *Alexander Marx Jubilee Volume on the Occasion of his Seventieth Birthday.* Eng. sec. ed. S. Lieberman. New York: Jewish Theological Seminary of America, 1950. **Gray, G. B.** *Studies in Hebrew Proper Names.* London: A. C. Black, 1896. **Gray, John.** "The Kingship of God in the Prophets and Psalms." *VT* 11 (1961) 1–29. **Grindel, J. M.** "Another Characteristic of the *Kaige* Rescension." *CBQ* 31 (1969) 499–513. **Hayes, J. H., and Miller, J. M.** eds. *Israelite and Judean History* Philadelphia: Westminster, 1977. **Hillers, D. R.** *Covenant: The History of a Biblical Idea.* Baltimore: Johns Hopkins Press, 1969. **Hodges, Z. C.** "Conflicts in the Biblical Accounts of the Ammonite-Syrian War [2 Sam. 10:6, 18 and 1 Chron. 19:6–7, 18]." *BSac* 119 (1962) 238–43. **Hornig, B.** "Das Prosagebet der nachexilischen Literatur." *TLZ* 83 (1958) 644–46. **Huffmon, H. B.** "The Exodus, Sinai, and the Credo." *CBQ* 27 (1965) 101–13. ———. "A Further Note on the Treaty Background of the Hebrew Yādā^c." *BASOR* 184 (1966) 36–38. **Hurvitz, A.** "The Evidence of Language in Dating the Priestly Code." *RB* 81 (1974) 24–56. **Janssen, E.** *Juda in der Exilzeit. Ein Beitrag zur Grage der*

Entstehung des Judentums. Göttingen: Vandenhoeck & Ruprecht, 1956. **Johnson, M. D.** *The Purpose of the Biblical Genealogies.* SNTSMS 8. Cambridge: University Press, 1969. **Jones, B. W.** "The Prayer in Daniel 9." *VT* 18 (1968) 488–93. **Kapelrud, A. S.** *The Question of Authorship in the Ezra-Narrative. A Lexical Investigation.* Oslo: J. Dybwad, 1943. **Kennett, R. H.** "The Date of Deuteronomy." *JTS* 7 (1905/06) 481–500. **Klein, R.** "Jeroboam's Rise to Power." *JBL* 89 (1970) 217–18. ———. "New Evidence for an Old Recension of Reigns." *HTR* 60 (1967) 93–105. ———. "Once More: 'Jeroboam's Rise to Power.' " *JBL* 92 (1973) 582–84. ———. "Supplements in the Paralipomena: A Rejoinder." *HTR* 61 (1968) 492–95. **Koch, K.** *The Growth of the Biblical Tradition.* Tr. S. M. Cupitt. New York: Scribner's, 1969. ———. "Das Verhältnis von Exegese und Verkündugung anhand eines Chroniktextes." *TLZ* 90 (1965) 659–70. **Köhler, L.** "Justice in the Gate." *Hebrew Man.* Tr. P. Ackroyd. London: SCM Press, 1956. 127–50. **Kraft, R. A.** "Barthelemy, les devanciers d'Aquilla." *Gnomon* 35 (1965) 474–83. **Kraus, H.-J.** *Worship in Israel.* Tr. G. Buswell. Richmond: John Knox, 1966. **Kropat, A.** *Die Syntax des Autors der Chronik.* BZAW 16. Giessen: Töpelmann, 1909. **Kutsch, E.** "Die Dynastie von Gottes Gnaden. Probleme der Nathanweissangung in 2 Samuel 7." *ZTK* 58 (1961) 137–53. **Laurentin, A.** "Wecattah–Kai nun. Formule caracteristique des textes juridiques et liturgiques." *Bib* 45 (1964) 168–97. **McCarthy, D. J.** "Covenant in the Old Testament: The Present State of Inquiry." *CBQ* 27 (1965) 217–40. ———. "2 Samuel 7 and the Structure of the Deuteronomic History." *JBL* 84 (1965) 131–38. **MacDonald, J.** *The Samaritan Chronicle II.* BZAW 107. Berlin: de Gruyter, 1969. ———. *The Theology of the Samaritans.* London: SCM Press, 1964. **MacKenzie, J. A. R.** "Valiant against All. From Text to Sermon on I Chron. 11:22, 23." *Int* 22 (1968) 18–35. **McKenzie, J. L.** "The Dynastic Oracle: II Samuel 7." *TS* 8 (1947) 187–218. ———. "Royal Messianism." *CBQ* 19 (1957) 25–52. **Maisler, B.** "Ancient Israelite Historiography." *IEJ* 2 (1952) 82–88. **Marsden, E. W.** *Greek and Roman Artillery I: Historical Development.* Oxford: Clarendon Press, 1969. **Mendenhall, G. F.** "The Census Lists of Numbers 1 and 26." *JBL* 77 (1958) 52–66. ———. *Law and Covenant in Israel and the Ancient Near East.* Pittsburgh: The Biblical Colloquium, 1955. **Miller, P. D. Jr.** "The Gift of God. The Deuteronomic Theology of the Land." *Int* 23 (1969) 451–65. **Moore, C. A.** Review of *Les Livres des Chroniques, d'Esdras et de Nehemie,* by Frank Michaeli. *JBL* 87 (1968) 210–212. **Moran, W. L.** "The Ancient Near Eastern Background of the Love of God in Deuteronomy." *CBQ* 25 (1963) 77–87. **Morgenstern, J.** "The Dates of Ezra and Nehemiah." *JSS* 7 (1962) 1–11. **Moriarity, F. L.** "The Chronicler's Account of Hezekiah's Reform." *CBQ* 27 (1965) 399–406. **Mowinckel, S.** "Erwägungen zum chronistischen Geschichtswerk." *TLZ* 85 (1960) 1–8. ———. "The Intercession of the Covenant Mediator (Exodus 33:1a, 12–17)." *Words and Meanings: Essays Presented to David Winton Thomas.* Eds. P. Ackroyd and B. Lindars. Cambridge: University Press, 1968. 159–81. **Muilenberg, J.** "The Form and Structures of the Covenantal Formulation." *VT* 9 (1959) 347–65. ———. "A Study in Hebrew Rhetoric: Repetition and Style." *VTSup* 1 (1953) 97–111. **Murtonen, A.** "The Use and Meaning of the Words *lebarek* und (*sic*) *berakah* in the Old Testament." *VT* 9 (1959) 158–77. **Myers, J. M.** "The Kerygma of the Chronicler." *Int* 20 (1966) 259–73. **Newman, M. L. Jr.** *The People of the Covenant.* New York: Abingdon, 1962. **North, R.** Review of *I Chronicles. II Chronicles. Ezra–Nehemiah,* by Jacob M. Myers. *CBQ* 28 (1966) 519–24. **Noth, M.** "Das Amt des 'Richters Israels.' " *Festschrift Alfred Bertholet zum 80. Geburtstag.* Ed. W. Baumgartner, et al. Tübingen: Mohr, 1950. 404–17. ———. "History and Word of God in the Old Testament." *The Laws in the Pentateuch and Other Studies.* Tr. D. R. Ap-Thomas. Edinburgh: Oliver & Boyd, 1968. 197–93. ———. "Jerusalem and the Israelite Tradition." *The Laws in the Pentateuch and Other Studies.* Tr. D. R. Ap-Thomas. Edinburgh: Oliver & Boyd, 1968. 132–44. **Pavlovsky, V.** "Die Chronologie der Tätigkeit Esdras." *Bib* 38 (1957) 275–305, 428–56. **Payne, D. F.** "The Purpose and Methods of the Chronicler." *Faith and Thought* 93 (1963) 64–73. **Payne, J. B.** "Validity of Numbers in Chronicles." *Near East Archaeology Society Bulletin* ns 11 (1978) 5–58. **Pederson, D. L.** Review of *Untersuchungen zur Theologie des chronistischen Geschichtswerkes*, by Rudolph Mosis. *JBL* 93 (1974) 603–5. **Pedersen, J.** *Israel. Its Life and Culture.* 4 vols. London: Oxford University Press, 1940. **Plöger, O.** *Theocracy and Eschatology.* Tr. S. Rudman. Oxford: Blackwell, 1968. **Pohlmann, K.-F.** *Studien zum dritten Esra. Ein Beitrag zur Frage nach dem ursprunglichen Schluss des chronistischen Geschichtswerkes.* Göttingen: Vandenhoeck und Ruprecht, 1970. **Porter, J. R.** "The Interpretation of 2 Samuel 6 and Psalm 132." *JTS* 5 (1954) 167. **Purvis, J.** "The Origin of the Samaritan Sect." Diss.: Harvard Divinity School, Cambridge, 1962. **Rad, G. von.** "The Beginnings of Historical Writing in Ancient Israel." *The Problem of the Hexateuch and Other Essays.* Tr. E. W. T. Dicken. New York: McGraw Hill, 1966. 166–204. ———. *Das Geschichtsbild des Chronistischen Werkes.* Stuttgart: Kohlhammer, 1930. ———. *Old Testament Theology.* 2 vols. Tr. D. N. G. Stalker. Edinburgh: Oliver and Boyd, 1962–65. ———. "The Preaching of Deuteronomy and Our Preaching." *Int* 15 (1961) 3–13. **Richardson, H. N.** "The Historical Reliability of Chronicles." *JBR* 26 (1958) 8–12. **Richter, W.** "Die nagid-Formel." *BZ* 9 (1965) 71–84; 10 (1966) 44–56. **Rinaldi, G.** "Quelques remarques sur la politique d'Azarias (Ozias) de Juda en Philistie" (2 Chron. 26, 6ss). VTSup 9 (1963) 225–35. **Rost, L.** "Zur Vorgeschichte der Kultusreform des Josias." *VT* 19 (1969) 113–19. **Rowley, H. H.** "The Chronological Order of Ezra and Nehemiah." *The Servant of the Lord and Other Essays.* 2d ed. Oxford: Blackwell, 1965. ———. "The Samaritan Schism in Legend and History." *Israel's Prophetic Heritage.* Ed. B. W. Anderson and W. Harrelson. New York: Harper and Row, 1962. ———. "Sanballat and the Samaritan Temple." *BJRL* 38 (1955) 166–98. ———. *Worship in Ancient Israel.* Philadelphia: Fortress, 1967. **Rudolph, W.** "Der Aufbau der Asa-Geschichte." [2 Chron. 14–16]. *VT* 2 (1952) 367–71. ———. "Problems of the Books of Chronicles." *VT* 4 (1954) 401–9. ———. "Zur Theologie des Chronisten." *TLZ* 89 (1954) 286. **Rylaarsdam, J. C.** "Recovery of Relevance (1 Chron. 29:11)." *Criterion* 5 (1966) 13–16. **Schumacher, J. H.** "The Chronicler's Theology of History." *The Theologian* 13 (1957) 11–21. **Schürer, E.** *The History of the Jewish People in the Age of Jesus Christ.* Rev. ed. G. Vermes and F. Millar, eds. Edinburgh: T. & T. Clark, 1973. **Seeligman, I. L.** "Der Auffassung von der Prophetie in der deuteronomistischen und chronistischen Geschichtsschreibung." VTSup 29 (1979) 254–84. ———. "Menschliches Heldentum und göttliche Hilfe. Die doppelte Kausalität im alttestamentlichen Geschichtsdenken." *TZ* 19 (1963) 385–411. **Steck, O. H.** "Das Problem theologischer Stromungen in nachexilischer Zeit." *EvT* 28 (1968) 445–58. **Swete, H. B.** *An Introduction to the Old Testament in Greek.* Rev. R. R. Ottley, Cambridge: University Press, 1914. **Thackery, H. St. John,** and **Marcus, R.** *Josephus: Jewish Antiquities: Books V–VIII.* Cambridge, MS: Harvard University Press, 1934. **Thomas, D. W.** "The Sixth Century B.C.: A Creative Epoch in the History of Israel." *JSS* 6 (1961) 33–46. **Torrey, C. C.** "The Chronicler's History of the Return under Cyrus." *AJSL* 37 (1920–21) 81–100. **Tsevat, M.** "House of David in Nathan's Prophecy." *Bib* 46 (1965) 353–56. ———. "Studies in the Book of Samuel III: The Steadfast House: What Was David Promised in 2 Samuel 7:11b–16?" *HUCA* 34 (1963) 71–82. **Vannutelli, P.** *Libri Synoptici Veteris Testamenti seu Librorum Regum et Chronicorum loci paralleli.* Two vols. Rome: Pontifical Biblical Institute, 1931–34. **Vaux, R. de.** Review of *Chronikbücher, Ezra, und Nehemia*, by W. Rudolph. *RB* 64 (1957) 278–81. **Vogt, H. C. M.** *Studie zur nachexilischen Gemeinde in Esra-Nehemia.* Werl: Dietrich Coelde, 1966. **Weinberg, J. P.** "Das Eigengut in den Chronikbüchern." *OLP* 10 (1979) 161–81. **Weinfeld, M.** "Deuteronomy—The Present State of Inquiry." *JBL* 86 (1967) 249–62. **Welch, A.** *Post-Exilic Judaism.* London: W. Blackwood and Sons, 1935. 185–216. **Wenham, J.** "Large Numbers in the Old Testament." *TynBul* 18 (1967) 19–53. **Westermann, C.** *Basic Forms of Prophetic Speech.* Tr. H. C. White. Philadelphia: Westminster,

1967. ————. "Die Begriffe für fragen und suchen im alten Testament." *KD* 6 (1960) 2–30. ————. *Der Segen in der Bibel und im Handeln der Kirche.* Munich: Chr. Kaiser Verlag, 1968. **Wevers, J. W.** "Principles of Interpretation Guiding the Fourth Translator of the Book of the Kingdoms (3 Kings 22:1–4 Kings 25–30)." *CBQ* 14 (1952) 40–56. **Whitley, C. F.** *The Exilic Age.* Philadelphia: Westminster, 1957. **Whybray, R. N.** *The Succession Narrative. A Study of II Sam. 9–20 and I Kings 1 and 2.* SBT 2/9. Naperville, IL: Allenson, 1968. **Yamauchi, E.** "The Reverse Order of Ezra-Nehemiah Reconsidered." *Themelios* 5 (1980) 7–13. **Zimmerman, F.** "Chronicles as a Partially Translated Book." *JQR* 42 (1951–52) 265–82, 387–412. **Zerafa, P.** Priestly Messianism in the Old Testament." *Angelicum* 42 (1965) 318–41.

The Genealogical Prologue (Chaps. 1–9)

Bibliography

Bowman, R. A. "Genealogy." *IDB* 2:362–65. **Brin, G.** "The Status of the Firstborn in Genealogical Lists." *BMik* 24 (1979) 255–59 (Heb.). ———. "The Story of the Birthright of Jacob's Sons." *Tarbiz* 48 (1978/79) 1–8 (Heb.). **Brown, R. E.** *The Birth of the Messiah*. Garden City, NY: Doubleday, 1977. **Brunet, A.-M.** "Le Chroniste et ses Sources." *RB* 60 (1953) 481–508 (and 61 [1954] 349–86). ———. "Paralipomenes." *DBSup* 6 (1960) 1220–61. **Cross, F. M.** "A Reconstruction of the Judean Restoration." *JBL* 94 (1975) 4–18. **Geus, C. H. J. de.** *The Tribes of Israel*. Assen: Van Gorcum, 1976. (Extensive bibliography.) **Gottwald, N. K.** "Israel, Social and Economic Development of." *IDBSup*, 465–68. **Japhet, S.** "Conquest and Settlement in Chronicles." *JBL* 98 (1979) 205–18. **Johnson, M. D.** *The Purpose of the Biblical Genealogies*. New York: Cambridge University Press, 1969. **Kallai, Z.** "Tribes, Territories of." *IDBSup*, 920–23. (With recent bibliography.) ———. "Judah and Israel—A Study in Israelite Historiography." *IEJ* 28 (1978) 251–61. **Malamat, A.** "King Lists of the Old Babylonian Period and Biblical Genealogies." *JAOS* 88 (1968) 163–73. ———. "Tribal Societies: Biblical Genealogies and African Lineage Systems." *Archives européennes de sociologie* 14 (1973) 126–36. **Mendenhall, G. E.** "The Census Lists of Numbers 1 and 26." *JBL* 77 (1958) 52–66. ———. "Tribe and State in the Ancient World: The Nature of the Biblical Community" *The Tenth Generation*. Baltimore: Johns Hopkins University Press, 1973. 174–97. **Michaeli, F.** *Les Livres des Chroniques, D'Esdras et de Nehemie*. Neuchatel: Delachaux & Niestle, 1967. 70–74. **Osborne, W. L.** "The Genealogies of 1 Chronicles 1–9." Diss.: Dropsie University, 1979. **Sasson, J.** "Genealogical 'Convention' in Biblical Chronology?" *ZAW* 90 (1978) 171–85. **Taber, C. R.** "Kinship and Family." *IDBSup*, 519–24. **Waetjen, H.** "Genealogy as the Key to the Gospel According to Matthew." *JBL* 95 (76) 205–30. **Waterman, I.** "Some Repercussions from Late Levitical Genealogical Accretions in P and the Chronicler." *AJSL* 58 (1941) 50. **Weinberg, J. P.** "Das bēit 'āḇōt im 6.–4. Jh. v. u. Z." *VT* 23 (1973) 400–414. **Wilson, R. R.** "Between 'Azel' and 'Azel': Interpreting the Biblical Genealogies." *BA* 42 (1979) 11–22. ———. *Genealogy and History in the Biblical World*. New Haven: Yale University, 1977. (Extensive bibliography.) ———. "The Old Testament Genealogies in Recent Research." *JBL* 94 (1975) 169–89. **Wolf, C. U.** "Tribes." *IDB* 4:698–701. **Zachmann, L.** "Beobachtungen zur Theologie in Gen. 5." *ZAW* 88 (1976) 272–74.

GENEALOGIES: DEFINITION AND TERMS

In view of the fact that 1 Chr 1–9 is composed in large part of genealogical material, it is essential to inquire into the nature of genealogies. "A *genealogy* is a written or oral expression of the descent of a person or persons from an ancestor or ancestors" (Wilson, *Genealogy*, 9). This expression may be found either included within the broader confines of a narrative in which much additional information is also included or it may be presented more succinctly in the form of a list, as is the common pattern in 1 Chr 1–9.

Genealogies may display *breadth* ("These are the sons of Israel: Reuben, Simeon, Levi, Judah, . . ." 1 Chr 2:1) and *depth* ("The sons of Solomon:

Rehoboam, Abijah his son, Asa his son, . . ." 1 Chr 3:10). If a genealogy displays depth alone, it is termed *linear*. It must by definition have a depth of at least two generations. Wilson has pointed out that biblical genealogies, like extrabiblical ones, are normally quite limited in depth, with even the linear genealogies rarely extending beyond ten to twelve generations; a range of four to six is more common. However, 1 Chr 2–9 is noted as the sole exception to this principle, possibly because the writer has simply joined together originally separate genealogies (*Genealogy*, 197). If a genealogy displays breadth as well as depth, it is termed *segmented*. Due to their more complex nature, segmented genealogies are normally more restricted in depth than are linear genealogies. In Chronicles multiple descendants of an ancestor are frequently named, but the descendants of only one line (or at least not all lines) are pursued in subsequent generations. Although the terminology may be imprecise, and is not used by Wilson, we have on occasion termed such genealogies *mixed*. Genealogies may proceed from parent to child, in which case they are termed *descending* (cf. 1 Chr 9:39–44), or from child to parent, termed *ascending* (cf. 1 Chr 9:14–16).

Linear and segmented genealogies differ substantially in their function. The linear genealogy commonly seeks to legitimize the position of the last-named person by relating him or her to an ancestor whose position is accepted as established; hence the various king lists of the ANE and the OT are uniformly linear in form. The segmented genealogy, on the other hand, has as its primary function the expression of the relationships existing between the various branches of individuals named. As such it points both to a commonality, in that those named are descended from a single individual, and to a divergency, in that respective branches are derived through different intermediate ancestors. Johnson points to 1 Chr 7:20–29 as an example of confusion arising from the fact that the author understood Num 26 to be linear in form rather than segmented (*Purpose*, 51). While genealogies may be distinguished as functioning in domestic, political, or religious spheres, these areas are often "multiple and interpenetrating" (Wilson, *Genealogy*, 38–45).

It is the essential purpose of the genealogy to point to kinship relations between various individuals and groups. Osborne ("Genealogies," 318) has pointed to four formulae through which this kinship relationship is expressed. (1) The most prevalent type is "The son(s) of PN₁: PN₂." According to Osborne, this formula is found only in segmented genealogies (but cf. 1 Chr 3:10–14). (2) "PN₁ begat (הוליד "caused to bring forth") PN₂." Since there is only a variation in verb forms, Osborne includes here also cases in which a woman is said to give birth to (ילדה) a child. Although differing more radically, we should include here also cases in which this same relationship is expressed nominally, i.e., "the father of" (אבי; cf. 2:49), although, as we shall note below, the relationship reflected here is at least at times figurative. (3) "PN₁, son of PN₂," which must always be in ascending order. (4) "PN₁, his son PN₂," always in descending order (contrary to Osborne, "Genealogies," 318) and surprisingly common in 1 Chr 1–9 (cf. 3:10–14; 7:25–27, etc.).

A genealogy is frequently terminated without the use of any determining feature. At other times, however, the termination "these are the sons/descendants of . . ." (בני [היו] אלה) is found. Since this formula may also be used at the beginning of a genealogy as an apparent variation of (1) above (cf. 2:1; 3:1), confusion can result. (Cf. 2:50a, which the Masoretic text understands as the introduction to a following listing, though more likely it concludes a previous one, as in rsv.)

In general, no significant difference has been seen to underlie the use of these various formulas in Chronicles, nor has their varied use contributed significantly to the understanding of the structure or history of 1 Chr 1–9. Although the second category named above is characteristic of P in the Pentateuch, no significance appears to be associated with it in Chronicles (cf. 1 Chr 9:39–44, where various formulae seem to be used interchangeably, with the הוליד "he brought forth" pattern broken [unnecessarily] for the multiple sons of Micah in v 41 and Azel in v 44, apparently for the sake of variation in style only). It is probably true that in given cases the use or non-use of a formula may be indicative of an earlier source (cf. the use of אבי "father of" and the reconstruction offered in Aharoni, *Land*, 225–27), but no compelling rationale has yet been found, and we must be content at present to say that such variations may result in part from the sources that lay at the writer's disposal, and in part to nothing more than a desire for variety.

THE PURPOSE OF GENEALOGIES

Johnson (*Purpose*, 77–82) has pointed to nine functions which genealogies serve in the OT. (1) The demonstration of existing relations between Israel and neighboring tribes, showing both a degree of kinship and a degree of distinction, seen especially in J (77). (2) The interrelating of previously isolated traditional elements concerning Israel's origins by the creation of a coherent and inclusive genealogical system (78). (3) The establishment of continuity over those periods of time not covered by material in the traditions. (4) As vehicles for chronological speculation concerning world cycles. (5) Some genealogies are military in content and purpose. (6) To demonstrate the legitimacy of an individual in his office or provide an individual of rank with connections to a worthy family or individual of the past. (7) In Ezra and Nehemiah only, genealogies are important for establishing and preserving the homogeneity of the race. (8) "Taken as a whole, the Chronicler's genealogical survey of 'all Israel' may be viewed as an attempt to assert the importance of the principle of the continuity of the people of God through a period of national disruption." (9) To exhibit "a sense of movement within history toward a divine goal" (80). The course of history is governed by a pre-arranged plan.

In general it may be seen that most of these purposes are closely related to the form of the linear and segmented genealogies noted above. It is also clear that many of these functions are interpenetrating and overlapping (e.g. 1, 2, 3, 7, and 8). 1 Chr 1–9 may on the whole be taken as an elaborate segmented or mixed genealogy whose major purpose is to demonstrate the relationships existing between the various components of the people of Israel in the past and relating them in part to those who claimed to be a part of Israel at the time of the writer(s).

As Wilson has indicated, such segmented genealogies reflect not only blood relationships, but geographical, social, economic, religious, and political realities as well. Since these factors vary from time to time, a genealogy extant at one time may differ substantially from that of another, although both are "correct" in expressing the relationships existing at their respective times. Genealogies therefore reflect what is commonly called *fluidity,* i.e., they change from time to time in response to ongoing changes in society, although significant parts of genealogies may become "frozen," after which no significant alteration occurs. Hence Israel's descendants are regularly seen in twelve tribes deriving from twelve sons in the canonical tradition, although the numbers and names of these sons and tribes differ in what we consider significant ways. The partition of the tribe of Joseph into Ephraim and Manasseh ill accords with the constant tradition of twelve tribes, as does the tradition of the "half-tribe" of Manasseh. Simeon was apparently absorbed by Judah at an early date, but continued to be counted among the twelve. Apparently the number twelve was sufficiently established that it was no longer a variable term, or, as the genealogists say, it was no longer genealogically functional. Dan and Zebulun, while present in the list of Israel's sons in 2:1–2, are not named in the present format of chaps. 1–9.

Examples of genealogical fluidity may be summarized under three types of headings: (1) there may be a change in the kinship relationship between the names; (2) additional names may be added; and (3) names may be deleted. The first of these may occur because a name loses its functional importance, or it may reflect changes within the structure of the lineage. The second often reflects a process of natural growth as new generations are added; but may also include the integration of persons into a genealogy not formerly related to it in any way. There may be many reasons for the loss of names, the most important of which is the loss of function of names in the middle of a lineage, resulting in what is commonly called telescoping (Osborne, "Genealogies," 113–14).

Examples of all of these are probably found in Chronicles, though divergent explanations can be given. Jerahmeel is in 2:9 the brother of Ram, in 2:25 his father. The genealogy of 7:6 lists only three sons of Benjamin, while 1 Chr 8:1–2 numbers five. 1 Chr 8:39 appears to add additional (later?) descendants attaching themselves to the end of Saul's line, while Caleb/Chelubai and the Kenites are in chap. 2 integrated into the line of Judah and the gatekeepers are merged with the line of Levi (cf. 9:17–27). 1 Chr 4:1, seen in the context of chap. 2, does not list four immediate sons of Judah, as a simple reading would indicate, but a telescoping of succeeding generations, from which indeed some of the most prominent members are omitted (cf. Caleb). Johnson has noted the anomaly that while Joshua is listed as the tenth (or eleventh) descendant of Ephraim (1 Chr 7:20–29), Moses is only three generations removed from Levi in the traditional lists (Johnson, *Purpose,* 51).

In many cases we must admit that we can no longer be certain of precisely what the relationship is between individuals named in a genealogy. George Mendenhall cites Hur in 1 Chr 2:19 and 4:1 as a beautiful example of processes "which combine the complexities of local tribal history with observations concerning the lineages of particular persons in such a way that it is doubtful that we can ever determine where the former ends and the latter begins" (*The Tenth Generation,* 178). Wilson cites an example of an Arabic genealogy devised after the advent of Mohammed whose function was to display the unity of all the Islamic people (*BA* 42 [1979] 18). So now in the same sense "all Israel" included all those people who in the course of time were a part of Israel.

At the same time, many of the genealogies of chaps. 1–9 are linear in form. At times such lists may amount to little more than establishing a list of all those who have held a certain office, such as the list of the high priests in 5:27–41 [6:1–15] or of the Davidic kings in chap. 3. At the same time, however, at least portions of these lists originally served to legitimate the office or authority of the last-named person by attaching him to an individual whose authority was accepted as legitimate. We may assume that this same kind of interest continued to be paramount in naming, e.g., the descendants of Zerubbabel (1 Chr 3:19–24) and of Shallum the gatekeeper and his kin (9:19, 31). The same is probably true also of instances where an unknown individual, often with a sizable family, stands at the end of an otherwise well-known line. (Cf. Azel's six sons in 8:38; 9:44, and the addition of an otherwise unknown family in 8:39.)

The purpose of chaps. 1–9 is thus complex. That it proposes to present a kind of historical overview of Israel and her history seems apparent, whether one chooses to call this a *Heilsgeschichte* or not. That at the same time it provides a literary connection with the demise of Saul recounted in 1 Chr 10 and a chronological connection with the returning exiles (cf. 1 Chr 9) seems no less apparent. I would also be willing to agree with those who feel that certain names have been included merely for the sake of completeness, a kind of genealogy for genealogy's sake (cf. Johnson, *Purpose,* 81–82). There is however a deeper significance to this lengthy recitation of the people of Israel. Genealogies may be used, Johnson notes (cf. no. 9, p. 3), to exhibit "a sense of movement within history toward a divine goal." We may see this in its simplest form in the priestly genealogy of 1 Chr 5:27–41 [6:1–15], where the as yet unnamed priest of the next generation may be expected to function in a new temple. But in more pregnant form, the marshalling of Israelites from throughout the ages, of north and south, faithful and unfaithful, points to an understanding of the God of Israel as the one who preserves and guides his people to the destiny which he holds in store for them. Whether the original work of the Chronicler ended with Israel in exile (cf. 2 Chr 36:20–21), with the advent of Cyrus (2 Chr 36:22–23; Ezra 1:1–3), the erection of the temple (Ezra 6), or at a still later point, that message spelled hope, and it spelled hope for all Israel.

GENEALOGICAL SOURCES

Much of the genealogical material used by the writer has been taken from other parts of the canonical text, with other material being of unknown origin. While it has often been stated by more critical scholars that much, if not all, of this additional material is fictional and has its origin only in the writer's imagination, a more balanced approach would suggest the likelihood that little if any of the material is to be so regarded. Comparison with the canonical accounts in some cases clearly suggests that related but divergent traditions were extant, either in oral or literary form or both. Wilson has demonstrated the antiquity and commonplaceness of genealogies in the ANE in both oral and literary form, and there is no reason to doubt their provenance in Israel. In addition to the family level at which genealogies function, Wilson has shown such genealogies to be at home also in domestic, social, juridical, religious, and political environs, in all of which claims may be based on genealogical ties, widely defined.

Johnson has pointed to a common pattern to be seen in a number of the genealogies which contain at least three kinds of information: (1) the basic core data of the genealogy; (2) a list of cities inhabited by the people named; and (3) additional data. The historicity of this "additional data" has often been questioned, and its place within the genealogical schema disputed. Johnson has pointed out, however, that such apparently insignificant remarks also characterize the genealogical material available to us in the Safaitic inscriptions (*Purpose*, 61). With reference in particular to the genealogies of Chronicles, much of this additional material can be seen to be of a military nature (cf. 5:18–22; 7:1–5, 6–12, 40; 8:40, etc.). In fact, military allusions are lacking in only four of the tribal genealogies—those "core tribes," Judah, Levi, Manasseh, and Ephraim (*Purpose*, 69).

Building upon the work of George Mendenhall, who had demonstrated that the regular context for such genealogical listings in the OT was in association with census lists drawn up for the purpose of military conscription, Johnson has also pointed to comparison with Assyrian military classes such as the *mariannu* to demonstrate that military leadership could be vested in certain groups of people in a hereditary way, thus justifying the genealogical setting as well (*Purpose*, 67). The prominence of military illusions, lists, etc., in Chronicles has often been noted in the past, and its significance debated. (See *Introduction*.)

It seems likely, although concrete evidence is lacking, that genealogical records of several sorts may have been available to the writer. Some of these may have been of an oral nature and in circulation at the writer's own time, though in my opinion little beyond current information should be sought in this way. In addition, however, we may assume that official documents of a civil and/or religious nature must have been in existence then as now. Chronicles refers to specific genealogical enrollments in the days of Hezekiah (4:41) and Jotham (5:17), and there is no obvious reason to consider such notices as fictional. The account of the return, in which certain individuals, including priests, were unable to prove their ancestry, indicates that material was on hand with regard to both priests and other citizens as well (Ezra 2:59–62). In general we must state that the nature of the material transmitted in our genealogies for which no OT tradition is extant is so devoid of tendentious overtones that there can be little reason for an author to have invented it.

At the same time, the general authenticity—and corresponding accuracy— of this material does not mean that the writer himself has not inserted or emphasized material of interest to himself from time to time, nor that the genealogies themselves as they are distributed before us do not have a tendentious nature. By way of historical remarks, we will call attention to the appearance of items common with the theology of Chronicles in the doctrine of warfare in 5:18–26; to prayer in 5:20; to retribution in 9:1; to the role of faith in 5:20, and the extension of the birthright to Joseph in 5:1–2.

Moreover, it seems likely that the author himself had inferred or devised genealogical links in some crucial cases where these were lacking, such as above all 2:9. More in the line of popular etymology, Hur-Uri-Bezalel are included among the descendants of Judah, as are Ethan, Heman, Calcol, and Darda (2:6), noted for their wisdom. Whether these and other similar attachments existed in the writer's sources or whether they were contributed by him cannot be said with certainty (cf. the gatekeeper Shallum in 9:19 and Ner in 9:36 [contrast 8:30]).

THE PEOPLE ISRAEL: KINSHIP TERMS IN ISRAEL'S GENEALOGIES

We have referred to some of the ways in which the basic genealogical relationship between father and children is expressed in the genealogies of Chronicles. Other expressions of tribal and family solidarity occur with some frequency as well, an understanding of which is significant for the material at hand.

The nuclear family is that kinship unit which lives together on a fairly continuous basis, and is commonly designated only after the name of its head. (Cf. Gen 12:1, where Abraham is commanded to leave his father's house and establish his own family.) The father's house (בית אב) represents the extended family, including not only the father, his wife or wives, and their unmarried children, but also their married sons with their wives, children, and servants (de Vaux, *Ancient Israel*, 8). The next largest grouping is the clan (משפחת), which essentially comprises all whom we would commonly designate relatives, and the largest subunit of Israel is the tribe (מטה/שבט), one of the roughly twelve units into which the people (עם) Israel divided itself. The essential hierarchy of these three terms—*father's house, clan,* and *tribe*—is clearly expressed in Josh 7:14–18. However, the terms are not always used with precision, cf. Num 4:18; Judg 20:12.

The father's house, or extended family, which appears as the largest functioning sub-group of the people is of particular prominence in 1 Chr 1–9. If many of the genealogies have a military background, we may assume that these "father's houses" would have been the basis through which military conscription was realized. Mendenhall has argued that the term אלף, traditionally translated "thousand," may also refer to a tribal sub-section, and then to a military unit taken from that sub-section (*JBL* 77 [1958] 60–63).

Also of importance in understanding the genealogies is the nature of the terms "father" (אב) and "son" (בן). The term "son" is used with various understandings. While commonly used to refer to one's immediate male offspring, it may at times include females also, and thus require the understanding "children." (At other times, however, sons and daughters are clearly distinguished, cf. 4:27.) At other times the meaning of בן is extended to include grandsons and great-grandsons, etc. (cf. 1 Chr 4:1). In still other cases, however, we must assume that the term includes all descendants of a person, and perhaps as well those who have become attached to the individual named through relationships other than blood. In this connection it is quite easy to see how a singular collective might be followed by more than one "son" (cf. the Hebrew of 2:50), and as well how the plural בנים or בני might be followed by only a single name. The individual named is viewed not as an individual, but as a designation for all of the individuals considered members of that social grouping (cf. 3:22, "the sons of Shecaniah: Shemaiah"). Such usages appear far too frequently to be uniformly dismissed as textual errors.

A similar situation is to be discerned in the use of the term "father." Aharoni has pointed to a series of instances in which the term "father" is applied to an individual as the founder of a city or the initiator of an occupation (*Land*, 225, and cf. especially 2:50–55; 4:14, 21–23).

Although Aharoni's reconstruction of the supposed source from which these various notices were supposedly derived, based upon the work of Noth, may not be compelling, the examples cited are another instance of the close and often indissoluble relationship between the genealogies and their social, political, and economic backgrounds. It is through such factors that בני ישראל, "sons of Israel," composed of diverse elements related to one another, at times to be sure by natural descent but by a host of other factors as well, has come to mean simply "Israelites."

The Tribes of Israel

As admitted by scholars of all persuasions, the genealogies of Israel are notoriously complex, dealing not only with matters of genealogy per se but with the understanding of early Israel's history as well. Since the author of 1 Chr 1–9, which may be viewed as the most extensive segmented genealogy in the OT, has in most cases drawn his material directly from other OT traditions, most of these matters lie beyond the scope of our study. Nevertheless, since the present form of chaps. 1–9 may well represent a purposeful statement of the relationship between the twelve tribes, it will be helpful to compare the order of the tribes of Israel in chaps. 1–9 and in 1 Chr 2:1–2 with other OT traditions and with other listings of the tribes in Chronicles as well.

Wilson finds the twelve tribes explicitly related genealogically in only four passages: (1) Gen 29:31–30:24; 35:16–20; (2) Gen 35:22b–26; (3) Gen 46:8–27, and (4) 1 Chr 2:1–2 (*Genealogy*, 183–84). The first of these (1), commonly ascribed to JE and considered the oldest, is a segmented genealogy in narrative form dividing Jacob's sons as follows: (a) the sons of Leah: Reuben, Simeon, Levi, Judah (29:32–35), Issachar, and Zebulon (30:17–20); (b) the sons of Bilhah, Rachel's maid: Dan and Naphtali (30:5–8); (c) the sons of Zilpah, Leah's maid: Gad and Asher (30:10–13); and (d) the son of Rachel: Joseph (30:22–24). (Rachel's second son, Benjamin, is recorded in 35:16–20.) In genealogical terms preeminence is here given to Joseph, the son of Jacob's favorite wife, Rachel. Her second son, Benjamin, also occupies a significant position, though inferior to Joseph. Leah's sons are also set apart from the remainder, who are born of concubines.

TRIBAL LISTS IN THE OT AND CHRONICLES

(1) Gen 29:31–
30:24; 35:16–20 　*(2) Gen 35:22b–26*　*(3) Gen 46:8–27*　*(4) 1 Chr 2:1–2*

	(1)	(2)	(3)	(4)
1.	Reuben	Reuben	Reuben	Reuben
2.	Simeon	Simeon	Simeon	Simeon
3.	Levi	Levi	Levi	Levi
4.	Judah	Judah	Judah	Judah
5.	Dan	Issachar	Issachar	Issachar
6.	Naphtali	Zebulon	Zebulon	Zebulon
7.	Gad	Joseph	Gad	Dan
8.	Asher	Benjamin	Asher	Joseph
9.	Issachar	Dan	Joseph	Benjamin
10.	Zebulon	Naphtali	Benjamin	Naphtali
11.	Joseph	Gad	Dan	Gad
12.	Benjamin	Asher	Naphtali	Asher

(5) 1 Chr 2–8　　*(6) 1 Chr 12:24–38 [23–37]*　*(7) 1 Chr 27:16–24*

(5)	(6)	(7)
Judah	Judah	Reuben
Simeon	Simeon	Simeon
Reuben	Levi	Levi
Gad	Benjamin	Judah
E. Manasseh	Ephraim	Issachar
Levi	W. Manasseh	Zebulon
Issachar	Issachar	Naphtali
Benjamin	Zebulon	Ephraim
Naphtali	Naphtali	W. Manasseh
W. Manasseh	Dan	E. Manasseh
Ephraim	Asher	Benjamin
Asher	Reuben	Dan
Benjamin	Gad	[No Gad]
[No Zebulon]	E. Manasseh	[No Asher]
[No Dan]		

The second (2), Gen 35:22b–26, which is from P, is segmented, in list form, and makes only one significant alteration. Rachel's children, Joseph and Benjamin, follow immediately upon Leah's, thus placing together the sons of Jacob's two wives. Wilson suggests (*Genealogy*, 187) that P may have been aware that this arrangement emphasizes the first position of Judah and Levi, and that the resulting order is related to the tradition which underlies all the twelve tribe lists which omit Levi, divide Joseph into Ephraim and Manasseh, and record the names Asher and Naphtali in that order. These lists may be divided into two groups, all stemming from P. (a) The first group (Num 1:5–15; 1:20–43; 13:4–15; 26:5–51) begins with Reuben, and may be derived from Num 1:5–15 (although Noth, *U.S.*, 187, opts for Num 26:5–51). Except for Asher and Naphtali, all follow P in Gen 35:22b–26 (replacing Joseph with Ephraim and Manasseh) and then either simply omit Levi or replace Levi with Gad. (b) The second group (Num 2:3–31; 7:12–

83; 10:14–28) is identical, beginning with Judah instead of Reuben. The tribes are separated into four groups, with three tribes being assigned to each compass point.

The third group (3) is the second P genealogy (Gen 46:8–27), which is also segmented, sometimes reaching a depth of four generations. This genealogy often lies closer to Chronicles, and introduces only one innovation. The children of each maid are introduced immediately following those of her mistress. Wilson considers this a logical arrangement of no apparent significance.

In the fourth group (4) 1 Chr 2:1–2, the explicit arrangement in four groups is abandoned. Leah's six sons are still listed together, as are the sons of Rachel and Zilpah. However, Dan has been separated from Naphtali and moved from ninth position in the list, where he occurs in Gen 35:25, to seventh position. Wilson (*Genealogy*, 189) views the significance of this move as unclear, with certainty being impossible. However, we believe that the mention of Dan may well have been omitted in an earlier stage of the text, even as is still the case in 1 Chr 7:14 (see below). A subsequent writer, finding the list incomplete, has restored Dan after Zebulon. If Dan would have instead been placed before Naphtali, the list would agree with that of Gen 35:22b–26.

Alternatively, 1 Chr 27 (see List 7) may point to a tradition in which Dan and Naphtali stood immediately after Leah's sons (as in List 1). However, Dan has been removed to the end of the list, with Gad and Asher lacking, and Joseph divided into Ephraim and Manasseh. In 1 Chr 12:24–38 also, which varies considerably from other listings, Naphtali and Dan (in that order) follow Issachar and Zebulon.

By way of contrast, the order in which the tribes are treated in 1 Chr 2–8 differs considerably. The order here seems to be in part one of preeminence, in part geographical, in part unknown. Hence Judah is listed first in view of its importance in the book, with Simeon, Reuben, Gad, and E. Manasseh attached to it by reason of geography. The placement of Levi next is also commonly associated with its significance in the book; after that point, however, there is less certainty. Although Issachar could be expected on the basis of 1 Chr 2:1–2, chaps. 2–8 do not even name the tribe of Zebulon or Dan. Since what appears to be a remnant of Dan is still to be seen in 7:12, followed by Naphtali in 7:13 as would also be expected, and our current text lists Benjaminite genealogies in both 7:6–12a and chap. 8, some have sought to understand 7:6–12a as the genealogy of Zebulon (cf. Curtis, 145–49), although it cannot be said that the evidence for doing so is compelling. Rudolph (69–71) has sought to reorder the entire pericope after Num 26. The omission of Dan and Zebulon, plus the double genealogy of Benjamin, rather suggests that more extensive revision has taken place over a period of time, based on understandings to which we are no longer privy. An earlier and briefer account may well have concluded with the notice concerning Benjamin followed by Ephraim and Manasseh as representatives of the northern tribes. A later writer or writers has omitted Dan (and Zebulon), perhaps added mention of other northern tribes, and above all added an expanded account of Benjamin (cf. chap. 8). With certain concessions made on the basis of geography and otherwise, the final form of the list is quite closely related to the list of 1 Chr 27, which ends with Ephraim and Manasseh, followed by Benjamin (with Gad and Asher being omitted), and with Dan trailing in last place, probably as an addendum. It may be, as suggested by Osborne, that the position of the north in chaps. 1–9 is unclear, as is also the case in, he believes, the narrative portion of the book. However, we believe this lack of clarity is more likely due to differing views of subsequent writers rather than to a single individual.

The degree to which 1 Chr 1–9 may be attributed to "the Chronicler" has been vigorously disputed, and it cannot be said that the last word on this subject has been spoken. Most recently F. M. Cross, Jr. has included chaps. 1–9 as a part of the contribution of the latest editor of the book, his so-called "Chr₃," dated about 400 B.C. (*JBL* 94 [1975] 11–14). Although Cross has not discussed this possibility, it would seem probable that if that were the case, chaps. 1–9 would have replaced or expanded upon an earlier text, since beginning a literary work with chap. 10, while possible, does not seem most probable. By way of contrast, other more recent studies, such as those of Williamson, Osborne, Johnson, Polzin, and Japhet, have continued to point to similarities in vocabulary, style, thought, and structure between chaps. 1–9 and 1 Chr 10–2 Chr 36, as evidence of a common authorship. Critical scholars such as Kittel, Rothstein, Noth, Rudolph, and Galling have usually considered the present form of chaps. 1–9 to be an expansion of an originally very brief format of Israel's ancestors, numbering perhaps less than a hundred verses (cf. Rudolph, 1–2), repeating the brief genealogies of, e.g., Gen 46 and/or Num 26 with few additions; more conservative scholars have with few exceptions defended the entire complex as the product of the Chronicler (cf., e.g., Keil, and to a great extent Curtis). Other more recent scholars, also of a critical persuasion, have tended to be more nuanced in their judgments, often admitting that while the text shows signs of successive alterations (rather than the single revision proposed by the two-edition theory of Rothstein and Galling), neither the nature nor extent of these revisions is fully understood (cf. Myers, Ackroyd, and most judiciously, Coggins, and Michaeli). It is in this last-named group that the present work too must fall.

An example of the type of data now becoming available which may at last provide additional insight into the unity and structure of 1 Chr 1–9 is that gleaned by Johnson from his study of the genealogical prologue. Johnson notes that: (1) Only four genealogies of 1 Chr 2–9 contain no military allusions. These are the "core tribes" of north and south, Judah, Levi, Manasseh, and Ephraim (*Purpose*, 69). (2) In chaps. 1–9, only sixteen out of some three hundred verses are given to the five "Galilean" tribes—Issachar (7:1–5); Naphtali (7:13), Zebulon (lacking), Dan (7:12b?), and Asher (7:30–40). (3) In comparing the immediate descendants of Israel's sons in these chapters with the lists of Gen 46 and Num 26, we observe that (a) the names associated with seven tribes (Judah, Simeon, Reuben, Levi, Issachar, Naphtali, and Asher) are essentially identical; (b) those of three tribes (Manasseh, Ephraim, and Benjamin) show a mixed relationship; and (c) Zebulon and Dan are absent, and the Gadite list (1 Chr 5:11–17) bears no relationship to the lists in Genesis and Numbers (*Purpose*, 45, 51–52).

Such data, together with the expressed interest in Levi, Judah, Benjamin, Ephraim, and Manasseh in 9:3 and the position of north and south elsewhere in the book, suggests that initial interest may well have fallen here, although it is impossible to determine to what degree other tribes may have been represented. The mixed nature of the notices concerning Benjamin may well point to a later interest in that tribe, as do the lengthy additions to Judah and Levi. The reason for the omission of Zebulon is not apparent; that of Dan (see on 7:12b) appears late and tendentious.

In our judgment, then, the opinions of Noth, Rudolph, etc., are probably overly critical, while those who seek to attribute all or the great bulk of 1 Chr 1–9 to the same author as the remainder of Chronicles tend to harmonize the disparate evidence and minimize the difficulties involved. That 1 Chr 1–9 are similar to the later chapters on many levels is certainly true. However, these similarities, in view of the differences which also surface, point not to a common authorship, but rather to a similarity in age, interest, and outlook on the part of the writers.

It is, however, in the last analysis, this final product, whether it be from the hand of a single writer or of many, that we are called upon to seek to understand as God's revelation to us, and to that task we now turn.

OUTLINE

The current form of these chapters may be outlined as follows:
I. From Adam to Israel, 1:1–54
   A. Descendants of Noah 1:4–27
   B. Descendants of Abraham 1:28–54
      1. Descendants of Abraham 1:28–37
      2. Sons of Seir 1:38–42
      3. Edomite Rulers 1:43–54
II. Descendants of Israel 2:1–9:44
   A. Israel's Sons 2:1–2
   B. Descendants of Judah 2:3–4:23
   C. Descendants of Simeon 4:24–43
   D. Descendants of Reuben, Gad, and half-Manasseh 5:1–26
   E. Levites 5:27–6:66 [6:1–81]
   F. Descendants of Issachar 7:1–5
   G. Descendants of Benjamin 7:6–12
   H. Descendants of Naphtali 7:13
   I. Descendants of (West-) Manasseh 7:14–19
   J. Descendants of Ephraim 7:20–29
   K. Descendants of Asher 7:30–40
   L. Additional descendants of Benjamin 8:1–40
   M. List of Returning Exiles 9:1–44
A more detailed outline of each of these units is included in the treatment of each of the units below.

From Adam to Israel (1:1-54)

Bibliography

Podechard, E. "Le premier chapître des Paralipomenes." *RB* 13 (1916) 363–86. **Rad, G. von.** *Genesis: A Commentary.* OTL. Tr. J. H. Marks. Philadelphia: Westminster Press, 1961. **Roehrs, W.** *Genesis.* Concordia Commentary. St. Louis: Concordia Publishing House, 1979. **Skinner, J.** *A Critical and Exegetical Commentary on Genesis.* ICC. 2d ed. Edinburgh: T. & T. Clark, 1930. **Speiser, E. A.** *Genesis.* AB 1. Garden City, NY: Doubleday, 1964.

Chap. 1 provides a kind of "preamble to the prologue" (Brunet, *RB* 60 [1953] 485) of chaps. 1–9, passing rapidly from Adam to Abraham, Isaac, and Israel (v 34), whose descendants are in chaps. 2–9 the principal interest of the writer.

In its present form, the material of this chapter, whose unity is disputed, is best divided as follows:

vv 1–23   from Adam to Noah and his sons;
vv 24–54   from Shem to Abraham and his sons.

Divided in this manner, each unit begins with an extremely terse listing in identical form of the ancestors of the individuals whose offspring are the chief item of interest (Noah, vv 1–4; Abraham, vv 24–27) and concludes with more extensive genealogies of the offspring of that individual in reverse order: Japheth, Ham, and Shem (vv 5–23); Ishmael, Keturah, and Isaac (vv 28–54). The listing of Isaac's sons Esau and Israel (v 34) prepares the way for the presentation of Isaac's offspring through Israel, which is the proper subject of chaps. 2–9 and indeed of the remainder of the work.

In the selection and arrangement of his material our author, like the traditions of Genesis upon which he is dependent, has arranged his material schematically. Israel's pre-history falls into two periods of ten generations each extending from Adam to Noah and from Noah to Abraham. The descendants of Noah's sons, Shem, Ham, and Japheth, are probably meant to number seventy, the traditional number of the families of the earth. Whether the writer of Chronicles recognized this schema or adopted it unknowingly may be argued; however, the pivotal position of vv 4 and 24 within the chapter suggests the former. It is possible that a similar pattern is to be seen in the listing of the descendants of Abraham (cf. W. Roehrs, 254), although this is no longer obvious.

In presenting such a picture of history the sacred authors have been unconcerned about the difficulties in picturing peoples and geographical areas as individuals (cf. Egypt and Canaan, v 8; Seir, v 38, etc.) with their own genealogical ancestors and descendants. The value of such portrayals, however, ought not be underestimated. The understanding of history as consisting of distinguishable blocks of time, separated by events of extraordinary significance, is a favorite way in which God's people have pictured graphically his purpose in history and his direction of it, as may be seen in the highly schematic ordering of the genealogy of Jesus into three periods of fourteen generations each in the genealogy of Matt 1:1–17. Similarly, the tracing of Israel's ancestors back to the first man, Adam, has its parallel in the Lucan genealogy of Jesus Christ which is also traced to the beginning of creation and even before (Luke 3:23–38). In both cases the point is to demonstrate by way of genealogy the integral relationship which existed between the person or nation whose genealogy is recounted and the Creator, whose plan for that person or nation is thus seen to form a part of his purpose from before the foundations of the world. Seen in that light, 1 Chr 1, and the chapters following it, do not recount dry genealogical data. Instead they speak of God's guidance and direction of all things, and particularly of his chosen people, Israel, to the goal which he has prepared for them.

From Adam to Noah and His Sons   (1:1–23)

Translation

¹ *Adam, Seth, Enosh,* ² *Kenan, Mahalalel, Jared,* ³ *Enoch, Methuselah, Lamech,* ⁴ *Noah,* ᵃ *Shem, Ham, Japheth.*

⁵ *The sons of Japheth: Gomer, Magog, Madai, Javan,* ᵃ *Tubal, Meshech, and Tiras.* ⁶ *The sons of Gomer: Ashkenaz, Diphath,* ᵃ *and Togarmah.* ⁷ *The sons of Javan: Elishah and Tarshish,* ᵃ *Kittim, and Rodanim.* ᵇ

⁸ *The sons of Ham: Cush and Egypt, Put, and Canaan.* ⁹ *The sons of Cush: Seba, Havilah, Sabta, Raama, and Sabteca. The sons of Raama:* ᵃ *Sheba and Dedan.* ¹⁰ *Cush also became the father of* ᵃ *Nimrod. He was the first* ᵇ *to be a mighty man.* ᶜ ¹¹ ᵃ *Egypt became the father of the Ludim,* ᵇ *the Anamim, the Lehabim, the Naphtuhim,* ¹² *the Pathrusim, and the Casluhim, from whom came the* ᵃ *Philistines and the Caphtorim.* ᵃ ¹³ *Canaan became the father of Sidon his first-born, Heth,* ¹⁴ *the Jebusite,* ᵃ *the Amorite, the Girgashite,* ¹⁵ *the Hivite, the Arkite, the Sinite,* ¹⁶ *the Arvadite, the Zemarite, and the Hamathite.*

¹⁷ *The sons of Shem: Elam, Asshur, Arpachshad,* ᵃ *Lud, Aram,* ᵇ *Uz, Hul, Gether, and Meshech.* ᶜ ¹⁸ *Arpachshad became the father of Shelah,* ᵃ *and Shelah became the father of Eber.* ¹⁹ *To Eber were born* ᵃ *two sons: the name of the one* ᵇ *was Peleg (because the earth was divided in his days), and the name of his brother was Joktan.* ²⁰ *Joktan became the father of Almodad, Sheleph, Hazarmaveth, Jerah,* ²¹ *Hadoram, Uzal, Diklah,* ²² *Ebal,* ᵃ *Abimael, Sheba,* ²³ *Ophir, Havilah, and Jobab. All these were the sons of Joktan.*

Notes

4.a. Gᴮ + "the sons of Noah," reflecting the obvious difficulty in including Noah's three sons without differentiation in a pattern identical to the preceding, in which the name of each parent is followed by that of only a single son.

5.a. G⁻ᴸ + Ελεισα "Eleisa," which both G and Heb. include in v 7 as one of Javan's sons.

6.a. Reading ריפת "Riphath" with *ca.* 30 MSS G Vg and Gen 10:3 for דיפת "Diphath." The confusion between ד and ר is a common scribal error (cf. n. 7.b.).

7.a. Reading תרשיש "Tarshish" for תרשישה "Tarshishah" with G Vg Gen 10:3. The ה may be misplaced from the preceding word, as suggested by Rudolph (6), or attracted from the following.

7.b. Read דודנים "Dodanim" for רודנים "Rodanim" with most MSS G Syr Gen 10:4.

9.a. RSV and JB "Raamah" reflects orthography of the Bomberg Bible and Masora. L reads רעמא "Raamah" in both occurrences within the verse.

10.a. The use of the qal of ילד in the sense "to beget," or "become the father of," is characteristic of the J source of the Pentateuch, upon which this verse is dependent (Gen 10:8). Cf. BDB, 408b. The same form occurs also in vv 11, 13, 18 (2x), 20, all similarly dependent upon J portions of Gen 10.

10.b. Cf. JB, TEV, von Rad (*Genesis*, 141). The customary translation of החל "he began" is meaningless in this context.

10.c. G + κυνηγὸς "to be powerful" = ציד, BDB, 844, "hunting"; cf. Gen 10:9.

11.a. G^B < vv 11–16, Rudolph (6) believes, because it was lacking in his *Vorlage*.

11.b. Q לודים "Ludim"; K Gen 10:13 לודיים "Ludiim."

12.a-a. Amos 9:7 also includes mention of the Philistines and Caphtor together, although there the Philistines are said to have their origin from Caphtor.

14.a. The gentilics of vv 14–16 are sg in form, in contrast to the pls of vv 11–12.

17.a. G^B omits the following to ארפכשד "Arpachshad," v 24 (by homoiotel).

17.b. G^A "the sons of Aram, Uz. . . ."

17.c. 6 MSS Vg α′ Gen 10:23 ומש "and Mash"; MT as in v 5.

18.a. G^{Aal} + "Arpachshad was the father of Kenan and Kenan was the father of Shelah."

19.a. Heb. ילד "he brought forth"; G Vg Tg read as pl. But Heb. frequently uses a sg vb preceding a compound subj; GKC, § 145o, 146d.

19.b. Or, "the first"; cf. Gen 1:5.

22.a. Gen 10:28 Syr nonn MSS עובל "Obal."

Form/Structure/Setting

Vv 1–23 are closely related to the genealogical data of Gen 1–10, all of which is in fact included in vv 1–23 with the exception of the genealogy of Cain in Gen 4:17–24. The more precise correspondencies may be indicated as follows:

	1 Chronicles	*Genesis*
From Adam to Noah's sons	1:1–4	5:1–32 (P)
Sons of Japheth	1:5–7	10:2–4 (P)
Sons of Ham	1:8–16	10:6–7 (P), 8 (J), 13–18 (J)
Sons of Shem	1:17–23	10:21–23 (P), 24–29 (J)

Vv 1–4, which like vv 24–27 consist only of a series of names placed together without so much as a conjunction, depend upon Gen 5 only in the individuals named and the sequence in which they are listed. However, vv 5–23 owe much of their form (e.g., "the sons of Japheth," v 5, cf. Gen 10:2; "and Egypt became the father of [ילד] the Ludim," v 11; cf. Gen 10:13) as well as their structure (e.g., the descendants of Noah's sons Shem, Ham, and Japheth are dealt with in the reverse order, though this is sometimes errone-ously attributed to the style of the author of Chronicles) to Gen 10. In addition, the degree to which the descendants of each of these three sub-lines is pursued is directly dependent upon the author's source in Gen 10.

The identity in form between vv 1–4 and 24–27 has suggested to many that vv 5–23 (or, more precisely, 4b–23) are not an original part of the work but are due to later expansion (cf. Rudolph, 6–7). Several arguments may be advanced to support this view. (1) Vv 5–23 differ in *form* both from the preceding and the following verses. (2) The listing of Noah's three sons in v 4 interrupts the regular sequence, in which the name of the father is followed only by that of the single son through whom the genealogy is continued. (3) G^B omits both vv 11–16 and 17b–23. While some view the omission(s) as simple scribal error (Curtis, 57; Noth, *Ü.S.*, 117), Rudolph (6–7) finds no logical reason for the omission of vv 11–16, and views the results as evidence for the continuing supplementation of the original text, which consisted only of vv 1–4a, by later hands. (4) Vv 17–23 do not blend easily with vv 24–27. In particular, Shem's lineage in v 17 differs from that in v 24, where the simple form of the list is resumed; and vv 20–23 name no less than 13 sons of Joktan, whose name is absent in vv 24–27. (5) Vv 24–27 will connect directly with nothing except vv 1–4a.

These arguments, while substantial, may not appear conclusive to many. It may be argued, for example, that vv 1–4, culminating with Noah's sons, and vv 24–27, concluding with Abraham, are stylistic devices used to point to the significance of these individuals in Israel's history. Such an arrangement would be suggested already by Genesis, in which the ten antediluvian and ten postdiluvian patriarchs form, in at least partial dependence upon Near Eastern parallels, recognizable units (see the Genesis commentaries). A similar use of structured genealogies may be seen in the Matthean version of Jesus' genealogy in Matt 1; cf. especially v 17. The listing of Noah's three sons may well be dependent upon the similar listing of Gen 5:32 (cf. also 11:26, both P). The evidence of G is admittedly susceptible to different interpretations.

Points 4 and 5, taken together with point 1, may provide the most substantial evidence. Here again, however, it may be argued that the likelihood that the original author, largely in dependence upon his sources, would include material within his work without bothering to resolve the divergencies differs only in degree, rather than in kind, from the likelihood of a later hand doing the same. (The inclusion of the disparate notices within Gen 10–11 itself is an indication of the latter.)

Whichever decision one makes (and the present writer is inclined to accept the probability that vv 4b–23 represent an addition to the precanonical textform), it is well to recognize that neither the purpose nor message of the unit is materially altered. The author's primary (sole?) purpose was to point a line from Adam, the father of mankind, to Abraham, the father of the faithful. The precise degree to which this line was supplemented, whether by the original writer or a later one, is of little importance, and can only be conjectured.

Comment

1–4 *From Adam to Noah.* The writer has taken his material from Gen 5, omitting all details. The names are identical in every respect to those of Gen 5, including the Masoretic vocalization. In the tradition represented in Gen 5 too, it should be noted, commonly assigned to the priestly strata of the Pentateuch and resumed in 10:1, the genealogical tree branches with Noah's sons, all of whom are listed. This suggests that the Heb. text of v 4 is correct, and the author unconcerned with our difficulty in understanding his failure to be consistent.

DESCENDANTS OF SHEM, HAM, AND JAPHETH

Gen 10, which forms the basis for this unit, is traditionally stated to include 70 descendants of Noah's sons, symbolizing the 70 peoples of the world. Although Rudolph (7) is right in his assertion that the number can be maintained only with difficulty, necessitating the omission of Nimrod, it is probable that such was its intention. Whether the same was in the mind of the compiler of these verses is questionable. He has, however, maintained the complete listing of 70 (or 71) names from Gen 10.

5–7 *Descendants of Japheth.* Virtually identical with Japheth's genealogy in Gen 10:2–4, with the minor differences cited in the notes. The remarks of 10:5, brief as they are, are nonetheless bypassed. That the author has pursued Japheth's line through his sons Gomer and Javan, and not through the remaining sons, is due to the author's source, and hence not to be attributed to any particular *Tendenz* on his part.

8–16 *Descendants of Ham.* The individuals named are again identical to those found in Gen 10:6–20. Since all names found in the source are included, it is difficult to agree with Myers' judgment (7) that the greater detail concerning Ham is due to the fact that the Hebrews had more dealings with this group than with the Japhethites. Once again, most of the extraneous detail from Genesis has been omitted (cf. 10:9–12, 18b–20) as apparently outside the author's purpose. However, one reference to Nimrod as a mighty man (גבור, v 10, cf. Gen 10:8) has been retained, the first example of such material in Chronicles. Retention of the genealogical terminology of his source (vv 10, 11, 13) also indicates a very close dependency upon the text in this unit, as does the retention of the reference to the origins of the Philistines and Caphtorim from the Casluhim (cf. Amos 9:7).

The mention of the nations of Egypt ("Mizraim," מצרים) and Canaan in the genealogy as if they were individuals, in agreement also with Gen 10, is a regular phenomenon of such genealogies, and a reminder that the term "sons" (בנים) must often be understood in a very broad sense. The biblical writers were often more desirous of sketching general relationships rather than providing genealogical data in the narrow sense.

17–27 *Descendants of Shem.* These verses are derived from Gen 10:22–29, from which they diverge only in minute detail. The omission of the opening verse of that genealogy, "To Shem also, the father of all the sons of Eber, the elder brother of Japheth, were born (children)," (Gen 10:21), is striking, since it could have been taken to emphasize Shem's role as the progenitor of the Hebrews and his senior status among Noah's sons. Perhaps such knowledge was assumed, however. The concluding verses of that genealogy (vv 30–32) have also been omitted.

Explanation

In initiating his book with Adam, the author's methodology is reminiscent of the genealogy of Jesus found in Luke 3:23–38, which also traces Jesus' parentage beyond Abraham to the beginning of creation in Adam and thus in God himself (Luke 3:38). In doing this, the chief emphasis lies upon God's purpose for and direction of Israel, which is thus portrayed as extending back to the dawn of creation. The existence of Israel is not incidental to God's purpose, but has formed the center of his plan from the beginning. This purpose is reflected in the linear genealogy of vv 1–4 (and 24–27) and in the division of Abraham's progenitors into two distinct groups represented in Genesis by the ten antediluvian and ten postdiluvian patriarchs. At the same time the genealogy as a literary device provides the briefest, if to our mind quite unsatisfactory, method of recalling Israel's history and her role among the nations of the world. It is for this purpose also that the segmented genealogies of vv 5–23 are particularly useful. Israel dwells among the nations of the world, yet for her God has a unique position and purpose.

From Shem to Abraham and His Sons   (1:24–54)

Translation

²⁴ Shem, ᵃ Arpachshad, Shelah, ²⁵ Eber, Peleg, Reu, ²⁶ Serug, Nahor, Terah, ²⁷ and ᵃAbram, who is ᵃ Abraham.

²⁸ The sons of Abraham were Isaac and Ishmael. ²⁹ These were their generations: ᵃ The firstborn of Ishmael, Nebaioth; then Kedar, Adbeel, ᵇ Mibsam, ³⁰ Mishma, Dumah, Massa, Hadad, Tema, ³¹ Jetur, Naphish, and Kedemah. ᵃ These were Ishmael's sons.

³² The sons of Keturah, Abraham's concubine: ᵃ she gave birth ᵃ to Zimran, Jokshan, Medan, Midian, Ishbak, ᵇ and Shuah. Jokshan's sons were Sheba and Dedan, ᶜ and Midian's sons were Ephah, Epher, Hanock, Abida, and Eldaah. All these were Keturah's sons.

³⁴ Abraham was the father of Isaac. The sons of Isaac: ᵃ Esau and Israel. ᵃ ³⁵ The sons of Esau: Eliphaz, Reuel, Jeush, Jalam, and Korah. ³⁶ The sons of Eliphaz: Teman and Omar, Zephi ᵃ and Gatam, Kenaz, ᵇ Timna, and Amalek. ᵇ ³⁷ The sons of Reuel: Nahath, Zerah, Shammah, and Mizzah.

³⁸ The sons of Seir: Lotan, Shobal, Zibeon, Anah, Dishon, ᵃ Ezer, and Dishan. ᵃ ³⁹ The sons of Lotan: Hori and Homan ᵃ ᵇ (Lotan's sister was Timna). ᵇ ⁴⁰ The sons of Shobal: Alian, ᵃ Manahath, and Ebal, Shephi ᵇ and Onam. The sons of Zibeon: Aiah and Anah. ⁴¹ The sons ᵃ of Anah: ᵇ Dishon. ᶜ The sons of Dishon: ᵈ Hamran, Eshban, Ithran, and Cheran. ⁴² The sons of Ezer: Bilhan, ᵃ Zaavan, ᵇ and Jakan. ᶜ The sons of Dishan: ᵈ Uz and Aran.

⁴³ These are ᵃ the kings who reigned over the land of Edom before any king of the sons of Israel ᵃ reigned: Bela, ᵇ the son of Beor, and the name of his city was Dinhabah. ⁴⁴ Bela died, and Jobab, the son of Zerah from Bozrah, reigned in his place. ⁴⁵ Jobab died, and Husham from the land of the Temanite reigned in his place. ⁴⁶ Husham died, and Hadad, the son of Bedad, ᵃ who smote Midian in the field of Moab, reigned in his place. (The name of his city was Avith.)ᵇ ⁴⁷ Hadad died, and Samlah of Masrekah reigned in his stead. ⁴⁸ Samlah died, and Shaul from Rehoboth of the Euphrates reigned in his stead. ⁴⁹ Shaul died, and Baal-hanan, the son of

Achbor, reigned in his place. ⁵⁰ Baal-hanan died, and Hadad ᵃ reigned in his place. The name of his city was Pai ᵇ ᶜ and the name of his wife was Mehetable, the daughter of Matred, ᵈ the daughter of Me-zahab. ᶜᵈ ⁵¹ Hadad died.

The chiefs of Edom were Chief Timna, ᵃ Chief Aliah, ᵇ Chief Jetheth, ⁵² Chief Oholibamah, ᵃ Chief Elah, Chief Pinon, ⁵³ Chief Kenaz, Chief Teman, Chief Mibzar, ⁵⁴ Chief Magdiel, and Chief Iram. ᵃ These were the chiefs of Edom.

Notes

24.a. G "the sons of Shem"; cf. perhaps n. 4.a.

27.a-a. Not in Gᴮ.

29.a. תלדותם. This is the first occurrence in 1 Chronicles of the familiar but problematic term around which the framework of the book of Genesis is built. While traditionally translated "generations," in Genesis the term regularly introduces not simply a genealogy but a pericope denoting the history of a man and his descendants (BDB, 410). Both for the sake of convenience and because that fuller meaning seems to be lost in Chronicles, the traditional translation has been retained here. Cf. 1 Chr 5:7; 7:2, 4, 9; 8:28; 9:9, 34; 26:31. The term is not found in Ezra-Nehemiah.

29.b. Heb. אדבאל "Adbeel"; Gᴮᴬ Ναβδε(αι)ηλ "Nabdeel" or "Nabdail."

31.a. Cf. Gen 25:15. 1 Chr 5:19 lists Jetur, Naphish, and one Nodab (נודב) as enemies of Reuben, Gad, and half Manasseh, along with the Hagrite.

32.a-a. > G.

32.b. G Σωβακ "Sobak."

32.c. Heb. דדן; Gᴮᴬ Δαιδαν Heb. and Gr. "Dedan"; Gᴸ Δαρδαν "Dardan."

34.a-a. Gᴮ Ιακωβ καὶ Ησαυ "Jacob and Esau"; Gᴬ Ησαυ καὶ Ιακωβ "Esau and Jacob." On the basis of the consistency with which Chronicles uses "Israel" instead of "Jacob," textual emendation here on the basis of G would be hazardous (cf. Williamson, *Israel*, 62, n. 3).

36.a. L צפי "Zephi"; *ca.* 30 MSS Syr Gen 36:11 צפו "Zepho"; Gᴮᴬ Σωφαρ (= צפר "Sophar").

36.b-b. Gᴮ καὶ τῆς Θιμνα Αμαληκ "and Timna, Amalek." Gᴬ and some other MSS read as in Gen 36:12.

38.a-a. Gᴮ Ωναν "Onan"; Gᴬᴸ ᴹˢˢ καὶ Ρισων "and Rison."

39.a. Gen 36:22 והימם; G καὶ Αιμαν; Heb. and Gr. = "and Homan."

39.b-b. Gᴮ καὶ Αιλαθ καὶ Ναμνα "and Ailath and Namna."

40.a. L עלין "Alian"; mlt MSS Gᴸ Gen 36:23 עלון "Alvan."

40.b. L שפי "Shephi." Some Heb. MSS + Gen 36:23 שפו "Shipho"; Gᴮ Σωβ "Sôb." Gᴬ Syr שפר "Shiphar." For a similar pattern of variants see n. 36.a.

41.a. MT בני "sons"; Seb and many commentators sg. The problem of the translation of the sg and pl forms of this word is constant throughout the genealogies of Chronicles, in view of the number of "children" named in subsequent verses, but it appears unreasonable to consider all such occurrences as scribal errors. Two other solutions seem possible: (1) to consider the use of the pl בני as purely mechanical and without significance (cf. Rudolph, 8); or (2) to understand בני in such contexts to have a broader meaning than "son" in its most literal sense, including on occasion daughters, male descendants of later generations, and possibly also individuals unrelated by blood who became attached to the family through various historical, geographical, and sociological circumstances. If this be the case, a more general term such as "kindred," "family," or "descendants" would be more precise. In most cases, however, we are ignorant of the precise relationship of those named, making the use of a term other than the conventional "sons" equally problematic.

41.b. Not the Anah of v 40, but Seir's son of v 38, as indicated by the structure of the entire pericope.

41.c. Gen 36:26 "Dishan." Gᴬᴸ + καὶ Ελιβαμα Θυγατηρ Ανα "and Elibamah was the daughter of Anah"; cf. Gen 36:25.

41.d. Again, not the "Dishon/Dishan" just mentioned in v 41, but Seir's son of v 38.

42.a. Heb. בלהן "Bilhan"; G Βαλααμ(ν) "Balaam(n)."

42.b. Heb. וזען "and Zaanan"; Gen 36:23 זון "Zoan"; Gᴮᴬ? Ζομκαμ "Zomkam."

42.c. Heb. יעקן "Jakan"; either prefix the conj ו (cf. Gᴸ Syr Vg) or read ועקן "and Akan" with Gen 36:27 α′ Gᴬᵃˡ.

42.d. Reading דישן "Dishan" with Gen 36:28 (unnoted in *BH³*, but cf. *BHS*), thus restoring the name of Seir's last-named son from v 38.

43.a-a. G^B "their kings."

43.b. Heb בלע "Bela"; Tg בלעם "Bilam"; G Βαλακ "Balak."

46.a. G^BA = ברד "Berad"; Gen 36:35 בדד "Bedad."

46.b. Q Gen 36:35 עוית "Avith"; K עיות "Ayuth" (?); G^BA MSS Γεθθα(ι)μ (= עתים "Athaim").

50.a. Most MSS Tg Gen 36:39 הדר "Hadar."

50.b. Heb פעי "Pai"; most MSS G^L Syr Vg Tg פעו "Pau"; G^BA Φογωρ "Pogor."

50.c-c. > G^B.

50.d-d. G^A Syr = בן "son"; cf. Gen 36 Syr G and Deut 1:1.

51.a. G^B Θαιμαν "Timan."

51.b. K עליה "Aliah"; Q many MSS Vg Tg Gen 36:40 עלוה "Alvah"; G^BA Γωλα "Gola" = עולה "Olah."

52.a. G Ελιβαμα "Elibama."

54.a. G^B Ζαφωειν "Zaphoein"; cf. Gen 36:43.

Form/Structure/Setting

The relationship of the materials of this unit with the genealogical portions of Genesis is again apparent from the following table:

	1 Chr 1	Genesis
Shem to Abraham	vv 24–27	11:10–26 (P)
Title	v 28	(cf. 25:9)
Ishmael	vv 29–31	25:12–16 (P)
Keturah	vv 32–33	25:1–3a, 4 (J)
Isaac	v 34a	25:19–26 (P)
Esau	vv 35–37	36:1–5, 10–19 (P)
Sons of Seir	vv 38–42	36:20–28 (P)
Kings of Edom	vv 43–51a	36:31–39
Chiefs of Edom	vv 51b–54	36:40–43 (P)

Vv 24–27 are parallel in form to vv 1–4, and may have originally been a direct continuation of them. Abraham's descendants are then presented according to their descent from Ishmael (vv 29b–31), Keturah (vv 32–33), and Isaac (vv 34–54). Of Isaac's descendants, those from Esau are listed in four separate units (vv 35–37, 38–42, 43–51a, and 51b–54). Isaac's descendants through Israel will then become the subject of 2:1–4.

The order of treatment of these various descendants is again noteworthy. As in Gen 25, Abraham's descendants through Ishmael precede those through Isaac. The inclusion of Keturah's sons is unexpected in view of the heading of v 28, where her name is absent, and also occupies an unusual place between Ishmael and Isaac. Of Isaac's sons, Chronicles considers Esau first, and the various sub-units listed with Esau follow the same order as in Gen 36. However, Genesis contains two separate listings of Isaac's sons, one preceding (Gen 35:23–26) and the other following (Gen 46:8–27) the genealogy of Esau. While it is evident that Chronicles' listing of Israel's sons is more clearly dependent upon the latter (see under 2:1–2), it is probably unwarranted to make literary judgments on that basis. Hence it can only be asserted that Chronicles, in agreement with or contrary to his sources as he read them, placed the descendants of Esau before those of Israel. The result is, however, that throughout chap. 1 the subsidiary lines are regularly treated first (Ackroyd, 31).

Many scholars consider the three units composing vv 38–54, and especially the latter two of these (vv 43–54), to be probable additions to an earlier form of the genealogy. Their reasoning deserves attention. First, a more brief presentation of Esau's descendants, ostensibly continued in these verses, has already been given in vv 35–37. The extensive listing of twenty-six descendants of "Seir," eleven kings of Edom, and eleven "chiefs" of Edom seems disproportionate in view of the intense brevity not only of vv 1–4, 24–27, but of vv 5–23 and 28–37 as well. Secondly, the mention of the "sons of Seir" in v 38 comes as an intrusion, since Seir's name is not found in any of the previous genealogies, including that of Esau, where, upon the basis of tradition and geography, it might be expected. (See Gen 36 and *Comment*, below). Instead we find a feature known in other portions of the OT, and more obviously apparent in this connection in Gen 36, in which the people inhabiting a given area are linked together genealogically as though derived from a common ancestor whose name the area bears. Finally, the manner in which the author of vv 43–51a has dealt with his source in Gen 36:31–39, retaining the more expansive style of the text there which mentions both the death of the earlier king and the accession of the latter, as well as bits of miscellaneous data such as the names of cities over which they ruled and the names of other relatives, stands in striking contrast to his methodology in earlier verses of the chapter.

That such additions and such a change in methodology could have been made by the original author is of course possible. It seems more likely, however, especially in view of the rather inconsequential position of Seir/Edom within the total purview of the work, that they owe their inclusion to a later attempt either to preserve for later readers as much of the genealogical materials of Genesis as possible, or to the importance which the Edomites, Israel's traditional enemy to the south, occupied for another writer later in the post-exilic period.

Comment

17–24 *From Shem to Abraham.* While vv 17–23 stemmed from the Shemite genealogy of Gen 10, vv 24–27 are dependent upon Gen 11:10–26. As in the case of vv 1–4, only the names of Shem's descendants are here left intact, chronological and other notations having been omitted. As noted above, these descendants from Shem to Abraham number ten, inclusive, as was the case also from Adam to Shem.

The genealogy of vv 24–27 extends beyond that of v 19 by including Reu, Serug, Nahor, Terah, and Abram/Abraham, apparently through the line of Peleg, which was in v 19 omitted in favor of that of his brother Joktan. This divergence, it has been noted, existed already in Gen 10 and 11, and may have been included here either by the original author or by a later hand. The name Abram is found in the same form (אברם) in Gen 11:26, where, however, two additional sons of Terah, Nahor and Haran, are also listed. (The P genealogies of both Gen 5 and 11 thus end with a triplet, Shem-

Ham-Japheth and Terah-Nahor-Haran.) In the continuing narrative of Genesis, the change of the name of Abram (אברם) to Abraham (אברהם) occurs
in conjunction with the priestly covenant of Gen 17 (cf. v 5). As a bridge,
therefore, between the genealogy of Gen 11, in which the name Abram is
used, and that of Gen 25, where we find the name Abraham, the author
has appended his own note, הוא אברהם "he is Abraham." It is thus in the
context of Abraham that the author has written the first words for which
he is not immediately dependent upon a source.

23–31 *Descendants of Ishmael.* The expression of v 28, "The sons of Abraham: Isaac and Ishmael," does not occur in this form in Genesis. However,
Isaac and Ishmael are listed together, and in this order, in connection with
the burial of their father in Gen 25:9. The title of v 29a, "these are their
generations: the firstborn of Ishmael, Nebaioth . . . ," is likewise a combination of terms derived from Gen 25:12–13 ("*These are* the names of the sons
of Ishmael by their names, according to their *generations: the firstborn of Ishmael,
Nebaioth . . .*"). The list of Ishmael's descendants (29b–31) is virtually identical
with that of Gen 25:13b–15, and, as far as it extends, even the closing note
of the genealogy (31a) is identical with the Genesis format (25:16a, through
Ishmael), including the rather striking "*these are* (אלה הם) the sons of Ishmael." Once again, the more extended termination of Gen 25:16–18 is omitted.

32–33 *Descendants of Keturah.* The account of Keturah's descendants is
derived from Gen 25:1–4. Both the names of the children and the sequence
in which they are given is identical. However, the slightly more narrative
style of Genesis is, as usual, abandoned, and the three sons of Dedan (Gen
25:3b) are omitted. (See n. 32.c.) It is striking also that that the sign of the
definite direct object (את) is omitted before all except the first name of the
list, Zimran, although occurring no less than eight times in the Genesis parallel. This might support the omission of the words ילדה את "she bore," with
Syr, although the textual evidence is otherwise weak.

Chronicles explicitly names Keturah as Abraham's concubine (פילגש), although this term is not found in Gen 25, where the vocabulary suggests a
second wife. However, Gen 25:5–6 does point to a difference between Isaac
and Abraham's other sons, and v 6 can be understood to include Keturah's
children among the sons of the concubines. Nevertheless, the terminology
of v 32 does represent an interpretative viewpoint of the writer.

As noted above, the enumeration of Keturah's children is unexpected in
view of her omission from the title of v 28, and the order in which the completed genealogy of Chronicles lies before us (Keturah's children following
those of Ishmael) is contrary to the order of Genesis. Hence the possibility
exists that the Keturah genealogy reflects a later desire to include all of the
genealogical information of Genesis. On the other hand, it can be argued
that the inclusion of a female within the genealogy, in addition to the more
disparate location of the various aspects of Abraham's genealogy in Genesis,
could easily have led to the reshuffling of positions.

34–37 *Descendants of Isaac: Esau.* The heading of v 34, which resumes
that of v 28 after inclusion of the genealogies of Ishmael and Keturah,
is unexpected and contrary to the writers' usual practice. However, v 34 is
dependent upon Gen 25:19, where too there is a backtracking to include the

parentage of Abraham, אברהם הוליד את יצחק, "Abraham begat Isaac," which Chronicles has rephrased in more classical form, ויולד אברהם את יצחק "and Abraham begat Isaac." In its subtitle, "the sons of Isaac: Esau and Israel" (v 34b), which Rudolph (7) would consider to be the direct continuation of v 31 prior to the insertion of the Keturah material, Chronicles has compressed the narrative of Gen 25:20–34, which recounted the birth of Jacob and Esau's despising of his birthright. Chronicles similarly has reduced the introductory verse of Esau's genealogy in Genesis, "these are the generations of Esau, who is Edom" (36:1) to the simple "the sons of Esau" (v 35a). The names of Esau's five sons are then derived from Gen 36:2–5, with omission of details relating to Esau's Canaanite wives. The names of the sons of Eliphaz (v 36) and Reuel (v 37) are taken from the parallel genealogy of Gen 36:9–14 (especially vv 11–13). However, the Timna who in Gen 36:12 was a concubine of Eliphaz and bore his son Amalek is listed in v 36 simply as another son of Eliphaz. A third parallel genealogy in Gen 36:15–19 agrees in principle on the names of six of the seven sons, but omits Timna and includes Korah (v 16). A Korah is also listed as a son of Esau's wife Oholibamah in Gen 36:5, 14, 18, cf. 1 Chr 1:35.

38–42 *Descendants of Seir.* Seir is not listed directly as a descendant of Esau in any of the genealogies available to us, and may better be understood as a geographical area rather than a person. However, in what appear to be redactional notices (Gen 36:1, 8, 9, 19), Esau is repeatedly identified with Edom or the father of Edom (Gen 36:9), and Edom's home is placed in the hill country of Seir. These "sons of Seir" are further identified with the Horite (Gen 36:20, 29, 30). (Cf. Gold, "Seir," *IDB* 4:262.)

Vv 38–42 are taken from Gen 36:20–28, with which the names are again identical in substance. Only a single name, that of Anah's daughter Oholibamah (Gen 36:25), has been bypassed by Chronicles. Once again, however, the writer has presented his material as briefly as possible, omitting most qualifying phrases and the historical note of 36:24.

43–51a *The Kings of Edom.* This list is taken from Gen 36:31–39, with which it is essentially identical. The author has used a somewhat different procedure in dealing with his source here, however. Where he regularly extracted only the names from the Genesis lists, this list retains a lengthier style in which the death of a king is noted, as well as the indication that the subsequent king ruled in his place. Chronicles has, perhaps for the sake of consistency, also recorded the death of the last king listed, Hadad (v 51a), not recorded in Genesis.

51b–54 *The Chiefs of Edom.* Once again the names and their order are identical with the source, Gen 36:40–43; however, Chronicles has abbreviated both the opening and closing formulas. This section of Genesis agrees with vv 15–19, a second (or third) listing of Esau's descendants, in applying the term אלוף, traditionally rendered "chief," or "chiliarch" (BDB, 48), to the family heads of Esau (cf. Exod 15:15; Zech 12:5–6; 9:7). The use of the parallel איל, "ram," in Exod 15:15 suggests, however, a derivation from אלף, "cattle," rather than "thousand," as does the striking parallel in the Ugaritic tablets, III K 4:6–8; 17–19; II Aq 5:16, where animal terminology is also applied to human rulers.

While eleven leaders of Edom/Esau are listed here, four share names with three sons and a wife of Esau's son Eliphaz, cf. v 36 and Gen 36:11, 12, 15, 18. Whether these names were so popular among prominent Edomites, or whether the four names point to the two lists as being more directly related, can only be conjectured. Once again the opening and closing notices are abbreviated, and where Genesis spoke of the chiefs of Esau (v 40) and the chiefs of Edom (v 43), apparently identifying them, Chronicles has changed the opening rubric to read "the chiefs of Edom." A closing statement identifying Esau with the father of Edom is also omitted.

Explanation

The second portion of our chapter moves rapidly from Shem to Abraham (vv 24–27), the father of the faithful (Gen 12:1–3). As is customary in the canonical form of the book, Abraham's descendants through the subordinate lines are traced first (vv 29–33), followed by the line of Isaac. Here too the line of Esau is listed first with the primary line of Israel (Jacob) postponed for the extensive treatment of 2:1–4:43.

While it is possible that sizable portions of this unit reflect later additions to an earlier core genealogy, it is also true that these additions are of similar content to the earlier material and do not materially affect its message. Abraham's descendants through Keturah (vv 32–34a) find a natural place beside the Arabs descended through Ishmael as do the inhabitants of Seir and Edom (vv 38–54) with the descendants of Esau traditionally identified with the same geographic area. The principal effect of these additions is therefore one of completeness rather than of change. To this extent the position of E. Podechard (*RB* 13 [1916] 362–86), adopted in substance by Johnson (*Purpose*, 74), that the chapter is the result of a genealogist's interest in "art for art's sake" in wishing to include all the genealogical data of Genesis, may be accepted. Only the material related to Cain (Gen 4:17–22) and Lot (Gen 19:30–38) has been neglected. The inclusion of this material, which may be considered a complex form of a segmented genealogy, does point to the ancient ties which bound Israel to the peoples surrounding her. At the same time, its inclusion does tend to obscure the clearness of the path from Abraham through Isaac to his son Israel, the proper subject of chaps. 2–9. At the end of a lengthy chain reaching back to Adam and Abraham stands Israel, God's chosen people, from one of whose sons will come David and Solomon, and in whose midst will be built a house of rest for him (1 Chr 28:2) for all ages.

Descendants of Israel and Judah   (2:1–4:23)

Bibliography

Aharoni, Y. "The Negeb of Judah." *IEJ* 8 (1958) 26–38. ———. "The Northern Boundary of Judah." *PEQ* 90 (1958) 27–31. **Beltz, W.** *Die Kaleb Traditionem im Alten Testament.* BWANT 98. Stuttgart: Kohlhammer, 1974. **Brunet, A.-M.** "Paralipomenes." *DBSup* 6. 1220–61. **Cohen, M. A.** "Judah, Formation of." *IDBSup.* 498–99. **Cross, F. M., and G. E. Wright.** "The Boundary and Province Lists of the Kingdom of Judah." *JBL* 95 (1975) 202–26. **Demsky, A.** "The Houses of Achzib." *IEJ* 16 (1966) 211–15. **Dijkstra, M.** "A Note on 1 Chr 4:22–23." *VT* 25 (1975) 671–74. **Elliger, K.** "Judah." *IDB* 2:1003–1005. ———. "Tribes, Territories of." *IDB* 4:701–710 (with extensive bibliography). **Kallai-Kleinmann, Z.** "Note on the Town Lists of Judah, Simeon, Benjamin and Dan." *VT* 11 (1961) 223–27. ———. "Tribes, Territories of." *IDBSup.* 920–23 (with recent bibliography). **Mendelsohn, I.** "Guilds in Ancient Palestine." *BASOR* 80 (1940) 17–21. **Noth, M.** "Die Ansiedlung des Stammes Juda auf dem Boden Palastinas." *PJ* 30 (1934) 31–47. (Also: *Aufsatze zur biblischen Landes und Altertumskunde.* Ed. H. W. Wolff. Neukirchen-Vluyn: Neukirchener Verlag [1971] 183–96.) ———. "Eine siedlungs-geographische Liste in 1 Chr. 2 und 4." *ZDPV* 55 (1932) 97–124. **Rothstein, J. W.** *Die Genealogie des Königs Jojachin und seiner Nachkommen.* Berlin: Reuther & Reichard, 1902. **Vaux, R. de.** "The Settlement of the Israelites in Southern Palestine and the Origins of the Tribe of Judah." *Translating and Understanding the Old Testament: Essays in Honor of Herbert Gordon May.* Eds. H. T. Frank and W. L. Reed. Nashville: Abingdon, 1970. 108–34. **Wellhausen, J.** *De Gentibus et Familiis Judaeis, quae 1 Chr 2, 4 enumerantur.* Göttingen: Officina Academica Dieterishiana, 1870. **Williamson, H. G. M.** "Sources and Redaction in the Chronicler's Genealogy of Judah." *JBL* 98 (1979) 351–59.

That there are serious difficulties in understanding this unit in its present form has long been recognized. The order of the descendants of Hezron's sons throughout chap. 2 does not correspond to the order in which they are listed in v 9—Jerahmeel, Ram, and Chelubai—nor is the name Chelubai in this verse found in this identical form elsewhere in the unit (cf. vv 18, 19, 42). The list of Jerahmeel's descendants begun in v 25 is apparently concluded in v 33, only to be continued in vv 33–41. Similarly, if the genealogy of Ram (2:10–17) is to be continued beyond David, it would be anticipated that this would follow immediately rather than in 3:1–24. The genealogy of Caleb (2:18–24), broken off by that of Jerahmeel, is resumed in vv 42–50a with appropriate opening and closing formulas, and again in vv 50b–55 as well as 4:2–7 without such formulas.

Although some (cf. Curtis, 82–84; Williamson, *infra.*) attribute the unit in its present form to the Chronicler himself, these duplications and the kind of inconsistencies usually associated with them have led most critical scholars to conclude that the unit has developed through a more complex pattern of supplementation which, they would argue, is understandable in view of the central position of the tribe of Judah in general and David in particular.

For example, M. Noth finds the work of the original author only in 2:1–5,

9 (in part) and 10–17 (*Ü.S.*, 119–20). Rudolph believes the original core was 2:1–9, 25–33, 10–17, 42–50aα, supplemented first by 2:21–23, 34–41, 50aβ–55, then by 3:1–4:23 and finally by 2:18–19, 24. (An even later addition is 2:20.)

The attempt to attribute these various components to specific sources has been described by Rudolph (13) as *"verlorene Liebesmühe,"* although marks of earlier sources have been isolated. Rothstein (73–74), as may be expected, traces the entire complex to two such sources. The opening and closing formulas of 2:25–33 and 42–50 are identical, cf. also 2:50b and 4:4b. The unusual form "X was the father of Y," in which Y represents not an individual but a city and its inhabitants, is found scattered throughout the unit (cf. 2:24, 42, 49–55; 4:16–19), and suggests an earlier source (cf. Noth, *ZDPV* 55 [1932] 100; *PJ* 30 [1934] 41–42), but it cannot be said that the attempt to reconstruct such a source from the materials at hand has met with success (see most recently Aharoni, *Land*, 225–27). Rudolph's theory of supplements, listed above, recognizes the difficulty in such reconstructions.

Most recently H. G. M. Williamson has renewed the investigation of Judah's genealogy and arrived at an analysis successful in explaining many of the duplications and inconsistencies in the unit which is at a minimum helpful in understanding the present form of the text (*JBL* 98 [1979] 351–59). Williamson, like Curtis (83–84), sees in the heart of the unit a chiastic arrangement which is the product of the Chronicler himself: The order of the first group of descendants:

A   2:9–17   Descendants of Ram (to David)
  B   2:18–24   Descendants of Caleb
    C   2:25–33   Descendants of Jerahmeel

is reversed in the second group:

    C'   2:34–41   Additional descendants of Jerahmeel
  B'   2:42–55   Additional descendants of Caleb
A'   3:1–24   Additional descendants of Ram (descendants of David)

Moreover, the unit is structured by a double inclusion, with 4:1–23 reverting in more general terms to descendants of Judah and Perez, recalling 2:3–8. Also, the unit concludes with the descendants of Shelah (4:21–23), the only surviving son of Judah mentioned in 2:3.

Williamson believes the Chronicler has here brought together various canonical and non-canonical sources, at least one of which had already passed through the hands of an earlier redactor (see below). The Chronicler has provided 2:9, which provides the organizing framework of 2:10–3:24 (*JBL* 98 [1979] 357). As keystones in his analysis, Williamson begins with the parallel formula of 2:25, 33 ("the sons of Jerahmeel: . . . . These were the descendants of Jerahmeel") and 2:42, 50 ("The son of Caleb: . . . . These were the descendants of Caleb.") However, a third similar introductory formula, "the sons of Hur" (v 50b), now finds its conclusion only in 4:4, "These were the sons of Hur" (*JBL* 98 [1979] 352–53). Closer analysis reveals the point at which the original insertion took place: the Haroeh (הרעה) of 2:52 represents a corruption of the name of Shebal's son, Reiaah (ראיה) in 4:2. Williamson thus argues reasonably that 2:53–55 and 4:1 represent an intrusion into a source listing the descendants of Caleb, encompassing originally 2:18–19, 24, 50b–52, 4:2–4, 5–7. The nature of this intrusion is close at hand: vv 53–55 represent an elaboration of the families of Kiriath-jearim mentioned in v 52. Seeing the resumptive nature of 4:1, the Chronicler has been led to introduce his list of David's descendants (3:1–24) at this point also.

Williamson believes the Calebite source used by the Chronicler already contained the intrusive vv 53–55. His reasons for so asserting are as follows: 4:1 resumes 2:52, but 4:1 does not belong to the Chronicler, since 4:1 does not agree precisely with 2:3–8. Note in particular the occurrence of "Carmi" (4:1) instead of "Caleb." Moreover, the Chronicler uses the formula "the sons of X" only to introduce brothers, and not a list proceeding from father to son, as does 4:1 (*JBL* 98 [1979] 356).

It is this same Calebite source, however, in which various other difficulties abound. Uri and Bezalel, the sons of Caleb's son Hur in 2:20, are not mentioned as Hur's children elsewhere in the unit (cf. 2:50–52, 4:1–4), but this is in harmony with Exod 31:2; 35:30; 2 Chr 1:5, where Bezalel, one of the chief architects of the tabernacle, is named "son of Uri, son of Hur, of the tribe of Judah." Williamson thus concludes that the Chronicler, in the interest of bringing together dynasty and temple, has included the appropriate genealogy. He has also added vv 21–23, perhaps attracted by the mention of Hezron's death in v 24 (*JBL* 98 [1979] 353). The troublesome phrase of v 24b, "and the wife of Hezron was Abijah," is difficult at best, and may best be understood as a misplaced gloss on v 21, where Hezron's wife is left unnamed (*JBL* 98 [1979] 354).

Williamson accordingly believes the Chronicler had at his disposal four basic sources or types of materials: (1) earlier biblical texts, or their near-equivalents; (2) 2:25–33, 42–50a, marked as a unit by their parallel opening and closing formulas; (3) 2:18–19, 24, 50b–52; 4:2–4, 5–7, to which 2:52–55 and 4:1 had already been added; and (4) miscellaneous fragments. The Chronicler has then compiled 2:(1–2) 3–8 on the basis of the biblical material, composed v 9, to which he has appended the ancestors of David (vv 10–17), again the basis of the biblical material. Using sources (2) and (3) above, he has placed together the genealogies of Caleb and Jerahmeel, adding v 20 from the tabernacle materials and vv 20–23 and 34–41 from the fragments. Chap. 3 was added prior to the obviously resumptive 4:1 and, after the conclusion of the second source in 4:2–7, additional fragmentary material is supplied in 4:8–23. Williamson's analysis serves well to explicate the arrangement of the form of the text before us. This is equally true whether with him we assert the Chronicler's hand in the construction of the total unit from a variety of sources available to him, or see the final form as emerging through the later integration of sources. Since it is 2:9 which stands as the structural entity upon which the unity of the following genealogies is based, it seems necessary to assert that, if any of the text is from the hand of the Chronicler, it was he who was responsible for attaching Ram, David's progenitor, to the line of Judah through Hezron. If v 9 in its present form as well as the remainder of the genealogy is from the same hand, however, the divergency in names between this verse—Chelubai—and the Caleb of vv 18–19, 42 is surprising, and the position of Ram as the second son of Hezron in v 9, although treated first in the subsequent genealogy, is no less so (Williamson himself has seen the difficulty inherent in his position, but apart from the possibility of textual error, can only suggest that Chelubai may have been the form of the name most common to the Chronicler, and that the placing of Ram in the second position may point to the desire to show his central significance). This is possible, of course, but hardly compelling. Both Chelubai and Jerahmeel could result from the work of a later writer, who wished to provide opportunity for the inclusion of other groups of peoples into the tribe of Judah. Vv 18, 25, and 42 would then stem from the same hand. Too, attributing various parts of the text to pre-Chronistic sources may alleviate some of the difficulties involved, but does not eliminate them. Difficulties of test or understanding still abound in the third source named, although the removal of a part of v 24 as a misplaced gloss on v 21 is certainly a help. Moreover, are the introductory and closing formulae to 2:25–33, 42–50aα, sufficiently distinct to separate them from, e.g., 2:50aβ 4:4bα? Is the very full form of 3:1 (ואלה היו בני דויד אשר נולד לו בחברון "these were the sons of David born to him in Hebron") to be ascribed to the same author as the אלה בני ישראל "these are the sons of Israel" of 2:1 or the even briefer בני יהודה "sons of Judah" of 2:3? Again, is the unusual construction of נולד לו (v 9), followed by three instances of the emphatic use of the particle את, to be paralleled with the נולד לו "were born to him" of 2:3, or 3:5 (ואלה נולדו לו "and these were born to him")?

Finally, is not the relationship between 2:51–52, 53–55, 4:1–24 more complex than Williamson's analysis suggests? The numerous occurrences of similar names (e.g., of the Zorites, the Menuhoth) seems indicative of the wedding of doublets. Again, the pattern "X was the father of Y," in which Y represents a city rather than an individual, is scattered throughout the unit (cf. 2:24, 51–52, 54; 4:5, 12, 14, etc.) and seems to point to a more varied integration of another source as does the mention of peoples and guilds in 2:53–55; 4:11–15, 21–23. Indeed, most of chap. 4 seems to reflect the style and interests of 2:53–55, and less obviously, other portions of chap. 2. The twofold chiasmus which Williamson sees between chap. 4 and the early part of chap. 2 may also be more apparent to some students than to others, who may view it as at best accidental.

In brief, certain portions of Williamson's analysis seem compelling, other portions less so. That it helps us understand the present form of the text and some of the steps involved in its composition is surely true; that the final stage of this composition was due to the individual we would name the Chronicler is possible, but seems less certain. As our more detailed analysis will indicate, the final author/editor, whoever he might have been, included a vast amount of information, some of it appearing to be contradictory, into his genealogy of the tribe of Judah.

Sons of Israel and Judah (2:1–8)

Translation

¹ *These are the sons of Israel: Reuben, Simeon, Levi, and Judah; Issachar and Zebulon;* ² *Dan, Joseph, and Benjamin; Naphtali, Gad, and Asher.*
³ *The sons of Judah: Er, Onan, and Shelah.* ᵃ *Three were born* ᵇ *to him by the daughter of Shua,* ᶜ *the Canaanitess;* ᵈ *but Er, Judah's firstborn was evil in Yahweh's eyes, and he killed him.* ᵉ ⁴ *Tamar, his daughter-in-law, bore him Perez and Zerah. So all Judah's sons were five.*
⁵ *The sons of Perez: Hezron and Hamul;* ᵃ ⁶ *and the sons of Zerah: Zimri,* ᵃ *Ethan, Heman, Calcol, and Darda,* ᵇ *five in all.*
⁷ *And the sons* ᵃ *of* ᵇ *(Zimri, Carmi; and the sons of)* ᵇ *Carmi: Achar, the troubler of Israel, who acted unfaithfully* ᶜ *in the matter of the devoted thing.* ⁸ *The sons of* ᵃ *Ethan: Azariah.*

Notes

3.a. G Σηλων "Selon."
3.b. The subj is grammatically sg, though pl by meaning. One MS reads וולדו "they were born." Cf. GKC, § 125a.
3.c. As necessitated by Gen 38:2. Gen 38:12, like the text here, is ambiguous and would permit "Bath-shua."
3.d. Shua is identified as a Canaanite in Gen 38:2, making Israel's early relationship with the Canaanites apparent.
3.e. The omission of any reference to Onan's death is unusual, since Gen 38 also mentions the latter, and at more length. Rudolph (10–15) assumes, though with only Tg as evidence, that Onan's death has been omitted by haplogr.
5.a. Gᴮᴬ (ι)ἐμουηλ "Hemouel" = חמואל "Hamul"; cf. Gen 46:12 *SamPent.*
6.a. Heb. זמרי "Zimri": Josh 7:1, 18 זבדי "Zabdi." Curtis (86) notes that the confusion between ב and מ is phonetic, while that between ד and ר is graphic. G reads Ζαμβρ(ε)ι "Zambr(e)i" in both Josh passages. In view of the divergent textual evidence, the author has probably chosen Zimri because of its relationship to temple music (זמר = "to make music," BDB, 274).
6.b. MT דרע "Dara"; ca. 40 MSS Syr Tg 1 Kgs 5:11 [4:31] ודרדע "and Darda," which should probably, in view of any apparent significance of the alteration, be accepted as the reading.
7.a. Retaining the pl בני, although only a single "son" is named. Since Carmi's parentage is not given, it is either necessary to speculate that the writer assumed a knowledge of the material at hand (cf. Curtis, 85) or, better, that the part of the genealogy reflected in Josh 7:1, 18, where Carmi is listed as the son of Zimri, has been omitted by haplogr.
7.b-b. עכר "Achar." Josh 7:1, 18 has "Achan." Already there, however, there is explicit connection with the root עכר "to trouble," preserved in the name "the valley of Achor" and explicated by Joshua in vv 24–26. Apparently our author has carried this play on words a step farther.
7.c. מעל "unfaithful." A favorite word in Chr and other priestly writings; see 10:13.
8.a. Seb ובן "and the son of."

Form/Structure/Setting

The enumeration of Israel's twelve sons (vv 1–2) connects with 1:34, from which it has been separated by the extended treatment of the sons of Esau (vv 35–37) and related information concerning Seir and Edom (vv 38–54).

With the sons of Israel, the author arrives at the principal item of his concern, which occupies the remainder of the genealogical material of chaps. 2–9, and the remainder of the work as well.

As we have noted, the order of the listing of Israel's sons found here is unique, agreeing neither with earlier OT traditions nor with the ordering of the tribes found elsewhere in Chronicles or other later traditions. It is closely akin, however, to that found in Gen 46, from which it may be derived. Israel's grandchildren are listed according to their descent from the daughter of Shua (v 3) and Tamar (v 4). Of Tamar's sons, the children of Perez, Hezron and Hamul, (v 5) precede the five of Zerah (v 6). The line of the first of these five, Zimri (see nn. 6.a., 7.b.) is followed two generations to Achar (v 7); of Zerah's second-named son, Ethan, only a single descendant is given (v 8). The stage is thus set for v 9, where Judah's main line through Perez will be resumed with Hezron.

The listing of Judah's five sons is derived from Gen 38; Perez' sons Hezron and Hamul are found in Gen 46:12. Zerah's line through Zimri/Zabdi (see n. 6.a.), Carmi, and Achar lay at hand in Josh 7:1, 18, although Chronicles has apparently resorted to some interpretative reconstruction here.

However, no other biblical tradition attaches Ethan, Heman, Calcol, and Darda to the Judahite Zerah. In 1 Kgs 5:11 [4:31] Ethan is designated "the Ezrahite (הָאֶזְרָחִי), outwardly reminiscent of Zerah (זֶרַח). W. F. Albright, however, believes the term *Ezrahite* refers not to parentage, but describes instead a pre-Israelite inhabitant of the land, an aborigine (*Archaeology and the Land of Israel*, 122–23), a meaning clear from Num 9:14, where the Ezrahite is contrasted to the sojourner (גֵּר). Heman, Calcol, and Darda are further identified in the Kings passage as "sons of Mahol" (בְּנֵי מָחוֹל), a designation which would prevent our understanding them as Ezrahites in the sense intended for Ethan. That these Ezrahites, whatever their origin, were related to the temple and its music seems assured by the superscriptions of Pss 88–89, where Heman and Ethan respectively are designated Ezrahites. It thus seems likely, as suggested by Albright, that certain temple guilds traced their origins to the pre-Israelite inhabitants of the land. In that connection Albright's further suggestion that the "sons of Mahol" (1 Kgs 5:11 [4:31]), understood by most versions and translations as a proper name, refers instead to "sons of the orchestral guild," i.e., musicians (*Archaeology*, 123, and 210, esp. n. 96). The root חוּל "to writhe, dance" and its derivatives מָחוֹל and מְחֹלָה are used for dance offered in praise of Yahweh (cf. Pss 149:3; 150:4; Exod 15:20; Ps 96:9; חוּל BDB, I, 296–98). It seems likely that the author, noting these striking coincidences and aware of the traditional association of a Heman and Ethan with the cult (in his own day?) has found for them a noble place within Israel's ancient records. Whether there was a tradition current or whether it reflects the writer's own ingenuity can only be surmised. At any rate, its inclusion here, like that of Bezalel in 2:20, brings together in a striking way the themes of dynasty and temple.

It can be protested that the author of Chronicles would not have identified the Heman and Ethan known to him as temple musicians with Judah, as does their inclusion at this point in the genealogy, since such activity was restricted to the Levites alone. However, another alternative ought to be considered. The tradition conveyed here may point to the (correct) understanding that the temple guilds were ancient and Canaanite in their origins. Albright points out that the names Ethan, Heman, Calcol, and Darda are all characteristic of names of the late Bronze Age (*Archaeology*, 123). The author may have ignored the contradiction which he was in a sense introducing into the record, considering the discovery of such a missing link more significant than consistency.

That the writer was interested in finding such musical associations might be reflected also in his choice of the name Zimri, meaning "to make music," for the textually dubious Zabdi, the son of Zerah, according to Josh 7:1, 18 (see n. 6.a.). That the author was not averse to giving priority to meaning over strict textual accuracy can also be seen in the continuing evolution of the Achan of Josh 7 into the Achar ("Troubler") of 1 Chr 2:7, although the evolution was already at hand in Josh 7:24–26 in its reference to the Valley of Achor.

Comment

(On the sons of Israel [vv 1–2], see above, pp. 7–12.)

The name Israel is used uniformly throughout Chronicles for Isaac's elder son, the more familiar Jacob of other sources is found only in 1 Chr 16:13, 17 in two passages taken from Ps 105:6, 23. No attempt is made to hide the checkered parentage of Judah's sons (vv 3–4), both their Canaanite mother and Judah's reprehensible conduct with Tamar (cf. Gen 38) being spoken of without apology. The mention of the wickedness and death of Er has been considered unusual in view of the omission of a similar reference to Onan, since Gen 38:7–11 speaks at considerably more length of the latter, and it is possible that Rudolph (10–15) is correct in assuming a loss due to haplography. No sons of Shelah, the sole surviving son through Shua's daughter, are given here; however, 4:21–23, which seems to balance the mention of Shelah here, suggests a structural concern as the reason (Williamson, *JBL* 98 [1979] 359).

Of Judah's two sons through Tamar, the sons of Perez are listed first, followed by the sons of Zerah (v 6). The inclusion of further descendants of Zerah at this point (vv 7–8) prepares for the concentration upon Perez' descendants through Hezron which forms the center of 2:9–4:23. No descendants of Hamul (v 5) are known, either in Chronicles or elsewhere in the OT. The sons of Zerah and Zimri have been dealt with in the tradition study above, where we have seen the probability that the writer has brought together data provided by Josh 7:1, 18 and 1 Kgs 5:11 [4:31] in such a way as to provide a suitable genealogical tradition for at least some temple musicians. A similar freedom is seen in the completed transformation of Achan into Achar, "Troubler," for whose transgression Israel was defeated before the men of Ai. Although מעל, "unfaithful," is a favorite term in Chronicles, its use in v 7, like that of חרם, "devoted thing," is probably due to Josh 7, cf. esp. 7:1. Ethan's son Azariah ("Yahweh has helped") is otherwise unknown, though the name is popular (cf. Schumacher, "Azariah," *IDB* 1:324–25, who lists no less than 24 such individuals).

Explanation

With the sons of Israel the writer has reached the central focus of his attention. The inclusion of all of Israel's sons, both in vv 1–2 and in the chapters to follow, indicates that "all Israel," both north and south, were included within his purview. With the listing of Judah and his descendants, however, a different arrangement seems to prevail. While subordinate lines are up to that point dealt with first, to be followed by the principal line (cf. Isaac's sons, Esau and Israel, 1:34–37; 2:1), from Judah on the principal line is regularly given first. Thus the descendants of Judah (2:3–4:23) are dealt with prior to those of his brothers; the sons of Perez (v 5) are listed prior to those of Zerah (vv 6–8); and of Hezron's sons, Ram (vv 9–17) assumes prior place. By both structure and content, the writer is pointing both to the inclusion of all the tribes of Israel within his "all Israel" and to the particular place which Judah and his descendants through Perez, Hezron, and Ram—from whose line is to come David—occupy within Israel.

From Hezron to David   (2:9–17)

Translation

⁹ *And the sons of Hezron* ᵃ *who were born to him:* ᵃ *Jerahmeel, Ram, and Chelubai* ᵇᶜ ¹⁰ *Ram* ᵃ *was the father of Amminadab, and Amminadab was the father of Nahshon, prince of the sons of Judah.* ¹¹ *Nahshon was the father of Salma,* ᵃ *Salma was the father of Boaz,* ¹² *Boaz was the father of Obed, Obed was the father of Jesse.* ¹³ *Jesse* ᵃ *was the father of his first-born Eliab, Abinadab* ᵇ *his second, Shimea* ᶜ *his third,* ¹⁴ *Nethanel his fourth; Raddai his fifth;* ¹⁵ *Ozem his sixth, David his seventh.* ᵃ ¹⁶ *Their sisters were Zeruiah and Abigail. The sons of Zeruiah were Abishai, Joab, and Asahel, three;* ¹⁷ *while Abigail bore Amasa. (The father of Amasa was* ᵃ *Jether the Ishmaelite.* ᵃ *)*

Notes

9.a-a. "Who were born to him"; cf. 2:3; 3:4, 5; and esp. 3:1. The use of the niph ptcp of ילד is a favorite in Chronicles; cf. Williamson, *JBL* 98 (1979) 358. Contrast 2 Sam 3:2; 5:13; and 14:27 for the more common construction.

9.b. כלובי "Chelubai." G reads Χαλεβ "Caleb," as in vv 18, 42.

9.c. *BH³* and *BHS* are incomplete. G⁻ᴸ speaks of four sons of Hezron, including both a Ram and an Aram. All G MSS list Aram as the father of Amminadab in v 10, as do Ruth 4:19; Matt 1:3–4. Gᴸ reads Aram instead of Ram in v 9 and does not read Aram at the end of the verse, as do the remaining G MSS.

10.a. See n. 9.c.

11.a. שלמא "Salma," consistently in Chronicles (2:11, 51, 54); Ruth 4:20 שלמה "Salmah"; Ruth 4:21 שלמון "Salmon."

13.a. Only here אישי "Jesse"; elsewhere uniformly ישי "Jesse" (as in v 12). The reason for this difference has not been satisfactorily explained.

13.b. G Αμιναδαβ "Aminadab."

13.c. שמה(ו) "and Shimeah" Syr 1 Sam 16:9; 17:13.

15.a. Syr השמיני דויד השביעי אליהו "Elihu, the seventh; David, the eighth"; cf. 1 Chr 27:18; 1 Sam 16:10.

17.a-a. הי\u200bשמעאלי יתר "Jether the Ishmaelite"; 2 Sam 17:25 הישראלי יתרא "Ithra the Israelite."

Form/Structure/Setting

By way of parallel to vv 6–8, v 9 lists Perez's grandchildren through Hezron. Vv 10–12 extend those descendants through Ram, listed in v 9 in central position between Jerahmeel and Chelubai. This genealogy is linear in form, in contrast to both the preceding and following, and encompasses eight generations from Ram to Jesse. Vv 13–15 number seven sons of Jesse, of whom David is the seventh and last, while vv 16–17 list Jesse's two daughters Zeruiah and Abigail and a total of four sons through them.

Comment

With the genealogy of Hezron Chronicles reaches the major point of the writer's concern. It is also at this point that sizable gaps occurred in the earlier traditions of the OT. Disregarding Ruth 4:18–22, which is probably derived from Chronicles rather than vice versa (cf. Noth, *Ü.S.,* 119–20; Rudolph, 16), the OT contains scant information on Hezron and his descendants to the time of David, and nothing which would link them directly to the genealogy of that king. Hezron is mentioned as Perez's son in Gen 46:12; Num 26:21, but no descendants are given in either place. However, the name Hezron is regularly associated with the southern portion of Canaan, in relation to not only Judah but also Reuben (Gen 46:9; 1 Chr 5:3). Josh 15:3 lists Hezron as a city between Kadesh-barnea and Addar (cf. Num 34:4, see also Kerioth-hezron [Josh 15:25]). The Jerahmeelites are mentioned as inhabitants of southern Judah in 1 Sam 27:10; 30:29. If Chelubai is to be identified with the Caleb of vv 18, 42, and the conquest tradition, as seems virtually assured to this writer, although denied by others (Myers, 14; Keil, 73), his association with the south is likewise assured, although other problems surface. The Caleb of the conquest tradition is regularly identified as the son of Jephunneh (Josh 14:6, 14, etc.), and he is furthermore named a Kenizzite (Josh 15:17; Judg 3:9). The Kenizzites, however, like the Jerahmeelites, Amalekites, and others, appear to be a non-Israelite people who moved into the Negeb prior to the conquest and continued to be associated with the area around Hebron (formerly, Kiriath-arba). (Cf. Josh 14:6–15; 15:52–54, and see Hicks, "Kenaz," *IDB* 3:6; Glueck, "Kenites and Kenizzites," *PEQ* 72 [1940] 22–24.) Their association with the Edomites can still be seen in the names in 1 Chr 1:36, 53. BDB notes that only P considers Caleb a full Judahite. The inclusion of Caleb as a son of Hezron, however, incorporates his descendants directly into Judah's mainstream, as is the case also with Jerahmeel.

The inclusion of Ram as a descendant of Hezron is even more significant. Apart from the parallel passage in Ruth 4:19, this Ram is otherwise unknown in the OT, unless it be as a descendant of Jerahmeel (cf. 2:25). The Salma through whom the genealogical link between Nahshon and Boaz is forged

is also unknown (but cf. 2:51). What the writer did know on the basis of
the OT traditions was that Nahshon, the son of Amminadab, was Judah's
tribal prince (נשיא) and contemporaneous with Moses and Aaron (Num 2:3;
Exod 6:23, both P) and that David's father was Jesse (1 Sam 16, etc.). We
may assume that he would also have been privy to the tradition that Jesse's
father and grandfather were Obed and Boaz; cf. Ruth 4:13–17. By including
Salma and Ram, the genealogist has provided a continuous, if fragmentary
(see below), line connecting David to Judah. Whether this connection was
extant in noncanonical forms of the traditions available to him or was his
own contribution can only be conjectured. The same is true for the attachment
of Jerahmeel to Judah through Hezron. The amalgamation of Caleb to Judah
in P, however (cf. Num 13:6; 34:39), suggests that the process by which foreign
strains were incorporated into Israel was not an unusual one. (For the possible
association of Caleb and Kenaz to the Hurrians, see Johnson, "Caleb," *IDB*
1:482–83; Bush, "Hurrians," *IDBSup*, 423–24, and the bibliographies there.)
In any case, the central significance of 1 Chr 2:9 in Chronicles is established,
whether that verse is the composition of the Chronicler himself (Williamson,
JBL 98 [1979] 357–58), a later writer, or an admixture of both (Noth, *Ü.S.*,
119, n. 4).

That even the resulting genealogy is fragmentary is apparent. Only nine
generations span the period between Judah and David (Perez, Hezron, Ram,
Amminadab, Nahshon, Salma, Boaz, Obed, Jesse), too few to span a period
of 430 years in Egypt (Exod 12:40) and 480 years from the Exodus to Solomon's temple (1 Kgs 6:1). Moreover, if Nahshon is accepted as a contemporary
of Moses and Aaron (Exod 6:23), only four generations are left to bridge
approximately three hundred years between the Exodus (ca. 1290 B.C.) and
the birth of David, ca. 1025 B.C. (?). This difficulty is only increased if one
holds to the fourteenth century date of the Exodus.

The genealogy of Jesse at hand (vv 13–17) also diverges from other canonical traditions in significant ways. Earlier tradition depicts David as the eighth
son of Jesse (1 Sam 16:10; 17:12–14); v 15 explicitly enumerates him as the
seventh. The reading of Syr, which lists an Elihu as the seventh son and
makes David the eighth, appears to be a conscious effort to bring the Chronicles tradition in line with Samuel and is based on 1 Chr 7:18, where, however,
G reads Eliab (as in 2:13) instead of Elihu. While a tradition diverging so
pointedly from the canonical norm is striking, it may be more easily understood where the number seven is involved in relation to King David. By
making David the seventh son, the writer may have wished to portray him
as a uniquely favored offspring. On the other hand, I know of no instance
in Chronicles (or Ezra-Nehemiah) of the symbolic use of the number seven,
or, indeed, of any number.

Nethanel, Raddai, and Ozem are not named in 1 Sam 16 and occur only
here as David's brothers. Raddai does not appear elsewhere in the OT. An
Ozem is listed as the fourth of Jerahmeel's sons in 2:25. Nethanel occurs in
a Judahite genealogy in 2 Chr 17:7–9 and frequently in Levitical genealogies.
That a source for the names of David's brothers and sisters may have been
available in either the temple or royal archives does not appear unlikely.

Zeruiah, listed in v 16 as David's sister, is named in 2 Sam 2:18 also as the mother of Joab, Abishai, and Asahel, counted as among David's servants in fighting against Saul's troops. Asahel is killed by Abner and buried "in the tomb of his father, which was at Bethlehem," suggesting a prominent family of Bethlehem (2 Sam 2:32). According to 2 Sam 17:25, Abigail's sister was Zeruiah, but her father was Nahash, not Jesse, although the latter is read by G[L]. Although according to v 17, Abigail mothered Amasa by Jether the Ishmaelite, 2 Sam 17:25 lists Amasa's father as Ithra the Israelite (see n. 17.a-a.). Harvey suggests that Jesse's wife was once married to Nahash, or that the name Nahash has been introduced into v 25 from v 27, or that a matriarchal form of reckoning is involved ("Zeruiah," *IDB* 4:956). Rabbi Kimchi suggested the statements might be harmonized by assuming that Ithra lived among the Ishmaelites (Beck, "Abigail," *IDB* 1:7). At any rate the genealogy before us makes it apparent that David invested leadership of his troops in his own relatives, and that Absalom's choice of Amasa to replace Joab (2 Sam 17:25) was similarly conditioned.

Explanation

Hezron's genealogy (v 9) is without parallel in the OT, and represents the framework around which the author has built the central part of the genealogy of the Judahites. Of Hezron's three sons, pride of place goes to Ram, perhaps indicated by his listing between Jerahmeel and Chelubai, though this is far from certain and in violation of the usual practice in Chronicles (cf. Williamson, *JBL* 98 [1979] 358), at the end of whose genealogy stands Jesse's seventh son, David, with his six brothers and two sisters. As our tradition study has indicated, the author has joined Amminadab to Hezron through the otherwise unknown Ram, and Boaz to Nahshon through the similarly unknown Salma. Although non-canonical records may have been at the author's hand, the nature of the linkages involved suggests an immediate dependence upon the canonical traditions, which have been utilized to serve the author's purpose. On the other hand, the data with regard to David's brothers and sisters is of a different nature, and more likely rests upon an alternative tradition found in the nation's archives.

Descendants of Caleb (Chelubai) and Jerahmeel (2:18–55; 4:1–7)

Translation

[18] *Caleb,* [a] *the son of Hezron, was the father* [b] *of Jerioth by Azubah his wife,* [b] *and these were her sons:* [c] *Jesher, Shobab, and Ardon.* [19] *Azubah died, and Caleb took for himself Ephrath,* [a] *who bore him Hur.* [20] *Hur was the father of Uri, and Uri was the father of Bezalel.*
    [21] *Afterward Hezron went in to the daughter of Machir, Gilead's father, and he took her . . .* [ab] *although he was sixty years old, and she bore him*

Segub. ²² Segub was the father of Jair, who had twenty-three cities in the land of Gilead. ²³ But Geshur and Aram took from them Havvoth-jair with ^a Kenath and its villages, sixty cities. All these were the sons of Machir, Gilead's father. ²⁴ After Hezron's death Caleb went ^a in to Ephrathah ^b ^c(and Hezron's wife was Abijah)^c and she bore him Ashhur, the father of Tekoa.

²⁵ The sons of Jerahmeel, Hezron's firstborn, were Ram, the firstborn, Bunah, Oren, Ozem, ^aand Ahijah.^a ²⁶ Jerahmeel also had another wife whose name was Atarah. She was the mother of Onam. ²⁷ The sons of Ram, Jerahmeel's firstborn, were Maaz, Jamin, and Eker. ²⁸ Onam's sons were Shammai and Jada, and the sons of Shammai were Nadab and Abishur. ²⁹ The name of Abishur's wife was Abihail. She bore him Ahban and Molid.

³⁰ The sons of Nadab: Seled and Appaim. Seled died without sons. ³¹ The sons of ^a Appaim, Ishi; the sons of ^a Ishi, Sheshan; the sons of ^a Sheshan, Ahlai.

³² The sons of Jada, Shammai's brother: Jether and Jonathan. Jether died without sons. ³³ The sons of Jonathan: Peleth and Zaza. These were the sons of Jerahmeel.

³⁴ Sheshan had no sons, but only daughters; but Sheshan had an Egyptian slave whose name was Jarha. ^a ³⁵ So Sheshan gave his daughter as a wife to his slave Jarha and she bore him Attai. ³⁶ Attai was the father of Nathan; Nathan was the father of Zabad; Zabad was the father of Ephlal; and Ephlal was the father of Obed; ³⁸ Obed was the father of Jehu; Jehu was the father of Azariah; ³⁰ Azariah was the father of Helez; Helez was the father of Eleasah; ⁴⁰ Eleasah was the father of Sismai; Sismai was the father of Shallum; ⁴¹ Shallum was the father of Jekamiah; Jekamiah was the father of Elishama.

⁴² The descendants ^a of Caleb, the brother of Jerahmeel: Mareshah, ^b his firstborn, who was the father of Ziph, and the sons of Mareshah, who founded Hebron. ^c ⁴³ The sons of Hebron: Korah, Tappuah, Rekem, and Shema. ⁴⁴ Shema begat ^a Raham, the father of Jokdeam, ^b while Rekem begat ^a Shammai. ⁴⁵ Shammai's son was Maon, and Maon was the father of Beth-zur.

⁴⁶ Ephah, Caleb's concubine, gave birth to Haran, Moza, and Gazez; Haran begat ^a Gazez.

⁴⁷ The sons of Jahdai: Regem, Jotham, Geshan, Pelet, Ephah, and Shaaph.

⁴⁸ Caleb's concubine Maacah gave birth ^a to Sheber and Tirhanah; ^{49 a}she also bore Shaaph, ^a the father of Madmannah, and Sheva, the father of both Machbenah and Gibea. ⁵⁰ These were the sons of Caleb. ^a

The sons ^b of Hur, the firstborn of Ephrathah, were Shobal, the father of Kiriath-jearim; ⁵¹ Salma, the father of Bethlehem; and Hareph, the father of Beth-geder. ⁵² Shobal, the father of Kiriath-jearim, also had sons, Reaiah, ^a ^bhalf of the Menuhoth. . . . ^b ⁵³ The families of Kiriath-jearim were the Ithrite, the Puthite, the Shumathite, and the Mishraite. From these descended the Zorathite ^a and the Eshtaolite. ⁵⁴ The sons of Salma: ^a Beth-lehem, the Netophathite, Atroth-beth-joab, and the half of the Manahathite, ^b the Zorite. ^c ⁵⁵ The families of the scribes ^a who inhabited ^b Jabez were Tirathites, Shimeathites, (and) Sucathites. These are the Kenites who came in from Hammath, the father of Beth-rechab. . . .

^{4:1} The sons of Judah: Perez, Hezron, and Carmi, ^a and Hur, and Shobal. ² Reaiah, Shobal's son, was the father of Jahath, and Jahath was the father of Ahumai and Lahad. These were the families of the Zorathite.

³ And these (. . .) ^a the father of Etam: Jezreel and Ishma and Idbash, and their

sister's name was Hazzelelponi. [b] [4]*And Penuel was the father of Gedor, and Ezer the father of Hushah. There were the sons of Hur, the firstborn of Ephrathah, the father of Bethlehem.*

[5]*Ashhur, the father of Tekoa, had two wives, Helah and Naarah,* [6]*Naarah bore him Ahuzzam and Hepher, and the* [a]*Temenite and the Ahashtarite.* [a] *These were Naarah's sons.* [7]*The sons of Helah: Zereth, Zohar,* [a] *and Ethnan.* [b]

Notes

18.a. Apparently to be identified with the Chelubai (כלובי) of v 9; cf. n.9.b. and v 42.

18.b-b. The text is problematic. One would expect the two uses of את to be coordinate and to introduce the dir obj; cf. JB: "became father of Azubah, Ishshah, and Jerioth," although JB also construes אשה "Ishshah" as a proper name without preceding את. However, the pronominal suff on the following noun, בניה "these are *her* sons," makes such an understanding difficult. (JB "these are *the* sons," hides the difficulty.) KJV and RSV coordinate Azubah and Jerioth but understand את as the prep "with" or "by": "had children *by* his wife Azubah and *by* Jerioth," ignoring the difficulty with the following בניה. NAB NEB TEV all understand the first את to be the prep and the second the obj marker and disregard the conj, thus making Azubah Caleb's wife, but Jerioth the daughter to whom the sg suff of בניה refers. This last reading has been adopted here in principle. Instead of ו אשה "wife and," read אשתו "his wife" with Syr Tg α', or simply אשה "wife." The unusual construction was guarded against misunderstanding perhaps by the original writer, but more likely later, by inserting אשתו after Azubah. The misunderstanding persisted, however, and the pronom suff was transferred to the following word, where it was wrongly taken as a conj. Alternatively, the conj may have been added simply to remedy an apparent deficiency.

18.c. "Her sons," i.e., sons of Jerioth, who is thus understood as a female. Perhaps this suff too derives from a misunderstanding of the verse. Curtis, 92, alters the text to בת יריעות "daughter of Jerioth," with Wellhausen.

19.a. אפרת "Ephrath." 1 Chr 2:24 אפרתה "Ephrathah." See n. 24.b.

21.a. See n. 24.c-c.

21.b. "He took her. . . " G[L] αὐτὸς Γαλαὰδ ἐλαβε τὴν Αχημ = lit., "he, Gilead, took Achem," understanding Gilead to be the subj and supplying Achem as the wife.

22.a. Understanding את as the prep. The alternative is to add the conj or to understand Kenath and its villages as identical to Havvoth-jair.

24.a. Reading בא כלב "Caleb went," with G Vg and most translations and commentaries.

24.b. V 19 אפרתה "Ephrathah." The connection between Bethlehem and this Ephrath(ah) is constant; cf. Mic 5:1 [5:2]; 1 Chr 4:4. The family of David were also called Ephrathites (Ruth 1:2; 1 Sam 17:12). Cohen suggests that Ephrathah was an older city, later absorbed into Bethlehem ("Ephrathah," *IDB* 2:122). It seems probable that the suff ה, in some instances (cf. Gen 35:16 and our passage) is to be understood as the *he*-directive, but this is impossible in others (cf. Ruth 1:2; 4:11). Perhaps the longer form ultimately became normative.

24.c-c. The usual emendation, deriving ultimately from Wellhausen, which omits the conj on ואשת, lit., "and the wife of," and reads אביהו "Abijahu" for אביה "Abijah," is, as noted by Williamson (*JBL* 98 [1979] 354), unsatisfactory and contradicts the tone of vv 18–23. However, if Abijah is understood as a proper name and female (cf. 2 Chr 29:1), the phrase is clear. Perhaps, as Williamson notes, it originated as a gl on v 21, where Hezron's wife is not named and was subsequently misplaced.

25.a-a. For אחיה "Ahijah," read perhaps אחיהו "his brothers" with G[BA]; Syr אחותם "your brothers"; Rudolph, 16; *BHS* מאחיה (reading the *mem* as haplogr; cf. v 26); Keil, 66; Curtis, 94.

31.a. MT is regularly pl ובני "and sons of" (Seb Vg: sg), although only a single "son" is named. It seems again apparent that an entire family or clan of descendants is being referred to by the name of its progenitor.

34.a. G Ιωχηλ "Jochel."

42.a. See n. 31.a. Textual problems make certainty here impossible, however.

42.b. The text is problematic and does not lend itself to simple reconstruction. Many emend

מישע "Mesha" to "Maresha" with v 42b and G (cf. Vg rsv); others assume that a parallel phrase which would make Ziph the father of Mareshah has dropped out. If, however, we assume that a city may be viewed both as the "child" of its founders and as the "father" of its inhabitants, who may themselves found still other cities, the present text is not impossible.

42.c. Heb. "the sons of Mareshah (were) the father of [אבי] Hebron." The phrase is unusual and heavy, but not impossible, and preferable to the alternatives offered.

44.a. The traditional translation of הוליד, "begat," has been retained to avoid confusion with the use of אב "father" throughout the pericope.

44.b. Reading "Jokdeam" with Josh 15:56, where, however, Gᴬᴸ reads Ιερ__ "Jer__." The location is uncertain.

46.a. See n. 44.a.

48.a. Read perhaps ילדה (fem) "she bore."

49.a-a. Heb. ותלד שעף "and she bore Shaaph" is abrupt, lacking the expected ויולד "and he fathered," and perhaps reflects a textual displacement; cf. v 47, "Shaaph." Vg ויולד.

50.a. Cf. v 33b. The verse division of MT is accordingly erroneous.

50.b. Heb. בן "son," although followed by multiple descendants, perhaps occasioned by the faulty verse division and attraction to Caleb.

52.a. Reading ראיה "Reaiah," with 4:2, instead of הראה "the seer."

52.b-b. חצי המנחות "half of the Menuhoth," without the conj and quite abrupt. The descendants of Salma in v 54 include וחצי המנחתי "and . . . ," which is perhaps the intended reading here. If Williamson's analysis is correct, vv 53–55 derive from a source, suggesting that the difficulty results either from an insertion of or an adjustment to a second source at this point. Note also the Zorathites (הצרעתי), v 53 and 4:2; and the Zorites (הצרעי), v 54.

53.a. V 54, "the Zorite."

54.a. Read perhaps אבי בית לחם "father of Bethlehem"; cf. v 51, and cf. Shobal in vv 50, 52.

54.b. See n. 52.b-b.

54.c. See n. 53.a.

55.a. Or possibly, if ספרים "scribes" does not refer to a scribal guild, "the families of the Siphrites," perhaps earlier dwellers of Kiriath-Sepher (Rudolph, 23).

55.b. Q שבי; K ישבו "they inhabited."

4:1.a. On the basis of chap. 2 (cf. vv 9, 18), the name expected would be Chelubai or Caleb, but there is no textual evidence for such reading here. Perhaps the name כרמי "Carmi" represents continuing difficulty concerning the position of both Carmi and Caleb in Judah's line. See 2:7, where in the present text Carmi's parentage is not given, and the variations in Caleb's name (כלובי "Chelubai," v 9; כלב "Caleb," vv 18, 42; cf. כלוב "Chelub," also in 4:11). On the other hand, the lack of textual variants in 4:1 is striking.

3.a. Heb. 'And these . . . the father of Etam." Some words are lacking. Most reconstructions either follow the versions (G "these are the sons of Etam"; Syr "and these are the sons of Aminadab") or the reading adopted here, after Rudolph, Rothstein, and Noth. In 2:51, however, Hareph is associated with Beth-gader, pointing perhaps to a more complex problem.

3.b. The unusual formation of the name, otherwise unknown, taken together with the following ופנואל "Penuel," suggests dittogr (Curtis, 108). Rudolph (30) believes the entire half-verse results from the inclusion in the text of a marginal gl explaining the order of the wives in vv 5-6.

6.a-a. Understanding the suffixed י to be that of the gentilic, as suggested by the article on "the Ahashtarite."

7.a. Reading וצהר "and Zohar," with Q G; K Vg יצחר "Izhar."

7.b. Tg + וקוץ "and," supported by Rudolph in BHS, supplying a connection with v 8. But that Tg alone would preserve the correct reading is hardly likely. The addition is also in harmony with Tg's tendencies to harmonize and conflate.

Form/Structure/Setting

(For general notes concerning the structure of this unit, see above.) One genealogy of Caleb, as we have seen, is found in vv 18–24, 50b–55, and 4:1–7. A second genealogy of Caleb is found in vv 42–50a. The two genealogies of Jerahmeel occur in vv 25–33 and 34–41 in the chiastic structure of the entire unit and are separated by the concluding formula of v 33b.

Though the genealogies of Jerahmeel are in good order, that of Caleb is much more complex. Even if vv 20 and 21–23 are regarded as supplements, some lack of uniformity pervades the remainder. Caleb's second wife is named Ephrath (אפרת) in v 19 and Ephrathah (אפרתה) in v 24 (where the termination may be directive) and v 50b (where the termination cannot strictly speaking be so). (Caleb's concubine Ephah in the other source, v 46, appears similar in English transliteration, but is not comparable in Hebrew.) Caleb's marriage to Ephrath results in the birth of Hur, v 19, and Ashhur, v 24, whose descendants are named in vv 50b–55, 4:1–4 (Hur) and 4:5–7 (?) (Ashhur). If the analysis outlined above is correct, Caleb's descendants as listed in chap. 2 encompass those of Jerahmeel in the overall chiastic form of the unit, while the final part of Caleb's genealogy (4:1–7), together with vv 8–23, balances 2:1–8.

Concerning the form of the various genealogies, it is impossible to say much. In contrast to vv 10–17, which are linear and extend to David in a single line, all genealogies of this sub-unit are branched, though descendants of only a single ancestor are frequently pursued. The genealogies make use of a wide range of genealogical terminology (e.g., "Caleb begat," v 18; "and she bore," vv 19, 24; "the sons of Jerahmeel were," (ויהיו), vv 25, 27; "the sons of Caleb," v 42, cf. v 47 and often; "there were sons *to* (ל) Shobal," v 52; "these were the sons of Hur," 4:4; and still others, which may represent an amalgam of styles reflecting various sources and authors. At present, however, no analysis of sources or authors seems possible on the basis of these usages. Similarly the inclusion of varying amounts of historical data is not susceptible to detailed analysis, although the emphasis upon cities, villages, and groups of craftsmen might indicate that such apparently secondary notices as 2:21–23, 42–50a, 52–55; 4:2–7 derive from common or similar origin.

It is perhaps through the incorporation of some such larger source into the genealogy of Caleb, rather than through progressive supplementation by isolated fragments, that the present shape of 2:18–55, 4:1–7 is due. The immediately following section, 4:8–23, exhibits interests similar to, e.g., 2:21–23, 53–55, and may derive from the same source.

Comment

18–24 *Descendants of Caleb.* (2:18–24, 42–50a, 50b–55; 4:1–7). None of the descendants of Caleb named here are otherwise known, although Shobab is also the name of one of David's sons (3:5; 14:4; 2 Sam 5:14). As indicated above (n. 18.b–b.), Jerioth is best understood as the daughter of Caleb and Azubah and the mother of Jesher, Shobab, and Ardon. It is perhaps for this reason that Caleb's ancestry is traced through Ephrath(ah), the mother of Hur (v 19), and Ashhur (v 24) in the sections which follow rather than through Jerioth or any of the sons named in v 18. Although it is possible that Ephrath(ah) had previously been the wife of Hezron, as indicated by many translations of v 24 (see n. 24.b.), such a view appears contrary to the understanding of vv 18–19. The adoption of Williamson's suggestion that the insertion of the name of Hezron's wife represents a misplaced gloss on v 21, where Machir's daughter is unnamed, is attractive (*JBL* 98 [1978] 355).

It was perhaps the mention of Hezron's death in v 24 which attracted the additional note concerning Hezron in vv 21–23. Through Hezron's marriage to the daughter of Machir (Abijah?; cf. v 24b), who is named the "father of Gilead" (v 21), Hezron's descendants of Judah are related through Segub to Jair and his possessions in Gilead (v 22), which are in v 23 named the Havvoth-jair ("villages of Jair"). Nothing else is known of this Segub (שׂגוב); in view of the frequent occurrence of Argob (ארגב) in conjunction with Jair in other passages (cf. Deut 3:14; 1 Kgs 4:13), it may be the result of textual corruption.

This relationship between Judah and Machir/Jair is not expressed genealogically elsewhere in the OT, where both are viewed as sons of Manasseh (Num 32:39–42). An enumeration of the cities of Jair in Gilead appears traditional; in addition to the twenty-three cities of v 22 and the sixty of v 23, we find a similar count of sixty in Deut 3:4 and perhaps a related count of thirty in Judg 10:4. The Aramean background of the cities and peoples of this area, which lay on the north and east fringes of Israel's territory, is well-known, and emphasized in v 23 by coupling Aram, indefinable as a geographical unit, with Geshur, Havvoth-jair, and Kenath. Geshur, together with Maacath, is included among the lands which Israel was not able to take for Manasseh (Josh 13:13). However, in the time of David a matrimonial alliance linked David with Geshur through the marriage of Maacah, daughter of Talmai, Geshur's king, to David. This alliance apparently persisted over the years. David's son by Maacah, Absalom (1 Chr 3:2; 2 Sam 3:3), fled to his grandfather Talmai in Geshur after avenging Tamar by having Amnon killed (2 Sam 13:37–38), and Abijah, Rehoboam's son through Absalom's daughter, also named Maacah, was named crown prince by his father (2 Chr 11:18–22) and succeeded him as king. The disparity of the biblical traditions concerning the parentage of this Abijah, as well as Asa (2 Chr 13:2; 1 Kgs 15:1–2, 9–10; cf. MacLean, "Abijah," *IDB* 1:8–9), suggests that there may have been a greater willingness at some times than others to emphasize the Aramean connections of the relationship of David's line. Cf. Myers (14), who suggests, however, only that our list may reflect an obscure relationship between David and the Trans-jordanian tribes. For Kenath, see also Num 32:42, where its conquest is ascribed to one Nobah, who gave the city his own name. As our passage would indicate, however, the older name of the city prevailed over a period of time. Concerning the date, nature, and effects of the incursion of Geshur and Aram into Gilead (v 23) we know nothing. It is not made apparent that the defeat is to be attributed to the writer's theology of retribution, though this is possible. (For v 24, see n. 19.b. and vv 50b–55 below. Vv 25–41, see below.)

42–50a *Additional descendants of Caleb.* This unit is sharply defined by its opening and closing formulas, which are identical with those of the similar unit relating to descendants of Jerahmeel in 2:25–33. In its content it has little or nothing to do with the Calebite genealogy begun in 2:18–24 and continued in 50b–55 and 4:1–7. Not a single one of the descendants listed in this unit is to be found in the other(s). Especially striking is the absence of Caleb's children, Jerioth (? v 18), Hur (v 19), and Ashhur (v 24), upon whom the other genealogies are structured.

The relationship of this unit to 2:9 (and therefore to 2:25–33, 34–41), is established by v 42, which alone names Caleb and Jerahmeel as brothers. At the same time, the absence of any mention in v 42 of Ram, from whom the Davidic line is derived, is striking. Perhaps v 42, at least in part, belongs to the editorial stage of the composition of the book, together with vv 9 and 25. Any views in this regard, however, can only be speculative.

This second genealogy of Caleb is composed of three parts. (1) *Caleb's sons by an unnamed wife (vv 42–45)*. The form of this part is mixed, partially linear and partially segmented, and a variety of genealogical terminology is employed. In addition, unless the text be altered with G (see n. 42.b.), the parentage of Mareshah (v 42b) is not given, resulting in a gap in the record. (2) *Caleb's descendants through his concubine Ephah (vv 46–47)*. We have included Jahdai's children (v 47) here on the basis of the overall form of the unit and the occurrence of the name Ephah also among Jahdai's children, although Jahdai's relationship to any of the individuals named in v 46 is not given. The form "X begat Y" is used both times in v 46; while v 47 takes the form, "The sons of X were . . . ." (3) *Caleb's sons through a second concubine, Maacah (vv 47–48)*. The form is again "X begat Y" (v 48) and "X begat Y, the father of Z." Unless the Shaaph of v 49 is identified with that of v 47, Shaaph's parentage is not given. V 49b, which lists Caleb's daughter as Achsah, as do also Josh 15:16–19 and Judg 1:11–15, is perhaps with Rudolph to be considered a gloss (Rudolph, 22).

Within this unit it is apparent that a different concept of genealogy is often involved in which a man is considered to be the "father" of a city rather than an individual. Many of these cities are known to us from the lists of cities allotted to Judah in Josh 15. Thus Ziph is named in Josh 15:55, and usually identified with Tell Ziph, about 5 miles southeast of Hebron, although V. Gold ("Ziph," *IDB* 4:961–62) identifies it with Khirbet-ez-Zeifeh, southwest of Kurnub. Mareshah is known as a chief city of the Shephelah (Josh 15:44) and identified with Tell Sandahanna, some 12 miles northwest of Hebron (Aharoni, *Land*, 381), although Rudolph (21) considers this location too remote. Hebron's relation to Caleb is well established (cf. Josh 14:15; 15:13), and the city's former name, Kiriath-Arba, reoccurs in post-exilic times (Neh 11:25). Korah (v 43) is known otherwise only as a Levitical name. Beth-Tappuah (Josh 15:53) is identified with Taffuh, 2 miles west of Hebron. Rekem, like Moza of v 46, is listed as a Benjaminite town in Josh 18:26–27, but is too far removed to apply here. The location of Shema, named in Josh 15:26, is unknown.

The name Shammai (v 45) is also associated with a descendant of Jerahmeel (1 Chr 2:28, 32). Maon (Josh 15:55) is Tell Main, 8 miles south of Hebron. Jorkeam (v 44) should perhaps be read Jokdeam with Josh 15:56 (see n. 44.b.), although the location is unknown.

Beth-zur (Josh 15:58) is Khirbet et-tubeka, about 4.5 miles north of Hebron. Of the names given in vv 46–48, only Beth-Pelet (Josh 15:27) is known by name, although its location is uncertain. The association of Caleb with a Maacah is, however, suggestive in view of Hezron's association with Geshur in 2:21–23. Madmannah (v 49) is listed next to Ziklag in Josh 15:31, and identified by Aharoni with Khirbet Umm ed-Deimneh (*Land,* 381), though replaced by Beth-marcaboth in Josh 19:5 (Cohen suggests the name was changed when the city became a center of chariotry under Solomon; "Madmannah," *IDB* 3:220). Machbenah is unknown. Gibea (גבעא) may be identical with the Gibeah of Josh 15:57, but the location suggested, el-Jeba, 7.5 miles southwest of Bethlehem, appears too far north to be associated with Caleb. Achsah is, as noted above, Caleb's daughter according to Josh 15:16–19; Judg 1:11–15, and the inclusion here may be a gloss designed to identify Caleb the son of Hezron with Caleb of conquest fame. The remainder of the names scattered throughout the unit are unknown and may refer to either individuals, cities, or both. The association of the cities known, so far as can be determined, with Caleb in the southern part of the territory Judah, is in harmony with what we know of Judah and Caleb from earlier canonical traditions and appears to represent reliable tradition.

50aβ–55 *Descendants of Caleb through Hur.* These verses form a logical and literary unit with 2:18–19, 24 (see above) and extend Caleb's genealogy through Hur, here designated the firstborn of Ephratha. However, in denoting each of Hur's three sons as the "father" of a well-known city, vv 50–52, 55b show a relationship with vv 20–23, 42–49 as well. According to our analysis above, vv 52–55 may be a pre-Chronistic addition. Shobal, a name borne by an Edomite chieftain (Gen 36:20, 23, 29; 1 Chr 1:38, 40), is credited with the formation of Kiriath-jearim, earlier called Kiriath-baal (Josh 15:60; 18:14) and located on Judah's northern border with Benjamin and Dan. (Its families are described more fully in v 53.) An individual named Salma is also listed as the father of Boaz (v 11), and his association here with Bethlehem is particularly noteworthy in that regard. (See n. 19.b. on Ephrath and its association with Bethlehem.) Salma's descendants are treated more fully in vv 54 and (?) 55. Hareph is otherwise unknown, and the city attributed to him, Beth-geder, unidentified, but its location in the vicinity of Bethlehem and the northeast Shephelah would be expected (Aharoni, *Land,* 227). At least in the present form of the text his descendants are not listed.

The listing of Shobal's descendants in vv 52 appears fragmentary, being interrupted perhaps by the insertion of vv 53–55, if Williamson is correct in a pre-Chronistic source. As in v 50, Shobal is again termed the father of Kiriath-jearim, and his descendants are named as Reaiah (n. 52.a.) and "half of the Menuhoth" ("resting places"?). These Menuhoth are otherwise unknown unless they are related to the "half of the Manahathites" in v 54, which appears to be etymologically related, both being derived from the root נוח "to rest." In 1:40 and Gen 36:23 the second son of the Edomite Chieftain Shobal is also named Manahath, pointing once again to the associations between Judah and its neighbors to the south.

Little is known of the families of Kiriath-jearim named in v 53. Two of David's mighty men are termed Ithrites (2 Sam 23:38; 1 Chr 11:40), but of the three remaining gentilics we have no knowledge. However, Zorah and Eshtaol are listed together in Josh 19:41 as the first cities of the Danites before their migration to the north, and are commonly identified located some 12 miles west of Jerusalem and 6 miles southwest of Kiriath-jearim. (Aharoni, *Land,* 296, map 26). In Josh 15:33 both are reckoned to Judah, to whom they apparently fell following the migration of Dan to the north. Samson was buried between the same two cities (Judg 16:31). Gold refuses to identify these Zorites of v 54, associated with Salma in the area of Bethlehem, with those of vv 53 or 4:2, identified with Shobal and Kiriath-jearim ("Zorah," *IDB* 3:963), although this would not seem impossible.

This Salma is termed the "father of Bethlehem" (v 51), and Bethlehem is also listed among his "sons" in v 54. (A Salma is also named as father of Boaz in v 11.) The Netophathites are associated with Bethlehem not only here, but in Ezra 2:21–22 and Neh 7:26 as well. Two of David's mighty men were also natives of this site (2 Sam 23:28–29; 1 Chr 11:30; 27:13, 15), which apparently served as a position of some prominence both before and after the exile. One Netophathite, Seraiah, was among the captains of the Judean forces gathered to Gedaliah in the last days before the fall of Jerusalem (2 Kgs 25:23; Jer 40:8–9), and fifty-six men who counted Netophah their ancestral home are among those who returned with Zerubbabel (Ezra 2:21–22; Neh 7:26). Netophah also served as a Levitical residence (1 Chr 9:16; Neh 12:27–28). Its location, only some 3 miles southeast of Bethlehem, would have made it a convenient locale for serving in Jerusalem. (Morton, "Netophah," *IDB* 3:541.) Atroth-beth-joab ("Crown of the house of Joab") is otherwise unknown, and whether the name may be also cited in any way with David's well-known general of that name or with other Judean "Joabs" (1 Chr 4:14; Neh 7:11; Ezra 2:6). For the Manahathites and the Zorites, see above and n. 52.b–b. The "families of the scribes" may have been scribal guilds (Myers, 16), but again the Jabez at which they are located is unknown (a Jabez is introduced abruptly in 4:9–10, with etymological explanation, but no lineage is given). Rudolph (25) believes them to have been inhabitants of Kiriath-sepher, resettled further north in post-exilic times. Curtis (98) suggests the scribal note points to post-exilic times, since it is doubtful whether families of them existed earlier. As early as Jerome the families of Tirathites, Shimeath-ites, and Sucathites have been understood to refer to groups of religious functionaries (Curtis), but there is nothing substantial upon which to base such a view. Whether the Hammath from which these peoples designated as Kenites came is to be identified with a person, place, or both is conjectural; nor does the reference permit us to say which of the preceding peoples are to be understood as Kenites. The Rechabites are known as a people championing a non-sedentary way of life in Jer 35, where however they are without genealogy. This association with Hammath has suggested, to M. Pope ("Rechab," *IDB* 4:15–16), that Hammath is to be identified with the city of that name in Naphtali (cf. Josh 19:35), near which, at Kedesh, one Heber the Kenite also settled (Judg 4:11, 17). That the Rechabites continued to be a factor after the exile may be seen from Neh 3:14, where one of their number is named administrator of one of the districts of Judah. The association of the Kenites, who seem to have been an ancient nomadic or semi-nomadic group, with Judah, especially at the time of David, is well-known (cf. Num 24:20–22; 1 Sam 15:6; 30:29), but we have no reference to them after that time. This genealogy too, like that of Caleb referred to earlier, would seem to reflect the ongoing amalgamation of previously unrelated tribal elements into the mainstream of Judah.

4:1–7 *Additional Calebites: Hur and Ashhur.* V 1, as suggested earlier, reiterates the earlier part of Judah's line, interrupted in a pre-Chronistic stage by 2:53–55 and now by chap. 3 as well. More precisely, v 2 appears to be the original (or a second) continuation of 2:53, both relating descendants of Shobal. The unusual Haroeh of that verse, we have seen, probably represents a corruption of the Reaiah of 4:2 (see n. 52.a.). Vv 3–4 are not directly related to v 2, but their inclusion within the formula of v 4, "these were the sons of Hur . . . ," makes Rudolph's emendation of v 3, which inserts Hur's son Hareph on the basis of 2:51, attractive. (Hareph's descendants are otherwise not given.) With the genealogy of Hur terminated, vv 5–7 continue with that of Asshur, Caleb's second (?) son; cf. 2:24. This source then is abruptly broken off by v 8 and what appears to be a multitude of unrelated genealogical fragments.

V 1 recounts Judah's line through to the point where it was discontinued in 2:52, naming Perez, Hezron, Carmi, Hur, and Shobal. This listing does not agree fully with that which might be expected on the basis of 2:1–9, 18–19, in that Hur's father is named Carmi (cf. 2:7) rather than Caleb or Chelubai, and has persuaded Williamson (*JBL* 98 [1979] 356) to attribute it to the person responsible for the insertion of 2:53–55 rather than to the original source or the Chronicler, to whom he, with most commentators, attributes 2:1–17. (Many would, without textual evidence, alter "Carmi" here to "Caleb." See n. 4:1.a.) It may be, as suggested by Williamson (*JBL* 98 [1979] 369, n. 18), that some confusion has resulted on the basis of Gen 46:9.

Of Reaiah's descendants mentioned here, Jahath is a common Levitical name in Chronicles (cf. 6:20, 43; 23:10–11; 24:22; 2 Chr 34:12), Ahumai and Lahad are unique. The Zorathites were among those named in 2:53 as descended from Shobal, but their line of descent is not clear. Since Zorah occurs here also as the final term in the genealogy, we may suppose that the author wished to elucidate their origin by tracing their descent more directly through Reaiah. Since Zorah is known to us as one of the cities said to be rebuilt by Rehoboam (2 Chr 11:10) and as a village inhabited by post-exilic Judeans (Neh 11:29), the demonstration of that link may have had particular significance for the author.

Vv 3–4a are in the MT unrelated to the previous verses and perhaps contain descendants of Hur's third son Hareph (cf. 2:51 and n. 3.a.). The Etam of which Hareph would then be the father is listed along with Tekoa (cf. 2:24; 4:5) and Zorah (2:54; 4:2) as cities fortified by Rehoboam (2 Chr 11:5–10), and in a passage not included in the MT but found in G of Josh 15:59a, is one of eleven cities in an apparent administrative district around Bethlehem (Aharoni, *Land,* 301–2; Gold, "Etam," *IDB* 2:152). Aharoni locates Gedor (v 4) just north of Beth-zur and west of Tekoa, and Hushan some 5 miles west of Bethlehem (*Land,* 249, map 19). Once again, two members of David's guard are listed as Hushites (2 Sam 21:18; 23:27; 1 Chr 11:29; 20:4; 27:11 (Curtis, 106). Jezreel may be the city referred to in Josh 15:56, and if so might indicate a northward migration of the families associated with that city (Myers, 28), but may be, as the remaining names of the verse appear to be, a personal name about whom nothing is known. V 4b is the concluding formula of Hur's genealogy begun in 2:50aα.

Vv 5–7 present the genealogy of Asshur, which would be expected following that of Hur, cf. 2:19, 24. Tekoa is the well-known home of the prophet Amos (Amos 1:1), six miles south of Beth-lehem. The names of Asshur's two wives do not occur elsewhere, although Naarah is a city on Ephraim's borders, Josh 16:7. Although nothing is known of the remaining names of vv 6–7, the southern connections of some seem apparent. Hepher is mentioned with Tappuah (Josh 12:17) and Socoh (1 Kgs 4:10), and hence evidently in southern Judah (Curtis, 106); the term *Temanite* refers to a southerner and is associated with Edom (Gen 36:11). Ethnan is often identified with Ithnan, a city of southern Judah, cf. Josh 15:23. Zohar is a name of Simeon's son (Gen 46:10). Hence we can at best affirm the southern orientation and the continuing and fluctuating relationships between these "clans of Judah." The Persian derivation of (Ha-) Ahastarite has been both posited and questioned (Torrey, "Medes and Persians," *JAOS* 66 [1966] 7–8; Myers, 28; Rudolph, 14). Rudolph believes it contains the Persian word *kšatra*, "*Reich, Heershaft*," and thus dates from Persian times.

2:25–33, 34–41 *Descendants of Jerahmeel.* The passage consisting of vv 25–33 is segmented in form and set apart by appropriate opening and closing formulas corresponding to that of Caleb in vv 42–50a; vv 34–41 are linear and include no such formulas. That the two portions stem from different sources is strongly suggested in that the same Sheshan who in v 31 is said to be the father of Ahlai is in v 34 said to have had no sons. Attempts to resolve this conflict by considering Ahlai a daughter (cf. Keil, 66–67) are harmonistic.

We know little of the clan of Jerahmeel, other than that in David's time it inhabited the Negeb of Judah (1 Sam 27:10; 30:29). Curtis (93) believes the names in vv 25–33 to be early in form and favors the antiquity and historicity of the list. Noth thinks the Jerahmeelites formed an amphictyony at Hebron with Judah, Caleb, Simeon, Othniel, and Kain (*ZDPV* 55 [1932] 97–124). Rudolph believes the similarity of a number of names with the Edomite genealogy of chap. 1 supports the contention of Meyer of connections between the Jerahmeelites and the Edomites (cf. Onam, v 26 and 1:40; Oren, v 25, and Aran, 1:42; Shammai, v 28, and Shammah, 1:37; Jether, v 32, and Jithran, 1:41). Beyond such speculations, however, little can be said. While some of the names occurring here are found elsewhere in the OT, it is unlikely that any of them belong to the individuals named elsewhere.

The superscription of v 25, which points to Jerahmeel as the firstborn of Hezron, is parallel to that of v 42, which names Caleb as Jerahmeel's brother, and would suggest also that Jerahmeel's position in v 9 is due to his status as the firstborn. Jerahmeel's sons of two wives are named in vv 25–26, but in the subsequent verses the line through the first (Ahijah?) is continued through only one of the four (or five) sons named, Ram, and that only for a single generation (v 27); the line through Atarah and her son Onam occupies the remainder of the notice (vv 28–33), extending in the case of Ahlai to the sixth generation beyond Onam. All of the names listed are to the best of our knowledge personal.

That the Sheshan with whose line vv 34–41 are concerned is to be identified with that of v 31 is not stated by the text. Once again nothing is known of any of the individuals named, including Jarha, Sheshan's Egyptian slave, to whom he is said to have given his daughter to continue his line (v 34), or Elishamah, who stands at the end of the genealogy and for whose sake the linear genealogy of fourteen generations would seem to exist. Commentators who assume the genealogical record to be complete number Sheshan as the tenth generation beyond Judah and place him near the time of the Exodus; an additional fourteen generations would then place Elishamah near the time of David (Keil, 67). Others more prone to point to the significance of Elishamah's pedigree for the author's own day are inclined to place him nearer the time to which they would ascribe the authorship of the book, or approximately 400 B.C. (cf. Rudolph, 19). Either procedure may be supported with some logic and, in the absence of additional evidence, the matter must remain open.

Explanation

The genealogist has brought together under Hezron's two sons, Jerahmeel and Caleb, a host of genealogical, geographical, and societal information, some of which may be seen to be derived from biblical sources and some whose origin is unknown. Since no Judeans other than the line of David are derived from Ram, the result is that all remaining data are gathered under the overarching rubric of Hezron's other sons, Caleb and Jerahmeel. The materials in this unit are without real parallel in other canonical traditions.

We may assume that the materials at hand are fragmentary and relate both to various ages and localities. Concerning the ages involved, the text tells us nothing. We cannot ascertain, for example, whether the Elishamah with whom Jerahmeel's line ends in 2:41 belongs to the time of David or the second temple or somewhere in between. Concerning the localities, we are at times provided information, at other times not. Hezron's offspring through Segub (vv 1–23) are at home in Gilead. Caleb's descendants in vv 42–50a are associated with Hebron; those of Hur's sons in vv 50b–55, 4:1–7 are clustered around two areas to the south-southwest and west of Jerusalem. The fact that Caleb and others traditionally associated with the extreme south of Judah are here removed to the center of the tribe's traditional territory may reflect some post-exilic interests, in which the misfortune of the exile has led to a resettlement and continued diffusion of earlier more independent and farther removed peoples.

The aim of the author or authors, however, is to attach all of these, in their diversity, to the tribe of Judah through Hezron and his descendants. We may assume that some honor, if not political, economic, and social advantages, derived from belonging to the only tribe restored to its territory by official decree. At the same time, if one result of the exile, at least in certain quarters, was to separate Israel from peoples surrounding her (cf. Ezra 4), a second effect, wrought perhaps less consciously, was the inclusion of heterogeneous peoples under the banner of the restored kingdom of Judah. While the inclusion of such a genealogy testifies to the first trend, a consideration of its contents witnesses equally strongly to the second. If members of all of the tribes of Israel belong to the chosen people, it is also true that many of those who came to be attached to the tribe of Judah attained that status not by birth but, as it were, by adoption. The present genealogy serves to legitimate that adoption.

Descendants of David   (3:1–24)

Bibliography

The material on the Davidic monarchy is voluminous, and much is irrelevant to the concerns most prominent here. The following materials may be most helpful.

Aharoni, Y. *Excavations at Ramat Rahel, Seasons 1959 and 1960.* Rome: Centro dei studi semitici, 1962. ———. *Excavations at Ramat Rahel, Seasons 1961 and 1962.* Rome: Centro dei studi semitici, 1964. **Albright, W. F.** *The Biblical Period from Abraham to Ezra.* New York: Harper Torchbooks, 1963. 81–89. **Avigad, N.** "A New Class of Jehud Stamps." *IEJ* 7 (1957) 146–53. ———. *A New Discovery of an Archive of Bullae from the Period of Ezra and Nehemiah.* Qedem IV. Monographs of the Institute of Archaeology. Jerusalem: Hebrew University, 1975. **Cross, F. M.** "Judean Stamps." *Eretz Israel* 9 (1969) 20–27. **May, H. G.** "King Jehoiachin in Exile." *BA* 5 (1942) 49–55. **Myers, J. M.** "David." *IDB* 1:771–82. **Stern, E.** *The Material Culture of the Land of the Bible in the Persian Period 538–332 B. C. E.* Jerusalem: Israel Exploration Journal, 1973. (Heb.) **Talmon, S.** "Ezra and Nehemiah." *IDBSup,* 314–28. **Wifall, W.** "The Chronology of the Divided Monarchy of Israel." *ZAW* 80 (1968) 319–37.

Translation

Children of David

[1a] *These were the sons of David born to him* [a] *in Hebron: the firstborn Amnon by Ahinoam the Jezreelitess; the second,* [b] *Daniel,* [c] *by Abigail, the Carmelitess;* [d] [2] *the third, Absalom,* [a] *by the son of Maacah, the daughter of Talmai, the king of Geshur; the fourth, Adonijah, the son of Haggith;* [3] *the fifth, Shephatiah, by Abital;* [a] *the sixth, Ithream,* [b] *by his wife Eglah.* [b] [4] *Six (children) were born* [a] *to him in Hebron, and he was king there seven years and six months, and he was king in Jerusalem thirty-three years.*

[5] *These were born* [a] *to him in Jerusalem:* [b] *Shimea,* [c] *Shobab, Nathan, and Solomon, four by Bath-shua* [d] *the daughter of Ammiel;* [e] [6] *as well as Ibhar, Elishama,* [a] [b] *Eliphelet,* [7] *Nogah,* [a] *Nepheg, Japhia,* [8] *Elishama, Eliada,* [a] *and Eliphelet, nine.* [9] *All (these were) David's sons, besides the concubines' sons, and* [a] *Tamar was their sister.* [a]

From Solomon to the Exile

[10] *The son* [a] *of Solomon: Rehoboam, Abijah his son, Asa his son, Jehoshaphat his son,* [11] *Joram his son, Ahaziah his son, Joash his son,* [12] *Amaziah his son, Azariah* [a] *his son, Jotham his son,* [13] *Ahaz his son, Hezekiah his son, Manasseh his son,* [14] *Amon his son, Josiah his son.*

15 *The sons of Josiah: the firstborn Johanan; the second, Jehoiakim; the third, Zedekiah; the fourth, Shallum.*

16 *The sons of Jehoiakim: Jeconiah his son; Zedekiah his son.*

Descendants of Jeconiah/Jehoiakim

17 *The sons* a *of Jeconiah, the prisoner:* b *his son Shealtiel,* 18 *Malchiram, Pedaiah, Shenazzar, Jekamiah, Hoshama, and Nebadiah.*

19 *The sons of Pedaiah:* a *Zerubbabel and Shimei.* b

The offspring c *of Zerubbabel: Meshullam and Hananiah, and their sister Shelomith;* 20 *Hashubah, Ohel, Berechiah, Hasadiah, (and) Jushab-hesed,* a *five.*

21 *The offspring* a *of Hananiah: Pelatiah, Jeshaiah, the sons* b *of Rephaiah, the sons* c *of Arnan, the sons* c *of Obadiah, (and) the sons* c *of Shecaniah.*

22 *The offspring* a *of Shecaniah: Shemaiah.* b *The sons of Shemaiah:* b *Hattush, Igal, Bariah, Neariah, and Shaphat, six.*

23 *The offspring* a *of Neariah: Elioenai, Hizkiah, and Azrikam, three.*

24 *The sons of Elioenai: Hodaviah, Eliashib, Pelaiah, Akkub, Johanan, Delaiah, and Anani, seven.*

Notes

1.a-a. "And these . . . were born," (אלה נולד). 2 Sam ויולדו "and they were being born" (Q); וילדו "and they were born," (K); cf. also 1 Chr 3:4 (ששה נולד "six were born") with 2 Sam 3:5 אלה ילדו "these were born").

1.b. שני "second." One would expect the article, as uniformly with the remaining ordinals in vv 1–3, G Tg. 2 Sam 3:3 reads משנהו "his second."

1.c. Daniel (דניאל). Syr כלב "Caleb," 2 Sam 3:3 כלאב "Chileab." That the difficulty is complex and prolonged is suggested by the Gr. readings of Chr (G^L α') Δαλουια(ς) "Dalouias"; G^B Δαμνιηλ "Damniel" and Samuel (G^B = Δαλουια "Dalouia").

1.d. "Abigail, the Carmelitess." 2 Sam 3:3 = "Abigail, the wife of Nabal, the Carmelite."

2.a. Absalom. Omitting the prefixed ל with 2 Sam 3:3, G Syr Tg and about 20 Heb. MSS. It is possible, however, that the ל is used loosely, according to the habit of Chronicles.

3.a. "By Abital"; 2 Sam 3:4 "the son of Abital."

3.b-b. "By his wife, Eglah"; Syr = "by Eglah, the wife of David" = 2 Sam 3:4.

4.a. נולד "were born"; see n.3:1.a-a.

5.a. נוּלְּדוּ "were born." The pointing is anomalous. The sense demanded is that of a niph pf; see GKC, § 69t, and 1 Chr 20:8. 2 Sam 5:14 הַיִּלֹּדִים (pl noun), 1 Chr 14:4 הַיְלוּדִים (qal pass ptcp).

5.b. בירושלים "in Jerusalem." The Masora calls attention to the fact this is one of only 5 occurrences in the OT in which "Jerusalem" is written *plene*.

5.c. שמעא "Shimea," Syr 1 Chr 14:4; 2 Sam 5:14 שמוע "Shamua."

5.d. "Four, by Bath-shua, the daughter of Ammiel." David's wife Bathsheba is given this name only here. The entire phrase is absent in the Syr; 1 Chr 14:4; 2 Sam 5:14. Also the name of one of Judah's wives, 1 Chr 2:3.

5.e. עמיאל "Ammiel." In 2 Sam 11:3, Bathsheba's father is Eliam (אליעם), with the two components of the name reversed.

6.a. אלישמע "Elishama." 1 Chr 14:5; 2 Sam 5:15 אלישוע "Elishua"; G^B Ελεισα. Another son, אלישמע, is listed in v 8.

6.b.-7.a. Eliphelet, Nogah. This pair of names is absent in 2 Sam 5:15, although present in 1 Chr 14:5, where, however, a distinction occurs in the spelling (14:5, אלפלט; 14:7, אליפלט) of the name on its second occurrence. The presence of the identical (or similar) name as another of David's sons in v 9 suggests dittogr, although it is impossible to say at which point in the history of the text this may have happened. The present form of the text in v 8 enumerates nine sons of David, exclusive of those born in Hebron and the children of Bath-shua, and thus requires the inclusion of both.

8.a. Eliadah. The original form of the name is probably that preserved in 1 Chr 14:7 בעלידע "Beeliadah." The alteration of names with a בעל-component is common in the OT (see Hos 2:19 [2:17], and cf. Judg 7:1 with 2 Sam 11:21).

9.a-a. The inclusion of this notice seems to have been occasioned by 2 Sam 13.

10.a. The Heb. is again sg, but 3 MSS G Syr read pl. It is possible here, however, in view of the structure of the unit, that ובן שלמה "and the son of Solomon" does not refer to the entire list following, but only to Rehoboam.

12.a. עֲזַרְיָה "Azariah." Most MSS עֲזַרְיָהוּ "Azariahu"; G^L $^{+MSS}$ Syr עֻזִּיָּה "Uzziah."

17.a. Seb. Syr sg. In this pericope alone, the sg בן "son" is followed by more than one son in vv 20, 21, 23; the pl בני by pl "sons" here (MT) and vv 19, 22b, 24; and the pl by only a single "son" in v 22. Note also the unusual use of the pl בְּנֵי 4x in v 21b.

17.b. אסר "prisoner." The absence of the article is striking, and in conjunction with Syr, which construes אסר as part of the following proper noun, has led some to consider "Assir" as a proper noun (cf. Keil, 80).

19.a. G$^{BA+10MSS}$ Σαλαθιηλ "Shealtiel"; cf. Hag 1:1; Ezra 3:2, 8, and *Comment* below.

19.b. G^B. Perhaps אסר originated as a marginal gl, or the article may have been dropped after the final ה of the preceding word.

19.c. Heb. sg; see n.17.a.

20.a. G^{Aal} suggests ישוב "Jashob." The absence of the conj suggests other minor textual problems.

21.a. Heb. sg.

21.b. MS G Vg בְּנוֹ "his son"; cf. n. 21.c.

21.c. G Vg בְּנוֹ "his son," understanding the names beyond "Pelatiah" to represent a continuing line of descendants rather than brothers of Pelatiah.

22.a. MT pl; Seb. G Syr Vg sg.

22.b-b. Delete? Cf. the numeral 6 at the end of v 22.

23.a. MT sg; Seb. nonn MSS G Tg pl.

Form/Structure/Setting

Vv 1–9, listing David's sons, which total nineteen, follow logically upon 2:9–17, which has traced Ram's descendants down to David and included his nephews on the side of his two sisters. This section is composed of two major parts: vv 1–3, David's sons born at Hebron, based upon 2 Sam 3:2–5; and vv 4–8, David's sons born in Jerusalem, found in 2 Sam 5:14–16 as well as 1 Chr 14:4–7. These two parts have been joined together by v 4 and concluded with v 9, which is reminiscent of 2 Sam 5:13–14.

Vv 10–14 trace the descendants of Solomon in a single line from Rehoboam through Josiah (died ca. 609 B.C.). With the exception of Rehoboam, each descendant is explicitly denoted as the son of the preceding through a following בנו "his son." (In v 17, the first of Jeconiah's descendants is so noted also, in contrast to the case with Rehoboam here.) This line comprises, with the exceptions noted below, the rulers of the southern kingdom during this period. In v 15, however, four sons of Josiah are named, at least three of whom ascended the throne, and v 16 lists two descendants of Jehoiakim, although the relationship between them, as we shall see, is questionable.

Vv 17–24 continue the Davidic line through Jeconiah for an apparent eight generations beyond the deportation. The practice begun with Josiah in v 15 of listing multiple sons of each father is continued. The familiar בנו "his son" occurs only with Jeconiah's first son Shealtiel, suggesting the possibility that one form of the list may have ended near this point. As the line is continued, however, we note the regular "mixed" pattern, in which further descendants are traced only through a single one of the sons previously listed, who does not necessarily appear to have been the eldest surviving (cf. vv 21–22). If the Hebrew text is maintained as we have done, v 21 is unique in that Hananiah's descendants are after the listing of two sons grouped according to more obvious families, "the sons of Rephaiah, the sons of Arnon," etc. With the exception of v 21, vv 20b–24 not only name but consistently enumerate the descendants named.

Comment

1–9 The listing of David's sons (vv 1–9) born at Hebron does not occur elsewhere in Chronicles, which is perhaps not surprising in view of the writer's general policy of omitting all references to David's rule over only a part of the land. (See below and on 1 Chr 29:27.) Here too the writer has avoided any suggestion that David's rule at Hebron was less than complete by excising statements that David's seven and one-half years at Hebron were "over Judah" while his subsequent rule in Jerusalem was "over all Israel and Judah" (2 Sam 5:5). Apart from minor textual variations and a tendency to simplify the descriptions of David's various wives (see the *Notes*), these verses do not differ substantially from the corresponding list of Samuel.

The list of David's sons born in Jerusalem differs more substantially from 2 Sam 5:14–16, as well as from the similar list in 1 Chr 14:3–7. Our passage is unique in counting the first four names (Shimea, Shobal, Nathan, and Solomon) and attributing them to Bath-shua (v 5b), and in including the count of the sons born in Jerusalem (nine, v 8). It also differs from 1 Chr 14:4 and 2 Sam 5:14 in naming David's first son born of Bath-shua, Shimea (שמאה, v 5) instead of Shammua (שמוע), and the second born at Jerusalem as Elishama (אלישמע, v 6), identical with the seventh son in all texts but differing from the other two which have here Elishua (אלישוע) for the second son. Our passage also includes mention of Tamar as David's sister (v 9), perhaps, as suggested by Rudolph (27) because she was the only sister about whom additional information was available.

The two Chronicles passages agree against Samuel in including the names Eliphelet (v 6) and Nogah (v 7), absent in Samuel, perhaps through haplography. At the same time, however, the naming of another Eliphelet in v 8 in agreement with the other two texts and the repetition of Elishama in v 8 and parallels raise the possibility that all of our lists result from an earlier conflation of lists of David's sons which duplicated some names. This textual history can no longer be reproduced. 1 Chr 14:7 probably reflects reliable tradition in naming David's eighth son as Beeliada, (בעלידע), rather than Eliada (אלידע), since the alteration of names compounded with Baal is otherwise well-attested (cf. n. 8.a.). The inclusion of the numbers four (v 5) and nine (v 8) as the sum of the sons born to Bathshua and David's remaining wives respectively in Jerusalem presumes the conflate text we have before us.

10–16 The listing of the kings of Judah in vv 10–16 is familiar to us from the books of Kings. That Athaliah is not mentioned (between Ahaziah and his son Joash) is to be expected, since she was not a Davidide. (Although the Deuteronomist states that "Athaliah reigned [מלכת] over the land"

[2 Kgs 11:3] he avoids the customary opening and closing notices within which he includes the account of other rulers.) Uzziah's throne name, Azariah, is used in contrast with 2 Chr 26, and Jehoiakim's son is Jeconiah, with the theophoric element reversed; contrast 2 Kgs 24:6–9; 2 Chr 36:9.

In listing Josiah's sons, however, our author, or his source, differs substantially from what we know from the books of Kings and elsewhere in Chronicles. The Johanan named as Josiah's firstborn (v 15) is otherwise unknown. It has been assumed either that he died before his father Josiah or that he should be identified with Jehoahaz, although Jer 22:11 identifies this Jehoahaz with Shallum.

Rudolph (27) has pointed out that, proceeding from 609 B.C. as the date of Josiah's death and using the figures available from the Deuteronomistic chronology, Josiah would have been born in 648 B.C., Jehoiakim in 634, Jehoahaz/Shallum in 632, and Zedekiah in 619 (2 Kgs 24:18, 598 + 21). That would mean that Josiah would have been only fourteen years old when Jehoiakim was born, so that it is difficult to assume Johanan to be an older son. However, this older son could have been born of a different wife, so that he might have been almost identical to Jehoiakim in age.

Another difficulty relates to the order in which Josiah's sons are listed as coming to the throne. That Johanan, the eldest, did not serve as king might be explained by assuming that Johanan preceded his father Josiah in death. That Jehoiakim might have been bypassed by the people of the land in favor of the slightly younger Jehoahaz/Shallum because of his pro-Egyptians tendencies seems possible in view of the fact that Neco subsequently deposed Jehoahaz and installed Jehoiakim/Eliakim in his place (2 Kgs 23:34; 2 Chr 36:4). This Jehoiakim then reigned until the land was besieged by Nebuchadnezzar, although 2 Kgs 24:1–7 seems to indicate that Jehoiakim died before the final siege, while 2 Chr 36:6–7 indicates that he was taken captive by Nebuchadnezzar at the same time a portion of the temple vessels were removed to Babylon(!). Both texts agree, however, that Jehoiakim was succeeded by his son, who is variously named Jehoiachin (2 Chr 36:9; 2 Kgs 24:6, 12, 17), Jeconiah (here and in Esth 2:6; Jer 24:1; 27:20; 28:4; 29:2), and Coniah (Jer 22:24, 28; 37:1), and that this son reigned only briefly (598–97 B.C.). (His age, given in 2 Chr 36:9 as eight, is probably erroneous, and should be read as eighteen; cf. 2 Kgs 24:8 [see May, "Jehoiachin," *IDB* 2:811–13].) His brief three-month rule was followed by that of Zedekiah.

At this point some confusion exists in our texts. Both 2 Kgs 24:17 Heb. G^L and the Greek of 2 Chr 36:10 consider this Zedekiah as the son of Josiah and hence Jehoiachin's uncle; however, 2 Chr 36:10 Heb. names Zedekiah as Jehoiachin's brother and 2 Kgs 24:17 G^B makes him the son of Jehoiachin himself. This latter reading is also the most probable understanding of 1 Chr 3:16, where the suffix "his son," attached to Zedekiah, should refer to the individual named immediately before, hence to Jeconiah/Jehoiachin, although this understanding is admittedly contradicted by v 17, which includes no such Zedekiah among Jeconiah's sons.

It seems likely on the basis of the evidence that there was a Zedekiah son of Josiah and also a Zedekiah son of Jeconiah, or perhaps of Jehoiakim. The texts reflect a confusion in understanding which of these was Judah's king. Historical accuracy is probably to be attributed to 2 Kgs 24:17 Heb. and G^L and to 2 Chr 36:10 G, which name Zedekiah as Josiah's son and Jehoiachin's uncle. It seems reasonable to assume either that the fact that Jeconiah also had a son named Zedekiah (v 16) has led to this confusion, which would have been increased by the chaotic times with which it deals, or conversely, that attributing such a son to Jeconiah, in apparent contradiction to v 17, may be the result of the uncertainty apparent in other texts. Which is more likely appears to be a toss-up.

The account of Jeconiah's exile and imprisonment is vividly attested to by the Babylonian Chronicles (cf. *ANET*, 308). In one of these tablets mention is made of five sons of Jehoiachin, in contrast to the seven mentioned here— perhaps the final two were born at a later date.

The list of Jeconiah's descendants, of significant importance for the post-exilic period, may best be viewed in the following genealogical chart:

Descendants of Jeconiah: 1 Chr 3:17–24

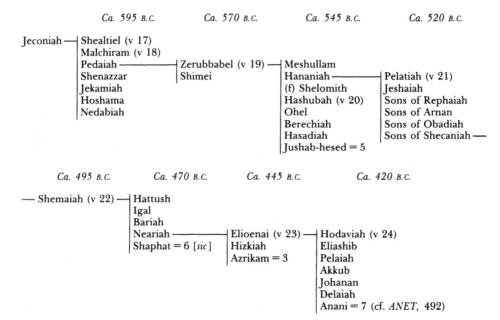

19–24 V 19 names Zerubbabel as the son of Pedaiah, while elsewhere (Hag 1:12, 14; 2:2, 23; Ezra 3:2, 8; 5:2; Neh 12:1) he is the son of Shealtiel (see n. 19.a. above). Keil maintains Zerubbabel may have been the son of Shealtiel's widow, taken in Levirate marriage by Pedaiah after Shealtiel's death, and thus officially reckoned as his son (81–82). (Keil explains the fact that Luke 3:27 makes Shealtiel the son of Neri, a descendant of David through Nathan rather than Solomon, as due to a similar Levirate marriage involving Jeconiah and Assir [v 17], understood by Keil as a proper name.) Dahlberg

("Zerubbabel," *IDB* 4:955–56) concludes either the writer is in error here or the reference may be to a later Zerubbabel who is the namesake of the former. The relationship between the Shenazzar (שנאצר) named here and the Sheshbazzar (ששבצר) denoted the leader of the returning exiles (Ezra 1:8, 11), as well as the relationship of both to Zerubbabel, has been much debated. Rothstein understands Shenazzar to be the Babylonian name of Pedaiah (*Die Genealogie*, 27–29). These data are commonly reconciled today by following the suggestion of Albright that Sheshbazzar and Shenazzar are to be identified, the two names representing variant transliterations of some such Babylonian name as Sin-ab-usur (Bright, *History*, 362; Dahlberg, "Shenazzar," *IDB* 4:325–27; Albright, *The Biblical Period*, 86–87). Additional support of this theory may be gained from the name Σαναβασσαρος ("Sanabassaros"), preserved in the Greek of 1 Esdr 2:12, 15; 6:18, 20, and Josephus, which reflects a closer transliteration of Sin-ab-usur, from which Shenazzar is then derived.

A similar difficulty surrounds the problem of the relationship of Zerubbabel to this Sheshbazzar/Shenazzar. Ezra 1:8, 11 make Sheshbazzar, named prince (שר) of Judah, responsible for the return of the temple vessels, and the Aramaic letter of Ezra 5:15–17 for the laying of the temple foundation. Ezra 2–3, however, ascribe the laying of the foundation to Zerubbabel working together with the high priest Jeshua, and the work is resumed by these same individuals after being interrupted by the peoples of the land (cf. Ezra 5:2). Although some have identified Sheshbazzar and Zerubbabel, it seems better to maintain that the writer has instead telescoped the work of these two individuals, and that Shenazzar/Sheshbazzar, who initiated work on the temple soon after Cyrus's decree of 538 B.C., was succeeded by his nephew Zerubbabel, either then or upon resumption of the work some years later.

Neither Zerubbabel's brother Shimei (v 19) nor subsequent descendants of Zerubbabel listed in vv 19–24 are named elsewhere in the Bible, including the genealogies of Jesus in Matthew and Luke. The inclusion of Zerubbabel's daughter Shelomith in the midst of the list of his children, coupled with the enumeration of five further sons of Zerubbabel in v 20, may support Rudolph (29) in his contention that Meshullam, Hananiah, and Shelomith were born in Babylon and their five brothers were born after the return in Judah. On the basis of a collection of bullae and seals published by Avigad and dated to the late sixth and early fifth centuries, however, some light may be shed on this prominent family after their return to Palestine. One seal reads לאלנתן פחוא "to Elnathan the governor." This Elnathan may be dated, it is held, by a second seal, יהד לשלמית אמת אלנתן "Judah: to Shelomith, the mother of Elnathan." This Shelomith, according to Avigad and Talmon ("Ezra," *IDBSup*, 325) is to be identified with the daughter of Zerubbabel by that name, and her husband (assuming "mother" to reflect court language) Elnathan was the governor of the independent province of Judah at that time. Similar impressions on storage jars at Ramat Rahel reading יהד חננה ("Judah: Hananiah") might then refer to Zerubbabel's second-named son. It is also possible that one Baruch ben Shimei, listed on eleven additional bullae, is the son of Zerubbabel's brother named in v 19.

In contrast to the name Zerubbabel ("Offspring of Babylon"), the names of Zerubbabel's children are suggestive of the hope of restoration which one would expect in their day: Meshuallam ("Restored"), Hananiah ("Yahweh is merciful"), Shelomith ("Peace"), Hashubah ("Yahweh has considered"), Ohel ("Tent [of Yahweh]"), Berechiah ("Yahweh has blessed"), Hasidiah ("Yahweh has had covenant love") and Jushab-hesed ("Covenant love returns").

We have no further information concerning the Davidides, although many of the names are common in the post-exilic period (see the listing in Myers, 21). If Jehoiachin was born about 616 B.C. and we allow 25 years for each generation, Hodaviah and his brothers would have been born about 420 B.C., and probably several years earlier. This permits the understanding that the Anani named in an Aramaic letter dated 407 B.C. (ANET 492) with the high priest Johanan and Anani's brother Ostanes and the nobles of the Jews could be the last name given among Solomon's descendants (v 24). Of course, this figure is lowered by almost a century if the text suggested by G in v 21 is read.

Explanation

In vv 1–9, which include names of nineteen sons of David, we see additional evidence of the desire to make the genealogical lists as complete as possible. The inclusion of only those sons of David born in Jerusalem within the main part of the book (1 Chr 14:4–7) is probably due to unevenness of composition; since the inclusion of events related to David's rule over Judah only at Hebron is not in harmony with the book, its inclusion here may be secondary. At the same time, the omission of crucial parts of 2 Sam 5:5 (see above) indicates the author was aware of this difficulty and adjusted for it accordingly.

This bipartite nature of vv 1–9 is doubtless dependent upon the sources; the inclusion of reference to Bathshua is probably due to the author and reflects two opposite trends. Since all mention of Bath-sheba is lacking in the center portion of the work (cf. 1 Chr 20; 2 Chr 1), its inclusion here is unexpected and not in harmony with the remainder of the book. At the same time, the use of the name Bath-shua, which occurs only here in the OT, instead of Bath-sheba may serve both to recall Judah's Canaanite wife of the same name (known only in 1 Chr 2:3) and to veil in some obscurity Bath-sheba's relationship to David and Solomon. The listing of Solomon as the last of Bath-shua's sons, contrary to what appears to be the intent of 2 Sam 12:24–25, may be an intentional device to place Solomon in a position of prominence. The placing of Solomon at the head of vv 10–14 may reflect a similar interest.

With the listing of no less than four sons of Josiah (v 15), the writer or his source seems either to have regained a more historical perspective, or at least to have discovered a more complete source. This fullness is characteristic also of vv 16–24, which appears to reach far into the post-exilic period.

This list of Davidides stretching for eight generations beyond the exile is both suggestively lengthy and tantalizingly cryptic. Our best available information suggests that the Davidic nobility played a prominent role in the early days of the restoration, and some messianic speculation may have been associated with them at that time (cf. Hag 2). However, the text before us is silent concerning any future hope of either a political or a theological nature that might have been attached to this line. As noted by Coggins (26), the naming of so many sons of David may suggest that later families were proud of their Davidic descent, but no hopes associated with the restoration of the Davidic king in Jerusalem seem to be implied. "The impression is that these names are recorded because of their distinguished ancestor, rather than that there is any expectation of a 'new David' to arise from among them."

(On 4:1-7, see above, p. 35.)

Additional Judahites   (4:8-23)

Translation

⁸ *Koz begat Anub and Zobebah,* ª *and the families of Aharhel, Harum's son.*
⁹ *Jabez was more honored than his brothers. His mother had called his name* ª *Jabez, saying, "Because I gave birth in pain."* ª ¹⁰ *Jabez called to the God of Israel, "May you indeed bless me,* ª *and increase my territory, and your hand be with me, and may you keep me from evil, so as not to hurt me."* ᵇ *And God brought about that which he had asked.*
¹¹ *Chelub,* ª *the brother of Shuhah,* ᵇ *was the father of Mehir, who was the father of Eshton.* ¹² *Eshton was the father of Beth-rapha* ª *and Paseah and Tehinnah,* ᵇ *the father of Ir-nahash.* ᶜ ᵈ *These were the men of Recab.* ᵉ
¹³ *The sons of Kenaz were Othniel and Seraiah. The offspring of Othniel: Hathath and Meonothai.* ª ¹⁴ *Meonothai was the father of Ophrah, and Seraiah was the father of Joab, the father of Ge-harashim,* ª *because they were craftsmen.* ¹⁵ *The sons of Caleb, the son of Jephunneh, were* ª *Ir, Elah,* ᵇ *and Naam; These were the sons of Kenaz.* ᶜ
¹⁶ *The sons of Jehallelel: Ziph, Ziphah, Tiria, and Asarel.* ª
¹⁷ *The offspring* ª *of Ezrah: Jether, Mered, Epher, and Jalon.* ᵇ *Jether begat* ᶜ *Miriam,* ᵈ *Shammai, and Ishbah, the father of Eshtemoa.* ¹⁸ *His wife, the Jewess,* ª *bore Jered the father of Gedor, Heber the father of Soco, and Jekuthiel the father of Zanoah. These were the sons of Bithiah,* ᵇ *Pharaoh's daughter, whom Mered* ᶜ *took: . . .* ᵈ ¹⁹ *The sons of Hodiah's* ª *wife, the sister of Naham, were* ᵇ *the father of Keilah the Garmite and Eshtemoa the Maacathite.*
²⁰ *The sons of Shimon: Amnon, Rinnah, Ben-hanan, and Tilon.* ª *The sons of Ishi: Zoheth and Ben-zoheth.*
²¹ *The sons of Shelah, Judah's son: Er the father of Lecah, Laadah the father of Mareshah, the families of the house of byssus-working* ª *at Beth-ashbea,* ²² *Jokim and the men of Cozeba, and Joash and Saraph, who ruled over Moab and returned to Bethlehem* ª *(The records are ancient).* ᵇ ²³ *They were the potters and the inhabitants of Netaim and Gederah. They dwelt there with the king for his work.* ª

Notes

8.a. *BH³* again suggests adding or reading יעבץ "Jabez," thus providing a link for Jabez in v 9. However, there is no textual evidence to support such a reading.

9.a-a. The play on words between יעבץ "Jabez," the root meaning of which is unknown and occurs only here, and עצב "pain" is popular rather than scientific.

10.a. אם ברך תברכני "may you indeed bless me." The form is that of the oath, in which the vow has been suppressed, resulting in an emphatic form of a wish or prayer. (Cf. GKC, § 1513, 167a.) Myers (28–29) suggests that the Chr may have rejected the idea of the vow, since the term does not occur in his writings.

10.b. עצבי "hurt me." Inf with suff, as suggested by לבלתי "so as not." Cf. GKC, § 114s.

11.a. "Chelub," i.e., Caleb; cf. G^BA Vg Syr. See n. 2:9.b. above. Rudolph (32), however, feels the two are to be distinguished.

11.b. "The brother of Shuhah." G reads πατηρ Ασχα(ς) "the father of Ascha(s)"; cf. Josh 15:16–17.

12.a. בית רפא. Either a place name, Beth-rapha, as translated here, or "house of a giant"; cf. 20:4. A Benjaminite Rapha is named in 8:2. The location of such a site has not been identified.

12.b. Tehinnah. G Θαιμαν "Timnah."

12.c. Ir-nahash, "Serpent-city" (cf. BDB, 638a; Aharoni, *Land,* 224), or perhaps "city of bronze," "city of smiths" (Myers, 29).

12.d. G adds "the Kenizzite," adopted by Rudolph (32).

12.e. Reading רכב "Recab," with G^BL. Heb. רכה "Recah." Cf. 2:55; Curtis, 108; Rudolph, 32. The families recorded in vv 11–12 were thus Rechabites.

13.a. Adding "Meonothai" with G^L Vg; cf. v 14, supported by בני of "the *sons* of Othniel." It is possible, however, that the reading represents an attempt to systematize the list.

14.a. Ge-harashim, "valley of craftsmen." Morton suggests the name may preserve the memory of a Philistine iron monopoly (1 Sam 13:19–20; "Ge-harashim," *IDB* 2:361).

15.a. Syr here lists 6 sons of Caleb; cf. BH³.

15.b. G, possibly correctly, understanding the concluding *waw* of עירו "Iru" as the conj, and placing it on the following noun, עיר ואלה "Ir and Elah."

15.c. The text is in disarray, ובני אלה וקנז "the sons of Elah and Kenaz." Seb reads בן "son" (sg); most MSS of G Vg Tg omit the conj before Kenaz. We have assumed a transposition of what was the demonstrative אלה "these" and read אלה בני קנז "these were the sons of Kenaz." Genealogical formulas would then enclose vv 13–15.

16.a. Curtis (110) has suggested that "Asarel" (אשראל) may be a variant of "Israel," ישראל.

17.a. Again, the Heb. is sg: בן "son."

17.b.-18.d. The text is corrupt beyond reasonable reconstruction. Two major types of solutions are commonly offered: (1) V 18b, "These were the sons of Bithiah, the daughter of Pharaoh, whom Mered took . . . ," is moved after v 17a, so that Bithiah becomes the subj of ותהר "conceived," which, as the text stands, is without subj. (2) Others, such as Kittel, Galling, and Rudolph, emend along lines suggested by G, which is itself, however, fraught with difficulties (Michaeli, 46). This procedure must assume that the names of Bithiah's children have fallen from the text (Curtis, 111). Rudolph (34) assumes in addition a larger omission at the beginning of v 18, but his argument is not compelling.

17.c. MT lacks a subj for ותהר, lit., "and she conceived"; read ויולד יתר "and Jether begat," with G.

17.d. Miriam is apparently a male offspring. The name is otherwise known in the OT only as Moses' sister. The names of Ezrah's (and Jether's) children diverge greatly in the various MSS of G; see Brooke-MacLean-Thackeray, *The Old Testament in Greek,* vol. 2, pt. 3, 403.

18.a. The text is again corrupt, since the sons here identified as offspring of an unnamed Jewish wife are later in the same verse attributed to Mered's wife Bithia, called a daughter of Pharaoh. For "Jewess," G^B reads αὐτή; read perhaps as המצריה "the Egyptian."

18.b. Bithiah: G^B Γελια; G^L Φαθθουια.

18.c. G^B Νωρωηλ, for Mered.

18.d. See n.17.b. above.

19.a. Perhaps read with G^A יהודיה "Hodiah"; G^B Ιδουιας "Idouias." Hence this textual problem and those of vv 17–18 are probably related.

19.b. Various G^MSS supply additional names to this verse, some of them including one reminiscent of the שימון "Shimon," who appears at the beginning of v 20.

20.a. K G^L תולון "Tolon"; Q G^A Vg Tg תילון "Tilon." V 20 in the Syriac suggests that some words have now dropped out; cf. *BH³*.

21.a. בוץ "linen, byssus" appears to be late (BDB, 101; Curtis, 28, #9). Of 8 occurrences in the OT, 5 are in Chronicles (cf. 15:27; 2 Chr 2:13; 3:14; 5:12), the remainder in Esth 1:6; 8:15; Ezek 27:16.

22.a. The Heb. וישבי לחם is untranslatable unless it is understood as a proper name parallel with Joash and Saraph, as does KJV. The commonly accepted emendation וישבו בית לחם "and they returned to Bethlehem," although admittedly strained in the absence of a meaningful context, could refer to some such situation as that reflected in Ruth.

22.b. והדברים עתיקים, translated above as "the records are ancient." The phrase is again too pithy for certainty. Rudolph (36) is possibly right in suggesting that it stems from a marginal gl pointing to the difficulty of the text in general. Perhaps עתיקים should bear the sense of "remote, obscure," rather than "ancient." (Cf. Dijkstra, "A Note on 1 Chr. IV 22–23," *VT* 25 [1975] 671–74.) Rudolph, with Rothstein and others, suggests an omission has occurred in v 22, since it is impossible to label such persons as Joash and Saraph leaders over Moab, as v 23 seems to do.

23.a. "For his work." Again, Rudolph's suggestion that במלאכתו ("for his work") was added to avoid misunderstanding "dwelt with the king" in a more honorific sense seems plausible.

Form/Structure/Setting

The shape of this material is obscure due to numerous lacunae and textual difficulties of other kinds. In its present form, it can only be described as isolated bits of materials attached to the tribe of Judah.

If the reading of G for v 7 is adopted (see n. 7.b. above), v 8 would be integrally related to v 7. However, this is far from certain. Vv 9–10 are in any case unattached to that which immediately precedes them and contain a popular etymology of the name "Jabez" (cf. 2:55). Vv 11–12, which again resume the "X was the father of Y" style, give the genealogy of Chelub (כלוב, G Χαλεβ); this raises still again the question of whether the various references to individuals of similar names refer to the same or different individuals (cf. 2:9, 18, 42). Since the references to Kenaz envelop vv 13–15, which include a second (?) section on Caleb, here identified as the son of Jephunneh, it is possible that vv 13–15 are a unit expanding upon the Caleb material of v 15.

V 16 has no obvious connection with either what precedes or follows. Vv 17–20 appear to be related, though textual difficulties make this less than certain. As reconstructed, vv 17–18 list the children of at least two wives of Jether; v 17 lists Mered's children through his Egyptian wife Bithiah. The relationship of v 19 is less apparent, and the textual confusion surrounding Hodiah (n. 19.a.) and its similarity to the equally problematic היהדיה ("the Jewess"; n. 18.a.) suggests ongoing difficulties in understanding these relationships.

V 20, the sons of Shimon and Ishi, is again a disconnected fragment according to MT. It may be related to the previous verse through Shimon as suggested by G, but this connection might equally well be secondary. Vv 21–23, descendants of Shelah, are again unattached to the preceding and seem to recall Judah's son of 2:3. Williamson has argued that they comprise a final part of the chiastic structure of the descendants of Judah.

Comment

8–16   Our knowledge of the people and places named in this portion of
Judah's genealogy is essentially nonexistent. Comparison with other biblical
data such as the genealogies of chap. 2 only heightens the difficulties. Of
the names associated with Koz (v 8), only Anub may be identified with Anab,
a city near Debir (Josh 15:50); the remainder are unknown.

The meaning of the name Jabez is unknown; the etymology of vv 9–10
associates it with the similar sounding עצב, "pain." In 2:55, Jabez is the
name of a city occupied by descendants of Hur's line through Salma. While
the etymology of v 9 is typical of folk etymology, that of v 10 is less so and
may rest upon a second tradition. The emphasis here is rather upon Jabez'
prayer to God and the fact that God heard that prayer and "brought about
that which he asked." This emphasis upon prayer is a marked feature of
Chronicles, and its inclusion here, whether by the Chronicler or another
writer, reflects an appreciation of that same interest. God's grace is always
available to those who turn to him in prayer.

The naming of Chelub (כלוב, v 11), with which compare especially Chelubai
(כלובי, 2:9), raises again the vexing problem of the identity of the persons
of these and similar names (see n. 2:9.b.). That the same individual is everywhere referred to seems probable, though the evidence is less compelling
here than in the remaining passages. However, G here, as elsewhere, reads
Χαλεβ, "Caleb," and its mention of Caleb's daughter Achsah (cf. n. 11.b.
and 2:49) in place of the unknown Shuhah of the MT indicates clearly that
here too it was the hero of the conquest to whom reference was being made.
The separate mention of Caleb the son of Jephunneh in v 15 and his association with Kenaz and the Kenizzites (v 15, cf. v 13) point to divergent traditions
which the author has related only by juxtaposition.

The parentage of Chelub is not given in this verse, and nothing is known
of Shuhah, Mehir, or Eshton. Noth believes vv 11–12 were once introductory
to 2:42–55 (*ZDVP* 55 [1932] 97–124), a view which Myers (29) calls "probably
the best interpretation available at present." Nor is anything known of the
people or places of v 12. (An earlier attempt to identify Beth-rapha with
the place mentioned in the Lachish ostraca [IV 5] seems now to have been
given up.) Glueck has connected Ir-nahash with the Arabah (*Rivers in the
Desert* [New York: Farrar, Strauss and Cudahy, 1959] 134–56) but this view
is not compelling either. Rudolph (34) comments aptly that the use of the
term אנשי before Recab, as emended, does point to this as a place name
rather than an individual, not clear from 2:55, and sees in G's addition "the
Kenizzite" (n. 12.d.) an indication that 2:55 speaks of Kiriath-sepher, which
was possessed by the Kenizzite Othniel. However, this seems like grasping
for straws.

Vv 13–15 are clearly centered on Caleb and Othniel. In two parallel passages, Josh 15:13–17 and Judg 1:11–15, Othniel is known as the son of Kenaz
and apparently the nephew (or possibly the brother) of Caleb who at Caleb's
request conquers Debir (= Kiriath-sepher) and is rewarded for doing so by
being given Achsah, Caleb's daughter, for a wife. It is these same two individu-

als, as noted again by Rudolph (34), who were involved in the conquest of Kiriath-sepher.

The mention of the Ge-harashim in Neh 11:35 in conjunction with Lod, Ono, and other cities inhabited by Benjamin after the return gives an approximate position for the otherwise unidentified locations of v 14 some 30 miles west-northwest of Jerusalem (Morton, *IDB* 2:361; Aharoni, *Land,* 363; 249, map 34). The occurrence of these references to Benjaminite possessions suggests that also Ophrah and Meonothai (v 13) (cf. Maon) may not be identified with those in the south (1 Chr 2:45), but with places by those names in Benjaminite territory (Rudolph, 35). It thus appears that the Kenites too in the course of history may have been displaced to positions farther and farther north.

Of the descendants of Jehallelel (v 16), only Ziph, which is located just south of Hebron and which would have lain outside of the boundaries of post-exilic Judah, is known. Ziphah, the feminine form of the same root, might be due to dittography.

17–20 *Descendants of Ezrah.* The list is again commonly considered preexilic due to the inclusion of cities which would have lain south of Judah's post-exilic border. Thus Eshtemoa lay some 20 miles south of Hebron (Aharoni, *Land,* map 32). The locale of Gedor, Soco, and Zanoah is disputed with some arguing for a southern location (Rudolph, 35; Myers, 29), others for one more to the west and north (Noth, van Selms), cf. Josh 15:34, 35, 48, 56. Otherwise nothing is known of the people or places listed in vv 17–18. Rudolph mentions that here as in 2:42–50aα, to which he believes this is a supplement, the center of the Calebites is Hebron.

Keilah (v 19) is a well-known site in both pre-exilic and post-exilic Judah (Aharoni, *Land,* maps 26, 34) just west of Beth-zur. That two individuals should be listed as the father of Gedor need not mean they are to be distinguished, since the references may be to different time periods. The reference to the marriage of Mered to one of Pharaoh's daughters, without negative connotations, might also be taken as a sign of an earlier rather than a later dating and point to the inclusion of Egyptian elements within Judah. However, Rudolph's (35) suggestion that an intentional comparison with Solomon is being made perhaps goes too far.

20 *Descendants of Shimon.* Nothing is known of those named.

21–23 *The Descendants of Shelah.* Shelah in 2:3 is listed as a son of Judah through the Canaanitess Bath-shua, but the note in Num 26:20 adds nothing to our knowledge of the history of his family. It is probable that the references to "the Shilonite" in 1 Chr 9:5; Neh 11:5 (MT = הַשִּׁילוֹנִי, הַשִּׁלֹנִי, respectively) should be emended to read "the Shelanite" (הַשֵּׁלָנִי), since the reference is specifically to Judahites (cf. Reed, "Shilonite," *IDB* 4:330). The name Er is known otherwise only as that of Judah's son and Shelah's brother (cf. again 2:3), but there is nothing improbable in naming a child after his uncle. Of the various localities named, the only one that can be identified with certainty is Mareshah (cf. 2:42) some 15 miles west of Beth-zur. In this earlier reference from Chronicles, Mareshah is related to Caleb, however, who in the Chronicler's genealogies is descended from Judah through Perez and Hezron

(1 Chr 2:5, 9, 18). This divergency might be related either to the different circles in which the genealogies were transmitted or reflect ages when different families were influential in that city. Other cities have been tentatively identified with far less certainty. (See the listing of the possibilities in Myers, 29–30; Rudolph, 36–37.)

The names Lecah, Laadah, Beth-ashbea, Jokim, Cozeba, Saraph, and Netaim (vv 21–23) are all unique to this passage in biblical literature. Because of their relationship to Judah, however, it is natural to look for them in the south, an expectation strengthened by their association here with Mareshah.

The mention of the crafts of byssus workers and potters in a genealogical table suggests that such professions were closely bound up with family ties and that trades tended to be kept "within the family." The relationship between king and potters has been demonstrated by numerous stamped jar handles that have emerged from the excavations in Palestine.

The reference to Judeans ruling in Moab (v 22) suggests pre-exilic times, since the only documented cases of such Israelite rulers stems from the ages of David (2 Sam 8:2) and Solomon (1 Kgs 5:1 [4:21]). Macalister (340–41) and others are probably right in seeing reminiscences of continuing Judahite/Moabite relationships in the post-exilic family of Pahath-Moab (Ezra 2:6; 8:4; 10:30, etc.). Myers remarks correctly that we have here more than genealogy in a strict sense of the word, but that the names of the founders of various guilds came to be associated with localities where the crafts were carried on for centuries.

Explanation

In this unit it is again apparent how flexible the lines between individuals and cities were in genealogical representations, and how easily even sociological relationships related to various crafts came to be presented in genealogical form (cf. vv 12, 14, 23). We see additional evidence in the fragments of information available to us that the fluctuating paths of history led from time to time to different understandings of the origins and relationships of peoples. The descendants of Caleb, as well as the members of his immediate family, are placed among the descendants of Judah, although the names and relationships of these individuals differ from place to place and frequently point to the Kenizzite backgrounds of that clan. Place is found for the inclusion within the line of Judah of elements even more foreign to Israel, e.g., Egypt (v 18). In placing next to each other what appears to be both pre-exilic and post-exilic locales for these families of Judah we have continuing evidence both for the varied ages of the genealogical materials that have come down to us and, though the material is scant, for the different understanding of the constitution of Israel following the exile.

Summary: The Descendants of Judah   (2:1–4:23)

To conclude this treatment of the descendants of Judah a summary of some of the principal interests follows here. It is apparent that to some degree these may seem to be in tension with one another; at the same time they faithfully represent processes at work within Israel's history and/or in the thought of the writer(s).

The very constitution of the unit as a whole is vivid witness to a concern for "all Israel." All of Israel's sons are named (2:1–2), and it is upon this basis that chaps. 2–9 are ordered. Nevertheless, pride of place here goes to the tribe of Judah, which is uncharacteristically dealt with as the first of Israel's sons, and of Judah's descendants it is above all those of the line of Hezron, and of Hezron's descendants those of the line of Ram, of whose lineage is David, upon whom Chronicles focuses.

This interest in Judah is so pervasive that it tends at times to distort and consume other concerns. Groups and individuals not originally related to Judah by blood are incorporated into Judah in such a way as to obscure earlier tribal diversity. Hence Caleb-Chelubai, whose non-Israelite background is apparent not only in other parts of the OT but in Chronicles as well (cf. 2:18, 49; 4:15), is placed among Hezron's sons, as are the Jerahmeelites. At the same time, however, references to Kenites (2:55) and Kenaz (4:13) remain, and Hezron's remote relationship to Gilead through Hezron is also affirmed (2:21).

More transparent references to foreign elements within Israel and Judah and to other relationships which might seem less than wholesome are also transmitted to us without embarrassment or apology. The births of Er, Onan, and Shelah (2:3) of Bath-shua, named a Canaanitess, are reported (2:3), and the incident with Tamar is not silenced (2:4). The same name, Bath-shua, is also found in 3:5 for the mother of Solomon and his brothers in an occurrence which is at least suggestive. (Note also a closely related reference to David's daughter Tamar in 3:9.) Similar references to integration of Egyptian blood within Judah are also made (cf. 2:34; 4:17).

In some instances this desire to incorporate divergent elements within Israel is paralleled by an interest in the temple and cult, but this remains quite subdued. We have noticed, however, that Ethan and Heman, whose names are associated with temple music but who appear to have been of Canaanite background, are according to 2:6 descended from Perez's son Zerah, and we have suggested that the name Zimri in the same verse may be a textual alteration made because of similar concerns with temple music. The attachment of Hur, Caleb's son, to Uri and Bezalel, probably reflects this same kind of concern.

Despite these interesting sidelights, emphasis is directed primarily toward the tribe of Judah, and particularly upon the place in this genealogy of David and his line. David's own relationship to Judah has been accomplished by the inclusion of two genealogical links, neither of which exists in earlier OT traditions. Through the otherwise unknown Ram (2:9–10), a bridge is con-

structed between Hezron and the age of the Exodus, exemplified by Amminadab and Nahshon; through the also unknown Salma a similar linkage is made
between Nahshon and the line of Boaz which concludes with Jesse and David
himself (2:10–15). David himself appears in Chronicles as Jesse's seventh
son, in contrast to earlier traditions, a position to which particular significance
may have been attached.

This interest in David, and perhaps in his son Solomon as well, is continued
in chap. 3 (cf. esp. vv 1, 10). The listing of David's children here is, in contrast
to 1 Chr 14:4–7, unusually full, making specific mention of the early and
fragmentary nature of his rule at Hebron (3:4), an event normally ignored
in the body of Chronicles. From Solomon to Josiah the listing of Judah's
monarchs is unexceptional; from this point on, however, we are greeted with
a fullness of information not always easily harmonized with the accounts of
the exile and restoration otherwise available to us. However, the relative
fullness of these references (3:15–24) is in itself eloquent testimony to the
interest in David's line in the post-exilic period, as are the profuse references
of chap. 4 to the interest in Judah.

In view of the interest in Judah in the post-exilic period and the prominence
in which at least for a time the Davidic line continued to be held, the attraction
of so many diverse elements under the all-embracing rubric of Judah is not
surprising. In effect this marks the continuation of an emphasis begun well
before the exile, in which disparate elements of the population, such as the
Calebites and Jerahmeelites, were absorbed into Judah. This emphasis would
have accelerated in the post-exilic period, when questions both of prominence
and legitimacy were attached to genealogical lines. The resulting records
thus reflect a bewildering array of genealogical, social, political, and theological motives. All Israel is the kingdom of God, yet that kingdom is realized
essentially in Judah. However, into this political and theological unity the
most diverse of elements are incorporated.

Questions concerning the original extent of this unit defy easy answers,
although the excellent analysis of Williamson supports the idea of a more
involved participation in the formation of the whole. On the other hand,
nothing more than 2:1–8, 10–17, and that part of v 9 relating to Ram is
required for the unit, and at least portions of the remainder, together with
the larger purview of 2:9, may represent additions from later sources. That
these additions sometimes ignore concerns of other parts of the book may
be true; but much more often they reflect continuing development of interests
and concerns already at hand. In the final form of the canonical text, then,
we have vivid testimony not only to the exclusiveness that is often considered
indicative of the post-exilic period, but to an inclusiveness that transcends
blood lines in the interest of a broader understanding of Judah and Israel.

Descendants of Simeon (4:24–43)

Bibliography

See the *Bibliography* under Judah also.

Aharoni, Y. "The Negeb of Judah." *IEJ* 8 (1958) 26–38. **Albright, W. F.** "Egypt and the Early History of the Negeb: The Topography of Simeon." *JPOS* 4 (1924) 149–61. **Elliger, K.** "Simeon." *IDB* 4:356. **Kallai-Kleinmann, Z.** "Note on the Town Lists of Judah, Simeon, Benjamin, and Dan." *VT* 11 (1961) 223–27.

Translation

24 *The sons of Simeon:* [a] *Nemuel* [b] *and Jamin,* [c] *Jarib,* [d] *Zerah,* [e] *Shaul,* [f] 25 *his son Shallum, his son Mibsam, his son Mishma.* 26 *The sons of Mishma: his son Hammuel, his son Zaccur, his son Shimei.* 27 *Shimei had sixteen sons and six daughters, but his brothers did not have many children, and none of their families became as numerous as the Judahites.* 28 *They dwelt in Beer-sheba,* [a] *Moladah, and Hazar-shual,* 29 *as well as in Bilhah,* [a] *Ezem, Tolad,* [b] 30 *Beth-uel,* [a] *Hormah, Ziklag,* 31 *Beth-marcaboth, Hazar-susim, Beth-biri,* [a] *and Shaaraim.* [b] *These were their cities until David was king.*

32 *Their villages were Etam and Ain, Rimmon,* [a] *Tochen, and Ashan, five cities,* 33 *as well as all their villages around these cities as far as Baal.* [a] *This was their habitation, and they kept a genealogical record.* [b]

34 [a] *And Meshobab, Jamlech, and Joshab the son of Amaziah,* [a] 35 *Joel, Jehu* [a] *the son of Joshibiah, the son of Seraiah, the son of Asiel,* 36 *Elioenai, Jaakobah, Jeshohaiah, Asaiah,* [a] *Adiel, Jesimiel,* [a] *Benaiah,* 37 *and Ziza the son of Shiphi, the son of Allon, the son of Jedaiah, the son of Shimri, the son of Shemaiah* [a] 38 *—these listed by name* [a] *were princes* [b] *over their families, and the house of their fathers* [c] *increased* [d] *abundantly.* [e] 39 *They went to the entrance of Gedor* [a] *as far as the east side of the valley to seek pasture for their flock.* 40 *They found fertile* [a] *and good pasture, and the land was spacious,* [b] *peaceful, and quiet, because* [c] *those who dwelt there formerly were from Ham.*

41 *But these indicated by name entered in the days of Hezekiah, king of Judah, and destroyed their tents, and the Meunim* [a] *found there, and annihilated* [b] *them until this day. They dwelt in their place, because there was pasture for their flock there.* 42 *Some of them* [a] *(i.e., some of the sons of Simeon),* [a] *five hundred men, went to Mount Seir with Pelatiah, Neariah, Rephaiah, and Uzziel, the sons of Ishi, at their head.* 43 *They smote the surviving remnant* [a] *of Amalek and have lived there until this day.*

Notes

24.a. Other lists of Simeon's sons occur in Gen 46:10 and Exod 6:15, where the names given are identical, and in Num 26:12–13, more similar to this passage. Specific differences are noted below.

24.b. MT נמואל "Nemuel"; Gen 46:10; Exod 6:15 ימואל "Jemuel."

24.c. Both Gen 46:10 and Exod 6:15 add after Jamin, אהד "Ohad."

24.d. "Jarib" (יריב). All parallels read יכין "Jakin."

24.e. MT זרח "Zorah"; Genesis and Exodus צהר "Zohar."

24.f. Gen 46:10; Exod 6:15 + "the son of a Canaanitish woman."

28.a. G + ושמע "and Shema"; cf. Josh 15:26; G^L + καὶ Σαμα "and Sama" after ומולדה "and Moladah."

29.a. Josh 15:29 בעלה "Baalah"; Josh 19:3 בלה "Balah."

29.b. Josh 15:30; 19:4 Syr אלתולד "Eltolad."

30.a. Josh 19:4 בתול "Bethul."

31.a. Josh 15:32 לבאות "Lebaoth"; 19:6 בית לבאות "Beth-lebaoth."

31.b. Josh 15:32 שלחים "Shilhim"; 19:6 שרוחן "Sharuhen."

32.a. That the expression עין רמון refers to a single well-known city, En-rimmon, is likely. However, the enumeration attached to the present text both here and in Josh 19:7 requires the expression to refer to two separate cities. Josh 15:32 adds the conjunction between the two words, but the enumeration there (36 cities are named, but only 29 counted) makes it impossible to reckon how they were counted.

33.a. G^B Βαλατ "Balat"; cf. 19:8.

33.b. RSV "they kept a genealogical record," והתיחשם להם is a substitute for למשפחתם "according to their families"; cf. Josh 19:8. All translations are according to sense, since the Heb. does not parse.

34.a-a. The translation of v 34 and its relationship to v 33 is problematic. The first three words of v 34 have traditionally been treated as proper nouns in the absence of a meaningful alternative; however, the beginning of the list is very abrupt and the form of the names is suggestive of verb forms (cf. משובב "Meshobab"; ימלך "he ruled") as understood by G^L ἐπιστρέφων ἐβασίλευσεν "returning, he ruled . . ."). Rudolph (40) suggests that Richter's attempt at reconstruction is an "unverbindliches Gedankenspiel," and the same might be said about Begrich's conjecture in BH^3, והתיחשו למשפחתם בימי המלך אמציה בן־יואש "and they were enrolled according to their clans in the days of King Amaziah, the son of Joash."

35.a. G^B "and he," reading והוא "and he" for ויהוא "and Jehu."

36.a-a. > G^B.

37.a. G^B שמעון "Simeon" and the reading שמעי "Shimei," proposed by many, appear to be attempts to attach this section more closely to vv 24–33 (cf. vv 24, 26) and thus to establish a unity the text otherwise lacks.

38.a. אלה הבאים בשמות "these coming in with names." Cf. the parallel expression of v 41 ויבאו אלה הכתובים בשמות "but these indicated by name entered" and the similar נקבו בשמות "who were designated by name" of Num 1:17; 1 Chr 16:41; 2 Chr 28:15; 31:19; Ezra 8:20.

38.b. The original amphictyonic connections of the term seem to be entirely lacking here.

38.c. For בית אבותם "house of their fathers," see the Introduction.

38.d. The root פרץ has connotations not only of multiplying but of spilling over, emptying (BDB), a sense which fits well here with vv 39–43.

38.e. לרוב "abundantly." A favorite usage in Chronicles, it is found in this sense otherwise only in Neh 9:25; Zech 14:14. See Curtis, 33, 105.

39.a. גדור "Gedor," emended by many to "Gerar" with G, since neither of the known Gedors appears to be appropriately located, while the area of Gerar is better situated with regard to the sons of Ham and its pasturage (v 40). However, as noted by Coggins (32), it is dangerous to identify an unknown place with a well-known one of similar name.

40.a. For שמן "fertile," cf. Num 13:20 (E); Ezek 34:14; Neh 9:25, 35.

40.b. Lit., "broad of hands." Cf. BDB, 390.

40.c. כי "because," or perhaps better, adversative, "but."

41.a. Q מעונים "Meunim"; K מעינים "Meinim." The מעונים are known in Chronicles also from the days of Uzziah (2 Chr 26:7), where they are listed along with the Philistines, Arabs, and Ammonites, all traditional enemies of Israel; and probably are meant also in 2 Chr 20:1 (reading מהמעונים for מהעמונים "the Ammonites") with G^BA, RSV, and most commentators (cf. Ezra 2:50 = Neh 7:52). These "sons of Meunim," listed among the Nethinim, are perhaps descendants of those mentioned in 2 Chr 26:7, now integrated into Israel.

41.b. Although in earlier writings חרם "annihilated" denotes a destruction for religious purposes (cf. Josh 6:18–19, 21; 7:1, 7–15), as contrasted with that which is קדש "holy" (Josh

6:18–19), it is doubtful whether such associations remain here. Cf. 2 Chr 20:23; 32:14; Ezra 10:8; 1 Chr 2:7.

42.a-a. The two expressions are parallel and have perhaps arisen through the conflation of synonymous variants.

43.a. שארית הפלטה "surviving remnant." The use of forms of both roots in Chronicles-Ezra-Nehemiah is not rare, but the exact construction is without parallel. Both nouns are used in Ezra 9:14, where, however, they are coordinated (לאין שארית ופליטה "neither surviving nor remaining"). More frequently a verbal form of שאר is used with the noun פליטה "to be left a remnant"; cf. 2 Chr 30:6; Ezra 9:8, 15; Neh 1:2. In 1 Chr 11:8; 16:41; 2 Chr 24:14, שאר seems to have only a nontheological meaning, "to be left." Otherwise, it is used in Chronicles, like פליטה in Chronicles-Ezra-Nehemiah, only of Israel; cf. 2 Chr 30:6; 34:9, 21; etc.

Form/Structure/Setting

This unit concerning Simeon is composed of three sub-units: (1) sons of Simeon, and a line of descent through Shaul (vv 24–27); (2) their settlements (vv 28–33); (3) "princes and conquests of Simeon" (vv 34–43) (Curtis, 116). Its tripartite form, as we shall see (cf. chap. 5), is typical of the information transmitted to us for several of the less significant tribes. Each of these units seems to be composite in itself, justifying Coggins's remark (31) that we have here a combination of genealogical information, geographical notes, and "miscellaneous scraps of tradition concerning particular individuals."

Other OT lists of sons of Simeon (v 24), who is regularly listed second in tribal enumerations in Chronicles and elsewhere, are found in Gen 46:10; Exod 6:15; and Num 26:12–13. The first two lists are identical and name six sons of Simeon (an additional son, Ohad, is listed as the third son after Jamin); Num 26:12–13 is more closely related to our text and names five sons. Chronicles is unique only in naming its third son Jarib, in contrast to Jachin of all other lists; the source of the Chronicler's text is unknown.

Vv 25–27, which trace a line of descent from Simeon's son Shaul, whose birth from a Canaanite mother is noted in both Gen 46:10 and Exod 6:15, to an otherwise unknown Shimei are without parallel elsewhere. The list of Simeonite cities and villages (vv 28–33), however, is closely related to the list of Josh 19:2–8 and more remotely to Josh 15:21–42, especially vv 28–36, 42. Aharoni (*IEJ* 8 [1958] 26–38) dates the list of Josh 19 as the earliest, followed by Josh 15, which stems from the period of Judah's greatest expansion; both are then earlier than our list, which is more accurate due to its infrequent copying. However, Elliger believes the list of Josh 19 is extracted from Josh 15 (*IDB* 4:356).

In any case, vv 25–27 are more closely related to Josh 19:2–8, which emphasize Simeon's inheritance *in the midst of* the tribe of Judah (vv 1, 9). In a parallel way, Chronicles contrasts the size of Simeon's descendants with the size of Judah (1 Chr 4:27). By way of contrast, Josh 15 includes in Judah the majority of the cities here allotted to Simeon, although most are named in a group "belonging to the tribe of Judah in the extreme south, toward the boundary of Edom" (Josh 15:21, RSV).

These parallel lists enable us to see once again the effects of continuing reshaping of the texts, although we may not be able to trace the tradition in detail. Josh 19 includes thirteen cities before inserting its first summary (19:6), "thirteen cities (ערים) and their villages." It is at this same point that Chronicles inserts its initial editorial remark that "these were their cities until David was king" (v 31). Josh 19:7 then enumerates four additional cities with their villages, and an additional comment, perhaps later, is appended referring to their villages "as far as Baalath-beer, Ramah of the Negeb" (v 8). Chronicles, however, seems either to have understood these four localities as the "villages" referred to in the earlier verses ("all their villages" at the beginning of v 8 should perhaps be omitted with G as a synonymous variant to "their villages" at the end of v 7) or does not distinguish between cities and villages. At any rate, in the final form of the text as it appears in Chronicles, the four (or five; see below) villages are later in the same verse labeled "five cities" (1 Chr 4:32b; cf. Josh 19:7b), which themselves have villages reaching "as far as Baal" (v 33). In this statement, the hand of the writer is clearly present, breaking off in the middle of a word the use of his source as it is found in Joshua, "until Baal-(at-beer, Ramah of the Negeb)" (Josh 19:8a).

A further indication of Chronicles' dependence upon Josh 19 is apparent in the enumeration of this second group of cities. Josh 19 counts four, appearing to consider En and Rimmon as two separate cities. Chronicles includes Tochen with its list and counts five, although, in agreement with Josh 19, no conjunction occurs on Rimmon. (RSV and NEB anomalously print Enrimmon as a single word, though counting it as two cities, in Josh 19:7; and as two words [Ain, Rimmon] in Chronicles.) In Josh 15, however, the anticipated conjunction is appended to Rimmon, although the text's enumeration of the larger group of south Judean cities, which counts twenty-nine cities for what appears to be thirty-five or thirty-six, makes further evaluation impossible. Curtis's argument (118) that Josh 19 retained the correct count, four, while erroneously omitting the fourth city, Tochen, is plausible.

The relationship of vv 34–37 to the preceding and following verses is quite obscure. Although the word is grammatically unrelated, it appears necessary to understand the אלה "these" of v 38 to refer to the names given in vv 34–37. These names themselves are often unrelated to each other except for the coordinating conjunctions, although the lineage of Joshab (v 34) is extended backward one generation; that of Jehu (v 35), three generations; and that of Zizah (v 37), five. Vv 39–40 are a historical note apparently reflecting movement of Simeonites into the region of Gedor (Gerar?; cf. n. 39.a.). V 41 speaks of a military action against the Meunim in the days of Hezekiah, perhaps identical with the movement in vv 39–40, and vv 42–43 note a similar action against Amalek in the region of Seir. This entire unit (vv 34–43) is without parallel elsewhere.

Comment

(For general background on Simeon, see K. Elliger, "Simeon," *IDB* 4:356.)
Nothing is known of the sons of Simeon except that both Gen 46:10 and Exod 6:15 tell us that the last-named, Shaul, whose line is continued in vv 25–27, was the son of a Canaanite woman. That reference is often taken to refer to Simeon's supposed earlier history in central Canaan (cf. Gen 34:25, 30). If that is so, the omission of the words by Chronicles may well be tendentious, since Shaul's descendants here include Mibsam and Mishma, otherwise

known to us as descendants of Ishmael (1 Chr 1:29–30; Gen 25:13–14), and in which the southern connections of Simeon would be apparent.

The dwelling places of Simeon (vv 28–33) are, as far as they have been identified, confined to the area near Beer-sheba. En-rimmon, Moladah, Ashan, and Hormah are each only a few miles distant. Aharoni identifies Ziklag with Tel esh-Shariah, some 12 miles northwest of Beer-sheba; and Shaaraim, if identical with Sharuhen, a city prominent in the Egyptian records already at the time of the Hyksos, is about 20 miles west of Beer-sheba (Aharoni, *Land*, 296, map 26). Ziklag is prominent as a city given to David by King Achish of Gath (1 Sam 27:6). The separation of the Simeonite cities into two groups, the first of which the writer probably means was Simeon's *until* the time of David, suggests that in his outlaw days David exercised authority over a considerable area of the Negeb, as indicated by Aharoni (*IEJ* 8 [1958] 26–38). If the Baal(-ath) of v 33 is identified with Ramah of the Negeb, as in Josh 19:8, it too is identified with cities related to David's earlier adventures (cf. 1 Sam 30:27). The names of certain of these cities, i.e., Moladah, Hazar-shual, Beer-sheba, Ziklag, and En-rimmon, also occur in Neh 11:26–29 with other cities inhabited by the returning exiles.

Concerning vv 34–43 we are again in the area little beyond conjecture. Of the names found in vv 34–37 we know nothing, although Gray (*Hebrew Proper Names*, 236, quoted in Curtis, 116) judges them to be of late formation on the whole. These individuals are characterized in v 38 as princes (נשיאים) of the clans of Simeon, a title commonly recognized as having amphictyonic overtones (cf. Rudolph, 40). To the difficulties in locating Gedor we have already referred (n. 39.a.). The descendants of Ham (v 40) could point to Egyptians, Ethiopians, or even Canaanites (cf. Gen 10:6; 1 Chr 1:8), and, even if the incursion of v 41 be understood to refer to the same incident as vv 39–40, the identification or location of the Meunim (see n. 41.a.), which Rudolph (42) relates to the Arabic *maʿan*, dwelling, and reads אהלי הם as "the tents of Ham," is uncertain. Aharoni, with most interpreters, reads Gerar, located near Gaza, with G for Gedor, and suggests actions against the Philistines to the southwest and against Edom to the southeast (cf. Mt. Seir, v 42) at the time of Hezekiah may be the point at issue (*Land*, 336–37). The "remnant of Amalek" (v 43) can only be identified as those who survived the attacks of Saul and David and perhaps others (cf. 1 Sam 14:48; 15:3; 2 Sam 8:12). On the other hand, the phrase "in the days of Hezekiah" (v 41), which provides the only firm date in the narrative, may refer either to the time of the invasion itself or to the writing down of the names, or to both if we envision a kind of enrollment preparatory to war.

In view of the difficulty of placing these incidents within the framework of Israel's known history, it is often suggested that the events recorded are the invention of the writer. This view may be supported by the seemingly archaizing use of certain terms in the narrative (cf. נשיא "prince" v 38; חרם "destroy" v 41, both without apparent earlier amphictyonic connotations) and by other phrases which appear to be characteristic of Chronicles or of late Hebrew in general (cf. אלה הבאים בשמות "these listed by name" v 38; ואלה הכתובים בשמות "but these indicated by name" v 41 and n. 38.a., אשר נמצאו שמה "found there," in the sense of "to be present," v 41). On the other hand, no motive is apparent to suggest that the events were anything other than historic, and it seems best to admit that the writer has included this brief account of otherwise unknown events simply because they were attached to other material concerning Simeon which came into his hands. It is then possible that the marks of later style referred to above are to be attributed to the later writer rather than his source. The same may be true of the phrase "to this day," vv 41, 43, but it seems more appropriately applied to the original source.

Explanation

The significance of the concept of "all Israel" and the attachment to the ideal of twelve tribes is clear in the place which Simeon continues to occupy in the tribal lists long after it has disappeared as a geographic or political entity. While Simeon's earlier history is obscure, its eventual settlement in southern Judah and its *de facto* incorporation into that tribe is assured (Josh 19:1).

Within this pericope, Simeon's fortunes are also bound up with those of Judah (cf. 4:27) and its relationship to other peoples on Judah's southern fringes apparent. Mibsam and Mishma, we have noted, are elsewhere associated with the descendants of Ishmael, i.e., the Arabs. The cities which can be identified lie in close proximity to Beer-sheba. The excursion at Mt. Seir against the Amalekites points us in a similar direction, as does perhaps the mention of Gedor/Gerar in v 39.

To what extent these Simeonites maintained a tribal identity in the years following their incorporation into Judah is impossible to determine. Since some of the cities named here are noted as resettled by returning exiles in Neh 11, although clearly lying south of the border of the restored Judean state, it appears their identity survived even the difficult years of the exile. When the restored captives returned to their land, they may have been greeted not only with the opposition of various inhabitants of the land, but also with the support and encouragement of other groups and individuals who recognized them as their relatives and offered them their support.

The Transjordanian Tribes: Reuben, Gad, East Manasseh (5:1-26)

Bibliography

Cohen, S. "Bashan." *IDB* 1:363–64. **Elliger, K.** "Gad." *IDB* 2:333–35. ———. "Manasseh." *IDB* 3:252–54. ———. "Reuben." *IDB* 4:53–54. **Mendelsohn, I.** "On the Preferential Status of the Eldest Son." *BASOR* 156 (1959) 38–40. **Noth, M.** "Beiträge zur Geschichte des Ostjordanlandes." *PJ* 38 (1941) 50–51. ———. "Israelitische Stamme Zwischen Ammon und Moab." *ZAW* 60 (1944) 11–57. ———. "Gilead and Gad." *ZDPV* 75 (1969) 14–73. **Simons, J.** "Two Connected Problems Relating to the Israelite Settlement in Transjordan." *PEQ* 79 (1949) 27–39.

Translation

The Reubenites

[1] *The sons of Reuben, Israel's firstborn (for he was the firstborn, but because he defiled the bed* [a] *of his father, his birthright* [b] *was given to the sons of Joseph, the son of Israel, but the genealogical listing* [c] *is not according to the birthright.* [2] *For although Judah prevailed over his brothers, and a leader* [a] *came from him, the birthright* [b] *was Joseph's.)* [3] *The sons of Reuben, Israel's firstborn: Hanoch and Pallu, Hezron and Carmi.*

[4] *The sons of Joel:* [a] *Shemaiah his son, Gog his son, Shimei his son,* [5] *Micah his son, Reaiah his son, Baal his son,* [6] *and Beerah his son, whom Tilgath-pilneser,* [a] *the king of Asshur, carried into exile. He was prince of the Reubenites.*

[7] *His kinsmen,* [a] *according to his families, were enrolled according to their generations:* [b] *the chief was Jeiel, then Zechariah* [8] *and Bela the son of Azaz, the son of Shema, the son of Joel, who lived* [a] *in Aroer and as far as Nebo and Baal-meon.* [9] *On the east, he dwelt as far as the beginning of the wilderness* [a] *which reaches to* [b] *the Euphrates River, because their cattle were very numerous in the land of Gilead.* [10] *In the days of Saul they made war on the Hagrites, who fell by their hand. So they lived in their tents throughout all the region east of Gilead.*

The Gadites

[11] *Next to them* [a] *were the Gadites; they lived in the land of Bashan as far as Salecah.* [12] *Joel was the chief and Shapham* [a] *the second, while Janai judged* [b] *in Bashan.* [13] *Their relatives,* [a] *according to fathers' houses, were Michael, Meshullam, Sheba, Jorai, Jacan, Zia, and Eber,* [b] *seven.* [c] [14] *These were the sons of Abihail, the son of Huri, the son of Jaroah,* [a] *the son of Gilead, the son of Michael, the son of Jeshishai, the son of Jahdo, the son of Buz* [b]— [15] *Ahi,* [a] *the son of Abdiel, the son of Guni, was chief of their father's house.* [16] *They lived in Gilead,* [a] *in Bashan* [b] *and its villages,* [c] *and in all the pasturelands of Sharon* [d] *to* [e] *their remotest limit.* [c] [17] *All these had their genealogies recorded in the days of Jotham,* [a] *king of Judah, and in the days of Jeroboam,* [b] *king of Israel.*

¹⁸ *The sons of Reuben, the Gadites, and the half-tribe of Manasseh, that is, the warriors,* ᵃ *who bore shield and spear and drew the bow and were trained for battle, numbered 44,760 warriors.* ¹⁹ *They waged war with the Hagrites, Jetur, Naphish, and Nodab.* ²⁰ *They were helped against them,* ᵃ *and the Hagrites and all who* ᵇ *were with them were given into their hand, for they cried out in the battle, and God let himself be entreated* ᶜ *by them, because they trusted in him.* ²¹ *So they seized their cattle (fifty thousand camels, two hundred and fifty thousand from their flocks, and two thousand asses), together with one hundred thousand men whom they took alive.* ²² *Many others fell slain, because the war was of God. Then they dwelt in their place until the exile.*

East Manasseh

²³ *The sons of the half-tribe of Manasseh also lived* ᵃ *in the land from Bashan* ᵃ *to Baal-hermon, Senir, and Mount Hermon. They were numerous.* ²⁴ *These were the heads of their father's houses: . . .* ᵃ *Epher, Ishi, Eliel, Azriel, Jeremiah, Hodaviah, and Jahdiel, valiant men, famous men, heads of their father's houses.*
²⁵ *They acted unfaithfully against the God of their fathers and played the harlot after the gods of the peoples of the land, whom God had destroyed from before them.* ²⁶ *So Israel's God stirred up the spirit of Pul, the king of Assyria,* ᵃ *the spirit of Tilgath-pilneser,* ᵃ ᵇ *the king of Assyria, and he led them into exile, i.e.,* ᶜ *the Reubenites, the Gadites, and the half-tribe of Manasseh. He brought them to Halah,* ᵈ *Habor, Hara, and the River Gozan* ᵈ *until this day.*

Notes

1.a. יְצוּעִי "bed of." The pl is that of extension (GKC, § 124a; cf. Curtis, 121), which the Heb. text also permits in Gen 49:4.
1.b. G εὐλογίαν αὐτοῦ "his blessing," suggesting בִּרְכָתוֹ "his blessing," rather than בְּכֹרָתוֹ "his birthright" (BDB, 114, "right of firstborn"). Cf. also n. 2.b. below. This reading is adopted by Rudolph in his commentary and in *BHS*.
1.c. See above introductory material.
2.a. לְנָגִיד, lit., "to a leader." The ל is problematic, as reflected by the Masora. It has been understood as emphatic; cf. Curtis, 121. Again, the reading might result from the conflation of the synonymous variants, וְנָגִיד מִמֶּנּוּ "a prince was from him," and some such phrase as לְנָגִיד הָיָה "he became a prince." The absence or presence of the def art is, of course, obscured due to the prefixed prep.
2.b. G again reads εὐλογίαν "blessing" (cf. n. 1.b.); Rudolph reverses the meaning of the passage by inserting לֹא "not"; לוֹ "to him"—"the blessing was *not* to him/his," citing Ps 78:67–68 (*BHS*). See *Comment* below.
4.a. "The sons of Joel." RSV "Jeul," thus obscuring a possible connection with a person by the same name in v 7. The readings of both Gᴸ (Ιωηλ υἱὸς αὐτοῦ, "Joel, his son") and Syr ("Joel, the son of Carmi") are attempts to integrate Joel into Reuben's line.
6.a. Most MSS read, with Gᴬ and Syr, the more common Tiglath (תִּגְלַת). No less than 4 variations are extant in 6 OT occurrences (2 Kgs 15:29; 16:10; 16:7; 1 Chr 5:6; 2 Chr 28:20, as here); 1 Chr 5:26 פִלְנֶסֶר "Pilneser." It is open to conjecture whether one or more of these forms might be the result of intentional malformation or whether all represent imperfect attempts to transliterate the Assyrian "*Tukulti-apil-Esarra*," also known by his Babylonian throne name "Pul" (2 Kgs 15:19; 1 Chr 5:26).
7.a. "His kinsmen," lit., "his brothers" (אֶחָיו). If vv 7–10 are read as a unit with the preceding, the antecedent of the suff is the exiled Beerah. Other difficulties within these verses, however— such as the designation of Beerah as נָשִׂיא "prince" in v 6 and that of his "brother" Jeiel as chief (הָרֹאשׁ) in v 7, the differing position of the two Joels (see *Comment*), and the obscurity of

v 7a—suggest that vv 7–10 may not be integrally related to the preceding. Rudolph accordingly reads אחר "after that" for אחיו "his brothers."

7.b. The translation is according to sense; cf. NEB "His kinsmen, family, as registered in the tribal lists. . . ."

8.a. "Who dwelt." The nearest antecedent is Bela. However, it seems likely that the dwelling places listed are those of the Reubenites in general. See *Comment.*

9.a. עד לבוא "until the beginning of." The inf phrase, as noted by Curtis (121), is common with the proper name Hamath; cf. Amos 6:14; Judg 3:3; Josh 13:5;, etc. The "wilderness" indicated would be that east of Moab and Gilead to the Euphrates.

9.b. The translation of למן הנהר פרת "which reaches to the Euphrates" is again according to sense. It seems unlikely that the writer here wishes to portray the Reubenites as inhabiting the entire desert to the Euphrates, although this is not impossible. Rather למן is construed to refer to the wilderness which extends to or from the Euphrates.

11.a. "Next to"—more lit., "in front of, opposite."

12.a. G^L Vg καὶ Σαφαν "and Saphan"; G^B καὶ Σαβατ "and Sabat." Cf. Tg.

12.b. M ושפט "and judge"; Tg דינא "judges, court"; G ὁ γραμματεύς "the scribe." Read שפט "judge."

13.a. Or, "their brothers" (אחיהם). See *Form* and n. 7.a.

13.b. A few MSS G^B read ועבד "and Obed." G^{Aal} καὶ Ιωβηδ "and Obed."

13.c. G^{B*} ὀκτω "eight."

14.a. G^B Ιδαι "Jedai"; G^A Αδαι "Adai"; G^L Αρουε "Aroueh"; Syr (α΄) zrḥ, Vg *Jara.*

14.b. G Ζαβουχαμ "Zabocham" (from בוז "Buz" + אחי "the brother of," v 15?); cf. G^{Aal} Αχιβουξ "Achibouz." See *Form* below.

15.a. > G* Syr; cf. n. 14.b.

16.a. "In Gilead" omitted by Syr.

16.b. "In Bashan"; Rudolph, *BHS* ביבש "in Jabesh."

16.c-c. > Syr.

16.d. Read perhaps "Sirion"; see *Comment.*

16.e. על "upon." Read עד "to/until"; cf. G Vg.

17.a. G^L Ιωας "Joash."

17.b. G^L + τοῦ Ιωας "of Joash."

18.a. מן־בני־חיל "from sons of strength."

20.a. עזר niph, "they were assisted." Cf. 2 Chr 26:15; Dan 11:34; Ps 28:7.

20.b. וכל שעמהם "and all who were with them." Reading שעמהם as ש being the degenerate form of אשר, the particle עם as "with," and הם as the 3d m pl suff "them."

20.c. ונעתור: niph inf abs used for a finite vb, "and he granted their entreaty." Cf. 2 Chr 33:13, 19; Ezra 8:23.

23.a-a. So M, G^B ἀπο Βασαν "from Bashan." It is customary to alter the text to place East Manasseh in Bashan, but the perspective of the chap. is quite consistent. Reuben occupies Gilead (at least in part), vv 9–10; Gad dwells in Bashan (v 11) and either in part of Gilead or Gilead understood as a larger area encompassing Bashan (v 16); Manasseh then occupies the land the author views as stretching from Bashan to Hermon.

24.a. Omitting the conj with Vrs. An alternative solution would assume an additional name or names to have fallen from the text before ועפר "and Epher."

26.a-a. It is again customary to assert that Chronicles, dependent upon 2 Kgs 15:19, 29, has understood the two names of Assyria's king to refer to two different individuals, and this possibility must be admitted. However, the conj may be explicative (cf. BDB, 252, 1.b,c), as suggested by the sg vb forms following.

26.b. See n. 6.a.

26.c. The ל is used to introduce an enumeration of objs contained within the previous obj suff; cf. BDB, 514 f(d). It is dubious whether any Aramaic influence is to be seen in this usage (*contra* Curtis, 35, n. 128). Cf. R. Polzin, *Late Biblical Hebrew* (Missoula, MT: Scholars Press, 1976), 67, who terms the usage "*lamedh* emphatic." The highly increased usage of this prep is one of the characteristics of Chronicles.

26.d-d. 2 Kgs 17:6; 18:11 בחלח ובחבור נהר גוזן וערי מדי "in Halah, and on the Habor, the river of Gozan, and in the cities of the Medes." The otherwise unknown Hara has probably resulted from duplication of נהר "river" (G^B also reads הר מדי "mountain of the Medes" at the end of the verse). Kings understands only the Habor as a river, designated "the river of

Gozan"; G, both the Habor and the Halah. Chronicles apparently understands Habor, Halah, and Hara as cities and the river of Gozan as a separate entity.

Form/Structure/Setting

Upon initial reading, this chapter appears to be composed of three independent units, each dealing with one of the three tribes traditionally occupying the territory east of the Jordan and each fittingly introduced with its own heading: Reuben (v 1), Gad (v 11), and East Manasseh (v 23). However, closer analysis indicates that these three groups are not being dealt with independently, as was Simeon in the previous section, but the entire chapter has been structured as a single entity including all three Transjordanian tribes.

This is apparent first of all in the introductory notices concerning Gad and half-Manasseh. Gad is said to dwell "next to them," (לנגדם, v 11), i.e., next to Reuben, implying a literary unity; and Manasseh also is said to have dwelt "in the land" (v 23). Three other marks may be noted which point in the same direction. (1) The geographical pattern of settlements exhibited throughout the chapter is schematized, reflecting its own understanding of the relative location of the Transjordanian tribes (see *Comment* below). (2) V 18 repeats the mention of Reuben and Gad from the previous sections but anticipates the mention of half-Manasseh in the following as well. The account of the Hagrite war (vv 19–22) appears to be a logical conclusion to the entire unit. (3) Vv 25–26, parallel in significance to vv 19–22 which follow the brief listing of half-Manasseh (vv 23–24), likewise make mention of each of the Transjordanian tribes and have as their purpose the application of a common exile to each.

That the entire chapter comes from the hand of a single author is unlikely in view of the unevenness of v 18 in the structure of the remainder of the chapter and the apparent duplication of vv 19–22 and 25–26, factors recognized also by more conservative scholars such as Williamson (*Israel*, 81–82). Two patterns seem to be apparent in the arrangement of the chapter as a whole. (1) In dealing with Reuben, Gad, and East Manasseh, the writer(s) has/have placed together all of those tribes inhabiting the Transjordanian area. (2) Within the first two of these notices (Reuben and Gad), each unit presents genealogical information proper, specifies particular cities inhabited by the tribe, and includes a brief mention of military encounters. In this respect the sub-units dealing with Reuben and Gad are identical in structure with that of Simeon noted above. In addition, the matter of exile, briefly noted in connection with Reuben (v 6), is repeated in v 22 and especially v 26.

1–10 *The Reubenites.* The Reubenite notice accordingly is composed of genealogical material (vv 1–8a) to which is appended a reference to the area occupied (8b–9). One historical note is attached to the person of Beerah (v 6) and another more generally to the conclusion of the unit (v 10). The genealogical notice itself is interrupted by a pointed statement explaining the position of Reuben (vv 1b–2); neither does it otherwise present a unified picture. The relationship of the Joel whose children are named in vv 4–5 to any earlier Reubenite is not given. Similarly, the antecedent of אחיו "his brothers/kinsmen" (v 7) and the nature of the relationship indicated by אח (brother?/kinsman?) remains obscure. Since Beerah (v 6) is referred to as "prince" (נשיא) of the Reubenites and Jeiel is also named "chief" (ראש, v 7), it seems likely that we are to think of these two groups of Reubenites as relating to two different periods of time.

The significance of the parenthetical remark concerning Reuben in vv 1b–2 has evoked considerable interest. Reuben's transgression is that referred to in Gen 35:22 (cf. 49:4) wherein he had intercourse with Bilhah, his father's concubine. There is disagreement, however, if not as to the basic intent, at least as to the clarity with which Gen 48 relates Reuben's fate to Joseph's two sons, Ephraim and Manasseh. Many commentators have maintained that though the term "birthright" does not occur in Gen 48, it was in fact this right to a double inheritance of the property (cf. Deut 21:15–17; I. Mendelsohn, *BASOR* 156 [1956] 38–40) which was being transferred to Joseph through his two sons. (Cf. most recently Myers, 35). The difficulties inherent in this understanding have recently been pointed out by Williamson, *Israel,* among others. (1) The OT nowhere else speaks explicitly of the transfer of the birthright to Joseph, nor is there any OT tribal listing that would reflect such a view. (2) The text of G in 5:1–2, upon which such an interpretation is often based (cf. Rudolph) appears to be conflate and suggests that the author/translator was attempting to make the best of a bad situation. (3) The reference to Ephraim and Manasseh becoming like Reuben and Simeon suggests a simple rite of adoption rather than a bestowal of the birthright, since the reference to Simeon would otherwise be pointless.

If Williamson's analysis is correct, our text is the *first,* and indeed *only,* explicit reference to the transfer of the birthright to Joseph. This is all the more remarkable, however, since Chronicles is commonly considered antinorthern in its orientation. Myers's observation that there is really no necessity to introduce Joseph at all is immediately muted by his indicating that the Chronicler felt Joseph's birthright had been nullified "by the apostasy of North Israel and the failure of the remnants [sic] to maintain their legal status (the Samaritans) and that the choice of David (the leader, or messiah) had indicated the shift of blessing and power . . ." (Myers, 36; the reference to Beerah's exile by Tilgath-Pilneser is cited as further confirmation of this shift). The simple reading of the text suggests rather that the author wished to affirm that the Joseph tribes, representing now the Northern Kingdom, had been given the birthright and apparently still enjoyed it, and that Judah also enjoyed preferential status by virtue of his prominence and the fact that "a leader" was to come from him.

Even if the privilege accorded to the Joseph tribes is described as a blessing (cf. G) rather that the transferral of the birthright, the essentially balanced and favorable treatment of the north remains. While we might find the relationships of the text between Reuben, Judah, and the Joseph tribes unclear, a similar lack of clarity is present in Gen 48–49, where pictures of Joseph's blessing and prosperity (cf. especially 48:15–16, 20; 49:22–26) exist side by side with that of a dominant Judah existing in paradisal bliss (49:8–12; cf. Skinner, *Genesis,* 524).

Reuben's four sons (v 3) are listed in Gen 46:9; Exod 6:14, and in a slightly more verbose way in Num 26:5–6. No other Reubenites named in our passage are found elsewhere in the OT. The text does not link Joel (v 4) into the genealogical structure. Whether this Joel is to be identified with the Joel listed as the great-grandfather of Bela in v 8 is unclear (although Dahlberg, "Joel," *IDB* 2:925, so understands him).

11–22 *The Gadites.* Vv 18–22 have the appearance of what was at one time a conclusion not only to Gad, but to all of the East Jordanian tribes (cf. v 18a); accordingly v 17 stands as the original conclusion of the Gadite notice, and is at least formally parallel to the historical notes of vv 6 and 10. V 16 includes a dwelling list, although no cities are named (unless "Sharon" be such a city; and cf. Salecah in v 11); vv 12–15 are the genealogical notice proper.

This genealogical material, which is beset with more than customary difficulties, has the appearance of isolated notes whose relationship to Gad would be unknown if it were not affirmed in v 11. The names of Gad's immediate children, known to us from Gen 46:16 and Num 26:15–17, are not included, perhaps because of the inclusion of the reference to the Gadites' dwelling place already in v 11. None of the descendants of Gad listed here is otherwise known in the OT. The specific relation to Gad in which the three (or four, see n. 12.b.) leaders named in v 12 stood is not noted, and the seven individuals listed in v 13 as אֲחֵיהֶם (lit., "their brothers") must be considered more distant relatives. V 14 sets out to enumerate the sons of Abihail, but the connection with what follows is obscure. The first name given after Abihail is "the son of Huri," suggesting either that a name has fallen out or that the following are to be understood as ancestors of Abihail rather than descendants. GNB, NAB, NIV, and NEB accordingly point the first words of v 14 back to the names of v 13, understand v 14 to refer to Abihail's ancestors, and take Ahi named in v 15 as chief of these; but this seems unnatural and without parallel (cf. KJV, RSV, JB). (G, for example, seems to understand אֲחִי as part of a proper name with בּוּז "Buz" of the preceding verse, see n. 14.b., and the Masoretic tradition indicates a break *before* v 14.) No satisfying solution is at hand, and we have chosen to indicate the problem by leaving the verses disconnected in our translation, assuming some degree of textual corruption.

The language of vv 18–22 is replete with military terminology, much of which will return later in the book. This repeated connection of the genealogical material with warfare gives substance to suggestions that such genealogies originally served a military function. (Cf. 4:41–42; 5:10, 24, and the *Introduction.*)

23–26 *East Manasseh.* Vv 23–24 are a briefer notice concerning East Manasseh, unexpected in view of the inclusion of the half-tribe of Manasseh in v 18 and what appears to be the summary notice of vv 18–23. V 23 parallels vv 9 and 11 in giving the extent of East Manasseh's territory. V 24 lists seven heads of fathers' houses and applies to them titles, which, if by now honorific, were military in origin. Again, none of Manasseh's sons named in the remainder of the OT are specified here (cf. Num 26:29; Josh 17:2), and none of those named here are found elsewhere in the OT.

Vv 25–26 now conclude both the Manassehite section and the chapter as a whole. The reason for the exile stands in the place of the earlier explication of holy war (vv 20–22), and the account of victory in battle following the requisite faithfulness there is here replaced with the implied defeat of the Transjordanian tribes and their exile because of unfaithfulness (vv 25–26). The details of this final notice have been woven together from various traditions. The term מעל, "to act unfaithfully," is almost exclusively a priestly word, with high concentration in P, Ezekiel, and Chronicles. However, in depicting the tribes' sin as harlotry (v 25b), the writer has adopted the terminology of the Deuteronomistic writer and has here in fact summarized 2 Kgs 17:7–23. His total picture is at the same time something of a composite, uniting elements of Tiglath-Pileser's earlier (ca. 734 B.C.) campaign to the west when Transjordan fell into his hands and the later campaign of Shalmaneser which ended with the fall of the north to Sargon (cf. Bright, *History*, 267–308). It is from this latter campaign that the list of the places to which the exiles were deported is derived.

Comment

1–10 *The Reubenites.* Vv 1–2 affirm that because of Reuben's transgression his birthright was transferred to Joseph. Nevertheless, it is Judah, and neither Reuben nor Joseph, from whom "the leader," i.e., David, came. The reference to the order of the genealogical listing (v 2b) may refer to a general principle or to the specific order in which either the author or his source is arranging his genealogical material. Perhaps it is above all an explanation for the priority of Judah in the chapters before us.

Other than Reuben's sons named in v 3, known to us from Gen 46:9 and elsewhere, we have no knowledge of other Reubenites mentioned here. On the basis of the text we can only affirm that one Beerah, seventh in the line of Joel, was prince of the Reubenites at the time of Tiglath-Pileser's deportation (vv 4–6). Myers (36) feels this note confirms the transfer of Reuben's birthright. It is quite possible that the note, despite its brevity, is an accurate reflection of Tiglath-Pileser's conquest of Gilead *ca.* 733 B.C. (cf. Bright, *History*, 273, and 2 Kgs 15:29). It may also be true, as suggested by R. J. Coggins (36), that the author was reflecting a theological judgment in writing that all ten tribes were carried away by the Assyrians.

Although the details included in vv 7–10 are obscure, the situation reflected here belongs to an earlier date, at which time one Jeiel was chief of Reuben (v 7). Aroer, Nebo, and Baal-meon are all listed in the Mesha inscription (*ANET*, 320–21) as taken from Israel in the days of Omri's son, i.e., in the last half of the ninth century B.C. Aroer is the well-known city on the Arnon that would here designate Reuben's southern boundary, while Nebo is located in Moab opposite Jericho (Deut 32:49), and Baal-meon, just a few miles south of Nebo, marks its northern limits (Aharoni, *Land*, 307 and map 27; Grohman, "Moab," *IDB* 3:409–19). All are also included within the cities allotted to Reuben in Num 32:34, 38; Josh 13:8–13). Jer 48 indicates they remained in Moab's hand at the time of the prophet.

The term "Gilead" (vv 9–10) is susceptible of both wider and narrower limits. In its narrowest sense it applies to territory in south-central Transjordan centered in the area between Amman and the Jabbok. In its widest extent, it may designate a much larger area extending from the Arnon to north of the Yarmuk; in Josh 22:9 it seems to refer to all of Israelite Transjordan as distinct from the "land of the Canaanite," i.e., Cisjordan. In its most common usage, Gilead refers to the area from the Arnon to just south of the Yarmuk (cf. M. Noth, *Old Testament World* [Philadelphia: Fortress Press, 1966] 62–63).

The reference to David's war with the Hagrites (v 10; cf. vv 19–20) is again without parallel. One of David's officers is designated a Hagrite (1 Chr 27:30), as is the father of one of his warriors (1 Chr 11:38; contrast 2 Sam 23:36). Ps 83:7 [6] names Hagrites with Moab, Edom, and Ishmaelites as among Israel's traditional enemies in Transjordan, and they probably are the Ἀγραῖοι referred to by the Greek geographers Strabo, Ptolemy, and Pliny (E. Meyer, *Die Israeliten und ihre Nachbarstamme*, 328; noted in R. F. Schnell, "Hagrite," *IDB* 2:511). Whether these Hagrites are to be seen as descendants of Hagar, also traditionally at home in Transjordan, remains conjectural.

11–22 *The Gadites.* The territory of Gad is described as north of and adjacent to that of Reuben, extending from Mt. Nebo near the north end of the Dead Sea to Salecah, some fifty miles to the northeast, and variously named as Bashan (v 11) or Gilead and Bashan (v 16). Since no other cities are mentioned, it is impossible to be more precise, or to surmise whether in using these names the author is reflecting popular terminology in a given period or his own understanding of the Transjordanian area. Normally Bashan extends no farther south than a few miles to the south of the Yarmuk, and its northern limit is Mt. Hermon. In that context, we should here perhaps read Sirion, an alternate name for Hermon found with Gilead, Bashan, and Salecah (!) in Deut 3:9–10; Ps 29:6, instead of Sharon in v 16. No Sharon is otherwise known east of the Jordan, although Mesha's inscription does make mention of a people of Sharon (*ANET*, 320–21). The Deuteronomy passage explicitly confines Reuben and Gad to the lower half of Gilead (v 12) with Manasseh receiving not only all of Bashan but half of Gilead as well (v 13).

Concerning the Gadites listed here we know nothing. Vv 12–17 can be understood as a single unit only with difficulty. It is better to consider Ahi (v 15)—if that be an individual's name—as another of those Gadites who, at an unknown time and place, rose to a position of some prominence in "their fathers' houses" (בית אבותם). The different spelling of this latter term here and in v 13 (בית אבותיהם) supports the view that these are gleanings from disparate sources.

The genealogical enrollment referred to in the days of Jotham of Judah and Jeroboam of Israel (v 17) could refer to all of the preceding list or only to a part of it. According to the Albright chronology Jeroboam is dated 786–46 B.C.; Jotham 742–35 B.C. However, 2 Kgs 15:5 makes it clear that Jotham served as regent when Azariah was stricken with leprosy, a period apparently to be included in the sixteen-year reign attributed to him in 2 Kgs 15:33; cf. 2 Chr 26:21; 27:1. (Rudolph [48, note 3] notes that Thiele's chronology does not consider our passage and does not allow for a contemporaneous reign.) The census referred to would then date from about 750 B.C., the last days of the revitalization of Israel and Judah. This enhances the possibility that the exile mentioned here is that of the Assyrian period rather than that of 587–86, as assumed, e.g., by Coggins (37). Although the term גולה "exile" normally refers to the latter, there is no a priori reason why it must do so, and both the preceding (v 6) and the following (cf. v 26) pericopes refer to the Assyrian crisis. There is to my knowledge no evidence that Judah exercised any control over the Transjordan after this period.

That a war of all the Transjordanian tribes—Reuben, Gad, *and* East Manasseh—should be included at this point in the narrative is surely striking and probably results from later editorial work. The enemy is once again the Hagrites (cf. v 10), joined now by Jetur and Naphish, to be understood as Arabian tribes by virtue of their derivation from Ishmael (Gen 25:15; 1 Chr 1:31) and Nodab, who is otherwise unknown. Whether this report is based upon a single historical encounter or whether it reflects ongoing and traditional hostility between the East Jordanians and their neighbors cannot be determined with certainty. Whatever its origins, however, the terminology applied both to the warriors themselves (v 18) and to the proper attitude toward, and conduct of, war closely approximates that met repeatedly throughout 1 and 2 Chronicles and represents the first explicit statement of the book's understanding of warfare. (For a more comprehensive treatment of this subject, see the *Introduction.*) Here we note only that the terminology applied to the warriors (v 18) is similar to that of 1 Chr 12 (cf. vv 2, 8, 24, 25, 33, 34, 39); that the size of the muster (44,760) is comparable to that in portions of chap. 12 (cf. especially vv 30–37, although the number named from Reuben, Gad, and East Manasseh in v 37 is the largest of all the figures given in chap. 12, i.e., 120,000); and that the theology and vocabulary of vv 19–22 is at least similar to such texts as 2 Chr 13:13–20; 14:8–14 [9–15]; 20:1–30, in all of which cases Judah trusts in the Lord and is rewarded with victory. Some of the terminology, however, is not that which we might anticipate; e.g., בטח "trust" occurs only here in the non-synoptic portions of Chronicles (2 Chr 32:10 is dependent upon 2 Kgs 18:19–21), which otherwise use שען "lean" in this context. Because Israel trusts in the Lord and "cried out" (זעק) to him, he allowed himself to be entreated by them (niph, עתר "praying"), they were "helped" (niph, עזר) by him, and the Hagrites were given into their hands. The mention of the large number of people and animals taken captive, together with those killed, gives concrete form to the theology expressed—it is God's war; those who trust in him will be victorious. However, a mention of the exile concludes this sub-unit, as it will also the next (cf. v 26).

23–26 *East Manasseh.* The sons of Manasseh are not named, perhaps by analogy with v 11, where the designation of the area inhabited by the tribe is found instead, or because Gen 46:20 includes no such list (but contrast Num 26:29; Josh 17:2), perhaps because Manasseh is dealt with also in 1 Chr 7:14–19 (see below). Its inclusion here is doubtless due to the desire to include all of the Transjordanian tribes together; cf. vv 18, 26.

The limits of East Manasseh are described as from Bashan on the south (see on v 11) to Baal-hermon, Senir, and Mount Hermon (v 23). Baal-hermon is otherwise known only from Judg 3:3, where many read Baal-gad. Its location is unknown. Although some would identify it with Baal-gad and modern Baalbek, this identification is usually rejected today (cf. Curtis, 125; Rudolph, 49) for a more easterly location, perhaps modern Baneas (Caesarea Philippi). Senir is, according to Deut 3:8–9, the Amorite name for Hermon/Sirion, perhaps so called after one of its prominent peaks or ridges (cf. Cant 4:8; Haldar, "Senir," *IDB* 4:270). While the precise location in which the writer places East Manasseh thus cannot be determined, it is clearly north of Bashan, which he attributes to Gad, and extends to the northernmost extremity of Israel's territory.

Concerning the seven [sic] tribal leaders named in v 24 we know nothing. The terms applied to them אנשים גבורי, חיל אנשי, שמות ראשים לבית אבותם "valiant men, famous men, heads of their fathers' houses" are common in Chronicles, where at least the first two regularly have military associations. This fact, together with other military terminology and information in the chapter, may indicate that the material stems from an old military source, that the author had a military interest, or both.

Since vv 25–26 appear to apply to all three tribal units and to serve as a conclusion for the total, the material on East Manasseh is very brief. Perhaps vv 25–26 function both as a conclusion for East Manasseh and for the larger unit as well.

If vv 20–22 portray the result of a battle in which Israel has been faithful to her God, vv 25–26 indicate the result of unfaithfulness as it is seen especially in 2 Chronicles. While the concept of retribution is characteristic of Chronicles, as is also some of the terminology here (cf. מעל, "to act unfaithfully," and "to stir up the spirit,". v 26; cf. 2 Chr 21:16; 36:22 = Ezra 1:1), the presentation here is strongly colored by that of the Deuteronomistic historian in 2 Kgs 17, of which it is almost a summary. This is most apparent in the depicting of the sin of the people as harlotry (v 25b), in the reference to the destruction of the peoples of the land, and in the enumeration of the places to which the tribes were exiled (see n. 26.d-d.).

Explanation

In keeping with the concern for all Israel which we have noted before, chap. 5 sets out the tribes whose traditional dwellings were east of the Jordan— Reuben, Gad, and the half-tribe of Manasseh. Each history includes names of prominent descendants, areas in which the tribe lived, and in at least two of the cases, brief notes concerning the military activity of the tribes.

It is in his dealings with Reuben that the writer's interest in the concept of "all Israel" is most obvious. Reuben was, like Simeon, a tribe whose significance had declined to the point where it possessed no independent territory but coexisted in the midst of Gad. The Mesha inscription knows only of Gad as Moab's neighbor to the north, and Ezekiel's vision too places Gad as the southernmost tribe. Since the writer speaks pointedly of Reuben's loss of the birthright, a theological explanation for Reuben's demise lay easily at hand. He could also have pointed out that among the descendants of Reuben were such individuals as Dathan and Abiram (Num 26:9), known chiefly for their rebellion against Moses. He passes by this incident in silence, however, and allots to Reuben for its own a portion of the land of Israel in the extreme south of Transjordan that extends to the fringes of the desert. In more schematic form than in the remainder of the OT, Gad lies immediately to its north, perhaps partially in Gilead but principally in Bashan, and East Manasseh to the north of Gad to Hermon.

Nor, it should be noted, does Reuben forfeit its birthright for the benefit of Judah. Although the writer is explicit that leadership belongs to Judah, the birthright becomes the property of the Joseph tribes Ephraim and Manasseh, whose opposition to Judah is paradigmatic. Apparently they continue to possess that right.

Into the midst of this presentation of the peoples of Transjordan, the writer(s) has (have) also inserted his (their) understanding of faithfulness toward God and its results in the lives of the people of Israel, particularly in warfare. Vv 19–22 present a positive example of victory attained when God's people display the requisite trust in him while vv 25–26 present a picture of the defeat that comes upon those who are unfaithful. In 2 Chronicles the reigns of numerous kings are divided chronologically into these same two periods. (Cf. Asa in 2 Chr 15–16.) So here too a chronological division is drawn. The precise nature of the "unfaithfulness" of Reuben, Gad, and East Manasseh is left undisclosed, as is commonly the case. The end result, however, is exile. Such is the case, the writer appears to say, with those who are unfaithful to God.

Sons of Levi   (5:27–41; 6:1–66 [6:1–81])

Bibliography

The material is voluminous, and only a brief selection is given here, including the older classical works and more recent works encompassing a variety of viewpoints. For an extensive bibliography, see Cody, *A History of the Old Testament Priesthood.*

Abba, R. "Priests and Levites." *IDB* 3:876–89. **Baudissin, W. W. G.** *Die Geschichte des alttestamentlichen Priestertums.* Leipzig: Hirzel, 1889. **Cody, A.** *A History of the Old Testament Priesthood.* Rome: Pontifical Biblical Institute, 1969. **Cross, F. M.** "The Priestly Houses of Early Israel." *Canaanite Myth and Hebrew Epic.* Cambridge, MA, and London: Harvard University Press, 1973. 195–215. ———. "A Reconstruction of the Judean Restoration." *JBL* 94 (1975) 4–18. **Gese, H.** "Zur Geschichte der Kultsänger am zweiten Tempel." *Abraham unser Vater.* Ed. O. Betz. Leiden: Brill, 1963. 222–34. **Gray, G. B.** "The Hebrew Priesthood: Its Origin, History, and Functions." *Sacrifice in the Old Testament.* Oxford: Clarendon, 1925. 179–270. **Greenberg, M.** "Levitical Cities." *EncJud* 11 (1971) 136–37. ———. "A New Approach to the History of the Israelite Priesthood." *JAOS* 70 (1950) 41–46. **Gunneweg, A. H. J.** *Leviten und Priester.* FRLANT 89. Göttingen: Vandenhoeck & Ruprecht, 1965. **Hanson, P. D.** "The Origins of the Post-Exilic Hierocracy." *The Dawn of Jewish Apocalyptic.* Philadelphia: Fortress Press, 1975. 209–79. **Haran, M.** "The Gibeonites, the Nethinim and the Servants of Solomon." *Judah and Israel.* Jerusalem: Magnes, 1957. 37–45. (Heb. with Eng. summary.) ———. "Studies in the Account of the Levitical Cities." *JBL* 80 (1961) 45–54, 156–65. ———, *et al.* "Priests and Priesthood." *EncJud* 13 (1970) 1069–88. **Hoonacker, A. van.** *Le sacerdoce lévitique dans la loi et dans l'histoire des Hébreux.* Louvain: J. B. Istas, 1899. **Japhet, S.** "The Supposed Common Authorship of Chronicles and Ezra-Nehemiah Investigated Anew." *VT* 18 (1968) 330–71. **Levine, B.** "The Netinim." *JBL* 82 (1963) 207–12. ———. "Priests." *IDBSup,* 687–90. **Milgrom, J.** *Studies in Levitical Terminology.* Vol. I. Berkeley: Univ. of California Press, 1970. **Mohlenbrink, K.** "Die levitischen Überlieferung des Alten Testaments." *ZAW* 52 (1934) 184–231. **Polk, T.** "The Levites in the Davidic-Solomonic Empire." *SBT* 9 (1979) 3–22. **Rehm, M. D.** "Studies in the History of the Pre-Exilic Levites." Diss.: Harvard University, 1968. **Smith, W. R.** and Bertholet, A. "Levites." *EB* 3 (1902) 2770–76. ———. "Priests." *EB* 3 (1902) 3837–47. **Speiser, E. A.** "Unrecognized Dedication." *IEJ* 13 (1963) 69–73. **Wellhausen, J.** *Prolegomena to the History of Israel.* New York: Meridian Books, 1957. 121–51, 171–227. **Welch, Adam.** "The Chronicler and the Levites." *The Work of the Chronicler.* London: Oxford University Press, 1939. 55–80. ———. "The Priesthood." *Post-Exilic Judaism.* Edinburgh: Blackwood, 1935. 172–84. ———. "The Priests and Levites." *Post Exilic Judaism.* Edinburgh: Blackwood, 1935. 217–41. **Williamson, H. G. M.** "The Origins of the Twenty-four Priestly Courses." VTSup 30. Leiden: E. J. Brill, 1979. 251–68.

These genealogical registers of the descendants of Levi, second in length of treatment only to that of Judah (2:3–4:23), are composed of four smaller units.

(1) A Levitical line extending from Levi to Aaron and his sons (5:27–30 [1–4]), mixed in nature, which then dovetails into a linear genealogy of the priestly line from Aaron to the exile (5:31–41 [5–15]).

(2) A list of three groups of Levites who traced their genealogies back to Gershom, Kohath, and Merari respectively (6:1–15 [16–30]).

(3) A listing of Levitical musicians installed in their offices by David, similarly divided along the lines of Kohath, Gershom, and Merari (in that order), at the head of which groups stand Heman, Asaph, and Ethan respectively (6:16–38 [31–53]). The activity of this group is distinguished both from that of other Levites (v 33 [48]) and from the Aaronic priests (v 34 [49]), whose names are again listed from Aaron's son Eleazar to Zadok's son Ahimaaz at the time of David (vv 50–53 [65–68]).

(4) A list of dwelling places of the priests and Levites (6:39–66 [54–81]), closely related to a similar list in Josh 21:1–42.

There is considerable agreement among critical scholars that much of this pericope is to be considered secondary. Noth considers only 6:1–4, 34–38 [16–19, 49–53] as original, although his reasoning (e.g., 6:16–33 [31–48] is secondary since the Chronicler, had he wished to include such material, *"sie unzweifelhaft im Zusammenhang mit I. Chr. 16,4 gebracht haben würde"* [*Ü.S.,* 121]) may be less than compelling. Galling (28–30) includes v 34 [49] as well. Rudolph (1) accepts 6:1–9, 14–15 [16–24, 29–30] as original. Myers (44–48) does not attempt to assign various parts of the unit, though referring to the possible work of editors. Curtis notes older views that the first list of high priests (5:27–41 [1–14]) is secondary, but himself opts for the contrary view that the second list (5:35–38 [50–53]) is secondary. With its removal, he maintains the remaining material is characteristic of the Chronicler's order: the genealogy of the high priests, the genealogy of the Levites, the duties of the Levites, and the duties of the priests; the cities of the priests and the cities of the Levites (Curtis, 127–28). While this is certainly true in respect to the final form of the book, it seems unlikely that it represents the order of the original author.

Several items suggest that various lists do not stem from the same hand. (1) The introductory phase, "The sons of Levi . . ." etc., occurs both at 5:27 [6:1] and at 6:1 [16]. (2) There are two lists of priests (5:27–41 [6:1–15]; 6:35–38 [50–53]). The second extends only to the time of David and seems to add nothing to the first. (3) Concerning the two lists of Levites, the first is less tendentious in nature (with the exception of the inclusion of Samuel in the line of Kohath), and the order of the treatment of the three Levitical families differs. (In 6:1–15 [16–30] it is Gershom-Kohath-Merari as in 6:1 [16]; in 6:16–33 [31–48] it is Kohath-Gershom-Merari.) (4) As will be noted below, the priority of Heman over Asaph and the placement of Ethan instead of Jeduthun at the head of Merari, as seen in 6:16–33 [31–48], both appear to be features of later strands of the work (cf. 15:17–19 with 16:41–42).

It is of course possible that all of these lists, despite their various differences, were compiled and/or composed by the same writer, but that seems less than likely. While admitting to the subjective nature of the decision, I would incline toward considering 6:1–15, 35–38 [16–31, 50–53] as the core of the unit. Extending beyond the introductory material gathered from Exod 6, these share the common "his son" and they both appear to reach also to the time of David. By way of contrast, the priestly list of 5:27–41 [6:1–15] is uniformly verbal in its genealogical formula (cf. "Eleazar begat . . . ," v 31 [46]) and vv 16–33 [31–48] move from son to father with the use of the literary formula denoting sonship (בֵּן, "son"; cf. v 29 [44], "Ethan the *son* of Nishi, *son* of Abdi . . . ," etc.). The position of Johnson (*Purpose*, 41) that 6:35–38 [50–53] "is a simple representation of the first half" of 5:27–41 [6:1–15] need not be sustained. 6:35–38 [50–53] can as easily be considered an abbreviated form of Ezra 7:1–15, breaking off before the offending Azariah, who is according to 1 Kgs 4:2 and 2 Sam 15:36 the *brother* rather than the son of Ahimaaz. Vv 39–66 [54–81] also show the order of treatment found in the final form of the total unit, with Aaron listed first followed by Kohath, Gershom, and Merari in that order, agreeing with vv 16–33 [31–48] rather than vv 1–15 [16–31], and may belong to the same or to a later stage of expansion.

The Sons of Levi: the High Priests (5:27–41 [6:1–15])

Translation

27[6:1]*The sons of Levi: Gershon,* [a] *Kohath, and Merari.* 28[2]*The sons of Kohath: Amram, Izhar, Hebron, and Uzziel.* 29[3]*The children* [a] *of Amram: Aaron, Moses, and Miriam.* [a] *The sons of Aaron: Nadab, Abihu, Eleazar, and Ithamar.*

30[4]*Eleazar was the father of Phinehas; Phinehas was the father of Abishua;* 31[5]*Abishua was the father of Bukki; Bukki was the father of Uzzi;* 32[6]*Uzzi was the father of Zerahiah; Zerahiah was the father of Meraioth;* 33[7]*Meraioth was the father of Amariah; Amariah was the father of Ahitub;* 34[8]*Ahitub was the father of Zadok; Zadok was the father of Ahimaaz;* 35[9]*Ahimaaz was the father of Azariah* [a] *(it was he who served as priest in the house which Solomon built in Jerusalem);* [a] *Azariah was the father of Johanan;* 36[10]*Johanan was the father of Azariah . . . ;* [a] 37[11]*Azariah was the father of Amariah; Amariah was the father of Ahitub;* 38[12]*Ahitub was the father of Zadok; Zadok was the father of Shallum;* 39[13]*Shallum was the father of Hilkiah; Hilkiah was the father of Azariah;* 40[14]*Azariah was the father of Seraiah; and Seraiah was the father of Jehozadak.* 41[15]*Jehozadak went into exile* [a] *when Yahweh carried Judah and Jerusalem into exile by the hand of Nebuchadnezzar.*

Notes

27.a. גֵּרְשׁוֹן "Gershon." Elsewhere in Chronicles, גֵּרְשׁוֹם "Gershom"; cf. 6:1, 2, 5, 28 [16, 17, 20, 40; 1 Chr 23:6–7]. The form here is regular in P; cf. Exod 6:16; Num 3:17; 26:57; Gen 46:11.

29.a-a. בְּנֵי as "children" is necessitated by the inclusion of Miriam. While this inclusion may be secondary (cf. Num 26:29; Exod 6:20, G Syr *SamPent*), it may equally well be authentic, and it is permitted by this wider meaning of בֵּן (cf. BDB, 121 ¶ 2, and references cited there).

35.a-a. The parenthetical expression most appropriately follows the Azariah of v 35 rather than v 37, as read. The Azariah who functioned as the first priest of Solomon's temple was the son of Zadok and brother of Ahimaaz; cf. 1 Kgs 4:2; 2 Sam 15:27, 36.

36.a. See n. 35.a-a.

41.a. MT simply הלך "went." Insert בגלה "into exile," or read בגלות as haplogr; cf. Tg Syr α'.

Form/Structure/Setting

This genealogy of the high priestly line begins with a listing of Levi's three sons. On the basis of the sources, multiple descendants of Kohath, Amram, and Aaron are listed (vv 27–29 [1–3]; cf. Gen 46:11; Exod 6:16–25; Num 3:1–4, 19; 26:57–60). However, the intention is to follow only the high priestly line itself, as becomes apparent with Eleazar's son Phineas (v 30 [4]). From that point on the genealogy lists only a single descendant in the form "X begat Y," interrupted only by the parenthetical remarks of v 35 [10] (or v 36, see n. 35.a-a.) and v 41 [15].

THE SONS OF LEVI
1 Chr 5:27–29 [6:1–3]

Levi ⟶	Gershom	Amram ⟶	Aaron ⟶	Nadab	
	Kohath ⟶	Izhar	Moses	Abihu	
	Merari	Hebron	Miriam (f)	Eleazar ⟶	Phineas, etc.
		Uzziel		Ithamar	(see chart p. 84)

The genealogy of 1 Chr 5:27–41 [6:1–15] is the most extensive of the priestly line found in the OT and is effectively the latest as well. The chart on p. 84, which includes other listings of the high priestly line, indicates the way in which the complex tradition represented here seems to have developed. Johnson is probably correct in seeing the lists of Neh 11:11 and 1 Chr 9:11 as the oldest, or at least as based upon the oldest sources (*Purpose*, 37–40). Zadok stands at the center of each list and in apparent harmony with 2 Sam 8:17, is descended from Ahitub. While textual and chronological difficulties abound in this verse (see F. Cross, *Canaanite Myth and Hebrew Epic*, 212–14; M. Rehm, "Zadok," *IDB* 4:976), the primary intent is surely to secure for the otherwise unknown Zadok a place within the Levitical line of Ahitub, whose grandson Abiathar was removed by Solomon from the priesthood (cf. 1 Sam 20–23; 1 Kgs 2:27). Hilkiah, it may be supposed, is to be identified with the priest of Josiah's reformation (2 Kgs 22; 2 Chr 34–35); Seraiah (Neh 11:11), named as chief priest at the time of the exile was put to death by the king of Babylon at Riblah (2 Kgs 25:18, 21). The parallel of 1 Chr 9:11 instead names Azariah here—a common name, especially among priests and Levites (cf. Schumacher, "Azariah," *IDB* 1:324–25, who includes twenty-five listings under that name). These two names are very similar in sound and, at least in some scripts, in appearance (Seriah = שריה; Azariah = עזריה). It is at least suggestive that they have been interchanged in other places as well: the Seraiah listed as accompanying Zerubbabel and Jeshua in Ezra 2:2 and 1 Esdr 5:8 is named Azariah in Neh 7:7; and the Azariah of Neh 10:3 [2] (which stands next to another Seraiah) seems to be identical with the Ezra of Neh 12:1. See also Ezra 7:1, where Ezra himself is the son of Seraiah, without intervening generations.

Ezra 7:1, like Neh 11:11, names only Seraiah after Hilkiah. (Both the chart and the discussion in Johnson, *Purpose*, 39, 41, are in error.) Our passage alone names both Azariah and Seraiah, a typical example of conflation. The Jehozadak who stands at the end of the genealogy as the son of Seraiah would then be identical with the Jehozadak named as the father of Joshua, the high priest of the return, whose career is coupled with that of Zerubbabel (cf. Hag 1:1; Ezra 3:2, etc.) and who obviously did not meet the fate of his father upon the fall of Jerusalem. Ezra would then need to be understood either as a (younger?) brother of Jehozadak, although of course the usual chronologies of the period would not permit this, or a later descendant of the same Seraiah, or a descendant of a later Seraiah of the same line.

HIGH PRIESTS OF ISRAEL

A Neh 11:10–11	B 1 Chr 9:11	C Ezra 7:1–5	D 1 Chr 5:29–41 [6:1–15]	E 1 Chr 6:35–38 [6:50–53]
			Levi	
			Kohath	
			Amram	
		Aaron	Aaron	Aaron
		Eleazar	Eleazar	Eleazar
		Phineas	Phineas	Phineas
		Abishua	Abishua	Abishua
		Bukki	Bukki	Bukki
		Uzzi	Uzzi	Uzzi
		Zerahiah	Zerahiah	Zerahiah
		Meraioth	Meraioth	Meraioth
			Amariah	Amariah
Ahitub	Ahitub		Ahitub	Ahitub
			Zadok	Zadok
			Ahimaaz	Ahimaaz
			Azariah	
			Johanan	
		Azariah	Azariah	
		Amariah	Amariah	
Meraioth	Meraioth	Ahitub	Ahitub	
Zadok	Zadok	Zadok	Zadok	
Meshullam	Meshullam	Shallum	Shallum	
Hilkiah	Hilkiah	Hilkiah	Hilkiah	
	Azariah		Azariah	
Seraiah		Seraiah	Seraiah	
			Jehozadak	
		Ezra (!)		

Of the two names remaining in the briefer genealogies (A and B), both Meraioth and Meshullam are prominent in post-exilic priestly circles. Meraioth is listed as a priestly house in Neh 12:15; Meshullam is a frequent priestly name and the leader of the house of Ezra in Neh 12:13. Their names have probably been included at earlier stages in the genealogy because of the prominence of those in the post-exilic period who traced their ancestry back to them.

The genealogy of Ezra 7:1–5 differs from A and B in several respects. First, the genealogy extends back all the way to Aaron, Eleazar, and Phineas, with data readily available from, e.g., Exod 6:16–25, but that was not included in the briefer materials. Second, six additional names are included between Phineas and Zadok, and Ahitub is drawn closer to Zadok by the removal of Meraioth to an earlier place in the list. We know nothing further of Abishua, Bukki, and Zerahiah, although Zerahiah also occurs as a layman in Ezra 8:4. However, Uzzi is a common post-exilic name. One such Uzzi is named as the head of the priestly family of Jedaiah at the time of the high priest Joiakim (Neh 12:19). The name Amariah is known both as a chief priest at the time of Jehoshaphat (2 Chr 19:11), and is also listed among the priests of the post-exilic period (Neh 10:4 [3]; 12:2, 13). Finally, the Ezra 7 list begins with Ezra, whose relationship to the priestly line is secured through attachment directly to Seraiah, without intervening generations. Such a construction would appear to make Ezra the priest of the return! It thus appears probable that the post-exilic nature of the priesthood is reflected in the additions to the earlier part of this list. At the same time, the addition of these extra names makes Zadok the twelfth high priest after Aaron, possibly by design.

Our list in 1 Chr 5 seems to assume this enlarged list of Ezra 7. At the same time, it prefaces the Levitical line from Levi to Aaron, and repeats a series of three priests (Amariah, Ahitub, and Zadok), the first still preceded by Meraioth and the second followed by Shallum exactly as in Ezra 7:1–5. While some have maintained the correctness of the lists (cf. Curtis, 129; Schumacher, "Amariah," *IDB* 1:102–3), it seems much more likely that the repetition reflects either accidental or intentional dittography. The reason for the insertions between the repeated series also appear clear. Ahimaaz was according to 2 Sam 15:27 et al. a son of Zadok, though there is no indication that he served as priest; Azariah was Zadok's son [sic!] who served as Solomon's priest (1 Kgs 4:2). It thus seems likely that the description "it was he who served as priest in the house which Solomon built" (v 36 [6:10]) should be inserted after the Azariah of v 35 rather than that of v 36 (see n. 35.a-a.). The name Johanan is unknown in earlier literature; however, it is exceedingly important in later priestly families (cf. Neh 12:22–23), and it figures prominently in the Elephantine papyri as well as in speculation concerning the chronological reconstruction of the Persian and Greek periods (see Dahlberg, "Johanan," *IDB* 2:920–30; F. M. Cross, *JBL* 94 [1975] 4–18).

The final list of priests, 1 Chr 6:35–38 [50–53] appears to be a direct abridgement from this list, and in the portion it covers (from Aaron to Ahimaaz, at the time of David), is identical with it (Johnson, *Purpose,* 41).

Explanation

In this most extensive list of priests in the OT, the writer has included twenty-six generations, with twenty-three extending from Aaron to the priest at the time of the captivity—Jehozadak. The *Form/Structure/Setting* section above has indicated that the genealogy has attained its present form through the selective inclusion and exclusion of various names. For example, we have no reason to believe that Ahimaaz functioned as priest, yet he is included in the list as Zadok's son and the father of Azariah, who, according to 1 Kgs 4:2, was actually Zadok's son. It may also be true that the writer would not hesitate to omit such apostate priests as Uriah, priest of the reign of Ahaz who erected the idolatrous altar and was thus responsible for the very closing of the temple doors themselves (2 Kgs 16:11; 2 Chr 28:24), but no reason is apparent for the omission of Jehoiada (2 Kgs 11:9; 2 Chr 22:11), for whom the Chronicler had only good to report (cf. 2 Chr 23:1; 24:2, 14–15). We have indicated above that some priests have probably been included in the genealogy because of the prominence of those who traced their ancestry to them in the post-exilic period. A second factor influencing the inclusion or exclusion of a given priest may well have been the desire to arrive at a theologically significant number. Such a pattern may have been in mind already in Ezra 7:1–5 (and in 1 Chr 6:35–38 [50–53]), where Zadok is the twelfth generation from Aaron. Our writer instead computes twelve generations from Aaron through Ahimaaz, and, if the textual emendation made above is appropriate (cf. n. 36.a-a.), as seems certain by comparison with 2 Kgs 4:2, Ahimaaz's "son," Azariah, is explicitly named as the one who served as priest in the temple that Solomon built. In 1 Kgs 6:1 the period from the Exodus to the building of the temple is set at 480 years, amounting to twelve generations of forty years each ($12 \times 40 = 480$). Our author seems to have envisioned a similar period of twelve generations from Solomon's temple to the restoration. Jehozadak, the priest of the captivity (5:41 [6:15]), marks the eleventh generation in this period, the twelfth of which may be expected to participate in the worship of the second temple. Whether this priest was already known at the time or whether the writer's vision could not yet see that far is questionable, although concluding the list with Jehozadak would seem to favor the latter opinion. Perhaps in the same manner in which Ezra's genealogy is connected directly to Seraiah, the priest put to death at the time of the deportation (Ezra 7:2), priestly speculation concerned itself at great length with the time and the person during whose high priesthood the worship of God would be restored to its Solomonic splendor.

The Levites *(6:1–15 [16–30])*

Translation

1[16] *The sons of Levi: Gershom,* a *Kohath, and Merari.* 2[17] *These are the names of the sons of Gershom: Libni* a *and Shimei.* 3[18] *The sons of Kohath: Amram, Izhar, Hebron, and Uzziel.* 4[19] *The sons of Merari: Mahli and Mushi.*
These are the Levitical families according to (their) fathers: a

^{5[20]}*Of Gershom: Libni his son, Jahath his son, Zimmah his son,* ^{6[21]}*Joah his son, Iddo his son, Zerah his son, Jeatherai* ^a *his son.*

^{7[22]}*The sons of Kohath: Amminadab* ^a *his son, Korah his son,* ^b *Assir,* ^{8[23]}*Elkanah, and Ebiasaph, his sons,* ^a *Assir his son,* ^{9[24]}*Tahath his son, Uriel his son, Uzziah his son, and Shaul his son.* ^{10[25]}*The sons of Elkanah: Amasai and Ahimoth,* ^a ^{11[26]}*his son* ^a *Elkanah, Zophai* ^b *his son, and Nahath* ^c *his son,* ^{12[27]}*Eliab* ^a *his son, Jeroham* ^b *his son, Elkanah his son,* ^c*Samuel his son.* ^c ^{13[28]}*The sons of Samuel: Joel* ^a *the firstborn and Abijah the second.* ^b

^{14[29]}*The sons of Merari: Mahli, Libni his son, Shimei his son, Uzzah his son,* ^{15[30]}*Shimea his son, Haggiah his son, Asaiah his son.*

Notes

1.a. See n. 5:27.a.

2.a. 1 Chr 23:7, 8; 26:21 לעדן "Ladan."

4.a. Exod 6:19 has לתולדתם "their generations"; Num 3:20 has לבית אבתם "house of their fathers" at the conclusion of its listing. Hence the phrase here applies more appropriately to the preceding verses than to the following.

5.a. The name is perhaps corrupt; cf. Rudolph, 56.

7.a. Read perhaps יצהר "Izhar"; cf. vv 3, 23 [18, 38], G^{AL}. Every other list of Kohath's sons includes Izhar; no other list includes an Amminadab. Rudolph's (54) extensive explanation of the source of the textual error is, as usual, ingenious.

7.b.-8.a. According to Exod 6:24, Assir, Elkanah, and Ebiasaph are all sons of Korah. (Cf. also 6:23 [38] below.) As noted by Rudolph, the conjunctive *waw* attached to Ebiasaph also favors that understanding, the omission of בנו "his son" after Elkanah by G^B and the presence of the conj on the second Assir resulting from the misreading of בניו אסיר "his son, Assir."

10.a. In both v 20 and 2 Chr 29:12 one מחת "Mahath" is listed as a *son* of Amasai, suggesting that the present reading אחימות "Ahimoth" arose as a gl (אחיו = "his brother") explaining that this was not the intended reading here.

11.a. Reading the K בנו "his son" (Q = בני "sons of") and omitting a second Elkanah with G Syr.

11.b. K ציף "Ziph"; צוף "Zuph"; G, 1 Sam 1:1 צוף "Zuph."

11.c. V 19 תוח "Toah"; 1 Sam 1:1 תהו "Tohu."

12.a. V 19 אליאל "Eliel"; 1 Sam 1:1 אליהוא "Elihu."

12.b. G^B Ιδεαρ "Idear"; G^{A min} Ιεροβοαμ "Jeroboam"; G^L Ιερεμεελ "Jeremeel."

12.c-c. Adding "Samuel his son" with G^L. The connection, however, may have been assumed by the writer.

13.a. Adding יואל "Joel" with 1 Sam 8:2.

13.b. Reading והשני אביה "Abijah the second"; cf. 1 Sam 8:2.

Form/Structure/Setting

V 1, like 5:27 [6:1], names Levi's three sons, however, vv 2–4 list the immediate sons of each of these, unlike 5:28–29 [6:2–3], which continued the priestly line of Kohath only. In subsequent verses, the genealogy appears linear in form, pursuing only a single line of each family. In the case of Gershom and Merari, this is the line of the eldest son, pursued for seven generations beyond the father named; in the case of Kohath, however (vv 7–9, 10–13 [22–24, 25–28]), it is not the line of the eldest son, Amram, from whose line the Aaronide priests traced their lineage (5:29 [6:3]), but the "Levitical" line of Amminadab, at least to be related to Izhar (see n. 7.a.), that is followed. Kohath's genealogy is more complex in other respects also. Even if Assir, Elkanah, and Ebiasaph are considered brothers, as in the translation above (see n. 7.b.–8.a.), Shaul represents the eighth generation beyond Kohath. However, vv 10–13 [25–38] do not appear to continue the line of Shaul, but instead seem to resume the line of Elkanah from v 8 [23] and extend this line approximately nine generations (the text is problematic) to Joel and Abijah, the sons of Samuel. These last verses, it will be seen, also appear most tendentious in nature.

Vv 1–4 [16–19] are identical in substance with Exod 6:17–19; Num 3:18–20, with minor variations cited in the notes. (Cf. also 1 Chr 23:6–23; 26:21.) Of the individuals named in the linear genealogies of vv 5–6, 7–9, 14–15 [20–21, 22–24, 29–30], we have no additional information, other than that the subsequent pericope (vv 16–33 [31–48]) makes it plain that the genealogy of Gershom is in fact a part of that of Asaph (vv 39–43 [54–58]), that of Kohath belongs to Heman the singer (vv 33–38 [48–53]); and, less obviously, that of Merari is that of Ethan (vv 44–47 [59–62]). Hence each of the Levitical groups named here is connected with the music of the temple. (For a further discussion of the Levites, see the *Introduction,* above.)

For vv 10–13 [25–28], which appear as an insertion in the line of Kohath, the writer had available to him 1 Sam 1:1, which traces the line of Elkanah, Samuel's father, back through Jeroham, Elihu, Tohu, and Zuph. This Elkanah is named an Ephraimite, in which some have seen only a geographical designation. However, there is no indication that this Elkanah is considered a Levite. In view of the writer's understanding of the nature of the temple functionaries, however, and noting the presence of an Elkanah both within the line of Kohath and the line of Samuel, he has been led to attach Samuel to the line of Kohath. Since Samuel's grandfather was known to be Jeroham, however, he has related Jeroham's line to an earlier Elkanah. Why yet a third Elkanah should be included one can only guess, save as a possible way of including Amasai and Ahimoth (cf. 2 Chr 29:12), who should, however, be dated centuries later.

The names of Samuel's sons are taken from 1 Sam 8:2. Samuel's firstborn, Joel, is in 1 Chr 6:18 [32] the connecting link between Samuel and Heman the singer.

Explanation

Next to Judah, the tribe of David, Chronicles devotes the greatest amount of attention to the Levitical functionaries of the temple. Among these the priests occupy pride of place formally. However, at least in its final form, Chronicles is more interested in the lower clergy such as the gatekeepers and, above all, the singers. Based on priestly tradition, all such functionaries are derived from one of the three clans of Levi: Gershom, Kohath, and Merari. Even Samuel, the writer seems to have deduced, must have been a Levite, since he exercised Levitical functions (cf. 1 Sam 2:11, 18, etc.). That the genealogies again seem to extend approximately to the time of David calls attention to their fragmentary character—the nine generations from Levi to Jeatherai, the last-named descendant of Gershom, or Asaiah at the end of the line of Merari, is hardly sufficient to span the centuries in Egypt and to the reign of David. Nevertheless, their presence continues to demonstrate the conviction that at the center of all Israel lay God's temple, with a ministry chosen by God himself and functioning in accordance with his will.

Additional Levites and Priests (6:16–38 [31–53])

Translation

^{16[31]}*And these are they whom David appointed* ^a *over* ^b *the music of Yahweh's house after the ark had attained its rest.* ^c ^{17[32]}*They ministered* ^a *before the tabernacle of the tent of meeting* ^b *with music until Solomon built Yahweh's house in Jerusalem. They served as appointed,* ^c *as was their right,* ^d *in their service.* ^e ^{18[33]}*Those who served,* ^a *and their descendants:*

Of the sons of the Kohathite: ^b *Heman the singer, the son of Joel, the son of Samuel,* ^{19[34]}*the son of Elkanah, the son of Jeroham,* ^a *the son of Eliel, the son of Toah,* ^b ^{20[35]}*the son of Zuph,* ^a *the son of Elkanah, the son of Mahath, the son of Amasai,* ^{21[36]}*the son of Elkanah, the son of Joel, the son of Azariah, the son of Zephaniah,* ^{22[37]}*the son of Tahath, the son of Assir, the son of Ebiasaph, the son of Korah,* ^{23[38]}*the son of Izhar, the son of Kohath, the son of Levi, the son of Israel.*

^{24[39]}*And his brother Asaph, who stood* ^a *on his right—Asaph, the son of Berechiah, the son of Shimea,* ^{25[40]}*the son of Michael, the son of Baaseiah, the son of Malchijah,* ^{26[41]}*the son of Ethni, the son of Zerah, the son of Adaiah,* ^{27[42]}*the son of Ethan, the son of Zimmah, the son of Shimei,* ^{28[43]}*the son of Jahath, the son of Gershom, the son of Levi.*

^{29[44]}*The sons of Merari, their brothers, upon his left hand: Ethan, the son of Kishi, the son of Abdi, the son of Malluch,* ^{30[45]}*the son of Hashabiah, the son of Amaziah, the son of Hilkiah,* ^{31[46]}*the son of Amzi, the son of Bani, the son of Shemer,* ^{32[47]}*the son of Mahli, the son of Mushi, the son of Merari, the son of Levi.*

^{33[48]}*Their brothers, the Levites, were dedicated* ^a *to all of the services of the tabernacle of the house of God,* ^b ^{34[49]}*but Aaron and his sons sacrificed* ^a *upon the altar of burnt offering and upon the altar of incense, as well as* ^b *all the work of the holy of holies, and made atonement* ^c *for all Israel, in accordance with all which Moses, God's servant,* ^d *had commanded.*

^{35[50]}*These are the sons of Aaron: Eleazar his son, Phinehas his son, Abishua his son,* ^{36[51]}*Bukki his son, Uzzi his son, Zerahiah his son,* ^{37[52]}*Meraioth his son, Amariah his son, Ahitub his son,* ^{38[53]}*Zadok his son, Ahimaaz his son.*

Notes

16.a. העמיד "appointed." See BDB, 764, עמד "appoint," Hiph. ¶ 5; Curtis, 89; Williamson, 42, ¶ E.2.

16.b. See BDB, 391, יד "over," ¶ 5h, and the examples given there, which point more to the idea of direction than of location. Cf. also Curtis, 85–86; Driver, 34; Williamson, 49, ¶ E13, for similar usages, though none cite the passage at hand.

16.c. For the broader significance of נוח "rest" in Chronicles, see 1 Chr 22:9, *Comment.* In that passage, however, rest is reserved for the age of Solomon, suggesting a slightly different concept here.

17.a. The periphrastic construction משרתים ויהיו, lit., "and they were the ones ministering," points to the *continuing* ministry exercised by the Levites; cf. GKC, § 116r.

17.b. The expression משכן אהל מועד "the tabernacle of the tent of meeting" is that of P, where the משכן designates the planks lined with tapestry, with the (אהל) tent over it; cf. Exod 39:32; 40:2, 6, 29 (BDB 1015, משכן, ¶ 2; 14, אהל, ¶ 3). The tent is placed by JE outside the camp; cf. Exod 33:7–11. See also 1 Chr 16:1, 39; 2 Chr 5:4–5.

17.c. This rare usage of עמד "appointed" here and in v 18, inadequately reflected in the lexica, appears to mean to stand to function as one has been appointed (cf. עמד hiph, n. 16.a.) and might best be translated "to minister" except for possible confusion with the technical priestly term שרת, which occurs in the same verse here with a similar meaning.

17.d. Or, "custom," since משפט has both connotations (BDB, 1049, משפט, ¶ 5, 6).

17.e. Curtis, 81; Williamson, 57, ¶ F25. In Chronicles, P, Ezekiel, עבודה "service" regularly designates service of a liturgical nature. See also Exod 2:23b (P), where this nuance might also be present.

18.a. See n. 17.c.

18.b. MT הקהתי "the Kohathite"; G Syr Vg קהת "Kohath."

19.a. G reads as in n. 12.b.

19.b. See n. 11.c.

20.a. See n. 11.b.

24.a. See n. 17.c.

33.a. נתונים "ones being dedicated." Cf. the Nethinim (נתינים), a later (?) technical term for one group of lower clergy, 1 Chr 9:2. Cf. Curtis, 79; Japhet, *VT* 18 (1968) 351–54; and the *Introduction*.

33.b. This is the only occurrence of עבודת משכן בית הא' "services of the tabernacle of the house of God" in the OT. The Chr's preference for אלהים "Elohim" rather than Yahweh is well known (cf. Curtis,-15; Williamson, 41, ¶ 13; Polzin, 13); of 51 occurrences of בית האלהים "house of God," no less than 33 are in Chronicles. For משכן יהוה "tabernacle of Yahweh," see 1 Chr 16:39; 21:29; 2 Chr 1:5; 29:6; and, most closely, with עבודת "service," Num 16:9.

34.a. This more general meaning of קטר "sacrificed" is obvious from the context and should probably be the translation in other cases as well; cf. 2 Chr 2:6 (RSV "to burn incense"; JB NEB more correctly "[burn] sacrifices").

34.b. For the Chr's prolific use of the prep *lamedh* (ל), see Curtis, 127–30, esp. the last, and Driver, 45. Kropat (*Syntax*, 6) considered this use of the so-called "*lamedh* emphatic" as resulting from Aramaic influences, although its wider distribution makes this more doubtful (cf. Polzin, 66–68, ¶ 4; Williamson, 43 ¶ D7).

34.c. ולכפר "made atonement." Inf constr with *waw*, a continuation of מקטרים "sacrificed"; GKC, § 114p. For the use in Chronicles of *lamedh* with inf to express intention, see Curtis, 129.

34.d. עבד האלהים "God's servant"; also in 2 Chr 24:9; Neh 10:30; Dan 9:11. Cf. n. 33.b. For the more common and older עבד יהוה "Yahweh's servant," see 2 Chr 1:3 and 24:6 as references under משה "Moses" (BDB, 602).

Form/Structure/Setting

This unit consists in the main of genealogies of Kohath (vv 18b–23 [33b–38]), Gershom (vv 24–27 [39–42]), and Merari (vv 29–32 [44–47]) akin to those met previously in 5:27–43 [6:16–30]. This time, however, the genealogies are supplied with an introduction (vv 16–18 [31–33]) which relates their office as temple musicians to the appointment by David (v 33 [48]) and a conclusion placing their activity within the broader context of the remaining Levites (v 33 [48]) and the Aaronide priests (vv 34–38 [49–53]).

In addition to the differences noted below, these genealogies differ from those given in 5:27–43 [1–15], as may be seen in the accompanying charts, in that each is extended by one or more generations and made to terminate with the patriarch of a family or group of singers. Kohath's line is extended but one generation beyond Joel, that of Heman himself (v 18 [33]), for a total of twenty names; while that of Gershom is longer by six generations, concluding with Asaph (v 24 [39]), and that of Merari appears to add four generations, for a total of twelve, terminating with one Ethan (v 29 [29]), otherwise known only from 1 Chr 15:17.

The relationship between the two sets of genealogies is closest in the case of Kohath, as may be seen from the following chart:

DESCENDANTS OF KOHATH

1 Chr 6:7–13 [22–28]		1 Chr 6:18–23 [33–38]	
			Israel
			Levi
7	Kohath	23	Kohath
		23	Izhar
	Amminadab		
	Korah		Korah
8	Assir, Elkanah, Ebiasaph		
			Ebiasaph
	Assir		Assir
9	Tahath	22	Tahath
	Uriel		Zephaniah
	Uzziah		Azariah
	Shaul		Joel
10	Elkanah	21	Elkanah
	Amasai, Ahimoth		Amasai
	("brother of Mahoth"?)		
			Mahath
11	Elkanah		Elkanah
	Zophai	20	Zuph
	Nahath		Toah
12	Eliab		Eliel
	Jeroham		Jeroham
	Elkanah	19	Elkanah
	(Samuel)		Samuel
	(Joel) and Abijah		Joel
		18	Heman the singer

Even here it is apparent that the differences lie deeper than may be ascribed to textual corruption alone, although that may be the case with the listing of Korah's sons (cf. n. 7.b.–8.a. above). The three links after Tahath all differ, although precedent for identifying Uzziah (v 9 [24]) and Azariah (v 21 [36]) can be found in the case of Judah's well-known king of the same names (cf. 2 Kgs 14:21; 2 Chr 26:1). Most tellingly, however, the break seen in the former genealogy between vv 7–9 and 10–13 [22–24 and 25–28], the descendants of Elkanah, does not occur here. Elkanah is here simply the son of Joel (vv 21–22 [36–37]), and his two sons Amasai and Ahimoth/Mahath (n. 10.a.) are included in the genealogy without comment as father and son. Amminadab (v 7 [22]) is replaced with Izhar (v 23 [36]). Other differences in detail may be seen from comparing the two lists.

These differences have led some to conclude that this second genealogy is a later variation of the first and directly dependent upon it (cf. Curtis, 134). In our opinion, however, the variations are more complex than that, and reflect differing perceptions, ages and conditions, of Israel's Levitical families. This opinion is strengthened when we compare the two genealogies of Gershom:

DESCENDANTS OF GERSHOM

1 Chr 6:5–6 [20–21]   *1 Chr 6:24–28 [39–43]*

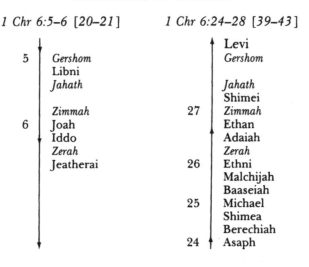

That the genealogy of vv 24–28 [39–43], although six generations longer than that of vv 5–6 [20–21], is itself incomplete is indicated by the omission of Libni, the well-known son of Gershom (cf. v 2 [17]; Exod 6:17; Num 3:21). Concerning the remainder of the list, little more can be said than that the differences outweigh the similarities, with Zimmah and Zerah the only names common between the two. It is of course possible that the author of the second list had additional information on the basis of which he has supplied further names which happened to be identical with other names that he has chosen to omit. But to admit to such harmonization and conflation is still to acknowledge that variant traditions were in existence and that the lists as we have them are at best incomplete, if not actually in contradiction with one another.

The relationship between the two genealogies is considerably more remote in their treatment of the sons of Merari, as can be seen from the following chart:

DESCENDANTS OF MERARI

1 Chr 6:14–15 [29–30]   1 Chr 6:29–32 [44–47]

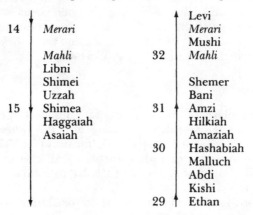

			Levi
14	Merari		Merari
			Mushi
	Mahli	32	Mahli
	Libni		
	Shimei		Shemer
	Uzzah		Bani
15	Shimea	31	Amzi
	Haggaiah		Hilkiah
	Asaiah		Amaziah
		30	Hashabiah
			Malluch
			Abdi
			Kishi
		29	Ethan

Only two names in the lists, Merari and Mahli, are completely identical. Moreover, Mahli is here the son of Mushi and hence the grandson of Merari, rather than Merari's son and Mushi's brother (cf. 6:4, 14 [19, 29]; Exod 6:19). This is of course quite possible. However, that none of the remaining names of vv 29–31 [44–46] is clearly the same as those of vv 4–5 [19–20] means that Ethan is depicted as having descended from Merari through a parallel line, and that the author of this genealogy cannot have been dependent upon vv 4–5 [19–20].

The genealogies have a similar form in that in each case the line is traced from son through father, rather than the opposite as in vv 1–15 [6:16–30]. For comparison with other traditions cf. the *Introduction*. Gese would place the tradition reflected here as the latest, since it considers Heman first and foremost, both in being listed first (cf. vv 1–16 [16–31]) and in being flanked by Asaphites on the right (v 24 [39]) and Ethanites on the left (v 29 [44]), and especially that Jeduthun, who is everywhere else except 1 Chr 15:19 listed as a family head together with Heman and Asaph, is here replaced by Ethan (H. Gese, *Abraham unser Vater*, 147–58; Williamson, VTSup 30 [1979] 263, who also considers this verse to stem from the hand of a reviser). Curtis's (136) argument that Heman is here not necessarily considered the chief is unconvincing. The view of R. J. Corney ("Jeduthun," *IDB* 2:809) that Ethan and Jeduthun might refer to the same person, with the name Jeduthun developed from the name of a psalm tone, לידי איתן (cf. BDB, 451) after the manner of Pss 32, 62, 77, is suggestive but would still point to the latter tradition as secondary.

The unevenness of the genealogies is further indicated in that, while each of the singers mentioned is apparently placed at the time of David (v 16 [6:3]; cf. 1 Chr 15:16, 19), the number of names in the various genealogies differs considerably, from twelve in the case of Ethan to fifteen with Asaph and twenty with Heman, significantly considered the foremost here.

The brief list of priests in vv 35–38 [50–53] has the appearance, as noted by Johnson (*Purpose*, 41), of a simple representation of the first part of the list of 5:27–41 [6:1–15], a list of the high priests who functioned up to the time of Solomon's temple. It has apparently been occasioned by the similar lists of the Levites in vv 18–32 [33–47] and by the statement of their position relative to the Aaronides in v 34 [49]. At the same time, they provide occasion for the lists of Levitical cities in vv 39–66 [54–81].

Comment

Concerning the place of the Levitical families of singers within Israel's traditions see above, *Form/Structure/Setting*, and the *Introduction*. Heman is here explicitly denoted as a "singer" or "musician" (המשורר, v 18 [33]), although the note appears somewhat intrusive. At least in its present form, 1 Chr 15:19 applies the same name, המשוררים, to Heman, Asaph, and Ethan (and in that order).

Concerning these families of singers, the editorial framework seeks to establish the following points. (1) The Levitical musicians were appointed to their posts by David himself when the ark was brought up to Jerusalem (1 Chr 15–16). There is here no idea apparently, as in 1 Chr 16:37–42; 2 Chr 1:2–6, that the ark and the tent or tabernacle were separated, with families of priests and Levites divided between the two. Although not stated directly, it seems to be assumed that with the erection of the temple their duties were transferred there. (2) Although the musicians are considered Levites, as evidenced by their genealogies (and cf. especially v 23 [38] with respect to Heman), their status is distinct from that of other Levites (v 33 [48]), whose task is less definite, "all of the service of the tabernacle of the house of God" (v 33 [48]). (3) The work of the Levites is also distinguished from that of "Aaron and his sons" (v 34 [49]), to whom has been given the prerogative of sacrifice and ministry within the Holy of Holies. Such a note is in harmony with other statements in the book which speak apologetically of specifically priestly duties (cf. 1 Chr 16:6; 2 Chr 29:16; 35:2) and may well be a later addition to the text. According to this understanding, the priests were established in their offices by Moses, the Levites owe at least their organization to David (cf. 1 Chr 15:2, 6; 16:4, 7, 37, 39; 2 Chr 8:14).

Explanation

The work of the temple is here seen as being performed by three separate groups: priests, musicians (themselves divided into three groups), and other Levites. All trace their origins to Levi (cf. 5:27 [6:1]), but it is here principally the musicians upon whom attention is focused.

Levitical pedigrees are given for three different groups of temple musicians who found justification for their existence in David's appointment of Heman, Asaph, and Ethan. Leadership is clearly vested in the family of Heman, of the line of Kohath. His genealogy is listed first (contrast 5:27 [6:1] and 6:1–15 [16–30]); he alone is specifically named "the singer" or "the musician" (v 18 [33]); his genealogy is the longest of those given; his line only is explicitly extended all the way back to Levi and Israel (v 23 [38]). The Asaphites are placed at his right (v 24 [39]) and the Ethanites at his left (v 29 [44]).

It was important for such groups that their Levitical backgrounds be demonstrable, and the genealogies given provide such a demonstration. Before the erection of the temple the groups specified functioned before the tabernacle or tent, the writer states, and implies that they later performed the same function in Solomon's temple.

Other Levites, termed "their brothers" (v 33 [48]), performed other functions in the temple, but the ministry of music was confined to these three groups. By the same token, the priestly functions proper, including the offering of sacrifices and the work around the Holy of Holies proper, was restricted by Moses' command to the sons of Aaron (v 34 [49]). Ten of the high priests of this line, reaching from Aaron to Ahimaaz at the time of David, are named in vv 35–38 [50–53]. It is the dwelling places of these priests and Levites which occupy the remainder of the unit (vv 39–66 [54–81]).

It is difficult, if not impossible, to determine whether the various concerns apparent throughout the pericope are all those of the same historical period or writer. Gese's study referred to earlier demonstrates the tradition in which Ethan replaces Jeduthun as the leader of the clan of Merari to be the latest of those having to do with temple musicians, and his relative dating is accepted by Williamson, who, however, refers this final strand to a period only a generation later than the main strand of the work (about 350 B.C.). It is our inclination, however, to date the main strand of the book earlier, and to see more variety in date and authorship of later supplements than does Williamson. (See the *Introduction.*) Nevertheless, it seems likely that this unit is to be placed at or near the end of the final composition of Chronicles, and hence not far from the end of the Persian period. It is quite possible that the priestly concerns of v 34 [49] belong to another hand of approximately the same period.

The Levitical Cities   (*6:39–66* [*54–81*])

Bibliography

Albright, W. F. "The List of Levitic Cities." *Louis Ginsberg Jubilee Volume.* New York: American Academy for Jewish Research, 1945. 49–73. **Auld, A. C.** "Cities of Refuge in Israelite Tradition." *JSOT* 10 (1978) 26–40. **Bright, J.** "Joshua." *IB* 2 (1953) 648–55. **Delakat, L.** "Zum Hebräischen Wörterbuch." *VT* 14 (1964) 13–23 (מגרש). **Greenberg, M.** "The Biblical Conception of Asylum." *JBL* 78 (1959) 125–32. **Haran, M.** "Studies in the Account of Levitical Cities." *JBL* 80 (1961) 161. **Mazar, B.** "The Cities of the Priests and the Levites." VTSup 7. Leiden: E. J. Brill, 1959. 193–205.

Translation

[39][54] *These are their* [a] *dwelling places according to their encampments in their territory:*

To the sons of Aaron, of the family [b] *of the Kohathites, because the lot* [c] *fell to them—* [40][55] *to them they gave Hebron* [a] *in the land of Judah and the common land* [b] *around it,* [41][56] [a] *although the field of the city and its villages they gave to Caleb, the son of Jephunneh.* [a] [42][57] *To the sons of Aaron they gave the cities* [a] *of refuge, Hebron, Libnah and its common land, Jattir,* [b] *Eshtemoa and its common land,* [43][58] *Hilen* [a] *and its common land, Debir and its common land,* [44][59] *Ashan and its common land,* [a] *Juttah and its common land,* [a] *and Beth-shemesh and its common land;* [45][60] *and, from the tribe of Benjamin,* [a] *Gibeon and its common land,* [a] *Geba and its common land, Alemeth* [b] *and its common land, and Anathoth and its common land. All the cities for their families* [c] *were thirteen cities.*

[46][61] *To the remaining sons of Kohath, from the family of* [a] *the half-tribe of Manasseh,* [a] *ten cities by lot.* [47][62] *To the sons of Gershom,* [a] *according to their families, from the tribe of Issachar, from the tribe of Asher, from the tribe of Naphtali, and from the tribe* [b] *of Manasseh in Bashan, thirteen cities.* [48][63] *To the sons of Merari, according to their families, from the tribe of Reuben, from the tribe of Gad, and from the tribe of Zebulon, twelve cities by lot.* [a]

[49][64] *So the sons of Israel gave the Levites the* [a] *cities and their common land.* [b] [50][65] *They gave by lot from the tribe of the sons of Judah, from the tribe of the sons of Simeon, and* [a] *from the tribe of the sons of Benjamin* [a] *these cities,* [b] *which they named by name.* [b]

[51][66] *With regard to the families of* [a] *the sons of Kohath, the cities allotted* [b] *them were from the tribe of Ephraim.* [52][67] *They gave them the cities* [a] *of refuge, Shechem and its common land in the hill country of Ephraim, Gezer and its common land,* [53][68] *Jokmeam* [a] *and its common land, and Beth-horon and its common land;* [54][69] [a] *from the tribe of Dan, Eltekah and its common land, Gibbethon and its common land,* [a] *Aijalon and its common land, and Gath-rimmon and its common land;* [55][70] *and from the half-tribe of Manasseh, Taanach* [a] *and its common land and Ibleam* [b] *and its common land, for the family of the sons* [c] *of Kohath who remained.*

[56][71] *To the sons of Gershom, from the family* [a] *of the half-tribe of Manasseh, Golan in Bashan and its common land and Ashtaroth* [b] *and its common land;* [57][72] *from the tribe of Issachar, Kishon* [a] *and its common land, Daberath and its common land,* [58][73] *Ramoth* [a] *and its common land, and Enanem* [b] *and its common land;* [59][74] *from the tribe of Asher, Mashal* [a] *and its common land, Abdon and its common land,* [60][75] *Hukok* [a] *and its common land, and Rehob and its common land;* [61][76] *and, from the tribe of Naphtali, Kedesh in Galilee and its common land, Hammon* [a] *and its common land, and Kiriathaim* [b] *and its common land.*

[62][77] *To the sons of Merari who remained:* [a] *from the tribe of Zebulon, Jokneam* [b] *and its common land, Rimmon* [c] *and its common land, Tabor and its common land, and Nahalal and its common land;* [b] [63][78] *and,* [a] *beyond the Jordan at Jericho,* [a] *to the east of the Jordan,* [b] *from the tribe of Reuben, Bezer in the wilderness and its common land, Jahzah and its common land,* [64][79] *Kedemoth and its common land, and Mephaath and its common land;* [65][80] *and, from the tribe of Gad, Ramoth in Gilead and its common land, Mahanaim and its common land,* [66][81] *Heshbon and its common land, and Jazer and its common land.*

Notes

39.a. The suff here must be prospective, referring to the groups following.

39.b. למשפחת "for the family of." Often altered to ממשפחת "from the families of," as in Josh 21:10, where, however, G Syr read sg. See also Josh 21:4 למשפחת. Our text appears to conflate these two verses. For additional use of משפחה as a close approximation to "tribe," see vv 46, 56 [61, 71].

39.c. Josh 21:10 + רישנה "the first," but the meaning is reasonably clear and emendation unnecessary (*contra* Rudolph, 58).

40.a. Chronicles lacks the explanatory phrase of Josh 21:11 (cf. Josh 14:15). Such brevity is characteristic of the writer's style in this pericope. Cf. A. G. Auld, *JSOT* 10 (1978) 26–40, who believes the Joshua text to be secondary.

40.b. For the significance of מגרש "common land," see Delakat, *VT* 14 (1964) 13–23.

41.a-a. Josh 21:2 inserts באחזתו "for his possession." The entire verse is probably a later insertion and is responsible for the double mention of Hebron in vv 40, 42 [55, 57].

42.a. Josh 21:13 את עיר מקלט הרצח "the city of refuge for the slayer." Many scholars wish to read the sg in Chronicles also, which would be technically correct, since of the cities named only Hebron is a city of refuge according to Josh 20:7–8. However, the understanding here may well be the author's own; cf. v 52 [67] with Josh 21:21. (Other cities designated as cities of refuge in the Josh 21 list [Golan, v 27; Kedesh in Galilee, v 32; Ramoth-gilead, v 38] are not so named in 1 Chr 6; cf. vv 56, 61, 65 [71, 76, 80]). Bezer is not designated a city of refuge in either list; cf. Josh 21:36; 1 Chr 6:63 [78].

42.b. Many would supply ומגרשה "and its common land" consistently throughout the narrative, but the writer himself may be responsible for the inconsistency.

43.a. *BH³* חילז "Hilez"; MSS חילן "Hilen"; Gᴮ Σελνα "Selna." Josh 15:51; 21:15 חלן "Holon"; Gᴬ Νηλων "Nelon." Many Gᴹˢˢ confuse this name and Jattir of v 42.

44.a-a. Adding ואת יטה ואת מגרשה "and Juttah and its common land"; cf. Gᴮ Syr Josh 21:16, necessary to arrive at the total of 13 cities (v 45).

45.a-a. Adding את גבעון ואת מגרשיה "Gibeon and its common land" with Josh 21:17; cf. n. 44.a-a.

45.b. עלמת "Alemath." Josh 21:18 עלמון "Almon"; Gᴸ Syr עלמות "Alemoth."

45.c. Josh 21:19 + ומגרשיהן "and their common land."

46.a-a. The text is untranslatable. Probably read with Josh 21:5, 25 (מ)מטה אפרים וממטה דן וממחצית מטה מנשה "(From) the tribe of Ephraim and from the tribe of Dan and from the half-tribe of Manasseh." The corruption may have arisen by the desire to omit mention of the tribe of Dan (cf. n. 54.a. and 7:12) and by the gl חצי on the unfamiliar מחצית (only here and Josh 21:25 [P] of a tribe).

47.a. Josh 21:6 גרשון "Gershon"; cf. n. 5:27.a.

47.b. Josh 21:6 מחצי מטה, perhaps to be read here also. However, the designation "in Bashan" may have been considered adequate.

48.a. Lacking in Josh 21:39, but cf. Josh 21:38, 40.

49.a. Josh 21:8 adds האלה "these."

49.b. The omission of Josh 21:8b, "as Yahweh had commanded by the hand of Moses," is striking.

50.a-a. Lacking in Josh 21:9, G*, but cf. v 4.

50.b-b. The stylistic differences from Josh 21:9 are considerable:

Josh 21:9   אשר יקרא אתהן בשם   "which he called them (f) by name"
1 Chr 6:50   אשר יקראו אתהם בשמות   "which they called them (m) by names"

The author's use of the impf is probably due simply to his retention of the text of Joshua.

51.a. Gᴸ Vg Josh 21:20 ולמשפחות, lit., "and to clans of."

51.b. Josh 21:20 גורלם "their allotment" (but G* גבולם "their border"). Cf. Auld, *JSOT* 10 (1978) 32.

52.a. See n. 39.b.

53.a. Josh 21:22 קבצים "Kibzaim." Mazar suggests Jokmeam is to be connected with a Levitical family of Hebron and that the change in name reflects the city's new population when Levites were settled there by Solomon (VTSup 7 [1959] 193).

54.a-a. Adding with Josh 21:23 וממטה דן את אלתקא ואת מגרשיה את גבתון ואת מגרשיה "and of the tribe of Dan, Elteke with its pasture lands, Gibbethon with its pasture lands." The omission of Dan here and in v 46, as well as in the total genealogical schema of chaps. 1–9, would appear to represent the unique view of a later writer. See chaps. 1–9 Introduction.

55.a. Read with Josh 21:25 תענך "Taanach"; cf. Albright, *Archaeology*, 208.

55.b. Read יבלעם "Ibleam"; cf. G^B Ιεβαθα "Iebatha." Josh 21:25 גת־רמון "Gath-rimmon."
55.c. Josh 21:26 pl. See n. 56.a.
56.a. Josh 21:27 ממשפחת הלוים מחצי "from the family of the Levites from the half"; cf.
6:46 [61]. M. Curtis (141) suggests that the use of *family* before the name of the tribe results
from the abbreviation of Josh 21:27, where the word is pl and refers to the Gershonites.
56.b. Josh 21:27 בעשתרה "Be-eshterah."
57.a. Read with Josh 21:28 קשון "Kishon"; cf. v 61 (Albright, *Jubilee Volume*, 208).
58.a. Josh 19:21 רמת "Remeth"; Josh 21:29 ירמות "Jarmuth." See *BHS*.
58.b. Read עין־ענם "En-anem." Josh 21:29 עין־גנים "En-Gannim (Albright, *Jubilee Volume*,
70–71).
59.a. Josh 19:26; 21:30 משאל "Mishal."
60.a. Josh 21:31 חלקת "Helkath."
61.a. Josh 21:32 חמות דאר "Hammoth-dor." G lists both cities correctly, according to Bright
(654). The additional city would result in a total of 4 from Naphtali also (see *Form*).
61.b. Josh 21:32 קרתן "Kartan."
62.a. The phraseology, inappropriate here (contrast v 20, where it indicated those Kohathites
not descendants of Aaron), is that of Josh 21:34.
62.b-b. Josh 21:34–35 lists 4 cities of Zebulon, in the following order: יקנעם "Jokneam";
קרתה "Kartah"; דמנה "Dimnah"; נהלל "Nahalal." קרתה is probably an incorrect repetition
from v 32 [47] (see n. 61.b.), דמנה a variant of Rimmon (n. 62.c.). The inclusion of Jokneam
and Nahalal is necessary to arrive at the total of 12 cities (v 48 [63]; cf. Josh 21:40) and again
results in 4 cities of Zebulon.
62.c. Josh 21:35 דמנה "Dimnah"; read as רמון "Rimmon" or רמונה "Rimmonah." Cf. *BH*³
on Josh 19:13.
63.a-a. The same phrase, absent from the Heb. text of Josh 21:36 (but present in G), also
occurs in conjunction with Bezer in Josh 20:8.
63.b. Josh 20:8 מזרחה "toward the east"; G^BA κατα δυσμάς.

Form/Structure/Setting

This section is closely related to, and by most scholars is considered directly
dependent upon, Josh 21:1–42. However, it is possible that both may be
traced to a common original (cf. Mazar, VTSup 7 [1959] 196), and most
recently A. G. Auld (*JSOT* 10 [1978] 26–40) has argued that Joshua is dependent upon Chronicles instead. However, other indications point to Chronicles'
dependence upon Joshua (cf. below, *Form/Structure/Setting*, on v 50 [65] and
Comment on v 45 [60]). It may well be that the two texts have continued to
influence each other throughout various stages of their development, as suggested by Auld, e.g., for 1 Chr 6:39–40 [54–55]. G^B in Joshua at times does
display a text between Chronicles and MT Josh, as noted by Albright and
Auld (*JSOT* 10 [1978] 33).

Noth and Alt believe that the original list of Levitical cities dates from
the time of Josiah and reflects the well known reforms initiated by that king
(cf. 2 Kgs 22–23; 2 Chr 34–35). (For the references, see Mazar, VTSup [1959]
4.) However, a consensus seems to be emerging which would date the original
in the reign of either David or Solomon. Cities named, such as Gezer, Taanach,
Jokneam, Ibleam, Nahalal, Eltekeh, and Gibbethon, were not in Israel's hands
until the time of David (cf. Judg 1:27–30). On the other hand, Gezer was
destroyed by Shishak late in the tenth century and not reoccupied until the
Persian period (Myers, 48), Golan and Ashtoreth would have been lost to
Ben-hadad early in the ninth century (1 Kgs 15:20), and Bezer was in ruins
when taken by Mesha of Moab in the mid-ninth century according to the
Moabite stone. The data as it exists then requires a date during the United

Monarchy, probably near the end of David's reign or the beginning of Solomon's.

That certain administrative changes were undertaken as a result of David's conquests is well documented (cf. 1 Kgs 4:7–19). Mazar has argued persuasively that the Levitical cities were actually provincial administrative centers, strategically located in occupied territory for the supervision of the royal estates and the collection of taxes and settled by loyalist Levites (VTSup 7 [1959] 196). He finds support for such a position in 1 Chr 26:30–32, where Levites deriving from Hebron are in the fortieth year of David given both civil and religious duties in Transjordan. Mazar's theory has the advantage also of being able to explain to more satisfaction than most the absence of Levitical cities in certain central areas of Judah and Israel (cf. deVaux, *Ancient Israel*, 367). Such administrative centers were concentrated in border areas and other places requiring special attention, which would have been unnecessary in central Judah (VTSup 7 [1959] 200) and contrary to the strong tribal tradition in Ephraim (202). On the other hand, the concentration of Levitical cities north of Jerusalem may be occasioned by the need for Levites functioning in the Jerusalem temple to be located nearby.

Although the Chronicles list is closely related to that of Joshua, its contents are arranged quite differently. Josh 21 first summarizes the number and source of the cities to be granted each of the four Levitical groups (vv 4–8), after which follows a detailed listing by name of these cities (vv 9–40). In both parts the Aaronide priests are listed first, followed by the remaining Kohathites, the Gershonites, and the Merarites.

In Chronicles, however, almost all summary data is lacking at the beginning (cf. v 39 [54] with Josh 21:4), and the writer proceeds immediately to the complete list of the cities set apart for Aaron's sons (vv 39b–45 [54b–60]). Once this listing has been completed the summary data which might be expected concerning the three remaining Levitical groups is presented (vv 46–50 [61–65], cf. Josh 21:5–9), after which follows the listing of the cities allotted each group.

That this procedure, executed somewhat carelessly, has led to certain difficulties in the text is readily apparent upon closer examination. This is especially apparent in v 50 [65], which in the context of Josh 21:9 occurred immediately following the summary introductions and introduced the detailed report of the Aaronide cities. The present structure of Chronicles has retained the position at the end of the various summaries, even though the list of Aaronide cities which it introduced in Josh 21 now no longer follows.

Whether this *non sequitur* occurs in the work of a single author or is indicative of another hand is a matter of judgment over which differences exist. The former position is held by Curtis (137), who refers to "similar infelicities" of the Chronicler elsewhere. While it may be true that the Chronicler himself sometimes excerpts and summarizes without careful attention to detail, it seems more reasonable to assume we are dealing with a text that has passed through one or more alterations (cf. Rudolph, 63), or that at a minimum v 50 [65] has been displaced from its original position after v 39a [54a] (cf. Keil).

Ongoing editorial revision of the pericope is also to be discerned in the canonical text with regard to the tribe of Dan. (See chaps. 1–9, *Introduction,* and the *Notes* on vv 46 and 54 [61, 69] above.) While the exclusion of Dan could be attributed to the original author, the textual corruption (v 46 [61]) and gaps (v 54 [69]) may be more easily explained if an original reference to Dan has later been excluded.

In working with these lists, it is difficult to avoid the impression that each tribe should have originally contributed four cities to reach the total of forty-eight, and that each group of Levites received twelve cities. Such a pattern can be largely restored through textual criticism (see *Notes* and *Comment*). The degree to which this pattern was ever realized is impossible to determine. The text of Joshua seems to reflect a stage when the cities of refuge and the Levitical cities were either confused or identified. This resulted in the inclusion of Shechem and Hebron on the list, which at the same time led to other misplacements and, to a degree, the obscuring of the original pattern. This process of obscuration continued because of normal difficulties of textual transmission and was hastened by the realities of history, in which cities and territories passed from the control of one tribe and nation to another. In the case of Chronicles, it appears that the original schema has been further obscured not only by similar circumstances but also by efforts of a later writer to remove the name of the tribe of Dan from the list.

Comment

39–45 [54–60]   *Cities of the Aaronides.* V 39a [54a] is the writer's own introduction to the list (contrast Josh 21:1–3, where the emphasis is upon the divine character of the allotments). The nine cities of vv 40–44 [55–59] are obviously to be viewed as the combined contribution of Simeon and Judah (cf. v 50 [65] and Josh 21:4, 9), though surprisingly this is not stated. Judah is mentioned only in connection with a reference to Hebron already considered secondary in Joshua by many (v 40 [55], cf. Josh 21:11). Simeon is not mentioned at all, although Ashan (v 44 [59]) is in Josh 19:7 attributed to Simeon. This doubtless reflects the early demise of Simeon as an independent tribal unit.

Apart from Beth-shemesh (accorded to Dan in Josh 19:41) and Libnah, the remaining seven cities all lie in the extreme south. (For locations of all of the cities mentioned, see the maps in J. Bright *IB* 2 [1953] 648–55 and Mazar, VTSup 7 [1959] 193–205). Since this territory did not belong to the restored Judah of post-exilic days, it would be erroneous to find the reason for the retention of the list in its immediate relevance to the post-exilic situation. The reference to Benjamin as the source of the four remaining cities (v 45 [60]) has been retained from Josh 21:17, although in a very prosaic manner. If the writer were the Chronicler himself, this failure to point more specifically to Judah and Benjamin as the source of the cities given to the Aaronide priests would seem difficult to justify, given this opportunity to bring together two themes about which he felt so strongly.

46–48 [61–63]   *Summary of Remaining Allotments.* This material is in general agreement with Josh 21, if the text is reconstructed as above (see *Note* on v 46 [51]).

49–50 [64–65] See *Form/Structure/Setting.*

51–55 [66–70] *Cities of the Remaining Kohathites.* Joshua lists four cities contributed by Ephraim, identical with the first four listed here except that Joshua includes Kibzaim instead of Jokmeam (see n. 53.a.). Aijalon and Gath-rimmon (v 54 [69]) are in Josh 21:24 from Dan, and that reference should be included in Chronicles also, together with Elteke and Gibbethon, probably omitted by error when the reference to Dan was expunged. Mazar believes the name of Kibzaim was changed to Jokmeam as a result of the settlement of Levites there, derived from a priestly family of a similar name settled in Hebron (VTSup 7 [1959] 198). Or, if the inclusion of Shechem is considered secondary as a city of refuge (and in Josh 16:6–8 assigned to Manasseh rather than Ephraim), perhaps both Kibzaim and Jokmeam were included in the original form of the list. Either alternative would arrive at the expected total of four cities. The two cities of half-Manasseh listed here are to be complemented with two additional cities (v 56 [71]) contributed to the Gershomites.

The resulting picture is that the two elements of the Kohathites, i.e., the Aaronides and the "remaining Kohathites" (v 55 [70]) have their allotted cities in the center of the land, that of the Aaronides in Judah and Benjamin and the "remaining Kohathites" (v 55 [70]) in Ephraim, Dan, and W. Manasseh.

56–61 [71–76] *Cities of the Gershomites.* Two cities of the remaining half-tribe of (E.) Manasseh, together with four each from Issachar and Asher and three from Naphtali, make up the Gershomites' allotment. (If Bright's reconstruction is correct [see n. 61.b.], Naphtali originally would have had four cities listed.) If the text is correct as we have reconstructed it, each tribe but Naphtali would have contributed four cities, with Naphtali's three counterbalanced by the nine of Judah and Simeon to reach the ideal total of forty-eight.

62–66 [77–81] *Cities of Merari.* The four cities of Zebulon must be reconstructed, as indicated in the notes. Four cities of Reuben and four of Gad are included, the locations of which indicate a similar fluidity in the boundaries of these tribes as we have seen in chap. 5. These cities, in agreement with Mazar's hypothesis (see *Form/Structure/Setting*), are concentrated along the Moabite boundary.

Explanation

The Aaronide priests, named as descendants of Kohath, stand at the head of the narrative, as in Josh 21. However, here their preeminent position is even more pronounced in that the details concerning their allotted cities precede all mention of the remaining Levitical groups. It is possible that one form of the text ended with summary material concerning the other tribes (vv 46–48 [61–63]), and that detailed information was added later to parallel that accompanying the Aaronide listing. The order in which the remaining Levitical groups are named, both in the summary and in the detailed listing, is identical to that in Josh 21, i.e., the remaining sons of Kohath, Gershom, and Merari.

Contrary to expectations, our writer gives less emphasis than Joshua to the point that the Levitical cities given to Aaron and his sons stem from Judah and Benjamin (and Simeon), who form the nucleus of the post-exilic kingdom. On the other hand, the retention of the listing of the various other tribes here, as in the overall picture of chaps. 1–9, shows the continued interest of the writer in all Israel. Only in the omission of the tribe of Dan, probably due to later editorializing, does there appear to be a conscious effort to exclude a northern tribe from its place in Israel's history.

Descendants of Issachar (7:1–5)

Bibliography

Elliger, K. "Issachar." *IDB* 2:770–71.

Translation

¹ *The sons of* ᵃ *Issachar: Tola and Puah,* ᵇ *Jashub* ᶜ *and Shimron, four.* ² *The sons of Tola: Uzzi, Rephaiah, Jeriel, Jahmai, Ibsam, and Samuel,* ᵃ *heads of the fathers' houses* ᵇ *of Tola, valiant men, according to their generations. Their number in the days of David was 22,600.*
³ *The sons of* ᵃ *Uzzi: Izrahiah, and the sons of Izrahiah—Michael, Obadiah, Joel, and* ᵇ *Isshiah, five, all of them chiefs.* ⁴ *Besides them,* ᵃ *according to the genealogy of* ᵇ *their father's house, were thirty-six thousand troops of war,* ᶜ *because they had many wives and children.* ᶜ ⁵ *Their brothers, all the clans of Issachar, were also warriors;* ᵃ *the total reckoning of them all was 87,000.* ᵃ

Notes

1.a. Heb. ולבני "and to the sons of"; cf. 1 Chr 6:47, 56, 62. Gᴬ Syr Vg αʹ "sons of."
1.b. Gen 46:13, Num 26:23 פֻּוָה "Puvah."
1.c. K ישיב "Jashib"; Q (G) Vg Syr ישוב "Jashub"; Gen 46:13 יוב "Job."
2.a. RSV "Shemuel," devising a (false) contrast with the famous prophet of the same name.
2.b. See *Introduction* and n. 4:38.c.
3.a. The Heb. is pl, though followed by only a single "son." We can assume again that the term has broader collective significance, such as "descendants, relatives," or that, since the enumeration "five" must include Izrahiah, here it refers to sons and grandsons together. Rudolph (64) omits "the sons of Izrahiah" as dittogr, thus restoring the text to a logically consistent form, although without textual support.
3.b. Reading ו "and."
4.a. Heb. ועליהם "and beside them," a rather rare meaning if correct; cf. BDB, 755, II.4.c., for על as "beside."
4.b. Understanding the suff as prospective and the *lamedh* as indicative of the genitive (cf. GKC, § 129a).
4.c-c. The significance of the phrase is dubious at best. Curtis (145) and others connect with the first word of v 5 and read as מאחיהם ". . . were more numerous *than* their relatives."
5.a-a. Implied by the context.

Form/Structure/Setting

Issachar is regularly listed with Zebulon in the OT after Leah's older sons (cf. Deut 33:18–19). For usage in Chronicles, see 1 Chr 12:33, 41 [32, 40]; 27:18; 2 Chr 30:18, where it is regularly listed before Zebulon somewhat as a symbol of the northern extremity of Israel.

This genealogy appears to extend only four generations beyond Issachar and is mixed in form. Although multiple sons are listed for Issachar, Tola, and Izrahiah, the line is traced only through the eldest son. Izrahiah and his four sons, however, are enumerated as a group (v 3).

It is possible to view v 1, based upon canonical sources (cf. Gen 46:13; Num 26:23-25), as standing alone; however, it seems preferable to consider the relationship between v 1 and v 2 as parallel to that between v 3a and v 3b. V 2 is separated from v 3 formally by the enumeration of v 2b, just as v 3 is concluded with that of v 4. The whole unit is then concluded with the broader enumeration of v 5.

Rudolph (65) has argued that the military terminology of this list ill accords with its genealogical format, and is to be attributed to the author of the Benjaminite genealogy of vv 6-11, where the enumerations are an organic part of the whole. V 2b (from לתולע "of Tola") and vv 4-5 probably stem from military records of the sort gathered in 1 Chr 12, where they are used for a more propagandistic purpose.

Only v 1 has parallels in earlier OT genealogies (cf. Gen 46:13; Num 26:23-25). However, Judg 10:1 names as a minor judge a man of Issachar, one Tola, the son of Puah, son of Dodo, who dwelt in Shamir in Ephraim. Curtis has imaginatively suggested that all four names included as Issachar's sons may be ultimately derived from this information with Shamir (שמיר) corresponding to Shimron (שמרון) and Jashub (ישוב) reflecting some such verbal form of the root ישב, "to dwell," as יושב. This would also explain in part the variant reading יוב, "Job" of Gen 46:13 (see n. 1.c. and Curtis, 144).

The first enumeration (v 2b) refers to a census in the time of David and has been thought to be related to David's census of 1 Chr 21 (cf. Keil, 131). No setting is given for the figures of vv 4-5, though they would appear to be essentially parallel figures. Similar but different figures are found in Num 1:29, where Issachar's warriors are numbered at 54,400, and Num 26:25, where the total is 64,300. Issachar's warriors are the only ones not numbered in 1 Chr 12:33 [32], which mentions instead only two hundred chiefs.

Comment

Since we have no parallel data with which to compare our list as a whole, and details of the text are open to various understandings, we shall content ourselves with broader observations. Twenty-two thousand, six hundred warriors of Issachar appear to be numbered at the time of David (cf. 1 Chr 12:33 [32]). Our writer has associated these with the sons of Tola, although, literally understood, two generations past Issachar would leave us centuries removed from David. Two additional census figures seem also to have been at the writer's disposal, and these have been included and brought into relationship with subsequent parts of the genealogy, the first as though enumerating the "sons of Uzzi," the second as including unnamed "remaining clans" of Issachar. That it would be inappropriate to sum up Issachar's descendants, stretching over even a few generations, as though they comprised a larger group of Issacharites would appear to have been of little concern to the author, who was concerned instead that Issachar be included among Israel's tribes and perhaps that no information available to him about this rather remote tribe be lost.

Explanation

The enumeration of Israel's northern tribes begins with Issachar, in agreement with the expected listing (cf. 2:1). Perhaps because the information available to the author was skimpy and encompassed no more than four generations, this has been supplemented, either by the original author or by a later hand, with material which appears to have been derived from military census lists (see *Introduction*). No *Tendenz* is apparent, although the occurrence of Shimron, related to Shamir (cf. Judg 10:1) and the later Samaritans, would have certainly provided ample opportunity for negative comparisons had the author chosen to draw them. Issachar seems to be included for the sake of completeness. All Israel, including Issachar, was to be included within the scope of the divine plan.

The Descendants of Benjamin, Dan (?) and Naphtali (7:6–13)

Bibliography

Elliger, K. "Benjamin." *IDB* 1:383–84. **Mazar, B.** "The Cities of the Territory of Dan." *IEJ* 10 (1960) 65–77. **Williamson, H. G. M.** "A Note on I Chronicles VII 12." *VT* 23 (1973) 375–79.

Translation

[6] *The sons of* [a] *Benjamin: Bela, Becher, and Jediael,* [b] *three.*

[7] *The sons of Bela: Ezbon, Uzzi, Uzziel, Jerimoth, and Iri, five—heads of father's houses, mighty warriors—their genealogical enrollment was 22,034.*

[8] *The sons of Becher: Zemirah, Joash, Eliezer, Elioenai, Omri, Jeremoth, Abijah, Anathoth, and Alemeth. All these were sons of Becher.* [9] *Their genealogical enrollment, according to their generations, heads of fathers' houses, mighty warriors, was 22,200.*

[10] *The sons of Jediael:* [a] *Bilhan. The sons of Bilhan: Jeush,* [b] *Benjamin, Ehud, Chenaanah, Zethan, Tarshish, and Ahishahar.* [11] *All these were the sons of Jediael, heads of (fathers') houses, mighty warriors, 17,200 who went out with the army to battle.* [12a] *. . . and* [b] *Shuppim and Huppim.* [b]

The sons of Dan: [c] *Hushim,* [d] [e] *the sons of Aher.* [ea] [13] *The sons of Naphtali: Jahziel, Guni, Jezer, and Shallum.* [a] *These were the sons of Bilhah.* [a]

Notes

6.a. Adding בני "sons of," with most MSS G[L] Vg Syr Tg, perhaps omitted by haplogr. But if the word Benjamin is not original here (see below), an original reading such as בני זבלון "sons of Zebulon" (Curtis, 147) may have contributed to the present confusion.

6.b. Syr ואשבל "and Ashbel" reflects harmonization here and in v 10; cf. Gen 46:21.

10.a. See n. 6.b.

10.b. K יעיש "Jeish"; Q G[BL] Vg Tg יעוש "Jeush." Cf. 1:35.

12.a-a. Cf. Gen 46:24–25, NEB, NAB, *Textual Notes on the New American Bible,* 357, and *Comment* below. The Heb. ושפים וחפים בני עיר חשם בני אחר is fragmentary and corrupt; lit., "and Shuppim and Huppim were the sons of Ir (?), Hushim, the sons of Aher (?)."

12.b-b. Gen 46:21 מפים וחפים "Muppim and Huppim"; Num 26:39 חופם . . . שפופם "Shephupham . . . Hupham."

12.c. Conjectural; cf. Gen 46:23. Heb. בני עיר "the sons of Ir."

12.d. Num 26:42 שוחם "Shuham."

12.e. Heb. בני אחר "sons of Aher"; probably a corrupt gl, perhaps related to the Benjaminite Ard (ארד, Gen 46:21) or Ahiram (אחירם, Num 26:38).

13.a-a. Cf. Gen 46:25; אלה בני בלהה "these were the sons of Bilhah," referring to Dan and Naphtali preceding.

Form/Structure/Setting

The overall structure of vv 6–11 is clear. Following the naming of three of Benjamin's sons (v 6) is a list of the sons of each, accompanied by an enumeration of the warriors of each of the three families.

Beyond this point, however, difficulties emerge. The beginning of v 6 (see n. 6.a.) is abrupt, if not fragmentary. Based on the other OT lists, one would expect here the genealogy of Zebulon. (Zebulon follows Issachar in 1 Chr 2:1; 12:34 [32]; 27:18; and, according to Curtis [147], in fourteen of seventeen OT lists). For the omission of Zebulon, see also the *Introduction* to chaps 1–9 above. In the same vein, it would be expected, according to the order of the tribes presented in both Gen 46 and Num 26, for Benjamin to be followed by Dan, likewise missing from chaps 2–9, and according to Gen 46, Naphtali, which is indeed the case in v 13.

At the same time, v 12 presents rather substantial difficulties as it now stands. The שׁפּים "Shuppim" and חפּים "Huppim" of this verse, it is commonly agreed, are to be identified with Benjamin's sons named מפּים "Muppim" and חפּים "Huppim" in Gen 46:21 and שׁפופם "Shephupham" and חופם "Huphim" in Num 26:39, and אחר "Aher" is at a minimum suggestive of Ard (ארד), the name of Benjamin's son following Muppim and Huppim in Gen 46:21, or Ahiram (אחירם) of Num 26:38. Most strikingly, however, the name of the single son of Dan listed in Gen 46:23, Hushim (חשים), occurs here near the end of v 12, ostensibly as a descendant of Benjamin, in the very place where Dan and his descendants are anticipated.

This situation, coupled with the fact that a still more extensive genealogy of Benjamin occurs in chap. 8, has convinced many that the present text has undergone one or a series of rearrangements resulting in the omission of Zebulon and of the name Dan. We may suggest that these alterations were suggested positively by the writer's concern for Benjamin, readily apparent throughout the book, and negatively by an aversion to Dan, which we have seen to be apparent also in 1 Chr 6:46, 54 [61, 69]. (Cf. Bertheau, found in Keil, 135–36, and Rudolph, 65–67.)

In contrast, Williamson, while admitting the fragmentary character of v 12 and its lack of connection with vv 6–11, has argued strongly against the understandings and the kinds of textual emendations usually offered in support of such a view. Working strictly on the basis of textual criticism, however, Williamson has offered no rationale for the omission of Dan or Zebulon from the total tribal listing. Moreover, the fact that Hushim is also found as a Benjaminite name in 1 Chr 8:8, 11, only partially negates the striking similarity of v 12 to Gen 46:21, 23, and the immediate succession of Naphtali in Gen 46:24 as here in v 13. That no precise textual emendation commends itself is not surprising when we consider that the scribes were forced to deal with a tradition already showing extensive variation (compare the number and names of Benjamin's sons listed below), which was now reduced to a meaningless fragment.

The source of the Benjaminite tradition present in vv 7–11 differs substan-

tially from other OT presentations, as may be seen from the following chart
on the sons of Benjamin and Bela.

SONS OF BENJAMIN AND BELA

Sons of Benjamin

Gen 46:21	Num 26:38	1 Chr 8:1–2	1 Chr 7:6
Bela	Bela	Bela	Bela
Becher			Becher
Ashbel	Ashbel	Ashbel	
			Jediael
Gera	Ahiram	Aharah	
Naaman		Nohah	
Ehi		Rapha	
Rosh			
Muppim	Shephupham		
Huppim	Hupham		
Ard			

Sons of Bela

Gen 46	Num 26:39–40	1 Chr 8:3–4	1 Chr 7:7
	Ard	Addar	Ezbon
	Naaman	Gera	Uzzi
		Abihud	Uzziel
		Abishua	Jerimoth
		Naaman	Iri
		Aloah	
		Gera	
		Shephuphan	
		Huram	

The three sons of Benjamin named here in 1 Chr 7:6–13 represent the
smallest number found in any OT genealogy and do not agree with any
other OT list of Benjaminites. Bela alone is common to all of the genealogies;
Becher occurs only here and Gen 46:21; a Benjaminite Jediael is unknown
outside our list, unless he be identified with David's mighty man of the same
name in 1 Chr 11:45. There are no lists of descendants of Becher and Jediael
with which to compare our text; but the list of Bela's sons also appears unrelated to other lists, which do include names such as Ard, Naaman, Gera,
Shephuphan, and Huran identical with or similar to names of Benjamin's
sons found in other OT traditions.

The source of our specific tradition seems relatively obvious. Each of the
three groups of Benjaminites is followed by a statement pointing to those
named as "heads of fathers' houses" and "mighty warriors" (vv 7, 9, 11).
The numbers given then must refer to the total number of warriors found
among each group, and we have, as indicated by Johnson, names and numbers

ultimately derived from censuses taken for military purposes (see the *Introduction*). These figures, it may be noted, appear to be in place and an integral part of the narrative here, which is not the case in 7:1–5 (see above). We might conclude, therefore, that an original genealogy of Benjamin based on Gen 46 has now been replaced with another based on a military census, which has also influenced the genealogy of Issachar preceding it. On the basis of such names as Anathoth, Alemeth (v 8), and Benjamin (v 10) Rudolph (65), in dependence upon Noth, concludes that the list used here is post-exilic in provenance.

The use of the term אבות בית אבות "fathers' house" with אבות in the plural, if belonging to the original list, also suggests a late date (cf. J. Weinberg, "Das Bēit 'Ābōth im 6.–4. Jh. v. U. Z.," *VT* 23 [1973] 400–414), as does the occurrence of such "biblical" names as Benjamin and Ehud (cf. Noth, *Die israelitischen Personennamen,* quoted by Myers, 53).

V 12, as we have indicated above, represents a fragment of an earlier genealogy of Benjamin and Dan related to Gen 46:21, 23.

The genealogy of Naphtali, included in this unit for convenience and because of its immediate association with the genealogies of Benjamin and Dan, may best be understood by comparing Gen 46:24–25. Apart from minor divergencies in orthography, Naphtali's sons are identical with those four named in Gen 46:24 and Num 26:48–49. The concluding phrase, however, ". . . the sons of Bilhah, " is meaningless in our context, unless Bilhah be understood as Naphtali's wife. Comparison with Gen 46:25 indicates that our text preserves a portion of the following verse, "the sons of Bilhah," a summary statement pointing to Dan (!) and Naphtali as Israel's sons through Rachel's concubine Bilhah.

Explanation

At the time of the census reflected in this pericope, the tribe of Benjamin was divided into three major families tracing their origins to Bela, Becher, and Jediael. The disruption of the text and the divergence of the names given from those of other OT traditions suggest that this was in post-exilic times. Individuals without lineage in the course of time took their names from the cities in which they were located, and their names were enrolled genealogically among the ancestors of Israel. The total number of warriors given is 61,434, compared with Benjaminite figures of 3,000 in 1 Chr 12:29 (see below), 35,400 in Num 1:37, and 45,600 in Num 26:41 (cf. Ezra 2:23; Neh 10:20). The late date of the Benjaminite material found here, like the expansive treatment of Benjamin in, e.g., chap. 8, points to the significance that the tribe had during the post-exilic period.

Concerning Dan and Naphtali we can add little. The genealogies attributed to them (vv 12b, 13) are identical to those in Gen 46 so far as we can determine, suggesting at a minimum that the author did not wish to elaborate upon them, that a longer tradition has been lost, or that no additional material was available. Their presence, however, even in such brief form, testifies to the tendency to include all of the tribes of Israel as a part of the people of Israel.

Descendants of Manasseh   (7:14–19)

Bibliography

Albright, W. F. "The Site of Tirzah and the Topography of Western Manasseh." *JPOS* 11 (1931) 241–51. **Elliger, K.** "Manasseh." *IDB* 3:252–54.

Translation

[14] *The sons of Manasseh, whom* [a] *his Aramean concubine bore:* [a] *Machir, the father of Gilead* [15a] *(he took a wife whose name was Maacah),* [a] *and whose second (son)* [b] *was named Zelophehad. (He had only daughters.)* [c] [16] *Machir's wife Maacah had a son and called his name Peresh, and that of his brother Sheresh. His sons were Ulam and Rakem.* [17] *The sons of Ulam: Bedan. These are Gileadites, descended through Machir, Manasseh's son.*

[18] *Gilead's sister, Hammolecheth, bore Ishhod, Abiezer, and Mahlah.*

[19] *Shemidah's sons were Ahian, Shechem, Likhi, and Aniam.*

Notes

14.a-a. MT "Asriel, whom his Aramean concubine bore; she also bore. . . ." Asriel is otherwise known only as a *son* of Gilead, Num 26:31; cf. Josh 17:1–3. Its occurrence here is probably due to dittogr; cf. (דה)יל אשר "whom she bore."

15.a-a. MT "Machir took a wife for Huppim and Shuppim, and the name of his sister was Maacah." Delete "Huppim" and "Shuppim" (cf. v 12). Maacah is the wife of Machir rather than his sister, though it is uncertain whether אחתו "his sister" represents a distortion of this idea or is a part of the misplaced reference to Huppim and Shuppim (cf. אחתם "their sister" of G[L] Tg).

15.b. The Heb. השני "the second" is masc and best refers to a second son of Machir (v 14) or, alternately, of Manasseh himself. Zelophehad is according to Num 27:1 a male, ruling out the idea (cf. G[B] השנית "the second_____") that this individual might be considered a second wife or sister of Machir.

15.c. Cf. Josh 17:3.

Form/Structure/Setting

Both the Hebrew text and the versions present great difficulties to the understanding of these verses, which seem to be in harmony neither with other OT traditions concerning Manasseh nor with each other, as admitted by scholars of all persuasions. Michaeli (60) lists several of the more obvious difficulties, as follows: (1) the reoccurrence of the unusual names Huppim and Shuppim; cf. v 12; (2) the question of who is the "second" of v 15; (3) the naming of Maacah in v 15 as the sister of Machir, but in v 16 as his wife; (4) the identification of the descendants of Machir in v 17 as sons of Gilead; (5) the problem of who is the Shemida whose sons are mentioned in v 19?

The text adopted above answers some, but not all, of these questions and has the advantage of avoiding complete textual reconstruction, as seen, e.g., in Rudolph (69–70), who rebuilds the entire unit on the basis of Num 26:29–34. This supposed dependence is questionable. Other OT traditions know only a single son of Manasseh—Machir, referred to as Manasseh's first-born in Josh 17:1 and to whom is allotted Gilead and Bashan (Josh 17:2; cf. Num 26:29). The line of descent in Num 26:29–34 and Josh 17:1–4 is as follows:

```
Manasseh-Machir-Gilead-Abi-ezer
                 Helek
                 Azriel
                 Shechem            Mahlah
                 Shemida            Noah
                 Hepher -Zelophehad- Hoglah
                                    Milcah
                                    Tirzah
```

According to Josh 17, Machir is given territory in Gilead and Bashan; the remaining "sons of Manasseh" are thus placed in the territory west of the Jordan, reflected in such names as Shechem and Tirzah (cf. Myers, 54, who notes that Shemida, Abiezer, Helek, Shechem, Hoglah, and Noah occur in the Samaria Ostraca).

The significant difference from our text, unless it simply be reconstructed to agree with other lists, is apparent. Machir's wife Maacah and the sons descended from Gilead through her (Peresh, Sheresh, Ulam, Raken, and Bedan) are unknown in other lists of Manasseh's descendants. The same is true of Gilead's sister, Hammolecheth, her son Ishhod, and Shemidah's sons Ahian, Likhi, and Aniam (although many identify Likhi with Helek and Aniam with Noah of Num 26:30 and 33; Josh 17:2–3; cf. Curtis, 152; Rudolph, 70). Despite these differences, the genealogy does reflect names commonly associated with Manasseh. Besides the familiar Machir and Gilead, Zelophehad is known in Num 26 and Josh 17 as Gilead's son, and Abiezer, Mahlah, Shemidah, and Shechem are all sons of Gilead in Num 26:30–32, as is "Asriel" of the Hebrew text of v 14 (cf. n. 14.a.). (Notice also that v 17 sums up the first part of the genealogy as being Gileadite.) Moreover, the name of Machir's wife, Maacah, is also that of an Aramean kingdom (Deut 3:14; Josh 12:5; 13:11, 13) which continued to exist in the midst of Israel and with whom relations continued into the time of David (cf. 1 Chr 19:6–9; A. Haldar, "Maacah," *IDB* 3:196, #10). Such a notice is then consistent with Manasseh's Aramean concubine (v 14), although Gen 50:23 at least implies the birth of Machir's sons in Egypt.

Beyond these associations, however, the present text appears independent of the others available to us. Since a tradition relative to descendants of Manasseh in Transjordan has already been met in 5:18–26, it would be anticipated that our text would restrict itself to West Manasseh. Tradition does refer the non-Machirite portion of Manasseh, and especially the inheritance of Zelophehad's daughters, to West Manasseh (cf. Josh 17:1–6), and such names as Shechem and Tirzah must refer to West Manasseh, though ascribed to Gilead in Num 26. However, the emphasis upon Machir and Gilead obvious throughout vv 14–17 indicates at least an equal interest in the eastern portions of the tribe.

Comment

Rudolph (70–71) has pointed to the reference to Manasseh's Aramean concubine as intending to reflect discredit upon Manasseh in general and the inhabitants of Shechem, with whom the later Samaritans are to be identified, in particular. It is doubtful, however, whether the reference is meant to be derogatory at all, or in what sense it would be more negative than the reference to Joseph's children as being born of the daughter of an Egyptian priest in Gen 46:20. The reference to Shechem itself is far from prominent. Rather we seem to have here a collection of names and places related to Manasseh in one way or another and brought together in a genealogical table which recalls both the eastern and western associations of the tribe. If Zelophehad is referred to as Machir's second son, rather than Manasseh's, we may see in Gilead the progenitor of the eastern tradition, in Zelophehad that of the west. That this may be the case is suggested by the inclusion of Gilead's sister in v 18, while Shemida (v 19) is elsewhere known also as a son of Gilead (Num 26:30–32). On the other hand, the descendants of Hammolecheth, Gilead's sister, and of his brother Zelophehad, and Shemidah, may be located in W. Jordan.

The Descendants of Ephraim
(and Manasseh)   (7:20–29)

Bibliography

Albright, W. F. "Ophrah and Ephraim." *AASOR* 4 (1922–23) 125–33. **Elliger, K.** "Ephraim." *IDB* 2:119–21. ———. "Tribes, Territories of." *IDB* 4:701–10 (with bibliography).

Translation

[20] *The sons of Ephraim: Shuthelah, his son Bered,* [a] *his son Tahath, his son Eleadah, his son Tahath,* [21] *his son Zabad, his son Shuthelah—and Ezer and Elead, (the two of) whom the men of Gath born in the land killed when they came down to take their possessions.* [22] *Ephraim their father mourned many days, and his brothers came in to comfort him.* [23] *He went in to his wife, and she conceived and bore a son. He called his name Beriah, because evil had come upon his house.*

[24] *His daughter was Sheerah, and she built Lower and Upper Beth-horon and Uzzen-sheerah*

[25] *his son* [a] *Rephah, Resheph, his son Telah, his son Tahan,* [26] *his son Ladan, his son Ammihud, his son Elishama,* [27] *his son Nun,* [a] *his son Joshua.*

[28] *Their possessions and their dwelling places were Beth-el and its villages, to the east Naaran,* [a] *and to the west Gezer and its villages and Shechem and its villages as far as Ayyah* [b] *and its villages,* [29] [a]*and, alongside* [a] *the sons of Manasseh, Beth-shean and its villages, Taanach and its villages,* [b] *Megiddo and its villages, and Dor and its villages. In these dwelt the sons of Joseph, the son of Israel.*

Notes

20.a. Num 26:35 Syr ‫בכר‬(‫ל‬) "(of) Becher."
25.a. A few MSS of G[L] + ‫בנו‬ "his son."
27.a. MT ‫נון‬ "Non" only here; elsewhere always ‫נון‬ "Nun."
28.a. Josh 16:7 ‫נערתה‬(‫ל‬) "(to) Naaratha."
28.b. Mlt MSS G[A] ‫עזה‬ "Azzah."
29.a-a. G καὶ ἕως ὁρίων "and as far as the borders."
29.b. G + καὶ βαλααδ καὶ αἱ κῶμαι αὐτῆς "and Balaad and its villages"; cf. Josh 17:11 (‫יבלעם‬).

Form/Structure/Setting

This pericope is composed of three major parts: (1) a genealogy extending from Ephraim to Joshua, vv 20–21a, 25–27; (2) a historical notice centering upon the birth of Beriah, vv 21b–24; and (3) a list of villages occupied by the sons of Joseph, vv 28–29, which in its present setting also serves to unite and conclude the notices concerning both Manasseh (vv 14–19) and Ephraim.

The genealogy that stretches from Ephraim to Joseph is recognized as a unity by its form (X, his son Y, his son Z), which is interrupted by the mention of Ezer and Elead in v 21b and resumed again abruptly in vv 25–27. (The antecedent of the first pronominal suffix "his" in v 25 is unclear.) This list is related to the only other genealogical list pertaining to Ephraim available to us (Num 26:35–36), but direct dependence is unlikely. In the Numbers passage, four families of Ephraimitic background are named: Shuthelah, Beker, Tahan, and Eran (ערן, תחן, בכר, שותלה). The first three are termed families (משפחות) of the "sons of Ephraim"; the last, Eran, is derived through Shuthelah. While Shuthelah occurs in our list twice (vv 20, 21), in form identical to that in Numbers, the following two sons have different but closely related names, Bered (ברד) and Tahath (תחת), the latter occurring twice in v 20. (A similar Tahan [תחן] is also found in v 25.) A name easily associated with Shuthelah's son Eran (ערן) is lacking in Chronicles, although some see similarities in Ladan (לעדן), v 26. An Elishamah, son of Ammihud, is the Ephraimitic representative involved in the census of Num 1:10, but nowhere else is Joshua or his father Nun (Josh 24:29) associated with other parts of the genealogy.

The repetition of various names in the genealogy (Shuthelah, Tahath) and the similarity in others (Bered, v 20, and Zabad, v 21; Eleadah, v 20, and Ladan, v 26; Tahath, v 20 *twice* and Taha, v 25) suggests that the present list may be a combination of two earlier lists that were parallel but divergent. This impression is strengthened when we note that according to the present form of the text (in which Bered and Tahath are considered the son and grandson respectively of Shuthelah rather than his brothers, as would appear to be the case in Num 26) Joshua would belong to the seventeenth generation of Ephraim, entailing a period much too long between Exodus and conquest. The occurrence of a single genealogy spanning seventeen generations would in itself be very unusual (see "The Genealogical Prologue" beginning on p. 1).

That the narrative beginning with Ezer and Elead (v 21b) lies outside this framework is shown both by the omission of the expected בנו "his son" after each and by the fact that they are viewed as sons of Ephraim (v 22) and not as his descendants of the ninth generation. The etiology of vv 24–25 may represent another originally independent fragment.

Vv 28–29 record dwelling places of Joseph, apparently divided between Ephraim (v 28) and Manasseh (v 29). The change of terminology introduced here (i.e., Joseph instead of Ephraim and Manasseh), coupled with the fact that he considers other such lists of possessions as later additions, has led Rudolph (73–74) to consider this one a later addition also. It is, however, at least plausible that the author who in 1 Chr 2:2 has spoken of Joseph rather than Ephraim and Manasseh has again joined the two through this more comprehensive terminology.

Comment

Ephraim was Joseph's younger son, born of Asenath, daughter of the high priest of On (Gen 41:52; 46:20), adopted by Jacob with his brother Manasseh, and treated, some say, as his firstborn (see on 5:1). (For the general history of the tribe, see Elliger, "Ephraim," *IDB* 2:119–21.)

In the listings of Chronicles, Ephraim precedes Manasseh in 1 Chr 12:31–32 [30–31]; 27:20; while Manasseh is first in 1 Chr 6:46–51 (dependent upon Josh 21:5–20); 7:20; and 2 Chr 34:9. Chronicles contains much special Ephraim material, much of it having to do with military expeditions and reform movements of Judean kings in the north (cf. Braun, *JBL* 96 [1977] 59–62).

The significance of the tribes of Ephraim in the Israelite confederacy can be seen from the names of some of the leaders of the tribe: Joshua, Samuel, Saul and Jeroboam. Elliger (*IDB* 2:120), who does not believe Shechem was an Ephraimite town, believes Ephraim's rise to special prominence began with the shift of the central sanctuary from Shechem to Shiloh. After the Syro-Ephraimitic conflict of 734–732 B.C., when Israel lost her more peripheral areas, Ephraim became synonymous with Israel, and the name Ephraim is often found as a designation for the entire northern nation (cf. Hos 7:1; 11:8).

20–21a, 25–27 The Ephraimite genealogy has as its goal the well known hero of the conquest, Joshua. We know nothing of the other individuals named prior to Ammihud, except for those who are or may be mentioned in Num 26. Their names are otherwise unknown in Ephraimite circles. Rudolph (72) may well be right in his contention that Resheph represents partial dittography of the preceding Rephah (note also the absence of בנו "his son" after Rehah). While Ammihud and Elishama are Ephraimites known from Numbers, as noted above, only here are they brought into the genealogy of Joshua.

21b–24 Ezra and Elead are set forth as "sons of Ephraim" (cf. v 20) killed in an attack upon Gath. The identification and location of this "Gath" is problematic, but sentiment seems to favor identification not with the better known Philistine Gath but with the Gittaim of 2 Sam 4:3 (cf. Mazar, "Gath and Gittaim," *IEJ* 4 [1954] 227–35; Stinespring, "Gath," *IDB* 2:355–56) as the locale and date to which the account should be assigned. Since Ephraim was born in Egypt (Gen 46:20), it is unlikely he was personally involved in such an event. The incident referred to would then have been one related to individuals who either subsequently or previously became identified with Ephraim, and may have occurred either in the patriarchal period or in the days of Joshua and the judges. The tribal character of the reference is apparent also in that Ephraim's "brothers" join him in mourning his deceased sons, although the biblical record knows of only a single brother of Ephraim, i.e., Manasseh. This event forms the basis, however, for the birth and naming of Beriah (בריעה), whose name is explained etymologically as related to this evil (רעה). This is not a scientific, but a folk etymology, as may be seen from the fact that the preposition ב "in" must be prefixed to the common רעה to secure a sound approximating that of Beriah. While v 24 may represent a completely separate genealogical fragment, in its present context Sherrah represents Beriah's daughter, who is uniquely named the founder of the two Beth-horons. On these cities, located on the south border of Ephraim (Josh 18:13–14), and their traditional association with Joshua, see Reed, "Beth-horon," *IDB* 1:393–94. See also 2 Chr 8:5; 25:13, which relates an attack by Ephraimites upon Beth-horon in the time of Amaziah. Uzzen-sheerah is otherwise unknown.

28–29 (For the specific locations, see Curtis, 154–55; Rudolph, 74; and the various entries in *IDB.*) The cities appear to represent the southern and northern limits of the combined territories of Ephraim and Manasseh according to the lists of Josh 16–18, although the content of vv 20–27 would lead us to expect a list of Ephraimitic cities only. This impression is heightened by the postscript of v. 29b, which encompasses both Ephraim and Manasseh as the "sons of Joseph, the son of Israel." Although vv 28–29 are not formally so divided (unless the nebulous ועל ידי בני מנשה "alongside the sons of Manasseh" of v 29 be so understood), v 28 appears in general agreement with cities allotted to Ephraim in Josh 16:5–10; v 29 is even more clearly related to those of Manasseh in Josh 17:11. Ayyah (v 28) is otherwise unknown. Although Bethel was conquered by the Joseph tribes (Judg 1:22), it lay on the border with Benjamin and was apparently assigned to the latter (Josh 18:22). The assignment of Shechem is problematic and doubtless reflects various historical periods. Although within the limits of Manasseh (Josh 17:7), it is apparently assigned to Ephraim (Josh 20:7; 21:21), perhaps, as suggested by Myers (56), on the basis of the curious notice of Josh 16:9, which refers to towns in Manasseh set aside for Ephraimites. More immediately, 1 Chr 7:19, as we have seen, relates Shechem to Manasseh, contrary to v 28, which groups it with other cities of Ephraim.

We are thus again faced with the difficulty of ascribing this unevenness either to a single author or of proposing ongoing editorial activity. Since the headings of neither vv 14 nor 20 anticipate such a conclusion, and vv 19 and 28 are not in harmony, the latter seems more likely. Moreover, since the beginning of v 29 is unclear, this wording too may result from the attempt to place a passage from another context into its present Ephraim + Manasseh = Joseph form, probably suggested by Num 26:37.

Explanation

Various snippets of information relating to Ephraim and Manasseh have here been assembled by the writer, or probably, writers, including a linear genealogy ostensibly stretching from Ephraim to Joshua, as well as brief historical notes and a list of tribal possessions. Especially this last item relates to both Ephraim and Manasseh, in accord with Num 26:37, just as the previous unit has dealt with both East and West Manasseh, although only the latter would be expected in view of the earlier treatment of East Manasseh (5:23–26). This lack of uniform perspective may be due to divergent sources utilized by a single writer or to different writers.

In view of the strong apologetic in favor of Joseph in 5:1–2, the scant information found here is surprising. Nevertheless, the writer(s) affirms, as has been his practice, that these tribes, composing the center of northern Israel, represent an essential ingredient in God's plan. Any supposed condemnation of the north based on the mention of Shechem, as seen, e.g., by Rudolph, is so subtle as to be pointless. Ephraim is the tribe of Joshua, the successor of Moses, who gave Israel its territory in Canaan. Ephraim and Manasseh, like Judah and Benjamin, continue to form the heart and core of the Chronicler's concern (cf. 2 Chr 31:1).

Descendants of Asher (7:30–40)

Bibliography

Abel, F.-M. "Une mention biblique du Birzeit." *RB* 46 (1937) 217. **Elliger, K.** "Asher." *IDB* 1:249–40. ———. "Tribes, Territories of." *IDB* 4:707–8.

Translation

30 *The sons of Asher: Imnah,* [a] *Ishvah, Ishvi,* [a] *and Beriah (Serah was their sister).*
31 *The sons of Beriah: Heber and Malchiel. (He was the father of Birzaith.* [a] *)*
32 *Heber was the father of Japhlet, Shomer,* [a] *Hotham, and their sister Shua.*
33 *The sons of Japhlet: Pasach, Bimhal, and Ashvath—these are the sons of Japhlet.*
34 *The sons of his brother* [a] *Shemer:* [b] *Rohgah, Jehubbah,* [c] *and Aram.*
35 *The son* [a] *of Helem* [b] *his brother: Zophah, Imna, Shelesh, and Amal.*
36 *The sons of Zophah: Suah, Harnepher, Shual,* [a] *Beri, Imrah,* [a] 37 *Bezer, Hod, Shamma, Shilshah, Ithran,* [a] *and Beera.*
38 *The sons of Jether:* [a] *Jephunneh, Pispa, and Ara.*
39 *The sons of Ulla:* [a] *Arah, Hanniel, and Rizia.*
40 *All these were descendants of Asher, heads of father's houses, chosen ones, valiant warriors, the heads of princes, and their military roster listed twenty-six thousand men.*

Notes

30.a-a. ישוה "Ishvah" and ישוי "Ishvi." Probably variants of the same name; cf. Num 26:44, which names only ישוי. Our text is based on Gen 46:17, which, however, includes both forms (see *Form* below).
31.a. Q ברזית "Birzaith"; K בְּרְזוֹת "Birzoth" (or בְּבְרָזוֹת[?]).
32.a. MT שׁומר "Shomer"; G^B Σαμερ "Samer" (cf. v 34).
34.a. MT שׁמר "Shemer"; MS G^A AL al Vg שׁומר. See n. 32.a.
34.b. Reading אחיו רהגה "his brother Rohgah" for MT (Q) אחי ורהגה "my brother and Rohgah."
34.c. Q וחבה "and Hubbah"; K יחבה "Jehubbah."
35.a. Seb nonn MSS G^L Vg ובני "and sons of."
35.b. Some read חותם "Hotham," as in v 32 (cf. Rudolph, *BHS*).
36.a-a. Heb. וברי וימרה "and Beri and Imrah." Read perhaps ובני ימנע "and the sons of Imna." Cf. v 35 and omission of conj on בצר "Bezer" (v 37).
37.a. Ithran (יתרן). Read perhaps יתר "Jether" as in v 38 (or vice versa).
38.a. See n. 37.a.
39.a. Ulla (עלא). Some would read ארא "Ara" (v 38), שׁועא "Shua" (v 32), or עמל "Amal" (v 35). Cf. Rudolph, 74.

Form/Structure/Setting

This genealogy of Asher consists of three parts. (1) The immediate descendants of Asher, vv 30–31a, which are derived from Gen 46:17. (2) Further descendants of Asher, vv 31b–39, for which we have no parallel source. (3)

V 40, the conclusion which characterizes those named as military men and gives their number.

That vv 30–31 are taken from Gen 46:17, rather than Num 26:44, may be seen from the following observations. (1) In Gen 46, Asher has four sons, while Num 26 names only three (see n. 30.a-a.). (2) Gen 46 lists Serah immediately after Asher's sons and terms her their sister (אחתם). (3) Num 26:46 instead lists Serah after Beriah's sons and designates her as Asher's daughter (בת). In neither case, however, does the lineage extend beyond Beriah's sons Heber and Malchiel.

There are no known parallels to the remainder of the list. Since Rudolph and Noth believe the original writer was always dependent upon Num 26, these facts confirm for them the view that the current section is secondary, the author's original genealogy of Asher standing in the "gap" of 7:12–13 (Rudolph, 75; Noth, Ü.S., 122).

For the location and history of Asher see the article of Elliger cited above. Asher usually follows his older brother Gad in the OT lists (cf. Gen 46:16). In P, Asher is usually separated from Gad, appearing instead at the end of lists between the sons of Rachel's maid, Dan and Naphtali (Elliger, IDB 1:250). 1 Chr 12:36, like our present list, places Asher last in the twelve-tribe series; however, 1 Chr 6:47, 59–60 [62, 74–75], dependent upon the list of Josh 21, places Asher between Issachar and Naphtali. The list of David's officials in 1 Chr 27 mentions neither Asher nor Gad. Asher is included in 2 Chr 30:11 with Manasseh and Zebulon as tribes who "repented" (נכנעו) and came to Jerusalem for Hezekiah's Passover, but his name is lacking in v 18 in a similar notice.

The form of vv 32–39 is what we have termed mixed, and the terminology generally parallels that of vv 30–31, i.e., "the sons of X: Y and Z." Subsequent listings continue the lineage through only one of the sons previously named, who may be, but is not necessarily, the eldest. The number of those listed in each generation varies from three to eleven. The following variations from this common pattern are noteworthy. (1) The first additional name included in our list, Birzaith, is added to the end of the list as known from Genesis (and Numbers) parenthetically in the form, "He was the father of Birzaith" (הוא אבי ברזית) (v 31 Q). (2) The notice concerning Malchiel's brother, Heber, takes the form "Heber begat . . . : (וחבר הוליד), which occurs nowhere else in this unit, but which is familiar to us from P in general and from previous portions of Chronicles, e.g., 2:10–13, 44; 4:2, 8; 5:30–41 [6:3–14]. (3) In the case of Heber (v 32), through whom all of Asher's descendants listed in vv 32–38 (39?) appear to be traced, parallel lines are traced through his sons Japhet (v 33), Shemer/Shomer (v 34), and apparently Helem (v 35), who is marked as "his (i.e., Shemer's) brother." Moreover, Heber's daughter Shua is also named (v 32), as was Asher's daughter Serah in v 30. (4) The Helem whose descendants (Heb. בן "son," singular only here in this pericope) are given in v 35 is not listed as Heber's son in v 32 (although some would read חותם "Hotham" here as in v 32; see n. 35.b.). (5) In at least two cases what appear to be different forms of the name of an individual occur in our text. (Cf. Shomer [v 32] with Shemer [v 34]; and Zophar's son Ithran [יתרן, v 37] and Jether [יתר] in the following verse.) (6) The Ulla

of v 39 is not related to the list in any way. Although many would alleviate
this difficulty through emendation (see n. 39.a.), this happens frequently
enough that it may be said to be a common feature of the genealogy (cf.
Shemidah in 7:19).

Such features suggest that the genealogy as we have it represents a collection of disparate notices unified loosely around the person of Heber. On
the basis of the variations in similar names, we may assume either that the
author(s) did not identify the names in question, and so has handed them
on as disconnected elements, or has chosen this rather unusual way to state
that the individuals in question, though known by various names, are in fact
the same.

The data of v 40 are couched in the terminology of the military census
list like that of 7:1–5, 6–12, and suggests that it too had its origin in a situation
such as we posited for 7:6–12, i.e., a military enrollment. Since there is no
ostensible reason for the invention of such material, it should be assumed
to rest upon ancient records.

Comment

For vv 30–31a see the Genesis commentaries listed in the *Bibliography* on
p. 13. Of the remaining names included here, we have no additional information. Birzaith (v 31b) has on the basis of the form (אֲבִי בִרְזָיִת) been taken
as a place name (cf., e.g., 1 Chr 2:50–55) and identified with modern Birzeit,
north of Tyre (Guthrie, "Birzaith," *IDB* 1:441; Abel, *RB* 46 [1937] 217).
The fact that Beriah is also known as an Ephraimite (v 23) has led some to
posit relationships between Asher and Ephraim (cf. Curtis, 155), but such a
conjecture seems hazardous. On the other hand, one Shemer is known as
the original owner of the hill upon which Omri built Samaria (1 Kgs 16:24),
and the name of his city, called שֹׁמְרוֹן "Samaria," shows the same variation
from that of its previous owner as does Shemer and Shomer in vv 32 and
34. (R. J. Coggins does not to my knowledge mention this possibility in his
discussion of Samaritan nomenclature; cf. *Samaritans and Jews*, 8–12.)

Explanation

Such full notice of a tribe of peripheral importance is surely striking, and
the reason for its inclusion is not clear. Perhaps some clue may be seen in
v 40, which, while similar to the notices of 7:4, 9, 11, also seems more extrava-
gant. The reference to the warriors as בְּרוּרִים ("chosen, select," only here
and 1 Chr 9:22, 16:41; Neh 5:18 with this meaning) is unique to this passage,
as is the title רָאשֵׁי הַנְּשִׂיאִים "heads of the princes." The notice of their
mustering is equally prolix, although the number counted (26,000) is small
contrasted with the figures of Num 1:40; 2:28 (41,500), Num 26:47 (53,400),
and 1 Chr 12:37 [36] (40,000). Perhaps the number originally referred only
to the sons of Heber (cf. 1 Chr 7:7, 9, 11).

Additional Descendants of Benjamin
(8:1–40)

Bibliography

(See *Bibliography* on 1 Chr 7:6–13)

Translation

[1] *Benjamin was the father of Bela his firstborn,* [a] *Ashbel the second, Aharah* [b] *the third,* [2] *Noah the fourth, and Rapha the fifth.* [3] *Bela also had sons: Addar,* [a] *Gera the father of Ehud,* [b] [4] *Abishua, Naaman, Ahoah,* [5] *Gera,* [a] *Shephuphan,* [b] *and Humram.* [c]

[6] *These are the sons of Ehud.* [a] *They are the heads of fathers' houses of the inhabitants of Geba, who were moved* [b] *to Manahath:* [7] . . . *and Naaman,* [a] *Ahijah, and Gera, who moved them* [b] *and became the father of Uzza and Ahihud.*

[8] *After* [a] *he had sent away his wives Hushim and Baara, Shaharaim had children in the territory of Moab.* [9] *Of his wife Hodesh he fathered Jobab, Zibia, Mesha, Malcam,* [10] *Jeuz, Sachia, and Mirmah. These were his sons, heads of fathers'* [a] *houses.* [11] *Of Hushim he fathered Abitub and Elpaal.* [12] *Elpaal's sons were Eber, Misham, and Shemed. (It was he who built Ono and Lod and its villages.)* [a]

[13] *Beriah* [a] *and Shema* [b] *were the heads of fathers'* [c] *houses of the inhabitants of Aijalon. They routed the inhabitants of Gath.* [14] *Their brothers* [a] *were Shashak and Jeremoth.* [b] [15] *Zebadiah, Arad, Eder,* [16] *Michael, Ishpah, and Joha were the sons of Beriah.* [17] *Zebadiah, Meshullam, Hizki, Heber,* [18] *Ishmerai, Izliah, and Jobab were the sons of Elpaal.* [19] *Jakim, Zichri, Zabdi,* [20] *Elienai, Zillethai, Eliel,* [21] *Adaiah, Beraiah, and Shimrath were the sons of Shimei.* [a] [22] *Ishpan, Eber, Eliel,* [23] *Abdon, Zichri, Hanan,* [24] *Hananiah, Elam, Anthothijah, Iphdeiah, and Penuel were the sons of Shashak.* [26] *Shamsherai, Shehariah, Athaliah,* [27] *Jaareshiah, Elijah, and Zichri were the sons of Jeroham.* [a] [28] *These were the heads of father's houses in their generations, chiefs.* [a] [b] *These dwelt in Jerusalem.* [b]

[29] *In Gibeon dwelt* [ab] *the father of Gibeon (his wife's name was Maacah),* [30] *his* [a] *firstborn Abdon, as well as Zur, Kish, Baal,* [b] *Nadab,* [31] *Gedor, Ahio,* [a] *and Zecher.* [bc] [32] *Mikloth was the father of Shimeah.* [a] *These also dwelt opposite their brothers, in Jerusalem* [b] *with their brothers.* [b] [33] *Ner was the father of Kish,* [a] *Kish was the father of Saul, and Saul was the father of Jonathan, Malchishua, Abinadab,* [b] *and Eshbaal.* [c] [34] *The son of Jonathan was Merib-baal,* [a] *and Merib-baal* [a] *was the father of Micah.* [35] *The sons of Micah: Pithrin, Melech,* [a] *Tarea,* [b] *and Ahaz.* [c] [36] *Ahaz was the father of Jehoaddah,* [a] *Jehoaddah was the father of Alemeth, Azmaveth, and Zimri, Zimri was the father of Moza,* [37] *and Moza was the father of Binea.* [a] *Raphah* [b] *was his son, Eleasah his son, Azel his son.* [38] *Azel had six sons, and these are their names: Azrikam, Bocheru,* [a] *Ishmael, Sheariah,* [b] *Obadiah, and Hanan. All* [c] *these were the sons of Azel.*

[39] *The sons of Eshek his brother: Ulam his firstborn, Jeush the second, and Eliphelet*

the third. ⁴⁰ *Ulam's sons were men valiant in warfare, bowmen, having many sons and grandsons, one hundred and fifty.* ᵃ

All these were sons of Benjamin.

Notes

1.a. Gen 46:21; 1 Chr 7:6 וּבֶכֶר "and Becher" is found. Perhaps the enumeration has here resulted from first misunderstanding (וּ) בֶכֶר as the common "firstborn" rather than as the proper name Becher, after which other ordinals were added, making a simple emendation impossible.

1.b. Num 26:38 וַאֲחִירָם "and Ahiram."

3.a. 9 MSS Gᴬ⁺ᴹˢˢ Gen 46:21, Num 26:20 אַרְד "Arad"; cf. 1 Chr 7:12 אַחַר "Ahar."

3.b. Gᴸ καὶ Αωα "and Aoa." Read perhaps אֲבִי אֵהוּד "father of Ehud"; cf. v 6a, which Rudolph (*BHS*) would transpose here. Judg 3:15 mentions one אֵהוּד בֶּן־גֵּרָא "Ehud, son of Gera" as a בֶּן־הַיְמִינִי "Benjaminite."

4.a. *BHS* אֲחִיָּה "Ahijah"; cf. Gᴮ Syr α′ and v. 7.

5.a. > Syr.

5.b. Num 26:39 שְׁפוּפָם "Shephupham"; Gᴮ Σεφφαμ "Seppham."

5.c. Syr Num 26:39 חוּפָם "Hupham."

6.a. Reading אֵהוּד "Ehud" for אֵחוּד "Echud"; cf. n. 3.b.

6.b. Understanding the 3 c pl וַיַּגְלוּם impersonally, "they were moved," i.e., emigrated. Cf. GKC, §§ 144f-g.

7.a. The text is difficult, and an omission has perhaps occurred. The presence of the conj makes it difficult to understand Naaman as the first of Ehud's sons, although this seems to be demanded by the context. Otherwise no sons of Ehud are listed, but cf. v 6a.

7.b. KJV "Gera, he removed them . . ."; RSV's "that is Heglam" is alone among modern translations in understanding הֶגְלָם "Heglam" as a proper noun.

8.a. מִן "after" is temporal with the inf; GKC, § 164g.

10.a. רָאשֵׁי אָבוֹת "heads of fathers"; see *Introduction*.

12.a. It is possible to understand those named in v 14 as Elpaal's sons also, but this seems less likely in view of the structure of vv 14–28. See *Form* below.

13.a. Many insert אֶלְפַּעַל "Elpaal" with v 18; cf. *BHS*.

13.b. V 20 שִׁמְעִי "Shimei."

13.c. See n. 10.a.

14.a. Reading אֲחִיהֶם "their brothers" with Gᴸ; Heb. וְאַחְיוֹ "and Ahio" (?). However, no sons for this "Ahio" are listed in the following verses, as is the case with the other four individuals of vv 13–14.

14.b. Read perhaps יְרוֹחָם "Jeroham"; cf. v 27, or vice versa. See also n. 28.b-b.

21.a. See n. 13.b.

27.a. See n. 14.b.

28.a. The repetition of רָאשִׁים "heads, chiefs" probably results from the conflation of two concluding formulas.

28.b-b. Rudolph (78) would transfer these words to the end of v 14.

29.a. G Syr יָשַׁב "he dwelt"(sg), but cf. 9:35.

29.b. 9:35 G Tg Vg Q + יְעִיאֵל "Jeiel"; K יְעוּאֵל "Joel."

30.a. G "her son."

30.b. Gᴬᵃˡ 9:36 + וְנֵר] "and Ner."

31.a. G וְאַחְיוֹ "and Ahio" (9:37 G καὶ ἀδελφός[-oι] "and brother[s]").

31.b. 9:37 וּזְכַרְיָה "and Zechariah."

31.c. 9:37 Gᴮ Syr Vg α′ + וּמִקְלוֹת "and Mikloth."

32.a. 9:38 שִׁמְאָם "Shimeam."

32.b-b. The phrase is parallel with נֶגֶד אֲחֵיהֶם "opposite their brothers" and may represent either the inclusion of an explanatory gl or the conflation of synonymous variants.

33.a. Some would read "Abner."

33.b. G Αμιναδαβ "Aminadab."

33.c. Syr יִשְׁוִי "Ishvi"; cf. 1 Sam 14:49, *BHS*.

34.a. Gᴮ (Syr) Μεριβααλ "Meribaal"; cf. 9:40 מְרִי־בַעַל "Meri-baal."

35.a. Gᴮᴸ καὶ Μελχ(ε)ηλ "and Melch(e)al" (9:41 Gᴮ και Μαλαχ "and Malach"; Gᴬᵃˡ Μαλωχ "Maloch"; Gᴸ Μελχιηλ "Melchial").

35.b. ‎ותחרע 9:41 "and Tahrea."
35.c. > 9:41.
36.a. Gᴮ Iαδα "Jada"; Gᴬᵃˡ Iωιαδα = ‎יהוידע "Jehoiadah." Cf. 9:42 ‎יערה "Jarah."
37.a. G Bα(a)να = ‎בענא "Baana."
37.b. G Pαφαι(a) "Raphai(ah)"; 9:43 ‎ורפיה "and Rephaiah."
38.a. MT ‎בָכְרוּ "Bocheru"; reading with some MSS G Syr as ‎בְכָרוֹ "Bochero."
38.b. Read as ‎עזריה ("Azariah")? Cf. Gᴸ BHS.
38.c. > 9:44.
39.a. Vv 39–40 are lacking after 1 Chr 9:44.
39.b. Gᴮ Aσηλ "Aseel."
40.a. Gᴬⱽ reads 90.

Form/Structure/Setting

As we have noted in the *Introduction* (pp. 10–12; see also under 7:6–12), the two (or three) separate listings devoted to Benjamin are exceptional and reflect the intense interest in Benjamin in the post-exilic period, which has occasioned ongoing editorial updating. The genealogy of 7:6–12, we have noted, already differs from that of Gen 46, although remnants of the latter are to be seen, e.g., in vv 6 and 12. Chap. 8 also shows evidence of continuing development, as indicated below. Comparison with the genealogy of Saul in 9:35–44, which seems appropriately placed in view of the narrative of Saul introduced in chap. 10, suggests that 8:29–38 is derived from chap. 9, rather than vice versa, although the opposite is maintained by some. In particular, it is difficult to account for the inclusion of 8:28 within the context of chap. 8 except to assume that is has been borrowed from chap. 9:34, where it is appropriate, at the time when the Saulide genealogy of 9:35–44 was appended to 8:29–32, probably because of the mention of Kish in 8:30. Vv 39–40 represent a continual elaboration of the Benjaminite line.

This chapter is commonly divided into four parts, each of which is marked by a discontinuity of names and perhaps by a different geographical setting:

vv 1–7, the sons of Benjamin and Ehud (vv 6–7) at Geba;
vv 8–12, the sons of Shaharaim in Moab, Ono, and Lod;
vv 13–28, the Benjaminites at Aijalon, Gath, and Jerusalem;
vv 29–40, the Benjaminites in Gibeon, and the genealogy of Saul.

While this division adequately reflects the final form of the chapter, the tradition-history of the chapter appears complex. Vv 1–7 appear to be a conflation of variants of the identical list (see below). One would expect v 10b to conclude the list of Shaharaim's sons, but the descendants of the Hushim "sent away" in v 8 follow in vv 11–12 and, if the "Elpaal" of these verses is identified with the individual of the same name, in vv 13–27 as well. Vv 15–27 have a common format: "X and Y were the sons of Z," in which the sons of each of the four brothers (?) listed in vv 13–14, plus Elpaal, are given. On the other hand, the unevenness of vv 13–14, as well as the absence of Elpaal, is apparent. While the names Beraiah and Shashak are identical in form in both parts of the unit, the Shema (‎שמע) of v 13 seems to be represented in v 21 by Shimei (‎שמעי), and the Jeremoth of v 14 (‎ירמות) by Jeroham (‎ירחם) in v 27. Moreover, Elpaal (v 18) is absent from vv 13–14, but present as a son of Shaharaim and Hushim in v 11.

In addition, at first glance vv 6–27 (and 29–32) appear to be parallel in listing settlements of Benjaminites at various localities throughout the land— Geba, Moab, Ono, Lod, Aijalon, and Gibeon. V 28, however, seems to contradict this pattern by bringing at least many of the Benjaminites listed previously together into Jerusalem. (A similar notice in v 32 is more easily understood.) This same v 28, which is apparently derived from 9:34 with the alteration of only one word, also appears to mark the conclusion of the pericope. While the shorter units above are noted as containing the "heads of fathers' houses" (vv 6, 10, 13), v 28 names them as "heads of father's houses in their generations, heads." In so doing, it appears that the list of Benjaminites in Gibeon (vv 29–32), including one Kish, has now been separated from the foregoing, to be joined with the remainder of Saul's genealogy (vv 33–38), probably occasioned by the mention of Kish.

The final effect of the imposition of this framework is that isolated references to Benjaminites dwelling at different places and perhaps at different times have been brought together under geographical rubrics such as 8:28, 32 (cf. 9:3), i.e., within the immediate confines of Jerusalem. With this in mind, it is perhaps pointless to seek to determine the historical period reflected in the list (cf. Rudolph, 77; Curtis, 157). The final form of the chapter must be as late as the exile, as evidenced by the 14 generations following Saul. Moreover, the prominent position of the cities referred to in the post-exilic period (see below in *Comment*) suggests that at a minimum the post-exilic situation governed the inclusion of these elements within the chapter.

Vv 1–2 differ from all other accounts of Benjamin's sons in that it names and enumerates five sons of Benjamin, not including Becher (cf. 1 Chr 7:6–13, *Form/Structure/Setting*), whose name, however, lies hidden in the "his firstborn" (בכרו) of v 1. Sons ascribed directly to Benjamin in some traditions are in others derived through Bela, but this practice is compounded here. Gen 46:21 attributes nine sons to Benjamin (five of whom, however, G derives through Bela), and 1 Chr 7:7 knows five (different) sons of Bela in addition to three of Benjamin. 1 Chr 8 shows continued elaboration of this tradition in listing five sons of Benjamin and eight (or nine) of Bela.

The complex nature of the tradition is nowhere more apparent than here. 1 Chr 8:1–5 cannot be derived directly from any other known tradition. Rather some of the names appear to be transcriptional variations of each other. Cf. Achrach (אחרח) and Ahoah (אחוח), variants of Ahiram (אחירם, Num 26:38); Nohah (נוחה) and Naaman (נעמן); Rapha (רפא) and Gera (גרא), whose name appears twice in the list of Bela's sons in vv 3–4 and still again as son of Ehud (?) in v 7. The names of Bela's sons Shephuphan and Huram continue the variations on the Muppim/Huppim of Gen 46:21 and the Shuppupham/Huphan of Num 26:39, and Addar (v 6) is probably the Ard of Gen 46:21 and Num 26:40. While any of these identifications can be disputed, still others can be proposed (cf. Curtis, 157–58). Taken as a whole, they indicate the long history of transmission in which variations of Benjamin's descendants were adjusted and related to both Benjamin and his son Bela. Only (Abi-)Ehud and Abishua are unrepresented in earlier lists. The inclusion of the former is doubtless due to the desire to include the famous Benjaminite judge of that time (Judg 3:15); that of the latter is more problematic (cf. Curtis, 158, who cites Gen 38:2 and 1 Sam 13:17 unconvincingly).

The names of Ehud's sons (vv 6–7), though textually dubious, continue this pattern of duplication and variation. Both Naaman and Gera are names of brothers of Ehud's father Gera, the latter named twice, as mentioned above. Ahijah is quite possibly a variant of Ahoah (v 4) (F. T. Schumacher, "Ahijah," *IDB* 1:67–68). Uzzah recalls Bela's son Uzzi of 1 Chr 7:7; Ahihud (אחיהד) perhaps pointed to Uzzah as Bela's son (cf. 1 Chr 7:7) and hence "brother of (Ahi-)Ehud."

Of the names of vv 8–27 little can be said, although the occurence of a Hushim in a Benjaminite genealogy, albeit as a female (vv 8, 11), is suggestive in view of 7:12. V 28, as indicated above, has been transposed to this location from 9:34.

Vv 29–32 may present a part of an abbreviated genealogy of Saul, but this is uncertain (see *Comment*). Besides Kish, only Zur (צור) may be identical to the צרור "Zeror" of 1 Sam 9:1. The parallel passage in 1 Chr 9:36–37 includes Ner as a brother of Kish, although this would appear to violate v 39, where Ner is father of Kish.

The mention of Kish, the name of Saul's father (cf. 1 Sam 9:1) has at any rate led to the inclusion of Saul's genealogy. In the genealogical data of Samuel, however, Ner and Kish are more easily understood as brothers, as in 1 Chr 9:36. 1 Sam 9:1 is clear in making Kish the son of Abiel, and 1 Sam 14:51 does the same for Ner (and probably Kish as well). Ner is then the father of Abner, probably the same as Saul's well-known captain, who would then be his first cousin. It is objected that 1 Sam 14:50 must refer to Abner as Saul's uncle, rather than Ner, but no convincing evidence has been cited as to why such an appositional phrase cannot modify either element within a construct chain. Attempts such as those of E. Dalglish ("Ner," *IDB* 3:536–37) and even Rudolph (81), which calls for emending the text of 1 Sam 9:1 by inserting "son of Ner" following Kish, appear to be concerned about a kind of consistency which we repeatedly find absent in the genealogical data before us.

Apart from the parallel in 9:39, all of Saul's four sons are not listed together elsewhere. 1 Sam 14:49 lists Jonathan, Ishvi (ישוי = יהוה איש "man of Yahweh" [?]; an alteration attesting a distaste for the name Baal corresponding to Ish-baal, "Man of Baal," in our text) and Malchishua; 1 Sam 31:2 (= 1 Chr 10:2) names Jonathan, Malchishua, and Abinadab as Saul's sons who died before the Philistines. Just as Ishvi/Ishbaal is otherwise known in the Deuteronomic history as Ishbosheth ("Man of Shame," 2 Sam 4:4), so Jonathan's son Meribbaal (מריב בעל here, but the reading of 9:40, מרי בעל "Hero of Baal," is probably correct) occurs regularly in the Deuteronomic history with the Baal component of the name altered to בֹּשֶׁת־, for the resulting Mephibosheth ("he who scatters shame" or "from the mouth of shame"). After Meribaal's son Micah, no parallel line of Saul's descendants is to be found in Scriptures.

The form of the genealogical note which serves as the basis for the structure of the chapter is "X begat Y"; cf. vv 1, 7, 8, 9, 11, 32, 33–37a. Other constructions occur within the smaller units, however, reflecting either their varied backgrounds or a simple desire for variation (cf. 3a, 6a, 39, 40 and especially vv 14–27, where the uncommon form "A, B, C, and D were the sons of

X"). Vv 39–40, however, resume the more common "the sons of X: A and B," and the military terminology of v 40, unique here within this chapter, suggests again an alternate source such as we found in 7:6–13. Other stylistic features of the chapter include the use of "(all) these were the sons of . . ." in a concluding rather than an introductory sense (cf. 10b, 38b, the all-inclusive 40b, and probably 6a); "these were the heads of fathers . . . (perhaps 6b, 10b, 13a at the beginning); and the concluding of a narrative with a brief historical note (cf. 12b, 13b, 6b [text difficult]).

Comment

1–5 For discussion of the sons of Benjamin and Bela, see the remarks under *Form/Structure/Setting* on 1 Chr 7:6–11. The name of Benjamin's son Becher, known to us from 1 Chr 7:6 and Gen 46:21 but absent from Num 26:38, lies hidden in "his firstborn" (n. 1.a.). Aharah, Nohah, and Rapha are otherwise unknown as sons of Benjamin, but probably represent variants of names known to us from Num 26 and Gen 46.

6–7 Ehud's sons are named in these verses as family heads of the inhabitants of Geba who were exiled or moved to Manahath. The reference is obscure. Geba (גבע) is a Levitical city of Benjamin (Josh 21:17; 1 Chr 6:60; Josh 18:24) which lay on the northern boundary of Judah six miles north-northeast of Jerusalem and was significant in the Philistine wars (W. Morton, "Geba," *IDB* 2:359). Geba was fortified by Asa (1 Kgs 15:22; 2 Chr 16:6) and occupied after the exile by Benjaminites (Ezra 2:26; Neh 7:30; 11:31; 12:29). Manahath is customarily identified with Malah, three miles southwest of Jerusalem (Aharoni, *Land,* 381, 296, map 26) (cf. 1 Chr 2: 52–54), although this is disputed by Rudolph (79), who insists upon a site in Edom (cf. 1 Chr 1:40). The short distance of the move suggests that we ought not think of an exile in the traditional sense, but of a less radical departure. The argument of Zobel ("גלה," *TDOT* 2:278) that the causative stems of גלה mean exclusively "to lead away into captivity" is not persuasive. The etymological data presented by Zobel himself (276) strongly suggests a simpler meaning "to emigrate." This also frees us from the difficulty of understanding why the name of the exiler is not given. The period and circumstances of the move are, however, obscure. In view of the activity of one Ehud, son of Gera, against the Moabites in the period of the judges (Judg 3:12–4:1), it is probably best to think of an event in that period (cf. v 8).

8–12 The details of these verses are equally sketchy. Rudolph (79) places the movement in the time of Josiah or better in the post-exilic period. The Hushim who figures so prominently in the textual difficulty of 1 Chr 7:12 and who is commonly assigned to Dan on the basis of Gen 46:23 appears here in the line of Benjamin (cf. Aharoni, *Land,* 222), although apparently as a female, the mother of Abitub and Elpaal (v 11). Of the individuals derived through Hodesh and Hushim we know nothing, although the association of Mesha with Moab is attested by the Moabite king of that name. The reference to the builder of Ono and Lod seems to connect most naturally to Shemed, although Curtis (160) refers it to Elpaal. Lod, the Lydda of Maccabean and NT times eleven miles southeast of Joppa, and Ono, seven miles southeast of Joppa, are well known in post-exilic times and were, together with Hadid, the home of 720 returning exiles (Ezra 2:33; Neh 7:37; 11:35), and seem to have been their westernmost dwelling (cf. Aharoni, *Land,* 356 and map 34; Avi-Yonah, *The Holy Land* [Grand Rapids: Baker Book House, 1966] 17–18). Ono was an ancient city, listed already in the Karnak list of Thutmose III, but the reference here could be to a rebuilding rather than to an initial foundation. However, it is not named in the Bible until Ezra-Nehemiah-Chronicles. Neh 6:2 assumes that Ono and Lod lay outside the jurisdiction of both Judah and Sanballat.

The ascription of Ono and Lod to Benjamin is difficult at any time, however, Myers (60) points to Josh 19:40–46, which places the border of Dan near Joppa. Perhaps when Dan fell into obscurity early (it is mentioned only two times in Chronicles), its territory was absorbed by Ephraim and Judah, and Judah and Benjamin then coalesced, as indicated by the emphasis upon Judah *and* Benjamin in Chronicles.

13–28 These verses speak of Benjaminites of Aijalon who "routed the inhabitants of Gath" (v 13), at least two of whom are listed as heads of families of Aijalon (v 13). Aijalon too is assigned to Dan (Josh 19:42), but lay on Ephraim's border and was dominated by it (Judg 1:35). As a Levitical city, it formed a portion of Dan's contribution in Josh 21:24, the reference to which is lacking in 1 Chr 6:54 [69]. Aijalon was fortified by Rehoboam (2 Chr 11:10) but was taken by the Philistines during Ahaz's reign (2 Chr 28:18). Though not mentioned in Ezra-Nehemiah, it would have lain within the territory of the restored Judah. However, of the cryptic reference to Gath (v 13) and of the families named we have no additional information. That the four individuals named in v 13 belong together in some sense seems apparent from the parallel way in which they, with Elpaal (v 18), are treated in the following sections. That they are brothers is possible if our reconstruction of the text is accepted (n. 14.a.). The most we can say is that the list intends to relate significant Benjaminite families at a certain period or periods of time and in various places, and that the various families seem to have traced their origins back to a common ancestor.

Taken in that connection, the summary note of v 28, which appears to contradict the obvious statements of vv 6, 8, 12, and 13 and place these miscellaneous groups in Jerusalem, imposes a certain unity to the whole. While it may be tempting at first to assume that v 28 referred only to various sons listed in vv 15–26, and not to vv 13 or 6–12, the all-inclusiveness of v 28 is clear. Previously we have read repeatedly of "heads of fathers' houses" (vv 6, 10, 13). Here, however, they are marked as *"heads of fathers according to their generations, chiefs,"* and, as if by way of a "trump card," their dwelling is placed in Jerusalem. Although this perspective may have been imported from 9:34, it is now the basic rubric covering all Benjaminite settlements (cf. 9:3 and the apparently meaningless but symbolic statements of 8:32 and 9:38).

29–32 The pattern of earlier sections of the chapter continues, listing Benjaminites dwelling in Gibeon. Gibeon is the well-known el-Jib six miles northwest of Jerusalem, assigned to Benjamin (Josh 18:25) and the site of Joab's battle with Abner (2 Sam 2:12–17). The men of Gibeon are also named among those who participated in rebuilding the walls of Jerusalem (Neh 3:7). Zur (צוּר) is perhaps to be associated with Zeror (צְרוֹר) in Saul's lineage in 1 Sam 9:1; and Kish is known as Saul's father from the same verse. The parallel in chap. 9 lists Ner (v 36) and Mikloth (מִקְלוֹת) (v. 37) among Jeiel's sons also. The other names listed here are unknown in connection with Benjamin or Saul; however, the retention of the name Baal (בַּעַל, v 30), the well-known Canaanite God, is noteworthy and suggests that the data of this list is either quite early or, more likely, quite late, when the threat of Canaanite syncretism was no longer strong (cf. Merib-baal, v 34). In apparent contradiction to v 29, v 32 places at least a part of this group of Benjaminites "next to" (נֶגֶד) their brothers in Jerusalem. While it may be possible to think of Gibeon as "next to" Jerusalem, this would not appear to be the most common understanding. Furthermore, the phrase added at the end of the verse, "with their brothers" (עִם־אֲחֵיהֶם), which may well have originated as a gloss, also seems to rule out that interpretation. However, such an understanding would fit in the total context of "those who dwelt in Jerusalem" of chap. 9, and it seems likely that the *non sequitur* here results from its problematic relationship to that chapter.

33–38 Saul's genealogy in vv 33–38 (9:39–44) was probably occasioned by the mention of Kish in v 30 (cf. 9:36) and, whether originally placed here or at the end of chap. 9, forms a bridge to the narrative of chap. 10 which begins with Saul's death in the Philistine war. At the same time, it reaches its goal in the family of Azel (v 38), whose six sons stand at the climax of the linear genealogy. The addition of Ner as a brother of Kish in 9:36 (see n. 30.a.) is probably an attempt to draw 29–32 and 33–38 closer together, as is the more explicit inclusion of Mikloth as his brother in 9:37 (n. 31.c.). (1 Chr 9:35 also adds the name of Jeiel as the father of Gibeon, pointing to a similar expansion of the tradition.) If vv 29–32 were originally conceived of as a genealogy of Saul, it would be expected that the locale indicated would be Gibeah (גִּבְעָה), Saul's birthplace, rather than Gibeon (גִּבְעוֹן); but perhaps Gibeon here reflects the original reading, or perhaps a change has been introduced reflecting the prominence of Gibeon in Chronicles as the site of the central sanctuary (cf. 2 Chr 1) or its significance in the post-exilic period (Neh 3:7). Moreover, the two sites are relatively close together and commonly confused in the OT.

Vv 33–38 comprise by far the most extensive genealogy of Saul in the Hebrew Scriptures, spanning fifteen generations. (For the earlier generations, see *Form/Structure/Setting* above.) Meribbaal's son Mica(h) is named also in 2 Sam 9:12, and his prominence is suggested here by the listing of his four sons, otherwise unknown, in v 35. The members of the following eleven generations are known to us only from this passage and its parallel in chap. 9. The genealogy ends with the six sons of Azel (v 38), who may be assumed to have been prominent in their day. This understanding, however, would seem to violate 1 Chr 10:6 which, in contrast to its *Vorlage* (1 Sam 31:6), makes the point that Saul, his three (!) sons, and his *entire house* perished. These fifteen generations, reminiscent of the genealogies of David and the Levites, would appear to bring us to the exilic or post-exilic period.

39–40 These verses are unattached to the preceding and differ also from the form predominant in most of the chapter. As appears to have been common in such genealogies, additional relevant data, although of a fragmentary character, was included as availability and interest dictated. In their present position, Eshek can be understood only as the brother of Azel, and that is of course possible. Alternatively, vv 39–40 may be understood as a disconnected fragment. The military vocabulary of v 40 suggests that this notice, like that of 1 Chr 7:6–13, stemmed from a military census list. Again, the listing of Eshek's three sons (v 39) would point to the prominence of his family.

Explanation

This extensive listing of Benjaminites reflects the widespread prominence and interest in that tribe seen in the book as a whole (see the *Introduction*) and recognized as central in the post-exilic period. Although most, if not all, of these genealogies stem from the more remote past, we may assume that the interest in such genealogies was keenest among those who wished to establish their own relationships to Israel through the tribe of Benjamin.

Individual notices within the chapter suggest that the genealogies reproduced here originally referred to Benjaminites living in certain specific localities, such as Geba, Moab, Ono, and Lod, and Gibeon. However, this understanding has been overlaid with another, apparently related to that seen in 9:1–34, which views the Benjaminites named as among those dwelling in Jerusalem (vv 28, 32b, cf. 9:7–9) in the post-exilic period. This may well have been the case with groups of those named, such as Azel and his sons (v 38).

The genealogy of the most prominent Benjaminite, Saul, has been included, even in contradiction of the view expressed in 10:6, because of its obvious relevance, because of the mention of Kish in v 30, and originally because of the need to provide a bridge to the narrative of Saul's wars with the Philistines in chap. 10. From the lengthy genealogy provided, we may see that centuries later there remained families of Israelites who pointed with pride to their descendancy from Israel's first king.

Inhabitants of Jerusalem (9:1–44)

Bibliography

For Benjamin, see 7:6–12 and 8:1–40. For Priests and Levites, see 5:27 and 6:1–38.

Batten, L. *The Books of Ezra and Nehemiah.* ICC. Edinburgh: T. & T. Clark, 1913. 267–75. **Damsky, Aaron.** "The Genealogy of Gibeon (1 Chronicles 9:35–44): Biblical and Epigraphic Considerations." *BASOR* 202 (1971) 16–23. **Myers, J.** *Ezra-Nehemiah.* AB 14. New York: Doubleday, 1963. 181–92. **Osborne, W.** The Genealogies of 1 Chronicles 1–9." Diss.: Dropsie University, 1979. 302–8. **Rudolph, W.** *Esra und Nehemiah.* HAT 1/20. Tübingen: Mohr, 1949. 181–91.

Translation

[1] *So all Israel was enrolled by genealogy, and behold, they are written in the book of the kings of Israel [a] and Judah. But Israel [a] and Judah were exiled to Babylon because of their unfaithfulness.*

[2] *Now the first [a] living [b] on their property in their cities were Israel, the priests, the Levites, and the Nethinim. [c]* [3] *Some of the sons of Judah, some of the sons of Benjamin, [a] and some of the sons of Ephraim and Manasseh [a] dwelt in Jerusalem:* [4] *Uthai, [a] son of Ammihud, [b] son of Omri, son of Imri, [b] son of [c] Bani, from [c] the sons of Judah's son Perez.* [5] *From the Shilonites: [a] Asaiah [b] the firstborn, and his sons.* [6] *From the sons of Zerah: Jeuel, [a] and their brothers, six hundred and ninety.*

[7] *From the sons of Benjamin: Sallu, [a] son of Meshullam, son of [b] Hodaviah, son of Hassenuah; [b]* [8] *Ibneiah, son of Jeroham; and [a] Elah, son [a] of Uzzi, son of Michri, and Meshullam, son of Shephatiah, son of Reuel, son of Ibnijah,* [9] *and their brothers, according to their generations, [a] nine hundred and fifty-six. [a] All these men were heads of their fathers' houses. [b]*

[10] *From the priests: Jedaiah, [a] Jehoiarib, Jachin,* [11] *and Azariah, [a] son of Hilkiah, son of Meshullam, son of Zadok, son of Meraioth, son of Ahitub, prince of the house of God,* [12] [a] *and Adaiah, son of Jeroham, son of Pashhur, son of Malchijah; Maasai, [b] the son of Adiel, [c] son of Jahzerah, [d] son of Meshullam, son of Meshillemith, [e] son of Immer;* [13] *and their brothers, heads of their fathers' houses, 1,760 valiant men in [a] the work of the service of God's house.*

[14] *From the Levites: Shemaiah, son of Hasshub, son of Azrikam, son of Hashabiah, [a] of the sons of Merari; [a]* [15] *Bakbakkar, [a] Heresh, Galal, and Mattaniah, son of Micah, son of Zichri, [b] son of Asaph;* [16] *and Obadiah, [a] son of Shemaiah, [b] son of Galal, son of Jeduthun; [c] and Berechiah, son of Asa, son of Elkanah, who dwelt in the villages of (the) Netophathite.*

[17] *The porters were Shallum, [a] Akkub, Talmon, Ahiman, [b] and their brothers. ([c] Shallum was the chief. [c])* [18] *Formerly they were in the King's Gate toward the east. They were the porters of the camps of the Levites.* [19] *Shallum, son of Kore, son of Ebiasaph, son of Korah, and his brothers of his father's house, the Korahites, were in charge of the work of the service, the keepers of the thresholds of the tent, as their fathers had been in charge of the camp of Yahweh, the keepers of the entrance.* [20] *(Earlier Phinehas, the son of Eleazar, had been their leader. Yahweh was with*

him.) [21] *Zechariah the son of Meshelemiah was the keeper of the entrance of the tent of meeting.* [22] *All of them chosen as the porters for the thresholds were two hundred and twelve. They were registered by genealogy in their villages. David and Samuel the seer established them* [a] *because of their faithfulness.* [b] [23] *So they and their sons were in charge of the gates of the house of Yahweh, the house of the tent, by watches.* [a]

[24] *The porters were at the four sides, east, west, north, and south,* [25] *and their brothers were in their villages* [a] *so that they might come in* [a] *for seven days from time to time with them.* [b] [26] [a] *Because of their faithfulness* [a] *the four* [b] *master gatekeepers* [b] *(they were Levites) were in charge of the chambers and treasuries of the house of God.* [27] *They slept around God's house, because it was their duty* [a] *and* [b] *they were in charge of opening (the temple)* [b] [c] *each morning.* [c] [28] [a] *Some of them* [a] *were in charge of the utensils for the service,* [b] *and* [c] *by number they would bring them in and by number they would take them out.* [29] *Others* [a] *were appointed over the* [b] *utensils and over all the holy vessels,* [b] *and over the fine flour, the wine, the oil, the incense, and the spices.* [30] *(Some of the priests mixed the ointment for the spices.)* [31] *Mattithiah, of the Levites, who was the firstborn of the Korahite Shallum, served faithfully* [a] *over the preparation of the flat cakes.* [32] *Some of the Kohathites, their brothers, were over the showbread and prepared it each Sabbath.*

[33] *These were the singers, heads of fathers' houses of the Levites, who were in the chambers (of the temple) free from other service,* [a] *since they were on duty day and night.*

[34] *These were the heads of fathers' (houses) of the Levites,* [a] *heads in their generations.* [a] *They dwelt in Jerusalem.*

[35] *In Gibeon dwelt* [a] *the father of Gibeon, Jeiel* [b] *(his wife's name was Maacah),* [36] *and his firstborn son Abdon, as well as Zur, Kish, Baal, Ner,* [a] *Nadab,* [37] *Gedor, Ahio, Zechariah, and Mikloth.* [a] [38] *Mikloth was the father of Shimeam.* [a] *They* [b] *too dwelt opposite* [c] *their brothers in Jerusalem,* [d] *with their brothers.* [d]

[39] *Ner was the father of Kish;* [a] *Kish was the father of Saul; Saul was the father of Jonathan, Malchishua, Abinadab,* [b] *and Eshbaal.* [40] *The son of Jonathan was* [a] *Merib-baal, and Merib-baal* [a] *was the father of Micah.* [41] *The sons of Micah: Pithon, Melech,* [a] *Tahrea,* [b] *(and Ahaz).* [c] [42] *Ahaz was the father of Jarah;* [a] *Jarah* [a] *was the father of Alemeth, Azmaveth, and Zimri; and Zimri was the father of Moza.* [43] *Moza was the father of Binea,* [a] *and Rephaiah* [b] *was his son, Eleasah his son, and Azel his son.* [44] *Azel had six sons, and these are their names: Azrikam, Bocheru,* [a] *Ishmael, Sheariah,* [b] *Obadiah, and Hanan.* [c] *These were the sons of Azel.*

Notes

1.a-a. Heb. "they are written in the book of the kings of Israel, and Judah was exiled. . . ." But the most common designation of this source is "the book of the kings of *Israel and Judah*"; cf. 2 Chr 27:7; 35:27; 36:8. The "book of the kings of Israel" occurs otherwise only in 2 Chr 20:34. (For the remaining references, see Eissfeldt, *Introduction*, 532–33.) Both G and Vg read "Israel" here, though not noted in *BH* or *BHS* (see Rudolph, 82). Since Israel is the subj of v 1 and the northern tribes are explicitly mentioned by the author in 9:3 (in contrast to Neh 11:3), it seems best to assume that the entire phrase, "Israel *and* Judah," has been omitted through haplogr (note the omission of the conj on הגלו "exiled" also). However, it is possible that only the exile of Judah was mentioned here, to be considered parallel to that of portions of the north in 5:6, 25–26.

2.a. Read perhaps with G (Syr α') προτερον "first" = בראשנה; cf. Neh 7:5.

2.b. Read perhaps השבים "those returning."

2.c. Neh 11:4 + ובני עבדי שלמה "the sons of Solomon's servants," perhaps from Neh 7:57 (Rudolph, 82).

3.a-a. > Neh 11:4.

4.a. Neh 11:4 עתיה "Ethaya."

4.b-b. Neh 11:4 אמריה "Amariah" (only); בן־אמרי "son of Imri" > G*.

4.c-c. K בן־בנימין "son of Banimin"; Q בן־בני מן "son of Bani from." Read Q.

5.a. Reading השלני "the Shilonites"; cf. 1 Chr 4:21; Num 26:20.

5.b. Neh 11:5 מעשיה "Maaseiah."

6.a. G^Aal Tg Ie(ι)ηλ = יאיאל "Jeial."

7.a. Neh 11:7 סַלָּא "Sallu"; Chr has סַלּוּא.

7.b-b. Cf. perhaps Neh 11:9 ויהודה בן הסנואה "and Judah son of Hassenuah."

8.a-a. Several MSS G^B ואלה בני "these are the sons of."

9.a-a. Syr has "99"; Neh 9:8 has "928."

10.a. Neh 11:10 בן יויריב "son of Joiarib," and cf. 24:7, 17, and *BHS*.

11.a. Neh 11:11 שריה "Seriah"; cf. 1 Chr 5:41[6:14].

12.a. Neh 11:12 + nonn vb.

12.b. Neh 11:13 ועמשסי "Amashsai"; cf. vv 5 and 11.

12.c. Neh 11:13 עזראל "Azarel."

12.d. Neh 11:13 אחזי "Ahzai."

12.e. Neh 11:13 משלמות "Meshillemoth."

13.a. Read perhaps חיל למ' "valiant men of . . ."; cf. G Tg Vg.

14.a-a. Neh 11:15 בן בוני "son of Bunni."

15.a. Cf. ? Neh 11:17 ובקביה "and Bakbukiah."

15.b. A few MSS Neh 11:17 זבדי "Zabdi."

16.a. Neh 11:17 ועבדא "and Abda."

16.b. Neh 11:17 שמוע "Shammua."

16.c. Neh 11:17 K ידיתון "Jedithun"; (Q ידותון "Jeduthun").

17.a. > Neh 11:19.

17.b. > Neh 11:19 (cf. ואחיהם "their brothers").

17.c-c. Neh 11:19 alliteration.

22.a. GKC, § 135a, n.1, considers this usage of המה "them" as an accusative to be perhaps due to Aramaic influence.

22.b. Or perhaps "in their office of trust"; see vv 26, 31, and cf. 2 Chr 19:9; 31:12, 15, 18; 34:12. The root meaning of אמונה "faithfulness" has to do with trustworthiness, but it seems possible that, like משמרות "faithfulness" (n. 23.a.), it came to symbolize an office itself rather than merely the faithful discharge of its duties.

23.a. Heb. למשמרות. The precise meaning of the term is uncertain, as is the syntax.

25.a-a. Cf. GKC, § 114k.

25.b. This unusual usage of אלה "them" as the obj of the prep עם "with" is not noted by GKC; cf. § 136.

26.a-a. Or perhaps "because they were in office . . ."; cf. n. 22.b. The translation supposes a very weak usage of כי "because of," as is found also in v 28, and a causal ב "in."

26.b-b. גברי השערים "master gatekeepers." The application of heroic terms in an honorific sense to less than heroic positions is still evidenced in political, religious, and social organizations today.

27.a. Or, "the watch was theirs." Cf. nn. 22.b., 23.a.

27.b-b. והם על המפתח, lit., "they were over the key." They were responsible for the security of the temple precincts.

27.c-c. Cf. GKC, § 123c.

28.a-a. The מן (usually trans. "from"; here, "some of them") is partitive, as also in vv 29, 30, and 32 (2x).

28.b. See n. 29.b.

28.c. This very weakened sense of כי as "and" seems necessitated by the context.

29.a. See n. 28.a-a.

29.b. The precise distinction between these כלים "utensils," left unspecified; the כלי העבודה "utensils for service" of v 28, which are carried in and out and counted; and the כלי הקדש "holy vessels" later in v 29, which quite probably refers to vessels or implements more directly connected to the temple rituals, is uncertain.

31.a. Again, באמונה "faithfully" may refer to an office; see n. 26.a-a.

33.a. Q פְּטוּרִים, K פְּטִירִים. Q represents the qal pass ptcp, K the Aramaic ptcp or adj with the same meaning. BDB (809) has "set free" from other duties.

34.a-a. The repetition of רֹאשִׁים "heads" is difficult and perhaps stems from the conflation of synonymous variants.

35.a. See n. 8:29.a.

35.b. > 8:29.

36.a. > 8:30.

37.a. > 8:31.

38.a. 8:32 שִׁמְאָה "Shimeah."

38.b. (הֵמָּה) 8:32 הֵם, both references to masc pl "they."

38.c. נֶגֶד "opposite."

38.d-d. An explanatory gl to נֶגֶד אֲחֵיהֶם "opposite their brothers."

39.a. See n. 8:33.a.

39.b. See n. 8:33.b

40.a-a. See n. 8:34.a.

41.a. See n. 8:35.a.

41.b. 8:35 וְתַאְרֵעַ "and Tarea."

41.c. 8:35 + וְאָחָז "and Ahaz" (haplogr).

42.a-a. See n. 8:36.a.

43.a. See n. 8:37.a.

43.b. See n. 8:37.b.

44.a. See n. 8:38.a.

44.b. See n. 8:38.b. Insert "Azariah"?

44.c. 8:38 + כֹּל "all."

Form/Structure/Setting

The basic structure of chap. 9 is dependent upon Neh 11, and may be outlined as the following shows.

Introduction (vv 1–2; Neh 11:3)
Judahites and Benjaminites in Jerusalem (vv 3–9; Neh 11:4–9)
   Introduction (v 3; Neh 11:4a)
   Judahites in Jerusalem (vv 4–6; Neh 11:4b–6)
   Benjaminites in Jerusalem (vv 7–9; Neh 11:4–9)
Priests (vv 10–13; Neh 11:10–14)
Levites (vv 14–16; Neh 11:15–18)
Gatekeepers (vv 17–27; Neh 11:19)
   Additional Levitical Functions (vv 28–32; cf. Neh 11:20–24)
Singers (v 33; cf. Neh 7:1, 73)
Conclusion (v 34; cf. Neh 11:20–21)
Benjaminites in Gibeon (?) and Jerusalem (vv 35–38; Neh 11:31–36)
Genealogy of Saul (vv 39–44)

Neh 11 exhibits the same outline, except that (a) Neh 11:1–2, which establishes the original function of the list within Nehemiah in the context of Nehemiah's efforts to populate Jerusalem in the days of the rebuilding of the walls (cf. Neh 7:1–5, 73), is replaced by 1 Chr 9:1, which serves as a linkage between chaps. 1–8, focusing upon Israel in pre-exilic days, and chap. 9, which is post-exilic in orientation; (b) the extensive material of 1 Chr 9:17–34, centering upon the gatekeepers and additional Levitical functions, is lacking in Neh 11 (cf. Neh 11:19–24); (c) Neh 11:25–36, which lists other dwellings of Judah and Benjamin outside Jerusalem, is omitted, replaced perhaps by (d), 1 Chr 9:35–44, two Benjaminite lists, which connect directly with the account of Saul's demise in 1 Chr 10.

Jacob Myers has pointed out that the order of the presentation of the elements within Israel apparent in the overall structure of these chapters—Israel (the laity), priests, Levites, gatekeepers—is identical and unique to these two passages (Myers, *Ezra-Nehemiah*, 175, 186). The close relationship between these two chapters may also be seen by comparing 1 Chr 9:2–3 with Neh 11:3–4a:

A COMPARISON OF THE TEXTS OF NEH 11:3–4A AND 1 CHR 9:2–3

Neh 11:3	ואלה ראשי המדינה אשר ישבו
1 Chr 9:2	והיושבים הראשנים אשר
Neh 11:3	בירושלם ובערי יהודה ישבו איש באחזתו בעריהם
1 Chr 9:2	באחזתו בעריהם
Neh 11:3	ישראל הכהנים והלוים והנתינים ובני עבדי שלמה
1 Chr 9:2	ישראל הכהנים והלוים והנתינים
Neh 11:4a	ובירושלים ישבו מבני יהודה ומבני בנימן
1 Chr 9:3	ובירושלים ילנו מן־בני יהודה ומן־בני בנימן ומן אפרים ומנשה

Neh 11:3–4a   "And these are the chiefs of the province who lived in Jerusalem and in the cities of Judah. Each lived on his property in their cities: Israel, the priests, the Levites, the temple servants and the descendants of Solomon's servants. And in Jerusalem lived the sons of Judah and the sons of Benjamin. . . ."

1 Chr 9:2–3   "Now the first living on their property in their cities were Israel, the priests, the Levites, and the Nethinim. Some of the sons of Judah, some of the sons of Benjamin, and some of the sons of Ephraim and Manasseh dwelt in Jerusalem."

As we have mentioned, both of these introductory passages mention the temple servants (הנתינים), although they are not referred to in subsequent portions of the chapters, and neither 1 Chr 9:3 nor Neh 11:3 mentions the gatekeepers, although they are included in Neh 11:10 and an elaboration of their duties forms a major part of 1 Chr 9:17–27 (cf. Neh 12:25). Neh 11:3 includes mention of the sons of Solomon's servants, perhaps in later dependence upon Neh 7 (= Ezra 2). Neither introductory passage names the singers, although 1 Chr 9:33 appears to anticipate such a list (and cf. Neh 7:1, 73; see also Neh 12:28, 45–47). While both passages refer to Benjaminites and Judahites living in Jerusalem, only 1 Chr 9:3 includes members of the northern tribes, Ephraim and Manasseh, among those dwelling there (see below).

That Neh 11 is composite is commonly recognized (cf. Rudolph, 181–84; Batten, 266). Since 1 Chr 9:2 reflects this same composite character (see below), Rudolph (183) is probably correct in stating that the author of 1 Chr 9 had before him Neh 11 in its present form.

Neh 11, in its present context, is a list of those dwelling in Jerusalem at the time of the rebuilding of the walls by Nehemiah, and connects most directly with Neh 7:4 (or 7:73). It is probably based upon a list of the inhabitants of Jerusalem at a particular time. Confusion has apparently resulted from the inclusion of 7:5–72, which incorporates a list of those returning from Babylon with Zerubbabel from Ezra 2 (cf. Neh 7:73). Neh 11:3a supposes that only the leaders of the provinces dwelt in Jerusalem, while the remainder of the people, laity, priests, and minor clergy (Neh 11:20) dwelt throughout the land (cf. Neh 11:36). The number of those counted, however, 486 (Neh 11:6), is too large to include only chiefs resident in Jerusalem. That the editorial introduction of v 3 does not correspond to the material included in the chapter is apparent in that the former does not mention the gatekeepers, though these are listed in v 19; it does include both the temple servants (הנתינים), mentioned only briefly in v 21 and as dwelling outside Jerusalem, and the descendants of Solomon's servants, not mentioned at all in the listing that follows. Under this influence the ראשים ("heads") of Neh 11:2, who dwelt in Jerusalem, became the first (הראשנים) to dwell on their particular property and in their cities (1 Chr 9:2). Both lists are complicated by this confusion. In general, however, the confusion in Neh 11 lies only in the editorial framework; that in 1 Chr 9 is more pervasive. (See *Comment*).

While the overall relationship of 1 Chr 9 to Neh 11 is clear, comparison of the two texts points to numerous differences. In general, it may be said that even these divergences attest to the fact that the lists are closely related; at the same time, however, they rule out the possibility of direct borrowing. Of the seven generations of Perez named in Neh 11:4, only two (Athaiah = Uthai, Amariah = Omri and/or Emri) are with probability named in Chronicles. Of the "Shilonites" of Neh 11:5, only the head, Maaseiah (מעשיה) can be seen in Chronicles. (On Asaiah [עשיה] see *Comment*.) Of the fourteen Benjaminite names of Neh 11, only the first two, Sallu and Meshullam, are clearly identical, although the correspondency between "Hodaviah the son of Hassenuah" (הודויה בן הסנאה] and "Judah the son of Hassenuah" (ויהודה בן הסנואה; Neh 11:7) is suggestive.

The correspondencies between the lists of the priests (vv 10–13) and Levites (vv 14–16) are, as might be expected, considerably closer. Chronicles lists six families of priests. As in Nehemiah, no pedigree is given for the first three, and the similarity of the lists is apparent:

Neh 11:10–14	*1 Chr 9:10–13*
Of the priests:	And from the priests
Jedaiah	Jedaiah
son of Joiarib (יויריב)	and Jehoiarib (יהויריב)
Jachin	and Jachin
Seraiah (שריה)	and Azariah (עזריה)
son of . . .	son of . . .
and Adaiah	and Adaiah
son of . . .	son of . . .
and Amashsai (עמששי)	and Maasai (מעשיה)
son of . . .	son of . . .

Chronicles lists six priestly families (understood as five in Nehemiah), to the first three of which no pedigree is attached. The line of Azariah/Seraiah is traced back through an identical list of five generations of what appears to be the line of the high priest (see *Comment*), and each is termed "prince" (נגיד) of the house of God (v 11, Neh 11:11). For the variation between Azariah and Seraiah see above on 5:40 [6:14]. The name of Chronicles' fifth priestly family, Adaiah, is identical with Nehemiah, as are the names of three of his progenitors, Jeroham, Pashur, and Malchijah. However, three other names found in the Masoretic text of Nehemiah (Pelihiah, Amzi, and Zechariah), for which G evidence is also poor, are lacking in Chronicles.

The divergences in the last-named priestly family are more striking, but the similarity is also apparent.

Neh 11:13	*1 Chr 9:12*
And Amashsai (ועמשסי)	And Maasai (ומעשי)
Azarel (עזראל)	Adiel (עדיאל)
Ahzi	Jahzerah
Moshillomoth (משלמות)	Meshullam (משלם)
	Meshillemith (משלימית)
Immer	Immer

Finally, Neh 11 includes an enumeration after each of the three families for whom a pedigree is given (vv 12, 13, 14), of which the total would be 1192. Chronicles mentions only a single total of 1760 at the end of the lists of priests.

14-16 *The Levites.* For the general presentation of the Levites and their relationship to the sub-Levitical groups, see the *Introduction*. The lists of 1 Chr and Neh 11 agree in that both list the Levitical families of Shemaiah (Neh 11:15; 1 Chr 9:14); Mattaniah (Neh 11:17; 1 Chr 9:15), and Obadiah (Neh 11:17 עבדא "Abda"; 1 Chr 9:16 עבדיה "Obadiah"), and that a pedigree of each is attached of four generations in the case of the first and three in the remaining two. Neh 11 may have intended these to represent the three major levitical groups, since Mattaniah's lineage is traced back to Asaph and Abdai's to Jeduthun (accepting the reading of *Q*, see n. 16.a.). The line of Shemaiah, however, concludes with a reference to an otherwise unknown son of Buni (בן בוני). This lack of definiteness is remedied by Chronicles, which reads instead "of the sons of Merari" (מן בני מררי). Otherwise the two pedigrees are identical. The same is true of the pedigrees of Mattaniah, except that Asaph's "son" in Neh 11:17 is Zabdi (זבדי), and in 1 Chr 9:15, is Zichri (זכרי, probably a textual error). The line of Obadiah/Abda also appears identical, with only a minor difference in spelling in the names Shemaiah (שמעיה, v 14) and Shammua (שמוע) (Neh 11:17). Beyond this, Chronicles contains no reference to two individuals, Shabbethia and Jozabad (Neh 11:16), or the description of their work; to the description of Mattaniah's (?) work at the conclusion of v 16; or to the enumeration of the Levites (284) in v 18. Instead, Chronicles adds, also without pedigree, the names Bakbakkar (strikingly similar to the name Bakbukiah listed as second in command to Mattaniah in Neh 11:17), Heresh (otherwise unknown), and Galal, included among the ancestors of Obadiah/Abda in both 1 Chr 9:16 and Neh 11:17.

These detailed similarities, including especially that of the introductory verse, lead us to conclude that Chronicles had before him a list of Nehemiah in its current framework. At the same time, however, he may have been privy to other traditions of unknown provenance, or he may have updated the lists available to him by the inclusion of other families prominent at the time at which he wrote.

In turning to the porters (vv 17–34) and additional detailing of Levitical functions (vv 17–32), it is apparent that at this point the concern of the writer (or writers) has led him to expand broadly upon the data of Nehemiah. Of the four heads named by Chronicles, Akkub and Talmon are listed in Neh 11:19, but the name Shallum, upon whom the major emphasis is placed in Chronicles does not occur. Ezra 2:42 (= Neh 7:45) lists six families of gatekeepers who returned from the exile—Shallum, Ater, Talmon, Akkub, Hatita, and Shobai—totaling 139 (138 in Neh). Neh 12:25 lists a Meshullam (משלם) with Talmon and Akkub (and perhaps three others) as "gatekeepers standing guard at the storehouses of the gates" in lists placed by the author "in the days of Joiakim, son of Joshua, son of Jozadak, and the days of Nehemiah the governor and of Ezra the priest and scribe" (Neh 12:25–26). It seems probable that the Shallum of v 19 and the Meshelemiah of v 21, together with the Meshelemiah of 1 Chr 26:1, the Shelemiah of 26:14, and the Meshullam of Neh 12:25 are one and the same (cf. Curtis, 174). The individuals in v 21 and in 1 Chr 26:2, 14 are all named as the father of Zechariah. It thus seems likely that all refer to the same individual, though certainty is impossible due to the frequency of both names in the post-exilic period and especially among the Levites (Mauch, "Zechariah" *IDB* 4:941–43, lists no less than thirty-three individuals in Scripture with the name Zechariah, although some are probably identical, and the listing under Shallum alone extends to fourteen.)

An Ahiman (אחימן) is otherwise unknown among the Levitical or sub-Levitical groups, and the name's occurrence here probably results from a confusion of the similar "their brothers" (אחיהם). In our context, however, v 26 strongly suggests that Ahiman be understood as a proper name.

Shallum's lineage is traced back to the Korahites, and his position here with the porters appears to reflect the ongoing struggles which that family experienced in relation to other priestly groups extending back, Num 16 maintains, to the wilderness period (see Mauch, "Korah," *IDB* 3:49–50). The Korahites traced their lineage to Levi through Kohath and his second son Izhar; in fact 1 Chr 26:1 includes the sons of Korah among the Asaphites of the temple choir (cf. also 2 Chr 20:19 and the superscriptions to Pss 44–49, etc.), but it appears they were replaced as singers by Heman, who computed his genealogy similarly (1 Chr 6:18–23 [33–38]). The Korahites were then relegated to lesser positions as porters (1 Chr 9:19; 26:1) and bakers of the sacrificial bread (9:31). (See the *Introduction.*)

The understanding of vv 17–22 is obscured by the way in which references to the writer's own period (v 17), to an undefined former period (ועד הנה, lit., "and until now," v 18), to the wilderness period (v 20), and to the age of Samuel and David (v 22) are combined. Strikingly, however, it is Phinehas rather than Moses whose precedent is cited for the wilderness period. The multiplicity of periods is matched by a prolific use of terms and titles for the porters and the task assigned to them, as if conscious effort were being made to omit none. The porters (שֹׁעֲרִים) are named "porters of the camp of the Levites" (v 18), "keepers (שֹׁמְרִי) of the thresholds of the tent" (v 19), whose fathers were "over the camp of Yahweh, keepers of the entrance" (v 19), and they are chosen as "porters of the thresholds" (v 22). Zechariah is "porter of the door of the tent of meeting" (v 21).

Such consistently varied terminology suggesting that an attempt is being made to point to the porter's functions at various times, is seen also in the reference to Phinehas, to Samuel-David, and the writer's own time. It is doubtful whether any should be taken too literally to refer to a specific time. "The camp of the Levites" (v 19) would most logically suggest a reference to the wilderness period (cf. Num 2:17), but the earlier reference in the verse clearly places it post-monarchy. The similar "camp of Yahweh" apparently refers to the outer courts of the temple in 2 Chr 31:2. Similarly the tent (אֹהֶל, v 19) and the tent of meeting (אֹהֶל מוֹעֵד, v 21) would also tend to recall the wilderness period (cf. Num 2:2) or in Chronicles, perhaps rather the tradition of the tabernacle at Gibeon or the "tent of David" (cf. 2 Chr 1:3; 5:2–5); here, however, it is used anachronistically of the time of Zechariah, the son of Shallum, i.e., the post-exilic period. Cf. also v 23, where the "house of Yahweh" and the "house of the tent" are analogous, if perhaps conflate, expressions.

The term "porter" (שֹׁעֵר) itself is, it should be noted, confined almost entirely to later OT traditions, with thirty-four of its thirty-seven OT occurrences in Chronicles-Ezra-Nehemiah (Curtis, 116; Driver, 46). (The only exceptions are 2 Sam 18:26; 2 Kgs 7:10–11.) Older traditions tend to speak rather of "keepers of the thresholds" (שֹׁמְרֵי הַסַּף) and to do so with reference to priests generally or to lower ranks of priests (cf. 2 Kgs 12:10 [9]; 23:4; 25:18; Jer 35:4).

As is often the case (see *Introduction*), the installation of these gatekeepers is attributed to David (v 22) despite the contrary reference to Phinehas. Phinehas's role is probably deduced from Num 25:6–13, where he dramatically exercises a responsibility for the temple precincts. The role of Samuel, on the other hand, may be related to the functions of the young Samuel in the temple, which were identified as being Levitical in nature. From beginning to end, however, the total import of the passage is that these porters, represented now particularly in the line of Shallum, have functioned in this role throughout Israel's history and continue to do so in the writer's day.

(For vv 24–27 and 28–32, see *Comment* below.)

The mention of the singers (v 33) is to be expected in view of their prominence in Chronicles-Ezra-Nehemiah although they are not named in Neh 11. (Cf. Neh 7:1, 73.) They are here clearly considered Levitical. That the anticipated list of singers does not occur is surely striking and suggests either an accidental omission, perhaps resulting from the addition of Saul's genealogy in vv 39–44, or a rigid type of dependence upon his *Vorlage*, which contained no such list.

For vv 34 and 35–44, see above under 8:28 and 29–40. V 34 parallels v 3, understanding all those included to dwell within Jerusalem (see also 8:28; 9:27, 33; 9:38 [= 8:33]). We have suggested above that Ner has been added to v 36, probably under influence of the presence of the name Kish, to point more clearly to the genealogy of vv 35–38 as that of Saul, which is then pursued in vv 39–44.

Comment

1   V 1a has been considered the conclusion of the lists of chaps. 1–8, and does round off the listings begun by 2:1 (see). However, v 1b, "Judah was exiled to Babylon because of her unfaithfulness," equally clearly anticipates the mention of the return in v 2, so that it is impossible to separate the two units sharply.

The contents or the nature of this "book of the Kings of Israel and Judah" (see n. 1.a-a.) in which the genealogies referred to are to be found can no longer be determined. That the reference is not to the canonical books is obvious, since such material is not found there. Regardless of whether a common author is posited for this verse and similar passages in 2 Chronicles, it seems certain that the reference here is to be understood in the same sense as those notices regularly concluding the accounts of the kings of Israel and Judah in, e.g., 2 Chr 27:7; 35:27; 36:8. Despite the varied forms of the references, Eissfeldt (532–33) is probably correct that only a single source is referred to by these various names. The repeated use of such a formula in Chronicles is probably due to the parallel usage in Kings, where the reader is regularly referred to "the books of the chronicles of the kings of Israel (and Judah)" for additional information. Whether a specific document is referred to or whether the reference might be more generally to official archives—royal, priestly, or both—cannot be determined. That the writer had available to him certain records of a genealogical nature cannot be seriously questioned. The content and interest of these records, in places where it is apparent, suggest sources of a military and priestly nature.

The terminology of the remainder of v 1 is also common in Chronicles. For התיחשם "enrolled" see 1 Chr 4:33 and Curtis, #49; for מעל "unfaithful," 1 Chr 2:7 and Curtis, #68. Although גלה "exiled" in the hophal is found only here in Chronicles (and otherwise only four times in Jeremiah and twice in Esther), the hiphil is found in 1 Chr 5:6, 26, 41; 8:6, 7; 2 Chr 36:20; Ezra 2:1; Neh 7:6. The concept of *all Israel,* present to at least a degree in any reading of v 1 and more emphatically if our emendation of v 1 is accepted (see n. 1.a-a.), and seen preeminently in the addition of Ephraim and Manasseh to the inhabitants of Jerusalem at the end of v 3, we consider to lie at the heart of the author's message (see the *Introduction*). In this connection we would argue that, just as Judah and Benjamin epitomize the South, so Ephraim and Manasseh stand not as tribes in their own right but as a designation for the entire northern kingdom (cf. Hos 11:8; Judg 10:9; Ps 78:9, 67–68; and cf. Rev 7:6, where it is Manasseh who stands beside Joseph). This usage is found also in 2 Chr 30:1 (cf. v 5), 10, and see especially 31:1; 34:9, where Ephraim and Manasseh are again paralleled with Judah and Benjamin.

2–3 These verses, as we have indicated (see *Form/Structure/Setting* above), are dependent upon Neh 11:3–4, which, however, is a listing of those who settled in Jerusalem at the time of the building of the walls by Nehemiah. In both lists there is a confusion between those who dwelt in Jerusalem (Neh 11:1a, 2, 3a, 4, 6, 9 [?], 18, 19, 22, 24, 36 [?]; 1 Chr 9:3, 34 [cf. v 38b]) and those who dwelt in the land (Neh 11:1b, 3b, 5 [?], 20 [!], 21, 25–35, 36 [?]; cf. 1 Chr 9:2, 5 [?], 16 [?], 35–38a). However, the twofold nature of the list is much more pronounced in Neh 11; cf. especially vv 3, 20, 25–36. The more obvious of these notices have been systematically removed in Chronicles, so that the total list is now enveloped by vv 3 and 34, which includes everyone within Jerusalem. Even the list of the inhabitants of Gibeon in 9:35–38 (cf. 8:29–32), which originally may have been parallel to the list of Benjaminites and Judahites dwelling in villages throughout the land (cf. Neh 11:25–36), has been altered to place these "Gibeonites" in Jerusalem. Although this policy has not been put to practice in the remainder of the chapter, Chronicles has expanded its outlook to include even Ephraim and Manasseh within the confines of Jerusalem (9:3).

4–6 *Descendants of Judah.* (See *Form/Structure/Setting* above.) Neh 11 considers all Judah's descendants to be descended from Perez (Neh 11:6) and lists their total as 468; Chronicles finds descendants there of Judah's sons Shelah and Zerah as well, and the corresponding number, which may however be understood in a different sense, is 690. The omission of the designation of Neh 11:6 אנשי חיל "warriors," is surprising in view of the apparent military background of the phrase and the occurrence of so much of that terminology elsewhere in Chronicles.

Neh 11 listed only two family heads of Judah, with a pedigree of seven generations (including Judah) for Othiah and seven for Maasaiah (not including Judah). Chronicles lists three family heads, one of each of Judah's surviving sons Perez, Shelah, and Zerah. The pedigree of Perez approximates that found in Neh 11, though ostensibly traced here through Perez' son Bani (v 4) rather than Mahalalel and Shephatiah (Neh 11:4). Bani is a common post-exilic name (cf. Schumacher, "Bani," *IDB* 1:346), although the consonants בני, which may also be read "sons of" or "my son(s)," have led to much confusion. If Asaiah (v 5) is to be identified with the Maasaiah of Neh 11:5, as appears reasonably certain, his seven-generation pedigree in Neh 11:5 is lacking here, where he is referred to only as "the firstborn" (הבכור), probably an error for or suggested by the name of Maasaiah's father Baruk (ברוך, Neh 11:5). Of the family of Jeuel, descended from Zerah, Nehemiah says nothing, although the name is known to us from Ezra 8:13, cf. 2 Chr 29:13 (of a Levite).

7–9 *Descendants of Benjamin.* Chronicles names four family heads, with a combined number of 956; Neh 11 five family heads (?) with a total of 928. The two lists have only their first two names in common, Sallu who is designated the son of Meshullam. Sallu is found as a Levitical house in Neh 12:7; beyond Meshullam, one of the most common names of the post-exilic period (see E. R. Achtemeier, "Meshullam," *IDB* 3:358, who lists no less than nineteen individuals with that name), the two lists differ completely. It is possible, as suggested by Curtis (171), that "Hodaviah son of Hassenuah"

(הודויה בן הסנאה) represents a corruption or derivation from "Judah son of Hassenuah" (ויהודה בן הסנואה) (Neh 11:9). The second of the family heads named by Chronicles, Ibneah (יבניה) has been seen in Gabbai (גבי), though this is far from certain. The two remaining family heads of Chronicles, Elah and a second Meshullam, have no parallel in Nehemiah.

10–13 *The Priests.* The dependency upon Neh 11 is here very pronounced, as indicated above. The six priestly families listed here all occur elsewhere among the priests of the post-exilic period. Jedaiah is said to have received the second priestly course from David (1 Chr 24:7), Jehoiarib the first (24:7), and Jachin the twenty-first (24:17). That these three are in some sense to be grouped is suggested both by the lack of separate pedigrees and by the single numerical total of Neh 11:12. Adaiah is given as a descendant of Malchijah, who held the fifth course (24:9), and Maasiah of Immer, who held the sixteenth (24:14) (Curtis, 171). A priest of the name of Seraiah, who probably represents the Azariah of v 11 (see n. 11.a.), is listed with those who returned with Zerubbabel (Neh 12:1), and a similar priestly family occurs in the list from the time of Joiakim (Neh 12:12).

The pedigree of this Azariah/Seriah is, with only minor variations, that of the high priest Seraiah, the father of Jehozadak who went into exile. The genealogy of 1 Chr 5:38–40 [6:11–14] lists Seraiah as the son of Azariah and the father of Jehozadak but is probably the result of conflation (see on that passage and cf. Neh 11:11). That the intent is to give the high priestly line seems to be supported by the title "prince of the house of God" (נגיד בית האלהים, 1 Chr 9:11; Neh 11:11). Another (?) Azaraiah, who is explicitly named high priest in the time of Hezekiah (2 Chr 31:10), also bears the title "prince of the house of God" in that chapter (v 13), but in 2 Chr 35:8 (the reference in Curtis, 172, is in error) the same title is given to three Levites.

It seems quite likely that some confusion or telescoping has entered the picture due to the multiplicity of these Azariahs. Three generations have dropped from the middle of Adaiah's genealogy, and that of Maasai (v 12), if identified with Amashsai (Neh 11:13) as we have done, differs consistently in detail from that of Nehemiah, although the similarity is obvious (see the listing under *Form/Structure/Setting* above). The total of all these priests is given as 1760, differing from the three separate figures of 822, 242, and 128 in Neh 11, which total 1192. In language by now familiar in Chronicles, these priests are termed "heads of fathers' houses" (ראשים לבית אבותם) and "valiant men" (גבורי חיל) (v 13, cf. Neh 11:14). However, this latter phrase, which seems to have its origin in military terminology, is qualified by the writer in 1 Chr 9:13 to apply to the particular work of the priests, by the use of "valiant men for *the work of the service of the house of God*" (מלאכת עבודת בת האלהים). (Cf. 6:33 [48] where similar terminology is used concerning the tabernacle; also 9:19 and frequently in Chronicles and P. Williamson, *Israel*, 57, #25, has noted that while עבודה occurs thirty-six times in Chronicles, it is found only once [Neh 10:33] in Ezra-Nehemiah.)

14–16 *The Levites.* For the general presentation of the Levites and their relationship to various sub-Levitical groups, see the *Introduction.* For the comparison of this list with Neh 11, see *Form/Structure/Setting* above. Chief emphasis here falls upon the families of Shemaiah, Mattaniah, and Obadiah, whose lineage is traced from the three chief Levitical families of Merari (v 14), Asaph (v 15), and Jeduthun (v 16). Chronicles here agrees closely with Neh 11, save that Neh 11 does not name Merari (see n. 14.a-a.). The only other exceptions are given in the notes. Of the families of Bakbakkar, Heresh, and Galal (v 15a) we know nothing. Chronicles has abbreviated the descriptive terminology concerning Asaph in v 15b (cf. Neh 11:17), though it would appear in harmony with his interests to have included it. Only Chronicles includes the family of Berechiah (v 16), who, like the three principal families, is provided with a brief genealogy. Guthrie ("Berechiah," *IDB* 1:385) rightly questions the identification of this Berechiah with the gatekeeper of the same name of David's era (15:23). Elkanah is a common Levitical name (cf. 6:23, 25, 26, 35; and 15:23) where he is listed with Berechiah as a gatekeeper of the ark. Netophah is closely identified with Bethlehem (cf. 2:54; Ezra 2:21–22 = Neh 7:26) and is commonly identified with a ruin some three and a half miles southeast of Bethlehem (W. Morton, "Netophah," *IDB* 3:541; Avi-Yonah, *The Holy Land,* 23). This village was associated with two of David's mighty men (1 Chr 11:30; 2 Sam 23:28–29) and was also the ancestral home of fifty-six men who returned with Zerubbabel (Neh 7:26; Ezra 2:22). Certain "sons of the singers" were also gathered from there for the dedication of the walls of Jerusalem (Neh 12:28). Elkanah is in 6:18–19 [33–34] a member of the family of Heman the Kehathite, whose family is otherwise not listed here. Perhaps the inclusion of v 16 is meant to remedy that deficiency. The total of these Levites, given as 284 in Neh 11:18, is omitted in Chronicles.

17–32 *The porters.* On vv 17–23, see *Form/Structure/Setting* above, where we have called attention to the emphasis upon the family of Shallum/Shelemiah/Meshullam, who is in v 17 termed the chief (הראש). The King's Gate (v 18) at which Shallum and his family served must have been the most prestigious location (cf. Ezek 46). As a descendant of Korah, Shallum was in fact of the same major branch of the tribe of Levi as was Aaron and the high priests (Exod 6:18–24), and just as his forefathers had served under immediate direction of Phineas, so his family too, we may assume, stood particularly close to the priestly office (vv 19–20). The mention of Zechariah, the son of Shallum/Meshelemiah (v 21) places us once again in the post-exilic period. However, the mention of their installation by David and Samuel (who would have been dead before David's accession), suggests that the tent of v 19 and the tent of meeting of v 21 are to be understood either as David's tent for the ark in Jerusalem (16:1) or as the tabernacle, placed by Chronicles in Gibeon (16:39; 2 Chr 1:2–6). Perhaps some telescoping or confusion has taken place in view of similar names borne by gatekeepers in various periods of their history. Of prime concern to the writer, no matter what age he was depicting, was the emphasis upon their association with, or rather their establishment in office by, Phineas in the age of Moses and Samuel and David at the time of the monarchy, with their office continuing into the post-exilic period.

Vv 24–32 elaborate upon the functions of the porters and other (?) Levites.

We have chosen to understand these verses as somewhat removed from
vv 17–23, though this is far from certain, or perhaps the new unit should
begin with v 23 or even v 22. However, the יִהְיוּ "they were," of v 24, coupled
with the וְהֵן "and they were" of v 26 and the יָלִינוּ "they slept" of v 27,
stand outside the nominal pattern more common in vv 17–23, and the syntax
of vv 24–32 seems to be even more tangled than that of vv 17–23, which
are already less than clear (cf. especially vv 22–23). There are three noteworthy
concerns here. (1) The gatekeepers, or at least their four heads, are named
as Levites (vv 26, 31). (2) Their functions, which necessitated their being
present around the temple twenty-four hours a day, are defined, including
not only security and janitorial concerns but the care of the sacred utensils
and the flour, wine, oil, incense, and spices of the temple services themselves.
Only the compounding of the spices is reserved for the clergy (v 30, Exod
30:22–38). (3) While at least the four "master porters" dwelt in Jerusalem,
some of their assistants resided in surrounding villages (v 25), from which
they commuted to fulfill their duties at the temple. This is, as noted by Curtis
(176), the only indication of gatekeepers living throughout the land (the same
is said of the singers in v 16) and stands in some tension with vv 3 and 34,
which point to the enclosed list as a register of those residing in Jerusalem.
The suggestion of Curtis (176–77) that the four principal porters lived in
Jerusalem, were considered Levites, and were installed in their office by Phinehas while their assistants lived outside the city, had been installed by Samuel
and David, and were not considered Levites, is more systematic than suggested
by the text. We should probably think instead of divergent traditions with
respect to the origins and nature of the porters' service.

This same divergence in traditions is also seen in v 31, where Mattithiah
is named Shallum's firstborn. In vv 19 and 21, as well as in 26:2, it is Zechariah
who holds that position. It thus seems quite possible that the text before
us (vv 17–32) was revised and updated through a period of at least three
generations (Shallum, Zechariah, and Mattithiah), in which the role of the
porters was undergoing substantial review.

V 33 is anomalous in referring to the singers, who have not before been
mentioned by name in the chapter (although vv 14–16 may be referred to
them). Perhaps a representative of this group, disappointed in the real or
apparent slight shown to him and his associates, wished to inform us that
they too were on constant duty in the temple, in a function so valued that
it released them from more menial chores.

V 34, we have seen (cf. *Form/Structure/Setting* above), points back to v 3
and understands the enclosed list as a roster of those returning from exile
and dwelling in Jerusalem, in contrast to Neh 11, where the distinction between those living in Jerusalem and those scattered throughout the remainder
of the land is more clear. We have suggested that the genealogy of Benjamin
(and Saul) here (vv 35–44) is prior to that of 8:29–38, since v 34, which
here concludes the previous unit, has been transferred together with vv 35–
44 to chap. 8 (cf. v 28) and in that context is inappropriate. Other more
elaborate explanations are possible, but it seems simplest to assume that
the person responsible for this transfer of the Benjaminite-Saulide list has
misunderstood v 34 to be a superscription rather than a postscript.

Explanation

As if by way of conclusion to the genealogical lists of chaps. 1–8, chap. 9 provides a listing of various groups whom we may assume to have been of special importance to the post-exilic period and who are named as the first to return to their possessions after the exile. Vv 1–3 provide the connecting point for these two groups of lists. V·1 looks principally backward, and points to the exile of the components of Israel and Judah just named as punishment for their unfaithfulness. Vv 2–3 look forward to the repopulation of the land and like Neh 11, with which it has been seen to be related, is followed by lists of Judahites, Benjaminites, priests, Levites, and gatekeepers who are said to have inhabited Jerusalem in post-exilic times. However, unlike Neh 11, Chronicles includes Ephraim and Manasseh, understood as a designation for all the northern tribes, among the inhabitants of Jerusalem (v 3), although no appropriate list of names follows; the list of gatekeepers and their functions is much expanded, and mention is made at least in passing of the singers (v 33), not noted in Neh 11. The list of the Benjaminites in Gibeon (vv 35–38), which has been attached somewhat haphazardly (cf. v 35, "in Gibeon," with v 38b, "these also dwelt opposite their kinsmen in Jerusalem,") may have been suggested by Neh 11:25–36, a list of Israelites dwelling throughout the land rather than in Jerusalem; and the genealogy of Saul (vv 39–44) may have been a part of the same list or may have been suggested either by its relationship to Benjamin, by the coming narrative of Saul (1 Chr 10), or both.

The primary point of the writer or writers is thus clearly one of continuity. Israel and Judah again dwell "in their possessions" (v 2), "in Jerusalem" (v 3). Our studies have indicated several interests which are attached to this larger concern: (1) The overall design of the writer, though executed imperfectly, is to place all of the lists of chap. 9 in the context of the inhabitants of Jerusalem, unlike Neh 11, which distinguished between inhabitants of Jerusalem and those who dwelt elsewhere in the land. (2) Ideologically and with special reference to Judah and the Levites, the lists have been made more systematically complete. Descendants of each of Judah's three surviving sons (Perez, Shelah, and Zerah) and each of the major Levitical clans (Merari, Asaph, and Jeduthun) are, in variance with Neh 11, named among those who inhabit the restored Jerusalem. (3) Various lists are updated, probably to reflect continuing developments and interests in post-exilic times. This is most apparent in the emphasis upon the gatekeepers in general (vv 17–32) and more specifically with the line of Shallum-Zechariah-Mattithiah, the chief family of the gatekeepers. In contrast to the brief treatment in Neh 11:19, Chronicles includes at least some of the gatekeepers among the Levites, and emphasizes both their close relationship to the clergy and the ancient roots of their office. It may be assumed that lesser variations in other lists, such as those of Benjamin and the priests, reflect similar post-exilic developments.

Whatever the ultimate origin of its diverse elements, chap. 9 sets before us a picture of Israel which in large measure is part and parcel with that of the remainder of Chronicles. All Israel, represented not only in Judah and Benjamin but also in Ephraim and Manasseh, is centered around Jerusalem, the site of the legitimate temple where priests, Levites, and other chosen cultic personnel function in accord with Yahweh's prescriptions. That some of these elements were of more importance to certain groups or individuals than to others goes without saying. Perhaps most strikingly absent is any apparent concern for a Judahite who may be connected with the Davidic ideal, which now looms most prominent in the narrative of Saul's demise and the rise of David.

David and Solomon   (Chaps. 10–29)

It is in this central portion of the Chronicler's work that his major interest is most apparent. While it is customary to relate 1 Chr 10–29 exclusively to David, and to define the writer's intentions almost exclusively with respect to him, our study indicates that the work of David and Solomon is to be considered a unity reaching its goal in the dedication of the temple. (Cf. Braun, *JBL* 92 [1973] 503–16; Williamson, *VT* 26 [1976] 351–61. This point is also noted by Ackroyd, 48, although he has failed to note the significance of Solomon's position in 1 Chr 22–29.) 1 Chr 22–29, as we have argued elsewhere, may best be seen as a transitional unit, whose function is to bring together and unite the chapters relating to David (1 Chr 10–21) and Solomon (2 Chr 1–9). Chaps. 23–27 consist largely of later insertions (cf. R. Braun, "Significance").

We may accordingly outline this larger unit as follows:

   I. The Davidic History (1 Chr 10–21)
      A. The Rejection of Saul's Kingship (1 Chr 10)
      B. The Rise of David (1 Chr 11–12)
      C. David, the Ark, and the Cult (1 Chr 13–17)
      D. David's Wars (1 Chr 18–21)
  II. Transitional Unit, 1 Chr 22 (23–27), 28, 29
 III. The Solomonic History (2 Chr 1–9)

In studying the content of these chapters, we are faced with a situation differing considerably from that of chaps. 1–9, in that extensive portions of these chapters have close—in many cases verbal—parallels in the books of Samuel, from which, it is commonly agreed, they are derived. For the fuller treatment of the contents of these synoptic portions, the reader is referred to the standard histories of Israel and the Samuel commentaries. It will be the primary task in this commentary to seek to understand these passages within the total context of the books of Chronicles.

It is my belief that the message of the writer is most apparent in those portions of the work where he has composed his narrative independently of other canonical sources, e.g., 1 Chr 10:13–14. At the same time, the comparison of Chronicles with Samuel-Kings in portions where the two are parallel, although fraught with more difficulties, cannot be ignored. When the text of Chronicles differs from that of its *Vorlage*, we may suppose that one of the following reasons is responsible: (1) *The author may have had a different text of Samuel before him.* Cases of this sort may be recognized at times by comparison of readings with Greek texts of the Lucianic tradition and with Hebrew texts of Samuel from Qumran where these are extant, both of which, with Chronicles, according to F. M. Cross, belong to the Palestinian tradition (*HTR* 57 [1964] 81–95). However, it is my judgment, based both upon Lemke's study of the synoptic portions of the work (*HTR* 58 [1965] 349–63) and my own studies that the results of such research are neither as numerous or as significant as one might expect. (2) *The writer may simply be abbreviating the text.* I believe this to be the case more frequently than has been recognized. (3) *The writer may add new information or alter old because of his own theological bias or Tendenz.* Such instances can often be identified by noting the similarity in vocabulary, syntax, and thought with other lengthier portions which appear to be of the writer's own composition.

Although it constitutes an argument from silence, it is impossible not to conjecture also upon portions of Samuel-Kings (some longer, some shorter) which have *not* been included in the work of Chronicles. It seems reasonable to assume that sometimes a section of no particular interest for the writer's purpose has been omitted for the sake of brevity while, on the other hand, such omissions may also have resulted from the writer's *Tendenz.*

The Death of Saul (10:1-14)

Bibliography

Mosis, R. *Untersuchungen zur Theologie des chronistischen Geschichtswerkes.* Freiburger theologische Studien 92. Freiburg: Herder, 1973. 17–43. **Myers, J. M.** "Saul, Son of Kish." *IDB* 4:228–33. **Willi, T.** *Die Chronik als Auslegung.* Göttingen: Vandenhoeck & Ruprecht, 1972. 9–12.

Translation

¹ Now the Philistines fought ᵃ against Israel, ᵇ and the men of Israel ᵇ fled from the Philistines and fell slain ᶜ on Mount Gilboa. ² The Philistines pursued Saul and his sons and killed Jonathan, ᵃ Abinadab, and Malchishua, Saul's sons. ᵇ ³ The battle was heavy against Saul, and he was struck by the archers and writhed ᵃ in pain because of the archers. ⁴ Saul commanded his armor-bearer, "Draw your sword and pierce me with it, so that these uncircumcised ones cannot come and ᵃ torture or ridicule ᵇ me." His armor-bearer refused, because he was terrified. Therefore Saul took the sword and fell upon it. ⁵ When his armor-bearer saw that Saul was dead, he too fell upon the sword and died. ᵃ ⁶ So Saul died, and his three sons, ᵃ ᵇ and all his house ᵇ—they all died together. ⁷ When all the men of Israel who were ᵃin the valley ᵃ saw that they had fled and that Saul and his sons were dead, they deserted their cities and fled, and the Philistines came in and occupied them.

⁸ On the next day the Philistines came in to strip the dead and found Saul and his sons fallen ᵃ on Mount Gilboa. ⁹ So they stripped Saul ᵃ and took his head and his armor and sent them throughout the surrounding land of the Philistines to make known the good news to their idols ᵇ and to their people. ¹⁰ They put his armor in the house of ᵃtheir gods ᵃ and ᵇdisplayed his skull in the house of Dagon. ᵇ

¹¹ When Jabesh-gilead heard all the Philistines had done to Saul, ᵃ ¹² all the warriors arose ᵃ and took the body ᵇof Saul and the bodies ᵇ of his sons ᶜ and brought them to Jabesh and buried their bones under the terebinth ᵈ in Jabesh. Then they fasted seven days.

¹³ So Saul died because of his unfaithfulness to Yahweh, since he did not obey the word of Yahweh, and, indeed, he even went so far as ᵃ to inquire of a necromancer. ᵃ ¹⁴ He did not seek ᵃ Yahweh, so he killed him and turned the kingdom over to David, the son of Jesse.

Notes

1.a. 1 Sam 31:1 נלחמים "fought." Cf. Mosis, *Untersuchungen,* 18–19.
1.b-b. 1 Sam 31:1 וינסו אנשי־ישראל "and the men of Israel fled." Cf. Kropat, *Syntax,* 11.
1.c. חללם "slain" = "pierced," i.e., by a sword. Cf. 10:8; 11:11, 20; 2 Chr 13:17.
2.a. 1 Sam 31:2 יהונתן "Jonathan"; otherwise uniformly יונתן.
2.b. Syr, in agreement with 8:33 and 9:39, adds "Ishbaal."
2.c. Read perhaps as וַיֶחֶל "he waited," from the root יחל "wait, tarry," or construe as an apocopated hoph of חלה "be sick, weak" (Rudolph). Cf. G Vg α'.
4.a. 1 Sam 31:4 + ודקרני "and pierce me."

4.b. The precise nuance of עלל "to deal with" is determined by the context; cf. Exod 10:2; 1 Sam 6:8. Saul is here pictured as preferring death to whatever fate the vengeful Philistines might visit upon him.

5.a. 1 Sam 31:5 + עמו "with him."

6.a. G (Syr) + "in that day"; cf. 1 Sam 31:6.

6.b-b. 1 Sam 31:6 וגם כל־אנשיו גם כליו ונשא "and his armor-bearer (and) also all his men." The alteration is significant; see *Comment*.

7.a-a. 1 Sam 31:7 adds ואשר בעבר הירדן העמק בעבר "who were beyond the valley and who were beyond the Jordan." The alteration is probably due only to a desire for brevity.

8.a. The time indicated by the act ptcp must be inferred from the context, and it is here clearly past; cf. GKC, § 116d.

9.a. Add perhaps ויראשוהו "and they beheaded him"; cf. 1 Sam 31:9.

9.b. 1 Sam 31:9 עצביהם בת "at the house of their idols"; cf. Syr Tg and a few Heb. MSS.

10.a-a. 1 Sam 31:10 עשתרות "Ashtaroth." The reason for this alteration is dubious; it may result from the desire to avoid mention of Astarte (cf. Michaeli, 77), or it may be a textual corruption (Rudolph, 92).

10.b-b. Cf. 1 Sam 31:10 שן בית בחומת תקעו ואת־גויתו "and his body they affixed to the wall of Bethshan." The reason for the alteration is again unclear, although it has frequently been related to the writer's supposed desire to avoid mention of the desecration of the body contrary to Jewish law; cf. Michaeli, 77. The root תקע (BDB [1075] "thrust, clap, give a blow") may be used to express the action of driving a weapon into a person (Judg 3:21; 4:21) or a tent peg into the ground (Isa 22:23, 25), etc.; it seems to be used here for the affixing of the body or head to a wall, etc., for display.

11.a. G + καὶ τῷ Ἰσραήλ "and to Israel."

12.a. 1 Sam 31:12 + כל־הלילה וילכו "and traveled all night."

12.b-b. 1 Sam 31:12 again includes mention both of the removal of the bodies from Bethshan (cf. n. 10.b-b.) and the burning of the bodies.

12.c. 1 Sam 31:12 + שם אתם וישרפו "and burned them there."

13.a-a. The style is heavy and the syntax unclear, although the meaning is apparent. Perhaps לדרוש "to a necromancer" (דרש "to resort to, seek," BDB, 205) should be omitted, either as a gl upon or a variant of לשאול "to ask" or as dittogr (cf. v 14). For the use of the inf constr as a finite vb, see GKC, § 114p.

14.a. In the pregnant sense, "to worship, have faith." See below.

Form/Structure/Setting

1 Chr 10:1–14 is drawn largely from 1 Sam 31:1–13, which comprises only a small part of the story of Samuel, Saul, and David related in 1 Sam 1–2 Sam 1. We may theorize that at least the general outline of the story was assumed to be known to the reader and that our writer thought it sufficient to begin with the account of Saul's last battle with the Philistines, culminating in the death of Saul and the end of his entire house (see below). Chapter 10 thus connects quite closely with the foregoing genealogy of Saul (9:35–44) and the following narrative of David proper in chapter 11.

The chapter may be outlined as follows:

vv 1–7   The death of Saul
vv 8–10   Saul's body displayed by the Philistines
vv 11–12 Saul's body retrieved by the men of Jabesh-gilead
vv 13–14 Reason for Saul's death

All of these portions are drawn from the narrative of 1 Sam 31:1–13, except for vv 13–14, which form the writer's interpretative comment.

It has been argued that 10:1 begins this larger portion of the work too abruptly, and does not connect easily to either 9:44, the preceding verse in the book as it now stands, or to 9:1, viewed as the preceding verse by those who assume 9:2–44 to be a later addition (cf. Rudolph, 94). This view of the fragmentary nature of chap. 10 appears at first to be supported by the presence of the conjunction *waw* on the first word of 10:1. However, it is questionable what kind of transition could relate the narrative of chap. 10 more smoothly to the genealogies of chaps. 1–9. Furthermore, the conjunction of ופלשתים "now the Philistines" is probably due to nothing more than the form extant in 1 Sam 31:1. (Rothstein, 200, and others who assume the integrity of 1 and 2 Chronicles with Ezra and Nehemiah point to Ezra 7:1 and Neh 1:1, where similar transitions occur [Noth, *Ü.S.*, 157; Mosis, *Untersuchungen*, 17, especially notes 5 and 6; Willi, 10].) It is only the death of Saul and the termination of the reign of his house that is of interest to the writer, and as Rudolph has expressed it, *"Aus dem Dunkel, in dem Saul versinkt, geht strahlend der Stern Davids* [Out of the darkness, in which Saul sinks, shines forth the star of David]" (96).

This point of view is not substantially altered by Mosis, who believes that Saul's reign also has paradigmatic significance for the author, considering his faithlessness and fate as symbolic of the results that always lead to punishment from God, most clearly apparent in the exile itself (*Untersuchungen*, 19–21, 41–42), or by Willi (9–12), who also sees here a close relationship among kingship, political independence, and the Chronicler's doctrine of retribution and who argues that chap. 9 is not only a *possible* but a *necessary* beginning of a historical work (12).

Comment

1–12 Saul met the Philistines for what was to be his last battle at Mt. Gilboa, located on the southern slopes of the Plain of Jezreel some six miles west of Beth-shan. The results were disastrous, as portended by the ghost of Samuel whom the medium at Endor summoned at Saul's request (1 Sam 28:18–19). Saul's men were routed and he and three of his sons died. Israel again appeared to be at the mercy of the Philistines (Bright, *History*, 190–91).

The account of Saul's final battle differs in detail in Chronicles from that in 1 Sam 31, despite wording which is often identical. Many of these differences are best considered stylistic (cf. v 1, where Chronicles reads נלחמו "they fought" instead of the participle נלחמים "fighting" and וינס איש־ישראל "the man of Israel fled" instead of וינסו אנשי ישראל "the men of Israel fled" [Kropat, *Syntax*, 11; Rothstein, 200; but see Mosis, *Untersuchungen*, 18–19, who views the differences as significant; cf. Curtis, 180], and the use of the later Hebrew גופה "body," instead of גויה "body, corpse" in v 12). Others are more clearly tendentious; still others are questionable.

Of greatest significance is the alteration introduced in v 6, where Chronicles states that not only Saul and his three (!) sons, but also *all his house* died before the Philistines. Instead of "all his house" Samuel reads "his armorbearer and all his men"; cf. n. 6.b-b. Curtis's (181) statement that the wording is "probably nothing more than a careless oversight" is incorrect. In the writer's plan not only Saul but *all* potential heirs to his throne met their end at Gilboa. That this is the writer's intention is clear from the omission of 2 Sam 2–4, which details the struggles of Abner to secure the throne for Saul's son Ish-bosheth, and the fact that there is in Chronicles no indication of opposition to the rule of David (or Solomon) from any quarter. That the genealogies of Saul in 1 Chr 8 and 9 name *four* sons of Saul and extend Saul's genealogy to later generations, perhaps to the exile itself (see on 9:39–40), suggests that these sections are not from the same hand as chap. 10.

Among the differences more difficult to explain are those of v 7, which restrict those fleeing from the battle to the inhabitants of the "valley" rather than including Galilee and Transjordan (cf. 1 Sam 31:7), and those relating to the treatment of the bodies of Saul and his sons. The account in 1 Sam 31 explicitly mentions that the Philistines cut off Saul's head (1 Sam 31:9), placed his armor in the temple of the goddess Ashtaroth, and hanged his body on the wall of Beth-shan (1 Sam 31:10), whence it was removed by dwellers of Jabesh-gilead after an all-night ride and subsequently burned. Chronicles does not explicitly mention Saul's beheading, omits mention of Ashtaroth (n. 10.a-a.), the over-night ride of the Jabesh-gileadites (n. 12.a.), and the burning of the bodies (n. 12.d.). The reason for these divergences is commonly assumed to be religious sensitivities of the writer, who wished to avoid mention of the desecration of the bodies and hesitated to so much as mention a Philistine goddess (cf. Rudolph, 95–96; Botterweck, *TQ* 136 [1956] 405–9). This tendency is extended by Mosis (*Untersuchungen*, 21–28), who views the flight of Saul and his men as typological for "all Israel" (it is for that reason that the geographical references to Galilee and Transjordan are obscured) and the removal of Saul's armor and head to Philistia as symbolic of the exile of faithless kings and their people from the land of Israel.

There may be some truth to this line of thought. However, while mention of Saul's decapitation is lacking in v 9, it is certainly assumed in both vv 9–10. The omission of "Ashtaroth" is striking, but, apart from textual corruption, how can the addition or retention of Dagon be explained? And, more fundamentally, why should the author feel compelled to preserve from desecration the body of Saul, whom he considers as having been put to death by Yahweh himself because of his unfaithfulness and by the Philistines, Israel's enemies, who (in the view of Mosis) represent all "pagan nations" (see below)? The situation may differ somewhat with reference to the inhabitants of Jabesh-gilead, since they are Israelites, but what has been said will suffice to indicate that the text has quite possibly been the object of over-interpretation. Some differences are probably due to the relative freedom with which the author has handled the text, resulting at times in abbreviation, at other times in alteration. Others may reflect the fact that the author had before him a text differing slightly from that now seen in 1 Sam 31 (cf. n. 10.a-a.). Still others may indeed be due to the religious scruples of the writer; judgment, however, is best withheld in the absence of supporting evidence, which is in this case lacking.

Particular mention should be made of the interpretation of Mosis, who understands the entire chapter as paradigmatic in nature (*Untersuchungen*, 17–43). One of the few remaining places where Dagon is mentioned in the OT is 1 Sam 4–7, where the ark of the covenant falls into Philistine hands and is placed in the temple of Dagon, who falls to the floor before it. The ark is then removed to Kiriath-jearim. Mosis relates here Israel's disobedience in the person of King Saul to death, defeat, and exile before the Philistines, who represent all pagan nations. It is as an example of the exile that Saul's armor and head are removed to the temple of Dagon in Philistia rather than to Beth-shan, which is to be understood as Israelite territory in 1 Sam 31 and such exile remains the result of disobedience throughout Israel's history. While Mosis' interpretation is problematic, especially in its interpretation of the books of Ezra and Nehemiah, which on his theory must be considered an integral part of the Chronicler's work, it is nonetheless true (though not mentioned by Mosis in this immediate text) that the first actions of David which the Chronicler will report following his securing of the throne are the capture of Jerusalem (11:4–9) and the removal of the ark from Kiriath-jearim (chap. 13).

13–14 These verses are the first lengthier insertion of the Chronicler within the narrative section of his work, and leave no doubt about the reason for recording Saul's death. God "killed him" (וימיתהו), v 14 states unequivocally, because (a) of his unfaithfulness (v 13, במעלו); (b) because he did not keep the word of Yahweh (v 13, על־דבר יהוה אשר לא־שמר), further explained as inquiring of a necromancer, v 13b (cf. Mosis, *Untersuchungen*, 39); and (c) he did not seek (דרש) Yahweh, v 14.

It is customary to relate this terminology to specific acts of Saul mentioned in 1 Samuel, in particular to his offering of a burnt offering (1 Sam 13, cf. v 13), to his disobedience in sparing some of the animals of the Amalekites (1 Sam 15), and especially in consulting the medium of Endor (1 Sam 28). This last act, to be sure, is readily suggested by v 13b, which, however, is of the nature of an explanatory gloss. The general terminology used here suggests the writer is more interested in picturing the *total* life of Saul as one of unfaithfulness rather than in pointing out specific sins. The unspecific use of מעל "unfaithfulness" in Chronicles is common knowledge (cf. 2 Chr 12:2; Curtis, 31, #68; Mosis, *Untersuchungen*, 29–33; and see on 1 Chr 5:25 above). The term שמר "keep, obey" is most readily associated with Deuteronomy and the Deuteronomistic history, and is found associated with Saul's disobedience in 1 Sam 13:13, 14; (1 Sam 15 uses שמע ב'; cf. vv 22–23); however, it is also very general in its orientation. Though less commonly recognized, this is also true of דרש, often translated mechanically as "to inquire of." But, as shown by Mosis in his excellent study of these three terms (*Untersuchungen*, 28–41), דרש too, whether occurring with the sign of the direct object את or the preposition ב, has a more general usage approaching "reverence, worship." (Cf. 2 Chr 11:16; 12:14, etc.) This sense is ignored by Wagner ("דרש," *TDOT* 3:293–307). See also 1 Chr 13:3; 15:13, where the pronominal object of דרש might better refer to Yahweh himself rather than the ark. (For all additional references see Curtis, 29, #23.) The reference to the medium in v 13b is an explanatory gloss, either by the original author or a later one. The final word of v 13, לדרוש, suggests textual difficulty, and is probably to be removed as dittography with the following: ולא דרש "and did not seek"; see n. 13.a-a. Understood in this manner, there is no need to defend the Chronicler against charges of falsifying the text in saying that Saul did not "seek Yahweh," when according to 1 Sam 28:6 he did so repeatedly (cf. also 1 Sam 14:37; 15:31), but received no answer. It was in his total behavior, not in isolated individual acts, that Saul showed himself to be unfaithful, and it was for that lack of faith that Yahweh rejected him and turned the kingdom over to David, the son of Jesse (v 14b).

Explanation

The kingship of Saul comes to an end because of his unfaithfulness. According to 1 Sam 13:13, Saul, like David, to whom our attention is now turned (cf. v 14), could have received an eternal dynasty, but because he did not keep Yahweh's word, he was rejected. Chronicles is much more explicit. Yahweh killed Saul, and turned the kingdom over to Jesse's son, David. Divine retribution (see *Introduction*) is visited upon Saul because of his unfaithfulness, and God in his free grace chooses another as the leader of his kingdom.

Such a message might be expected to have two immediate applications to the writer's audience and to today. (1) God may punish unfaithfulness; his people, whatever the age, are called to faithful obedience. (2) From the ashheap of failure, God raises up in grace a new leader, around whom he may gather a new people. And through David, he has promised a kingdom that will endure forever (2 Sam 7).

The Rise of David   (Chaps. 11–12)

The Beginning of the Rise of David   (11:1–9)

Bibliography

Elliger, C. "Die dreissig Helden Davids." *PJ* 31 (1935) 29–75. Mazar, B. "The Military Elite of King David." *VT* 13 (1963) 311–20. Mendenhall, G. "The Census Lists of Numbers 1 and 26." *JBL* 77 (1958) 52–66. Stinespring, W. "Eschatology in Chronicles." *JBL* 80 (1961) 209–19. Vaux, R. de. "Titres et fonctionnaires egyptiens à la cour de David et de Salomon." *RB* 48 (1939) 394–405. Williamson, H. G. M. "We Are Yours, O David." *OTS* 21 (1981) 164–76. Zeron, A. "Tag für Tag, kam Mann zu David, um ihm zu hilfen." *TZ* 30 (1974) 257–61.

Translation

[1a] *All Israel* [a] *gathered* [b] *to David at Hebron, saying, "Behold, we are your own relatives.* [2] *Formerly, even when Saul was king, you* [a] *were the one who led Israel out and in (to war), and Yahweh* [b] *your God* [b] *promised you, 'You will shepherd my people Israel, and you will be prince over* [c] *my people* [c] *Israel.'"* [3] *So all the elders of Israel came in to the king to Hebron, and David* [a] *made a covenant with them at Hebron before Yahweh, and they anointed David king over Israel* [b] *according to the word of Yahweh (which came) through Samuel.* [bc]

[4a] *David and all Israel* [a] *went to Jerusalem* [b] *(i.e., Jebus),* [b] *where the Jebusites were who inhabited the land.* [5] *The Jebusites told David, "You will not enter here,"* [a] *but David took the fortress of Zion (which is the city of David).* [6] *David said, "Anyone who smites the Jebusites* [a] *first will become chief and prince,"* *and Joab the son of Zeruiah went up first and became chief.* [a] [7] *Then David dwelt in the stronghold, so they named it "the city of David."* [8] *He* [a] *built the city* [b] *round about from Millo . . . ,* [b] [c] *while Joab restored the remainder of the city.* [c] [9] *David was continually becoming greater, because Yahweh Sebaoth was with him.*

Notes

1.a-a. 2 Sam 5:1 כל־שבטי ישראל "All the tribes of Israel" (cf. n. 4.a.).

1.b. Chr ויקבצו "now they gathered"; 2 Sam 5:1 ויבאו "now they came." Rothstein, 208, relates this difference to the author's supposed messianic hopes.

2.a. 2 Sam 5:2 (היית(ה "you were"; G ησθα "you had been."

2.b-b. > 2 Sam 5:2 ויאמר יהוה לך "Yahweh said to you"; Chr ויאמר יהוה אלהיך לך "Yahweh your God said to you."

2.c-c. > 2 Sam 5:2 פזג "a prince over Israel"; Chr נגיד על־ישראל "a prince over Israel"; Chr נגיד על עמי ישראל "prince over my people Israel."

3.a. MS G Syr + המלך "the king," as in 2 Sam 5:3.

3.b-b. 2 Sam 5:3 does not include this phrase.

3.c. Cf. 2 Sam 5:4–5 (1 Chr 3:4) for material not in this passage.

4.a-a. G* 2 Sam 5:6 המלך ואנשיו "the king and his men" (cf. n. 1.a-a.)

4.b-b. 2 Sam 5:6 אל היבסי ישב "against the Jebusites, inhabitants."

5.a. 2 Sam 5:6 adds "but the blind and the lame will ward you off." Cf. n. 6.a-a.

6.a-a. Cf. 2 Sam 5:8 which reads differently.

8.a. 2 Sam 5:9 + דוד "David."

8.b-b. ועד־הסביב "in complete circuit," RSV; 2 Sam 5:9 וביתה "inward," RSV.

8.c-c. 2 Sam 5:9 (cf. n. 6.a-a.) makes no mention of Joab, as in 2 Sam 5:8 and v 6, a different reading.

Form/Structure/Setting

These verses are dependent upon the narrative of 2 Sam 5. The outline of this unit and its relationship with Samuel is as follows.

1 Chronicles	2 Samuel	
———	(2 Sam 1–4)	(see below)
11:1–3	5:1–3	David made king at Hebron
(cf. 1 Chr 3:4)	5:4–5	Summary of David's rule
11:4–9	5:6–10	Conquest of Jerusalem and David's building

The Chronicler continues his interpretation of Israel's history by jumping forward to the anointing of David as king over all Israel at Hebron. The most obvious feature of the Chronicler's presentation is the omission of the contents of 2 Sam 1–4, which recount events following the death of Saul, including the death of the Amalekite who claimed to have slain Saul, David's lamentation over Saul, his rule at Hebron over Judah only, and his struggle with the remnants of Saul's family and kingdom. The omission of 2 Sam 5:4–5 from the Chronicler's narrative at this point (which has the same information included in 3:4) and the change of wording when the same topic is broached in 29:27 make it apparent that this omission is in keeping with the writer's understanding, first evidenced in 1 Chr 10:6 (see above), that Saul's entire house fell in his final battle with the Philistines. David therefore experiences no opposition from that quarter or any other in his rise to power.

This same interest is also apparent in several of the variations in the text of Chronicles when compared with Samuel, and suggests strongly that these alterations belong to the author of our text. The כל־ישראל "all Israel" of 1 Chr 11:1 is to be sure only slightly more inclusive than the כל־שבטי ישראל "all the tribes of Israel" of 2 Sam 5:1. However, the same cannot be said for the substitution of "David and all Israel" (1 Chr 11:4) for "the king and his men" (2 Sam 5:6) and for the omission of all mention of David's seven and one-half year reign over Judah only at Hebron found in 2 Sam 5:5.

A second interest of the writer, seen already in 10:13, is to indicate complete agreement between Yahweh's word and will and the events as they transpired.

This is apparent at the end of v 3, where he adds that David was anointed "according to the word of Yahweh through (ביד "by the hand of") Samuel." It seems probable that no specific "word" is referred to here. It is rather to the general principle that reference is made.

A third major difference between Chronicles and Samuel involves the role of Joab in the conquest and "rebuilding" (see below) of Jerusalem. Samuel makes no mention of Joab at all in this connection, and some of its references are at best obscure (cf. the references to the lame and the blind in 2 Sam 5:6, 8 and the description of David's building activity (מן־המלוא וביתה "from the Millo and inward") in v. 9. However, Chronicles attributes Joab's role as chief and commander (לראש ולשר) of David's army to the fact that he, in response to David's offer, went up first against the Jebusites (11:6). Perhaps too much should not be made of the fact that Chronicles then has Joab participate also in the "rebuilding" (חיה, piel v 8) of the city with David, although some (cf. Mosis, *Untersuchungen*, 45–47) find here an indication that the author pictured Jerusalem as completely destroyed and then restored, in conscious parallelism to the fate of Jerusalem at the time of the exile.

Other differences found in v 8 in contrast to 2 Sam 5:9 are probably due to the author's desire to bring understanding to a difficult text, perhaps in harmony with the topography of Jerusalem as he understood it some half a millennium later. (See the evidence cited by Welten [*Geschichte und Geschichtsdarstellung in dem Chroniksbüchern*] and Rudolph, 96–99.) The identification of the earlier name of Jerusalem as "Jebus" (v 4; cf. 2 Sam 5:6), is in accord with P (cf. Josh 15:8; 18:16, 28), but is contrary to the evidence of the Amarna letters of earlier centuries, where the term Jerusalem is regularly used.

Explanation

Immediately following the death of Saul, David is anointed king by "all Israel" at Hebron in accordance with God's word. As his first act, King David, again with the support of "all Israel," proceeds to the capture of Jerusalem, destined to be the home of the dynasty and the temple.

Many of the emphases of Chronicles were already present in Samuel-Kings. This is true of the emphasis upon all Israel's participation in David's reign (cf. 2 Sam 5:1; 6:5, 15) and of the choice of David as being in accord with the divine will (cf. 2 Sam 5:2). In 2 Samuel also, David's first act after his coronation at Hebron is the capture of Jerusalem.

Chronicles has heightened these points by stating them more clearly and by omitting material which might contribute to an opposite understanding. In effect, the writer has brought out the implications of 2 Sam 5:10, with which he also concludes this section (v 9): "David was continually becoming greater, because Yahweh Sebaoth was with him." Thus he wants his readers, and us, to understand the blessings which flow from faithful obedience to the Lord.

David and His Mighty Men (11:10–47)

Bibliography

Driver, S. R. *An Introduction to the Literature of the Old Testament.* New York: Meridian Books, 1956. ———. *Notes on the Hebrew Text and the Topography of the Books of Samuel.* 2nd ed. Oxford: Clarendon Press, 1960. **Gehrke, R. D.** *1 and 2 Samuel.* St. Louis: Concordia Publishing House, 1968. **Grintz, J. M.** "The Life of David in Samuel and Chronicles." *BMik* 1 (1956) 69–75. (Heb.) **Hertzberg, H. W.** *I & II Samuel.* OTL. Tr. J. S. Bowden. London: SCM Press, 1964. **Kennedy, A. R. S.** *Samuel.* The Century Bible 6. London: Caxton, n.d. **Smith, H. P.** *A Critical and Exegetical Commentary on the Books of Samuel.* New York: Scribner's, 1902. **Vaux, R. de.** *Les Livres de Samuel.* La Sainte Bible. Paris: Les Éditions du Cerf, 1961.

Translation

[10] *These are the heads of David's mighty men who supported him strongly [a] in his kingdom [b] with all Israel to make him king [b] according to Yahweh's word concerning Israel.* [11][a] *This is the roster [a] of David's mighty men: Jashobeam, [b] a Hachmonite, [c] was chief of the three. [d] On one occasion [e] he brandished his spear [e] against three [f] hundred slain at one time.* [12] *After him came Eleazar, son of Dodo, the Ahohite. He was included with the three mighty men.* [13] *He was with David at [a] Pasdammim, [a] when the Philistines gathered there for battle. . . . [b] A portion of the field was full of barley, [c] and the people fled [d] from the Philistines.* [14] *But they gathered [a] in the midst of that portion and held [a] it and defeated [a] the Philistines, and Yahweh gave them a great victory.*

[15] *Three chiefs [a] of the thirty went down to the refuge [b] to David at the cave of Adullam when the Philistines were camping in the vale of Sorek.* [16] *David was in the stronghold at that time, and the Philistine garrison [a] was at Bethlehem.* [17] *And David was very thirsty [a] and said, "If only I had a drink of water from the well at the gate of Bethlehem!"* [18] *So the three broke through the Philistine camp and drew water from the well at Bethlehem's gate and took and brought it to David. David refused to drink it, but poured it out before Yahweh,* [19] *saying: [a] "Far be it from me, my God, [b] to do this. Shall I drink the blood of these men at the cost of their lives?" [a] [c] Since they had brought it at the cost of their lives, David refused to drink it. [c] These were the exploits of the three mighty men.*

[20] *Abishai, Joab's brother, [a] was chief among the thirty. [b] He brandished his spear against three hundred, and his name was listed [c] with the three.* [21] *He was more honored than the thirty, [a] [b] and became prince to them, but he did not attain to the three.*

[22] *Benaiah from Kabzeel, the son of Jehoiada, a warrior [a] mighty in deeds—he smote the two leaders [b] of Moab, and he went down and smote a lion [b] in the midst of a pit on a snowy day.* [23] *He also smote an Egyptian, a huge [a] man [b] five cubits tall, [b] in whose hand was a spear [c] like a weaver's beam. [c] He went down to meet him with a stick, and tore the spear from the Egyptian's hand and killed him with his own spear.* [24] *These were the deeds of Benaiah, Jehoiada's son, and his fame*

was [a] *like that of the three mighty men.* [25a] *He was more highly honored than the thirty, but he did not attain to the three, and David placed him over his guard.* [a]

[26a] *The mighty men were* [a] *Asahel the brother of Joab,* [b] *Elhanan the son of Dodo from Bethlehem,* [27] *Shammoth* [a] *the Harorite* [bc] *Helez the Pelonite,* [d] [28] *Ira the son of Ikkesh the Tekoaite, Abiezer the Anathothite,* [29] *Sibbecai* [a] *the Hushathite, Ilai* [b] *the Ahohite,* [30] *Maharai the Netophathite, Heled the son of Baanah the Netophathite,* [31] *Ithai* [a] *the son of Ribai, from Gibeah of the Benjaminites, Benaiah* [b] *the Pirathonite,* [32] *Hurai* [a] *from the wadis of Gaash, Abiel* [b] *the Arbathite,* [33] *Azmaveth the Baharum-ite,* [a] *Eliahba the Shaalbonite,* [34] *. . .* [a] *Hashem* [b] *the Gizonite,* [c] *Jonathan* [d] [e] *the son of* [e] [f] *Shagee the Hararite,* [f] [35] *Ahiam the son of Sachar* [a] *the Hararite,* [b] *Eliphal* [c] *the son of Ur,* [d] [36] *Hepher* [a] *the Mecherathite,* [b] [c] *Ahijah the Pelonite,* [c] [37] *Hezro* [a] *the Carmelite, Naarai* [b] [c] *the son of Ezbai,* [c] [38] *Joel* [a] [b] *the brother of* [b] *Nathan,* [c] *Mibhar the son of Hagri,* [c] [39] *Zelek the Ammonite, Naharai the Beerothite, the armor-bearer* [a] *of Joab the son of Zeruiah,* [40] *Ira the Ithrite, Gareb the Ithrite,* [41] *Uriah the Hittite,* [a] [b] *Zabad the son of Ahlai,* [42] *Adina the son of Shiza the Reubenite, chief of the Reubenites, and thirty with him,* [a] [43] *Hanan the son of Maacah, and Joshaphat the Mithnite,* [a] [44] *Uzzia the Ashterathite, Shama and Jeiel* [a] *the sons of Hotham the Aroerite,* [45] *Jediael the son of Shimri and Joha* [a] *his brother, the Tizite,* [b] [46] *Eliel the Mahavite, and Jeribai and Joshaviah, the sons* [a] *of Elnaam, and Ithmah the Moabite,* [47] *Eliel and Obed and Jaasiel the Mezobaite.* [a]

Notes

10.a. The hithp of חזק "to be strong" is a favorite term in non-synoptic portions of Chronicles; cf. Curtis, #38; Williamson, *Israel*, 54 § F.5.

10.b-b. Syr (α' Vg) על־כל־ישראל להמלכו "over all Israel, to make him king."

11.a-a. 2 Sam 23:8 אלה שמות "these are the names."

11.b. Gmin Ιεσεβααλ/Ισβααλ "Ishbaal"; 2 Sam 23:8 ישב־בשבת "Joshab-basshebeth"; BHS ישבעל "Yishbaal."

11.c. חכמוני "Hachmonite"; 2 Sam 23:8 תחכמני "Tah-chemonite."

11.d. Reading without enthusiasm השלשה "the three" for השלושים "the thirty"; cf. GL both here and in 2 Sam 23:8, where MT reads השלשי (as in 2 Sam 23:18 K also), probably a military term, "captains" (cf. KJV, NIV, RSV footnote). The confusion among these same three terms, apparent also in vv 20, 21, 24, 25, is no doubt heightened by the composite nature of the list already in 2 Samuel. Judgments are arbitrary, since it appears that both "three" and "thirty" are designations which have lost their literal meaning. (The list of David's mighty men is concluded in 2 Sam 23:39 with the enumeration "thirty-seven," although that number can be counted in the preceding lists only with difficulty; cf. Elliger, *PJ* 31[1935] 30–36.) At any rate, the inclusion of 16 additional names in 1 Chr 11:41b–47 raises the total well above any literal meaning of "thirty."

11.e-e. 2 Sam 23:8 (Q נ') הוא עדינו העצנו : obscure.

11.f. 2 Sam 23:8 שמנה "eight."

13.a-a. 2 Sam 23:9 בחרפם בפלשתים "when they taunted the Philistines."

13.b. 2 Sam 23:9–11 adds the exploits of Eleazar and introduces "Shammah, the son of Agee, the Hararite," apparently as the third of the three. The episode related in 1 Chr 11:13b–14 is then in 2 Samuel attached to this Shammah.

13.c. 2 Sam 23:11 עדשים "lentils."

13.d. See n. 14.a.

14.a. The verbs are in 2 Sam 23:12 uniformly sg with the collective sg subj העם "the people."

15.a. ראש "chief, head" here and in 2 Sam 23:13 is sg; GL reads the pl. Perhaps ראש arose as a gl identifying the three with the three leaders in the preceding verses.

15.b. Lit. "rock, cliff" (צור).

16.a. 2 Sam 23:14 reads ומצב "garrison, outpost" for ונציב "post, refuge."

17.a. Hithp אוה "to long for, desire."

19.a-a. The text of this verse is confusing and incomplete here and in 2 Sam 23:17, although the meaning is clear enough. David refuses to drink water brought to him at the risk of men's lives.

19.b. Reading אלהי(מ) as vocative. 2 Sam 23:17 reads יהוה "Yahweh" for מאלהי "from my God."

19.c-c. This explanatory gl suggests the author or a later reader also found the previous line less than satisfying.

20.a. 2 Sam 23:18 + בן־צרויה "son of Zeruiah."

20.b. Reading השלושים "the thirty" for השלושה "the three," with Syr and most translations. 2 Sam 23:18 השלשי "captains." The reading "three" would seem to contradict vv 21–27.

20.c. K לא "not"; 2 Sam 23:18 Q לו "to him" (and cf. vv 24–25). The meaning, determined by the context, must be that, despite his reputation, he was not in some sense classed with the three.

21.a. Again reading שלשים "thirty" with Syr (see n. 20.b.), BHS, Rudolph.

21.b. Omitting בשנים "with the two," with Syr, BHS, Rudolph.

22.a. Omitting בן "son of" as a variant of איש "man"; cf. 2 Sam 23:20 Gᴮᴬᴬ.

22.b-b. אריאל "leaders," but lit., "lion of God" (BDB, 72), is not to be understood as a proper name, leading to the other supposed deficiencies in the text. Rather it is a technical term applied to foreign military leaders; cf. Mesha Inscription, line 12 (KAI I, 33) and the Canaanite inscriptions. Note also the retention of אלוף "chief" of the leaders of Moab in 1:51–54. Perhaps the constr pl ending should be added.

23.a. איש מדה "a huge man"; 2 Sam 23:21 מראה "good-looking."

23.b-b. > 2 Sam 23:21; cf. 1 Sam 17:4.

23.c-c. > 2 Sam 23:21; cf. 1 Sam 17:7.

24.a. See n. 20.c.

25.a-a. See n. 20.c.

26.a-a. > 2 Sam 23:24.

26.b. 2 Sam 23:24 + בשלשים "was with the thirty."

27.a. שמות "Shammoth." 2 Sam 23:25 שמה "Shammah."

27.b. 2 Sam 23:25 החרדי "the Harodite."

27.c. 2 Sam 23:25 + אליקא החרדי "Elika, the Harodite."

27.d. 2 Sam 23:26 הפלתי "the Palite" (pro הפלוני "the Pelonite").

29.a. 2 Sam 23:27 מבני "Mebunnai" (pro סבכי "Sibbecai").

29.b. 2 Sam 23:28 צלמון "Zalmon" (pro עילי "Ilai").

31.a. 2 Sam 23:29 אִתַּי "Itai" (pro איתי "Ithai").

31.b. 2 Sam 23:30 בניהו "Benaihu" (pro בניה "Benaiah").

32.a. 2 Sam 23:30 הדי "Hiddai" (pro הורי "Hurai").

32.b. 2 Sam 23:31 אבי־עלבון "Abi-albon" (pro אביאל "Abiel").

33.a. 2 Sam 23:31 הברחמי "the Barhumite" (pro הבחרומי "the Baharumite").

34.a. Delete בני "sons of" as dittogr? (Cf. v 33 השעלבני "the Shaalbonite.")

34.b. 2 Sam 23:32 בני ישן "sons of Jashan" (pro בני השם "sons of Hasham").

34.c. > 2 Sam 23:34.

34.d. 2 Sam 23:32 יהונתן "Jonathan."

34.e-e. > 2 Sam 23:32; BH³ suggests adding בני and moving verse division.

34.f-f. 2 Sam 23:33 שמה ההררי "Shammah the Haharite."

35.a. 2 Sam 23:33 שרר "Sharar" (pro שכר "Sachar").

35.b. 2 Sam 23:33 האררי "the Ha'arite" (pro ההררי "the Hararite").

35.c. 2 Sam 23:34 אליפלט "Eliphelet" (pro אליפל "Eliphal").

35.d. 2 Sam 23:34 אחסבי "Ahasbai" (pro אור "Ur").

36.a. > 2 Sam 23:34.

36.b. 2 Sam 23:34 בן־המעכתי "son of Maacai" (pro המכרתי "the Mecherathite").

36.c-c. 2 Sam 23:34 אליעם בן־אחיתפל הגלני "Eliam son of Ahithophel the Gilonite."

37.a. 2 Sam 23:35 K חצרי "Hezro"; Q חצרי "Hezrai" (pro חצרו "Hezro").

37.b. 2 Sam 23:35 פערי "Paarai" (pro נערי "Naarai").

37.c-c 2 Sam 23:35 הארבי "the Arbite" (pro בן־אזבי "son of Ezbai").

38.a. 2 Sam 23:36 יגאל "Igal" (pro יואל "Joel").

38.b-b. Gᴮˢ 2 Sam 23:36 בן נתן "son of Nathan"; not אחי נתן "the brother of Nathan."

38.c-c. 2 Sam 23:36 מצבת בני הגדי "from Zobah son of the Gadite" (pro מבחר בן־הגרי "Mibhar son of Hagri").

39.a. G^L Tg 2 Sam 23:37 K pl.

41.a. 2 Sam 23:39 + כל שלשים ושבעה "thirty-seven in all."

41.b. 2 Sam 23 lacks vv 41b–47.

42.a. Or "thirty over him" or "over thirty" (cf. Syr).

43.a. G^B ὁ Βαιθανει (G^S Βεθαναι) "the Bethanite."

44.a. K ויעואל "and Juel"; Q mlt MSS G Tg Vg ויעיאל "and Jeiel"; Syr עמיאל "Amiel."

45.a. G^BA και Ιωαξαε "and Johazah."

45.b. G^AL ὁ Θωσαι or החוצי "the Tozite."

46.a. G (Syr) υἱὸς αυτοῦ "his son" = בְנוֹ.

47.a. *BHS* suggests reading either הַמְצֹבָה "the Mezobite" or הַצֹּבָתִי "the Zobathite."

Form/Structure/Setting

This unit can be outlined and placed in relationship to Samuel as follows.

Chronicles	2 Samuel	
1 Chr 11:10	——	Writers's introduction
11:11–14	23:8–14	Three chief men
11:15–19	23:13–17	An exploit of the three
11:20–25	23:18–23	Two additional heroes
11:26–41a	23:24–39	List of David's mighty men
11:41b–46	——	Additional mighty men

Most of this unit (vv 11–41a) is what we have agreed to call narrative (see *Introduction*, "Literary Forms in Chronicles") parallel to 2 Sam 23:8–39, is composite, and is probably derived from it, although textual variants (see the *Notes*) may point to a more complicated relationship. By contrast to its position in Samuel as an appendix to the book, it is found in Chronicles in a new position near the beginning of David's reign.

The reason for this is made abundantly clear in v 10, which is unique to Chronicles and is replete with his vocabulary and themes. This gathering of the lists of David's leaders and warriors demonstrates the unanimity of Israel's support for David (cf. 11:1, 4; 12:23, 29 [22, 29]), as does chap. 12 also.

The origin of vv 41b–47, without parallel in the OT, is problematic. Although it is possible that the names found here have been dropped from the end of the same list in Samuel (the conclusion of the list with Uriah the Hittite is at a minimum suggestive in view of 2 Sam 11), it seems more likely that the additional names found here have been appended from another source. That this is so is suggested by both form and content. Formally, vv 41b–47 differ from vv 26–41a in their use of the conjunction "and" and the more profuse information contained (cf. v 42 and the frequent pairing of brothers), both of which are lacking in the earlier section. With respect to content, Bertheau (216) has already noted that while vv 26–41a refer mostly to Judah and Benjamin, vv 41b–47 are associated with places which are either

unknown or which lie east of the Jordan. While there is some evidence that
the form of the names in vv 41b–47 is post-exilic, the fact that they refer to
places either unknown or east of the Jordan (Reuben, Aroer, Moab, Ashteroth,
Mahanaim) would seem to rule out a simple derivation from post-exilic Judah.
Whatever its source or date, we may assume its inclusion here points to a
desire to make the list of those supporting David's kingship more complete.
Noth calls attention also to the fact that the origin of *every individual* named
in the first part of the list is cited while this is not the case in the latter
part (*Ü.S.,* 136).

The confusion, both textual and otherwise (cf. n. 11.d.), surrounding the
use of the similar terms "three," "thirty," and "captains" both in Samuel
and in Chronicles, is probably due to the composite nature of the lists, to
ongoing changes in the nature of David's "Thirty," and perhaps to ignorance
of שׁלישׁ as a term meaning a military official, now well established. Some
of those named "chiefs" may well date from different periods of time (notice
that David's general, Joab is not named at all save as the brother of Abishai,
v 20), these officials may at times have been included among the "Thirty,"
at other times considered above it; and the name "Thirty" itself became a
designation of a military group without strict regard to literal numerical
strength. The difficulties of text and understanding result from attempts to
understand as a literary unit items not originally so intended.

In that sense, the retention of the translation "captains" and "officers"
by the KJV and NIV in v 11 and in 2 Sam 23:8 (and cf. JB's "three") in Samuel
only may well be justified. The *kethib* variant of 1 Chr 11:11 has emended
this to "thirty" either out of ignorance or in view of his larger scope; the
qere variant is an amalgam of both traditions. Similarly, the *qere* and *kethib*
variants of v 20 (K לֹא "not," Q לוֹ "to him") reflected the concern as to
whether Abishai (and Benaiah, v 24) should or should not be classified with
the three or the Thirty.

Comment

V 10, unique to Chronicles, provides the rubric according to which the
following lists are to be understood. Already at Hebron (cf. 11:1; 12:24 [23])
these warriors joined with "all Israel" in their support of David. (For חזק
"to be strong" see Curtis, 29, #38; Williamson, *Israel,* 54; Driver, *Introduction,*
538, #8.) The all Israel theme clearly enunciated here has already been
stated in 11:1, 4 and will be repeated often; likewise the agreement of events
with God's will seen in conjunction with Saul's death (10:13–14) is here repeated. Those individuals referred to in the remainder of chaps. 11 and 12
are mustered as evidence for the unanimity of Israel's support of David's
kingship, which expressed itself even prior to his coronation at Hebron.

Since vv 11–41a relate directly to 2 Sam 23, they will be dealt with here
more briefly and as a unit, although their composite nature is apparent.
Vv 11–14 are apparently meant to list three of David's mighty men, as in
2 Sam 23:8–12. However, several lines have been dropped from the text

(see n. 13.b.), resulting in the omission of some of the exploits of Eleazar and (the name) Shammah, with the resulting attribution of some of Shammah's exploits to Eleazar. Vv 15–19 speak of a specific event carried out by a nameless threesome, which it would seem most natural to identify with the three introduced in vv 11–14, although some would deny this.

Vv 20–25 (cf. 2 Sam 23:18–23) add two additional heroes, Abishai and Benaiah, whose exploits are well known (cf. 1 Chr 2:16, 1 Sam 26:6; 1 Kgs 2:35), who apparently are understood to occupy a position of prominence somewhere between the "three" and the "thirty."

2 Sam 23:24–39, parallel to vv 26–41a, is apparently meant to include 32 names, which together with the 5 of vv 8–12, 18–23, would total the 37 mentioned in v 39. However, the condition of the text, especially in vv 32 and 34, makes certainty impossible. It seems that the text of Chronicles, even with the omission of "Elika" of 2 Sam 23:25 in 1 Chr 11:27, has in general been transmitted more accurately, though it too is not without difficulty (cf. the *Notes* on v 34) in that the addition of 16 additional names by Chronicles in vv 41b–47 puts the total number named significantly above the 37 mentioned in 2 Samuel. It is probably for that reason that the enumeration found in 2 Sam 23:37 has been dropped in Chronicles.

The relationship between the two lists can be seen more clearly when they are placed side by side.

2 Sam 23	1 Chr 11
Josheb-basshebeth	(11) Jashobeam cf. 1 Chr 27:2
Eleazar	Eleazar
Shammah	(12) . . .
Abishai	(20) Abishai
Benaiah	(22) Benaiah
Asahel	(26) Asahel
Elhanan	Elhanan
Shammah	(27) Shammoth
Elika	
Helez	Helez
Ira	(28) Ira
Abiezer	Abiezer
Mebunnai (LXX^L Sibbecai)	(29) Sibbecai
Zalmon	Ilai
Maharai	(30) Maharai
Heleb	Heled
Ittai	(31) Ithai
Benaiah	Benaiah
Hiddai	(32) Hurai
Abielbon	Abiel
Azmaveth	(33) Azmaveth
Eliahba	Eliahba
(sons of) Jashem	(34) (sons of) Hashem

Jonathan	Jonathan
Shammah	(the son of)Shagee
Ahiam	(35) Ahiam
Eliphelet	Eliphal
	(36) Hepher
Eliam	
son of Ahithophel	Ahijah
Hezro	(37) Hezro
Paarai	Naarai
Igal	(38) Joel
Bani	Mibbar
Zelek	(39) Zelek
Naharai	Naharai
Ira	(40) Ira
Gareb	Gareb
Uriah	(41) Uriah
	Zabad
	(42) Adina
	(43) Hanan
	Joshaphat
	(44) Uzziah
	Shama
	Jeiel
	(45) Jediael
	Joha
	(46) Eliel
	Jeribai
	Joshabiah
	Ithmai
	(47) Eliel
	Obed
	Jaasiel

Nothing is known of most of the individuals named here—for details, see the Samuel commentaries. Of special interest for Chronicles is the fact that the first twelve names mentioned are mentioned again in 1 Chr 27:2–15 as monthly commanders of David's army.

Explanation

As expressed clearly in v 10, these lists provide substance to Israel's support of David in his rise to kingship. As leaders of Israel, these warriors are representatives of the fact that *all Israel* was enthusiastic in its support of David's kingship, which was of course according to God's plan. In that sense details concerning those named are insignificant. It is not the individuals, but the cumulative effect of their more than fifty names which points to God's pleasure and Israel's full participation in the rise of King David, whose chief task will be the construction of a house of rest for his God in Jerusalem. So God's leaders and those who support them in every age are bound together as one to accomplish his will.

David at Ziklag and the Stronghold (12:1-23)

Bibliography

(See above at 11:1–9 and 11:10–47.)

Translation

¹ *These are the men who came to David at Ziklag, while he was still in hiding because of* ᵃ *Saul, the Son of Kish. They were with the mighty men, and they assisted in the warfare.* ² *They were archers and could sling stones or shoot arrows with either the right hand or left. From Saul's kinsmen, from Benjamin:* ³ *Ahiezer the chief, and Joash, sons* ᵃ *of Shemaah of Gibeah; Jeziel and Pelet the sons of Azmaveth; Berachah* ᵇ *and Jehu the Anathothite;* ⁴ *Ishmaiah the Gibeonite, a mighty man among the thirty and over the thirty;* ⁵ᵃ *Jeremiah, Jahaziel, Johanan, and Jozabad the Gaderathite;* ᵃ ⁶[⁵] *Eluzai, Jerimoth, Bealiah, Shemariah, and Shephatiah, the Haruphite;* ᵃ ⁷[⁶] *Elkanah, Isshiah, Azarel, Joezer, and Jashobeam, the Korahites;* ⁸[⁷] *Joelah* ᵃ *and Zebadiah, the sons of Jeroham* ᵇ *from Gedor.* ᵇ

⁹[⁸] *From the Gadites these defected to David at the stronghold* ᵃ *in the wilderness,* ᵇ *mighty men, warriors who could handle shield and spear.* ᶜ *They were as strong as lions* ᶜ *and as swift as gazelles upon the mountains:* ¹⁰[⁹] *Ezer the chief, Obadiah the second, Eliab the third,* ¹¹[¹⁰] *Mishmannah the fourth, Jeremiah the fifth,* ¹²[¹¹] *Attai the sixth, Eliel the seventh,* ¹³[¹²] *Johanan the eighth, Elzabad the ninth,* ¹⁴[¹³] *Jeremiah the tenth, Machbannai the eleventh.* ¹⁵[¹⁴] *These were Gadites, chiefs of the army. The least was over* ᵃ *a hundred, and the greatest over a thousand.* ¹⁶[¹⁵] *These were the men who crossed the Jordan in the first month when it was overflowing all the inhabitants of the valleys* ᵃ ᵇ *to the east and to the west.* ᵇ

¹⁷[¹⁶] *Some* ᵃ *Benjaminites and Judaites also came in to David at the stronghold.* ¹⁸[¹⁷] *David went out to them* ᵃ *and said* ᵃ *to them, "If you have come to me peacefully to help me,* ᵇ *my heart will be one with you, but if (you have come) to betray me to my enemies, although there is no violence in my hands, may the God of our Fathers see and judge."* ¹⁹[¹⁸] *And the Spirit clothed Amasai, the chief of the thirty:* ᵃ

"We are yours, David,
and we are with you, son of Jesse.
Peace, peace be with you, and peace be to him who helps you,
For he who helps you is your God."
So David received them, and put them at the head ᵇ *of his troops.*

²⁰[¹⁹] *Some from Manasseh also defected to David when he came in with the Philistines for the battle against Saul. They* ᵃ *did not help them however, because by counsel the Philistine lords sent him away, saying: "He will defect to his master, Saul,* ᵇ *and it will cost us our heads."* ᵇ ²¹[²⁰] *When he went to Ziklag there defected to him from Manasseh, Adnah,* ᵃ *Jozabad, Jediael, Michael, Jozabad, Elihu,* ᵇ *and Zillethai, heads of the clans of Manasseh.* ²²[²¹] *They assisted David* ᵃ *against the raiding bands,* ᵃ *because all of them were valiant men, princes over the army.* ²³[²²] *So day by day they kept streaming in to David to help him, until there was a great army, like the army of God.* ᵇ

Notes

1.a. Or "banned from the presence of" Saul (NEB).

3.a. MSS G$^{BA^R}$ בן "son of"; Syr בנו "his son."

3.b. Read perhaps as ברכיה "Berachiah" with G^{BAL}.

5.a-a. Ev 4b, resulting in different versification for the remainder of the chapter. Eng. verse numbers (in brackets) will regularly follow the Heb. verse numbers.

6.a. K G^B הַחֲרִיפִי "the Hariphite"; Q G^A Vg הַחֲרוּפִי "the Haruphite."

8.a. Syr יואח "Joah"; G^B Ἐλια "Eliah."

8.b-b. Perhaps delete as dittogr; cf. v 9.

9.a. למצד "stronghold" is not in G, suggesting deletion.

9.b. The ה is directive (cf. GKC, § 90c), perhaps in a weakened sense here (cf. GKC, § 90c).

9.c-c. Lit., "their faces were the faces of lions."

15.a. Or perhaps "was equal to."

16.a. K גדיתיו; Q גדותיו "valleys."

16.b-b. Or perhaps the reference is to the waters filling the lowlands and displacing the inhabitants; however, then no exploit of the Gadites would be named other than that of crossing the flooding Jordan.

17.a. The prep (מן) is partitive; see BDB, 580–81, ¶3.

18.a-a. Lit., "and answered and said."

18.b. לאזרני "to help me" is not in G$^{BA^R}$.

19.a. K G Syr Vg read השלושים "the thirty"; Q השלישים, adding לאמר "the thirty, saying."

20.a. Read perhaps as "he"; cf. G$^{AL·l}$ Vg.

20.b-b. ב of price or value. See BDB, 90, III.3.a.

21.a. A few MSS read עדנה "Adnah."

21.b. G^{BS} καὶ Ἐλίμουθ "and Elimouth"; G^A ^{min} καὶ Ἐλίουδ "and Elihud."

22.a-a. Or "with his troops."

22.b. Or perhaps, with אלהים used adjectivally, "a mighty army."

Form/Structure/Setting

This pericope consists of four smaller units, each without parallel, diverse formally but united under the general heading of tribal groups who joined in support of David before his coronation at Hebron, while he was a fugitive from Saul at the "stronghold" in the wilderness (vv 9 [8], 17 [16]) and later at Ziklag (vv 1, 21 [20]):

(1) Benjaminites who came to David at Ziklag, vv 1–8 [1–7];
(2) Gadites who came to David "at the stronghold in the wilderness," vv 9–16 [8–15];
(3) Benjaminites and Judahites at the stronghold, vv 17–19 [16–18];
(4) Manassehites who defected to David upon returning to Ziklag from the Philistine encounter with Israel, vv 20–23 [19–22].

Each of these units is introduced with a formal statement providing a setting for the list; the second contains a closing statement as well. The third unit differs from the others in that it contains only a single name, and emphasis falls upon the *words* of this Amasai, uttered under prophetic inspiration. While the terminology of the framework appears to be that of the Chronicler, the form of the lists themselves differs significantly (cf. vv 3–5 e.g., with 5–8 [7], and both with the method of enumeration in vv 10–14 [9–13] and the simple style of v 21 [20]). It appears that the Chronicler has here joined together lists of varying origin to support his point of widespread support for David.

V 1 may perhaps best be considered introductory both to the first unit and to the entire pericope, while v 23 [22] functions similarly to conclude the final unit and the pericope as a whole.

Comment

12:1–8 [7] *Benjaminites at Ziklag.* Ziklag is the Philistine city given David by Achish, King of Gath, in return for his loyalty (1 Sam 27:6). Hence this list (as well as those following) has its setting in David's "outlaw" days preceding his anointing at Hebron and chronologically precedes 11:1–9.

This list of twenty-three individuals from Benjamin probably occurs first to emphasize the support given David by Saul's own tribe. Since the faithfulness of Benjamin to Saul's house even after his death is a matter of record (cf. 2 Sam 2–4), it is unlikely that large numbers of Benjaminites defected to David while Saul was still alive. The writer, however, in keeping with his *all Israel* theme, states through this list that Benjaminites were also among those who supported David's kingship from the very beginning.

That Benjaminites were frequently left-handed is an oddity noted elsewhere as well (Judg 3:15; 20:16). It is unlikely that any of the individuals named here is otherwise known in the OT, although Azmaveth (v 3) could be David's hero named in 11:33. Ishmaiah, listed here as head of the "Thirty," is not included in the list of chap. 11. While Gibeah, Azmaveth, Gibeon, and Anathoth (vv 3–4) can be located within the narrow boundaries of Benjamin, the same is not true of Gadera, Haruph (if a place), Korah, or Gedor (vv 5–8 [4–7]). (Since this is a Benjaminite list, Korah ought not refer either to the Levitical clan or the Calebite Korah of 2:43.) As a consequence, some believe these latter verses actually contain a list of Judah (Curtis, 196 and cf. v 17 [16]), while others have maintained they were a list of Benjaminites living in Judah (Keil, 183). With others, it would appear preferable to withhold judgment at this time (Rudolph, 104; Myers, 96).

9–16 [8–15] *Gadites at the stronghold.* The inclusion of Gadites so far south is striking since they are a more northern tribe. Moreover, unlike Manasseh listed below (v 20 [19]), interest in Gad is minimal throughout Chronicles. (Apart from the lists of chaps. 1–9, the name Gad is found in Chronicles only three times in this chapter plus 1 Chr 26:32). It is doubtful whether any particular "stronghold" is envisioned, though some have thought of Engedi (1 Sam 24:1) as providing the most opportune place for such a defection. The use of בדל "separate oneself," niphal, in this sense is almost limited to Chronicles-Ezra-Nehemiah—of ten occurrences of the stem in the OT, only Num 16:21 (P) is not found here. Similarly only Chronicles uses מצד "stronghold" in the sg. (cf. also 11:7; 12:17 [16]), and Samuel uniformly chooses the plural (1 Sam 23:14, 19; 24:1 [23:29]) or a form of מצודה "fastness, stronghold."

Eleven Gadites are named with an enumeration following each after the manner of 1 Chr 2:13–15; 3:1–3. The military terminology applied to them, as well as the figures for strength and speed, are traditional (cf. 2 Sam 1:23). Of those named, and their exploit in v 16 [15], we have no further knowledge.

17–19 [16–18] *Benjaminites and Judahites at the stronghold.* Although Benjamin has been listed previously (v 9 [8]), its inclusion with Judah, as here, as the two component tribes of the Southern Kingdom is a common feature of Chronicles. Unlike the remainder of this unit, only a single individual, Amasai, called a chief of the thirty, is named, however. The emphasis is instead upon the message uttered by Amasai (v 19 [18]).

The setting is again the indefinite "stronghold" (v 9 [8]; v 17 [16], cf. v 9 [8]). David's restraint at accepting these new recruits would have been justified in view of previous attempts at deception (cf. 1 Sam 21–26). Though the terminology "the Spirit clothed . . ." is ancient (cf. Judg 6:34), the frequency of its appearance in Chronicles, and also among the members of the Levitical choir, is characteristic of the Chronicler's understanding of prophecy (see the *Bibliography* above, and most recently Petersen, *Late Israelite Prophecy* [Missoula, MT: Scholars Press, 1977], with whose conclusions regarding David I disagree; see also 2 Chr 15:1; 20:14; 24:20; 36:22).

Amasai's utterance professes both that God is with David to help him and that his help comes as well to those who help David, i.e., God's blessings flow upon his people through his chosen king (cf. Gen 12:3). The use of עזר "help" is again characteristic of Chronicles, with 25 of some 81 usages in the OT being found here (and only 2 in Ezra-Nehemiah). For a parallel thought, expressed however in terms of blessing, see Gen 12:3.

20–23 [19–22] *Supporters from Manasseh at Ziklag.* Seven chiefs of Manasseh are named, without mention of family or place of origin. Again nothing more is known of these individuals.

Support from such a distant northern tribe, as with Gad, is surprising. However, Manasseh is often used in Chronicles as representative of the north (cf. 2 Chr 15:9, where Ephraim and Manasseh of the north parallel Judah and Benjamin of the south). Striking also is the prominence of Manasseh in the accounts of the passovers of Hezekiah (2 Chr 30:1, 10, 11, 18; 31:1) and Josiah (34:6, 9).

The Philistine incident in v 20 [19] is that referred to in 1 Sam 29. Although it is clear there that David did not participate in the battle with his own countrymen, the writer here does seem to go to considerable length to make this clear (v 20 [19]). The "raiding bands" against which they helped David might well refer to the Amalekites of 1 Sam 30 or similar groups of desert raiders.

The writer's purpose in including these verses is clear from v 23 [22], which is replete with terminology common in Chronicles: "so day by day they kept streaming to David to help him, until there was a great army, like the army of God." While the final phrase could mean only a mighty or numerous army (cf. n. 22.b.), the degree to which the Chronicler's conception of warfare verges upon that of holy war suggests that the possibility of understanding David's army as nothing less than the army of God ought not be lost here (cf. 2 Chr 13:13–18; 14:9–15 [and note the terminology of v 13]). For עזר in the sense of "military help," see v 19 [18] above; for יום ביום "day by day," see Curtis, 40, #38. The use of the term מחנה "camp" or "battle," also used of the Lord's "camp," is also unusually common in Chronicles (cf. 1 Chr 9:18–19; 2 Chr 31:2; 14:12 [13]), as well as in priestly portions of the Pentateuch (cf. Num 2).

Explanation

The author has moved immediately from the death of Saul (1 Chr 10) to David's coronation by all Israel at Hebron (11:1–10). Bypassing David's conflict with Saul in the process, these verses indicate the author's (and reader's) knowledge of the period when David was hiding from Saul and later set up a more permanent base of operations at Ziklag through his association with King Achish of Gath. By means of a literary flashback, he returns us to those days, not to catalog opposition to David's reign, but instead to do the opposite. Already in this period individuals from Saul's own tribe, Benjamin, together with two more remote northern tribes, Gad and Manasseh, and of course the inhabitants of Judah, come to David to give him the recognition, support, and military aid to which he was entitled by divine decree. The word of the Lord first expressed by the prophet Samuel (11:3, 10) is reiterated by the soldier become prophet, Amasai:

> We are yours, David,
> and we are with you, son of Jesse.
> Peace, peace be with you,
> and peace to him who helps you,
> For he who helps you is your God!

No small wonder then that "from day to day men kept coming to David to help him, until there was a great army, like the army of God." (v 23 [22]).

The Rise of David, Concluded (12:24–41 [23–40])

Bibliography

(See above at 11:1–9 and 11:10–47)

Corney, R. W. "Zadok the Priest." *IDB* 4:928–29. **Cross, F. M. Jr.** "The Priestly Houses in Early Israel." *Canaanite Myth and Hebrew Epic.* Cambridge: Harvard University Press, 1973. 195–215.

Translation

[24][23] *These are numbers* [a] *of the heads of the men equipped for battle. They came to David at Hebron to turn over the kingdom of Saul to him according to Yahweh's command.* [25][24] *The sons of Judah, armed with shield and spear, 6,800 equipped for battle.* [26][25] *Of the sons of Simeon, valiant men of the army, 7,100.* [27][26] *Of the sons of Levi, 4,600.* [28][27] *Jehoiada was prince of the house of Aaron, and with him were 3,700.* [29][28] *Although Zadok was still a young man, he was a mighty warrior.*

His father's house counted twenty-two princes. [30[29]]*Of the sons of Benjamin, relatives of Saul, 3,000; most of whom had previously been loyal to the house of Saul;* [31[30]]*Of the sons of Ephraim, 20,800 valiant warriors, famous men of their fathers' house;* [32[31]]*Of the half-tribe of Manasseh, 18,000 who had been designated by name to make David king;* [33[32]]*Of the sons of Issachar, wise men who understood the times and what Israel should do, two hundred chiefs, and all their relatives* [a] *at their command;* [a] [34[33]]*From Zebulon, experienced troops, equipped for battle with every instrument of war, 50,000* [a] *who came together* [a] [b] *with a single purpose;* [b] [35[34]]*Of Naphtali, a thousand commanders, and 37,000 with them with shield and spear.* [36[35]]*Of the Danites 28,600 equipped for battle;* [37[36]]*Of Asher, experienced troops in carrying on warfare, 40,000;* [38[37]]*From Transjordan, of the Reubenites, Gadites, and the half-tribe of Manasseh, with all the implements of war,* [a] *120,000.*

[39[38]]*All these warriors, equipped for battle,* [a] *came to Hebron with perfect heart to make David king over all Israel. And also all the rest* [b] *of Israel was of one mind to make David king.* [40[39]]*They were there with David three days eating and drinking, because their relatives had made provision for them.* [41[40]]*Also their neighbors as far as Issachar, Zebulon, and Naphtali were bringing in food* [a]—*food on asses, camels, mules, and oxen. There was an abundance of flour, fig cakes, raisin cakes, wine, oil, cattle, and sheep, for there was joy in Israel.*

Notes

24.a. G τα ονοματα/שמות "the names."

33.a-a. G μετ' αὐτῶν "with them."

34.a-a. A few MSS ולעזר "to help"; (G + דויד "David"); G Syr Vg α' omit the conjunction. It seems preferable to retain the more difficult text (and cf. v 39), of which the meaning, if not the syntax, seems reasonably clear. For עדר, cf. Curtis, 32, #83.

34.b-b. בלא־לב ולב "without a divided heart"; cf. GKC, § 123f. G οὐ χεροκένως "the ones not handling idly" (Rudolph, ἐκ οὐχ ὁμχερκενῶς "not with rebellion" = MT).

38.a. G deletes צבא "war, warfare."

39.a. Cf. v 34.

39.b. Cf. GKC, § 23f, for the omission of א.

41.a. G להם "to them," whereas Chronicles has לחם "bread" or "food."

Form/Structure/Setting

The nucleus of this unit is an extensive listing of the numbers from the various tribes of Israel who came to David at Hebron to make him king. An introduction (v 24 [23]) and an exuberant conclusion (vv 39–41 [38–40]) enclose the tribal list itself, which is the most extensive found in Scripture. The outline can be construed as follows:

v 24   Introduction
vv 25–38   Israelites who came to David at Hebron
v 39   Conclusion: Celebration at Hebron

These verses are quite commonly denied to the Chronicler, since in a sense they repeat the lists of the earlier part of the chapter. Noth writes, for example, that if the Chronicler would have known this list he could have spared himself the effort to introduce the numerous individuals named in

11:10–47 as supporters of David's enthronement, with vv 12:1–23 (*Ü.S.*, 115–16; see also Myers 95, and most scholars). At the same time it should be noted that the goal of the writer(s) seems to be to amass a volume of material in support of his primary thesis that all Israel was in support of David's kingship, so that overlapping lists perhaps presented him with no difficulty.

The number of tribes named in vv 25–38 [24–37] is the most extensive found in Scripture, which is in itself indicative of the thoroughness with which this thesis is supported. Although the tribe of Levi is retained in the listing (considered by Rudolph, 109, as a later addition), Joseph's line is found in both Ephraim and Manasseh, of which both the eastern and western halves are named, resulting in a list of no less than thirteen (or fourteen) tribes. This retention of Levi with Ephraim and Manasseh is found also in 1 Chr 2–8; 27:16–22; and Deut 33, all of which however lack other tribes. (I am indebted to my former colleague, Dr. Merlin Rehm, of Concordia College, Bronxville, NY, for this observation.) See chart, page 9.

For all of its completeness, the list itself is not without difficulty. The numbers involved, as conventionally translated, are extremely large (see *Comment* below). In addition, there is a marked difference in both form and content between the southern tribes in vv 25–30 [24–29] and those of the North and Transjordan in vv 32–38 [31–37]. In the first place, the number of those defecting to David in the first part of the list are much smaller, numbering well below ten thousand per tribe, thereafter all are larger than twenty thousand, with Zebulon reaching 50,000 and the three east Jordan tribes arriving with a total of 120,000. Second, there is much more and a greater variety of information included with the second group of tribes also (cf., e.g., the attributes of Issachar in v 33 [32] with those of Judah and Simeon in vv 25–26 [24–25]). This suggests that, whether entered here by a single author or more, the material originally stemmed from different sources. If it should be concluded that all of the first part of chap. 12 was later, it might also be maintained that the conclusion, vv 39–41 [38–40] originally stood at the end of chap. 11 since they are replete with the terminology and emphases of Chronicles and have their proper setting at Hebron (12:39 [38]; cf. 11:1). Note also the manner in which 12:39 [38] seems to resume 11:10.

Comment

24 [23] This verse returns us to Hebron, the setting of 11:1–3 (and perhaps 11:10–47). Again we are dealing with warriors, "heads of the men equipped for battle." Their specific objective is to turn over Saul's kingdom to David (cf. 11:3, 10, and especially the use of סבב "turn about"; hiph here and in 10:14). The course of events is described as in accord with God's wishes (10:14), with emphasis upon the word as in 10:14; 11:3, 10. It is noteworthy here only that it is the *warriors* who turn over Saul's kingdom to David, whereas in 10:14 it is Yahweh himself who does so.

25–37 [24–36] We have indicated before that the tribal list of vv 25–37 [24–36] is the most extensive in the OT. The component tribes of Israel are here listed in geographical order from south to north, concluding with the Transjordanian tribes. The results are that Judah, Levi, and Benjamin, obviously of particular interest to the writer, are listed first, together with Simeon, usually found second (after Reuben) preceding Levi and Judah (cf. the lists of Gen 29, 35, 46, and 1 Chr 2:1–2).

Particularly striking is the listing of Levi (vv 27–29 [26–28]), in that it (or at least the Zadokite branch) is pictured as a typical group of warriors (*contra* Rudolph, 111) and two prominent Levites, Jehoida, termed "the prince (נגיד) of Aaron," and Zadok, "a young man," but apparently already noted for his prowess, are mentioned. It can be argued that these differences, together with the inclusion of Ephraim and Manasseh later in the list, suggest that the mention of Levi does not belong to the original form of the list (cf. again Rudolph, 109–10).

The debate about the origins of Zadok, who became priest under Solomon with the banishment of Abiathar, is well known (see R. Corney, *IDB* 4:928–29; F. M. Cross, Jr., *Canaanite Myth,* 195–215). Some have questioned whether this Zadok is to be identified with Solomon's priest, but it would seem most natural to do so (note the linkage of Benaiah, Jehoiada, Zadok, and Abiathar in 1 Kgs 2:35). Jehoiada has been identified by many (cf. Curtis, 201) with the father of Benaiah, (cf. 27:5) 11:22, who, in my opinion, it can be plausibly argued, could be assumed to be a Levite since it was in the temple of the Lord that he slew Joab (1 Kgs 2:28–29). Moreover, it is not unreasonable to connect the twenty-two commanders (שׂרים) ascribed to Zadok with the twenty-two (or twenty-four) priestly classes of later days (cf. Neh 12:1–7; 1 Chr 24:7–18); others, however, deny these possibilities (cf. Rudolph, 110) and point to the fact that we know of no high priest of Israel named Jehoiada except one of the time of Joash much later (cf. 2 Kgs 11; 2 Chr 23).

Benjamin's contingent is again described directly as Saul's kinsmen (v 30 [29], cf. 12:2), with mention that most had previously been faithful to Saul. The use of military terminology here, as elsewhere in the book, suggests that one source of the list would have been tribal lists at least relating to conscription for military service.

It has been mentioned above that the numbers in this list, particularly in reference to the northern and Transjordanian tribes, are very large. A total of 339,600 warriors can be counted, an immense army for any time and seemingly out of the question for David's retinue at Hebron. George Mendenhall has suggested that the term אלף, conventionally translated "thousand," ought to be understood here not in that sense, but as a tribal sub-unit of a smaller and more flexible size (*JBL* 77 [1958] 52–66). This would result in a drastic change in the understanding of the pericope (see Myers, 97–99). As Myers indicates, such a translation does not seem to answer all of the difficulties involved—Ephraim's twenty units would total only 800 men while four units of Levites numbered 600. It may be true that the author no longer understood the original connotation of some of these terms, but by and large it would appear most reasonable to assume here that he wished to state, either by hyperbole or as a theological principle, that vast numbers of Israelites—in fact, "all Israel," supported David in his kingship. To that end the tribal lists used provided a concrete evidence of a theological truth.

40–42 [39–41] The more prosaic materials of much of chaps. 11–12 are concluded by vv 40–42 [39–41], which mount to new heights in their assertion of all Israel's enthusiasm at David's coronation. Not only the immense number of those listed who came to Hebron, but also "all of the rest of Israel" were for David, and their devotion to his cause was complete: they came to Hebron "with perfect heart" (v 39 [38]), an expression especially dear to Chronicles (cf. 1 Chr 28:9; 2 Chr 19:9; 25:2, elsewhere only five times in the OT). Not only those near, but "neighbors" as far away as Issachar, Zebulon, and Naphtali participated by sending food for the three-day feast, which Stinespring (*JBL* 80 [1961] 209–19) considers so contrived that it can be described as a "messianic banquet" and an expression of the author's eschatological faith. With the statement that there was "great joy" in Israel, we come to a phrase with which the writer will highlight those occasions which for him are the epitome of joyous religious experience: the appointment of the Levite singers (1 Chr 15:16); Solomon's coronation (29:9, 17, 22); Asa's covenant with Yahweh (2 Chr 15:15); Jehoshaphat's victory celebration (20:27); the death of the apostate Athaliah (23:13–18); the offerings for repairing the temple (24:10), and, no less than six times, events connected with Hezekiah's reform (2 Chr 29:30, 36; 30:21, 23, 25, 26). In a sense only the presence of the Levitical singers is lacking (and that will be taken care of in the following sections).

Explanation

In what is the strongest statement of the "all Israel" theme yet found (see *Introduction*), the Chronicler lists groups of warriors from all the tribes of Israel, north and south, who come to David at Hebron to transfer Saul's kingdom to him. They, together with the remainder of Israel, were unanimous and undivided in their loyalty to David and his kingship, and his coronation takes on a festive air. For no less than three days the assembled warriors eat and drink lavishly and with "great joy"—another common theme of the writer. Such unanimity and joy were appropriate, since their actions were in accord with "Yahweh's command" (v 24 [23]).

David's coronation is described in such expansive terms that some scholars have seen here a prefigurement of a messianic banquet. While we judge this unlikely, the writer is certainly speaking to the subject of the support due to God's chosen leader, and to the joyous fellowship which surrounds obedience to him. The elaboration upon this theme found in the theme of the messianic banquet in Judaism and Christianity (and the Lord's Supper which prefigures it in the latter) is certainly a development of the same theme. The ultimate establishment of God's righteous rule will introduce an era of unlimited joy for all his people.

David, the Ark, and the Cult
(Chaps. 13-17)

With David's position secured, the Chronicler turns immediately to his chief concern, the ark of the covenant, and less directly, the temple in which it will be placed. Although he remains dependent upon his *Vorlage* (See *Form/Structure/Setting* below), his intention is obvious and governs in large measure his choice and arrangement of material. Only chap. 14, which appears somewhat as an interlude, breaks the progression of the first and second attempts to bring the ark to Jerusalem. Chaps. 15–16 include details of Levitical arrangements and ceremonies appropriate for such an occasion, after which the dynastic oracle of chap. 17 puts all in readiness for David's heir, Solomon, to appear as temple builder.

David, the Ark, and the Cult (a)   (13:1-14)

Bibliography

Japhet, S. "Conquest and Settlement in Chronicles." *JBL* 98 (1979) 205–18. **Mosis, R.** *Untersuchungen zur Theologie des chronistichen Geschichtswerkes.* Freiberger theologische Studien 92. Freiburg: Herder, 1973. 51–52.

Translation

[1] *Then David consulted with the commanders of the thousands and hundreds, with every* [a] *leader.* [2] *David said to all the assembly of Israel: "If it seems good to you, and if it is . . .* [a] *from Yahweh our God, let us send to our brethren who remain* [b] *in all the lands* [c] *of Israel, together with the priests and* [d] *the Levites in the cities of their pasture lands, that they may gather to us,* [3] *and let us bring back the ark of our God to us, because we did not seek it* [a] *in the days of Saul."* [4] *All the assembly said to do so, for the thing was right in the eyes of all the people.*
   [5] *So David assembled all Israel,* [a] *from the Shihor of Egypt to the entrance of Hamath,* [a] *to bring the ark of God from Kiriath-jearim.* [6] *And David and all Israel went up to Baalah, to Kiriath-jearim of Judah, to bring up from there the ark of Yahweh who sits enthroned upon the cherubim,* [a] *where his name is named.* [a] [7] *They carried the ark of God upon a new cart from the house of Abinadab, while Uzza and his brother* [a] *were directing on the cart* [8] *and David and all Israel were rejoicing before God with* [a] *all their strength with songs,* [a] *lyres, harps, tambourines,* [b] *cymbals, and trumpets.* [b] [9] *When they had gone as far as the threshing floor of Nacon,* [a] *Uzza put out his hand to steady the ark, because the oxen had stumbled.* [10] *Yahweh was angry with Uzza and smote him, because he put his hand on the ark, and he died*

there before God. ¹¹ *Then David became angry, because* ᵃ *Yahweh had "broken out"* ᵇ *against Uzza, and he named that place Perez-uzza to this day.* ¹² *And David was afraid of God* ᵃ *that day and said, "How can I bring the ark of God* ᵃ *in to me?"* ¹³ *So David did not bring back the ark to him,* ᵃ *to the city of David,* ᵃ *but left it at the house of Obed-edom the Gittite.* ¹⁴ *So the ark of God stayed with* ᵃ *the house of Obed-edom* ᵇ *in its house* ᵇ *three months, and Yahweh blessed* ᶜ *the house of* ᶜ *Obed-edom and all which he had.*

Notes

1.a. For the force of *lamedh,* which is essentially appositional, see BDB, 514, ¶5e(d). The usage in Chronicles is frequent; cf. Curtis, 35, #128. For כל "every, all," see Curtis, 35, #124.

2.a. The only evidenced meaning of פרץ (cf. v 11) is "to break through, spread," a meaning difficult to relate to the context here. G εὐοδώθη "prosper" might suggest reading נרצתה "be favorable" (cf. *BH³*). NEB "if the Lord our God opens a way" is ingenious but not compelling. Cf. Rudolph, 110.

2.b. That נשארים has in mind the post-exilic "remnant" is possible but far from certain; cf. 12:39; 2 Chr 30:5–6; and Mosis, 52.

2.c. G sg. The use of the pl in this sense is late; Driver, *Introduction,* 536 ¶14.

2.d. G > cop., = "the levitical priests" after the manner of Deuteronomy.

3.a. Or, "we did not inquire of it" or "we did not inquire of *him,* (God)" or even "we did not worship him." Cf. 1 Chr 10:13–14. דרש displays a wide range of meaning in Chronicles, of which the more common is "to worship"; cf. LXX^BA "they did not worship him/seek it."

5.a-a. This phrase is lacking in 2 Sam 6:2.

6.a-a. One would expect אשר נקרא שמו שם "where his name is named there"; cf. also G. The phrase is absent from 2 Sam 6:3 and possibly reflects a later addition.

7.a. אחיו may also be vocalized "his brother" or "his brothers."

8.a-a. 2 Sam 6:5 בכל עצי ברושים "with all instruments of fir," probably erroneously.

8.b-b. 2 Sam 6:5 ובמנענעים ובצלצלים "rattles" (BDB, 631) and "cymbals" (BDB, 853), a *h.l.* Chronicles perhaps omits the first "noisemaker" as rare (found only here), substitutes the more common (later?) ובמצלתים "cymbals," and adds חצצרות "clarion, horn," the instrument of the priests par excellence, out of personal preference (cf. Num 10:8; 1 Chr 15:28; 2 Chr 29:26–27; Ezra 3:10; Neh 12:35, 41).

9.a. 2 Sam 6:6 נכון, which might be construed either as a proper name "Nacon" (RSV) or a niph ptcp of כון "be established." (Cf. NEB "a certain.")

11.a. 2 Sam 6:8 על אשר "because"; Chronicles כי "for."

11.b. פָרַץ "he broke out," thus justifying the name "Perez-uzza."

12.a. 2 Sam 6:19 reads יהוה "Yahweh" in both cases; the Chr's preference for אלהים "Elohim-God" is well established.

13.a-a. The setting appears to be Jerusalem (cf. 2 Sam 5–6) and not Hebron, as in 1 Chr 12.

14.a. > 2 Sam 6:11. See n. 14.b-b.

14.b-b. 2 Sam 6:11. The writer apparently wishes to avoid the impression that the ark was placed in an ordinary house. The addition of the prep עם "with" (see n. 14.a.) serves a similar purpose.

14.c-c. > 2 Sam 6:11.

Form/Structure/Setting

Bypassing for the moment the contents of 2 Sam 5:11–25, the writer proceeds to the narrative of David's concern for the ark found in 2 Sam 6:1–11, prefixing it in vv 1–4 with his own commentary. We may view this relationship in outline as follows.

1 Chronicles	2 Samuel	
———	5:11–25	(See 1 Chr 14)
13:1–4	———	David directs Israel to bring up the ark
13:5–14	6:1–11	The ark brought from Kiriath-jearim to the house of Obed-edom

It will be seen, however, from the *Notes* above and the *Comment* below, that the variations between 2 Sam 6:1–11 and 1 Chr 13:5–14 are more substantial than is frequently the case in such synoptic sections.

Comment

1–4 The significance of these verses is best seen by contrast with v 5, which is taken from 2 Sam 6:1 and describes in a straightforward manner David's decision to bring the ark from Kiriath-jearim. By the addition of vv 1–4 the writer emphasizes: (1) David's decision is made in consultation and agreement with *all* Israel's leaders; (2) these leaders also agree to invite "all their brethren who remain in all the land of Israel," with particular mention of priests and Levites, to join them in securing the ark; (3) it is this enlarged assembly which is then seen to be the "all Israel" of v 5, in contrast to "all the chosen men of Israel, thirty thousand" of 2 Sam 6:1.

While a certain military perspective is retained by Chronicles, this is overlaid with a second view which sees Israel as a religious community (קהל "assembly, congregation") with its priests and Levites brought together by David to undertake a religious activity pleasing to God, in contrast with the negative examples of Saul's day (cf. n. 3.a.).

5–14 These verses are dependent upon 2 Sam 6, but the variations are numerous, especially in vv 5–9. Some of these are clearly tendentious, such as the reading of ויקהל (v 5, "and David assembled") for ויסף (apparently for ויאסף or ויסף "and David gathered"), which lends itself more readily to an ecclesiastical interpretation (see below). The reference to the thirty thousand chosen men of 2 Sam 6:1 is inappropriate in view of the concentration upon "all Israel" in vv 1–4; the addition of the limits of this Israel as "from the Shihor of Egypt" (identified by Lambdin with the easternmost of the Delta branches of the Nile, and not simply with the "brook of Egypt," i.e., the Wadi el-Arish ["Shihor," *IDB* 4:328]) "to the entrance of Hamath" adds geographical breadth to a more nebulous reality, the most extensive description of the Holy Land in the Bible (see S. Japhet, *JBL* 98 [1979] 208–11, who believes that the Chronicler here is making a statement upon the geographical scope of the conquest and [v 2] upon the question of the priestly and Levitical cities).

Other variations probably reflect changing names over the centuries, such as the various names for Kiriath-jearim. In still others we may assume that the writer is simply trying to understand a text which is obscure (cf.

the substitution of כידון "Chidon" for נכון "(n. 9.a) and the addition of את־ידו "his hand" in v 9). In still other cases the writer is simply abbreviating the text (cf. the omission of parts of 2 Sam 6:3 and all of 6:4 from 1 Chr 13:7).

While the vocabulary and themes present in this section are of importance throughout Chronicles, particular importance needs to be called to evidences of patterning found here in the account of the removal of the ark and in other events of special importance for the writer. David "took counsel" (ויעץ, niphal) with his constituents, as will Hezekiah in conjunction with his Passover (2 Chr 30:2, 23). Though קהל (hiphil) may simply mean "assemble," and the noun refer to any assembly, the view of the assembly here is closely related to that of D and especially P, where the קהל is in fact the "congregation of God" (cf. Num 16:3; 20:4; Deut 23:2–9; 1 Chr 28:8). This meaning is close at hand already in the Kings account of Solomon's erection of the temple (cf. 1 Kgs 8:1, 65), which the writer has probably used as his model (cf. Mosis, 53), and is noteworthy in other significant sections of Chronicles (cf. David's summons in 1 Chr 28:1; 29:1, 10, 20; and Hezekiah's in 2 Chr 30:1–13, 23–27; 31:1). Note also the correspondence between "it was right in the eyes of the people" (13:4) and "the thing was right in the eyes of the king and all the congregation" (2 Chr 30:4). The "all Israel" theme found in the idea of an invitation distributed throughout the land is also present in Hezekiah's passover (cf. 2 Chr 30:1) and is inherent also in the Kings account of the temple dedication (cf. 1 Kgs 8:65–66.) A related thematic unity is seen in the depiction of the limits of Israel as from "the Shihor of Egypt to the entrance of Hamath" (v 5). Mosis has pointed out that similar limits are found in Chronicles only three times, those again in conjunction with the dedication of the temple (2 Chr 7:8 = 1 Kings 8:65), "from the entrance of Hamath to the brook (נחל) of Egypt," and with Hezekiah's Passover (2 Chr 30:1, 5) "from Beersheba to Dan."

While the Chronicler has transmitted most of vv 4–14 without substantive change, his interest in things religious has prompted him to make significant alterations in the names of the musical instruments attending the procession of the ark (v 8; see *Notes*), and in the disposition of the ark at Obed-edom's house (see nn. 14.a., b-b.). It is in keeping with this same interest in preserving the sanctity of the ark that 1 Chr 15:18, 24 will enroll Obed-edom among the Levitical gatekeepers.

Explanation

David's first concern following his coronation at Hebron is for the ark of the covenant. Though it is not mentioned, the earlier history of the ark that left it at Kiriath-jearim is presupposed (cf. 1 Sam 7:1). The effort that follows, however, is not described as that of a king and his men, but an act undertaken with the support and encouragement of all Israel, including priests, Levites, and at a minimum, representatives of "all Israel from the Shihor of Egypt to the entrance of Hamath'' (v 5). Their participation is once again willing and enthusiastic.

With such seemingly complete obedience, the question naturally arises as to why the mission did not succeed or at best was left incomplete. While one explanation of this is given in vv 9–14, derived from Samuel, a second will be found in 15:2, 13—the failure to deal with the ark in the prescribed way. The writer thus adheres consistently to the dogma of retribution: disobedience to Yahweh and his word (15:13–15) cannot go unpunished and, in the same way, failure may always be explained by disobedience. Since the Chronicler here is interpreting past history, it may be from that perspective that no mention is made of the penitent heart which would find God's forgiveness.

David, the Ark, and the Cult (b)   (14:1–17)

Translation

¹ Hiram, ª king of Tyre, sent messengers to David, as well as cedar, masons, and carpenters to build him a house. ² David knew that Yahweh had established him as king over Israel, because ª his kingdom was exalted ᵇ greatly, ᶜ on account of his people Israel.

³ David took more ª ᵇwives in Jerusalem, and had more ª sons and daughters. ⁴ These are the names of the children which he had in Jerusalem: Shammua, Shobab, Nathan, Solomon, ª ⁵ Ibhar, Elishua, ª Elpelet, ᵇ ⁶ Nogah, ª Nepheg, Japhia, ⁷ Elishama, Beeliada, ª and Eliphelet. ᵇ

⁸ The Philistines heard that David had been anointed king over all ª Israel, and all the Philistines came up to seek David. When David heard of it, ᵇ he went out to meet them. ᵇ ⁹ The Philistines came in and made a raid in the valley of Rephaim. ¹⁰ And David inquired of God, ª "Shall I go up against the Philistines? Will you give them into my hand?" Yahweh ᵇ answered him, "Go up, and I will give them into your hand." ¹¹ He ª went up to Baal-perazim, and David smote them there and said, "God has broken through my enemies by my hand, like a breaking through of water''; therefore they called the name of that place Baal-perazim. ¹² The Philistines ª had abandoned their gods ᵇ there, ᶜand David gave command, and they were burned with fire. ᶜ

¹³ The Philistines made yet another raid ª in the valley. ¹⁴ David again inquired of God, and God said to him, "You shall not go up after them; go around them and come in against them from before the baca-trees. ª ¹⁵ When you hear the sound of steps in the tops of the baca-trees, ª then ᵇyou will go out into the battle, ᵇ because God has gone out before you to smite the army of the Philistines." ¹⁶ David did as God had commanded him, and they smote the army of the Philistines from Gibeon ª to ᵇ Gezer. ¹⁷ ªDavid's fame spread through all the lands, and Yahweh put his fear upon all the nations. ª

Notes

1.a. Q MSS חורם "Huram"; K G Syr Vg α' חירם "Hiram."

2.a. 2 Sam 5:12 reads וכי "and that," perhaps significantly.

2.b. נשאת "was exalted," niph ptcp fem; נשא 2 Sam 5:12 reads as a niph pf, "He (God) had been exalted."

2.c. In this significant and characteristic form found *only* here and in 1 Chr 22:5; 23:17; 29:3, 25; 2 Chr 1:1; 16:12; 17:12; 20:19; 26:8. See Curtis, 32, #87; Japhet *VT* 18 (1968) 357–58. Polzin suggests this may be "a mere stylistic entry without any chronological significance" (*Late Biblical Hebrew*, 140–41, #46).

3.a-a. עוד "again," copied from 2 Sam 5:13, presupposes the listing of wives and sons at Hebron, given earlier in 2 Sam 3:2–5 (cf. 1 Chr 3:1–4 and *Comment*), but omitted in this portion of Chronicles.

3.b. 2 Sam 5:13 + פלגשים "concubines."

4.a. 1 Chr 3:5 + ארבעה לבת־שוע בת־עמיאל "four by Bath-Shue, the daughter of Ammiel."

5.a. 1 Chr 3:6 + ואלישמע "and Elishama."

5.b. 2 Sam 5:15, but cf. v 16.

6.a. > 2 Sam 5:15.

7.a. 1 Chr 3:8 and 2 Sam 5:16 + ואלידע "and Eliada."

7.b. 1 Chr 3:8 + תשעה "nine"; cf. n. 4.a.

8.a. > 2 Sam 5:17.

8.b-b. 2 Sam 5:17 וירד אל־המצודה "and he went down to the stronghold."

9.a. 2 Sam 5:18 וינטשו "they spread out."

10.a. 2 Sam 5:19 ביהוה "of Yahweh"; cf. n. 13:12.a.

10.b. 2 Sam 5:20 יהוה "Yahweh; cf. n. 10.a.

11.a. G Syr and 2 Sam 5:20 suggest the sg ויעל "he went up" and ויבא דויד "and David came."

12.a. Heb. "they."

12.b. Tg 2 Sam 5:21 עצביהם "their idols."

12.c-c. 2 Sam 5:21 וישאם דוד ואנשיו "and David and his men *picked them up*."

13.a. 2 Sam 5:22 as in n. 9.a.; 2 Sam 5:23 אל־אחריהם "to their rear."

14.a. בכאים; KJV and rabbis "mulberry"; RSV JB "balsam"; NEB "as pens." Cf. J. Trever, "Balsam," *IDB* 1:344.

15.a. See n. 14.a.

15.b-b. 2 Sam 5:24 תחרץ "you will pay attention."

16.a. 2 Sam 5:25 מגבע "from Geba."

16.b. 2 Sam 5:25 עד־באך "until you come."

17.a-a. 2 Sam 5 does not include this material.

Form/Structure/Setting

The Chronicler interrupts his interpretative narrative of the fortunes of the ark with this story of David's family and fortunes taken from 2 Sam 5:11–25, which follows directly upon the capture of Jerusalem (2 Sam 5:6–10). The writer had apparently wanted to proceed immediately from the capture of Jerusalem to David's decision to bring the ark to Jerusalem, though in a sense this connection is interrupted by the lists of David's supporters inserted in 11:10–12:41 [40]. Having introduced the ark narrative in chap. 13, however, he now returns to his source to recount David's relationship with King Hiram of Tyre (vv 1–2), his family in Jerusalem (vv 3–7), and strife with the Philistines (vv 8–16).

The outline of this passage and relationship to 2 Samuel is as follows.

2 Samuel	1 Chronicles	
5:11–12	14:1–2	David and Hiram David's kingdom established
5:13–16	14:3–7 (cf. also 1 Chr 3:5–8)	David's children
5:17–25	14:8–16	Philistine raid on Rephaim
————	14:17	Summary: David's fame

The question of *why* the author has chosen to incorporate this material at this particular point has been discussed in great detail by Mosis (55–61), who feels it is meant to illustrate a theological point. David, unlike Saul, has shown his care for the ark (13:3). By incorporating at this point indications of David's prosperity, especially as seen in his victory over the Philistines (unlike Saul; see chap. 10), he has shown God's blessing upon that faithfulness, just as Saul's defeat was a result of his unfaithfulness (chap. 10).

This may well be so; there are many examples of such a theology throughout Chronicles, especially in the post-Solomonic kings. Many of these thoughts (like the "all Israel" pattern to which we have referred repeatedly) are found, at least in germ, in the Deuteronomic history; thus, what Chronicles has done is to deduce a principle from such data and to apply it "religiously." As will be seen in many of the comments below, the reigns of faithful kings are frequently associated with building operations, family, and victory in war (cf. 2 Chr 26:1–15). At the same time it is quite possible in this case that the writer, having bypassed this material earlier to demonstrate David's immediate concern for the ark, has now simply inserted it at the first appropriate time, i.e., in the "gap" indicated by the three-month period in which the ark was at the house of Obed-edom. Since his work is not chronological, to say this would not need to suggest that the events happened within that three-month period.

Comment

Since these verses are largely parallel with 2 Sam 5, we will restrict our comments to points of particular significance for understanding Chronicles.

1–2 *Hiram's delegation and assistance to David.* According to the Albright chronology (cf. Bright, *History,* 199) Hiram ruled *ca.* 969–936 B.C., and thus only the last decade of his reign would have coincided with that of David (*ca.* 1000–961 B.C.). Hence the inclusion of the notice at this point in the narrative is, it might be noted, as misleading in Samuel as in Chronicles. The writer apparently is not troubled by David's friendship with Hiram. If not the result of a simple reproduction of his source, the Chronicler has probably understood it as one example of the prosperity which Yahweh gives to his faithful people, i.e., recognition, respect, and gifts from foreign peoples (cf. the account of the Queen of Sheba in 2 Chr 9, taken from 1 Kgs 10, and more pointedly, 2 Chr 17:10–12; 26:8, 15; 32:23). To say that Hiram is pictured here as David's vassal rather than his ally, as does Mosis (65–66), perhaps goes too far, but it is clear that the relationship between Solomon and Hiram in 1 Kgs 5 is significantly recast by Chronicles, cf. 2 Chr 2. Yahweh's favor upon David, it should also be noted, is *because of* his people Israel (v 2).

3–7 (See also the notes and commentary on 1 Chr 3:6–9.) Striking here is that this list is sometimes in agreement with 2 Sam 5:14–16 (cf. the reading "Shammua" vs. "Shimea" and "Elishua" vs. "Elishama"), sometimes in agreement with 1 Chr 3:5–8 (the addition of "Elpelet" [though with differing vocalization] and "Nogah"), and sometimes differs from both ("Beeliada" vs. "Eliada"). The two uses of עוד in v 3 ("David took *more* wives . . . *more* children") presuppose the narrative of 2 Sam 3:2–5; (cf. 1 Chr 3:1–4) which has, however, been omitted from the main narrative of Chronicles, probably as placing undue emphasis upon David's seven-year rule over only a part of Israel at Hebron (cf. also the omission of 2 Sam 5:4–5 for the same reason). Mosis (77) perceives the omission of the conjunction before "Nathan" as resulting in an emphasis upon Solomon, though this is not apparent to me. In Chronicles remarks concerning a sizable family are regularly indicative of God's blessing; cf. 2 Chr 11:18–23.

8–12, 13–16 *Encounters with the Philistines.* Through his addition (n. 8.a.) the Chronicler again emphasizes David's reign over *all* Israel. The role of the Philistines as Israel's traditional enemy *par excellence* is well known, and is made more emphatic in 1 Chronicles (cf. 18:1 and 20:4, both with parallels in Samuel) but more pointedly in 2 Chronicles, where they, together with the Egyptians, Ethiopians, and Arabs in particular are typical of Israel's enemies (cf. 21:16; 26:6), over whom victory is a sign of God's blessing, defeat before whom a certain indication of his displeasure. David's faithfulness before the Philistines is exemplary. He inquires of God concerning the disposition of the battle and follows his instructions, and victory is forthcoming—all in pointed contrast to Saul (cf. 10:13–14; 13:3). The alteration of the text seen in n. 8.b-b. may be due to the Chronicler's attempt to preserve David's faithfulness more nearly intact, or it may be due simply to the desire to clarify an ambiguous text; perhaps, as suggested by Mosis (65), it is to bring the narrative more into harmony with Isa 28:21, where two battles of Yahweh for his people are juxtaposed (see below). That the root פרץ "to break through," had something of a special meaning for the author seems apparent from its repeated occurrence in different contexts (cf. 13:2, 11; 14:11), although the nature of that importance has not been found (see Mosis, 64–65, for one explanation). The reason for the alteration in v 12 (see n. 12.c-c.) seems apparent. Though the fact that Chronicles would designate the idols of the Philistines as "gods" is striking (LXX's reading in 2 Sam 5:21 suggests that the less suggestive עצביהם "idols" found there is secondary), David and his men do not "pick them up," i.e., as booty; rather at David's command his men destroy them by burning (cf. Deut 7:5; 12:3).

Vv 13–16 report a second encounter with the Philistines. The sounds of steps in the tree-tops is David's sign that God has marched before him into Holy War and he is to follow. That the writer placed this battle, geographically or symbolically, at Gibeon is suggested by his alteration in v 16 (cf. n. 16.a.) dependent upon Isa 28:21.

17 This verse, framed entirely by the writer, is a summarizing statement concluding this narrative of David's deeds. Under God's blessing and in keeping with David's faithfulness, David's fear and fame spread to *all the* nations. Such summary statements may have been suggested by the earlier history of David. (See 1 Sam 18:14; 2 Sam 5:10 = 1 Chr 11:9, 2 Sam 5:12 = 1 Chr 14:2; 2 Sam 7:1; for Solomon, see 1 Kgs 5:1 [4:21]; 8:56; 10:23–29.) They become characteristic and expanded at the hand of the Chronicler (1 Chr 29:25; 2 Chr 11:12–17; 17:5; 26:15; 32:23), who incorporates them as an important part of his understanding of Israel's history under God.

Explanation

The three types of incidents reported in chap. 14—Hiram's friendship which resulted in plans for a building, the listing of David's sons, and victory in battle—are regular ways in which Chronicles portrays the prosperity resulting from God's blessing upon the faithfulness of his king and people. Their inclusion here is fully in keeping with David's concern for the ark expressed in his first attempt to remove the ark to Jerusalem, the successful completion of which will now be reported in chaps. 15–16. David, and all Israel with him, are moving toward the establishment of God's house in Jerusalem, that he may take up his rest among them (1 Chr 28:20). As long as they do so, their success and prosperity is assured. Even so—the writer would certainly have us believe—faithfulness to God is regularly rewarded with not only spiritual blessings, but with material prosperity—buildings, family, and victory. That such results do not always follow, i.e., that God's children do not always find such blessings, presents a theological dilemma with which all religions have been forced to wrestle. One answer has been, of course, to transfer the expected blessings to the afterlife. Another has been to find God-pleasing purpose even in suffering and deprivation (cf. John 9:3). In an imperfect world, where the powers of evil still exist, God does not will, but sometimes permits, his children to suffer.

The Transfer of the Ark to Jerusalem   (15:1–16:43)

After the delay occasioned by the death of Uzza when attempting to move the ark the first time—a delay bridged by the writer in presenting the materials related to David's prosperity in chap. 14—the narrative of the transfer of the ark is again undertaken, with David, all Israel, and Levitical functionaries in place.

Bibliography

For priests and Levites, see the bibliography at 1 Chr 5:27.

Butler, T. C. "A Forgotten Passage from a Forgotten Era (1 Chr xvi. 8–36)." *VT* 28 (1978) 142–50. **Hill, A. E.** "Patchwork Poetry or Reasoned Verse? Connective

Structure in 1 Chronicles xvi," *VT* 33 (1983) 97–101. **Polk, T.** "The Levites in the Davidic-Solomonic Empire." *SBT* 9 (1979) 3–22.

Translation

¹ *David erected buildings for himself in the city of David, prepared a place for the ark of God, and pitched a tent for it.* ² *Then David gave command that no one should carry the ark of God except Levites, because Yahweh had chosen* ᵃ *them to carry the ark of Yahweh and to minister to him* ᵇ *forever.* ³ *Then David assembled* ᵃ *all Israel to Jerusalem to bring up the ark of Yahweh to its place which he had prepared for it.*

⁴ *David gathered* ᵃ ᵇ *the sons of Aaron and* ᵇ *the Levites:*

⁵ *Of the sons of Kohath, Uriel the chief, and a* ᵃ*hundred and twenty* ᵃ *of his brothers.*

⁶ *Of the sons of Merari: Asaiah the chief, and* ᵃ*two hundred and twenty* ᵃ *of his brothers.*

⁷ *Of the sons of Gershom: Joel the chief, and a hundred* ᵃ *and thirty* ᵇ *of his brothers.*

⁸ *Of the sons of Elizaphan, Shemaiah the chief, and two hundred* ᵃ *of his brothers.*

⁹ *Of the sons of Hebron, Eliel the chief, and eighty of his brothers.*

¹⁰ *Of the sons of Uzziel, Amminadab the chief, and a hundred and twelve of his brothers.*

¹¹ *David summoned* ᵃ*Zadok and Abiathar the priests, and* ᵃ *the Levites Uriel, Asaiah, Joel, Shemaiah, Eliel, and Amminadab,* ¹² *and said to them, "You are the heads of the fathers (houses) of the Levites. Sanctify yourselves, you and your brothers, and bring up the ark of Yahweh, the God of Israel, to (the place)* ᵃ *I have prepared for it.* ¹³ ᵃ*Because you were not with us the first time,* ᵃ *Yahweh our God broke out against us, because we did not inquire of him* ᵇ *according to the custom."*

¹⁴ *So* ᵃ*the priests and* ᵃ *the Levites sanctified themselves to bring up the ark of Yahweh, the God of Israel.* ¹⁵ *The sons of the Levites carried the ark of God, just as Moses had commanded, according to the word of Yahweh,* ᵃ*on their shoulders* ᵃ *with poles upon them.*

¹⁶ *David also commanded the chiefs of the Levites to install their brothers* ᵃ*as musicians to play musical instruments (harps, lyres, and cymbals) and to sing joyfully.* ᵃ ¹⁷ *So the Levites installed Heman the son of Joel and Asaph the son of Berechiah from his relatives; and from their relatives, the sons of Merari, Ethan, the son of Kushaiah,* ᵃ ¹⁸ *and with them as assistants* ᵃ *their relatives Zechariah,* ᵇ *Jaaziel,* ᶜ *Shemiramoth, Jehiel, Unni, Eliab, Benaiah, Maaseiah, Mattithiah, Eliphelehu,* ᵈ *and Mikneiah; and Obed-edom and Jeiel* ᵉ ᶠ*were the doorkeepers.* ᶠ ¹⁹ *The musicians Heman, Asaph, and Ethan were to play on bronze cymbals,* ²⁰ *Zechariah, Aziel,* ᵃ *Shemiramoth, Jehiel, Unni, Eliab, Maaseiah, and Benaiah (were to play) on harps* ᵇ*according to Alamoth,* ᵇ ²¹ *and Mattithiah, Eliphelehu,* ᵃ *Mikneiah, Obed-edom, Jehiel, and Azaziah* ᵇ *were to lead* ᶜ *with lyres* ᵈ*according to Sheminith.* ᵈ ²² *Chenaniah,* ᵃ *leader of the Levites in music,* ᵇ*should direct* ᶜ *the music,* ᵇ *for he understood it;* ²³ *Berechiah and Elkanah were to be gatekeepers for the ark.* ²⁴ *Shebaniah, Joshaphat, Nethanel, Amasai, Zechariah, Benaiah, and Eliezer, the priests, should blow* ᵃ *the trumpets before the ark of God.* ᵇ*Obed-edom and Jehiah also were to be gatekeepers for the ark.* ᵇ

²⁵ *So David* ᵃ*and the elders of Israel and the chiefs of thousands* ᵃ *were going to*

bring up the ark of the covenant of Yehweh from the house of Obed-edom with joy. [b]
[26a] And because God helped the Levites [a] who bore the ark of the covenant of Yahweh,
[b] they sacrificed seven bulls and seven rams. [b] [27] David [a] was clad [b] in a byssus robe, [a]
as were all the Levites who bore the ark, and the musicians, and Chenaniah [c] the
leader of the music of the singers, [c] [d] and David wore a linen ephod. [d] [28] And [a] all
Israel [a] was bringing up the ark of the covenant with shouting, [b] and with the sound
of the horn, and with trumpets, and with cymbals, playing on harps and lyres. [b]

[29] When the ark of the covenant was coming in to the city of David, Michal,
Saul's daughter, looked out the window and saw King David [a] dancing and laughing, [a]
and she despised him in her heart.

[16:1] They brought in the ark of God and left it in [a] the midst of the tent David
has prepared for it and [b] presented burnt offerings [b] and peace offerings before God.
[2] When David had finished sacrificing the burnt offerings and peace offerings, he blessed
the people in Yahweh's name. [3] He allotted to each Israelite, man and woman, a
loaf [a] of bread, [b] a date-cake, [c] and a raisin cake.

[4] David [a] also placed Levites as ministers before the ark of Yahweh to commemorate, [b]
to give thanks, and to praise Yahweh, Israel's God.

[5] Asaph was the chief. His assistants [a] were Zechariah, Jeiel, [b] Shemiramoth, Jehiel,
Mattithiah, Eliab, Benaiah, Obed-edom, and Jeiel, with harps and lyres, and Asaph
with cymbals to play, [6] and Benaiah and Jahaziel the priests with trumpets continually
before the ark of the covenant of God.

[7] On that day David first decreed that thanks should be given to Yahweh by Asaph
and his relatives:

[8] Give thanks to Yahweh, call upon his name,
   make known his deeds among the peoples.
[9] Sing to him, make music to him,
   meditate upon his wonderful deeds.
[10] Glory in his holy name,
   let the heart of those who seek Yahweh be glad.
[11] Seek out Yahweh and his strength,
   seek his face continually.
[12] Remember his wonderful deeds which he has done,
   his wonders, and the words of his mouth.
[13] O seed of Israel, [a] his servant, [b]
   O sons of Jacob, his chosen ones!
[14] He is Yahweh our God,
   his judgments are in all the earth.
[15] Remember [a] forever his covenant,
   the word he commanded to the thousandth generation,
[16] (the covenant) which he made with Abraham,
   his vow to Isaac. [a]
[17] And established it as a statute for Jacob,
   for Israel as an eternal covenant, saying,
[18] "To you I will give the land of Canaan,
   the portion of your inheritance."
[19] When you [a] were few in number,
   almost as nothing, and sojourners in it,

20 *They wandered about from nation to nation,*
   and (their) kingdom belonged to another people,
21 *He did not permit anyone* [a] *to oppress them;*
   he reproved kings concerning them.
22 *"Do not touch my anointed ones;*
   *do not wrong my prophets." * [a]

23 [a] *Sing to Yahweh, all the earth;*
   proclaim his deliverance from day to day. [a]
24 *Recite his glory among the nations,*
   his wonderful deeds among all the people,
25 *For Yahweh is great, and greatly to be praised,*
   and wonderful above all gods.
26 *Because all the gods of the peoples are idols,*
   but Yahweh made the heavens.
27 *Splendor and grandeur are before him;*
   strength and joy [a] *are in his place.* [b]
28 *Give to Yahweh, O families of the peoples;*
   give to Yahweh glory and strength.
29 *Give to Yahweh the glory due his name;*
   bring an offering and come before him.
30 *Worship Yahweh in holy array;*
   tremble before him, [a] *all the earth.*
   [b] *Yea, the world is established;*
   it cannot be tottered. [b]
31 *Let the heavens rejoice, and the earth be glad,*
   [a] *and let them say among the nations,*
   *"Yahweh is king." * [a]
32 *Let the sea and all that is in it roar;*
   Let the field [a] *and all in it rejoice.* [b]
33 *Then* [a] *the trees of the forest will sing before* [b] *Yahweh,*
   because he comes [c] *to judge the earth.* [d]
34 [a] *Give thanks to Yahweh, for he is good,*
   for his steadfast love lasts forever.
35   [a] *And say:*
   "Save us, [b] *God of our salvation,* [b]
   gather us and [c] *deliver us* [c] *from the nations,*
   that we may give thanks to your holy name,
   that we may bow down praising you. [a]
36 *Blessed be Yahweh, the God of Israel,*
   from eternity and to eternity.
   Then all the people said, [a] *"Amen," and* [b] *praised the Lord.* [b]
37 David left there [a] before the ark of the covenant of Yahweh Asaph and his brothers to minister before the ark continually [b] as each day required, [b] 38 and Obed-edom and his [a] sixty-eight relatives [b] (Obed-edom the son of Jeduthun and Hosah were gatekeepers), [b] 39 and (he left) [a] Zadok the priest and his relatives the priests before the tabernacle of Yahweh on the high place which was at Gibeon 40 to offer

up sacrifices to Yahweh upon the altar of burnt offerings continually morning and evening and as prescribed in the law of Yahweh which he had commanded Israel. [41] *With them were Heman and Jeduthun and the rest of those selected* ᵃ *and designated by name* ᵃ *to give thanks to Yahweh "because his steadfast love is forever."* [42] *And with them,* ᵃ *Heman and Jeduthun,* ᵃ *were trumpets and cymbals for playing, and instruments for sacred music,* ᵇ ᶜ *and the sons of Jeduthun were at the gate.* ᶜ [43] *And all the people went away, each to his house, and David returned to bless his house.*

Notes

2.a. For the significance of בחר "choose," here with "them," i.e., "the Levites," as obj, see on 28:5.

2.b. Or "it," i.e., the ark; cf. Deut 18:5; Num 1:50.

3.a. For קהל "assemble," hiph, in similar context, see 13:5; 28:1.

4.a. Cf. 23:2; 2 Chr 29:4, 15, 20.

4.b. LXX "and"; cf. 13:2. Mention of the priests here and in vv 11, 14, 24; 16:6 is considered secondary by many; cf. Williamson, 123; Rudolph, 115.

5.a-a. G^BS numbers 110.

6.a-a. G^BR numbers 250.

7.a. A few MSS מאתים (dual) "hundreds."

7.b. G^BR numbers 50.

8.a. One MS reads שמנים "80."

11.a-a. See n. 4.a.

12.a. Read (or understand) המקום אשר "the place which"; cf. v 3.

13.a. The text is probably corrupt, although the meaning is quite clear. Some consider למבראשונה as a combination of למה (in the sense of "because") and בראשנה "at the head"; "because you were not (employed) for what was at first" (BDB, 533, 1.d.e). G^L ὅτι οὐκ ἐν τῷ πρότερον ὑμᾶς εἶναι ἑτοίμους (G^B > ἑτοίμους "be prepared"); Rudolph reads למה and inserts אתנו "with us." It is probably best to render as an accumulation of prepositions not significantly affecting the meaning: "Because you were not (with us) at first" or "at the head" (i.e., of the procession).

13.b. The similarity to 10:13–14 and 13:3, where the text is also dubious, is suggestive.

14.a-a. Cf. n. 4.b.

15.a-a. LXX κατὰ τὴν γραφήν "according to the writings" (= ככתוב "as written").

16.a-a. The meaning is clear, but this is not the case with the syntax or the musical terminology—or both. Note, however, that the familiar משררים refers to musicians in general rather than singers only, and that שמע "sound aloud" in the hiph simply means "to play (an instrument)" (BDB, 1034, 1.b).

17.a. G "Kishiah"; cf. 6:29 קישי "Kishi" (pro קושיהו "Kushaiah").

18.a. המשנים = "the second," i.e., in command or rank.

18.b. MT adds בן "son."

18.c. יעזיאל "Jaaziel"; LXX Οζιηλ "Oziel" (cf. v 20 עזיאל "Uzziel"), 16:5 יעיאל "Jeiel."

18.d. G^A καὶ Ἐλιφαλὰ "and Eliphala."

18.e. G + οξιας (ועזיה) insert with v 21 ועזזיהו "Azaziah"?

18.f-f. Rudolph, BHS gl from v 24b.

20.a. Cf. n. 18.c.

20.b-b. עלמות "Alamoth," a technical musical term (cf. Ps 46:1; 48:15) traditionally associated with soprano voices (cf. עלמה "young woman, virgin").

21.a. G^Aal Ἐλιφαλαις "Eliphalais"; cf. n. 18.d.

21.b. > v 18 + 16:5.

21.c. לנצח "to oversee, lead," used only in Chronicles, Ezra, and Psalms as a musical title (cf. BDB, 663–64).

21.d-d. על־שמינית "upon the sheminith"; cf. Ps 6:1; 12:1; a technical musical term of unknown meaning, traditionally associated with "octave" (cf. שמנה "eight," hence "bass").

22.a. G Vg וכניה "and Conaniah"; a few MSS ובניהו "and Beniah."

22.b-b. The meaning is doubtful, but the phrase most likely refers to the lifting up of voices in song (cf. נשא "to lift up, bear"). Since משא "music" is also used of the prophetic oracle and since Chronicles also considers the Levitical singers as prophets (cf. 2 Chr 24:27), that meaning is also possible here, as is the more prosaic one of lifting up, or bearing, the ark, preferred by Curtis (216), KB, and others. Cf. G "song"; Vg "prophecy."

22.c. Considered by BDB as a qal inf abs of יסר "to instruct"; by KB as a noun, "instructor" (*h.l.*).

24.a. Q מַחְצְרִים; K מַחְצְצרִים "blow."

24.b-b. Considered by many a later gl based on v 18 (cf. vv 21, 23).

25.a-a. > 2 Sam 6:12.

25.b. The note of joy, like other emphases in Chronicles, is found also in Samuel.

26.a-a. 2 Sam 6:13 reads otherwise. See Lemke, *HTR* 58 (1965) 352–53.

26.b-b. 2 Sam 6:13 reads ויזבח שור ומריא "and he sacrificed an ox and a fatling."

27.a-a. 2 Sam 6:14 reads ודוד מכרכר בכל־עז "so David danced with all his might."

27.b. For מכרבל "clad," cf. 2 Sam 6:14 מכרכר "dancing," and Curtis, 219.

27.c-c. The Heb. שר המשא המשררים "*the* leader of *the* music of *the* singers" is grammatically impossible. Read either שר המשא "leader of the music" or שר במשא "*the* leader i*n* the music" (cf. v 22) and omit המשררים "the singers," or omit המשא "the music" with G[L].

27.d-d. A later insertion from 2 Sam 6:14, now conflicting with the alteration made earlier in the verse.

28.a-a. In the form וכל־ישראל "and all Israel." The all-Israel theme found here is already in Samuel; cf. 2 Sam 6:15, 19.

28.b-b. > 2 Sam 6:15.

29.a-a. 2 Sam 6:16 מפזז ומכרכר לפני יהוה "leaping and dancing before Yahweh."

16:1.a. 2 Sam 6:17 + במקומו "in its place" (cf. 1 Chr 15:1).

1.b-b. 2 Sam 6:17 ויעל דויד עלות "David presented offerings; cf. 1 Chr 16:1 וקריבו עלות "they presented offerings."

3.a. 2 Sam 6:19 חלת (חַלָה) "a kind of cake"; cf. Exod 29:2).

3.b. 2 Sam 6:19 the numeral "one," used as an indefinite article, here and with the two remaining nouns in the verse.

3.c. After KB, rsv "a portion of meat." The meaning of the word, found only here and in 2 Sam 6:19, is uncertain.

4.a. Heb. > "David."

4.b. Heb. ולהזכיר "to cause to remember." Cf. Ps 38:1. The precise nuance is unclear. Curtis, 220, and Welch *The Work of the Chronicler*, 67–68, connect the word with a liturgical practice associated with sacrifice (see Isa 66:3, and cf. the related אזכרה "memorial-offering" of Lev 2:2, 9, 16; 5:12; 6:8; Num 5:26). Williamson relates the construction with a psalm of lament (127). A similar passage in 2 Chr 31:2 omits this description of the Levites' function.

5.a. See n. 15:18.a.

5.b. See n. 15:18.a.

13.a. Ps 105:6 2 MSS Syr אברהם "Abraham."

13.b. G shows pl.

15.a. Ps 105:8 זכר "he remembers"; G[AL] μνημονεύων "remembering."

16.a. Ps 105:9 לישחק "to Isaac" (with ש).

19.a. Ps 105:12 בהיותם "when they were."

21.a. Ps 105:14 אדם "no one," lit., "not a man"—a variation of איש.

22.a. Ps 105:15 ולנביאי "and to my prophets."

23.a-a. Using only two of the four lines of Ps 96:1–2.

27.a. Ps 96:6 ותפארת "and renown" (BDB, 802).

27.b. Ps 96:6 במקדש "in his sanctuary" (cf. 15:1).

30.a. Ps 96:9 מפניו "from before him," lit., "from his face."

30.b-b. Cf. additional lines in Ps 106:10.

31.a-a. = Ps 96:10a.

32.a. Ps 96:12 שָׂדַי "field, land"; Chronicles השדה "the field."

32.b. Ps 96:12 יעלז "exult"; Chronicles יעלץ "exalt."

33.a. Ps 96:12 + כל "all."

33.b. Ps 96:13 לפני "before him" (cf. n. 30.a.).

33.c. Ps 96:13 repeats כי בא "for he comes."

33.d. Ps 96:13 adds other words.

34.a. V 34 = Ps 106:1.

35.a-a. Vv 35–36 = Ps 106:45–48.

35.b-b. Ps 106:47 יהוה אלהינו "Yahweh our God."

35.c-c. > Ps 106:47 (!).

36.a. Ps 106:48 ואמר "and say"; G Chr ἐρεῖ "he shall say."

36.b. Ps 106:48 הללו־יה "praise Yah" or "halleluja" (impv pl); G Chr ᾔνεσαν.

37.a. The *lamedh* indicates the dir obj, as in Aramaic.

37.b-b. Lit., "according to the thing of a day in its day."

38.a. MT ואחיהם "their brothers."

38.b-b. The phrase is probably a late interpolation based on different conceptions of Obed-Edom's office; cf. 5:18, 21, 24; 16:5.

39.a. The sentence continues the ויעזב "and he left" of v 37, which is not present here; the dir obj is marked by את (cf. n. 37.a.).

41.a-a. Perhaps an expression after the manner of Chronicles; cf. 12:32; 2 Chr 28:15; 31:19; also Ezra 8:20.

42.a-a. Probably a gl meant to clarify the roles of the minor clergy. One would expect the trumpets especially to be allotted to the priests.

42.b. MT שיר האלהים "sacred music," lit., "a song of God."

42.c-c. The position of the gatekeepers appears to have remained problematic.

Form/Structure/Setting

These two chapters may be viewed as follows:

15:1–3	Preparations for the ark
15:4–10	Levitical families
15:11–13	Priests and Levites instructed
15:14–15	Preparations concluded
15:16–24	Levitical musicians
15:25–29	The ark brought to Jerusalem
16:1–3	Celebration for the ark
16:4–6	Levites placed around the ark
16:7–36	A psalm of praise

Following chap. 14, which appears somewhat intrusive, the writer returns to the narrative of the transfer of the ark to Jerusalem. Instead of the dozen verses required by Samuel to narrate this successful transfer, however, Chronicles utilizes no less than seventy-one. For Chronicles, the moving of the ark becomes occasion for the organization and installation of the Levitical families, and in particular the temple musicians (15:1–24). The arrival of the ark in Jerusalem (15:25–16:3) is celebrated by a gathering of all Israel and marked by the inclusion of a lengthy hymn by the Asaphites (16:4–36), after which the priests and Levites are assigned to their various duties either before the ark in Jerusalem or before the tabernacle and altar of burnt offering at Gibeon (16:37–42). With the ark now in Jerusalem, the scene is set for a new stage in the history of the ark, David, and Israel.

Biblical parallels to portions of chaps. 15–16 are as follows:

1 Chronicles	Other Literature
15:25–29; 16:1–3, 43	2 Sam 6:12b–20a
16:8–22	Psalm 105:1–15
16:23–33	Psalm 96:1–13a
16:34–36	Psalm 106:1 (?), 47–48.

The remainder of the two chapters consists of narratives commonly assigned at least in part to the Chronicler (15:1–3, 11–15; 16:4, 37–42), into which various lists of priestly and Levitical personnel have been worked, either by the Chronicler or a later writer.

The extent of the supposed additions differs markedly from commentator to commentator. Noth, for example (*Ü.S.*, 116), considers 15:4–10, 16–24; 16:5–38, 41–42, as late, and is followed largely by Rudolph (2, 115–29) and many critical scholars. Others, however, are more inclined to accept other portions as original, especially in chap. 16 (cf. Myers, 119–23; Butler, *VT* 28 [1978] 142–50), but also in chap. 15 as well (the older commentators such as Keil, 201–8 as well as Williamson, 119–32), although allowing for smaller insertions and textual errors (cf. Keil, 219, on 16:38; Williamson, 11, 14, on 15:4).

That at a minimum the various lists included do not comprise a unity but reflect different interests or periods seems apparent. The same six Levitical heads named in 15:11 are named also in 15:4–10, but with the enumeration of their family group. The names in 15:17–18 recur in 15:19–24 with minor differences (see chart and *Comment* below) but separated according to musical instruments and with additional functionaries added. Moreover, the first part of the same list is repeated, again with minor differences, in 16:5–6. That we are dealing here not simply with varying usages of the same list is clear from the textual discrepancies and other variations. Obed-edom and Jeiel are named in 15:18 as gatekeepers, but in v 21 and 16:5 they are included among the musicians. (The second list concludes with another naming of Obed-edom and a strikingly similar Jehiah as gatekeepers, 15:24.) To propose that the lists refer to two Obed-edoms is a counsel of despair that ignores the structure of the lists as a whole and the history of Levitical developments (see pp. xxxi–xxxii). The desire to include Obed-edom with the Levites, and not just with the gatekeepers, and as well to include all gatekeepers as Levites, is further seen in 16:38, 41, 42, where Jeduthun replaces Ethan among the Levitical leaders, the sons of Jeduthun are gatekeepers, and Obed-edom is also a son of Jeduthun. (V 38 is a conflation.)

Other differences pointing to a different occasion for varying data in the two chapters might be mentioned. Mention of the priests in such passages as 15:4, 11, and 14 appears to be out of character with the narrative as a whole, which concentrates fully upon the Levites, and has suggested to many a "priestly redactor" (cf. Rothstein; Welch, *Post-Exilic Judaism*, 65; Rudolph; Williamson). The trumpets, which are in 15:24; 16:6 (as in the priestly strand of the Pentateuch; cf. Num 10:1–10) the prerogative of the priests, are in 16:42 ascribed to Heman and Jeduthun without further comment. And as mentioned above, the fact that in 16:41–42 Jeduthun rather than Ethan stands next to Heman is itself a clear indication of changes in the historical situation, or at a minimum, if it is argued that the two names denote the same individual, of differing textual or traditional circles.

For discussion of developments among priests, Levites, and singers, see the *Introduction*. Having said this, the question remains of how many of the discrepancies (and developments) can or should be removed by textual emendation; how many of them might be attributable to the Chronicler himself in extracting from and using various lists; and how many need to be assigned to later writers. That opinions differ here goes without saying. At present I consider it most reasonable to assume that 15:4–10 is a later addition (I find uncompelling the argument of Talmon ["Ezra and Nehemiah," *IDBSup* 322]; Welten, *Geschichte,* 150–91; and Williamson, 121–22, that repetition is a literary device signaling an insertion by the original author.) The same is also true of vv 16–24 and portions of 16:38–42 (most probably vv 38b, 42, and perhaps 41) which seek to make the list more complete (the addition of still more cultic personnel), more up to date (the varying fortunes of the gatekeepers), or more in accord with the writer's concept of how things were or ought to have been (inclusion of the priests, the Levitical genealogy of Obed-edom). I would assign 16:5–6 to an intermediate tradition due to its unusual relationship to 15:17–24, and 16:6 to a priestly revisor. The question of 16:8–36 may be left open—but I see no reason to conclude, whether the words were placed here by the Chronicler or a later writer, that they do not represent extractions from the Psalms as we know them rather than a specific composition for the occasion (against Keil, 217–18) or another composition or hymn parallel to the psalms (against Ackroyd, 44–45).

Comment

1–3 In these verses unique to the Chronicler, we find again three of his major emphases: (1) the ark and its tent, which is to form the major focus of the temple; (2) the role of the Levites in ministering to the ark, v 3; and (3) the reassembling of all Israel, v 3, cf. 13:5.

The nature of David's preparations for the ark is not detailed. In 2 Sam 6:17 it is noted only that the ark was put "in its place (בִּמְקוֹמוֹ) in the midst of the tent which David had pitched for it" (cf. 1 Chr 16:1). The tradition of the tent shrine for the ark is an ancient one, probably adopted and magnified also in the tabernacle tradition. Whether the tent here is to be understood as one in which the ark was kept with Obed-edom (cf. the textual addition in 13:14) or as a new construction by David, as seems more likely in view of the fact that no tent is mentioned in connection with the earlier journeys of the ark (2 Sam 5:1–7:2; the nature of the בֵּית־יהוה "house of Yahweh" at Shiloh [1 Sam 1:24] is problematic; cf. 1 Sam 2:22) or with either attempt to move the ark from Obed-edom's house, cannot be said with certainty. It appears that David's tent is in 1 Kgs 8:4 (reproduced thoughtlessly in 2 Chr 5:5) identified with the tent of meeting; however, the Chronicler's unique separation of the tent of meeting, apparently to be identified with the tabernacle and placed by him at Gibeon prior to its removal to Jerusalem for the dedication of the temple (cf. 16:39; 21:29; 2 Chr 1:3–6), makes that understanding impossible for him.

David's command that the Levites alone are to carry the ark is based upon Yahweh's divine choice (בָּחַר) of the Levites to carry the ark and, perhaps more significantly, "to minister to him forever." The role of the Levites as presented in Deut 10:8; 18:5 is reflected here. Although the text of v 13 is difficult, it appears obvious that the failure of the Levites to carry the ark the first time its removal to Jerusalem was attempted was the reason for the failure of that attempt.

David again assembles *all* Israel, as had been done at his coronation (11:1; cf. 12:39 [38]) and at the first attempt to transport the ark (13:1 [in contrast to 2 Sam 6:1], cf. also 15:28 and 2 Sam 6:15). Not only David and the prescribed Levitical personnel, but the entire people support this act by their presence.

4–10 All or much of these verses is quite commonly denied to the primary author of Chronicles (see above), and it seems likely that the text has undergone expansion, although Williamson (120–22) has argued that these verses stem from a time prior to the Chronicler and were incorporated by him. However, once again the change has been in the nature of expansion and elaboration in keeping with the Chronicler's basic emphasis. Six basic groups of Levites are represented, the chief of each is named, and their number, varying from 80 to 230, is given. These six groups represent, as expected, the three basic Levitical families of Kohath, Merari, and Gershom (see on 5:27–6:33 [6:1–48]), but they name also families of Elizaphan, Hebron, and Uzziel (vv 8–10), represented by Shemaiah, Eliel, and Amminadab respectively. These three families all are derived from Kohath. An Elizaphan is named in Exod 6:22 as a grandson of Kohath through Uzziel; both Hebron and Uzziel are listed as sons of Kohath (Exod 6:18; cf. 1 Chr 5:28 [6:2]; 6:3 [18]), while Elizaphan is a grandson through Uzziel (Exod 6:22, though not named in the genealogies of 1 Chr 5:27–6:33). This sixfold division of the Levites is otherwise unknown, and has led some (e.g. Williamson, 123) to conclude that it represents a historical stage prior to the time of the Chronicler. Elizaphan is also mentioned as a Levitical division in 2 Chr 29:13, joined with the three traditional families (Kohath, Merari, Gershom) and three characteristic families of Levitical singers, Asaph, Heman, and Jeduthun. As for the six chiefs mentioned, Uriel is named in the Kohathite genealogy of Elkanah in 1 Chr 6:9 [24] and is probably listed first here as noted by Curtis (213), because the Kohathites in Num 4:15 are given responsibility for carrying the sanctuary furniture. The name Asaiah is found in 6:15 [30]; a Gershonite Joel is found in 1 Chr 23:8; the entry "Shemaiah" occurs no less than 28 times in the entry under that name in *IDB* (4:322–23); an Eliel is found as a descendant of the Kohathite Heman in 1 Chr 6:19 [34]; and Amminadab is found as a son of Kohath in 6:7 [22], where it is commonly considered a textual error for Izhar (see Williamson, 71; Rudolph, 54 and n. 6:7.a.). This might mean that the present passage was so late as to be dependent upon the error already found in 1 Chr 6. The total of those numbered reaches 862, to whom apparently the six leaders are to be added.

11–15 V 11 names the same six heads of Levitical families as vv 5–10, albeit without designation of their families or numbers, and includes also the names of the priests Zadok and Abiathar, not found in v 4. Since the priests are not generally involved in the proceedings to be reported, their mention here is quite commonly considered secondary (see *Form/Structure/ Setting*, above), and as also noted above, the listing of the Levites in v 11 is often seen as the occasion for the insertion of vv 4–10, which are an elaboration upon them. The Levites are instructed to "sanctify themselves"—i.e., to refrain from the common and profane (cf. Gen 35:2; Exod 19:10–15, probably involving at a minimum bathing and abstention from sexual intercourse [1 Sam 21:5])—and to bring up the ark to the place David had prepared for it (see on v 1).

While the details of v 13 are somewhat ambiguous, v 15 strongly suggests that it was either the absence of the Levites (see on 13:2, although they are not so much as mentioned in the procedures which follow) or the manner in which they carried the ark—perhaps on a wagon rather than on poles, as prescribed in Exod 25:10–15; 37:1–5—that was responsible for the earlier failure.

16–24 *Installation of the Levitical musicians.* David, somewhat unusually, gives commandment to the chiefs of the Levites to install some of their number as musicians, and they respond by doing so. Three instruments named in v 16 (see on 13:8) are commonly named in Chronicles (cf. 16:5; 2 Chr 5:12; 29:25; Neh 12:27).

The three leaders are named (v 17), followed by eleven assistants (v 18) and two doorkeepers (v 18). Essentially these same personnel are repeated in vv 16–22 with the addition of the instruments upon which they are to play. However, this time the list is also extended with ten additional names (see chart below), included among whom are two priests (vv 22–24). (See also 1 Chr 16:5–6.)

LEVITICAL PERSONNEL (1 CHR 15–16)

A. 15:17–18	*B. 15:19–24*	*C. 16:5–6*
Heman	Heman	
Asaph	Asaph	Asaph (cymbals—see below)
Ethan	Ethan (cymbals)	
Zechariah	Zechariah	Zechariah
Jaaziel	Aziel	Jeiel
Shemiramoth	Shemiramoth	Shemiramoth
Jehiel	Jehiel	Jehiel
Unni	Unni	Mattithiah
Eliab	Eliab	Eliab
Benaiah	Maaseiah	Benaiah
Maaseiah	Benaiah (harps/Alamoth)	
Mattithiah	Mattithiah	
Eliphelehu	Eliphelehu	
Mikneiah	Mikneiah	
	Obed-edom	
Obed-edom	Jeiel	Obed-edom
Jeiel (gatekeepers)	Azariah (lyres/Sheminith)	Jeiel (harps and lyres)
	Chenaniah (direct music)	(Asaph-cymbals)
	Berechiah	
	Elkanah (gatekeepers)	
	Shebaniah	
	Joshaphat	
	Nethanel	
	Amasai	
	Zechariah	
	Benaiah	Benaiah
	Eliezer (priests/trumpets)	Jahaziel (priests/trumpets)
	Obed-edom	
	Jehiah (gatekeepers)	

It is apparent that we have here three closely related but substantially different lists, reflecting at a minimum three different layers of tradition. List

B is identical with List A except that the second assistant is Aziel (עֲזִיאֵל)
rather than Jaaziel (יַעֲזִיאֵל) (cf. also Jeiel [יְעִיאֵל] in List C); the names Benaiah
and Maaseiah are reversed, and Obed-edom and (another) Jeiel, who are in
List A as gatekeepers, are upon the first mention in List B (and C) musicians.
List B also adds an additional musician, Azariah, a "director" (see nn. 22.a.,
b-b., c.), names two additional gatekeepers, seven priests, and concludes with
what appears to be a repetition of Obed-edom and Jeiel/Jehiah, but now
named as gatekeepers. List C is briefer in every respect save the mention
of musical instruments. Only Asaph is listed as a leader, playing cymbals,
supplemented by seven persons named in List A and Obed-edom and Jeiel
on harps and lyres and the priests Benaiah and Jahaziel on trumpets.

It is quite apparent that we have here a collection of related lists, assembled
and supplemented by one or more writers. List B, which is in every way
the most extensive, appears to be also the most complex, as indicated both
by the systematic distribution of instruments, the inclusion of Obed-edom
and Jeiel/Jehiah both among the musicians and the gatekeepers, the naming
of other gatekeepers as well, and the listing of priests. However, it is difficult
to date the list. If Gese's conclusions are correct, the inclusion of Ethan
instead of Jeduthun as the third Levite family places both Lists A and B
among the latest OT Levitical traditions. List C could appear to stand between
Lists A and B in time, since it names Obed-edom and Jeiel as musicians
but does not apportion the instruments so clearly. It may owe its abbreviated
form to the desire to reflect the conditions of 16:37, where only Asaph and
his relatives are left at Jerusalem.

15:25–16:3 *The transport of the ark completed.* The writer returns to his *Vorlage*
in 2 Sam 6:12b–19 to recount the successful transport of the ark to Jerusalem.
The notation of Samuel that Yahweh had blessed Obed-edom's house because
of the ark is lacking in Chronicles, though probably too much is made of
this by many commentators. Other alterations made in Chronicles are common
to his work. (a) The addition of the "elders and princes of thousands" (see
n. 25.a-a.) transforms what appeared to be a private and singular act of David
into that of the people Israel, v 15 (but cf. "all the house of Israel"). (b)
The role of the Levites (not the priests), both in the sacrifices (vv 26–27)
and in the music (v 28) is made at least more explicit. Samuel had spoken
only of "the bearers of the ark" (2 Sam 6:13) and "(with a) shout and the
sound of the ram's horn" (v 15). Chronicles makes it explicit that it was
the Levites who bore the ark (vv 26, 27) and adds mention of the singers,
their leader (v 27), and the full panoply of instruments usually associated
with Levites and priests (v 28). (c) The priestly acts of David are omitted
or at least somewhat curtailed. The sacrifices offered by David both at the
beginning and the conclusion of the transport are ascribed at least in the
first instance to the Levites (vv 26; 16:1) (though the wording of 2 Sam 6:18
is retained in 16:2, "David finished offering" and "and David blessed the
people"). The linen ephod (אֵפוֹד בַּד) with which David is clothed in 2 Sam
6:14b appeared to the writer to be the same as that reserved for priests,
and is replaced with a byssus tunic (מְעִיל בּוּץ) v 27. (The occurrence of
אֵפוֹד בַּד "linen ephod" in v 27 must be due to a later writer.) (d) The
divine approval of the entire operation is plainly indicated in v 26, where
God's help of the Levites is stated. (e) Chronicles does not allow the festivities

to be interrupted by the account of David's conversation with Saul's daughter Michal (cf. 2 Sam 6:20b–23). It seems likely that we ought not make too much of this, save he did not want the dedication festivities interrupted or to end on a negative note. This section, parallel to a degree with 15:4–10 and 15:16–24 (see the chart there), lists Levites placed by David before the ark as ministers (משרתים). Their ministry is described as that of "commorating, praising, and giving thanks" to Yahweh (see n. 4.b.); terms which, with the exception of the first, will recur in describing their activity. (It is, however, probably being too precise to attach each word to a type of Psalm, as does Williamson, 127.) Only Asaph is named here as leader, and we are apparently to understand that the Levitical groups headed by Heman and Jeduthun were assigned to the tabernacle placed by Chronicles at Gibeon (see vv 37–42). The first seven assistants named to Asaph are identical with those named in 15:17–18, save that Mattithiah is moved up to replace Unni (see above-mentioned chart). Moreover, Obed-edom and Jeiel, set apart in 15:18 as gatekeepers, are here included without further mention with the (other) Levites. These nine are without further division assigned to harps and lyres, while Asaph as the leader plays the cymbals and the priests Benaiah and Jahaziel play the trumpets before the ark.

V 7 established more pointedly the role of Asaph and his kinsmen, and that their appointment goes back to David on that day. In 1 Chr 25:2 Asaph's work is identified with prophesying; and in 2 Chr 29:30 he is termed "Asaph the Seer" (החזה). Members of his family will be named in almost every celebration described by the writer. (See *Introduction.*) That priests are named here, but not in v 4, suggests that they may be a later addition.

8–36 These verses, denied to the Chronicler by most but accepted by others (see *Form/Structure/Setting* above), appear to be composed of portions of three psalms (Ackroyd's suggestion [64–65] that the three composed a single psalm otherwise known to the writer is possible, but seems unlikely—at any rate, the process of composition would have been the same.) Vv 8–22 correspond to Ps 105:1–15, the first part of a psalm of thanksgiving. However, 105:16–45 have been passed over, probably as limiting unnecessarily the focus of the psalm upon the past. Ps 105:1–6 are a summons to give thanks to God, based in particular upon his covenant with the fathers which culminated in the gift of the land of Canaan (vv 7–11). Vv 12–15 in that context (= 1 Chr 16:19–22) refer specifically to the wanderings of the patriarchs, and are followed in vv 16–45 with further examples of Yahweh's gracious protection spanning the ages from Joseph through the descent into Egypt, the Exodus, and the age of the wilderness wanderings, climaxing with the gift of the land. By concluding with v 15 of the psalm, the writer has permitted vv 12–15 (= 1 Chr 16:19–22) to stand more in the nature of a timeless principle applicable therefore in his own day: *It is the people Israel, reduced in number and without a homeland, which is protected by God.* The appropriateness of such a message, it must be agreed, is obvious during the exilic or post-exilic periods.

In this connection attention should be called to the alterations of the text indicated in n. 13.a., where the change from Abraham to Israel suggests more strongly that the addresses are to Israel, and in n. 15.a. (both erroneously corrected by RSV to agree with the Psalm), where the imperative is addressed to his audience. The writer is speaking to the current Israel, reminding them of their role as God's people. Specifically, he is calling upon them to remember Yahweh's covenant. The alteration of the suffixes from a third- to a second-person form (see n. 19.a.) suggests the same desire to make the text speak more directly: "When *you* were few in number. . . ." And as noted correctly by Butler (*VT* 28 [1978] 144), the "anointed ones" and "prophets" are certainly two groups of particular concern to the writer.

23–33 Apart from the minor items indicated in the notes, these verses are identical to Ps 96. No reason is apparent for the minor changes indicated: the omission of the reference to Yahweh's kingly reign in v 30 (cf. Ps 96:10) is found in v 31. This psalm is a psalm of praise to Yahweh the king, a summons to worship him on the basis of his superiority over all the peoples of the earth and their gods, which are in fact only idols (v 26), and in view of his coming judgment (v 33). The writer apparently found these verses adequately reflected his thoughts.

34–36 V 34 repeats the refrain so characteristic in Chronicles (cf. v 41) and is usually said in view of the following verses to be derived from Ps 106:1, though this is far from certain in view of its repeated use. Vv 35–36, however, do reflect the end of Ps 106, i.e. vv 47–48, which include a prayer that the Lord would gather Israel from among the nations (v 47) and the concluding doxology to Book IV of the Psalms (v 48). Significantly omitted is the remainder of the psalm, a long recitation of Israel's sinful nature in the period from slavery to Egypt to the promised land, culminating in Yahweh's anger and his handing them into the hands of the enemies (vv 40–43), as well as the assurance of the continuance of his steadfast love and the statement that "he caused them to be pitied by all those who held them captive" (Ps 106:46–48). Perhaps the mention of a part of the psalm was meant to arouse these thoughts in the minds of the worshipers.

37–43 These verses present final arrangements for the disposition of priests and Levites. Again, it seems likely that various literary levels are reflected. As in vv 5 and 7, Asaph and his relatives stand apart and are left at Jerusalem to minister before the ark of the covenant (v 37), accompanied only by "Obed-edom and his sixty-eight brethren" (v 38), for whom no genealogy is given. On the other hand, Zadok and his brethren the priests are placed with the tabernacle and the altar of burnt offerings at Gibeon (cf. 2 Chr 1:2–6). Either the original writer or a later one places Heman and Jeduthun (the latter not named in chap. 15, and usually considered earlier than Ethan, cf. 15:17, 19) with Zadok and the priests at Gibeon. It is not clear whether the priest Abiathar (cf. 15:11; but contrast 29:22) is to remain in Jerusalem, but that would appear to be likely.

A second Obed-edom, identified as a son of Jeduthun, and an otherwise unknown Hosah, are left as gatekeepers at Jerusalem (v 38), while other unnamed sons of Jeduthun are assigned to the gate at Gibeon (v 42). Hence priests, Levites, musicians, and gatekeepers are designated by David for the cultic centers at both Jerusalem and Gibeon until such time as the two are united in Solomon's temple at Jerusalem.

It has commonly been held that the placement of tabernacle and altar at Gibeon is a construct of the Chronicler, since no other OT tradition speaks of what by all rights ought to be a most important item. In the light of a greater appreciation of the Chronicler's historical accuracy, there have been some attempts to gather support for the accuracy of the Chronicler's presentation. Such efforts seem to me misplaced. To say, for example that 2 Sam 7:6 shows continuing respect for a tent shrine, and that it is therefore possible that it might have been at Gibeon, or to the point to the proximity of Gibeon to Nob, is a far cry from demonstrating any tradition analagous to that to which the Chronicler refers here. Also, to say that the Kings account (1 Kgs 3:3–5) is "as polemical against the legitimacy of Solomon's worship at Gibeon as the Chronicler is positive about it" (Williamson, 131) does not fit the fact that the Deuteronomist's evaluation of such worship prior to the erection of the temple differs markedly from that later, as shown from the fact of Yahweh's appearance to Solomon at Gibeon with the blessing of wealth, wisdom, and honor (1 Kgs 3:5–14) and the difference in the result of high place worship in 1 Kgs 11. Polk, wishing to associate Zadok with the Korahites, indicates the association could easily be maintained if Zadok could be shown to be a Gibeonite priest (*SBT* 9 [1979] 9), but concludes the evidence is tendentious (10). It therefore remains most likely that the Chronicler, wishing to present Solomon as without fault, has concluded in the light of Solomon's worship at Gibeon that tabernacle and altar must (or should) have been there at that time.

Explanation

David, once again with the support and participation of all Israel, and the Levites attending to the transfer of the ark properly, brings the ark without incident into Jerusalem to the tent which he has prepared for it, where it will remain until the temple has been built. In doing so, David affirms the unique role of the Levites in carrying the ark and ministering to Yahweh (15:2) and undertakes arrangements for the temple musicians (15:16–23; 16:4–7). In particular the Asaphites are appointed as musicians for the Jerusalem temple, with Obed-edom and his brethren at the gates (16:38), while Zadok, Heman and Jeduthun are assigned to the tabernacle at Gibeon. The lengthy psalm of chap. 16 provides an example of the work of the Levitical musicians, as well as illustrating the relevance of older hymns for a new day and situation. With ark and cultic personnel in place, the writer is now ready to approach more directly the central questions of the Davidic dynasty and the erection of the Jerusalem temple.

It is of course true that many have difficulty in seeing the relevance for today of the temple, and especially the elaborate Levitical organization detailed here. At the time of the exile, however, with God's presence and blessing so closely associated with the reestablishment of the temple in its place, that was not at all the case. And even today, we must wonder whether that kind of expression of devotion which gives little attention to worship—also the formal aspects of worship—has not gone far astray from the mark. The charge to give thanks to the Lord and to sing to his name (16:8–9) still rings out among his people. And his people still say "Amen" and praise the Lord (16:36).

The Promise to David   (17:1-27)

Bibliography

The material on the dynastic oracle is voluminous. For a broader and more extensive bibliography, see the bibliographies in the following three entries.

Carlson, R. A. *David, The Chosen King. A Traditio-historical approach to the Second Book of Samuel.* Tr. E. J. Sharpe and S. Rudman. Stockholm: Almquist & Wikseil, 1964. **Clements, R. E.** *God and Temple.* Philadelphia: Fortress, 1965. **Cross, F. M., Jr.** "Ideologies of Kingship in the Era of the Empire." *Canaanite Myth and Hebrew Epic.* Cambridge: Harvard University Press, 1973. 219–73.

For a fuller discussion of the Chronicles text, see the following entries.

Botterweck, G. J. "Zur Eigenart der chronistischen Davidsgeschichte." *TQ* 136 (1956) 402–35. **Braun, R.** "Solomonic Apologetic in Chronicles." *JBL* 92 (1973) 503–16. ———. "Solomon, the Chosen Temple Builder: The Significance of 1 Chronicles 22, 28, and 29 for the Theology of Chronicles." *JBL* 95 (1976) 581–90. **Brunet, A. M.** "Le Chroniste et ses Sources." *RB* 60 (1953) 481–508. **Loretz, O.** "The Perfectum Copulativum in 2 Sam. 7:9–11." *CBQ* 23 (1961) 294–96. **Williamson, H. G. M.** "Eschatology in Chronicles." *TynBul* 28 (1979) 115–54.

Translation

[1] *When David* [a] *had taken up residence in his house,* [b] *he* [a] *said to Nathan the prophet, "See, I live in a house (made of) cedar, but* [c] *the ark of the covenant of Yahweh* [c] *is beneath* [d] *curtains."* [2] *So Nathan said to David,* [a] *"Do whatever is in your heart, for God* [b] *is with you."*
    [3] *That night God's* [a] *word came to Nathan:* [4] *"Go and say to David my servant, 'Thus says the Lord: You* [a] *will not build me* [b] *this house* [b] *to dwell in,* [c] [5] *for I have not dwelt in a house from the day* [a] *I brought up* [ab] *Israel* [c] *until this day, but I have been* [d] *going about* [d] [e] *from tent to tent and from tabernacle to tabernacle.* [e] [6] *Wherever I went throughout Israel, did I speak a word with one of Israel's judges* [a] *whom I commanded to shepherd my people,* [b] *saying, "Why have you not built me a house of cedar?" '* [7] *Now thus you shall say to my servant David: 'Thus says Yahweh Sebaoth: I took you from the pasture, from following the flock, to be prince over my people Israel* [8] *and I was with you wherever you went and destroyed all your enemies before you. And* [a] *now I will make* [a] *your name famous* [b] *like the name of the great ones who are upon the earth.* [9] *I will establish a place for my people Israel and plant them* [a] *and they* [a] *will dwell in their* [a] *place and will no longer be disturbed, and* [b] *wicked men* [b] *will no longer oppress* [c] *them* [a] *as before,* [10] [a] *from the days when* [a] *I established judges over my people Israel.* [b] *I will subdue* [b] *all your enemies and* [c] *I declare to you* [c] *that a house Yahweh will build (for) you.* [11] [a] *When the time comes* [a] *for you to go* [b] *with your fathers to die, I will raise up your seed after you,* [c] *who will be one of your sons,* [c] *and will establish his kingdom.* [d] [12] *He will build a house* [a] *for me,* [a] *and I will establish* [b] *his throne* [b] *forever.* [13] *I will be a father to him, and he will be a son to me,* [a] *and* [b] *I will not take* [b] *my steadfast love from him, as I removed it* [c] *from him who* [c] *was before you.* [14] [a] *I will establish him over my house*

and over my kingdom ᵃ *forever; his throne* ᵇ *will be made sure forever.'* " ¹⁵ *In accordance with all these words and all this vision, so Nathan spoke to David.*

¹⁶ *King David went in and sat before Yahweh and said, "Who am I,* ᵃ *Yahweh God,* ᵃ *and who is my house that you have brought me to this point?* ¹⁷ *But this was a small thing in your eyes, O God* ᵃ—*you have spoken concerning your servant's house for a long time to come* ᵇ *and have shown me future generations,* ᵇ ᶜ *Yahweh God.* ᶜ ¹⁸ *How can David* ᵃ*give you more honor,* ᵃ *for you know* ᵇ *your servant.* ¹⁹ *Yahweh,* ᵃ *for your* ᵇ *servant's* ᵇ *sake and according to your heart you have done this great thing, to make known all this greatness.* ᶜ ²⁰ *Yahweh,* ᵃ *there is none like you; there is no God except you, according to all we have heard with our ears.* ²¹ *And who is like your people Israel, one nation on the earth whom God has gone* ᵃ *to redeem for himself as a people, to give you* ᵇ *a name great and wonderful, to drive* ᶜ *out nations* ᵈ *before your people whom you have redeemed from Egypt?* ²² *And you made* ᵈ *your people Israel a people to yourself forever, and you, Yahweh, became their God forever.*

²³ *"Now, Yahweh,* ᵃ *let the word which you have spoken concerning your servant and his house be established* ᵇ *forever, and do as you have spoken,* ²⁴ *that your name* ᵃ*may be established forever* ᵃ *and great, saying, 'Yahweh Sebaoth is* ᵇ *God of Israel* ᵇ *and Israel's God forever,' and the house of David your servant is established before you.* ²⁵ *Because you,* ᵃ*my God,* ᵃ *have* ᵇ*revealed to your servant* ᵇ *that you will build him a house, your servant has found courage* ᶜ *to pray before you.* ᵈ ²⁶ *And now, Yahweh,* ᵃ *you are God,* ᵇ *and you have spoken concerning your servant* ᶜ*this good thing.* ᶜ ²⁷ *And now* ᵃ*you have begun to bless* ᵃ *the house of your servant to be before you forever, for you, O Yahweh,* ᵇ *have blessed,* ᶜ *and it is blessed forever."*

Notes

1.a,a. 2 Sam 7:1 reads המלך "the king" in both places; Chronicles דויד "David."

1.b. 2 Sam 7:1 + "and Yahweh had given him rest" (הניח־לו) "from all his enemies roundabout. . . ." Cf. n. 10.b-b.

1.c-c. 2 Sam 7:2 וארון האלהים "the ark of God."

1.d. 2 Sam 7:2 בתוך "in the midst."

2.a. 2 Sam 7:3 המלך "the king"; cf. n. 1.a.

2.b. 2 Sam 7:3 יהוה "Yahweh"; contrast n. 1.c-c.

3.a. 2 Sam 7:4 יהוה "Yahweh"; cf. n. 2.b.

4.a. 2 Sam 7:5 האתה "(would) you" (interrogative).

4.b-b. 2 Sam 7:5 הבית "the house" (G 2 Sam 7:5 בית "house"); G בית לשבתי בו "a house to dwell in."

4.c. 2 Sam 7:5 G לשבתי "for me to dwell."

5.a-a. 2 Sam 7:6 העלתי "I brought up" (inf with suff).

5.b. 2 Sam 7:6 בני "descendants."

5.c. 2 Sam 7:6 + ממצרים "from Egypt."

5.d-d. Reading מתהלך "going about," with 2 Sam 7:6.

5.e-e. Insert אל משכן "to the tabernacle"; G 2 Sam 7:6 באהל ובמשכן "in the tent and in the tabernacle."

6.a. 2 Sam 7:7 שבטי "tribes" (but cf. v 10, with שפטי "scribes").

6.b. 2 Sam 7:7 + את־ישראל "Israel" as dir obj.

8.a-a. LXX καὶ ἐποίησα "and I have made" (past). Verb tenses here through v 10 are problematic; cf. Mosis, *Untersuchungen,* 282–87, who maintains the past throughout, as do Hertzberg and others in 2 Sam 7. The insertion of the future here is in keeping with the theology of Chronicles, in which peace and rest have not been fully attained (cf. *Form/Structure/Setting* below); it seems less appropriate in Samuel. It has not to my knowledge been suggested that the present confusion may be due to alterations first introduced into Chronicles and then carried back in part to Samuel. The question of tenses is not dealt with in Cross's otherwise very complete treatment.

8.b. 2 Sam 7:9 + גדול "great."

9.a. The pronominal prefixes and suffixes are sg to agree with the collective עם "people."

9.b-b. Heb. בני־עולה "sons of unrighteousness."

9.c. 2 Sam 7:10 לענותו "to afflict them."

10.a-a. 2 Sam 7:11 ־היום ולמן "from the day."

10.b-b. 2 Sam 7:11 והניחתי לך "and I will give you rest"; cf. n. 1.b.

10.c-c. G = ואגדלך "and I will make you great"; 2 Sam 7:11 והגיד לך יהוה "and Yahweh declares to you."

11.a-a. Lit., "When your days have been filled up."

11.b. G^BA 2 Sam 7:12 ושכבת "and you lie."

11.c-c. G and 2 Sam 7:12 אשר יצא ממעיך "who will come out from your loins."

11.d. 2 Sam 7:12 ממלכתו "his kingdom."

12.a-a. 2 Sam 7:13 לשמי "for my name."

12.b-b. 2 Sam 7:13 את־כסא ממלכתו "the throne of his kingdom."

13.a. 2 Sam 7:14 אשר בהעותו והכחתיו בשבט אנשים ובנגעי בני אדם "whom, when he commits iniquity, I will correct with the rod of men, and the stripes of the sons of men."

13.b-b. 2 Sam 7:15 וחסדי לא־יסור "But my steadfast love will not depart."

13.c-c. 2 Sam 7:15 מעם שאול אשר "from Saul whom."

14.a-a. 2 Sam 7:16 ונאמן ביתך וממלכתך "and your house and your kingdom will be established."

14.b. 2 Sam 7:16 כסאך "your throne."

16.a-a. 2 Sam 7:18 אדני יהוה "my Lord Yahweh."

17.a. 2 Sam 7:19 אדני יהוה "my Lord Yahweh" (cf. n. 16.a-a.).

17.b-b. Heb. obscure. 2 Sam 7:19 וזאת תורה האדם "and this is the law of man." See Rudolph for proposed emendations, none of which is convincing.

17.c-c. 2 Sam 7:19 אדני יהוה "my Lord Yahweh"; cf. v 16.

18.a-a. Chr אליך לכבוד "to give honor to you"; 2 Sam 7:20 לדבר אליך "to speak to you." Read perhaps לְכַבֵּד "to give honor" (cf. G).

18.b. In the sense of בחר "choose"; cf. Rudolph.

19.a. 2 Sam 7:20 אדני יהוה "my Lord Yahweh."

19.b-b. Read perhaps כלבך "your dog"; cf. Lachish Letters, *KAI* vol. 1, #192.

19.c. Omitting the second כל־הגדלות "all this greatness" as dittogr, 2 Sam 7:22; cf. G^BA^N על־כן גדלת "therefore you are great."

20.a. 2 Sam 7:22 יהוה אלהים "Yahweh God."

21.a. 2 Sam 7:23 הלכו "they have gone." In Samuel, the relative clause qualifies the foreign gods; in Chronicles, Yahweh.

21.b. 2 Sam 7:23 לו "to him."

21.c. 2 Sam 7:23 לארצך "for your land"; Chronicles G לגרש "to drive out."

21.d. 2 Sam 7:23 ואלהיו "and its gods."

22.a. 2 Sam 7:24 ותכונן "and you established."

23.a. 2 Sam 7:25 יהוה אלהים "Yahweh God."

23.b. 2 Sam 7:25 הקם "established" (cf. nn. 14.a-a., 24.a.).

24.a-a. 2 Sam 7:26 > ויאמן "and may it be established"; cf. n. 23.a.

24.b-b. > 2 Sam 7:26.

25.a-a. 2 Sam 7:27 יהוה צבאות אלהי ישראל "Yahweh Sebaoth, God of Israel."

25.b-b. Lit., "you have uncovered the ear."

25.c. 2 Sam 7:27 adds את־לבב "his heart."

25.d. 2 Sam 7:27 + את התפלה הזאת "this prayer."

26.a. 2 Sam 7:28 אדני יהוה "my Lord Yahweh."

26.b. 2 Sam 7:28 + ודבריך יהיו אמת "and your words are true."

26.c-c. In the sense of a covenant promise, as noted by Cross, *Canaanite Myth*, 254, #21; cf. Josh 23:14.

27.a-a. 2 Sam 7:29 הואל וברך "be pleased and bless," impv.

27.b. 2 Sam 7:29 אדני יהוה "my Lord Yahweh."

27.c. 2 Sam 7:29 דברת "you have spoken."

27.d. 2 Sam 7:29 adds some words. The future translation of RSV is erroneous; cf. NEB.

Form/Structure/Setting

This most significant chapter may be viewed as follows:

>   vv 1– 2   Introduction: David's plan
>   vv 3–15   Nathan's oracle
>   vv 16–27   David's prayer

This chapter is again narrative by almost universal consent (see the exceptions noted in Williamson, 132–33) considered to be directly dependent upon 2 Sam 7. We shall accordingly concern ourselves primarily with differences between our text and 2 Sam 7, reflecting the interpretation of Chronicles. For the background of 2 Sam 7 and its significance within the Deuteronomistic history, see the Samuel commentaries and most recently F. Cross, *Canaanite Myth,* 219–73, with the voluminous bibliography included there.

As noted by Cross, 2 Sam 7 consists of two major parts, vv 1–14, and vv 16–27. Vv 1–14 is itself composite, consisting of (1) vv 1–7, Nathan's oracle; (2) vv 11b–16, the oracle of the divine decree; and (3) vv 8–11a, the Deuteronomistic linkage between the two, which incorporates some earlier materials. While much Deuteronomistic terminology is embodied in vv 1–14 (see Cross's listings on 252–54), vv 16–27 are completely Deuteronomistic. 2 Sam 7 thus exhibits a unity imposed upon it by the Deuteronomistic historian, and is in that form adapted by the Chronicler.

Numerous divergencies in the two texts are not tendential in nature, and may be passed over more rapidly. Among these are alterations in vocabulary and style, such as the use of the first person pronoun אני instead of אנכי (consistently in Chronicles, Ezra, Nehemiah), the use of various combinations of prepositions, and vocabulary (note that מלכות is used for ממלכת "kingdom" in vv 11 and 14). Included here too should probably be the many variations in the divine name found in both the Hebrew and Greek texts throughout the chapters, so varied here as to suggest the near impossibility of determining the original reading. In some cases Chronicles probably had before him a better text (cf. שפטי "scribes" in v 6); in still others his text may belong to a tradition differing slightly from that found in Samuel (see the *Introduction* and Lemke).

Some divergencies, however, are completely in keeping with the *Tendenz* of the writer, and are best attributed to him:

(1) The concept of *rest* in the Deuteronomistic history (see especially Deut 12:9–11; Josh 21:43–45; 1 Kgs 8:56) permits the generalized statement that God had given (2 Sam 7:1) or would give (2 Sam 7:11) rest (hiphil, נוח; מנוחה) to David. However, since David did not in fact build the temple, Chronicles omits the statement of 2 Sam 7:1 that Yahweh had given rest to David (n. 1.b.), and has in v 10 altered the text of 2 Sam 7:11 from והניחתי ("I will give rest . . .") to והכנעתי ("I will subdue . . .") (see n. 10.b.). In the mind of the Chronicler, David is disqualified as temple builder because of his warfare (22:8; cf. 28:3); Solomon, on the other hand, is a man of peace, as designated both by his name (which means *peace*) and by the divine oracle itself (cf. Braun, *JBL* 95 [1976] 581–90; Williamson, *TynBul* 28 [1979] 138–42). His conduct, in sharp contrast to the presentation in Kings, is viewed in Chronicles as completely blameless (Braun, *JBL* 92 [1973] 503–16). Accord-

ingly we would expect greater emphasis to fall upon Solomon throughout the pericope than in Samuel. It is then, as noted by Williamson, incorrect to point to the removal of *rest* from 2 Sam 7 as due to David's wars recounted in chaps. 18–20, as if these served only to delay the beginning of the temple, which remained David's primary work. David was a "man of war," a "bloody man," and hence unfit to build the temple! What is required is for "one of his sons" (v 11) to come forth, who will both build the temple and through whom David's house will be established forever.

(2) Fittingly, somewhat more emphasis is placed on the choice of David's *seed*, and correspondingly less upon David. Whereas Nathan in 2 Sam 7:5 asks David, "Will you build me a house . . . ?", Chronicles states emphatically, *"You* will not build me this house . . ." (v 4). The same point may be argued from v 11, where I find "who will be one of your sons" at least as explicit as 2 Sam 7:12, "who will come out from your loins" (see n. 11.c-c.). However, due to possibilities of varying translations (see Williamson, *TynBul* 28 [1979] 135; *contra* von Rad, *Geschichtsbild,* 123–24) and textual difficulties (G of Chronicles reads ἐκ τῆς κοιλίας "from your loins"), it is probably best to consider the two phrases as essentially identical. The same point is at any rate made twice incontrovertibly in v 14, where the third-person suffixes ("I will appoint *him* [i.e., Solomon] . . . and *his* throne will be established") replace the second-person suffixes referring to David in 2 Sam 7:16 (see nn. 14.a-a., b.).

(3) In line with the theocratic thought of Chronicles, the same verse indicates more clearly in Chronicles that the kingdom itself is the Lord's, and that David's son will be established over *his* (i.e. Yahweh's) house, and over his kingdom (Williamson, *TynBul* 28 [1979] 136).

(4) Since Chronicles presents Solomon consistently as without fault, the omission indicated in n. 13.a. is, at a minimum, suggestive. While it is true that the omission does not materially affect the meaning of the passage, it is simplest to conclude that the words "whom, when he commits iniquity, I will correct with the rod of men, and the stripes of the sons of men," were omitted in deference to the writer's attitude toward Solomon (*contra* Williamson, *TynBul* 28 [1979] 135).

Other lesser points have been noted whose interpretation is more problematic. The omission of the name Saul (n. 13.c-c.) is striking, but the text even in its present form cannot possibly refer to anyone else, and the style of Chronicles is at least in the eyes of Rudolph preferable. The mention of the Exodus is dropped from v 5 (see n. 5.c.), but its retention in v 21 militates against placing too much emphasis upon that fact.

The certainty of Yahweh's blessing is, if that be possible, made more sure in Chronicles. What was in 2 Sam 7:29 presented as a desire and possibility becomes in v 27 a statement of fact and confession of faith: "you have begun to bless . . . for you, O Yahweh, have blessed, and it is blessed forever."

Explanation

The dynastic oracle here, as in 2 Samuel 7, incorporates two major thoughts. (1) Not David, but one of his descendants, will build Yahweh's house, i.e., the temple. Already in Samuel, but especially in Chronicles, the individual in mind is clearly Solomon. However, his roll here is made more explicit in that the "rest" which was the prerequisite for the construction of the temple is removed from David's reign.

(2) God will build a house for David, i.e., will establish his dynasty, forever. More specifically, it is here that God's kingdom will be established (v 14), and it is here that through David's seed (v 11), one of his sons, the throne would be established forever (v 14), i.e., through Solomon. No possibility is entertained that this covenant will be abrogated, or will need to be abrogated (v 13); no less than five times the writer repeats that it will be forever.

David's prayer in response does not differ significantly from Samuel except for its greater emphasis upon the fact that in pronouncing his promise, Yahweh has already begun to impart his blessing (v 27). After what may seem to be an intermission (chaps. 18–20), plans for the direct preparation of the building of the temple will be continued.

The significance of this message for biblical thought, Judaism, and Christianity can hardly be overestimated. From this time forward it will be impossible for the Messiah to be considered anything less than David's descendant, and when messianic thoughts are expressed, it will be most commonly in terms related to David and his family (cf. Isa 11:1–5; Jer 17:24–27; Ezek 34:20–24; Amos 9:11–12; Micah 5:2–4, etc.). It is in that light that the New Testament pictures Jesus as the son of David (cf. Matt 1:1) and relates his birth in Bethlehem (Matt 1:6). It is in that faith too that the Church celebrates the rule of Jesus the Christ, whose kingdom will have no end.

David's Wars (Chaps. 18-20)

Bibliography

Botterweck, G. J. "Zur Eigenart der chronistischen Davidsgeschichte." *TQ* 136 (1956) 423–27. **Goslinga, C. J.** "De Parallelle Teksten in de Boeken Samuel en Kronieken." *GTT* 61 (1961) 108–16. **Kapelrud, A. S.** "König David and die Söhne des Saul." *ZAW* 66 (1954) 198–205.

1 Chr 18–20 represent a distillation of a much larger body of material in 2 Sam 8–21. There are no larger blocks of material unique to Chronicles in this unit. 1 Chr 18 is parallel to 2 Sam 8 and 1 Chr 19 to 2 Sam 10; but 1 Chr 20 reflects briefer excerpts from 2 Sam 11, 12, 13, and 21. The following table of parallels better expresses the relationship between the two books.

1 Chronicles	2 Samuel
1 Chr 18	2 Sam 8
———	2 Sam 9
1 Chr 19	2 Sam 10
1 Chr 20:1a	2 Sam 11:1
———	2 Sam 11:2–27
———	2 Sam 12:1–25
1 Chr 20:1b	cf. 2 Sam 12:26
———	cf. 2 Sam 12:27–29
1 Chr 20:2–3	cf. 2 Sam 12:30–31
———	2 Sam 13:1–21:14
———	2 Sam 21:15–17
1 Chr 20:4–8	2 Sam 21:18–22

While it is interesting to speculate upon the specific reasons for the inclusion of this material, interest is heightened by first noting portions of 2 Samuel not included by Chronicles. This includes first of all 2 Sam 9, which would seem to reflect positively upon David in recounting his kindness to Jonathan's lame son Mephibosheth. However, Chronicles, unlike its source, has indicated that Saul and his sons and *all his house* died together at Gilboa (1 Chr 10:6); accordingly his dealings with Mephibosheth have been omitted.

The vast majority of 2 Sam 11–12 has also been omitted. The framework of this narrative is provided by the Ammonite war, which is retained by Chronicles, but it is more significantly the story of David's adultery with Bathsheba and his murder of her husband Uriah in the battle with the Ammonites that is the focus of attention here, together with the accompanying condemnation by Nathan. Moreover, chaps. 13–21 describe in vivid detail the "evil from his own house" (cf. 2 Sam 12:11) visited upon David as a result of his transgression. It is thus clear that Chronicles has in effect omitted David's major transgressions (but cf. chap. 21 below), together with the punishment resulting from them.

What is retained of 2 Sam 8–21 are accounts of wars conducted victoriously by or on behalf of David against Philistia, Moab, Aram, and Ammon (cf. 1 Chr 18:11) and, again, Philistia. If we ask the reason for the inclusion of this material, various reasons may be given. (1) That these chapters do *not* reflect punishment visited upon David seems apparent both from the fact that his major transgressions are omitted, as well as by the positive evaluations of David included throughout the narrative; cf. 18:6, 13, 14; 19:13; 20:3, 4, 8. (2) It has also been stated that the wars are included because it was through the wars that funds were provided for the construction of the temple. While this is true to a small degree (cf. 18:8, 11 with 22:3, 14; 29:3), it appears to be a secondary emphasis. (3) It is true to a greater degree that the wars described in these chapters explain why David himself did not build the temple, i.e., they either mark him as a warrior (cf. 22:8; 28:3), or, as stated more programmatically by Mosis (98), they picture David's age as an age of warfare as contrasted with the age of rest in which Solomon will build the temple. (4) It needs also to be stated that, in part, the account of David's wars was doubtless included here simply because they occupied the same position following the dynastic oracle in Samuel. The author does not carry out every implication of his position in every instance. Since little in these chapters dealing with David's wars was alien to his view of David, he has retained them, using them at the same time to illustrate God's approval of David and the warfare which was characteristic of him, as well as to prepare for the further introduction of the temple itself.

David's Wars (a)   (18:1–17)

Bibliography

(See the *Introduction* to chaps. 18–20 above.)

Translation

18:1*After this David smote the Philistines and subdued them, and took* ªGath *and its villages* ª *from the hand of the Philistines.* 2*He also smote Moab,* ª *and they became David's slaves* ᵇ *and brought tribute.* ᵇ 3*David also smote Hadad-ezer,* ᵃᵇ *the king of Zobah* ᶜ*at Hamath,* ᶜ *when he came to* ᵈ*establish his rule* ᵈ *at the Euphrates River.* ᵉ 4*David took from him a thousand chariots,* ª ᵇ*seven thousand* ᵇ *horsemen, and twenty thousand foot soldiers. He hamstrung all the chariot horses, leaving only a hundred chariots operational.* 5*When Aram of Damascus* ª *came to help Hadad-ezer, king of Zobah, David also smote twenty-two thousand men of Aram.* 6*Then David put garrisons* ª *in Aram of Damascus, and Aram became David's slaves and brought tribute. Yahweh gave victory to David wherever he went.* 7*David took the shields* ª *of gold which the servants of Hadad-ezer had and brought them to Jerusalem.*

⁸*David took* ᵃ*very much* ᵃ *bronze from Tibhath and Cun,* ᵇᶜ *cities of Hadad-ezer.* ᵈ*With it Solomon made the bronze sea and the pillars and all the brass utensils.* ᵈ

⁹*Tou,* ᵃ *king of Hamath, heard that David had smote all the army of Hadad-ezer,* ᵇ*king of Zobah,* ᵇ ¹⁰*so he sent his son Hadoram* ᵃ *to King David* ᵇ*to greet him* ᵇ *and to congratulate him because he had fought against Hadad-ezer and won. Tou himself was a warrior* ᶜ*(who had been fighting with)* ᶜ *Hadad-ezer.* ᵈ*As for all* ᵈ *the items of gold, silver, and bronze,* ¹¹*David sanctified them to Yahweh, together with the silver and gold he had taken* ᵃ *from all the nations—from Edom,* ᵇ *Moab, the Ammonites, the Philistines, and Amalek.* ᶜ

¹²ᵃ*Abishai, the son of Zeruiah,* ᵃ *smote Edom in the Valley of Salt, eighteen thousand.* ¹³*He put garrisons in Edom,* ᵃ *and all Edom became slaves to David. Thus Yahweh gave David the victory wherever he went.*

¹⁴*So David ruled as king over all Israel and executed justice and righteousness for all his people.* ¹⁵*Joab, Zeruiah's son, was over the army, and Jehoshaphat, the son of Ahilud, was recorder.* ¹⁶*Zadok, the son of Ahitub, and Ahimelech,* ᵃ *the son of Abiathar, were priests, and Shavsha* ᵇ *was scribe.* ¹⁷*Benaiah, the son of Jehoiada, was over* ᵃ *the Cherethites and the Pelethites, and* ᵇ*David's sons were the* ᶜ*chief deputies* ᶜ *of the king.* ᵇ

Notes

1.a-a. 2 Sam 8:1 אֶת־מֶתֶג הָאַמָּה "Methegh-ammah," perhaps a proper name (cf. W. F. Stinespring, "Methegh-ammah," *IDB* 3:368), but the meaning is uncertain. It is possible that the phrase, which has been translated "bridle/authority of the mother city," refers to the concept of Philistine domination (BDB, Rudolph). Concerning Gath, see Williamson, 138.

2.a. 2 Sam 8:2 adds, "and measured them with a line, making them lie down on the ground; two lines he measured to be put to death, and one full line to be spared."

2.b-b. Heb. נֹשְׂאֵי מִנְחָה, lit., "ones bringing tribute."

3.a. In 2 Sam 8:3 *ca.* 55 MSS read הֲדַרְעֶזֶר "Hedarezer," reflecting less exactly the name of the god Hadad.

3.b. 2 Sam 8:3 + בֶּן רְחֹב "the son of Rehob."

3.c-c. > 2 Sam 8:3ᴷ Syr α′.

3.d-d. 2 Sam 8:3 לְהָשִׁיב יָדוֹ "to restore his power."

3.e. Lacking in the Q variant of 2 Sam 8:3.

4.a. > 2 Sam 8:4.

4.b-b. 2 Sam 8:4 וְשֶׁבַע מֵאוֹת "and seven hundred."

5.a. 2 Sam 8:5 דַמֶּשֶׂק "Damascus." MT at 1 Chr 18:5 reflects Syr orthography.

6.a. Supplying נְצִיבִים "garrisons" with 2 Sam 8:6; cf. LXX φρουδάν "garrison."

7.a. The meaning is uncertain. NEB "quivers."

8.a-a. 2 Sam 8:8 הַרְבֵּה מְאֹד "very much."

8.b. 2 Sam 8:8 מִבֶּטַח "from Betah"; cf. Syr. But Tibhath and Cun are known from Egyptian texts of the Empire (Bright, *History,* 199, n. 47).

8.c. G καὶ ἐκ τῶν ἐκλεκτῶν "and from the chosen ones" = וּמִמִּבְחַר, questionable (*BHS*); 2 Sam 8:8 וּמִבֵּרֹתַי "and from Berothai."

8.d-d. > 2 Sam 8:8(!); but cf. 2 Samᴳ.

9.a. 2 Sam 8:9 תֹּעִי "Toi."

9.b-b. > 2 Sam 8:9.

10.a. Chronicles' הֲדוֹרָם "Hadoram" is preferable to 2 Sam 8:10 יוֹרָם "Joram"; cf. Gˢᵃᵐ Ἰεδδουραν "Jedduran." An Aramean name with a Yahweh component would be unexpected.

10.b-b. Or "to seek terms of peace."

10.c-c. The Heb. appears to be conflate.

10.d-d. 2 Sam 8:10 וּבְיָדוֹ הָיוּ "and in his hand were."

11.a. 2 Sam 8:11 הִקְדִּישׁ "dedicated."

11.b. 2 Sam 8:12 מארם "from Aram."

11.c. 2 Sam 8:12–13 + "and from the plunder of Hadadezer, the son of Rehob, king of Zobah. So David made himself a name."

12.a-a. 2 Sam 8:13 reads בשבו מהכות את־ארם "when he (David!) returned from smiting Aram."

13.a. 2 Sam 8:14 + בכל־אדום שם נצבים "in all Edom he placed garrisons."

16.a. Read with G Syr Vg α′ 2 Sam 8:17 ואחימלך "Ahimelech." NEB further corrects to "Zadok and Abiathar, son of Ahimelech, son of Ahitub," but cf. 1 Chr 5:34, 38.

16.b. 2 Sam 8:17 שריה "Seraiah"; cf. 1 Kgs 4:3.

17.a. 2 Sam 8:18 MT lacks "was over."

17.b-b. Rather than "the eldest sons of David were." Cf. NEB.

17.c-c. 2 Sam 8:18 adds כהנים היו "were priests"; Wenham ("Were David's Sons Priests?," ZAW 87 [1975] 79–82) believes "Samuel" may be corrupt.

Form/Structure/Setting

1 Chr 18 is, as noted above (see the introductory discussion to chaps. 18–20, pp. 201–2) identical in its setting and largely in content with 2 Sam 8, to the commentaries of which the reader is referred for general matters of geography and history. The chapter is to be outlined as follows.

1 Chr 18	2 Sam 8	
vv 1–8	vv 1–8	David's wars with the Philistines, Moab, and Syria.
vv 9–11	vv 9–12	Tribute brought to David
vv 12–13	vv 13–14	Victories in Edom
vv 14–17	vv 15–16	Davidic officials

The textual differences are pointed out in the notes. Some probably reflect a text better preserved in either Samuel or Chronicles; some may once again point to a different text-type utilized by Chronicles (see the Introduction, "Text"); others may result from preferences in style. In some cases Chronicles may have wished to update a geographical reference or at least to clarify an obscure phrase (cf. n. 1.a.).

Other divergencies, however, are probably (or at least possibly) dependent upon the unique views of the writer. Among these, the following five suggestions should be included. (1) The omission of a part of 2 Sam 8:2 depicting David's harsh treatment of defeated Moabites (v 2) may well be due to the belief that, although David was a warrior and was for that reason disqualified as a temple builder, such harshness reflected poorly upon him. (2) The reading "a thousand chariots and seven thousand horses/horsemen" (v 4) is suspect in view of Chronicles' tendency to elevate figures for the aggrandizement of his heroes. However, the retention of the same number of foot soldiers as in Sam (20,000) and the textual evidence of G makes that judgment problematic. The writer may have had a different text before him. (3) The note added by Chronicles in v 8 to the effect that Solomon used the plunder gathered by David, and especially the bronze, for the construction of the temple and its implements is certainly in keeping with the writer's equating of David and Solomon. Although once again the G of Samuel reflects a text similar to Chronicles, it seems most likely that this emphasis is original to Chronicles and its presence in the G variant of Samuel is due to secondary influence of Chronicles upon Samuel (cf. Williamson, *VT* 26 [1976] 357–58, n. 17, *contra* Lemke, *HTR* 58 [1965] 349–63). (4) It is at least interesting, in view of the common assessment of Chronicles' idealization of David, to note the omission of 2 Sam 8:13a, "David made a name for himself," as well as Chronicles' reading of v 12 (2 Sam 8:13) which effectively removes at least some of the victories from David and transfers them to Abishai. (5) Chronicles probably found the statement that "David's sons were priests" offensive, although it has been argued that Samuel is corrupt here (cf. n. 17.c-c. and note the double mention of priests in the pericope).

Explanation

While it is true that Chronicles will use David's wars to disqualify him from building the temple, the retention of the account of David's victories over the Philistines, Moab, Aram, Ammon, and Edom (cf. v 11), together with the positive view of David stated and implied in v 13 ("Yahweh gave David victory wherever he went") and v 14 ("David ruled as king over all Israel and executed justice and righteousness for all his people"), indicates that the primary thrust of this chapter is to portray the victory and success which David continued to enjoy by Yahweh's blessing. At the same time, emphasis is heightened that the plunder from his wars will benefit the temple to be built by Solomon.

We thus meet at the same time the significant themes of retribution (God's blessings upon the righteous David) and the temple, which even within this framework of Davidic victories remains in focus. The tribute brought by enemy nations may best be understood in this context, and need not suggest to us the subservience of other nations to Israel or to Christian nations.

David's Wars (b) (19:1–19)

Translation

¹ *After this Nahash,* ª *the king of the Ammonites, died, and his son* ᵇ *became king in his place.* ² *Then David said, "I will deal loyally with Hanum, the son of Nahash, because* ª *his father dealt loyally with me." So David sent messengers to console him concerning his father. But when David's servants came to the land of the Ammonites,* ᵇ *to Hanum to console him,* ᵇ ³ *the princes of Ammon said to Hanum, "Do you think David is honoring your father, because he has sent to console you? Have not his servants come to you to explore,* ª ᵇ*destroy, and to spy out* ᵇ *the land?"* ⁴ *So Hanum took David's servants and shaved them* ª *and cut their garments in half at the buttocks* ᵇ *and sent them away.* ⁵ *Some* ª *came and told David* ᵇ*concerning the men,* ᵇ *and he sent to meet them, because the men were very much ashamed, and the king said, "Stay at Jericho until your beards grow; then you can return."* ⁶ *When the Ammonites*

knew they had offended ᵃ *David, Hanum* ᵇ *and the Ammonites sent* ᶜ*a thousand talents of silver* ᶜ *to hire* ᵈ ᵉ*from Aram-naharaim,* ᵉ ᶠ*from Aram-maacah, and from Zobah* ᶠ ᵍ*chariots and horsemen.* ᵍ ⁷ᵃ *They hired for themselves thirty-two thousand chariots* ᵃ *and the king of Maacah* ᵇ*and his people,* ᵇᶜ ᵈ*and they came in and fought before Medeba, and the Ammonites also were gathered from their cities and came in to the battle.* ᵈ

⁸ *When David heard of it, he sent Joab and all the army of the mighty men,* ⁹*and the Ammonites gathered from their cities and set the battle line* ᵃ*at the gate of the city,* ᵃ ᵇ*while the kings who had come in* ᵇ *were opposite them in the field.* ¹⁰ *Joab saw that the battle was set against him to the front and to the rear, and he selected some of Israel's finest and deployed them to meet Aram.* ¹¹ *He put the rest of the people in the hand of his brother Abishai, and they took their positions to meet the Ammonites.* ¹² *He (Joab) said, "If Aram is stronger than I, you will help me; but if the Ammonites are stronger than you,* ᵃ*I will help you.* ᵃ ¹³ *Be strong, and let us conduct ourselves valiantly* ᵃ *for our people and for the cities of our God, and Yahweh will do that which is good in his eyes."*

¹⁴ *Joab and the people who were with him drew near Aram to the battle, and they (Aram) fled before him.* ¹⁵ *When the Ammonites saw that Aram had fled,* ᵃ*they also* ᵃ *fled before Abashai his brother, and they came in to the city,* ᵇ*and Joab came in* ᵇ *to Jerusalem.* ¹⁶ *When Aram saw they had been defeated before Israel,* ᵃ ᵇ*they sent messengers so that the Arameans who were beyond the river were dispatched,* ᵇᶜ *with Shophach, prince of Hadad-ezer's army, at their head.* ¹⁷ *When David was told, he gathered all Israel and crossed the Jordan and came in* ᵃ*to them.* ᵃ *David* ᵇ *set the battle to meet Aram,* ᶜ *and they fought with him.* ¹⁸ *Aram fled before Israel, and David killed* ᵃ*seven thousand* ᵃ *charioteers and forty thousand* ᵇ*foot soldiers.* ᵇ *He also killed Shophach, prince of the army.* ¹⁹ *When* ᵃ *the servants of Hadad-ezer saw they had been defeated before Israel, they made peace* ᵇ*with David* ᵇ *and became his servants, and Aram* ᶜ*was not willing* ᶜ *to help the Ammonites any longer.*

Notes

1.a. > 2 Sam 10:1.
1.b. 2 Sam 10:1 + חנון "Hanun" (cf. v 2).
2.a. 2 Sam 10:2 כאשר "as."
2.b-b. > 2 Sam 10:2. The appearance is that of a conflation.
3.a. 2 Sam 10:3 + את־העיר "the city."
3.b-b. 2 Sam 10:3 in inverse order.
4.a. 2 Sam 10:4 + ויגלח את־חצי זקנם "and he cut off half of their beard."
4.b. 2 Sam 10:4 שתותיהם "buttocks."
5.a. The subj is impersonal.
5.b-b. > 2 Sam 10:5.
6.a. 2 Sam 10:6 נבאשו "they became odious."
6.b. > 2 Sam 10:6.
6.c-c. > 2 Sam 10:6.
6.d. 2 Sam 10:6 וישכרו "and they hired."
6.e-e. 2 Sam 10:6 את־ארם בית רחוב "Syrians of Beth-rehob."
6.f-f. 2 Sam 10:6 ואת־ארם צובה "and Syrians of Zobah."
6.g-g. 2 Sam 10:6 עשרים אלף רגלי "twenty thousand foot soldiers."
7.a-a. > 2 Sam 10:6.
7.b-b. > 2 Sam 10:6.
7.c. + 2 Sam 10:6 אלף איש ואיש טוב שנים עשר אלף איש "a thousand men, and the men of Tob, twelve thousand men."

7.d-d. > 2 Sam 10:6. Medeba is in the land of Moab and would appear to be too far south for this engagement. Rothstein and Hänel accordingly reads מי רבה as "waters of Rabbah" (351–52).

9.a-a. 2 Sam 10:8 פתח השער "entrance of the gate."

9.b-b. 2 Sam 10:8 וארם צובה ורחוב ואיש טוב ומעכה "and the Syrians of Zobah and of Rehob, and the men of Tob and Maacah" (cf. v 6).

12.a-a. 2 Sam 10:11 והלכתי להושיע לך "then I will come to help you."

13.a. 2 Sam 10:12 ונתחזקה "and let us conduct ourselves valiantly."

15.a-a. 2 Sam 10:14 > גם הם "they also."

15.b-b. 2 Sam 10:14 וישב יואב מעל בני עמון ויבא "then Joab returned from fighting against the Ammonites and came."

16.a. 2 Sam 10:15 + ויאספו יחד "and they gathered together."

16.b-b. 2 Sam 10:16 וישלח הדרעזר ויצא "and Hadar-ezer sent and brought."

16.c. 2 Sam 10:16 + ויבאו חילם "and they came to Helam."

17.a. 2 Sam 10:17 חלאמה (K); חֶלָמָה (Q), "to Helam."

17.b. 2 Sam 10:17 ארם "Aram."

17.c. 2 Sam 10:17 דוד "David."

18.a-a. 2 Sam 10:18 שבע מאות "seven hundred."

18.b-b. 2 Sam 10:18 פרשים "horses" or "horsemen."

19.a. 2 Sam 10:19 + כל המלכים "all the kings."

19.b-b. 2 Sam 10:19 את ישראל "with Israel."

19.c-c. 2 Sam 10:19 ויראו "they feared."

Form/Structure/Setting

(For the general setting and the omission of 2 Sam 9, see the introductory discussion to 1 Chr 18–20 above.)

Chap. 19 may be outlined as follows:

1 Chr 19	2 Sam 10	
vv 1–7	vv 1–6	Ammonites offend David
vv 8–13	vv 7–12	Joab sets the battle
vv 14–19	vv 13–19	Joab/David victorious

For this portion of its account of David's wars with the Ammonites, Chronicles is dependent upon 2 Sam 10, with which it is often in verbatim agreement. Apart from the customary differences due to minor textual errors and style (see the *Notes*) and the desire to update the text (cf. Aram-naharaim in v 6 and n. 6.b.) the writer has shown relatively little interest in the narrative. Indeed, some alterations adopted for the sake of brevity appear to be rather clumsily done, and have the effect of confusing the text (cf. nn. 15.b-b. and 16.b-b.). Otherwise, the only *Tendenz* apparent is that of somewhat magnifying David's stature: (1) By placing him in a somewhat more aggressive light (v 17). (2) By adding to the value and number of the forces opposed to him and the numbers which fell to him. Hence Chronicles adds a thousand talents of silver used by the Ammonites to hire their Aramean allies (v 6) and with them they secure, not just thirty-three thousand footsoldiers (רגלי as in Samuel) but thirty-two thousand chariots (רכב), apparently plus other unnumbered people (v 7). Chronicles also speaks of David's destruction of "seven thousand charioteers and forty thousand footsoldiers" (v 18), while Samuel lists seven *hundred* charioteers and forty thousand horsemen (v 18). (3) By indicating that the Arameans made peace, not with Israel (2 Sam 10:19), but with David himself (v 19).

Apart from this tendency toward hyperbole, other indications of the writer's *Tendenz* are noticeably absent.

Explanation

Although not made explicit here, Chronicles recounts David's wars primarily to indicate God's blessing upon him. The only significant alterations to the text point in that same direction. Thus the theme of retribution (see *Introduction*) continues. God blesses David for his faithfulness, and that blessing is seen in his military victories.

Once again, we must realize that we are here dealing with a stereotype, with theology expressed in narrative form, and that we cannot conclude from this that every battle won is due to the victor's faithfulness, nor that every battle lost is due to the loser's unfaithfulness. We must be content with the general principle that God blesses his people and punishes those who disobey him. To go farther agrees neither with the principle of the analogy of faith nor with human experience.

David's Wars (c)   (20:1-8)

Translation

^{1a} *At the turn ^b of the year, at the time kings go out (to battle),^a ^cJoab led out the army ^c and laid waste the land of the Ammonites. He came and laid siege to Rabbah, while David stayed in Jerusalem. ^d ^eJoab smote Rabbah and destroyed it. ^{ef}*

²*David took the crown of Milcom ^a from his head and found ^b its weight a talent of gold, and ^cin it ^c was a precious jewel. It was on David's head, and he also brought out very much booty from the city.* ³*He brought out the people who were in it, and ^aput them to work ^a with saws and hoes of iron and axes of iron.^{bc} So David did to all the cities of the Ammonites. Then David and all the people returned to Jerusalem.*

⁴*Afterward a war arose ^a at Gezer ^b with the Philistines. Then Sibbecai the Hushathite smote Sippai ^c (and took it) from the children ^d of the Rephaim, ^e and they were subdued.^f* ⁵*Again there was war ^a with the Philistines, and Elhanan ^bthe son of Jair ^b smote Lahmi,^c ^dthe brother of^d Goliath the Gittite, the staff of whose spear was like a weaver's beam.* ⁶*There was still another war at Gath, and there was a huge ^a man,^a with ^bsix fingers on each hand and six toes on each foot ^b—twenty-four in all—and he too was born ^c to the Rephaim.^d* ⁷*He taunted Israel, and Jonathan, the son of Shimea,^a the brother of David, killed him.* ⁸*These ^a were born ^b to the Rephaim at Gath, but they fell at the hand of David and by the hand of his servants.*

Notes

l.a-a. I.e., in the spring; cf. Exod 12:2. Israel also knew of an autumnal new year.

l.b. 2 Sam 11:1 > לְעֵת "at time of."

l.c-c. 2 Sam 11:1 + וישלח דוד את־יואב ואת־עבדיו עמו ואת־כל־ישראל "and David sent Joab (!) and his servants with him and all Israel."

l.d. Cf. 2 Sam 11:2–27; 12:1–25, lacking in Chronicles.

l.e-e. 2 Sam 12:26 וילחם יואב ברבת בני עמון וילכד את עיר המלוכה "and Joab fought against Rabbah of the Ammonites and took the royal city."

l.f. Cf. 2 Sam 12:27–29, lacking in Chronicles.

2.a. MT מַלְכָּם "their king," perhaps correctly. Cf., however, 1 Kgs 11:7 and the double reading of G, Μολχὸμ (τοῦ) βασιλέως αὐτῶν "of Molkom their king" in both Samuel and Chronicles.

2.b. > 2 Sam 12:30.

2.c-c. > 2 Sam 12:30.

3.a-a. Reading without enthusiasm וישם "and he put," with 2 Sam 12:31, RSV, NEB. Chronicles וישר may perhaps be derived from שור "to saw" (cf. BDB); שרר "to rule"; or even יסר "to discipline." וישם is doubtless the easier reading, but 2 Sam 12:31 והעביר אותם במלכן "he caused them to pass through the brick-yard/kiln (?)" suggests something more harsh than forced labor. Moreover, in view of his treatment of 2 Sam 8:2 in 18:2, we would not expect Chronicles to have the harsher reading.

3.b. Reading מגזרת הברזל "axes of iron," with 2 Sam 12:31 (or omit ובמגרות).

3.c. 2 Sam 12:31 + (Q במלבן) והעביר אתם במלכן "he caused them to pass through the brick-kiln."

4.a. 2 Sam 21:18 ותהי־עוד "there was again."

4.b. 2 Sam 21:18 בְּגוֹב "in Gob"; G^Sam ἐν Γεθ "in Geth" (cf. v 6). Gob is otherwise unknown (Myers, 141). Chronicles may be clarifying an obscure location. (See n. 5.b-b.) Or might the usage be at least partially programmatic? Cf. 1 Chr 14:16, " . . . to Gezer."

4.c. 2 Sam 21:18 את־סף "Saph."

4.d. 2 Sam 21:18 אשר בילדי "who was a descendant of."

4.e. 2 Sam 21:18 הרפה "the Rephaim," as also only in 21:16, 20, 22, and here. The variation in Chronicles may be merely orthographic, or it may be an attempt by the author to identify these individuals more directly with the רפאים "giants" of the OT (cf. Gen 15:20; Deut 2:11, and some MSS of Chronicles; see also n. 6.d.).

4.f. > 2 Sam 21:18. G καὶ ἐταπείνωσεν "and he humbled (him)"; Rudolph (*BHS*) proposes מן־כנען "from Canaan," a gl. See below.

5.a. 2 Sam 21:19 + בגוב "in Gob"; see n. 4.b.

5.b-b. 2 Sam 21:19 בן־יערי (Q יעיר) ארגים "son of Jaareoregim," probably corrupt; cf. 1 Sam 17:7.

5.c. 2 Sam 21:19 בית הלחמי "the Bethlehemite."

5.d-d. 2 Sam 21:19 אֶת, making Goliath the victim of the slaying.

6.a-a. 2 Sam 21:20 Q מדין, K מדין "of great stature" (RSV).

6.b-b. Cf. 2 Sam 21:20 for the fuller form. The use of שש ושש "six and six" is distributive; cf. GKC, § 134q.

6.c. 2 Sam 21:20 יֻלַּד "was born," a qal passive (G. Beer, *Hebräische Grammatik* [ed. R. Meyer; Berlin: de Gruyter, 1952–55] 28, #68.3c). See also n. 8.b.

6.d. 2 Sam 21:20 להרפה "to the Rephaim"; see n. 4.e.

7.a. 2 Sam 21:21 K שמעי, Q שמעה "Shimei."

8.a. 2 Sam 21:22 את ארבעת אלה "these four"; see below.

8.b. 2 Sam 21:22 יֻלְּדוּ "were born"; see n. 7.c.

Form/Structure/Setting

For the broader context see above in the introductory discussion to chaps. 18–20. The unit outline reveals how much more selectively the Chronicler has dealt with his material here in interpreting this portion of Israel's history.

1 Chronicles	2 Samuel	
20:1a	11:1	Introduction
20:1b	12:26	Joab's Ammonite victory
20:2-3	12:30-31	Disposition of the booty
20:4-8	21:18-22	Other wars of David

It is clear that Chronicles in this chapter has dealt much more selectively with the material. It includes only the beginning and ending of the Ammonite war (20:1-3; cf. 2 Sam 11:1; 12:26, 30-31), omitting David's affair with Bathsheba, his murder of Uriah, and his condemnation by the prophet Nathan. By-passing also a significant portion of the so-called "Court History of David" in 2 Sam 13-21, it concludes its account of David's wars by proceeding to 2 Sam 21:18-22, which deals with the defeat of the Philistines and three giants, descendants of the Rephaim (vv 18-22).

The omission of David's transgressions with Bath-sheba and Uriah are the strongest evidence of Chronicles' desire to present David, if not as blameless, at least as more upright than he was. The details of 2 Sam 13-20 may well have seemed inappropriate to Chronicles' broader sweep of history, but those details also included the "evil out of your own house" that was to come upon David as a result of his transgressions. At the same time, they would stand in opposition to the basic premise of Chronicles, i.e., that David in his rise to and exercise of kingship was supported and accepted without exception by *all Israel,* including the king's own sons (cf. 11:1-3; 12:39-41 [38-40], and especially 29:23-24). Thus just as 2 Sam 9 conflicted with Chronicles' view of the demise of *all* of Saul's house in his final battle with the Philistines and was accordingly omitted; also 2 Sam 13:1-21:14 has been omitted. Perhaps the first part of the report of the Philistine war (2 Sam 21:15-17) was simply uninteresting to the writer, or perhaps its more restrained view of David's prowess was uninviting (cf. v 15, "David grew weary . . . ," his deliverance through Abishai, and the admonitions of his men that David should no longer engage directly in warfare, v 17).

At any rate, the omission of the death of Ishbibenob (2 Sam 21:16-17) necessitated an alteration in 2 Sam 21:22. (Botterweck, *TQ* 136 [1956] 427, suggests that the incident may have appeared to cast doubt upon God's promise to David and his descendants.)

Lesser differences have been included in the notes. Contrary to his usual custom, Chronicles seems to have minimized David's initiative in the Ammonite encounter (n. 1.c-c.). In addition, his rather mechanical method of extracting from the text of 2 Samuel has resulted in a sudden and unexpected appearance of David upon the scene (v 2). Uncertainties of text and interpretation prevent our being able to say with any certainty whether the variations in v 3 can be laid to the author's *Tendenz* or not.

In vv 4 and 5, Chronicles has probably first omitted (n. 4.b.) the otherwise unknown Gob, and upon its second appearance replaced it with the better known Gezer (n. 5.a.). The addition of ויכנעו "and they were subdued" (n. 4.f.), revives the note of the victories promised David by Yahweh (see on 1 Chr 17:10), though, like the former passage, refusing to attribute to David that "rest" required for the construction of the temple. (Rudolph's proposed emendation מִ[כְּ]נַעַן, "from Canaan" gives inadequate weight to this point.) Through the alteration in v 5, Chronicles has so arranged the text (perhaps building upon difficulties already inherent in the text; cf. Williamson) that Elhanan smote *Lahmi*, the *brother* of Goliath, rather than Goliath himself, as in 2 Sam 21:19, where this statement was allowed to stand despite the tension created with the account of David's battle with Goliath in 1 Sam 17. Chronicles reading of הרפא(ים) for הרפה (nn. 4.e., 6.d.) may represent only orthographic variation, or could be an attempt to identify David's enemies more closely with the better known Rephaim of the OT (cf. Gen 15:20; Deut 2:11). The uncommon qal passives in 2 Sam 21:6, 8 have been replaced with more conventional niphals (see nn. 6.c. and 8.b.). Finally, the omission of the numeral "four" from the conclusion of his account was necessitated by the fact that Chronicles has omitted the account of the first of the four giants (2 Sam 21:15–17) out of possible deference to David (n. 8.a.).

Explanation

Bypassing David's personal faults and family history, Chronicles concludes its account of David's wars with excerpts from Samuel noting his victories over the Ammonites and Philistines. The concluding sentences of vv 3 and 8, already present in his *Vorlage*, together with the addition of כבע, "to subdue," in v 4, point to these victories as a fulfillment of God's blessing upon David's work and provide a fitting climax to David's work prior to the more direct consideration of the temple in chap. 21.

It would be, as we have said, inappropriate to use these accounts of David's wars as a commentary upon the viability of warfare today. The points are again general and programmatic: The Lord is faithful to his word, and David's reign is blessed with victory as a result of his (David's) faithfulness. That the Chronicler himself saw some difficulty in the specifics of this formula can be seen from the fact that he passes by in silence the account of David's infidelity with Bathsheba. Nothing is permitted to interrupt God's design to have for himself a house in Jerusalem where he may dwell among his people. Thus are God's plans always brought to fruition, despite the frailties of those through whom he does his work.

David's Census   (21:1–22:1)

Bibliography

Botterweck, G. J. "Zur Eigenart der chronistischen Davidsgeschichte." *TQ* 136 (1956) 402–35. **Brunet, A. M.** "Le Chroniste et ses sources." *RB* 60 (1953) 481–508. **Cross, F. M. Jr.** "The History of the Biblical Text in the Light of the Discoveries of the Judean Desert." *HTR* 57 (1964) 281–99. ———. *The Ancient Library of Qumran.* Rev. ed. Garden City, NY: Anchor Books, 1961. **Dillard, R. B.** "David's Census: Perspectives on 2 Samuel 24 and 1 Chronicles 21." *Through Christ's Word.* Ed. R. Godfrey and J. Boyd. Phillipsburg, NJ: Presbyterian and Reformed, 1985. **Klein, R. W.** *Textual Criticism of the Old Testament.* Philadelphia: Fortress Press, 1974.

Translation

[1a] *Satan stood up against Israel* [a] *and incited David* [b] *to take a census of Israel.* [c] [2] *Then David* [a] *said to Joab* [b] *and the princes of the people,* [b] *"Go,* [c] [d] *take a count* [d] *of Israel* [e] [f] *from Beer-sheba to Dan* [f] [g] *and bring it to me* [g] *that I may know their number."* [3] *Joab said, "May Yahweh add* [a] *to his people* [a] *a hundred times* [b] *as many* [b] *—are not all of them, my lord the king, servants of my lord? Why does my lord desire this?* [c] *Why will he become an object of guilt to Israel?"* [c] [4] *But the king's word was insistent against Joab,* [a] *and he went out* [b] *and* [c] *passed through* [c] *all Israel* [d] *and came in* [e] *to Jerusalem.* [5] *And Joab gave the report of the census of the people to David.* [a] *All* [b] *Israel numbered* [c] *one million, one hundred thousand* [c] *men able to bear arms* [d] *[and Judah* [e] *four hundred and seventy* [f] *thousand* [e] *men able to bear arms].* [d] [6a] *As for Levi and Benjamin, no census was taken among them, because the king's word was abhorrent* [b] *to Joab.* [a] [7a] *This thing was wrong in God's eyes,* [a] [b] *and he smote Israel.* [b]

[8] *Then David said to God,* [a] *"I have sinned greatly, because I have done* [b] *this thing.* [b] *Now* [c] *remove, I pray, the guilt of your servant, for I have acted very foolishly."* [9ab] *So Yahweh spoke to Gad, David's seer,* [b] *saying,* [10] *"Go* [a] *and say to David: 'Three things I* [b] *offer* [c] *you. Choose one of them,* [d] *and I will do it to you.' "* [11] *So Gad came in to David* [a] *and said to him,* [b] *"Thus Yahweh has said: 'take* [b] [12] *either* [a] *three* [b] *years of famine,* [c] *or three months' flight* [d] *before your adversaries* [e] *with the sword of your enemies overtaking you,* [e] *or three days* [f] *of the sword of Yahweh* [f] *and pestilence in the land,* [g] *with the angel of Yahweh destroying throughout all the territory of Israel.* [g] *Now* [h] *consider what answer I shall take back to the one who sent me."*

[13] *Then David said to Gad, "I am in great distress.* [a] *Let me* [b] *fall into the hand of Yahweh, because his mercy is very* [c] *great, and do not let me fall* [d] *into the hands of man."* [14] *So Yahweh brought a pestilence upon Israel,* [a] *and seventy thousand* [b] *Israelites fell.* [bc] [15a] *God also sent an angel* [a] *to Jerusalem* [b] *to destroy it,* [b] *but while he was destroying it, Yahweh looked* [c] *and changed his mind concerning the evil, and said to the destroying angel,* [d] *"Enough; now withdraw your hand," and the angel of Yahweh* [e] *was standing* [e] *at the threshing floor of Ornan* [f] *the Jebusite.*

[16a] *David lifted his eyes and saw the angel of Yahweh standing between earth and heaven, with his sword drawn in his hand, stretched out against Jerusalem,*

and David and the elders fell down with sackcloth covering their faces. [a] [17]*David said to God,* [ab] *"*[c]*Did I not give command to count the people?*[c] [d]*I am the one who has sinned* [d] [e]*and acted very wickedly.* [e] *But these are the flock—what have they done?* [f]*Yahweh my God,* [f] *let now your hand be against me and my father's house,* [g]*and not for a plague against your people."* [g]

[18a]*Then the angel of Yahweh told Gad to tell David* [a] [b]*that David should go up to erect an altar to Yahweh* [b] *on the threshing floor of Ornan the Jebusite.* [19]*David went up, according to the word of Gad* [a]*which he had spoken in Yahweh's name.* [a] [20]*Ornan turned and saw the angel* [a] (*[b]four of his sons* [b] *who were with him hid themselves,* [c]*but Ornan was threshing wheat*).[c] [21a]*David came in to Ornan, and Ornan looked and saw David,* [a] [b]*and he went out from the threshing floor* [b] *and bowed down* [c]*before David,* [c] *face to the ground.* [d] [22]*David said to Ornan,* [a]*"Give me the site of the threshing floor, that I may build an altar to Yahweh on it.* [a] [b]*Give it to me at the full price,* [b] *that the plague may be kept back from the people."* [23]*And Ornan said,* [a]*"Take it,* [a] *and let my lord the king do* [b] *what is good in his eyes. See,* [c]*I give* [c] *the cattle for the burnt offering and the threshing-sledges* [d] *for the wood* [e]*and the wheat for the grain offering;* [e] *I give everything."* [fg] [24]*And David* [a] *the king said to Ornan, "No,* [b]*but I insist on buying it* [bc] [d]*at the full price,* [d] *because I will not offer* [e] *to Yahweh* [f]*what is yours,* [f] [g]*nor sacrifice a burnt offering at no cost."* [g] [25a]*So David gave Ornan* [a] [b]*six hundred shekels of gold* [b] [c]*for the place.* [c] [26]*David built there an altar to Yahweh and sacrificed burnt offerings and peace offerings.* [a]*Then he called to Yahweh, who answered him with fire from heaven upon the altar of burnt offering.* [a]

[27a]*Then Yahweh spoke to the angel, and he returned his sword to its sheath.* [a] [28a]*At that time, when David saw that Yahweh answered him at the threshing floor of Ornan the Jebusite* [b]*when he sacrificed there—* [b] [29](*the tabernacle of Yahweh which Moses had made in the wilderness and the altar of burnt offering was at the high place at Gibeon at that time,* [30]*but David was not able to go before it to worship God, because he was terrified of the sword of the angel of Yahweh)—* [22:1]*David said, "This is the house of Yahweh God, and this is the altar of burnt offering for Israel."*

Notes

1.a-a. 2 Sam 24:1 ויסף יהוה לחרות בישראל "Yahweh was again angry with Israel."

1.b. 2 Sam 24:1 + בהם "against them."

1.c. 2 Sam 24:1 + ואת־יהודה "and Judah."

2.a. 2 Sam 24:2 המלך "the king!"

2.b-b. 2 Sam 24:2 שר החיל אשר אתו "the commander of the army which was with him"; cf. n. 4.a.

2.c. 2 Sam 24:2 שוט־נא = "pass through"; cf. n. 4.c-c.

2.d-d. > 2 Sam 24:2 (cf. n. 2.g-g.).

2.e. 2 Sam 24:2 (ב)כל־שבטי ישראל "all the tribes of Israel."

2.f-f. 2 Sam 24:2 has the reverse order. For the south-to-north orientation, cf. Williamson, 144.

2.g-g. 2 Sam 24:2 ופקדו את העם "and count the people." (Cf. n. 2.d-d.)

3.a-a. 2 Sam 24:3 אל־העם "to the people."

3.b-b. 2 Sam 24:3 כהם וכהם, lit., "like them and like them."

3.c-c. > 2 Sam 24:3.

4.a. 2 Sam 24:4 + ועל שרי החיל "and against the commanders [sic] of the army"; cf. n. 2.b-b.

4.b. 2 Sam includes vv 4b–7. Chronicles has simply abbreviated its source.

4.c-c. 2 Sam 24:8 וישטו "and they wandered around"; cf. n. 2.c.

4.d. 2 Sam 24:8 הארץ "the land," instead of Israel.

4.e. 2 Sam 24:8 + "at the end of nine months and twenty days."

5.a. 2 Sam 24:9 המלך "the king."

5.b. > 2 Sam 24:9.

5.c-c. 2 Sam 24:9 שמנה מאות אלף איש "eight hundred thousand men." See the following notes.

5.d-d. This phrase is commonly considered a later addition in view of Chronicles' treatment of Israel and Judah as a unity; cf. n. 1.c. and below.

5.e-e. 2 Sam 24:9.

5.f. LXX "eighty."

6.a-a. > 2 Sam 24:9. The exclusion of Levi from a census is understandable in view of such passages as Num 1:49. The reason for Benjamin's exclusion is not apparent, although usually it is explained as being the locale of either Jerusalem (but Chronicles places Jerusalem at the heart of Judah) or, more probably, Gibeah. Mosis (110), following Galling (61), believes the text originally read "Judah and Benjamin" and reflects the desire to separate these two components of post-exilic Israel from the guilt of the census.

6.b. G^B κατίσχυσεν "was dominant"; G^L κατετάχυνεν "was swift."

7.a-a. > 2 Sam 24:9.

7.b-b. 2 Sam 24:10 ויך לב־דוד אתו אחרי־כן ספר את־העם "David's heart smote him after he had numbered the people."

8.a. 2 Sam 24:10 יהוה "Yahweh"; cf. n. 8.c.

8.b-b. > 2 Sam 24:10.

8.c. 2 Sam 24:10 + יהוה "Yahweh" (cf. n. 8.a.).

9.a. 2 Sam 24:11 + ויקם דוד בבקר "David arose in the morning."

9.b-b. 2 Sam 24:11 ודבר־יהוה היה אל־גד הנביא חזה דוד "the word of Yahweh came to the prophet Gad, David's seer."

10.a. 2 Sam 24:12 הָלוֹךְ "go," qal inf abs.

10.b. 2 Sam 24:12 אנוכי "I."

10.c. 2 Sam 24:12 G^{BL} and some MSS נוטל " . . . I am imposing."

10.d. 2 Sam 24:12 מהם "(one) of them," masc.

11.a. 2 Sam 24:13 + ויגד־לו "and he told him."

11.b-b. > 2 Sam 24:13.

12.a. 2 Sam 24:13 התבוא "will there come?"

12.b. 2 Sam 24:13 שבע "seven."

12.c. 2 Sam 24:13 + בארצך "on your land."

12.d. 2 Sam 24:13 נסך "to flee," inf; read נסכה.

12.e-e. 2 Sam 24:13 והוא רדפך "and he pursues you."

12.f-f. > 2 Sam 24:13.

12.g-g. > 2 Sam 24:13.

12.h. 2 Sam 24:13 + דע ו "know and."

13.a. G^{Chr} + καὶ τὰ τρία "and the three."

13.b. 2 Sam 24:14 נפלה־נא "let us fall." (Cf. v 14b אפלה "let me [not] fall.")

13.c. > 2 Sam 24:14.

13.d. 2 Sam 24:14 אל־אפלה "let me not fall," lengthened cohortative.

14.a. G^{Sam} 24:15 + מהבקר ועד־עת מועד "from morning until the appointed time."

14.b-b. 2 Sam 24:15 וימת מן־העם " . . . died before the people."

14.c. 2 Sam 24:15 + מדן ועד־באר שבע "from Dan to Beersheba" (cf. v 2).

15.a-a. 2 Sam 24:16 וישלח ידו המלאך "and the messenger stretched out his hand."

15.b-b. 2 Sam 24:15 לשחתה "to destroy it," piel inf.

15.c-c. > 2 Sam 24:15.

15.d. 2 Sam 24:16 + בעם "(the angel who was destroying) among the people."

15.e-e. 2 Sam 24:16 היה "was (present)." Cf. Josh 5:13 and Mosis, 115.

15.f. 2 Sam 24:16 K הארונה, Q 2 Sam 24:20 ארונה, "Araunah." The form in Chronicles (אָרְנָן "Ornan") is linguistically later.

16.a-a. > 2 Sam 24 (but of 4Q^{Sam}, cf. Cross, Ancient Library, 188–91).

17.a. 2 Sam 24:17 יהוה "Yahweh."

17.b. 2 Sam 24:17 + בעם המכה המלאך את בראתו "when he saw the angel smiting among the people" (cf. v 16).

17.c-c. > 2 Sam 24:17.

17.d-d. 2 Sam 24:17 חטאתי אנכי הנה "Behold, I have sinned."

17.e-e. 2 Sam 24:17 העויתי ואנכי "and I have done evil." Read perhaps הרעה ואני "I am the shepherd"; cf. G, *BHS*.

17.f-f. > 2 Sam 24:17.

17.g-g. > 2 Sam 24:17.

18.a-a. 2 Sam 24:18 לו ויאמר ההוא ביום דוד אל גד ויבוא "and Gad came that day to David, and said to him."

18.b-b. 2 Sam 24:18 מזבח ליהוה הקם עלה "Go up, establish an altar to Yahweh."

19.a-a. 2 Sam 24:19 יהוה צוה כאשר "as Yahweh commanded"; cf. 1 Chr 10:3, 10.

20.a. 2 Sam 24:20 המלך "the king"; cf. v 21.

20.b-b. 2 Sam 24:20 עליו עברים עבדיו ואת "and his servants passing over towards him." The "four sons" of Chronicles would appear to be Ornan's, but if we read המלך "the king" as in n. 20.a., they may be David's. On that basis some (cf. Galling, 113) have argued that since Solomon was David's fourth son according to 1 Chr 14:4, the intent was to have Solomon present on the site of the future temple at the time of its designation. This interpretation, if accurate, is probably secondary.

20.c-c. > 2 Sam 24:20, but present, according to Cross, in 4Q[Sam] (*HTR* 57 [1964] 294).

21.a-a. > 2 Sam 24:20.

21.b-b. 2 Sam 24:20 ארונה ויצא "and Araunah went out."

21.c-c. 2 Sam 24:20 למלך "to the king."

21.d. 2 Sam 24:21 עבדו אל המלך אדני בא מדוע ארונה ויאמר "and Araunah said, 'Why has my lord the king come to his servant?'"

22.a-a. 2 Sam 24:21 ליהוה מזבח לבנות הגרן את מעמך לקנות "to buy from you the threshing floor to build an altar to Yahweh."

22.b-b. > 2 Sam 24:21. Cf. Gen 23:9.

23.a-a. 2 Sam 24:22 יקח "May he take it," jussive.

23.b. 2 Sam 24:22 ויעל "may he offer."

23.c-c. > 2 Sam 24:22.

23.d. 2 Sam 24:22 + הבקר וכלי "and the things (= yokes) of the oxen."

23.e-e. > 2 Sam 24:22 (!).

23.f. 2 Sam 24:23 למלך (?) המלך ארונה נתן הכל "Araunah (the king?) gave everything to the king."

23.g. 2 Sam 24:23 + ירצך אלהיך יהוה המלך אל ארונה ויאמר "And Araunah said to the king, 'May Yahweh your God accept you.'"

24.a. > 2 Sam 24:24.

24.b-b. 2 Sam 24:24 אקנה קנו-כי "I will surely buy."

24.c. 2 Sam 24:24 + מאותך "from you."

24.d-d. 2 Sam 24:24 במחיר "for a price."

24.e. 2 Sam 24:24 אעלה "I will (not) offer."

24.f-f. > 2 Sam 24:24.

24.g-g. 2 Sam 24:24 חנם עלות "offerings which cost me nothing."

25.a-a. 2 Sam 24:24 דוד ויקן "and David bought."

25.b-b. Syr 2 Sam 24:24 חמישים שקלים בכסף "for fifty shekels of silver."

25.c-c. 2 Sam 24:24 הבקר ואת הגרן את "the threshing floor and the oxen."

26.a-a. > 2 Sam 24:25. Cf. 1 Kgs 18:38.

27.a-a. 2 Sam 24:25 ישראל מעל המגפה ותעצר לארץ יהוה ויעתר "then Yahweh heeded supplications for the land, and the plague was averted from Israel."

28.a. Vv 28–30; 22:1 > 2 Samuel.

28.b-b. The apodosis of the sentence comes, not with v 28b, but with 22:1, as seen correctly by Curtis and Rudolph.

Form/Structure/Setting

The outline of 1 Chr 21, which is essentially narrative drawn from 2 Sam 24, is as follows.

1 Chr 21	2 Sam 24	
21:1–4a	24:1–4a	David decrees a census
——	24:4b–7	Census itinerary
21:4b–7	24:8–10	Results of the census
21:8–12	24:11–13	Punishment chosen
21:13–18	24:14–17	The punishment stayed
21:18–27	24:18–25	The temple site secured
21:28–22:1	——	Conclusion

The Chronicler doubtless thought that 2 Sam 24, which he interpreted to result in the selection of the site of the Jerusalem temple, marked a fitting climax to this phase of David's activity. At the same time, there is in 2 Sam 24:1 ("*Again* the anger of the Lord was kindled") a reference to the events of 2 Sam 21:1–14, which likewise have to do with atonement for guilt. Though these verses are omitted by the Chronicler, he has here precedent for linking 2 Sam 21 and 24 (cf. also 21:14 with 24:25) both in content and vocabulary.

The Chronicler accordingly omits the material of 2 Sam 22 (The Song of David) and 2 Sam 23:1–7 (The Last Words of David), which together with the remainder of chaps. 21–24 form a series of appendices to Samuel (Noth, *Ü.S.*, 65). The list of David's mighty men has been incorporated into his work earlier to buttress the numbers of those who showed their support of David at the beginning of his reign (1 Chr 11:10–41a). The relationship between the two books can be seen in the following table.

1 Chronicles	2 Samuel
——	22:1–51 (= Psalm 18)
——	23:1–7
(11:11–41a)	23:8–39
21:1–27	24:1–25
21:28–30; 22:1	——

Since the variations between Samuel and Chronicles in this section are more numerous than usual and often reflect no clear *Tendenz* on the part of Chronicles, scholars have suggested that the Chronicler had before him here a different text type than that reflected in Samuel (Curtis, 245–46). Although we ought not overestimate the nature or the import of the differences, preliminary reports of as-yet-unpublished materials from Qumran do indicate at least some readings of Samuel in agreement with readings previously found only in Chronicles (cf. Cross, *Ancient Library*, 188–91; R. W. Klein, *Textual Criticism*, 42–50; see also Williamson, 147). The following eight variations should be recognized as the most significant.

(1) Satan (שָׂטָן) "Adversary," without the article, rather than God, is the instigator of David's census. Such a figure does not appear elsewhere in Chronicles (or Ezra-Nehemiah); indeed, only in Job 1–2 and Zech 3:1 does a somewhat similar figure appear. In both of these cases, however, the definite article is attached (הַשָּׂטָן "*the* adversary") so that the text of Chronicles probably represents the final stage in the OT's development of a figure of Yahweh's heavenly council who not only brings charges against his people but actually

incites them to evil. Since such a figure does not appear elsewhere in Chronicles, it probably reflects the commonly held piety of the day, which hesitated to speak of God as the direct cause of evil. The part which Persian dualism had in influencing this development in Israel is widely disputed. (See T. H. Gaster, "Satan." *IDB* 4:224–28.)

(2) Numerous alterations seem actually to increase David's guilt in calling for the census. His initial decision to conduct such a census is, e.g., disputed by Joab—who even refers to David's becoming an אשמה "a cause of guilt" to Israel (v 3)! (This same Joab is given credit for not counting Levi and Benjamin.) David's confession of guilt, while not substantially different, is stated more emphatically (vv 8, 17). Even in an unfavorable context, Chronicles frequently changes the simple המלך "the king" of Samuel to the more pointed דויד "David." Cf. vv 2, 5, etc.

(3) The initiative of God is also made more pointed throughout the narrative. Yahweh speaks directly to Gad, David's seer (v 9); Yahweh himself sends the destroying angel and instructs the angel to withdraw (v 15, but textually problematic). Yahweh himself answers David from heaven with fire upon the altar (v 26).

(4) If David's guilt in the matter of the census is emphasized, so is his uprightness in securing the site of the future temple and the value of that site. Although offered the site and all that was necessary for the sacrifice (v 23) *gratis* by Ornan, David insists on paying the full price (v 22)—the term used is reminiscent of that used for Abraham's purchase of the cave of Machpelah in Gen 23:9. In what would appear to be the clearest case of hyperbole in the chapter, David then pays Ornan, not the *fifty* shekels of *silver* named in Samuel, but no less than *six hundred* shekels of *gold*. (It is to miss the writer's point to explain the larger sum as due to the fact that Chronicles pictures the purchase of a larger site while Samuel pictures only that of the threshing floor and oxen, or as derived from a kind of head tax upon the various tribes of Israel.) To glorify the temple was to glorify God, and one way to glorify the temple was to escalate the cost of the site upon which it was built.

(5) The entire account of the "angel of Yahweh" is expressed more dramatically in Chronicles. This could reveal the *Tendenz* of the author, and would harmonize well, e.g., with his emphasis upon direct divine intervention and holy war (cf. the *Introduction*). On the other hand, this emphasis might be original to the text type being utilized by the author (Klein, *Textual Criticism*, 45) and due in part to the developing angelology of the period. Whatever its origin, there is no doubt that it represents the original text of Chronicles.

(6) Concerning the varying enumerations of "Israel" in Samuel and Chronicles it is impossible to speak with certainty. The total number of potential warriors counted in Israel and Judah (1,570,000) in Chronicles would exceed the total of 1,300,000 listed for Israel and Judah in 2 Sam 24:9, though not exorbitantly. However, in view of the alteration made by Chronicles in v 1 (see n. 1.a-a.), where the name Judah has been omitted, and in view of the general use of Israel to refer to the faithful in both north and south (cf. Williamson, *Israel*, 95–96), it is probable that v 5b is due to a later hand. Attempts to explain the specific numbers used in Chronicles are questionable. Something like that proposed by Williamson may be nearest to the mark.

Considering Ephraim and Manasseh as separate tribes, the total of 1,300,000 for the thirteen tribes represents a general figure of 100,000 per tribe. Since Chronicles (alone) states that Benjamin and Levi were not counted, the writer has accordingly reduced the total for his Israel to 1,100,000. The other figures were arrived at by the later writer on the basis of 2 Sam 24:9, with the reduction of 30,000 for Benjamin (Williamson, 145).

(7) The divine acceptance of David's offering is made explicit in that his prayer and offering, like Elijah's (1 Kgs 18) was answered by fire from heaven (v 26). That approval then becomes the basis for David's declaration that Ornan's threshing floor is to be the future site of both the temple and the altar of burnt offering.

(8) In a more subtle manner, our narrative seems to be overlaid with allusions to other OT events. (a) The figure of the angel of the Lord is related to that in Josh 5:13–15 (Mosis, 115–16), as seen most clearly in the sword and the association with a holy place. (Cf. also the use of the participle of עמד "was standing" [n. 15.e-e.].) (b) The reference to the "full price" in v 22 recalls the purchase of the cave of Machpelah by Abraham, also for the "full price." (c) Yahweh's answering of David through fire from heaven is reminiscent of the appearance of fire in connection with Elijah's contest with the prophet's of Baal in 1 Kgs 18:38. (d) The figure of Ornan threshing wheat (v 20) recalls Gideon (Judg 6; Willi, 157).

It is striking that all of these incidents are closely associated with altars and holy places. The use of such common themes was no doubt felt to draw them more closely together. (Cf. also the identification of Ornan's threshing floor with Mount Moriah [Gen 22] in 2 Chr 3:1.) On the other hand, Rudolph's assertion (148) that 22:1 stands as a clear rebuttal to the Samaritans, in view of Gen 22:1 and 28:17, is far from apparent.

Explanation

Despite David's guilt in calling for a census of Israel, his sin leads to the designation of the threshing floor of Ornan as the place of Yahweh's choosing for his altar and temple. It is quite clear here, as remarked by Rudolph and Williamson, that God's grace stands in the forefront—a point that David himself is at pains to make (v 13). The pestilence of God which had already slain seventy thousand Israelites (v 14) is stayed short of Jerusalem (v 15), the chosen city. Echoes of various portions of the OT, such as Abraham's purchase of the cave of Machpelah, make especially clear the significance of this moment. With the ark in Jerusalem and priests and Levites set apart to minister before it (chap. 16), with Solomon designated as temple builder (17:11–12; cf. 22:5, 8–10), and with the site for the temple declared and approved, our attention will be focused even more sharply upon the temple as the central feature of the Chronicler's message.

That same grace of God which triumphed over David's sins and led to the establishment of God's house remains God's principal attribute available to human beings. Available through repentance and reaching out to draw and sustain the weak, God himself always takes the lead in lifting up the fallen.

Transitional Unit (Chaps. 22–29)

Though these chapters are normally included as a part of the David history, they are set apart here because of the significant part they play in the total work of the Chronicler, and in particular for the manner in which they bind the works of David and Solomon together into one unified whole (see the *Bibliography* below). I have chosen to view chaps. 23–27 as an insertion (see the details at 23:1, *Form/Structure/Setting,* and 28:1). The intent of the whole is to designate Solomon as the divinely chosen temple builder and to secure the support of "all Israel" for his kingship and for the erection of the temple to which it will be dedicated.

David's First Speech (22:2–19)

Bibliography

Braun, R. L. "Solomon, the Chosen Temple Builder: The Significance of 1 Chronicles 22, 28, and 29 for the Theology of Chronicles." *JBL* 95 (1976) 581–90. ———. "The Significance of 1 Chronicles 22, 28, and 29 for the Structure and Theology of Chronicles." Diss.: Concordia Seminary, St. Louis (1971) 14–39. ———. "Solomonic Apologetic in Chronicles." *JBL* 92 (1973) 503–16. **Carlson, R. A.** *David the Chosen King: A Tradition-historical Approach to the Second Book of Samuel.* Stockholm: Almqvist & Wiksell, 1964. **Lohfink, N.** "Die deuteronomistische Darstellung des Übergangs der Führung Israels von Moses auf Josue. Ein Beitrag zur altestamentliche Theologie des Amtes." *Scholastik* 37 (1962) 32–44. **Margain, J. L.** "Observations sur 1 Chroniques, xxii à propos des anachronismes linguistiques dans le Bible." *Semitica* 24 (1974) 35–43. **McCarthy, D. J.** "An Installation Genre?" *JBL* 90 (1971) 31–41. **Porter, J. R.** "The Succession of Joshua." In *Proclamation and Presence: Old Testament Essays in Honor of G. Henton Davies.* Eds. J. Durham and J. Porter. Richmond: John Knox. 1970. 102–32. **Rad, G. von.** "There Remains Still a Rest for the People of God." In *The Problem of the Hexatuech and Other Essays.* Tr. E. W. T. Dicken. New York: McGraw-Hill, 1966. 94–102. **Williamson, H. G. M.** "The Accession of Solomon in the Books of Chronicles," *VT* 26 (1976) 351–61.

Translation

²*David then gave command to gather* [a] *the resident aliens who were in the land of Israel and appointed* [b] *masons who would cut hewn stones for building the house of God.* ³*And David made provision* [a] *for much iron for the nails for the doors of the gates and for the clamps, and so much bronze it could not be weighed,* ⁴*together with cedar wood without* [a] *limit, for the Sidonians and Tyrians brought much cedar to David.* ⁵*For David had said, "Solomon my son is young and immature,* [a] *and the house which is to be built for Yahweh must be exceedingly* [b] *great, an object of*

renown and splendor for all lands. Therefore I will provide for it." So David made elaborate provisions before his death.

⁶*Then he summoned Solomon his son and commanded him to build a house for Yahweh, the God of Israel.* ⁷*And David said to Solomon ᵃhis son,ᵃ "So far as I was concerned, I had my heart set on building a house for the name of Yahweh my God.* ⁸*But the word of God came to me, 'You have shed very much blood and waged great wars. You shall not build a house for my name, for you have shed much blood on the ground before me.* ⁹*Lo, a son will be born to you. He will be a man of rest, and I will give rest to him from all his enemies on every side. For his name will be Solomon, and ᵃI giveᵃ Israel peace and quiet in his days.* ¹⁰*He will build a house for my name, and he will be my son, and I ᵃwill beᵃ his father. I will establish the throne of his kingdom over Israel forever.' "*

¹¹*"Now, my son, may Yahweh be with you, that you may prosper and build the house of Yahweh your God, as he has spoken concerning you.* ¹²*Only may Yahweh give you intelligence and understanding [. . .]ᵃ that you may keep the Torah of Yahweh your God.* ¹³*Then you will prosper, if you observe to do the statutes and the judgments which Yahweh commanded Moses for Israel. Be strong and be courageous; do not be afraid and do not be terrified!"* ¹⁴*And behold, ᵃby my hard workᵃ I have provided for the house of Yahweh one hundred thousand talents of gold, a million talents of silver, bronze and iron beyond weighing (it was so much). Timber and stones also I have provided, and you shall add to them.* ¹⁵*And with you in abundance are workmen, hewers and gravers of wood and stone, and every (kind of) skilled workman for every work* ¹⁶ᵃ*of gold, silver, bronze, and iron, beyond reckoning.ᵃ Rise and act, and may Yahweh be with you."*

¹⁷*And David commanded all the princes of Israel to help Solomon his son:ᵃ* ¹⁸*"Is not Yahweh your God with you, and has he not given you rest on every side? For he has given into myᵃ hand the inhabitants of the land, so that the land is subdued before Yahweh and before his people.* ¹⁹*Now, give your heart and soul to seek Yahweh your God, and rise and build the sanctuary of Yahweh God to bring in the ark of the covenant of Yahweh and Yahweh's holy vessels to the house which is to be built for the name of Yahweh."*

Notes

2.a. G + πάντας "all"; cf. 2 Chr 2:16.

2.b. Gᴸ + αὐτούς "them"; Syr + mnhwn = מהם "from them"; cf. 2 Chr 2:17.

3.a. For the hiph of כון "provided" in Chronicles, cf. Curtis, #54; Williamson, *Israel*, 53.

4.a. For לאין "without," see Curtis, #132; Williamson, *Israel*, 50.

5.a. The phrase נער ורך "young and immature" is repeated in 1 Chr 29:1. The translation here reflects the fact that in 2 Chr 13:7 Rehoboam appears to be excused for his part in the disruption of the kingdom because he was נער ורך לבב "young and immature of heart." Cf. Deut 20:8; Jer 1:6.

5.b. For למעלה "exceedingly," see Curtis, #87; Williamson, 55.

7.a-a. Reading בנו "his son" with K, against Q and Vrs. Cf. the usage in 28:6; 29:1, and esp. at the beginning of direct discourse in 28:20.

9.a-a. 2 MSS Syr read יהיה "(there) will be."

10.a-a. A few Heb. MSS, Gᴬ, and other Gr. MSS, Syr Vg + אהיה "I will be," impf.

12.a. The present text is untranslatable and may well represent either an error that has crept into the text (cf. G, which reads κατισχύσαι "strengthen" for MT's ויצוך "when he puts you in command") or a later insertion. See Rothstein and Hänel 2:396. To retain the present text, most modern translations consider ויצוך to introduce a temporal clause, "when he sets you (over Israel)." *BHS* proposes ויצר רך "and delicate form" or ויצר יציב "and a flat form."

14.a-a. The precise nuance of עני ("poverty, pain, affliction, work, humility") is questionable. Cf. 29:2. It is possible that the thought is moving into the area suggested by the similar ענותו "his hardships" of Ps 132:1, which verges upon David's piety.

16.a-a. This phrase probably represents a later addition (cf. the enumeration given in v 14 and *Comment* below).

17.a. G^min (Vg) + λέγων "saying"; G^L + καὶ εἶπεν "and he said."

18.a. G^Aa1 Syr Vg have the 2d pers pl suff.

Form/Structure/Setting

Chapter 22 consists of three major portions, the first (vv 2–5) primarily narrative in form, the second and third in the form of speeches of David. The chapter may be outlined as follows:

A. David's arrangements for the temple, vv 2–5
B. David's first speech to Solomon, vv 6–16
   1. David designates Solomon as temple builder, vv 6–13
   2. David's provisions for the temple, vv 7–16
C. Exhortation to the princes, vv 17–19

This last section (vv 17–19) has been quite commonly denied to the Chronicler (cf. Rudolph, 151–52; Noth, *Ü.S.,* 112), although the reason given is usually restricted to the fact that the section appears to be a doublet of chap. 28. However, it should also be noted that there is here no indication of the prior convening of the princes addressed in these verses (cf. v 17), nor is there real reason to suppose that they were present for David's previous address to Solomon. Rudolph correctly notes that chap. 28 does not request the assembly to assist Solomon in the building of the temple apart from the offering to defray its cost. The insertion of an exhortation to the princes here could have been occasioned by the later insertion of chaps. 23–27 (see below), which gave the appearance of separating David's private address to Solomon from the public address of chap. 28 by a considerable period of time.

Vv 14–16 have been accepted by most scholars as an integral part of the speech of vv 7–13. They are excluded from the work of the original author by Rudolph, who gives the following reasons. (1) The figures listed for the gold and silver are so high and stand in such poor relationship to the other figures listed by Chronicles (cf. 29:4, 7; 2 Chr 9:13) that one can with justification assume that we have here a later addition of one who considered it impossible to overvalue the worth of the temple (2) That David placed numerous workers at Solomon's disposal for every conceivable kind of temple work is a heightening of v 15. (3) And v 13 presents a clear conclusion beyond which nothing else is expected (Rudolph, 151).

The following points would support Rudolph's conclusion. (1) The looseness of the connection between v 14 and the preceding והנה "and behold." (2) The disjointed character of the verses as a whole. In addition to the כי לרב היה "it was so much" of v 14, where the author seems to forget that he was quoting David in the present tense, the gold, silver, bronze, and iron mentioned in v 14 are repeated in v 16. This is all the more striking since the gold and silver enumerated in v 14 are in v 16 said to be "without reckoning." (3) In vv 2–4 there is no mention of workmen available to Solomon other than masons, or of gold and silver. It is typical of the expansion of Chronicles' text to insert notice of all kinds of preparations, such as workmen, building materials, and lay support, into each portion of the original narrative rather than presenting the narrative as a progressive one in which new preparations and arrangements are introduced at successive steps. The influence of the narrative of the construction of the tabernacle is often especially strong in these additions. (4) Finally, the note of David's prior contributions in 29:3 may well have led to their insertion here, since a later author saw room for a possible discrepancy.

The brief quote of v 5 (and of v 1) is an excellent example of the "royal edict" used by Chronicles with some frequency to lend authority to certain cultic institutions. The longer speech of vv 6–13 is similar to other speeches by kings in its use of the vocative and what amounts to a historical retrospect (vv 7–10), and its basic hortatory character is apparent in the jussive and imperatives of vv 11, 12, and 13. Like most such speeches, it is directly related to the cult. It differs from the remaining speeches, however, in that in it alone the king addresses his son and successor, in the use of the lengthy indirect quotation of vv 8–10, in the manner in which this prophetic oracle is used to "prove" Solomon's right to build the temple, and, as we shall now see, in the more extensive use which it makes of the form for the induction of a leader into his office (vv 11–13).

On the basis of various passages referring to the commissioning of Joshua, N. Lohfink has isolated three elements of what he has termed *"eine Art Gattung der Amtseinsetzung,"* or form for the induction of an individual into an office: (1) The *Ermutigungsformel,* or formula of encouragement, חזק ואמץ "be strong and courageous"; Josh 1:6. (2) The description of the task to which the individual is inducted, Josh 1:6, introduced here by כי אתה "for you." (3) The *Beistandsformel,* or formula of accompaniment, of which the central element is כי עמך יהוה "because Yahweh is with you"; Josh 1:9.

These same elements are found in the second part of David's speech, 1 Chr 22:11–13. The formula of accompaniment is represented by יהי יהוה עמך "may Yahweh be with you" (v 11). The task with which Solomon is charged is the building of the house of Yahweh (v 11). The formula of encouragement is represented by the fourfold imperative of v 13: חזק ואמץ אל תירא ואל תחת "be strong and be courageous; do not be afraid and do not be terrified." These same three elements will also be found in David's second speech, 1 Chr 28:20. Moreover, the description of the task and a variant of the formula of encouragement חזק ועשה "be strong and act" is found in 28:10. (See also 28:20; 2 Chr 19:7, 11; 25:8; Ezra 10:4.)

While some reservations have been expressed concerning Lohfink's study, especially with regard to the terminology involved (cf. McCarthy, *JBL* 90 [1971] 31–41), and it may be dubious whether we are here dealing with a form in the strictest sense of the term, the evidence that 1 Chr 22 and 28 are directly dependent upon Josh 1 is so strong that we can at any rate say without hesitation that Chronicles took Joshua's commissioning as the model for describing that of Solomon. This conclusion is established by the following six observations.

(1) The inclusion of the concern for the keeping of the law (1 Chr 22:12, 13; 28:7, 9) points to the influence of Josh 1:7–8. The only other passage in which a similar relationship is found is that referring to David's commissioning of Solomon in 1 Kgs 2:1–4, which also has literary affinities with Josh 1 (cf. Braun, *JBL* 95 [1976] 587).

(2) The introduction of the thought of prosperity (1 Chr 22:11, 13) points to the same dependence. Apart from the incidental use in 1 Kgs 22:12, 15 and Deut 28:29, Josh 1:8 provides the only example of the use of the hiphil of עלח "prosper" in Deuteronomy or the Deuteronomistic History.

(3) The fourfold division of the formula of encouragement "Be strong, be courageous; do not be afraid and do not be terrified" (v 13) likewise points to Josh 1:9. These same four terms in the same order occur only in 2 Chr 32:7, and with the order reversed in Josh 10:25. However, the same sequence is found in Josh 1:9 and Deut 31:6, but with a form of ערץ "tremble" instead of ירא "fear." The use of ערץ is rare (only in Deut 1:29; 20:3; 31:6; Josh 1:9), and it seems likely that for this reason Chronicles has replaced it with the more common ירא.

(4) While the formula "may Yahweh be with you/Yahweh is with you" is common in the OT and its use here without additional supporting evidence would be inconclusive, a large number of uses are clustered around two individuals, Joshua and David, who may on other grounds be shown to be of particular importance for the deuteronomistic historian (Cross, *Canaanite Myth and Hebrew Epic*, 252).

(5) As noted by McCarthy, the sequence between 1 Chr 28 and 29 "almost gives the impression that the Chronicler has studied Deuteronomy-Joshua with great care" (*JBL* 90 [1971] 36). While McCarthy follows most traditional commentators on Chronicles by overemphasizing the role of David at Solomon's expense, he correctly notes that the sequence between 1 Chr 22 and 1 Chr 28 is like that between Deut 31 and Josh 1 and 13. In chap. 22 David commissions Solomon to build the temple in what seems to be a private audience (v 6). Then he publicly commands the fulfillment of the same task in chap. 28. McCarthy also suggests that this twofold commissioning reflects an actual tradition. That may well be, but there is no evidence for such a tradition, and it seems more likely that Chronicles has indeed studied Deuteronomy-Joshua with great care (as the use of the מנוחה "resting" concept also indicates) and has used the twofold commissioning of Joshua (Deut 31:14–15; Josh 1:2–9) as the model for his account of the commissioning of Solomon.

(6) Williamson's observation that in the cases of both Joshua and David the obedience of the people is noted (Deut 34:9; 1 Chr 29:23) and reference is made to Yahweh's "magnifying" Joshua and David before all Israel (Josh 3:7; 1 Chr 29:25) makes the dependency even more apparent (*VT* 26 [1976] 355).

We have already had occasion to call attention to the unique treatment of the concept of rest (נוח/מנוחה "resting") in Chronicles in connection with the dynastic oracle of 1 Chr 17. It is, however, in vv 7–10 that the full significance of this term for Chronicles is made clear. David has "spilled much blood, and waged great wars" (v 8), and hence is explicitly disqualified from building the temple. (Cf. 28:3, where David is called a "man of war," איש מלחמה.) By way of contrast, David has been told he will have a son, who will be an איש מנוחה "a man of rest" (v 9), who will build the temple.

In drawing this conclusion, the writer is dependent upon 1 Kgs 5:17–19 [3–5], where David's earlier failure to build the temple is viewed as the natural result of the fact that he was engaged in warfare and did not have sufficient time to accomplish such a building activity. Chronicles reinterprets the text so that the construction of the temple is not left to historical chance, but is based upon divine decree and Yahweh's explicit choice of Solomon.

It should be noted here that already within Deuteronomy and the Deuteronomistic History the concept of rest and its connection with the unification of the cult and the erection of the temple is prominent. Throughout Joshua the completion of the conquest as fulfillment of Yahweh's promise is frequently described in terms of rest (נוח/מנוחה; cf. Josh 1:13, 15; 22:4; 23:1 and especially 21:44). "Rest," although of a less permanent type denoted by forms of the root שקט "be at peace" is characteristic of the work of the judges under Yahweh's blessing (cf. Judg 3:11, 30: 8:28, etc.). Above all, Deut 12:8–11 makes it clear that when the conquest was complete and God had given Israel rest (הניח, v 10) from all her enemies, Israel's offerings would be brought to the one place "where the Lord your God will choose to make his name dwell," i.e., the temple to be erected in Jerusalem. This connection between temple building and rest may also be seen by reading Josh 11:23 in connection with Josh 18:1, where the former passage indicates that the land had rest (שקטה), and the latter, following immediately upon the apportionment of the land described in chaps. 12–17 in the final form of the book, relates that the people assembled at Shiloh to set up the tent of meeting, since the land lay subdued (נכבשה) before them. However, for the Deuteronomistic historian it was in 2 Sam 7:1, 11; 1 Kgs 5:17–19 [3–5]; 8:56 that he gave final if imprecise expression to the concept of rest. It was when David enjoyed rest (2 Sam 7:1, 11; 1 Kgs 5:18 [4]) that he raised the question of building the temple; it was because of his warfare that he had been prevented from doing so earlier (1 Kgs 5:17 [3]). Above all, Solomon's dedicatory prayer points to the rest attendant upon the completion of the temple as the fulfillment of all God's promises to Israel (1 Kgs 8:54–61; cf. especially v 56, and Josh 21:44).

Chronicles adopts this motif of rest and temple-building for his own and adapts it to his own more precise understanding of the relationship between rest and temple and of the role of David and Solomon in the divine plan. Passages that ascribed rest to David are omitted (2 Sam 7:1; 1 Kgs 5:17–19 [3–5]) or altered [2 Sam 7:11]; cf. 1 Chr 17:1, 10; 2 Chr 2:1–2). On the other hand, the fact that 1 Kgs 5:17–19 and 1 Kgs 8:54–61 do not occur in Chronicles cannot in any sense be said to be due to the writer's lack of interest in them or disagreement with them, but must be due to his admittedly unusual practice of omitting certain passages which can be shown to have the greatest significance for him and giving expression to their thoughts in more detailed fashion elsewhere (cf. also the matter of obedience to the law and the disposition of the heart in 1 Kgs 8:57–58, 61 with 1 Chr 28:9–10). His further development of the concept of rest beyond this point lies in two areas. (1) As noted by von Rad (*The Problem of the Hexateuch and Other Essays*, 97–99), the temple now becomes the place where Yahweh himself takes up his "rest" in the midst of his people; cf. 28:2; 2 Chr 6:41 = Ps 132:8. (2) Later kings in particular favor with the Chronicler are said to have enjoyed Yahweh's rest as a part of the prosperity which marked their reigns when they were faithful to Yahweh, specifically, Asa (2 Chr 14:5; 15:15, plus שׁקט in 2 Chr 13:23, 14:4–5 [14:1, 5–6]), Jehoshaphat (2 Chr 20:30), and Hezekiah (2 Chr 32:22, reading וינח להם "he gave them rest" as suggested by G and Vg instead of וינהלם "and led to rest").

The concern which Chronicles wished to express by its dependence upon the narrative of Joshua's commissioning and its use of the concept of rest is thus clear beyond a doubt: Solomon is the "man of rest," divinely appointed to build the temple.

To our knowledge there is no tradition to the effect that David made the preparations ascribed to him in vv 2–5 (but compare 1 Kgs 7:51 [= 2 Chr 5:1]), although this subject is of considerable importance for Chronicles. In v 5, Chronicles has dealt explicitly with the reason for David's preparations, which it states is due to the disparity between Solomon's youth and inexperience and the immensity of the task lying before him. (See n. 5.a.). Many of the details of the section appear to be derived from the Solomonic portion of Kings. David's gathering of the aliens (v 2) is probably patterned upon Solomon's similar act (1 Kgs 5:27 [13]; 9:15, 22; cf. the addition in 2 Chr 2:16 [17], where the parallel between the censuses of David and Solomon is explicitly drawn.) The mention of cedar, especially in connection with the Tyrians and the inhabitants of Sidon, recalls Solomon's arrangements with Hiram of Tyre (1 Kgs 5:15–32 [1–19], esp. vv 22–24 [8–14] and v 32 [18]) and the extensive use of it in 1 Kgs 6:14–22. While the Kings account makes no mention of provisions for bronze, there is much emphasis upon the bronze articles constructed by Tyrian craftsman-artist Hiram (1 Kgs 7:14–47). There is no mention of iron in Kings, but considerable attention is given to the doors (1 Kgs 6:31–34; 7:50; Ezek 41:21–26); and the gates, also absent in Kings, are mentioned many times in Ezekiel's vision in Ezek 40–48. The statement of the purpose of the temple as being לשׁם ולתפאארת "an object of renown and splendor" recalls such passages as Deut 26:19; Jer 13:11; 33:9; and Zeph 3:19–20, in all of which cases, however, it points to God's elect people as a "name and glory" rather than to the temple, as here.

Accordingly we may conclude that Chronicles has introduced David's preparations for the temple primarily to magnify the temple, and second, to provide David a place alongside Solomon in the preparation for Israel's major cultic institution.

Comment

2–5 David gathers workmen and materials for the temple. (See the *Notes* and *Form/Structure/Setting* above). The resident aliens (גרים, v 2) were free men, who had however no legal rights. The statement here is probably to be read as a correction upon 1 Kgs 5:27 [13], where Solomon's levy appears to be laid upon Israelites. (See also 1 Kgs 9:22.) Specific mention of most

of the materials gathered is found in the account of the temple construction—
see *Form/Structure/Setting* above. Tyre and Sidon (v 4) are the two well known
cities of the Phoenicians, associated loosely also in 1 Kgs 5:15, 20 [1, 6]
and joined also in Ezra 3:7. (In 1 Chr 1:13 Sidon is listed as Canaan's firstborn,
but was later surpassed by Tyre.) Hiram of Tyre is surprisingly not listed
here, cf. 14:1 (= 2 Sam 5:11; 2 Chr 2, and 1 Kgs 5). V 5 is most significant
(a) in pointing to the elaborateness of David's provisions, (b) which is in
keeping with the splendor of the temple and (c) is occasioned by Solomon's
youth and immaturity (see n. 5.a.).

Despite the restricted vocabulary of the section, the style and vocabulary
of Chronicles is much in evidence, cf. לרב "in abundance," vv 3, 4, 5 (Curtis,
#105; Williamson, *Israel,* 45; Kropat, 58); לאין "without," vv 4, 5 (n. 4.a.);
למעלה "exceeding," v 5 (n. 5.b.); כון "provided," hiphil (v 3; see n. 3.a.),
and, omitting a single conjunction, the list of seven words in a row beginning
with the preposition ל "to" in v 5. (Cf. Curtis, ##127–134.)

6–10   David charges Solomon to build the temple. The "house for the
name of Yahweh (v 7) is reminiscent of Deuteronomy (cf. Deut 12:11) and
the Deuteronomic history (1 Kgs 8:16, 19, 20, 29). Significant in v 8 is the
explicitness of God's word forbidding David to build the temple; equally
significant is the direct manner in which the dynastic oracle of vv 9–10 is
attached directly to Solomon (contrast 2 Sam 7:13; but cf. 1 Kgs 5:18–19
[4–5]), where the idea is close at hand. With the insertion of the name Solomon
into the oracle, it is now the throne of *his* (i.e., Solomon's) kingdom that
Yahweh promises to establish forever.

11–16   The use of the form for the installation into office (see *Form/Struc-
ture/Setting* above) also sets Solomon aside as temple builder. For "intelligence
and understanding" (v 12) see 2 Chr 2:11, also of Solomon and without
parallel. Note, here, however, that this wisdom is directed toward the keeping
of the Torah and is to result in prosperity, items found also in Josh 1:7–8,
upon which Chronicles is dependent here (see *Form/Structure/Setting* above).
This note of obedience to the law will provide the basis for the doctrine of
retribution, expressed more extensively and more in keeping with the Chronicler's terminology in 28:9, upon which the interpretation of much (if not
all) of the history of the post-Solomonic kingdoms is modeled (see *Introduction*
on "Retribution").

14–16   These verses probably reflect a later addition to the text, as do
vv 17–19 (see *Form/Structure/Setting*). The hundred thousand talents of gold
and million talents of silver (v 14) are by any reckoning astronomical. (The
weight of a talent was most commonly about seventy-five pounds and the
so-called light talent about half of that.) By way of comparison, Solomon's
fleet brought back from Ophir 420 talents of gold (G, 120 talents), and Solomon's annual revenue is said to have been 666 talents (1 Kgs 10:14). It
would be pointless to try to express the value of such an amount of silver
and gold in terms relevant to today. Vv 15–16 appear to emphasize again
the volume of metals present, although it is at least possible that the emphasis
here is rather upon the workmen. V 16b restates two elements of the form
for installation, those of encouragement and divine presence, although espe-

cially the former (קום ועשה "rise and act") varies considerably in its wording (cf. 28:10, חזק ועשה "be strong and act").

17–19 These verses enlist the princes to help Solomon (cf. 28:1 and 23:2). In v 18, God's presence is now affirmed with the people, as it has been with Solomon, and the rest before ascribed to Solomon is ascribed to the people as a whole, who are further described as the people of the Lord. They too are to "seek the Lord" (cf. 28:9), to "rise and build" the temple (cf. 28:10) that the ark of the covenant and the holy vessels may be brought into it (v 19).

Explanation

David's provisions for the construction of the temple include above all the gathering of materials and workmen, and the commissioning of Solomon to perform that work. In the case of the materials, we may see a reflection of such passages as 18:8; however, there ought to be seen here also the desire to make David and Solomon equal participants in the total work of planning and building (cf. especially 2 Chr 2). Apologetically, the major thrust of the chapter is to legitimatize Solomon as the temple builder. Through the use of the concept of rest and its incorporation into the dynastic oracle, Solomon is pointed to as the divinely chosen temple builder, while David is disqualified because of his warfare. Like Joshua of old, Solomon is encouraged to undertake this task with the assurance of God's presence; like Joshua before him he is pointed to obedience to the Torah, in Solomon's case both as the result of God's gift of wisdom (v 12) and the cause of prosperity (v 13). Later portions of the chapter heighten the amount of both materials and workmen for the temple (vv 14–16) and include Israel's leaders in the God-given rest accorded Solomon, in the call to "seek Yahweh," and in helping Solomon in the erection of the temple itself (vv 17–19), anticipating many of the themes of chaps. 28–29.

While it is impossible because of our lack of knowledge of a date (see the *Introduction*) to determine the specific audience of the writer, the scope of the message is clear. The Jerusalem temple is the legitimate temple, built by David and Solomon at God's behest and with the assurance of God's presence and aid with them. In every age, therefore, there would have been the divine imperative to support that command and, of course, if the temple was in ruins, to gather to it and rebuild it. In support of this common task Israel would find both unity and blessing.

David's Organization
of the Levites (Chaps. 23-27)

These chapters, as noted below, are considered a later addition by most recent scholars. Obviously written over a period of time, or drawn from sources dating to different periods, they appear to present elaborate Levitical arrangements of a later day as dating from the time of David. In doing so they obviously build upon the tradition that it was David who was responsible for much that came to be associated with the temple, including above all priests, Levites, and temple song. Just as all Torah is then associated with Moses and all wisdom with Solomon, so it is David who was viewed finally as responsible for *all* of the details of the temple and its cult. A simplified outline of these chapters would be as follows:

    I. Divisions of the Levites (chap. 23)
    II. The Priests (chap. 24)
    III. The Singers (chap. 25)
    IV. The Gatekeepers (chap. 26)
    V. Other Appointees of David (chap. 27)

In their final form, these chapters are highly composite, presenting a collection of genealogies and lists (themselves often based on genealogy) sometimes linked by editorial statements and speeches attributed to David (cf. 23:2, 4, 6, 25; 25:1), at other times only by juxtaposition (cf. 24:1; 26:1); or, as at 27:1, the simple statement "This is the list. . . ."

Genealogy and Duties of the Levites (23:1-32)

Bibliography

(See also the general *Bibliography* on Priests and Levites at 5:37.)

Welch, A. *The Work of the Chronicler, Its Purpose and Date.* London: Oxford University Press, 1939. 81–96. **Williamson, H. G. M.,** "The Origins of the Twenty-four Priestly Courses." VTSup 30. Leiden: E. J. Brill, 1979. 251–68.

Translation

    [1] *When David was old and full of days, he made his son* [a] *Solomon king over Israel.* [2] *He gathered all the princes of Israel and the priests and the Levites.* [3] *The Levites thirty years old and up were numbered,* [a] *the number of their males* [b] *was thirty-eight thousand.* [4] [a] *Of these,* [a] *twenty-four thousand were to be over* [b] *the work*

of Yahweh's house, six thousand officers and judges, [5a]four thousand gatekeepers,[a] and four thousand praising Yahweh upon instruments made[b] for giving praise to the Lord.[c] [6]David [a]assigned them[a] to divisions corresponding to Levi's sons, Gershon, Kohath, and Merari.

[7]To the Gershonites (were allotted) Ladan and Shimei. [8]The sons of Ladan were Jehiel, the chief, Zetham,[a] and Joel, three; [9](while the sons of Shimei[a] were also three: Shelomoth,[b] Haziel,[c] and Haran). [d]These were the heads of the fathers' (houses) of Ladan.[d]

[10]The sons of Shimei[a] were Jahath, Zina,[b] Jeush, and Beriah. These were the sons of Shimei, four. [11]Jahath was the chief, and Zinah[a] the second. Since Jeush and Beriah did not have many children, they became a father's house,[b] a single roster.

[12]The sons of Kohath were Amram, Izhar, Hebron, and Uzziel, four. Amram's sons were Aaron and Moses. [13]Aaron and his sons were set apart forever to sanctify the most holy things, to sacrifice before Yahweh, to minister to him, and to bless by his name forever, [14]while Moses, the man of God, and his sons would bear the name of the tribe of Levi. [15]The sons of Moses were Gershom and Eliezer. [16]The sons of Gershom had Shebuel[a] as chief. [17]The sons of Eliezer had Rehabiah as chief. Eliezer had no other children, although the sons of Rehabiah were very numerous. [18]The sons of Izhar had Shelomith[a] as chief; [19]the sons of Hebron had Jeriah[a] as chief, with Amariah the second, Jahaziah[b] third, and Jekameam fourth. [20]The sons of Uzziel had Micah as chief and Isshiah second.

[21]The sons of Merari were Mahli and Mushi; Mahli's sons were Eleazer and Kish. [22]Eleazer died having no sons but only daughters, so the sons of Kish, their relatives, married them. [23]Mushi's sons were Mahli, Eder, and Jeremoth, three.

[24]These were the sons of Levi according to their fathers' houses, the heads of the fathers' (houses) according to their registration, with the listing of the names of their heads, who should do[a] the work of the service of the house of Yahweh, from twenty years old and upward. [25]For David had said, "Yahweh, the God of Israel, has given rest to his people and has taken up his dwelling in Jerusalem forever. [26]Therefore the Levites too are not to carry the tabernacle nor any of its things for its ministry. [27a]By the last words of David, the sons of Levi were numbered from twenty years old and upward,[a] [28a]but their position[a] should be at the side of the sons of Aaron for the ministry of Yahweh's house, over the courts and over the chambers and over the cleansing of everything that is holy, and the work[b] of the ministry of God's house, [29]as well as the showbread, the flour of the cereal offering, the wafers of unleavened bread, [a]the griddle cakes,[a] the mixed breads,[b] and indeed for [c]every kind of weight and measure.[c] [30a](They were)[a] to stand each morning to give thanks and to praise Yahweh, and likewise at evening, [31]and whenever[a] offerings were offered to Yahweh—on Sabbaths, new moons, and the appointed festivals—by number, according to their custom, continually before Yahweh. [32]They would follow the prescribed regulations[a] of the tent of meeting and the [b]holy things[b] and the directives of the sons of Aaron their relatives for the ministry of the house of Yahweh.

Notes

1.a. LXX + תחתיו "instead of him."
3.a. LXX[BA] reads the active voice.

3.b. The use of גלגלת in the sense of "head, poll" (otherwise in Chronicles only in v 24) is found, according to BDB, only in P and late (cf. Num 1:2, 18, 20, 22). The more usual meaning is "skull"; cf. 1 Chr 10:10.

4.a-a. > G.

4.b. For לנצח "be over, direct," see n. 15:21.c.

5.a-a. > Gᴮ.

5.b. The text is uncertain. Heb. עשיתי "I made," 1 pers sg; Gᴮ Vg 3 pers sg; Syr omits.

5.c. Reading τῷ κυρίῳ "to the Lord," with G.

6.a-a. MT וַיֶּחָלְקֵם "assigned them," niph; cf. 24:3. Read perhaps וַיְחַלְּקֵם, piel; cf. BDB.

8.a. Syr ויותם "and Jotham."

9.a. The text appears to be conflate and/or corrupt. Cf. v 10, which lists a second line of Shimei, and v 9b, which appears out of place. NEB omits v 9b.

9.b. K Syr α′ שלמות "Shelomoth"; Q mlt MSS G Tg Vg שלומית "Shelomith."

9.c. Gᴮ καὶ Ἰήλ "and Joel"; Gᴬᵃˡ Αζιήλ "Aziel."

9.d-d. Cf. n. 9.b.

10.a. Cf. n. 9.b.

10.b. Reading זינא "Zina," with v 11 (cf. 4:37), MS G Vg (Syr zbd' both here and v 11), Heb. זינה.

11.a. Cf. n. 10.b.

11.b. Insert אחד "one"? (Cf. Vg).

16.a. Reading שובאל "Shubael," with 24:20 for שבואל "Shebuel"; cf. G Σουβαήλ "Subael."

18.a. G Σαλωμώθ "Salomoth"; cf. n. 9.b.

19.a. Gᴮ Ἰδούδ "Idoud"; Gᴸ Ἰεδδί "Jeddi"; Syr יורה "Jurah."

19.b. Gᴮ Ὀζιήλ "Ozeel."

24.a. MT עֹשֵׂה, "who should do" many MSS pl, עֹשֵׂי.

27.a-a. V 27 is considered by most to be an explanation of v 24 in terms of v 3 and hence misplaced. See *Form/Setting/Structure* below.

28.a-a. G (Syr) ἔστησεν αὐτούς "he appointed them." For מעמד "standing," see 2 Chr 9:4.

28.b. G καὶ ἐπὶ τὰ ἔργα "and by the works."

29.a-a. Elsewhere מחבת "griddle cakes" denotes a griddle for roasting and frying (cf. Lev 2:5; 7:9; Ezek 4:3), but here the reference is to that prepared upon such a griddle.

29.b. Hoph ptcp of רבך "mix, stir," referring to stirred or mixed dough. Cf. Lev 6:14; 7:12.

29.c-c. משורה "weight" denotes a measure of liquid capacity (only here and Lev 19:35; Ezek 4:11, 16); מדה "a measure of size." The inference would seem to be that the Levites were in charge of the measuring and mixing of all the sacred elements. If reference is to the civil role of the Levites, which seems less likely, there is perhaps a note that the Levites had in their charge the official standards of weights and measures.

30.a-a. Heb. ולעמד "and to stand." The very long and syntactically indistinct sentence has been rephrased for the sake of the English.

31.a. The reference is probably not to their offering of sacrifices (cf. KJV), but to their attendance upon the priests at such sacrifices.

32.a. While משמרת "regulations" often suggests a measure of privilege and dominance, the connotation of obedience and responsibility to another is basic. In view of the Levites' subservience to the Aaronides here, a translation such as "to have or keep the charge of" would be misleading.

32.b-b. Or, "holy place," i.e., the sanctuary (cf. NEB). The two meanings are often more difficult to distinguish than many translations would suggest.

Form/Structure/Setting

Chapter 23 consists of three major units: (1) vv 1–6, a list of duties ascribed to the Levites by Davidic decree; (2) vv 7–23, three lists of Levitical heads; (3) vv 24–32, a statement of Levitical duties, again ascribed to Davidic decree.

Chapter 23 is commonly considered part of a later expansion to the original work of the Chronicler by most recent scholars. In addition, some find earlier and later strata mingled within the present chapter. Others, most recently Williamson, ascribe one or more of these strata to the Chronicler and consider the remainder later (Williamson [128] for example, considers 23:13b–14, 25–32 as later). We feel the preponderance of the evidence suggests that chaps. 23–27 as a whole form a later supplement to Chronicles, which itself exhibits earlier and later strata.

Among specific reasons which may be cited for considering chap. 23 as late and/or composite are the following. 1. V 2 appears to be a duplicate of 28:1, suggesting that the intervening chapters are a later addition. 2. Internal discrepancies. In v 3 the Levites are numbered from age thirty up; in v 24 from the age of twenty (and cf. v 27, often considered a misplaced gloss on v 24). There are two sets of sons of Shimei (vv 9, 10). 3. Discrepancies with other parts of Chronicles. For example, the Levitical genealogies of vv 7–23 differ from those in 1 Chr 6. The name Gershom/n is variously spelled throughout the work (cf. on 5:27 [6:1]); and his first son is uniformly Libni (cf. 6:2 [17]) except for here and 26:21. (See additional instances below.) 4. Despite the emphasis upon the Levites in vv 3–23, the position accorded them in vv 24–32 is that of subordination to the Aaronide priests. Moreover, the duties accorded them in vv 24–32 do not correspond to their divisions in vv 3–6. For these reasons we consider it most likely that chap. 23 is a later addition to the Chronicler's work, and is itself a composite of two or more writers. It is possible, however, that the chapter represents a selection from divergent sources by the same writer, who left discrepancies appearing in his various sources intact.

(For vv 1–2, see the *Introduction* to chaps. 23–27 and on 28:1.) V 1a is at the same time an echo of 1 Kgs 1:1. The remainder of vv 1–6 also exhibit a composite of traditions. The age at which the Levites entered service varies in the OT from thirty (as in v 3, and see Num 4:3, 23, etc.) to twenty-five (Num 8:23–26) to twenty (vv 24, 27; 2 Chr 31:17; Ezra 3:8). Although it has been common to picture a steadily decreasing age of service in view of the declining number of Levites available for service (e.g., in the post-exilic period) it is impossible to trace a single line of development in the materials available to us in this regard. All that can be said is that the number obviously fluctuated from time to time, due at least in part, we may surmise, to the law of supply and demand and probably in part to vacillating Levitical claims.

The total number of Levites over thirty found here is admittedly large by comparison with numbers found elsewhere. By comparison, the number of males over one month old at the time of Moses is given as twenty-two (or twenty-three) thousand (Num 3:39; 26:62).

The number of Levites defecting to David at Hebron is given as 4,600 (1 Chr 12:27) as 7,580 (Num 4:36, 40, 44) at the time of Moses, and the Levites returning in Ezra 2, even with the inclusion of the temple servants and sons of Solomon's servants, number only 733.

Of these 38,000 the fourfold division in v 4 is striking. The vast majority (24,000) is assigned to "direct the work of Yahweh's house." If vv 3–5 is a

unity, this number would seem to refer to supervisory work over the construction of the temple (cf. 2 Chr 34:12–13, where the term לְנַצֵּחַ "director,"
usually referring to leadership in musical activities, is also used of leadership
in construction activities [but where the Levites remain musicians]). It is possible, however, that the reference is rather to their responsibility for more
mundane facets of regular temple service. The number twenty-four thousand,
it should be noted, is identical with the number in each of the divisions
into which the king is said to have divided his administration (27:1–15) and
corresponds in a sense with the twenty-four divisions of priests (24:18), musicians (25:31), and probably the gatekeepers (cf. 26:12, 17–18).

Striking also is the allotment of six thousand as "officers and judges," a
role given the Levites clearly in 2 Chr 19:4–11; 34:13 and seemingly reflected
also in 1 Chr 26:29; 27:1 (and cf. Deut 17:8–13).

At the same time, the four thousand gatekeepers (here obviously considered
Levites) and four thousand musicians conclude the listing, numbers surprisingly small in view of the prominence accorded these groups in chaps. 15–
16.

For Gershon, Kohath, and Merari (v 6b) (probably to be joined here with
vv 7–23 rather than 3–6a) see on 5:27 [6:1]. Apart from vv 6, 7; 26:21, and
5:27 [6:1], the first name appears elsewhere in Chronicles, as in the remainder
of the OT, as Gershom, again pointing to divergent traditions or authorship.
The name of Gershom's first son elsewhere is Libni (cf. 6:2 [17], Exod 6:17;
Num 3:21), not Ladan, as only here and 26:21. Otherwise too the names
here have little in common with the genealogies of 6:5–6, 24–28 [20–21,
39–43]. See the Chart on Gershom at 6:24–28 [39–43]. This may not be
particularly significant, since both genealogies of chap. 6 are linear in form,
while the form here is segmented.

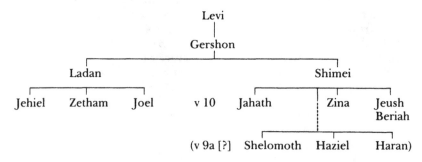

None of the names attached here to Ladan is listed in the earlier genealogies,
but Jehiel, a Gershonite of Ladan's house, named as being over the temple
treasuries, whose sons are given as Zetham and Joel (26:21–22). Shimei is
also attached to Jahath in 6:27 [42], although the order is reversed. The
remaining names attached here to Shimei do not otherwise occur in Gershonite lists.

The position of v 9b, as indicated in the *Notes*, is problematic, since it is
preceded by three sons of a Shimei whose relationship to Ladan, if assumed,
is not noted. (For proposed solutions, see Curtis, 264.) However, if v 9a is

removed as a second listing of families tracing their ancestries to Shimei (cf. NEB), the problem is resolved. The notation that the houses of Jeush and Beriah were merged (v 11) points to the role which historical circumstance played in genealogical structure.

Concerning the line of Kohath (vv 12–20), see also the chart at 5:27–41 [6:1–15]. The genealogy there is again essentially linear, concentrating upon the line of the high priest, though Kohath's four sons (Amram, Izhar, Hebron, and Uzziel) are given there, identical with those listed here. From that point, however, attention falls entirely upon the Aaronide side of Amram's family, to which the priestly genealogy is attached. In our passage, the priestly line is left aside (cf. chap. 24), and Amram's line is pursued through Moses, whose grouping with the Levitical (rather than the priestly) families is made explicit (v 14).

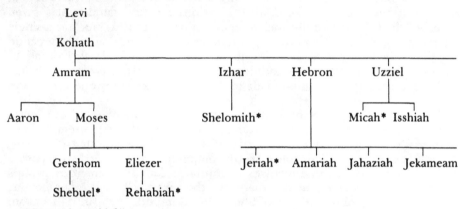

* Denoted as "chief."

Two family heads are named attaching themselves to Amram through Moses, one to Izhar, one to Jeriah with at least three additional sub-groups, and one to Uzziel with a secondary leader also named. There are therefore a total of five "chiefs" named, with four additional families or sub-families. These same nine heads are also named in 24:20–25. Shebuel is also listed as head of the treasuries in 26:24; and Rehabiah in 26:25 (and a Shelomoth apparently descended from him in vv 25–26). In the remainder of that list, Uzzielites are not mentioned, but the Izharites and Hebronites are, although apparently attached to duties in the king's service outside the temple. Only one Jerijah (יְרִיָּה, v 31) of the Hebronites is evidently to be identified with the Jeriah (see n. 19.a.) of our list.

Concerning the sons of Merari (vv 21–23) see also on 6:14–15 [29–30], 44–47 [44–47], with chart. Mahli and Mushi are everywhere uniformly the two sons of Merari (cf. 6:4 [19] 24:26; Exod 6:19; Num 3:33). Apart from Mushi's son Mahli, the other names here are found only in 24:29–30. This Mahli, grandson of Merari, is named also in 6:14, 32 [29, 47] and 24:30. A total of five families is attached to Merari, as seen in the following chart.

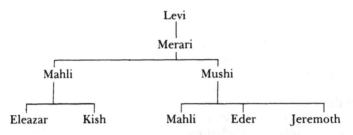

Since Merari's family contains names of only two additional generations, as is apparently also the case with Gershom, and the line of Kohath additional names of only three generations, with the exception of the two lines traced through Moses which extend to a fourth generation, it is apparent that we have here not a genealogy in the strict sense of the term but a listing of what must have been the heads of the various Levitical families at a given time, attached directly to the ancient genealogies without so much as a single intervening generation in most cases. In other words, genealogical connection is being affirmed; it is however in no case demonstrated. In this situation, 24:20–26 has appended one additional generation to the end of each list, perhaps indicating an addition made to the list approximately one generation later.

Since the total number of family heads named can be counted as twenty-three (nine each of Gershon and Kohath and five of Merari), attempts have been made to adjust the text to arrive at a total of twenty-four (see Curtis, 263, for examples). All of these are uncompelling, and indeed to secure a total of even twenty-three involves counting as families numerous groups which would appear to be designated in the text itself as sub-families, as well as including all of the sons of Shimei listed in both vv 9–10. Williamson, in addition, has argued that the twenty-four priestly courses actually developed a generation later (VTSup 30 [1979] 251–68). To attempt to find twenty-four generations would accordingly appear to be either pointless or fruitless.

Comment

1   With its "old and full of days," this verse places David with OT heroes of the faith such as Abraham (Gen 25:8), Isaac (Gen 35:29), and Job (Job 42:17) (and cf. Deut 34:7). While it seems misleading to view v 1 as a title to chaps. 23–27 in view of its relationship to 28:1 and the later development of chaps. 23–27, it is true that David's death (and Solomon's coronation) are not related until 29:22–30. Nothing of the weakness of body or spirit seen in the David of 1 Kgs 2 will be found in the narrative. The three segments of Israelite society noted as gathered by David—princes, priests, and Levites (v 2)—will in the chapters following be dealt with in reverse order, a characteristic often noted in Chronicles (cf. Curtis).

3–6a   These verses, which provide the context for the subsequent lists according to Williamson (158), give the total number of Levites above age thirty at 38,000 and attributes to David their division into four types of labor (see *Form/Structure/Setting*). Specific mention of divisions corresponding to

Levitical families (vv 6b, 7–23) would then belong to a different strata. (See further, *Form/Structure/Setting* above.)

V 24 appears to be a conflation of v 4 and v 28 (note the מלאכת בית יהוה "work of the house of Yahweh" in v 4 and the לעבדת בית יהוה "service of the house of Yahweh" of v 28) and v 27 a misplaced explanation of the "twenty years" of v 24 in terms of the thirty years of v 3. (For the concept of "rest," see on 22:9.) Note that here the rest to be enjoyed by Solomon, which will result in the construction of the temple, is already present. The usage of שכן "to dwell" is not characteristic of Chronicles, being found otherwise only in 1 Chr 17:9 (= 2 Sam 7:10) (where it is used of Israel rather than Yahweh) and in 2 Chr 6:1 (= 1 Kgs 8:12), where it more closely approximates the thought of 28:2.

26–32 The changing duties of the Levites following the erection of the temple are explained in vv 26, 28. Since they are no longer to be involved in carrying the tabernacle (note the connection between the שכן of v 25 and the משכן of v 26), they will henceforth serve "at the hand of the sons of Aaron" (v 28); i.e., as assistants to the Aaronide priests. A statement very similar in content is found in conjunction with Josiah's Passover (2 Chr 35:3), where the reason for its restatement has not been satisfactorily explained. In vv 28–32 the emphasis is not upon the prerogatives of the Levites and their ministry but rather upon their subservient role to the priests. Only in v 29 is their role as temple musicians asserted, but there too it is largely obscured by the recitation of other duties. For a similar list of duties, see 9:28–32 (also late). In Num 3:21–37 the families of Gershon and Merari are entrusted with the duties of carrying the tabernacle itself, and Kohath, more closely related to Aaron's family, with the ark, lampstands, and temple vessels directly under the supervision of Eleazar the high priest.

Some have found inconsistencies in v 32, understanding especially the reference to the Levites' responsibility for the temple or holy vessels (הקדש) to lie outside the scope of the Levites, especially in a passage emphasizing priestly prerogatives. However, in addition to the question of the translation of הקדש (see n. 32.b.), משמרת (conventionally translated "watch" or "charge") has to do not so much with privilege but with the responsibility for carrying out delegated responsibilities. In Ezek 44:8, it may be noted, the Levites are similarly delegated more menial temple service because they had not kept the "charge of my holy things" (משמרת קדשי), yet they remain "keepers of the charge of the temple, and all its service" (שמרי משמרת הבית לכל עבדתו, v 14).

Furthermore, while Num 18:1–7 restricts both use and care of parts of the temple/tabernacle to the Aaronide priests, this is expressed less rigidly in Num 3:5–9, 31, where one may perhaps speak of a delegation of responsibility of Aaronide duties to Kohathite Levites. Therefore a distinction between the Levitical charge to the tent (מועד אהל "tent appointment"; v 32) and a supposed Aaronide charge over the temple (understanding הקדש in that sense), while appearing at first suggestive in terms of Chronicles' separation of tent and altar (see on 16:37–42; 21:29; 2 Chr 1:2–6) is to be rejected; cf. NEB. It is not required by the text, is a result of a misunderstanding of vocabulary applied to the Levites, and is not suggested by the passages above, which assign groups of both priests and Levites to the care of both tent and temple site. The reference throughout these verses is instead upon the various duties which the Levites are to discharge under the general supervision of the priests.

Explanation

Under the leadership of David, thirty-eight thousand Levites are assembled and assigned to four types of labors. Their further organization arranges them in family groups which traced their ancestry to the traditional Levitical groups of Gershom, Kohath, and Merari.

With the building of the temple, Levitical responsibility for care of the tabernacle is terminated, and the Levites are assigned numerous duties in the temple under the supervision of the Aaronide priesthood (vv 24–32). The unique privileges of Aaron and his sons over against even Moses is made even more explicit in vv 13–14. These later two sections probably reflect the views of a later reviser of the text.

While the details of this and subsequent chapters may appear to us to be quite irrelevant and even trivial, they would have been of great importance to the writer and to at least part of the post-exilic audience. The details of God's relationship with his people are always significant. We who argue today about such issues as the ordination of women and orders within the church should recognize the need for other ages and people also to secure and maintain a clear understanding of God's will in present circumstances. Faithfulness in any age demands no less.

Divisions of the Priests   (24:1-31)

Bibliography

See at 5:27.

Translation

¹ *The divisions of the sons of Aaron: Aaron's sons were Nadab and Abihu,* a *Eleazar and Ithamar.* ² *Nadab and Abihu died before their father and had no sons, so Eleazar and Ithamar were the priests.* ³ *David apportioned them* a *(i.e., Zadok of the sons of Eleazar and Ahimelech of the sons of Ithamar) to their office for their work.* ⁴ *Since the sons of Eleazar were found* a *to be more numerous in chief men than the sons of Ithamar, the sons of Eleazar were divided into sixteen fathers' houses, and the sons of Ithamar into eight fathers' houses.* ⁵ *They apportioned them both* a *by lots, because whether of the sons of Eleazar or of* b *the sons of Ithamar, they were all holy princes, and* c*princes of God.* c ⁶ *Shemaiah, the son of Nethanel, the scribe, of Levi,* a *wrote them down before the king, the princes, Zadok the priest, Ahimelech the son of Abiathar, and the heads of the fathers of the priests and the Levites.* a *One father's house* b *was taken for Eleazar and one* c *was taken for Ithamar.*

⁷ *The first lot came out for Jehoiarib, the second for Jedaiah,* ⁸ *the third for Harim, the fourth for Seorim,* ⁹ *the fifth for Malchijah, the sixth for Mijamim,* ᵃ ¹⁰ *the seventh for Hakkoz, the eighth for Abijah,* ¹¹ *the ninth for Jeshua, the tenth for Shecaniah,* ¹² *the eleventh for Eliashib, the twelfth for Jakim,* ᵃ ¹³ *the thirteenth for Huppah, the fourteenth for Jeshebeab,* ᵃ ¹⁴ *the fifteenth to Bilgah, the sixteenth to Immer,* ¹⁵ *the seventeenth to Hezir,* ᵃ *the eighteenth to Happizzez,* ¹⁶ *the nineteenth to Pethahiah, the twentieth to Jehezkel,* ¹⁷ *the twenty-first to Jachin, the twenty-second to Gamul,* ¹⁸ *the twenty-third to Delaiah, the twenty-fourth to Maaziah.* ¹⁹ *Of these the duty of their ministry was to enter Yahweh's house according to the rubrics established by Aaron their father, as Yahweh the God of Israel had commanded him.*

²⁰ *For the remaining sons of Levi: for the sons of Amram, Shubael; for the sons of Shubael, Jehdeiah.* ²¹ *For Rehabiah: for the sons of Rehabiah, Isshiah the chief.* ²² *For the Izharites: Shelomoth; for the sons of Shelomoth, Jahath.* ²³ ᵃ *The sons of Hebron:* ᵃ *Jeriah the chief,* ᵇ *Amariah the second, Jahaziel the third, Jekameam the fourth.* ²⁴ *For the sons of Uzziel: Micah; for the sons of Micah, Shamir.* ᵃ ²⁵ *The brother of Micah, Isshiah; for the sons of Isshiah, Zechariah.* ²⁶ *The sons of Merari: Mahli and Mushi,* ᵃ *and sons of* ᵃ *Jaaziah* ᵇ ᶜ *his son.* ᶜ ²⁷ *The sons of Merari by Jaaziah, his son:* ᵃ ᵇ *Shoham, Zaccur, and Ibri.* ²⁸ *Of Mahli: Eleazar,* ᵃ *who had* ᵇ *no sons.* ²⁹ *Of* ᵃ *Kish: The sons* ᵇ *of Kish, Jerahmeel.* ³⁰ *The sons of Mushi: Mahli, Eder, Jerimoth. These were the sons of the Levites, according to their fathers' house.* ³¹ *They also cast lots alongside of their relatives, the sons of Aaron, before David the king and Zadok and Ahimelech and the heads of the fathers of the priests and Levites, the chief of the fathers alongside of his youngest brother.*

Notes

1.a. G καὶ Ἀβιούδ "and Abiud," as in 5:29.
3.a. See 23:6. Read perhaps hiph, as in vv 4, 5.
4.a. Note this usage of מצא "were found," niph; completely parallel to the similar English expression.
5.a. Heb. אלה עם אלה "these with these."
5.b. Many MSS ומבני "and from the sons of."
5.c-c. Or, "mighty princes," understanding האלהים as superlative in import.
6.a-a. A few MSS הלוים "(of the) Levites."
6.b. A few MSS G Syr Vg אחד "one (each)."
6.c. Read with a few MSS G Syr Vg ואחד "and one."
9.a. G τῷ Βενιαμιν "for Benjamin."
12.a. Gᴬᵃˡᵃˡᵃˡᵃˡᵃˡᵃˡᵃˡᵃˡ τῷ Ἐλιακιμ "for Eliakim."
13.a. Gᴮ, Gᴬᵃˡ.
15.a. Gᴮ τῷ Χηξεω "for Hazein"; Gᴬᵃˡ τῷ Ιεξ(ε)ιρ "for Jazir"; Syr (α') ᵓḥzjᵓ = לאחזיה "for Ahaziah."
23.a-a. 2 MSSᵐᵍ ובני חברון "and the sons of Hebron," which read (cf. 23:19). G καὶ (> B) υἱοί "and sons"; Gᴸ τοῖς υἱοῖς Χεβρων "the sons of Hebron."
23.b. Cf. 23:19.
24.a. K שמור "Shamur"; Q most MSS Vrs שמיר "Shamir."
26.a-a. Reading ובני "and sons of," with Vrs, NEB. Vv 26–27 are so problematic, both in text and content, that certainty is impossible. BHS suggests בבניו "with his sons"; BH³ וגם "and moreover." The confusion is heightened by the fact that בנו may be understood as a proper name.
26.b. G Ὀξια "Ozia."
26.c-c. > Gᴮ, Gʳᵉˡ υἱοί Βοννι "sons of Bonni"; Vg Βεννο. Cf. v 27.
27.a. G pl. For vv 26–27, see *Form/Setting/Structure* below.
27.b. G lacks "and."
28.a. G + καὶ Ἰθαμαρ· καὶ ἀπέθανεν Ἐλεαξαρ "and Ithamar; and Eleazar died."

28.b. Many MSS היו, pl of "to be."
29.a. *BHS* suggests וקיש "and Kish."
29.b. A few MSS Vg בן "son," sg.

Form/Structure/Setting

Chapter 24 is composed of two major units: (1) vv 1–19, listing twenty-four priestly courses; and (2) vv 20–31, a list of additional Levitical personnel.

The genealogical material concerning Aaron's sons in vv 1–2 is that of Num 3:2–4, although here the more unseemly details surrounding the deaths of Nadab and Abihu are omitted, probably out of deference to the priesthood. Regarding Zadok's place in the priestly genealogy, see on 5:27–41 [6:1–15], where Zadok is similarly incorporated into the line of Eleazar.

The inclusion of Ahimelech as Zadok's associate in Ithamar's line is suspect on two accounts. First, while there is frequent confusion concerning the relationship of Abiathar and Ahimelech, the evidence is quite conclusive that Ahimelech was Abiathar's father rather than the reverse, as indicated here. (See on 18:16, and cf. 1 Sam 22:20; 23:6.) It was this Abiathar who was active in the reign of David (cf. 1 Chr 15:11) and whom Solomon removed from the priesthood (1 Kgs 2:27) and replaced with Zadok (1 Kgs 2:35). Whether Ahimelech stands here as a simple error in textual transmission or represents a judgment of the writer upon Abiathar's unfaithfulness in supporting Solomon's rival Adonijah cannot be said with certainty. But that Ahimelech/Abiathar is said in vv 3, 8 to be descended from Ithamar, while earlier tradition connects the two names rather with the same Ahitub through whom Zadok's linkage with Eleazar is established, surely represents an attempt to subordinate his line to that of Zadok. (Rudolph, incidentally, believes Ezra 8:2 is the first statement of priestly privilege linked with Ithamar.)

(On the development of the twenty-four priestly classes, see Williamson VTSup 30 [1979] 251–68; and Rudolph, 163.) While there is agreement that the arrival at twenty-four courses marks the termination of the development of the priesthood in the OT, there is no agreement concerning the date at which this final step occurred. Williamson, for example, arrives at a date about a generation following the work of the Chronicler, whom he places at *ca.* 350 B.C. Rudolph, on the other hand, opts for a time approaching the era of the Maccabees due to the naming of Jehoiarib as the first of the twenty-four courses in 1 Chr 24:7 (cf. 1 Macc 2:1). Such a late dating seems unlikely, however, in view of the fact that a fragment of Chronicles has been discovered at Qumran (Myers), and is at any rate certainly not required by the text. Similar lists include Neh 12:12–21, which according to Rudolph's analysis consists of seventeen courses with six additional added in a supplement and dates from about 460 B.C., and Neh 10:3–9, listing twenty-one courses and dated by Rudolph about 430 B.C. It would thus seem probable that the number reached twenty-four not far after the time of Ezra, although the evidence indicates that the specific names of those courses continued to vacillate. The New Testament priest Zechariah is assigned to the course of Abijah (Luke 1:5), and this same pattern of twenty-four courses is still evidenced at the time of Josephus.

The list of Levites in vv 20–31 is marked as a supplement to 23:6–23 both by its heading ("The *remaining* sons of Levi," v 20) and by its content. The principal differences lie in the omission of all reference to Gershom and his sons (cf. 23:7–11), and in the extension of six of the Levitical families beyond the representatives named in chap. 23 by a single generation. The line of Moses through Gershom is extended beyond Shebuel to Jehdaiah and through Eliezer beyond Rehabiah to Isshiah, the line of Izhar adds Jahath, Uzziel's two families add Shamir and Zechariah, and Kish adds Jerahmeel. Within the family of Merari (vv 26b–27a) and before the place occupied by Eleazar in 23:22, is now found Jaaziah and his sons (Beno?) Shoham, Zaccur, and Ibri. Textual difficulties do not warrant speculation, but it appears that a new son has been added to Mahli, or that a name has been given to the family of Eleazar, who himself had no sons but whose line was continued through Kish (cf. 23:22). While no reason for the omission of Gershom's line is apparent, the other variations suggest the work of an author who wished to bring the Levitical lines into harmony with developments at a later date, probably a generation later than the same list in chap. 23 (Williamson).

Comment

1–6 Vv 1–2 point to the fact that, despite Aaron's four sons, only two priestly lines were to be counted. In the process of apportionment by lot which follows, in contrast with chap. 23, where the process seems to have been by royal decree (cf. Williamson), the line of Eleazar is represented by Zadok, the line of Ithamar by Ahimelech (v 6). Although those priestly families tracing their lineage to Eleazar are said to be more numerous than those claiming descent from Ithamar, resulting in a total of sixteen divisions for the former and only eight for the latter, the genealogical ties of the twenty-four courses which follow (vv 7–19) are not indicated. The development of these twenty-four priestly courses enumerated here seem to have marked the final development of OT priestly arrangements, a division which persisted also into NT times (see *Form/Structure/Setting*). That the house of Eleazar was preeminent we may deduce both from the attachment of Zadok to it and to its superiority in numbers. At the same time, however, v 5 appears to ascribe theoretical equality to both families. All are "holy princes, princes of God," designations probably not meant to indicate specific priestly offices but rather to point to their general acceptability for the priesthood.

The casting of lots itself is described as having taken place before the king, Zadok, Ahimelech, and the heads of both lay and clergy families (v 6), and its results were written down by an otherwise unknown Levite, Shemaiah. Problems of both text and understanding of grammar make it unwise to speculate on the order used in casting the lots.

7–19 Of the priestly families given in vv 7–18, the names Seorim, Huppah, Jeshebeab, Happizzez, Gamul, and Delaiah do not occur elsewhere, while Jakim and Pethahiah occur only here as names of priests. We have already noted that Jehoiarib's family is that to which the Maccabees were attached (1 Macc 2:1). This same Jehoiarib, together with Jehaiah and Jachin, are also named with those returning to Palestine in 1 Chr 9:10. Jehoiarib, Jedaiah, Harim, Malchijah, Mijamin, Abijah, Shecaniah, Bilga, and Maaziah occur in one or both lists of priests in Neh 10:3–9 [2–8] and 12:1–7. Descendants of

Jedaiah, Harim, and Immer also returned from the exile under Zerubbabel (Ezra 2:36–39 = Neh 7:39–42). That same list notes that the children of Hakkoz were debarred from the priesthood after the return because they could not find their record in the genealogies. Their inclusion here, which should probably be dated subsequent to that time, suggests they were later successful in having their claims recognized. Certainty concerning Jeshua and Eliashib is impossible due to the high frequency of those names (cf. Ezra 2:36 = Neh 7:39; Neh 3:1). Jehezkel is also the name of the well-known priest and prophet, son of Buzi (Ezek 1:3; 24:24).

The purpose of v 19 is to establish the activities of the priests as prescribed not merely by David, but by "Aaron their father" and ultimately by Yahweh himself.

20–30 For these verses, see on 23:7–23. Of the additional names, Jahath occurs also in 4:2; Shamir as a place name in Judg 10:1–2; Josh 15:48. Zechariah is very common. The difficulties attending vv 26–27 have been pointed out in the notes. By position alone, Jaaziah must be either an otherwise unknown son of Merari or the name of a family tracing its ancestry to him. While most commentators consider the former to be at best unlikely (cf. Curtis), that possibility would certainly not seem to lie outside the realm of the possible in view of the use to which genealogical innovation is used elsewhere in Chronicles (cf. e.g., the relationship between Ahimelech, Abiathar, and Ithamar in vv 4–6). Certainty is, however, impossible. Of Jaaziah's three (or four) sons, the name Shoham occurs nowhere else and Ibri only as the gentilic of Hebrew, Zaccur (and, if to be understood as a proper name, Bani), are common post-exilic names (cf. T. Mauch, "Zaccur," *IDB* 4:1927–28; F. Schumacher, "Bani," *IDB* 1:346), though it is impossible to identify any of the others bearing these names with individuals referred to here.

V 30b is an evidence of the copying of this section from chap. 23, cf. vv 23–24, and is less appropriate here. Of those mentioned in v 6 at Shemaiah's writing, only the princes (והשרים) are not renamed in v 30, resulting in a ceremony even more narrowly religious for the lot casting of the Levites. Although the comparison here with the priests would imply that twenty-four courses of Levites were ordered, it is impossible to derive that number either in chap. 23 or here. The phraseology of v 31 ("the head of each father's house and his younger brother alike") is similar to that of 25:8; 26:12–13, "at the side of" or "corresponding to," (this relatively rare preposition עמה occurs only in Chronicles in these passages and 26:16, and see Neh 12:24). All such passages, according to Williamson's analysis, belong to the later strand of chaps. 23–27.

Explanation

Vv 1–19 recount the organization of the Aaronide priests, corresponding formally to the organization of the Levites in 23:7–23. Unlike the latter, however, there are no groupings by family expressed beyond Zadok and Ahimelech, who are related to Eleazar and Ithamar respectively; the Aaronides are divided into twenty-four expressed courses, and the division here, unlike that of chap. 23, takes place by David through lots and with the participation of Zadok and Abiathar (v 3). David's initiative appears to be further curtailed in that the duties of the Aaronides are those given them by God through Aaron (v 30). In chap. 23, David appears to function alone, and the use of lots is at least not indicated.

Vv 20–30 update the list of Levitical families by extending five of the families named in 23:7–23 by an additional name, and by adding an otherwise unknown branch of Merari's family, Jaaziah, and three (or four) sons of his. The closing verse indicates that the Levites too were assigned their positions by lots in the presence of both David and a larger assembly of priestly and Levitical heads.

The Musicians (25:1–31)

Bibliography

(See the *Bibliography* on Priests and Levites at 5:27–41.)

Albright, W. F. "A Catalogue of Early Hebrew Lyric Poems." (Psalm LXVIII) *HUCA* 23 (1950–51) 1–39. **Böhmer, J.** "Sind einige Personennamen in 1 Chr 25:4 'kunstlich geschaffen'?" *BZ* 22 (1934) 93–100. **Haupt, P.** "Die Psalmverse I Chr 25:4." *ZAW* 34 (1914) 142–45. **Johnson, A. R.** *The Cultic Prophet in Ancient Israel.* Cardiff: University of Wales, 1962. **Pedersen, D. L.** "Chronicles and Levitical Prophets." In *Late Israelite Prophecy; Studies in Deutero-Prophetic Literature and in Chronicles.* SBLMS 23. Missoula, MT: Scholars Press, 1977. 55–96. **Rad, G. von.** *Das Geschichtsbild des chronistischen Werkes.* Stuttgart: Kohlhammer, 1930. 81–118. **Torczyner, H.** "A Psalm by the Sons of Heman." *JBL* 68 (1949) 247–49. **Welch, A.** *Post-Exilic Judaism.* London: W. Blackwood and Sons, 1935. 172–84, 217–41. ———. *The Work of the Chronicler, Its Purpose and Date.* London: Oxford University Press, 1939. 42–96. **Williamson, H. G. M.** "The Origins of the Twenty-Four Priestly Courses." VTSup 30. Leiden: E. J. Brill, 1979. 251–68.

Translation

[1] *David and the* [a]*chief ministrants* [a] *also set apart for ministry the sons* [b] *of Asaph, Heman, and Jeduthun,* [c] *who would prophesy* [d] *with lyres, harps, and cymbals. Their roster* [e] *of workmen for their ministry:* [2] *Of the sons of Asaph: Zaccur, Joseph, Nethaniah, and Asharelah,* [a] *Asaph's sons, at the side of Asaph, who prophesied* [b] [c]*at the side* [c] *of the king.*

[3] *Of Jehuthun: The sons of Jeduthun, Gedaliah, Zeri,* [a] *Jeshaiah, Shimei,* [b] *Hashabiah, and Mattithiah, six,* [c]*at the side of* [c] *their father Jeduthun,* [d]*who prophesied with the lyre* [d] *to* [e] *thank and praise Yahweh.*

[4] *Of Heman: The sons of Heman, Bukkiah, Mattaniah, Uzziel,* [a] *Shebuel,* [b] *Jerimoth,* [c] *Hananiah,* [d]*Hanani, Eliathah,* [e] *Giddalti, Romamti-ezer, Joshbekashah, Mallothi, Hothir, and Mahazioth.* [5] *All these were the sons of Heman, the king's seer by the words of God, to raise up a horn. God gave Heman fourteen sons and three daughters.* [6] *All these were* [a]*at the side of* [a] *their father with music at the house of Yahweh with cymbals, harps, and lyres* [b]*for the service of the house of God,* [b] *and* [c]*Asaph, Jeduthun, and Heman were at the king's side.* [c] [7] *Their number, with their*

brothers, trained in singing to Yahweh, every one who was skilled, was two hundred and eighty-eight.

⁸ᵃ *They cast lots* ᵇ *for their duties,* ᶜ *both small and great, the teacher with the student.* ⁹ *The first lot for Asaph* ᵃ *went out for Joseph,* ᵇ *Gedaliah the second,* ᶜ *he, his brothers, and his sons, twelve.*

¹⁰ *The third Zaccur, his sons and his brothers, twelve;*

¹¹ *the fourth for Izri,* ᵃ *his sons and his brothers, twelve;*

¹² *the fifth, Nethaniah, his sons and his brothers, twelve,*

¹³ *the sixth, Bukkiah, his sons and his brothers, twelve;*

¹⁴ *the seventh, Jesharelah,* ᵃ *his sons and his brothers, twelve;*

¹⁵ *the eighth, Jeshaiah, his sons and his brothers, twelve;*

¹⁶ *the ninth, Mattaniah, his sons and his brothers, twelve;*

¹⁷ *the tenth, Shimei,* ᵃ *his sons and his brothers, twelve;*

¹⁸ *eleventh, Azarel,* ᵃ *his sons and his brothers, twelve;*

¹⁹ *the twelfth, for Hashabiah, his sons and his brothers, twelve;*

²⁰ *thirteenth, Shubael, his sons and his brothers, twelve;*

²¹ *fourteenth, Mattithiah, his sons and his brothers, twelve;*

²² *fifteenth, for Jeremoth,* ᵃ *his sons and his brothers, twelve;*

²³ *sixteenth for Hananiah, his sons and his brothers, twelve;*

²⁴ *seventeenth, for Joshbekashah,* ᵃ *his sons and his daughters, twelve;*

²⁵ *eighteenth, for Hanani, his sons and his brothers, twelve;*

²⁶ *nineteenth, for Mallothi, his sons and his brothers, twelve;*

²⁷ *twentieth, for Eliathah,* ᵃ *his sons and his brothers, twelve;*

²⁸ *twenty-first, for Hothir,* ᵃ *his sons and his brothers, twelve;*

²⁹ *twenty-second, for Giddalti, his sons and his brothers, twelve;*

³⁰ *twenty-third, for Mahazioth, his sons and his brothers, twelve;*

³¹ *twenty-fourth, for Romamtiezer, his sons and brothers, twelve.*

Notes

1.a-a. Cf. Curtis, 279.

1.b. The *lamedh* is the sign of the accus, after the Aramaic manner.

1.c. G (Vg) καὶ Ἰδιθων "and Jedethon" (cf. 3:6).

1.d. Reading with Q, many MSS, G Vg Tg הַנִּבָּאִים; K הַנְּבִיאִים "the prophets" (see n. 2.b.).

1.e. G + κατα κεφαλὴν αὐτῶν "according to their polls" (Gᴸ ανδρῶν "of men").

2.a. A few MSS וְאָשׁ "and *Ash* . . ."; Rudolph (*BHS*) וְאַשְׂרְאֵל אַרְבָּעָה אֵלֶּה "and Asarel, these four" (cf. vv 3, 5). Pedersen, *Late Israelite Prophecy*, 91, n. 65.

2.b. A few MSS LXX הנביא "the prophet"; cf. n. 1.d.

2.c-c. Or, "at the direction of"; cf. vv 3, 6.

3.a. V 11 (לְ)יצרי "(to) Izri." Cf. Pedersen, *Late Israelite Prophecy*, 91, n. 65.

3.b. Inserting ושמעי "and Shimei," with v 17, as required by the number "six."

3.c-c. Or, "at the direction of"; cf. v 6.

3.d- d. The word order should perhaps be reversed.

3.e. The עַל "to" appears to be used here almost as a substitute for the *lamedh* regularly attached to the infinitive of purpose. To my knowledge, this construction does not occur otherwise.

4.a. Gᴮ Ἀζαράηλ "Azarael"; cf. v 18 עזראל "Azarel."

4.b. V 20 and 24:20 G שובאל "Shubael."

4.c. V 22 ירמות "Jeremoth."

4.d. Syr omits from the following word to the end of v 6.

4.e. V 27 אליתה "Eliathah."

6.a-a. Or, "under the direction of"; cf. vv 3, 6.

6.b-b. > LXX.

6.c-c. The phraseology is complex and suggests editorial work. Rudolph considers "Asaph, Jeduthun, and Heman" a misplaced gl to "all these" at the beginning of the verse, but to understand these musicians to be "at the side of their father (who was) at the side of the king" seems unwieldy and unlikely. No satisfactory solution is apparent. JB attaches Asaph, Heman, and Jeduthun to v 7, which seems equally unlikely.

8.a. LXX + καὶ αὐτοί "and they."

8.b. Repoint perhaps וְגֹרָלוֹת "lots"; cf. LXX.

8.c. A few MSS Tg + משמרת "duties."

9.a. Added?

9.b. Insert בניו ואחיו שנים עשר "his sons and his brothers, twelve," as elsewhere in vv 9b–31.

9.c. LXX + Ηυια "Enia," perhaps a double reading of השני "the second."

11.a. V 3 וצרי(ו), "and Zeri."

14.a. Cf. n. 2.a.

17.a. 2 MSS Vg שמעיה "Shemiah"; cf. n. 3.b.

18.a. LXX^L Οξιηλ "Ozial"; Syr עָזִיאֵל "Uzziel"; cf. n. 4.a.

22.a. V 4 יְרִי "Jerimoth"; see n. 4.c.

24.a. Syr אלישב "Elishab."

27.a. V 4 אליאתה "Eliathah"; see n. 4.e.

28.a. Syr יתר "Jothar"; but cf. v 4.

Form/Structure/Setting

Chap. 25 speaks of the temple musicians, who in vv 8–31 are arranged in twenty-four courses, as the priests have been in chap. 24. In its present form the chapter shows two major sections: (1) vv 1–7, a listing of sons of Asaph, Heman, and Jeduthun, interlaced with assigned duties and other laudatory comments; and (2) vv 8–31, a list of the assignment of twenty-four lots. While the names in vv 1–7 are in most cases easily identifiable with those in vv 8–31, there are sufficient differences to suggest the composite nature of the chapter (see *Notes*).

Pedersen (*Late Israelite Prophecy*, 67) has concluded that, while vv 1–7 are primary, the form of the names in vv 8–31 is actually based on an earlier source. That vv 8–31 are secondary appears clear in the manner in which the names given in vv 8–31 relate to those in vv 1–7. The list has been analyzed by Rothstein, as seen in the following chart.

Asaph	*Jeduthun*		*Heman*
1. Joseph	2. Gedaliah		———
3. Zaccur	4. Izri		———
5. Nethaniah	———		6. Bukkiah
7. Jesharelah	8. Jeshaiah		9. Mattaniah
	10. Shimei		11. Azarel
	12. Hashabiah		13. Shubael
	14. Mattithiah		15. Jeremoth
		16. Hanahiah	17. Joshbekashah
		18. Hanani	19. Mallothi
		20. Eliathah	21. Hothir
		22. Giddalti	23. Mahazioth
		24. Romamti-ezer	

As noted by Williamson, it is difficult to believe that a pattern of such regular alternation, and one which results in the retention of all of the names of v 4b at the end of the list, can be independent of the order of the names in vv 1–6. At the same time this suggests that some of those same names may have been seen to be required and added by the author of vv 8–31.

We have also noted before that the use of lots, such as found in 24:7–19, is a characteristic trait of the latest strata of these chapters (cf. Williamson, VTSup 30 [1979] 251–68).

At the same time, vv 1–7 also show traits of composite authorship. (1) The order of the Levitical divisions in v 1 is Asaph, Heman, and Jeduthun; in v 6 and in the listing of vv 2–5 it is Asaph-Jeduthun-Heman. (2) The form of the names of Heman's last nine sons (from Hananiah on) differs considerably from that of his first five sons (see below). (3) The total number of musicians given in v 7 (i.e., 288 = 24 × 12) presupposes both the twenty-four sons named and/or numbered in vv 2–6 and the twelve members of each course described in vv 9–31.

Additional minor variations are noted by Pedersen, who concludes that vv 1–7 exhibit three strata. The first variation was probably concerned only with Asaph, the separation of his sons by David, and the listing of his sons (vv 1–2). (This would account for the numeral attached to Heman and Jeduthun, but omitted from Asaph.) The second stage involved the threefold singer schema, and would have included most of vv 1–4, 6–7. The third and final stage included additional sons of Heman (v 4b), the understanding of the singers as prophets, the division into twenty-four courses, and other minor adjustments to the earlier text. (Pedersen, *Late Israelite Prophecy*, 66–68). With some reservations (e.g., at least portions of the threefold scheme may be original, as may be the designation of at least Asaph as a prophet), this analysis seems credible.

The understanding of chap. 25 is beset with other questions related to some of the most difficult problems in OT tradition studies.

1) The Levitical divisions here are Asaph, Heman, and Jeduthun, reflecting stage III.A of Gese's synthesis (see p. xxxi). While Asaph retains pride of place in order and perhaps other respects as well (cf. the phraseology of v 2b), Heman would appear to be clearly in the ascendancy as indicated by the fourteen courses allotted to him. This would point to a period near the end of period III.A., since Jeduthun has not yet been replaced with Ethan.

2) It has for many years been noted that the form of the names of the last nine of Heman's sons differs from the first five and from the form in which one might expect to find Hebrew names. Forms such as גִדַּלְתִּי and רֹמַמְתִּי ("I have made great" and "I have exalted"), e.g., are verb forms of the first common singular perfect. Essentially three explanations of the origin of the names or their use in this place have been given. (a) The words now read as names originally formed part of a psalm verse, used in the manner of 16:8–36 as an example of the activity of the singers. While varying somewhat in form, the reconstruction of Rudolph is characteristic:

V 4b	*Rudolph*
חֲנַנְיָה חֲנָנִי	חָנֵּנִי יה חָנֵּנִי
אֱלִיאָתָה	אֵלִי אַתָּה
גְּדַלְתִּי וְרֹמַמְתִּי עֶזֶר	גִּדַּלְתִּי וְרֹמַמְתִּי עֹזֶר
יָשְׁבְּקָשָׁה מַלּוֹתִי	יֹשֵׁב קָשָׁה מַלּוֹתִי
הוֹתִיר מַחֲזִיאֹת	הוֹתִיר(ה) מַחֲזִיאֹות

Be gracious to me, O Yahweh, be gracious to me;
You are my God.
I exalt (you), I praise (my) Helper.
Sitting in adversity I said, [or, Fulfill my request]
Clear signs give plentifully.

(For other recent comments and reconstructions, see Myers, 172–73; Pedersen, *Late Israelite Prophecy*, 65 and notes.) While many scholars support minor alterations in the above (see the *Bibliography*), Torczyner, for example, arguing for a reconstruction based upon the order in which the names occur in vv 23–31, the above represents a reasonable consensus.

(b) The words did not compose a single psalm verse, but represent rather a series of *incipits*, or beginnings, of various psalms, and so present a kind of directory of psalms. (Cf. Myers, 173, with a bibliography of relevant studies.) This view suffers from the fact that no satisfactory psalms are apparent in our psalter for the last two groups of names.

(c) Related to (b), it has been suggested that individuals or groups of singers may actually have taken their names from psalms which were especially sung by them (Rudolph). Pedersen (*Late Israelite Prophecy*, 65–66) finds unconvincing the Sumerian parallels that are quoted.

There is little doubt, however, that whatever their origin, the words cited above are used in v 4 as proper names and as necessary to complete the full complement of fourteen sons of Heman as given in v 5. Whether the alteration involved (if any) reflected a mere misreading of the text or represents an intentional adaptation of another sort cannot be said with certainty.

3) The Levites, or at least their leaders, are here referred to with prophetic terminology. (Cf., e.g., נבא "to prophesy" [vv 1, 2, 3] and חזה "to see" [v 5].) Such a development is in agreement with 2 Chr 20:14; 29:25; 35:15, where Levitical singers are similarly referred to with prophetic terminology or speak words of prophecy. See also 1 Chr 15:22, 28, where we have noted that משא "music" or "prophetic oracle" (cf. n. 15:22.b-b.) may refer to prophetic activity, and 2 Chr 34:30, where "the priests and the prophets" of 2 Kgs 23:2 is altered to "the priests and the Levites." While there has been some attempt to understand this development as flowing from either cultic prophecy (Rudolph, 171; Johnson, *The Cultic Prophet*, especially 69–74; Williamson, 166) or classical prophecy (Pedersen, *Late Israelite Prophecy*, 85, 87), it is questionable whether such a distinction would have been germane to the writer. Rather we are to understand that for the writer the instructive and hortatory words of religious personnel such as Levites and priests (2 Chr 24:20) have become at least one way in which God reveals his will to

his people, much as, for example, some measure of divine authority is some-times attributed to Christian preachers today. That temple personnel, and especially the singers, should have aspired to such a claim is certainly not unexpected in view of their efforts not only to be considered Levites, but apparently as pre-eminent among the Levites (cf. chaps. 15–16).

Comment

1–7 David, assisted by the leaders of the Levites (n. 1.a-a.), sets apart three groups of Levitical musicians. Asaph, Heman, and Jeduthun (v 1) are also listed in v 6 in the order Asaph-Jeduthun-Heman, the same order in which their families are listed in vv 2–5. (On the three families of Levitical singers, see p. xxxi and 1 Chr 6; 15:16–24; 16:4–7, 41–42.) The lyres, harps, and cymbals are found in the reverse order in v 6, cf. also 1 Chr 13:8; 15:16, 28; 16:5–6. Note that in this verse the prophesying is explicitly connected with the musical instruments, as with Jeduthun in v 3, but perhaps not with Asaph in v 2 or Heman in v 5. Of the four sons of Asaph (v 2), only Zaccur is mentioned elsewhere (Neh 12:35). Of the six sons of Jeduthun (adding Shimei with v 17, cf. n. 3.b.), only Mattithiah is mentioned in another place; cf. 1 Chr 15:18, 21; 16:5; but there he is not called a son of Jeduthun (Curtis). The remaining names of the sons of Jeduthun and Heman are common in post-exilic writings but cannot be identified with other personages, see Curtis, 277–78. "List" or "roster" is, as noted by Williamson, a legitimate translation of מספר (vv 1, 7), and hence is not in itself a sign of composite authorship. The terminology שר הצבא "chief of the ministers" (v 1) and עבדה "ministry" (v 1), is reflective of P (cf. Num 4:3, 23; 8:24, 25, etc.; also Curtis). While Jeduthun is apparently specifically attached to the lyre (v 3), association with a specific instrument is otherwise lacking (cf. 15:19–21).

All of the designations of v 5 emphasize the position of Heman. He is the king's seer (חזה), as is Gad in 21:9. (Cf. Williamson, who notes that Asaph in 2 Chr 29:30 is also named a "seer," as is Jeduthun in 35:15.) That no specific "words of God" are known pronouncing Heman the king's seer does not detract from what is here stated about him, but may rather enhance it (cf. Pedersen, *Late Israelite Prophecy*, 90, n. 43). The suggested translation of Rothstein and Curtis, "in religious matters," appears too weak despite the supposed parallel in 26:32. See also Rudolph, who seeks (unsuccessfully) to join the phrase with the following, "to raise up a horn," rather than "seer of the king." Heman's fourteen sons and three daughters are probably a specific example of God's blessing to exalt Heman, literally "to raise up (his) horn" (1 Sam 2:10; Ps 89:18; Ps 148:14, etc.). The "all these" of v 6 could refer to the sons of all the Levitical families, but the position of the phrase, together with the singular "their father," attaches it most directly to Heman. As indicated in the notes, it is difficult to determine here (and throughout the pericope) whether the phrase על ידי "at the hand of" is to be understood of mere proximity or rather of responsibility to, i.e., "at the direction of." However, since the general thrust of the unit is to magnify the position of the Levitical singers, and particularly their leaders, the former choice seems preferable. The number of singers, two-hundred and eighty-eight, represents the twenty-four courses of twelve each.

8–31 These verses present in detail the casting of the lots. The terminology of v 8 is similar to that of 24:31 and 26:13 in pointing out that the procedure covered everyone. Included in the phrase "the teacher with the student" is the fact that some sort of instructional program for the singers was apparently active, though we have no knowledge of that program. On the order of the lots, see *Form/Structure/Setting* above. The phraseology of vv 9–31 is similar, if the text is correct, save that in v 9 the family of Asaph is named. Asaph thus seems formally to have retained pride of place at this time, although outnumbered both by the sons of Jeduthun and especially the sons of Heman.

Explanation

The three families of Levitical singers are set apart for service. This work in v 1 is ascribed to David and the heads of the Levitical families, and takes place according to v 8 by the casting of lots. The three family heads are Asaph with four sons, Jeduthun with six, and Heman with fourteen. That the family of Asaph continues to be accorded pre-eminence among the families of singers is apparent in that he is regularly listed first; that Heman is in the ascendancy seems equally apparent. The work of the singers is classified as prophesying with lyres, harps and cymbals (v 1), indicating the desire of the writer to understand their work as placing them in a special relationship with God.

Once again, though we may find little of relevance in this material, it was obviously of significance in the arrangement of the worship of the post-exilic congregation. While the intent may seem restrictive, it is interesting to note the large number of people and groups associated directly with Israel's worship. As such, we may view it from another perspective as preparatory for the time when all of God's people are priests (cf. Exod 19:5–6; 1 Pet 2: 9–10).

Doorkeepers and Other Levites   (26:1–32)

Bibliography

(See also the *Bibliography* on Priests and Levites at 5:27–41.)

Albright, W. F. "The Judicial Reform of Jehoshaphat." In *Alexander Marx Jubilee Volume on the Occasion of his Seventieth Birthday*, ed. S. Lieberman. New York: Jewish Theological Seminary, 1950. 61–82. (Eng. sec.) **Mazar, B.** "The Cities of the Priests and the Levites." VTSup 7. Leiden: E. J. Brill, 1959. 193–205. **Polk, T.** "The Levites in the Davidic-Solomonic Empire." *SBT* 9 (1979) 3–22.

Translation

¹ *With reference to the divisions of the gatekeepers:*
Of the Korahites, Meshelemiah, ᵃ *the son of Korah, of the sons of Abiasaph.* ᵇ
² *Meshelemiah had sons: Zechariah the firstborn, Jediael the second, Zebadiah* ᵃ *the third, Jathniel* ᵇ *the fourth,* ³ *Elam the fifth, Jehohanan* ᵃ *the sixth, Eliehoenai* ᵇ *the seventh.*
⁴ *Obed-edom also had sons: Shemaiah the firstborn, Jehozabad the second, Joah the third, Sachar the fourth, Nethanel the fifth,* ⁵ *and Ammiel the sixth, Issachar the seventh, Peullethai the eighth, for God had blessed him.* ⁶ *Sons were also born to his son Shemaiah.* ᵃ *They ruled* ᵃ *over their father's* ᵇ *house, for they were* ᶜ *good men.* ᶜ ⁷ *The sons of Shemaiah: Othni, Rephael, Obed,* ᵃ *and Elzabad and his brothers,* ᵃ ᵇ *good men,* ᵇ *and* ᶜ *Elihu and Semachiah.* ᵈ ⁸ *All these were of the sons of Obed-edom, they and their sons and their brothers,* ᵃ *good men* ᵃ *with the ability to serve, sixty-two* ᵇ *belonging to Obed-edom.*
⁹ *Meshelemiah had sons and brothers,* ᵃ *good men,* ᵃ *eighteen.*
¹⁰ *Hosah of the sons of Merari had sons: Shimri the chief (although he was not the firstborn, his father made him chief),* ᵃ ¹¹ *Hilkiah the second,* ᵃ *Tebaliah* ᵇ *the third, Zechariah the fourth. All Hosah's sons and brothers were thirteen.*
¹² *These, the divisions of the gatekeepers, the male leaders, had tasks* ᵃ *beside their brothers, to minister in the house of Yahweh.* ¹³ *They cast lots, whether small and great in their fathers' houses, gate by gate.* ¹⁴ *The lot for the east (gate) fell to Shelemiah.* ᵃ *As for Zachariah his son,* ᵇ *a prudent man,* ᵇ *they also cast lots, and his lot came out for the north;* ¹⁵ *for Obed-edom, the south; and for his sons,* ᵃ *the storehouse;* ᵇ ¹⁶ *for* ᵃ *Hosah, the west, at the gate of Shallecheth* ᵇ *on the road that goes up, watch corresponding to watch.* ¹⁷ *On the east there were six* ᵃ *each day,* ᵃ *to the north four each day, to the south four each day, and for the storehouses, two each;* ¹⁸ *for the Parbar* ᵃ *to the west, four for the road, two for the Parbar.* ¹⁹ *These were the divisions of the gatekeepers, of the Korahites* ᵃ *and the sons of Merari.*
²⁰ *Their fellow* ᵃ *Levites, over the treasuries of God's house and the treasuries of the sanctuary:* ²¹ ᵃ *The sons of Ladan, the sons of the Gershonite belonging to Ladan, the heads of the fathers of Ladan the Gershonite:* ᵃ *Jehieli.* ²² *The sons of Jehieli: Zetham and Joel his brother were over the treasuries of Yahweh's house.* ²³ *With regard to the* ᵃ *Amramites, the Izharites, the Hebronites, and the Uzzielites:* ᵃ ²⁴ *Shebuel* ᵃ *the son of Gershom, the son of Moses, was chief over the treasuries,* ²⁵ *and his brothers* ᵃ *on Eliezer's side: Rehabiah his son,* ᵇ *and Jeshaiah* ᶜ *his son,* ᶜ *Joram* ᶜ *his son,* ᶜ *Zichri* ᶜ *his son,* ᶜ *and Shelomoth* ᵈ ᶜ *his son.* ᶜ ²⁶ *This* ᵃ *Shelomoth* ᵇ *and his brothers were over all the treasuries of the consecrated gifts which David the king, and the heads of the fathers and* ᶜ *the princes of thousands, and hundreds, and the princes of the army had consecrated.* ²⁷ *From the wars and from the booty they consecrated gifts to maintain* ᵃ *the house of Yahweh.* ²⁸ *All which Samuel the seer, and Saul the son of Kish, and Abner the son of Ner, and Joab the son of Zeruiah had consecrated* ᵃ— *all that which was consecrated was in the custody of Shelomoth* ᵇ *and his brothers.*
²⁹ *Of the Izharites: Chenaniah* ᵃ *and his sons (were designated) for the outside work over Israel as officials and judges.*
³⁰ *For the Hebronites: Hashabiah and his brothers, good men, a thousand and seven hundred, were over the administration of Israel, from beside the Jordan westward, with respect both to all Yahweh's work and the king's service.* ³¹ *Jerijah* ᵃ *was also*

chief of the Hebronites according to his fathers' generations. In the fortieth year of David's kingdom, search was made in the genealogies of the fathers of the Hebronites, and valiant men were found among them in Jazer of Gilead. [32] *His brothers,* ᵃ*good men,* ᵃ *were* ᵇ*two thousand* ᵇ*seven hundred* ᶜ*heads of fathers.* ᶜ *David the king appointed them over Reuben, Gad, and the half-tribe of Manasseh, for all the matters of God and the king.*

Notes

1.a. Gᴮ Μεσολαηλ "Mesolael"; Gᴬ Μεσολλαμ "Mesollam."

1.b. Read אביאסף "Abiasaph" (cf. Gᴮ Αβιασαφ(αρ) "Abiasaph(ar)"; 9:19 אביסף "Ebiasaph." Asaph was a Gershonite (6:24–28 [39–43]), while Abiasaph was descended from Kehath through Korah (cf. 9:19–20; 6:7–8 [22–23]); Exod 6:16, 18, 21.

2.a. A few MSS Gᴮ Syr זכריה "Zechariah."

2.b. Gᴸ Ναθαναηλ "Nathanael"; cf. Syr.

3.a. Gᴮ Ιωνας "Jonas"; Gᴸ Ιωναθαν "Jonathan."

3.b. Syr ידעי "Jedai."

6.a-a. Gᴮ τῶν πρωτοτόκου Ρωσαι "the firstborn Rosai" (Gᴬᵃˡ similar), meaning dubious. *BHS* proposes הם משלים "they were ruling."

6.b. A few MSS Tg אב(ו)תם "their fathers" (pl).

6.c-c. Heb. גבורי חיל, normally translated "warriors" or "valiant men." Here, however, it is apparent that the title has become honorific (cf. also vv 7, 8).

7.a-a. Read ואלזבד ואחיו "and Elzabad and his brothers"; cf. MSS G.

7.b-b. See n. 6.c-c.

7.c. One MS 'אֱ "and Elihu."

7.d. G καὶ Ισβακωμ "Isbakom" (or similar).

8.a-a. See n. 6.c-c.

8.b. 16:38 reads "sixty-eight."

9.a-a. See n. 6.c-c.

10.a. G⁽⁻ᴸ⁾ τῆς διαιρέσεως—τῆς δευτέρας "the second"; cf. *BHK* notes.

11.a. > G.

11.b. Gᴸ Ταβεηλ "Tabeel."

12.a. MT משמרות "watches of."

14.a. Vv 1, 2 משלמיהו "Meshelemiah."

14.b-b. MT יועץ בשכל "a shrewd counselor" (RSV).

15.a. G κατέναντι = לפני "in the presence of" (*BHS*).

15.b. Syrᴬ = הספים "the snatching place."

16.a. Delete as dittogr of the preceding (G⁹ᴹˢˢ). Gᴮᴸ 'εις δεύτερον = לשנים "the second"; Gᴸ + τοῖς προθύροις = לספים "to the doorkeepers"; cf. v 15.

16.b. The name of this gate is found only here. G παστοφορίου = לשכה "chamber room"; Vg *quae ducit* = ש + לכת.

17.a-a. Reading חה- ליום for MT למזרח הלוים "to the east, the Levites"; cf. G.

18.a. The meaning of the word is unknown. G εἰς διαδεχομένους; Vg *in cellulis*. The contextual meaning, apparently supported now by the Temple Scroll from Qumran (Williamson), appears to be a road, other outside area, or room adjacent to the temple.

19.a. Gᴮ Κααθ = קהת "Kaath."

20.a. Cf. G. Heb. אחיהם = "their brothers."

21.a-a. This and either or both of the following phrases may be synonymous variants.

23.a-a. The syntactical connection of these four gentilics is unclear, though one would expect them to parallel ללעדן "of Ladan" in v 21.

24.a. Read perhaps ושובאל "and Shubael"; cf. G and 23:16.

25.a. G καὶ τῷ ἀδελφῷ "and to his brother" = ולאחיו.

25.b. G* υἱός "a son."

25.c-c. > Gᴸ, *BHK* editor proposes deletion.

25.d. Q some MSS Gᴸ Syr Tg Vg ושלמית "Shelomith"; K Gᴮᴬᵃˡ ושלמות "Shelomoth."

26.a. The demonstrative here precedes the noun, contrary to classical style.

26.b. L = שלמות "Shelomoth," according to *BHS*; שלמות "Shelimoth," according to *BHK*. Many MSS as in v 25.

26.c. Reading וְשָׂרֵי "and princes of"; cf. G Vg and 29:6. If לְ "to" is to be retained, it would introduce phraseology apparently meant to identify the heads of the fathers with the various princes, though the meaning could be appositional.

27.a. G τοῦ μὴ καθυστερῆσαι "not to maintain"; Heb. לְ קחִל "to maintain the house of Yahweh."

28.a. Reading הַמֻּקְדָּשׁ or הַמֻּקְדָּשׁ "consecrated."

28.b. G Σαλωμωθ "Salomoth"; cf. nn. 25.d., 26.b.

29.a. G Vg 'כֹ "Chonaniah."

31.a. A few MSS ידיה "Jedaijah"; cf. 23:19.

32.a-a. See n. 6.c-c.

32.b-b. G^AV χίλιοι "a thousand"; cf. v 30.

32.c-c. Gl? Cf. v 30 and Rudolph, 176.

Form/Structure/Setting

Chapter 26 in its present form contains two major units: (1) vv 1–19, a genealogically based list of gatekeepers (vv 1–11) and their duties (vv 12–19); and (2) vv 20–32, a further listing of Levites and their duties. Each of these units is itself structured around major Levitical families. The gatekeepers are composed of the sons of Korah (vv 1–3, 9), i.e., Kohathites through the line of Izhar (6:7–10 [22–25]), and the sons of Obed-edom (vv 4–8), for whom no genealogical connection with the Levites is provided, and sons of Merari (vv 10–11). Vv 12–19 then recount the apportionment of gates by lot to representatives of these three groups. In addition to Gershonites of Ladan's line (vv 20–22) the listing of other Levites in vv 20–32 is regulated chiefly by the four families of Kohathites named in v 23, i.e., Amram, Izhar, Hebron, and Uzziel. Amram's line is represented by descendants of both of Moses' sons, Gershom and Eliezer (vv 24–28), the family of Izhar by Chenaniah (v 29), and the Hebronites by Hashabiah west of the Jordan (v 30) and in the Transjordan by Jeriah (vv 31–32). The family of Merari is absent from this listing.

The first of these units (vv 1–19) is commonly considered composite. The details of the sons of Obed-edom (vv 4–8) interrupts the account of the sons of Meshelemiah, which is concluded in v 9. Moreover, Obed-edom, while showing the largest number of families, sixty-two, is not provided with a Levitical genealogy. Vv 12–19 are secondary once again in that they recount the apportionment by lot of gates to these three families (cf. 24:7–19; 25:9–31). Moreover, the leader of the Korahites whose name is given in vv 1–2 as Meshelemiah in v 14 is named Shelemiah. V 19, which speaks of only two families, Korahites (i.e. Kohathites) and Merarites, could have been the original end-piece of vv 1–3, 9–11.

For the second unit (vv 20–32), we have noted that no descendants of Merari are found. The emphasis clearly falls upon the four families of Kohathites (vv 22–32). Of two listings of Hebronites (vv 30, 31–32), the latter is clearly exceptional in. its division of the family west of the Jordan (v 30) and east of the Jordan (vv 31–32). This latter unit is in other respects also unique (see Comment).

For other lists of gatekeepers in Chronicles, see 9:17–32; 15:18, 24; 16:38. In chap. 9 it appears neither gatekeepers nor singers were originally reckoned as Levites (cf. vv 10, 14, 17, 33, but also vv 18–21). In 15:18 Obed-edom is listed as a gatekeeper with Jeiel (יחיאל), probably to be identified with the

Jehiah (יחיה) of v 24; and in 16:38 Obed-edom is called the son of Jeduthun
and linked with Hosah (as here, v 10) as gatekeepers. 1 Chr 9:17 lists four
families of gatekeepers returning from the exile with a total of two hundred
and twelve gatekeepers (9:22). Shallum, Akkub, Talmon, and Shiman: Shallum
is named as the chief (v 17), and is probably to be identified not only with
Mattithiah's father Shallum (v 31) but also with Zechariah's father Meshelemiah (v 21, see above on chap. 9). This Shallum in v 19 is connected with
the Levitical line of Kohath through Korah (cf. vv 31–33). Ezra 2:42 (= Neh
7:45) lists six families—Shallum, Ater, Talmon, Akkub, Hatita, and Shobai—
with a total of 138 (or 139) persons. Neh 11:19 names only Akkub and Talmon
with 172 persons. Neh 12:23 has three families—Meshullam, Talmon, and
Akkub. According to Ezra 10:24, Shallum and Telem (Talmon?) had married
foreign wives. Myers (177) concludes that our list is best seen as a combination
of those in chaps. 9 and 16, with additions to bring it up to the age of the
compiler. Chaps. 9 and 26 in their final forms would appear to be the latest,
in view of the Levitical genealogies supplied there. The number of gatekeepers
given in 26:1–11 (ninety-three) is surprisingly small and would appear to
point to a continuing decrease.

For the history of the Korahites, see T. Mauch, "Korah," *IDB* 3:49–50,
who points to the composite nature of the tradition in Num 16, where according to his analysis Korah is a Levite only in the portions added by the P
redactor. (Cf. also the genealogy of Exod 6:24 with 1 Chr 6:7–8, 22 [22–
23, 37]). The Korahites are named alongside the Kohathites as singers in 2
Chr 20:19 and are named in the superscriptions of Psalms 42, 44–49, 84–
85; 87–88. Their name is omitted, however, in what are usually considered
later lists of singers, which name Heman, Asaph, and Ethan (or Jeduthun;
cf. 1 Chr 6:18–33 [33–48] and *Introduction*, "Priests and Levites"). In 1 Chr
9:19, as here, the Kohathites are gatekeepers (though this may represent
the development of a parallel line rather than a demotion) and bakers of
sacrificial bread (9:31). The families of both Korah and Obed-edom apparently
found their place within Levitical genealogies only with difficulty, and were
classified (or sought to be classified) from time to time both as singers and
as gatekeepers.

Comment

1–9 On the gatekeepers and Korah, see *Form/Structure/Setting*. On Shallum, Meshelemiah, Shelemiah, Meshullam, see v 14 and 9:17, 19; and Neh
12:25. Seven sons of Meshelemiah are enumerated (v 2), of whom the firstborn
is Zechariah, prominent also in 9:24 and designated as a man with special
talents in v 14. The other sons named are otherwise unknown. In v 9
the total number of "sons" and other relatives attached to Meshelemiah is
eighteen.

Obed-edom (see *Form/Structure/Setting*, vv 4–8) has eight sons named and
enumerated (v 5). Four sons of his eldest son Shemaiah are also given, with
two additional relatives (v 7), which would appear again to bring the list up
to date. The translation "good men" for בני חיל reflects the fact that an
ancient military title is being used in an honorific or formal sense. The total
of those attaching themselves to Obed-edom is given as sixty-two, compared

with sixty-eight in 16:38, by far the largest number of gatekeepers despite Obed-edom's lack of a Levitical genealogy (v 8). Of the sixteen names given in these verses, none is otherwise known, although some of the names are not uncommon (Curtis, 283). Semachiah, for example (slightly changed), is a Levitical family in 2 Chr 31:13.

10–19 Hosah (v 10) is also listed as a gatekeeper with Obed-edom in 16:38. Here four sons are named and enumerated, and the total contingent of Meraites is given as thirteen, bringing the total number of gatekeepers (18 + 62 + 13) to ninety-three. One may question whether these ninety-three are to be considered all of the gatekeepers or, as seems more likely, only their chiefs, since the introductory verses of chap. 23 saw no less than four thousand gatekeepers (23:5).

Vv 12–19 recount the casting of lots for gatekeeper assignments, as has been done earlier with the priests and singers (chaps. 24–25). On the phraseology "great and small alike" (v 13) cf. 24:31; 25:8. The predominance of Shelemiah is shown in that he is placed in charge of the east, or most important gate. Furthermore, since it is necessary to distribute the gates corresponding to the four compass points among only three families, (Me-)Shelemiah's son Zechariah, who is termed a "prudent man" (n. 14.b-b.), is placed at the north gate. Obed-edom is placed at the south, and his sons are placed over the store-houses (בית האספים), probably understood as the treasuries listed below. The lot for the Shallecheth Gate (found only here, cf. n. 16.b.) falls to Hosah and his brethren. Vv 17–18 appear to enumerate the daily watches. These included at a minimum six on the east, four on the north, and four on the south. The remaining verses are both textually difficult and geographically obscure and may reflect also the attempt to arrive at a total of twenty-four daily assignments. If the storehouses of v 17 are identified with the two treasuries of v 20, resulting in a total of four guards, and four are placed on a west road, and two on the "Parbar" (n. 18.a.), this goal is attained. While it has been questioned whether a gate on the south existed at this time due to the position of the king's palace (cf. Ezek 43:8), such a question is probably irrelevant. As the Levites surrounded the Tabernacle of old (Num 1:47–54), so their descendants cared for the temple (cf. 9:19).

V 19, as we have noted (see *Form/Structure/Setting*) may originally have served as the endpiece for vv 1–3, 9–11. Its position now suggests that the sons of Obed-edom also are being attached to the Kohathites through Korah.

20–32 "Other Levites." In a manner somewhat analogous to 9:22–32, where the duties of the gatekeepers are expanded upon and the four chief gatekeepers are given charge of temple chambers and treasuries (9:26), so here too Levites are placed in charge of the "treasuries of the house of God and the treasuries of the dedicated gifts" (v 20). While the text is again less than clear, it appears that Gershonite Levites of the family of Ladan were in charge of the former, which would have included temple vessels and other supplies (together, we may assume, with some money), while Kohathite Levites of Amram's line were in charge of the dedicated gifts, which included, according to vv 26–28, the offerings of military leaders from the spoils of battle (cf. 1 Chr 18:6–8). Jehiel alone is named in 29:8 as receiving precious stones given by the people; the textual difficulties of vv 21–22 suggest a revision reflecting a slightly later period when Jehiel had been succeeded by Zetham and Joel, who are named with him in 23:8. All of those named in v 23 (Amramites, Izharites, Hebronites, and Uzzielites) are Kohathites. The unity of vv 23–32, at least in its present form, is governed by the fact that the Amramites alone are in charge of the treasuries of dedicated gifts, while the Izharites and Hebronites (vv 29–32) are given other duties (see below). The lack of any mention of the Uzzielites in the following, on the other hand, probably points to the composite nature of the listing.

Vv 20–32 present many difficulties, and Welch (93–94), for example, concludes they represent a group of unrelated fragments (cf. Rudolph, 177). Since the Gershonites, who form the center of vv 20–22, are notably absent in vv 1–19, it is perhaps best to see them in the "brothers" of v 20. In that case the Kohathites and Merarites are placed at the temple gates, while the Gershonites were over the two types of treasuries (vv 20, 22). A later (or at least different) strand gave this charge also to the Kohathites of Amram (cf. vv 23–28, and especially v 24). Indeed, vv 29–32 extend the function of the Kohathites through Izhar and Hebron to duties throughout the land.

Within the "treasuries of God's house," we are to include probably the temple vessels and other supplies more directly associated with the cult (cf. 9:26–32; 23:26–32); the nature of the dedicated gifts is expounded in vv 26–28. V 21, as noted by Rudolph, is surely overloaded (note the three-fold naming of Ladan), probably the result of conflation—any of the three phrases could in fact stand by itself. Gershon's son here as in 23:7–9 is Ladan rather than Libni (see on 23:9), and the family head is Jehieli, who is to be identified with the Jehiel of 23:7 and 29:8. It would seem, however, that the subordination of Zetham and Joel expressed in 23:8, where they are most easily understood as Jehiel's brothers, is carried further here, where they are his sons (v 22), who may well have replaced him at a later date.

V 23 names the four families of Kohathites, although the Uzzielites are not named in the following verses. Here it is the Amramites who are placed in charge of the treasuries, under their chief officer Shebuel of the line of Moses' son Gershom (v 24; cf. n. 24.b. and 23:6; 24:20). These treasuries here in their final context probably are to be understood as the "treasuries of the house of God" in v 22, although it is possible that oversight of all the treasuries is intended, since in vv 25–26 the parallel line of Amramites, through Moses' second son, Eliezer, headed by Shelomoth, is named in charge of the treasuries of dedicated gifts. This Shelomoth is not to be identified with the Shelomoth of 23:9, who is a Gershonite, or of 23:18, 24:22, a son of Izhar (cf. T. Mauch, "Shelomoth," *IDB* 4:320). Neither this Shelomoth nor the other four descendants of Eliezer named here are otherwise known. Their charge consisted of the "dedicated gifts" offered from the spoils of war to maintain the house of the Lord (see 26:8, and on 18:8). V 28 is unique and appears to be all-inclusive in listing those associated with David and his wars. Its inclusion above all of Saul, apparently in a favorable light, contrasts strongly with 10:13–14, and is thus another indication of the supplementary nature of these chapters.

Kohathites of Izhar's line (v 29) are appointed to "outside work" (למלאכה החיצונה) over Israel as officers and judges (לשטרים ולשפטים; cf. 23:4). Their leader, Chenaniah, is otherwise unknown, although a man with the same name is in 15:22, 27 a Levitical leader of song. Whether this "outside work" (see also Neh 11:16) is to be identified with the "service of the king" to which the Hebronites are assigned in v 30 or the "business of the king" in v 32 cannot be said with certainty, although it would appear likely. Contrary to Williamson (173) the appointment of both Izharites and Hebronites to similar types of activities would not be unreasonable. Furthermore, if these "outside matters" be understood to refer to matters beyond the immediate area of the temple itself, it would appear at least possible that the "work of the Lord" (v 30) and the "business of God" (v 32) could also be included.

Since there is little information in Scripture relating to such "outside activity" of Levites, the tendency has been to see such assignments as retrospections from a later date. This tendency has been heightened by the difficulty of finding an appropriate historical period in which Levitic activity in East Jordan would have been possible, making dates later than the period of the United Monarchy or earlier than the Maccabees difficult if not impossible. Since the Jazer of v 31 was a prominent city in Maccabean times (cf. 1 Macc 5:8), and both Maccabees (1 Macc 2:17) and Josephus (*Ant.* IV.viii.14) know of a Levitical authority throughout the land, it is tempting to point to our passage as late and approaching the concept which will be attained in Maccabean times. While there might be some truth to such a point, however, it ignores the more complex (and admittedly unclear) evidence that points rather in the direction of an ancient and broader concept of Levitical roles. Jazer, for example, is one of the Levitical cities, and the tendency is to see the establishment of the Levitical cities as administrative centers established to at least some degree during the United Monarchy (see the articles by Mazar and Polk in the *Bibliography* above). Old Testament evidence, while skimpy, suggests a much broader definition and role of the Levites and points to their role as teachers (Deut 33:10), judges (Deut 17:9), and warriors (Gen 49:5). It is significant that in Chronicles, concentrating as it goes upon the sacred functions of the Levites, that side of the tradition which pictures Levites as "officers and judges" (as in 23:4 and here) and warriors (12:27–29 [26–28] and cf. 2 Chr 23:7) is also present. Particular attention should be called to the account of Jehoshaphat's actions in 2 Chr 19:1–11, where something of a secular/sacred role of Israel's judges is sketched (albeit under the direction of the king), and such passages as 2 Chr 24:1–10; 34:9, where the "religious" duties of the Levites include collecting the temple tax throughout the area. Without accepting all the evidence supplied by Polk (*SBT* 9 [1979] 3–22) it is tempting to see in this fact the Levites' activities in the service of temple and palace. (Cf. Albright, *A. Marx Jubilee Volume*, 61–82.)

In that connection, then, the Hebronite Hashabiah and 1700 of his relatives are assigned duties west of the Jordan and 2700 Hebronites under the leadership of Jerijah a similar position over Reuben, Gad, and Half-Manasseh in East Jordan. These proportions, it must be admitted, seem inappropriate in view of the greater population and larger number of tribes in the west. On Jazer, see S. Cohen, "Jazer," *IDB* 2:805–6. David's action here with regard to Jazer is otherwise unattested. While the name of Hashabiah, "Jahweh has taken account," is common, especially among the Levites (cf. 9:14; 25:3; 19; 27:17; 2 Chr 35:9, etc.), it is unlikely that any of the others so named are to be identified with the Hashabiah named here. Jerijah, however, is also listed as a Hebronite leader in 23:19; 24:23. The fortieth year of King David is his final regnal year (29:27).

Explanation

Following upon the division of the priests and Levitical singers (chaps. 24–25), the gatekeepers are assigned their allotted tasks according to three major families, of which that of Obed-edom (vv 4–8) appears to be a later addition. A total of twenty-four watches is called for, corresponding in a sense to the twenty-four courses of priests and singers. In the final analysis, Shelemiah the Kohathite is responsible for ten guards, Obed-edom (without Levitical genealogy) for eight, and Hosah the Merarite for six.

Of the "other Levites" in vv 20–32, some are placed over the temple treasuries (vv 20–28), while others are given other "outside duties." At first, it appears, charge of some of the temple treasuries was given to Gershonite Levites (vv 20–22), significantly absent from vv 1–19. However, in the final form of the chapter this task is at least shared with Kohathites of Amram's line, the line closest to Aaron, where duties are shared by Moses' two sons Gershom and Eliezer (vv 23–25). Vv 26–28 make the point strongly that the dedicated gifts of *all* Israel's leaders from the time of Samuel down to David (and including Saul) were brought and placed in the hands of the Levites for the service of the temple, a thought not far from the "all-Israel" theme seen so frequently earlier.

Two additional families of Kohathites, those of Izhar and Hebron, are given "outside duties" west and east of the Jordan respectively. What these specific assignments included we are not aware of. However, that such Levites served to bridge the gap between temple and king seems apparent. At the same time such a passage, like 2 Chr 19, reflects a much broader role for Levites than that of subordinate temple servants.

In addition to the attempt to regulate the details of the temple cult more precisely, and to specify more exactly who had the right of access to the temple and its precincts, these verses point to duties outside the temple as falling within the limits of Levitical activity. It may well be that such a notice derives from earlier rather than later Levitical practice. It is, at any rate, another pointer to a broadened view of God's kingdom which includes diverse kinds of people engaged in diverse activities.

Other Officials of David   (27:1–34)

Bibliography

On David's Mighty Men, see the *Bibliography* at 1 Chr 11–12.

Aharoni, Y. *The Land of the Bible.* Tr. E. F. Rainey. Philadelphia: Westminster Press, 1967. 263–80. **Albright, W. F.** "The Administrative Districts of Israel and Judah."

JPOS 5 (1925) 17–54. **Alt, A.** "Israel's Gaue unter Salomo." *KS* II (1953) 76–89.
Cross, F. M. and G. E. Wright. "The Boundary and Province Lists of the Kingdom
of Judah." *JBL* 75 (1956) 202–26. **Mettinger, T. N. D.** *Solomonic State Officials: A Study
of the Civil Government Officials of the Israelite Monarchy.* CBOTS 5. Lund: Gleerup, 1971.
Vaux, R. de. *Ancient Israel.* Tr. J. McHugh. New York: McGraw-Hill, 1961. 115–38.
Wright, G. E. "The Provinces of Solomon." *EI* 8 (1967) 58–68. **Yadin, Y.** *The Art
of Warfare in Biblical Lands.* 2 vols. Tr. M. Pearlman. New York: McGraw-Hill,
1963.

Translation

¹ *This is the list of heads of fathers and princes of thousands and hundreds, and
their officers who served the king* [a] [b]*with respect to every matter of the divisions* [b]
*which entered and left month by month each month of the year. Each division numbered
twenty-four thousand.*

² *Over the first division, for the first month, was Jashobeam,* [a] [b]*the son of Zabdiel,* [b]
with [c] *his division, twenty-four thousand.* ³ *He was from the sons of Perez, the chief
of all the army officers for the first month.*

⁴ *Over the division of the second month was Dodai,* [a] *the Ahohite,* [b]*(Mikloth was
the chief)* [b]*—with his division, twenty-four thousand.*

⁵ *The third chief* [a] *of the host for the third month was Benaiah, the son of Jehoiada,
the chief priest, with his division, twenty-four thousand.*

⁶ *This Benaiah was mighty man of* [a] *the thirty and over the thirty, and over* [b]
this division was Ammizabad his son.

⁷ *The fourth, for the fourth month, was Asahel, the brother of Joab, and Zebadiah
his son* [a]*was after him,* [a] *with his division, twenty-four thousand.*

⁸ *The fifth,* [a] *for the fifth month, was prince Shamhuth,* [b] *the Izrahite,* [c] *with his
division, twenty-four thousand.*

⁹ *The sixth, for the sixth month, was Ira, the son of Ikkesh, the Tekoite, with his
division, twenty-four thousand.*

¹⁰ *The seventh, for the seventh month, was Helez the Pelonite, of the sons of Ephraim,
with his division, twenty-four thousand.*

¹¹ *The eighth, for the eighth month, was Sibbecai the Hushathite, of the Zerahite,
with his division, twenty-four thousand.*

¹² *The ninth, for the ninth month, was Abiezer the Anathothite,* [a]*of the Benjaminite,* [a]
with his division, twenty-four thousand.

¹³ *The tenth, for the tenth month, was Maharai the Netophite, of the Zerahite,
with his division, twenty-four thousand.*

¹⁴ *The eleventh, for the eleventh month, was Benaiah the Pirathonite, of the sons
of Ephraim, with his division, twenty-four thousand.*

¹⁵ *The twelfth, for the twelfth month, was Heldai* [a] *the Netophathite, of Othniel,
with his division, twenty-four thousand.*

¹⁶ *Over the tribes of Israel:*

> *For Reuben, chief, was Eliezer the son of Zichri;*
> *for Simeon, Shephatiah the son of Maacah;*

¹⁷ *for Levi, Hashabiah the son of Kemuel;*

> *for Aaron, Zadok;*

¹⁸*for Judah, Elihu,* ª *one of David's brothers;*
for Issachar, Omri, the son of Michael;
¹⁹*for Zebulon, Ishmaiah,* ª *the son of Obadiah;*
for Naphtali, Jeremoth the son of Azriel; ᵇ
²⁰*for the sons of Ephraim, Hoshea the son of Azaziah;* ª
for the half-tribe of Manasseh, Joel the son of Pedaiah;
²¹*for the half* ª *of Manasseh (in) Gilead, Iddo the son of Zechariah;* ᵇ
for Benjamin, Jaasiel, the son of Abner;
²²*for Dan, Azarel the son of Jeroham.* ª

These were the princes of the tribes of Israel. ²³*David did not number those twenty years old and below,* ª *because Yahweh had promised to make Israel as numerous as the stars of the heavens.* ²⁴*Joab, the son of Zeruiah, began to number, although he did not finish; and because of this anger came upon Israel and the number was not entered* ª*in the book of* ª ᵇ *the chronicles* ᵇ *of King David.*

²⁵*Over the storehouses* ª *of the king* ᵇ *was Azmaveth the son of Adiel, and over the storehouses in the fields, the cities, the fortified cities, and the towers was Jonathan the son of Uzziah.* ²⁶*Over those who did the work of the field, the tilling of the soil, was Ezri the son of Chelub.* ²⁷*Shimei the Ramathite was over the vineyards,* ª *and Zabdi the Shiphmite* ᵇ *was in charge of* ᶜ*the grapes* ᶜ *and the wine cellars.* ᵈ ²⁸*Baal-hanan the Gederite* ª *was over the olive and mulberry* ᵇ *trees which were in the Shephelah, and Joash was over the stores of oil.* ²⁹*Over the cattle pastured in Sharon was Shitrai* ª *the Sharonite, and over the cattle in the valleys was Shaphat the son of Adlai.* ³⁰*Obil the Ishmaelite was over the camels, Jehdeiah* ª *the Meronothite was over the she-asses, and* ³¹*Jaziz the Hagrite was over the flocks. All these were stewards of the property of King David.*

³¹*Jonathan, David's uncle, was advisor—he was a wise and learned man. Jehiel the son of Hachmoni was with the king's sons.* ³³*Ahithophel was also an advisor of the king, while Hushai the Archite* ª *was the King's Friend.* ³⁴*After Ahithophel was Jehoida,* ª *Benaiah's son, and Abiathar, while Joab was chief of the king's army.*

Notes

1.a. G τῷ λαῷ καὶ "the people and."
1.b-b. G reads otherwise.
2.a. Read perhaps יִשְׁבָּעַל "Ishbaal"; cf. 11:11.
2.b-b. 11:11 בֶּן־חַכְמֹנִי "son of Hachmoni."
2.c. For this significance of עַל "with," see BDB, 755, II.4.c.
4.a. 11:12 אֶלְעָזָר בֶּן־דֹּדוֹ "Eleazar the son of Dodo"; cf. 2 Sam 23:9.
4.b-b. > Gᴮ. Gl to דּוֹדוֹ "Dodo" because of 11:12 (Rudolph). Omit וּמַחֲלֻקְתוֹ as dittogr or synonymous variant.
5.a. Read הָרֹאשׁ "the chief"; cf. 2 Chr 31:10; Ezra 7:5.
6.a. Many MSS 'בַּשׁ "among/over the thirty."
6.b. Adding וְעַל "and over" with G Vg.
7.a-a. G καὶ οἱ ἀδελφοί "and the brothers."
8.a. L הַחֲמִישִׁי; most MSS 'הַחֲ "fifth, *the* fifth."
8.b. 11:27 שַׁמּוֹת "Shammoth."
8.c. 11:27 הַהֲרוֹדִי "of Harod"; *BHS* reads הַזַּרְחִי "Zerahites" (cf. vv 11, 13).
12.a-a. K לַבְּנִימִין; Q ימיני לבן "of the Benjaminite."
15.a. 11:30 חֵלֶד "Heled."

18.a. G Ἐλιαβ "Eliab"; cf. 2:13; 1 Sam 16:6; 17:13.

19.a. G Vg 'שׁ "Shemaiah."

19.b. G^ALal Ὀξιηλ "Oziel."

20.a. A few MSS + G עזיהו "Uzziah."

21.a. A few MSS G Vg + שבט "tribe," as in v 20.

21.b. G^-L ובדיהו "Zabediah."

22.a. G Ζαβδιου = ובדיהו "Zabediah."

23.a. Read perhaps ומעלה "and upwards." Cf. Num 1:3. Some confusion may have resulted among those wishing to absolve David of his guilt in relation to the census.

24.a-a. Reading בספר "in the book of," with G.

24.b-b. The translation reflects the fact that the phrase is identical to that of the names of the books of Chronicles.

25.a. The word אצרות may mean equally "treasury" or "storehouse," the distinction not being as rigid then as now. (Cf. 26:20.) Obviously not only gold and silver and other metals are included, but items of lesser value and of less exotic nature.

25.b. Insert בעיר הממלכה "in the city of the kingdom"? Cf. v 25b and 1 Sam 27:5 (BHS).

27.a. Read 'הַכְ? Cf. G.

27.b. G^BA ὁ τοῦ Σέφνι "the Sepnite."

27.c-c. Lit., "that which was in the vineyards." BHS deletes as a gl.

27.d. See W. L. Reed, "Gideon," Archaeology and Old Testament Study (ed. D. Winton Thomas; Oxford: Clarendon, 1967), for this meaning (Williamson, 177).

28.a. G הגדרי "Gedorite."

28.b. MT השקמים "mulberry," conventionally tr. as "sycamore," but not to be classed with American sycamores. The reference is to a tree of the fig family, but bearing smaller, less desirable fruit like the mulberry. Cf. J. Trever, "Sycamore," IDB 4:470–71.

29.a. Reading Q MSS G^B Tg שרטי "Shirtai"; K שטרי "Shitrai.'

30.a. Syr^A יהודא "Jehuda."

33.a. G (ὁ) πρῶτος "the first" (cf. 'αρχι--; "archi—").

34.a. 2 MSS reverse the names.

Form/Structure/Setting

This chapter is composed of four separate, probably originally unrelated lists: (1) vv 1–15, commanders of the monthly courses; (2) vv 16–24, tribal heads; (3) vv 25–31, stewards of David's property; and (4) vv 32–34, Davidic advisors.

Since chap. 26 has concluded with Levites assigned to semi-secular duties throughout the land, chap. 27 moves naturally to other non-Levitical military and administrative personnel. In doing so, it appears to go beyond the scope of the heading of 23:2–6; it is considered secondary also by some who accept the authenticity of parts of chaps. 23–27. V 1 may be viewed as a title to the entire chapter, but it appears more likely that it is the heading to vv 1–15 alone. At any rate, it is impossible to say whether the materials of this chapter were found in a single unit by its author or (as seems more likely) were first joined together by him.

The term "officers" (שטריהם) in v 1 is at least reminiscent of the Levitical officers referred to in 23:4 (and cf. 26:29). The names of the twelve heads of David's divisions are among those found in the list of David's mighty men of 1 Chr 11:10–47, itself dependent upon 2 Sam 23:8–39. The following chart is instructive in viewing the similarities and differences between the two lists.

1 Chr 27:2–15	*1 Chr 11:10–31*
1. Jashobeam the son of Zabdiel from the sons of Perez	1. Jashobeam *the Hachmonite*
	2. Eleazar the son of Dodo (דודו) the Ahohite
	3. Abishai, vv 20–21
2. Dodai (דודי) the Ahohite	
3. Benaiah the son of Jehoiada, the chief priest (Ammizabad his son)	4. Benaiah, the son of Jehoiada of Kabzeel
4. Asahel the brother of Joab (Zebadiah his son)	5. Asahel the brother of Joab (v 26)
	6. Elhanan the son of Dodo from Bethlehem
5. Prince Shamhuth (שמחות) the Izrahite	7. Shammoth (שמות; 2 Sam 23:25, שמה) the Harodite
6. Ira the son of Ikkesh, the Tekoite	8. Helez the Pelonite
7. Helez the Pelonite of the sons of Ephraim	9. Ira the son of Ikkesh the Tekoite
8. Sibbecai the Hushathite of the Zerahite	10. Abiezer of Anathoth
9. Abiezer the Anathothite of the Benjaminite	11. Sibbecai the Hushathite
	12. Ilai the Ahohite
10. Mahari the Netophite of the Zerahite	13. Maharai (מהרי) the Netophite
11. Benaiah the Pirathonite of the sons of Ephraim	14. Heled (חלד) the son of Baanah Netophah
	15. Ithai the son of Ribai of Gibeah of the Benjaminites
12. Heldai the Netophathite of Othniel	16. Benaiah of Pirathon

That the two lists are closely related is apparent in that the twelve names of 1 Chr 27 are found among the first sixteen names of 11:10–47, and in a generally recognizable order. Minor differences, however, are noteworthy, as seen in the following. (1) Jashobeam is here named a son of Zabdiel and descendent of Perez (i.e., of the tribe of Judah); 11:11 terms him only "the Hachmonite." (2) For Dodai the Ahohite (v 4, the second part of which is obscure) 11:12 lists "Eleazar the son of Dodo" the Ahohite. (3) Abishai (11:20–21) is omitted here. (4) "Benaiah, the son of Jehoiada, the chief priest" (v 5), in 11:22–25 is the son of Jehoiada, a valiant man of Kabzeel, and the head of David's bodyguard. On Jehoiada as chief priest, see also v 34. His son Ammizabad is included with him. (5) V 7 adds the name of Zebadiah to that of his father Asahel. (6) "Elhanan, the son of Dodo" (11:26) is omitted. (7) On Shamhuth, see nn. 8.b. and 8.c. Also, the name "Izrahite" replaces "The Harorite/the Harodite" of 11:27. (8) Ira (v 9) precedes rather than follows Helez, who in 11:27 lacks the designation, "of the sons of Benjamin." (9) Sibbecai precedes rather than follows Abiezer, and a further description of each is added. (10) Ilai, the Ahohite (11:29), is omitted. (11) Mahari (v 13) is further designated "of the Zerahite." (12) Ithai (11:31) is omitted, and Benaiah precedes rather than follows Haldai/Heled. Moreover, a further designation is added to each.

These variations demonstrate that vv 2–15 are not directly dependent upon 11:10–47 (or 2 Sam 23). Other characteristics of the list have been cited as a demonstration of its artificial nature. These include the twelve divisions of twenty-four thousand each, reminiscent again of the other groupings of twelves and twenty-fours, and the three-part pattern exhibited in the last six names (name, gentilic, plus a further description). While 1 Kgs 4:7–19 indicates that Solomon organized a force of officers to provide for the needs of the king's household, one for each month, the author of this section has transposed and elaborated this idea into the age of David, placing no less than 288,000 men under conscription to do the king's bidding.

The order of the tribes in vv 16–24 does not correspond exactly with any other listing in the Old Testament. Correspondents have been seen with the list of 1 Chr 2:1–2 and Numbers 1, especially vv 20–42. Those comparisons can be seen in the following chart.

1 Chr 27	1 Chr 2	Num 1
Reuben	Reuben	Reuben
Simeon	Simeon	Simeon
Levi	Levi	Gad
Aaron		
Judah	Judah	Judah
Issachar	Issachar	Issachar
Zebulon	Zebulon	Zebulon
Naphtali	Dan	
Ephraim	Joseph	Joseph/Ephraim
Half Manasseh (east)		Manasseh
Half Manasseh (west)		
Benjamin	Benjamin	Benjamin
Dan	Naphtali	Dan
	Gad	
	Asher	Asher
		Naphtali

Apart from the inclusion of Aaron after Levi, the most obvious divergencies from 1 Chr 2 are the replacement of Dan with Naphtali and the moving of Dan to the end of the list, the extension of Joseph into the three (!) tribes of Ephraim and East and West Manasseh, and the omission of Gad and Asher from the end of the list. In Num 1 Levi is absent from the list proper (but cf. 1:47–54), Naphtali stands at the end of the list preceded by Asher, and the full number of twelve tribes is attained by dividing Joseph into Ephraim and Manasseh, as is more customary.

While it is impossible to assert a direct relationship in such a case, it would appear that 1 Chr 27 is closer to 1 Chr 2 than to Num 1. The position of Naphtali is a problem under any conditions; other variations between 1 Chr 27 and 1 Chr 2, such as the addition of the mention of Aaron-Zadok and the expansion of the Joseph tribes, are reasonable enough. The last two tribes of 1 Chr 2, Gad and Asher were probably omitted merely to keep the number of tribes at twelve. This arrangement has the result of placing the six Leah tribes first, followed by the Rachel tribes.

Certain features of these verses, including reference to David's census in vv 23–24, have suggested that ideas found in Num 1 may nevertheless lie behind our narrative. The matter of the order of the tribes has been mentioned above, although a direct dependence has been questioned. V 23 specifically mentions the age of those counted as ranging from twenty years and up, as does Num 1:3; and the rather unusual listing of Aaron as a separate entity among the tribes might be explained by his involvement in the same verse. More explicitly, Num 1:4 calls for the involvement of the head of each tribe in the census, quite possibly viewed here as the occasion for the listing of the twelve tribal heads. The fact that no census figures are included then occasions the explanation of vv 23–24, i.e., that out of obedience to David's wishes and in accord with his faithfulness to God's command those below twenty were not numbered, although that fact would not really explain the absence of the numbers of those above twenty.

In this connection it is quite apparent that David and Joab are here treated much differently than in 1 Chr 21, where it is David who gives command to number Israel (v 2) and Joab is opposed to the undertaking (vv 3–4, 6). Here the author has desired to absolve David of all blame for the census, and it is rather Joab upon whom the blame for the census falls (v 24). The mention of the resulting wrath (קֶצֶף) upon Israel is a final connection with the narrative of Num 1 (cf. v 53).

The list of David's administrators in vv 25–31 has no parallel in the OT. On vv 32–34, the judgment of Mettinger (*Solomonic State Officials*, 9), Rudolph, and others appears correct that the reference is here not to a roster of those holding official government positions, as in 18:14–17, but of those who served David in a less official way as advisors and enjoyed his confidence.

Our knowledge of administrative organization and procedures during David's reign is minimal, with direct evidence restricted to the lists of officials in 1 Chr 18:14–17 = 2 Sam 8:15–18; 20:23–26. On the other hand, more far-reaching administrative activity in the reign of Solomon is apparent (cf. 1 Kgs 4–5, 9–10; de Vaux, *Ancient Israel*, 115–38). However, it is widely held that the abortive census of 1 Chr 21 (= 2 Sam 24) was carried out with

some administrative changes in mind, the implementation of which may have
begun under David (cf. Bright, *History*, 201). Cross and Wright have argued
that the list of towns in Josh 15:21–62 reflects the organization of Judah
during the days of the United Monarchy, and might go back to David himself
(*JBL* 75 [1956] 202–26). Albright dates the list of the cities of refuge of
Josh 20 to the time of David, while placing the institution itself much earlier
(*JPOS* 5 [1925] 17–54). For similar views, see Aharoni, *Land*, 263–80, and
Yadin, *Warfare*, 279–84. While certainty is again impossible, the balance of
probability would suggest that in many of these areas at least initial developments were undertaken in the time of David, with fuller implementation at
a later date. Perhaps in some of these cases the final form envisioned by
the writer had never been achieved, but was seen as an ideal to be striven
for or attained in an age yet to come.

Comment

1–31 On vv 1–15, see above, *Form/Structure/Setting*, as well as for major
parts of vv 16–24. As seen there, all of the names of vv 1–15 are related to
those listed in 1 Chr 11. On the other hand, only five of the twenty-five
found in vv 16–24 can be identified with reasonable certainty with other
known individuals. Zadok, David and his brother Elihu/Eliab, and Abner the
cousin of Saul are well known, and Hashabiah (v 17) is probably the same
person mentioned in 26:30. Most of the remaining names are common but
impossible to identify with those named here. (For the possibilities, see Curtis,
292.)

Vv 15–31, as noted above, are without parallel in the OT. The officials
named fall naturally into three groups: (a) those responsible for the king's
storehouses, v 25 (or treasuries; see n. 25.a.); (b) those associated with agriculture and agricultural products, vv 26–28; (c) those associated with livestock,
vv 29–31.

On the significance of the royal estates, see de Vaux, *Ancient Israel*, 124–
26. It is again striking that exactly twelve officials are named here, although
the number may be accidental. We have no mention of taxation during the
reign of David, so we should probably assume that at least the major part
of the empire's revenue during his reign came from properties won, pur-
chased, or confiscated by the king.

Of the officials named here, it is again unlikely that any are referred to
elsewhere in the OT, although several of the names occur elsewhere. Supervision of the king's storehouses is shared by Azmaveth (a name found also in
11:33 as one of David's heros), who is in charge of those in Jerusalem, and
by Jonathan, who is not the well-known son of Saul, but an otherwise unknown
son of Uzziah (cf. J. Knox, "Jonathan," *IDB* 2:967–68). The Ezri who is placed
over the farmlands is otherwise unknown, as are the remaining officials. The
larger area of agriculture is divided into agriculture proper (v 26), vineyards
(v 27), grapes and wine (v 27), olive and mulberry trees (v 28), and the
stores of oil (v 28). In both vv 27 and 28 there is a division of responsibility
between the cultivation of grapes and orchards and the handling of the resulting product, i.e., wine and oil.

Vv 29–31 reflect the characteristic division of livestock into cattle (בָּקָר,

designating larger animals such as the ox and cow, responsibility for which is again divided into the rich grazing lands of Sharon and the remainder of the valleys), camels, she-asses, and flocks (צאן), among which are included both sheep and goats.

The presence among the officials named in this list of David's officials of the Ishmaelite Obil, whose name means "camel driver," and the Hagrite Jaziz, both of whom are associated with the Arabian territories to the south of Judah, has been taken by some (e.g., Rudolph, Williamson) to point to the early nature of the list. Others understand the name to be a sign of the list's artificiality if not actually late character, since Obil means "camel driver" (Curtis). It may well be, however, that preference was simply given to the most qualified person at whatever age the list was composed, and that in these two areas this entailed men of foreign background. Certainty is impossible, but there is no obvious reason for considering the list itself as late.

There is here then a rather complete listing of products central to the nation's economic health, and at least suggestive of greater administrative organization under David than is commonly recognized. See further *Form/Structure/Setting* above.

32–34 *David's Advisors.* As noted above (see *Form/Structure/Setting*), it appears we have here a list of those who enjoyed a close personal relationship with David, perhaps serving as his personal advisors in areas of their expertise.

The identity of the "Jonathan" who was David's דוד "uncle" or "friend" is questionable. In view of the fact that Saul's son Jonathan died before David's reign began (10:2), it seems preferable to consider this Jonathan as an otherwise unknown uncle of David, or, more loosely construed, "friend" or "relative" of David's. One of these might be David's nephew Jonathan, the son of his brother Shimea (20:7), despite the concept of youth suggested in the relationship. Jehiel the Hachmonite is otherwise unknown. Ahithophel is the well-known counselor of David who committed suicide when his counsel was not accepted (cf. 2 Sam 16:23; 17:23). Hushai the Archite is also clearly associated with David (cf. 2 Sam 15:32–37). Whether the designation given him as "king's friend" referred at this time to a specific office, as in Egypt and later under Solomon, is unclear (cf. 1 Kgs 4:5 and Mettinger, *Solomonic State Officials*, 63–69). While v 34 refers to Ahithophel's successor as Jehoiada the son of Benaiah, we elsewhere know only of a Benaiah the son of Jehoiada (v 5; 11:22–24; 18:17 and cf. 12:28 [27]). It would appear that the military activities of some Levites (or the priestly activity of some warriors) resulted in some difficulties in genealogical sequences—cf. also the juxtaposing here with the priest Abiathar. It is possible that this Jehoiada is for chronological reasons viewed by the author as the grandson of the earlier Jehoiada. While the mention of Joab seems out of place, his close association with David is well documented, or, as suggested by Williamson, a later scribe may have inserted his name from 18:15.

Explanation

With the listing of four groups of secular officials, the writer concludes his catalog begun with chap. 23 of those placed in their offices by David. It seems unlikely that these chapters come from the hand of the Chronicler, or that the chapters themselves come from the hand of a single person. The final collection, however, of Levites, priests, musicians, gatekeepers, and secular officials presents, in admittedly somewhat unattractive literary form, a compelling statement of the belief that Israel's total religious and governmental structure was to be attributed to David. At the same time we are surely to understand the structures inaugurated by David were the preferable, and, in at least the priestly-Levitical areas, divinely approved ones, for later ages as well.

Addressed to the exilic or post-exilic period, such materials thus presented a concrete picture of the legitimate community of God, established in accord with God's command, as passed on through David. While detailed renderings of this sort may seem to our day restrictive and "undemocratic," they also present an orderly arrangement which may have its own kind of beauty. At the same time, since these arrangements varied from age to age, they present a view of synagogue and church which is in fact not as static as a first reading may suggest, and which is open to the possibility of evolution and development. For Judaism, the growth of the synagogue marks another stage, while for Christians, a new era has been introduced by Jesus, who identified himself with the temple (John 2:21) and pointed to a worship in spirit and truth which would supersede that of the temple (John 4:21–26).

David's Second Speech   (28:1–21)

Bibliography

See the *Bibliography* at 1 Chr 22:2–19.

Translation

¹ *David assembled all the princes of Israel—* ᵃ *the princes of the tribes* ᵇ *and the princes of the divisions who served the king and the princes of thousands and the princes of hundreds* ᶜᵈ *and the princes of all the king's property and cattle, as well as his sons,* ᵈ *with the eunuchs and the mighty men, even every warrior—to Jerusalem* ᵃᶜ ² *and David the king rose to his feet* ᵃ *and said, "Hear me, my brothers and my people. So far as I was concerned,* ᵇ*it was* ᵇ *in my heart to build a house of rest for the ark of the covenant of Yahweh, for the footstool of our God, and I made provisions for building.* ³ *But God said to me, 'You shall not build a house for my name, for you are a warrior and have shed blood.'* ⁴ᵃ *Yahweh, the God of Israel, chose me out of all my father's house to be king over Israel forever. For he chose Judah as preeminent, and in the house of Judah (he chose) my father's house, and in my father's house he took pleasure in me, to make me king over all Israel.* ⁵ *And out of all my sons—for Yahweh has given me many sons—he has chosen my son Solomon to sit upon the throne of the kingdom of Yahweh over Israel.* ⁶ *And he said to me, 'Solomon your son, he is the one who will build my house and my courts,* ᵃ *for I have chosen him as my son, and I will be his father.* ⁷ *I will establish his kingdom forever, if he will be strong to do my commandments and my judgments as this day.'* ⁸ *And now, before all Israel,* ᵃ *the assembly of Yahweh,* ᵇ*and in the ears of our God, keep and* ᵇ *follow all* ᶜ*the commandments of Yahweh* ᶜ *your* ᵈ *God, in order that you may possess the good land and cause your sons to inherit it after you for ever.* ᵉ ⁹ *And now,* ᵃ *Solomon my son, know the God of your fathers* ᵇ *and serve him with a perfect heart and a willing spirit, for Yahweh examines all hearts and understands* ᶜ*every thought.* ᶜ *If you seek him, he will be found by you; but if you forsake him, he will reject you forever.* ¹⁰ *See now that Yahweh has chosen you to construct a temple for the sanctuary. Be strong and act!"*

¹¹ *Then David gave Solomon his son the pattern of the temple* ᵃ *and its rooms, its treasuries, its upper chambers, its inner chambers, and the room for the mercy seat,* ¹² *the pattern of all which he had in mind* ᵃ *concerning the courts of the house of Yahweh and concerning all of the chambers round about, the treasuries of the house of God and the treasuries for holy things;* ¹³ *and concerning the divisions of the priests and the Levites and all the work of the service of Yahweh's house* ¹⁴ *—for the gold by weight for* ᵃ*all the vessels of* ᵃ *gold, for every vessel for every service; for all the vessels of silver, by weight, for every vessel for every service,* ¹⁵ *the weight of the golden lampstands and their lamps, even of each lampstand and its lamps, according to the usage of its lampstand,* ¹⁶ *and the gold for the tables of showbread, for each table, and silver for the tables of silver,* ¹⁷ *and pure gold for the forks, the basins, and cups; for the golden bowls, the weight of each bowl, for*

the silver bowls, the weight of each; [18] and for the refined gold by weight for the incense altar; also for the gold for the model of the chariot of the cherubim that spread their wings and covered the ark of the covenant of Yahweh. [19] All he (David) made plain to him in a writing from the hand of Yahweh, [a] including all the details of the pattern.

[20] And David said to Solomon his son, "Be strong, be courageous, and act; do not be afraid and do not be terrified, for Yahweh God, [a] my God, is with you. He will not abandon you and he will not forsake you until all of the work of the service of the house of Yahweh is finished. [b] [21] And here are the divisions of the priests and the Levites for all the service of God's house. And with you for all the work will be every workman skilled for every kind of work, [a] and the princes and all the people will be at your command."

Notes

1.a-a. These words have sometimes been considered a later expansion; cf. Welch, *The Work of the Chronicler,* 26. For the various princes, see 27:1–22, 25–31. The mention of the warriors was probably occasioned by 29:24, as was also the mention of the king's sons.

1.b. G^AB τῶν κριτῶν = השפטים "the judges."

1.c-c. G reads differently in part.

1.d-d. Or, "the princes of all the property and cattle of the king and of his sons." The ל "of" may either be parallel to that on למלך "of the king," or it may represent the common appositional explicative usage familiar in Chronicles.

2.a. G ἐν μέσῳ τῆς ἐκκλησίας "in the midst of the assembly."

2.b-b. Understanding or reading היה "it was," with G Syr and 22:7.

4.a. On the unity of vv 4–8, see *Form/Structure/Setting* below.

6.a. G^-L sg.

8.a. > G^B.

8.b-b. > G^B.

8.c-c. Syr "his commandments."

8.d. G Vg suff 1 pl.

8.e. See n. 4.a. The use of pl vb forms throughout v 8 is again indicative of later expansion in a speech which at every other point has Solomon as its obj. See also the four previous notes.

9.a. Reading עתה "now," with G καὶ νῦν "and now." Perhaps with the addition of v 8 and its introductory ועתה, the identical form at the beginning of v 9 was altered.

9.b. Reading pl with G.

9.c-c. For יצר מח' "every thought," see Gen 6:5. G^L ἐνθύμημα "reflection" or "thought."

11.a. Reading τοῦ ἱεροῦ "the temple," with most MSS of G. MT אולם = "porch"; cf. 1 Kgs 6:3.

12.a. So with G and most older commentaries. Since Rothstein, it has been common to see here a reference to inspiration, but the ground cited (that the position of עמו "in his" shows it should be understood as a relative clause modifying רוח "mind" and therefore separate from it) is not compelling. The references to the use of עם in such passages as 1 Kgs 11:11 seem to favor the translation given above rather than one referring to inspiration. It should also be noted that Chronicles' portrayal of inspiration elsewhere is considerably more dynamic than here; cf. 1 Chr 12:8; 2 Chr 15:1; 10:14; 24:20. Rudolph adds that, for Chronicles, רוח never means the human spirit, an argument adopted also by Myers. His certainty is surprising in view of such passages as 2 Chr 21:16 and 36:22 (= Ezra 1:1). Both Rothstein and Rudolph have been influenced unduly here by the tabernacle narrative, which pictures Bezalel as inspired by God (Exod 35:30–35), and by v 19, which does attribute inspiration to the plans.

14.a-a. Reading לכל כלי הזהב "all the vessels of gold" with *BHS*; cf. v. 14b.

19.a. The text is awkward, and no completely suitable solution has been found. The most extensive discussion is that of Rothstein and Hänel, 503–6. Most translations have taken Yahweh as the subject of השכיל "make plain" and have understood עליו "unto him" (to which עלי

"unto me" must seemingly be altered in any case) to refer to David, or else have read עליו (cf. G) and connected it with מיד יהוה "from the hand of Yahweh." But on the basis of G (ἔδωκεν Δαυιδ Σαλόμων) it is possible to understand David as the subj: "He (David) taught him (Solomon) everything in a writing from the hand of Yahweh," thus requiring only a single textual change.

20.a. > G.

20.b. G adds words similar to vv 11–12a.

21.a. The combination (ל)כל נדיב בחכמה "all willing, skilled men" has been suggested by כל נדיב לבו "whoever is generous in his heart" of Exod 35:5 and כל חכם לב "every able-hearted man" of Exod 35:10. In this context, חכם "able, skilled" regularly refers to skilled craftsmen, thus suggesting the rendering here. See Curtis, 301.

Form/Structure/Setting

Chap. 28 resumes the thought of chap. 22, which has been interrupted by chaps. 23–27 (see at 23:1). Like chap. 22, chap. 28 consists primarily of a speech of David, but one that is interrupted by the narrative of the transfer of the plans for the temple from David to Solomon and extended by a verse in which David places various people at Solomon's disposal for work on the temple. The chapter may be outlined as follows:

David's Second Speech, vv 1–21
1. Framework, vv 1–2a.
2. Speech: David presents Solomon as temple builder, vv 2–10.
   a. The address, v 2a
   b. David forbidden to build the temple, vv 2b–3
   c. Choice of Solomon, vv 6–7
   d. First exhortation, vv 9–10
3. Transfer of the temple plans, vv 11–19
4. Concluding exhortation, vv 20–21

In both content and structure this speech is closely related to that of chap. 22, as can be seen from the following table.

Chapter 28		*Chapter 22*
28:2	Note of assembly	22:6
28:2	Formula of address	22:7
28:2	David's desire to build the temple	22:7
28:3	David's prior preparations	22:2–5
28:3	David forbidden to build	22:8
28:6	Solomon chosen to build	22:9
28:7	Dynastic promise	22:10
28:9,10,20	Exhortation to Solomon	22:11–13
28:9	Introduction by ועתה "and now"	22:11
28:9	The vocative of בני "my son"	22:11
28:10,20	Designation of the task	22:11
28:9 (cf. v 6)	Concern for keeping the law	22:12,13
28:9	Resulting prosperity	22:11b,13a
28:9b,20	Yahweh's presence assured	22:11
28:10,20	Formula of encouragement	22:13

While the similarities throughout the two chapters are striking, they are particularly noticeable between 22:7–9 and 28:2, 3, 6, which rehearse David's plans to build the temple and the subsequent choice of Solomon to do so, and between 22:11–13 and 28:9, 10, 20, where, despite differences in vocabulary and conceptions which are quite striking, the underlying form for the induction of an individual into office is readily apparent.

Despite these many similarities, chap. 28 also reflects significant differences in structure. David's preparations for the temple, which in 22:2–5 stood as a kind of prelude to his discourse with Solomon, are here introduced into the body of the speech itself, 28:3. The introduction of the speech in 28:2 is much more formal than in 22:7, as would appear proper before a large assembly. The two direct quotations of Yahweh in vv 3 and 6 mark the major divisions of the first part of David's discourse. Not only is the exhortation marked at its beginning with the particle ועתה, "and now" (v 9, see n. 9.a.), but v 10 is clearly marked as the first conclusion of the speech not only by the emphatic ראה עתה ("see now") with which it is introduced, but also by its restatement of Solomon's task as temple builder (cf. v 6) and by the formula of encouragement, חזק ועשה "be strong and act," which recalls the חזק ואמץ "be strong and be courageous" of 22:13. This exhortation is repeated in more extended form in v 20, which in other ways as well shows its final character. With the loose connective והנה "and behold" v 21 introduces for the first time the subject of the active involvement of the people in the work with Solomon.

Like David's earlier speech, this one also contains the introductory vocative (v 2) and the historical retrospect (vv 2b–3, 6–7) and has a hortatory nature (vv 9, 10, 20). It differs in that its setting is before the princes of the people rather than Solomon, and, corresponding to this, the introduction appears rather more formal. For more on speeches in Chronicles, see the *Introduction* and chap. 22.

V 1 probably reflects later expansion on the basis of chaps. 23–27, as pointed out by Welch (*Work*, 26) and others. The mention of the warriors and king's sons was probably occasioned by 29:24. Vv 4–5 appear to be a later expansion of the idea of election found in vv 6–10. This is suggested by the following items. (1) The connection between vv 6 and 10 is interrupted by vv 4–5. (2) The concern elsewhere in this pericope is with Solomon as templebuilder, not, as here, with Solomon as king. (3) Several other items, while not contradicting the views of the Chronicler, are expressed here in an unusual way. (a) The omission of כל "all" before Israel in both vv 4 and 5 (although "all Israel" does occur one time in v 4) seems strangely reticent for the Chronicler in this connection, cf. 29:21–26. (b) The reference to an election of *Judah* is unparalleled elsewhere in Chronicles. (c) The root רצה "to be pleased," used here of the election of David, occurs in Chronicles otherwise only in the difficult 29:3, where its meaning is entirely different. (d) The reference to the "throne of the kingdom of Yahweh over Israel," while in general agreement with the Chronicler's thought (cf. 29:3), is unusually extended and verbose as compared with the simpler "throne of Yahweh" of that verse, as well as the direct מלכותו "his kingdom" of v 7. On the other hand, our study is not affected if the verses are original, since the major themes found here are also found elsewhere in Chronicles.

The use of plural verb forms throughout v 8 is also indicative of expansion of a speech which at every other point has Solomon as its object. An additional problem arises in that those who are addressed in the plural in v 8 are at the same time urged to keep the law "before all Israel," and therefore must be the princes assembled in v 1, although most commentators ignore this part of the problem. Rothstein and Hänel (XVIII, 496–500) connects v 7b directly with v 9, as has been done in the translation above. Rudolph accepts the arguments of Rothstein, but believes that v 8a is the original introduction to Solomon's admonition, following which some such phrase as "hear my words" has fallen out. The variations found in the Septuagint confirm the conflate character of v 8 (e.g., G^B reads "in the face of" instead of "before the eyes of," omits the word "Israel" before "the assembly of Yahweh," and omits "and in the ears of our God," and "hear all" before "the command-ments of Yahweh," as well as the significant difference in v 9 seen in n. 9.a.). Moreover, the concluding phrase of v 8 speaks of Israel's "caus-ing her children to inherit the land" in a manner unparalleled elsewhere in Chronicles.

There is no agreement concerning the authenticity or integrity of vv 12b–18. While numerous modern commentaries view the entire chapter as a unity from the hand of the Chronicler (Williamson), others see in the section the mark of two or more hands. If one can speak of a critical consensus, it would be that of Rothstein and Hänel and Rudolph, both of whom consider vv 1b, 13a, and 14–18 as secondary. Others consider v 19 to be later on the basis that vv 10 and 20 are doublets, although Rothstein and Hänel preserves v 19 for the Chronicler by considering it originally to have stood after v 21.

Despite the subjective nature of the argument, it appears that the lengthy description of the temple vessels in vv 14–18 is secondary. (Cf. the comments of Rudolph, 185.) Attention must also be given to the grammatical difficulties involved in vv 14–18. These verses do not in fact constitute any recognizable grammatical construction, and can be translated only by taking liberties with the text. If vv 14–18 are an insertion, it is difficult to see why v 12ab, which is largely repetitive of v 11, and v 13b, whose emphasis upon the temple vessels is lacking elsewhere in chaps. 22, 28, and 29, should not likewise be omitted. Then v 12a connects directly with v 19.

In contrast to 22:7–13, where David speaks to Solomon in private, this second speech has its setting before "all the princes of Israel" (v 1). That such assemblies belong to Israel's tradition at least from the time of the tribal league and throughout her history appears certain (cf. Judg 5:14–18; 20:1–2; 1 Sam 7:5; 8:4; Deut 1:1; 29:1 [2]; 31:1; Josh 22:12; 24:1; 1 Sam 12:1; 2 Sam 5:1; 1 Kgs 8:1; Exod 12:3; 35:1; Lev 8:4; Ezra 10:1, 5; Neh 8:1; 9:1, etc.). That such assemblies would commonly be the setting for the delivery of extensive discourses may have led the Chronicler to assume that they should be present also for his discourses of a more literary nature. The convening of such assemblies provides a favorite means by which the Chroni-cler expresses the involvement of the people in political and religious activities of which he approved (cf. 1 Chr 12:24, 39; 13:1; 2 Chr 1:2; 13:4; 30:23; 31:1, etc.).

While the first part of the speech (vv 2–7) corresponds largely with David's private speech to Solomon in chap. 22, the Chronicler has here utilized a further development of the concept of rest, an extension of the formula of induction, and applied to Solomon a unique election tradition to express Solomon's unique role as temple builder. Moreover, vv 9, 10, 20 are filled with new concepts which play a significant role in expressing the Chronicler's own point of view. The theme of rest (נוח, מנוחה) has been discussed above (see on 22:9), where we have seen that "rest" was the prerequisite for the construction of the temple, and that the Chronicler attributed that "rest" only to the reign of Solomon. The description of the temple here as a "house of rest for the ark of the covenant of Yahweh and for the footstool of our God" (v 2) noticeably shifts the connotations of that "rest." While before it had been Yahweh who had promised and given rest to his people, here it is the ark, and Yahweh who may be assumed to be present with it in some sense, which finds its own resting place in the temple, and accordingly in the midst of Jerusalem and the people. This same tradition is present in Psalm 132, which shares many features with Chronicles. Here too it is David's desire to build the temple (vv 3–5), the movement of the ark into the temple is described (vv 6–8), and the concern for David's dynasty is also central (vv 10–12). But above all, vv 8, 14, unlike any other passages in the OT, refer to the temple as God's resting place:

> [8]"Arise, O Yahweh, and go to your resting place (למנוחתך)
> you and your mighty ark . . .";
> [14]"This is my resting place (מנוחתי) for ever;
> here I will dwell, for I have desired it."

That Psalm 132 had a special meaning for the Chronicler is apparent in that he had added vv 8–9 to the conclusion of Solomon's dedicatory prayer in 2 Chr 6:41–42.

Of course, it is not necessary to see these two concepts of rest—the one referring to Israel's rest in the promised land and the other to Yahweh's rest in the temple—as contradictory. They belong instead to a development which is completely in accord with the theology of the Chronicler. For if such God-given rest was the prerequisite for the construction of the temple, it follows that after its construction and with the entrance of the ark into the temple God would take up his abode with Israel in a sense in which he had not done so previously. Both of these ideas may seem to stem from such a tradition as that recorded in Num 10:33–36, where the ark both goes forward to seek out a resting place (מנוחה) for Israel (v 33) and when it rests (ובנחה), Yahweh rests with it (v 36).

The Deuteronomic tradition developed its concept of rest without reference to the ark, which it viewed as a container for the tablets of the covenant rather than a symbol of the divine presence. Closely related to this, the Deuteronomist considered the temple as a place for the *name* of Yahweh to dwell rather than a place where Yahweh himself dwells, but where, after Israel has found rest in the promised land, the one legitimate cult with its sacrificial system is found. The tradition found in Ps 132:8 and utilized in 1 Chr 28:2 views the ark as much more integrally related to Yahweh's dwelling in the temple, and in agreement with Num 10:35 pictures the ark as the place where

Yahweh dwells with his ark. (See also von Rad, "The Tent and the Ark," *Old Testament Theology* [Tr. D. N. G. Stalker; Edinburgh: Oliver and Boyd, 1962] 1:234–41.)

The new element introduced in v 6 to emphasize anew Solomon's right to build the temple is the use of the root בחר "to choose." Confining ourselves to those instances in which בחר has God for its subject, we see that בחר is used in the Tetrateuch only three times, and always of the election of the Levites (Num 16:5, 7; 17:20, all P). Deuteronomy uses the verb בחר frequently, but the only objects are Israel, the site which Yahweh will choose for his name (both frequently), the Levites (Deut 18:5; 21:5), and one time "the king whom Yahweh will choose" (Deut 17:15). (For these references, see S. Driver, *Deuteronomy* [ICC 5; New York: Scribner's, 1902] xxx, #23.) Within the Deuteronomic history the divine choice is referred only to Kings Saul (1 Sam 10:24) and David (2 Sam 6:21; 1 Kgs 8:16; 11:34; and cf. 1 Sam 16:8–10). The only other object of Yahweh's choice is the city of Jerusalem (1 Kgs 8:44, 48, etc.). Hence God's election in the Deuteronomic history is predicated only of Saul, David, and Jerusalem. It *never* refers to the Levites, or to any king after David.

In the latter prophets, the use of בחר with Yahweh as subject has as its object *only* Israel (Isa 14:1; 44:1, etc; Ezek 20:5), the Davidic and Levitical families (Jer 33:24), and Jerusalem (Zech 1:17; 2:16 [12]; 3:2). Usage in the Psalms is quite rare, including only Yahweh's people (Ps 33:12); Jacob (78:68; 135:4), Zion (78:68; 132:13), and David (Ps 78:70). Of particular importance here is Ps 78:67–70, parallel in many respects to Psalm 132, where God's election of Judah, Mount Zion, and David is linked directly with the building of the sanctuary. (See H. J. Kraus, *Psalmen* [BKAT 15/1; Neukirchen: Neukirchener Verlag, 1960] i, Psalm 78 in loc., and Excursus VI to Psalm 132; and R. Clements, *God and Temple*, 48–55.)

It is then in stark contrast to every other OT usage that the Chronicler applies the term בחר to Solomon at least three times (28:6, 10; 29:1; and 28:5, which may be late; see above). The usage is unique, and gains in significance since the Chronicler places no more emphasis upon any other object of God's election than do previous traditions. Von Rad has expressed himself very critically of what he terms the Chronicler's "disjointed" election of the king, the cult site, and Levi (*Old Testament Theology*, vol. 1, 352–53). His criticism is difficult to understand, since only Deuteronomy places a significant emphasis upon the election of Israel as a whole. Moreover, the very objects von Rad enumerates—king, cult, Levites (and we might add Jerusalem)—are for the Chronicler a closely related, most significant group centering in the temple.

George Mendenhall has pointed out as well that in every case of the election of an individual except Solomon in Chronicles, the individual obtains his office "by means other than regular, socially established conventions" ("Election," *IDB* 2:79). It could therefore be argued that the Chronicler has taken a term that applied to a certain kind of choice, such as that evidenced by charismatic endowment, and applied it, at least in Solomon's case, to dynastic succession.

Vv 11, 12a, 19, which relate the transfer of the plans for the temple and

its precincts to Solomon, are patterned upon the tabernacle narrative. This
is indicated by the use of the word תבנית "pattern" (vv 11, 12, 19), recalling
Exod 25:9, 40, in both of which cases it has references to a pattern which
Yahweh "showed" Moses of the tabernacle and its furnishings. Although
the analogy is not developed, the Chronicler seems to assert briefly that as
the plans for the tabernacle were delivered by inspiration to Moses, who
transferred them to Bezalel, so the plans for the temple were given to David,
who transmitted them to Solomon. However, in contrast to Exodus, the
Chronicler devotes little attention to this aspect of the preparations. Vv 12b–
19, which we have judged as late, seek to fulfill what its author considered
a felt need in that respect and, as is quite characteristic of such additions,
is more heavily dependent upon the tabernacle narrative.

Vv 20–21 also contain items derived from the tabernacle pericope, Exod
25–31 and 35–40. This is true first of all of the terms used to describe the
work on the temple, כל־מלאכת עבודת בית־יהוה "all the work of the service
of the house of Yahweh" (v 20) and the עבודת בית האלהים "the service
of the house of God" (v 21). Both מלאכת and עבודת occur frequently in
the tabernacle narrative (the former twenty-eight times, the latter eleven),
but it is even more significant that the combination מלאכת עבודה occurs
of work on the sanctuary only in Exod 35:24; 36:1–3 outside of Chronicles.
(The meaning in Lev 23 and Num 28 and 29 is less technical, "laborious
work.") The phrase לכל נדיב בחכמה "all willing, skilled men" likewise
points directly to the tabernacle narrative, in that the concepts embodied
in נדיב and חכם "able, skilled" here are otherwise unique to that portion
of the OT. The Chronicler, like the priestly writer before him, wished to
show the generous participation of Israel in building the temple, and utilized
the example of the tabernacle pericope to express his own *Tendenz* in this
regard. (For נדיב, cf. Exod 25:2; 35:5, 21, 22, 29. For חכם, see Exod 28:3;
31:6; 35:10, 25; 36:1, 2, 4, 8. For חכמה, see Exod 28:3; 31:3, 6; 35:26, 31,
35.) The use of this wisdom terminology is of a different sort than that found
in much of the OT. In the tabernacle pericope חכם and חכמה are used
some sixteen times with reference to the "wise of heart," i.e., the skilled
workers employed on the tabernacle and its furnishings. The noun itself in
particular is used in the sense of Yahweh's "putting wisdom" into the craftsmen, resulting in a concept very close to that of inspiration. It is this usage
which the Chronicler has adopted, and which he will develop still further
in relating the details of the construction of the temple (cf., e.g., Hiram in
2 Chr 2:6–13 [14]).

Finally, the two portions of the conclusion of this second speech, vv 10,
21, and 22, reflect again the form of the *Amtseinsetzung*, or induction into
office, which we have met in the first speech (see above, chap. 22). All three
of the elements isolated by Lohfink are present here, two of them in both
vv 10 and 20. For the formula of encouragement, compare the חזק ועשה
"be strong and act" of v 10 with the more complete formula, also extended
by ועשה, in v 20. (The use of עשה which may be translated "do," "act," or
"build," is common in Chronicles as a parallel or alternative to the words
expected in the formula of encouragement; cf. 2 Chr 19:11; 25:8, and the
unusual development in Ezra 10:4, as well as 22:16, 19, which may be later.)

The mention of the specific task for which Solomon is inducted is also reflected, both in v 10—"See now that Yahweh has chosen you *to construct a house* for the sanctuary"—and somewhat less directly in v 20—"until all of the work of the service of the house of Yahweh is finished." The formula of accompaniment, "Yahweh God, my God, is with you," is also found in v 20. Such detailed repetition of the components of the form, while at the same time introducing variations in order and vocabulary, would suggest that the author recognized fully the significance of the form he was using and was not simply repeating it out of dependence upon Joshua.

The variations introduced into the form here point again to a greater literary skill than is often associated with the Chronicler. The first of these, "He will not abandon you and he will not forsake you" (v 20), is actually an explanation of the accompaniment formula, further expanding upon Yahweh's presence. The same phrase is found in Josh 1:5, which in view of the Chronicler's strong dependence upon Josh 1:2–9 is probably the source of the quotation here (the only other occurrences are in Deut 31:6, 8, where they also are a part of Joshua's induction). In light of v 9 (see below) such an unconditional pledge of the divine presence is unexpected. However, the Chronicler's addition, "until all the work of the service of the house of Yahweh is finished," really serves to point to the *goal* of the divine presence, the construction of the temple. The apparent disharmony should be no more surprising here than in the case of the Deuteronomic historian, who did the same in Josh 1:5 and 7, upon which the writer was dependent.

V 9 introduces a number of concepts of great significance for Chronicles and concludes with a parallel statement expressing a cardinal tenet of the Chronicler's theology: "If you seek him, he will be found by you; but if you forsake him, he will reject you for ever" (v 9). The first part of this phrase is closely related to Deut 4:29 and Jer 29:13. Von Rad ("The Levitical Sermon," *The Problem of the Hexateuch*, 276) believes it to be based on Jeremiah, apparently because of the use of the niphal of מצא "find" there (which is, however, lacking in many versions); other factors, such as the heart/soul picture and the frequent use of Deuteronomy by Chronicles, would support the opposite conclusion. In any case, the manner in which the Chronicler has handled the tradition is exceptional. In both Jeremiah and Deuteronomy the reference is primarily, if not exclusively, to the "forsakenness" of the exile, and the "seeking" refers to the necessity for Israel's repentance, which will result in her being "found" or accepted again by Yahweh. Such thoughts are totally foreign to the Chronicler. He has indicated his interpretation of the first phrase by appending to it a second not found in either Deuteronomy or Jeremiah: "but if you reject him, he will reject you forever." The complete statement then states both positively and negatively the doctrine of God's retribution which became such a burning issue in post-exilic Judaism.

The import of the whole statement is heightened by the addition of לעד "forever." It may well be significant that among the infrequent occurrences of this word, found only nine times in the OT, are Ps 132:12, 14, quoted previously, where it is used of Yahweh's promise to David's and the Lord's "rest" in Jerusalem, and Ps 89:30 [29], where it likewise refers to the eternal promise to David. Therefore in one sense the Chronicler has balanced his statement of Solomon's eternal election with at least the possibility of an eternal rejection! That has already been suggested in v 7, where the permanence of Solomon's kingdom was qualified by the necessity for obedience to the law. This dogma of retribution, it should be noted well, is the single most important concept for the Chronicler's presentation of the post-Solomonic kings (see *Introduction*).

Comment

1–2a *Framework.* V 1 again pictures the great assembly, cf. 11:1; 13:1–2, 5, here described as the "princes" (שׂרים) of the people. The list of officials in v 1 has probably been revised to include those named in chaps. 23–27 (cf. especially 23:1–6 and chap. 27). To see David "rising to his feet" (v 2) is probably not to be understood as a sign of his infirmity, but a mark of the more formal occasion of the speech.

2b–10 *David's speech.* שׁמעוני "Hear me" is a mark of the speech in Chronicles. The contents of the speech are very similar to that in chap. 22, see above, *Form/Structure/Setting.* Here, however, the temple is designated a "house of rest for the ark of the covenant of the Lord, and for the footstool of our God," a significant movement in the Chronicler's thinking (see *Form/ Structure/Setting*). The designation of David as a "man of war(s)" and one who has spilled blood (v 3) disqualifies David as temple builder and leads to the election of Solomon instead (v 6). (Vv 4–5, which transfer this election from Judah through David and his family to Solomon, we have judged to be a later expansion, although not affecting the meaning). Vv 6–7 repeat with added emphasis the basis of the Davidic covenant, here transferred to Solomon—He is God's chosen son, and God is his father (cf. 2 Sam 7:14; 1 Chr 22:10)—although here phrased conditionally. It is above all this conditional nature of the covenant, or more properly understood, an emphasis upon obedience to the law, which forms the center of v 8, where the results of obedience—the possession of the "good land" and "causing your sons to inherit the land"—are reminiscent of the emphasis of Deuteronomy (cf. Deut 5:33; 6:1–3).

In vv 9–10 a number of concepts important to the Chronicler are introduced in addition to the concept of retribution (see *Form/Structure/Setting* above), which we have not met previously. Solomon is here exhorted to "know" (ידע) the God of his fathers. The only other occurrence of an imperative of ידע in the OT with a deity as its object is instructive: "No longer shall each man teach his neighbor and each his brother saying, 'Know the Lord,' for they shall all know me" (Jer 31:34). Jeremiah's reference indicates that "to know Yahweh" was a common exhortation, and that when the new covenant was inaugurated there would be no further need for exhortation. Studies in Hittite and Accadian treaties assure us of the usage of "to know" to denote the mutual legal recognition of suzerain and vassal and the binding nature of treaty stipulations (cf. H. Huffmon, "The Treaty Background of Hebrew *Yāda‘*," *BASOR* 181 [1966] 31–37). Biblical passages cited by Huffmon such as Amos 3:2; 2 Sam 7:20 (= 1 Chr 17:18); Hos 8:2; 13:4–5; Deut 9:24; and Psalm 14:4 wholly support the view that we are dealing here with conventional covenant terminology which exhorts Solomon to recognize Yahweh as his covenant lord and to conduct himself in accord with his stipulations. The parallel use of עבד "serve," which has cultic overtones for the Chronicler (cf. 2 Chr 24:18; 30:8; 33:16; 34:33; 35:3), suggests that this knowledge and service finds its best expression in obedience to the divine precepts associated with the cult (cf. 2 Chr 30:8).

The exhortation to serve Yahweh "with a perfect heart and a willing spirit" (v 9) occurs as frequently in Chronicles as in the remainder of the OT (1 Chr 12:39 [38]; 28:9; 29:9, 19; 2 Chr 15:7; 16:9; 19:9; 25:2; 1 Kgs 8:61; 11:4; 15:3, 14; 2 Kgs 20:3; Isa 38:3). The same emphasis is found also in "with all the heart," common in both Deuteronomy and Chronicles (cf. in the non-synoptic portions 2 Chr 6:14; 15:15; 22:9; 31:21; 32:31). (For the Deuteronomy references see S. R. Driver, *Deuteronomy*, p. lxxxii, #51.) Further emphasis upon the necessity for actions to flow from a perfect, undivided heart can be found in such phrases as לב אחד (1 Chr 12:39 [38]; 2 Chr 30:12), לב יחד ("one heart," "a single heart," 1 Chr 12:18 [17]), and נפש חפצה "a willing heart," used here in parallel with לב שלם "a perfect heart." In the phrase that Yahweh "examines all hearts and understands every thought" the writer unites his "theology of the heart" with a conception of Yahweh's omniscience found in such passages as Ps 7:10; 139:1; 1 Sam 16:7; and Jer 11:20, while at the same time using one of his favorite vocables, דרש "seek." The parallel phrase וכל-יצר מחשבות מבין "and understands every thought," clearly echoes Gen 6:5; 8:21. (On the use of the formula for induction into office in vv 10, 20–21, see above, *Form/Structure/Setting* and chap. 22.) These observations suggest that in this brief verse the Chronicler has gathered together myriad quite diverse traditions to which he wholeheartedly subscribed. (See further Braun, "The Significance," 169–99).

11–19 Vv 11, 12a, 19, relate the transference of the plans for the temple from David to Solomon. (On the concept of inspiration here see nn. 12.a. and 19.a.) Just as the "pattern" (תבנית, vv 11–12) recalls the tabernacle narrative (Exod 25:9, 40), so this greater elaboration is strongly dependent upon the same and presents a picture similar to that of the restored temple in Ezek 40–48. On the various parts of the temple (v 3), see 2 Chr 3. The emphasis upon the treasuries may stem from their special position in 1 Chr 26:22–28. The mention of the "divisions of the priests and Levites" has probably been influenced by 1 Chr 23–27, although, as noted by Williamson, a reference to them in a general statement such as this is not inappropriate. The emphasis upon the temple vessels and the vast amounts of gold and silver utilized in their construction is a mark both of the tabernacle narrative (cf. Exod 39:32–43) and of the significance which the writer wished to place in them. P. Ackroyd ("The Temple Vessels—A Continuity Theme," VTSup 23 [1972] 166–81) notes that this emphasis upon the cultic vessels is a mark of the period of the second temple. (For specific references, see Curtis-Madsen, 299, and 2 Chr 3–4.) In this expansion David, like Bezalel of old (Exod 31:3; 35:31), is provided by God with plans in detail for all the temple, its furnishings, and its personnel, that nothing may be left to chance.

20–21 *Concluding exhortation.* See again *Form/Structure/Setting* for the elements of the form for induction into office here. In v 21 for the first time the *total* people are placed at Solomon's disposal for work on the temple. The combination נדיב בחכמה "skilled men," as we have noted, also stems from the tabernacle pericope (cf. Exod 35:9–10). That trained artisans should be referred to in terms suggestive of Israel's wise men is itself indicative of the position the temple occupied in the mind of the writers of both pericopes.

Explanation

Having outlined to Solomon his divinely decreed task as temple builder and encouraged him to zeal and faithfulness in carrying out that task (1 Chr 22:7–13), David assembles Israel's leaders and informs them of the same details. Solomon is again explicitly designated as the temple builder, this time expressed through the use of the concept of election (vv 6, 7). Since Solomon's future is determined by his obedience to the law (v 7), David exhorts him to perfect service with two arguments not previously stated: (1) the omniscience of Yahweh, which examines not only the deeds of the hand but the spirit in which those deeds are done; and (2) the correspondence between Solomon's relationship to Yahweh and Yahweh's relationship to him, which is expressed in terms of retribution (vv 8, 9). However, in those portions of the speech influenced by the form for the induction into office, the emphasis again falls upon Yahweh's unconditional assistance, which will not fail until the temple has been completed (vv 10, 20).

In terms borrowed largely from the tabernacle pericope, David's preparatory role for the temple construction continues to be highlighted. The plan of the temple is given to David by inspiration (v 11) and conveyed to Solomon by him. David continues his preparations by placing at Solomon's disposal various other people to assist him: the priests and Levites, who will be necessary for the actual operation of the temple, the princes who must support the project, and even "all the people" (v 21) who, for the Chronicler, must be involved in every significant act involving cult or kingdom. With these important but preliminary arrangements taken care of, the stage is set for David's final speech.

The significance for its original audience of this pericope, with its emphasis upon the centrality of the temple and the Davidic/Solomonic role in its construction, has been pointed to before—the temple stands as the unifying point for all Israel. (See also the *Introduction.*) For God's people of all ages, the pericope points to that basic tension between God's free grace—amply illustrated here in the form for the induction into office with its "I am with you" and the use of the election concept—and the necessity for human response and obedience seen in the call for obedience to the law and the concept of retribution in general. This is in fact the same tension that exists throughout the OT between those covenants that are unconditional in their formulation, such as those with Abraham and David, and those that are conditional, such as that at Sinai. But, as Paul will argue later, God's grace—represented in his covenant with Abraham—always comes first, and that grace alone is determinative for salvation. The human response must, however, follow out of loving response to God's grace (Gal 3:1–14; Eph 2:8–10).

David's Third Speech (29:1-9)

Bibliography

See the *Bibliography* at 1 Chr 22:2–19.

Translation

¹ *Then David the king commanded all the assembly: "Solomon my son, whom alone* [a] *God has chosen, is* [b] *young and immature,* [b] *but the work is great, for the palace* [c] *is not for man but for Yahweh God.* ² *With all my power I have made provision for the house of my God—gold for (the objects of) gold, silver for those of silver, bronze for those of bronze, iron for those of iron, and wood for those of wood,* [a] *stones of onyx, (stones for) setting,* [a] *stones of antimony,* [b] *variegated cloth [. . .]* [c] *and fine linen in abundance.* ³ [a] *Moreover, I have a* [b] *personal treasury,* [b] *both gold and silver. Because of my delight in the house of my God,* [a] *I give to the house of my God above and beyond that which I have (already) provided for the* [c] *holy house* [c] ⁴ *three thousand talents of gold from the* [a] *gold of Ophir* [a] *and seven thousand talents of refined* [b] *silver for plating* [c] *the walls of the rooms;* ⁵ *yea, gold for the things of gold and silver for the things of silver and for all the work by the hand of craftsmen.* [a] *So who* [b] *will give generously,* [b] [c] *consecrating himself freely* [c] *today to Yahweh?"*

⁶ *Then the* [a] *princes of the fathers,* [a] *and the princes of the tribes of Israel, and the princes of thousands and hundreds, and* [b] *the princes over all the king's work gave freely.* [c] ⁷ *They gave to the service of the house of God five thousand talents and ten thousand darics* [a] *of gold,* [b] *ten thousand talents of silver, eighteen thousand talents of bronze, and one hundred thousand talents of iron.* [b] ⁸ *And whoever had* [a] *(precious) stones gave them to the treasury of Yahweh's house in the care of Jehiel* [b] *the Gershonite,* ⁹ *And the people rejoiced* [a] *over their* [b] *generous contributions,* [b] *for it was with a perfect heart that they had made these generous contributions to Yahweh; David the king also rejoiced with great joy.* [a]

Notes

1.a. Rudolph is probably right in stating that there is no valid reason to omit the rather difficult אחד "alone" or to alter it to אשר "which." LXX, contrary to the note in *BH³*, does not favor the omission but supports the text as it stands.

1.b-b. Cf. n. 22:5.a.

1.c. בירה, commonly considered late and a loan word, is found only here and in 29:19 in the sense of "temple"; cf. Polzin, *Late Biblical Hebrew*, 130, #12.

2.a-a. שהם "onyx" occurs no less than seven times in Exod 25–39, in three of these with מלאים "setting": Exod 25:7; 35:9, 27.

2.b. Cf. 2 Kgs 9:30; Jer 4:30, where the word is used for eye-shadow, and Isa 54:11, where it is used of dark cement for setting off stones; however, Wellhausen would read נפך "ruby," also a precious jewel, as would Keil here. נפך is also found in Exod 28:18 and 39:11 of a stone in the high priest's breastplate.

2.c. Omitting כל אבן יקרה "every precious stone" as a gl to the difficult פוך "antimony" later inserted into the text at the wrong place and occasioning also the introduction of אבני "stones" into the text before שיש "alabaster" (Curtis, 303). It is possible these changes were introduced deliberately by Chronicles, which otherwise states that the precious stones to be used for the high priest's vestments in the tabernacle narrative were to adorn the walls of the temple (2 Chr 3:16). The translation of רקמה "variegated cloth" reflects the fact that throughout the OT, with the single exception of Ezek 17:3, the word refers to woven or embroidered material.

3.a-a. The order of the two clauses of v 3a has been reversed to clarify the meaning. However, it is unnecessary to conclude that the unusual order marks the passage as later (cf. Rothstein and Hänel 2:508).

3.b-b. Only here and Eccl 2:8 in this sense, which BDB terms "very late"; elsewhere always of the people of Israel (Exod 19:5 + 5x).

3.c-c. בית הקדש "holy house" occurs only here in Chronicles, which is extremely prolific in its use of different names for the temple. (Cf. BDB, 109, col. A). Cf. also בית קדש קדשים "most holy house," 2 Chr 3:8, 10; and בית מקדשׁם "house of holiness," 2 Chr 36:17.

4.a-a. The exact phrase is again unique to Chronicles. For זהב אופיר "gold of Ophir," cf. Isa 13:12; Job 28:16; Ps 45:10. For Ophir, see 2 Chr 8:18 = 1 Kgs 9:28.

4.b. In the pual as here, only in 28:18; Isa 25:7; Ps 12:7; piel Mal 3:3.

4.c. Only here in Chronicles, otherwise only P and Ezekiel (BDB).

5.a. Cf. 4:14; 14:1; 22:15; 29:5; 2 Chr 24:12; 34:11. Among the usages are again those associated with the tabernacle; cf. Exod 28:11; 35:35; 38:23.

5.b-b. Curtis, 31, #70; Polzin, *Late Biblical Hebrew*, 135, #30. See also vv 6, 9 (2x), 14, 17 (2x); 2 Chr 17:16; Ezra 1:6; 2:68; 3:5; Neh 11:2, and in Aramaic Ezra 7:13, 15, 16. (The citation in Polzin is erroneous.) Polzin describes the meaning 'to offer free-will offerings" as late. The earlier meaning "to volunteer for holy war" is found only in Judg 5:2, 9.

5.c-c. That the term "to fill the hand" is a technical one associated with the induction of a priest to his office is well known; cf. de Vaux, *Ancient Israel*, 346–48. Its precise significance is unknown; de Vaux believes its original meaning was already lost to Israel. Its extended use may be seen in Ezek 43:26, where it occurs in connection with the inauguration of an altar, as well as in the passage before us, despite the objections of A. S. Herbert ("I and II Chronicles," PCB, 357–69), who believes it improbable "that a term so closely related to the priestly office would be used by the Chronicler in this vague metaphorical sense." However, Herbert's criticism ignores other places where Chronicles has shifted the meaning of a phrase; cf. n. 2.c. above.

6.a-a. That v 6 has been expanded seems probable in view of 28:2, but the original reading is difficult to conjecture. That suggested by Rothstein and Hänel, שרי ישראל "princes of Israel," is perhaps most likely. Rudolph assumes "die Oberen die Familien," for which one would, however, expect ראשי האבות "heads of the fathers" rather than שרי האבות "princes of the fathers."

6.b. For the use of the so-called "*lamedh* emphatic" before the last noun in a list as reflecting Aramaic influence, see Polzin, *Late Biblical Hebrew*, 66–68.

6.c. See n. 5.b-b.

7.a. See Curtis, 29, #22; Williamson, 42, ##10 and 50, #24 (C.10 and E.24), Polzin, *Late Biblical Hebrew*, 133, #21. The form with the prosthetic *aleph* occurs only here and in Ezra 8:27. The word is anachronistic here. The daric was a Persian coin weighing 130 grains, first issued by Darius I. Myers (190) computes that 5,000 talents of gold weighed 188-plus tons; 10,000 darics of gold, 185-plus pounds; and he notes that this passage and Ezra-Nehemiah are the first in the Bible to mention coined money. H. Hamburger (*IDB* 1:769) suggests that in the Persian period any gold coin might be called a daric. See also Williamson, *TynBul* 28 (1977) 123–26.

7.b-b. Myers computes 10,000 talents of silver at about 377.5 tons; 18,000 talents of bronze at about 679.5 tons; and 100,000 talents of iron at about 3,775 tons.

8.a. For מצא, niph, in the sense of "to be present," see Curtis, 31, #69; Williamson, *Israel*, 57, #23. The remainder of ten usages in Chronicles are all in the second book; in Ezra-Nehemiah only in Ezra 8:25.

8.b. This Jehiel is mentioned before only in the lists of 23:8; 26:21. Since Williamson considers the latter a part of the original strand of chs. 23–27, he feels no need to consider this passage a later addition as does Rudolph.

9.a-a. For the combined notes of joy and the perfect heart, see 1 Chr 12:39–41; for the note of joy on significant moments in Chronicles, cf. 1 Chr 15:16, 29; 2 Chr 7:10; 29:30, 36;

30:21, 23, 25, 26. See also Ezra 3:12, 13; 6:22; Neh 8:12, 17; 12:43. For the perfect and undivided heart, see also 28:9; 29:19; 2 Chr 15:12, 15; 19:9; 22:9; 25:2; 31:21; 32:31; 34:31.

9.b-b. See n. 5.b-b.

Form/Structure/Setting

The occasion and audience ostensibly remain the same as in David's second speech. This unit also is composed of a speech of David (vv 1–5), to which the people's response is added in vv 6–9.

In contrast with the first two speeches, where the logical progression was marked with literary features such as הנה "behold" and עתה "now," the third speech lacks such elements. In fact, each of the logical divisions within the speech begins only with the conjunction "and"; vv 2, 3, 5b, 6, 9.

The first two verses illustrate how closely this speech is related in content to the previous two.

Chap. 29		*Chaps. 22, 28*
29:1	Solomon's election	28:6, 10, cf. 22:9
29:1	Solomon as a נער ורך "inexperienced boy"	22:5
29:1	Greatness of the task	22:5
29:2	David's provisions	22:2–5, 28:3

At the same time, an obvious progression is noticeable. The emphasis upon Solomon's election, which formed the major thrust of the first two speeches, is here assumed and introduced almost parenthetically in v 1. David's provisions, which stood in the framework in 22:2–5 and were inserted briefly in 28:3, here become the central point, and are expanded to include jewels and fabrics (29:2).

In describing David's preparations for the temple, the author has continued his dependency upon the tabernacle pericope, Exod 25–31 and 35–40. This is clear from the following three notations. (1) The similarity of the building materials provided and contributed in the two sections. In addition to the gold and silver (vv 3–5), David's preparations included bronze, iron, wood, onyx stones, stones for setting, antimony, variegated cloth, and linen (v 2); and the people's contribution included gold, silver, bronze, iron, and precious stones (vv 7–8). All of these materials except iron are found in the tabernacle pericope, where iron would be anachronistic (iron is also lacking in the account of the temple's construction in Kings, but included loosely by the Chronicler, cf. 2 Chr 2:6, 13 [7, 14]). In addition to frequent mention of individual items, comprehensive lists of materials occur in Exod 25:3–7; 35:5–9, 22–28. Particularly striking is the mention of the otherwise rare onyx (Exod 25:7; 28:9, 20; 35:9, 27; 39:13), otherwise found in the OT only in Gen 2:12; Ezek 28:13; Job 28:16; variegated cloth (eight of nine occurrences of the cognate participle רקם are found here); "stones for setting" (Exod 25:7; 35:9, 27; cf. Exod 28:17, 20; 39:13), and linen (thirty-three times in the tabernacle narrative, only five in the remainder of the OT. פוך "antimony" is absent from the tabernacle narrative, although נכף "a precious jewel" (cf. BDB, 656), read here by some scholars, occurs as one of the jewels in the high priest's vestments in Exod 28:18; 39:11. (See n. 2.b.) (2) The use of חרש "engraver, artificer," recalls Exod 28:11; 35:35; 38:23. (Cf. also 1 Kgs 7:14.) (3) The fourfold use of נדב (hithpael) "to give generously" repeats a root that Chronicles has introduced in 28:21 in another sense. The priestly writer used the root five times (Exod 25:2; 35:5, 21, 22, 29) to refer to the generosity of the Israelites in making their contributions for the tabernacle. Curtis (301) correctly notes that as Moses appealed to the people for freewill offerings (Exod 35:4–9; cf. 25:1–8) and as they later responded to that appeal (Exod 35:20–29), so David is presented as appealing to the princes of Israel and receiving their gifts.

Attention should be called again to the freedom with which the Chronicler has used the material available to him, however. He has avoided mention of those items most closely connected with the priests and their vestments, such as the majority of the kinds of cloth, the oil, spices, and precious stones, and as well those items whose use would have been limited to the tabernacle, such as the goat and ram skins. In vocabulary, the Chronicler has worked with some freedom, preferring, e.g., the hithpael of נדב "give generously" to the qal used in Exodus. Moreover, while in Exodus the actual participation of the people in the building itself, and not just in contributions, is emphasized (Exod 35:25–26; 36:8–9), that element is lacking in Chronicles, perhaps because of the view that only Levites are permitted in the temple (cf. 2 Chr 23:6).

Note also that the writer in v 9 has woven together the closely related themes of generosity, a perfect heart, and joy. (On the "perfect heart," see 28:9.) All three concepts are also to be found in 12:39–41 [38–40], although a vocable corresponding to נדב "give generously" is lacking. Taken together, these three concepts epitomize the Chronicler's understanding of the faithful response of God's people—generosity and joy flowing from a fully committed heart.

Explanation

Just as Moses has solicited the contributions of the people and received them from generous worshipers, so David does the same. David also serves as a model in making his own contribution from his personal treasury, and his example is followed by both leaders and people. The immense amounts of the offerings are but another way of showing the writer's wholehearted dedication to his subject matter. (See n. 7.b-b.) The generous and joyful response of the people flowing from a perfect heart and directed toward the temple accurately portrays the Chronicler's understanding of the response God's people ought to make toward him.

This call to respond to God's grace and guidance with both generosity and joy is of course characteristic of all of God's revelation. The gift of the Torah, as the rabbis taught, is itself an occasion for joy, and the birth of Jesus in the New Testament is heralded by the angels as "good news of a great joy which shall come to all the people" (Luke 2:10). For generosity flowing from a cheerful heart, see further 2 Cor 9, especially vv 6–8, 11.

David's Blessing   (29:10–19)

Bibliography

See the *Bibliography* at 1 Chr 22:2–19.

Translation

¹⁰ Then David blessed ^a Yahweh before all the assembly. David said: ^b "Blessed are you Yahweh ^b our father, ^c the God of Israel, ^dfrom eternity even to eternity. ^d ¹¹ To you, Yahweh, is the greatness, the might, the splendor, the eminence, and the majesty—indeed, ^a everything in the heavens and on the earth. The sovereignty is yours, Yahweh, who art exalted ^babove everything as head. ^b ^{12 a} Riches and wealth ^a come from you, and ^byou rule over everything; in your hand is power and might, ^b and it is in your hand to make everything great and strong.

¹³And now, our God, ^awe give thanks ^a to you and praise your glorious ^b name. ¹⁴ But who am I, and who is my people, that we should be able ^a to give generously ^b like this? For everything comes from you, and we have given to you (only what we have received) from your hand. ¹⁵ For we are sojourners before you, and pilgrims ^a like all our fathers; ^bour days upon the earth are like a shade; ^b there is no hope. ^c ¹⁶ Yahweh our God, all this abundance ^a which we have provided ^b to build a house for you for your holy name is ^c from your hand; everything belongs to you. ¹⁷And I know, my God, that you examine ^a the heart and delight in righteous deeds. I, in the uprightness ^b of my heart, have freely contributed ^c all these. And now, I have seen your people who are present here ^d give freely ^c to you with joy. ^d ¹⁸ Yahweh, God of Abraham, Isaac, and Israel, ^a preserve forever ^bthe frame of the thoughts of the heart ^b of your people, and establish ^c their heart toward you. ¹⁹And as for Solomon my son, give him a ^aperfect heart, ^a that he may keep your commandments, your testimonies, and your statutes . . . , ^b and thus build the palace ^c for which I have made provision." ^d

Notes

10.a. For the expression "PN blessed Yahweh," found only in Gen 24:48; Deut 8:10; Josh 22:33 prior to Chronicles, see J. Sharbert, "ברך *brk*; ברכה *berakhah*," *TDOT* 2:292. In Chronicles, cf. v 20 and 2 Chr 20:26; 31:8.

10.b-b. For the formula "Blessed (are you) Yahweh," see Sharbert, *TDOT* 2:285–86, who points to the late and cultic use of the expression. In Chronicles, all usages of the qal pass ptcp except the one at hand occur also in parallel texts; cf. 1 Chr 16:36 = Ps 106:48; 2 Chr 2:11 [12] = 1 Kgs 5:21 [7]; 2 Chr 6:4 = 1 Kgs 8:15; 2 Chr 9:8 = 1 Kgs 10:9.

10.c. In contrast to Rudolph, Hänel (who completed Rothstein's work from 29:10 to the end), Myers, and all modern translations, which specify "the God of our father Israel" as Jacob. Such a translation gives too much weight to the admittedly similar phrase "the God of Abraham, Isaac, and Israel" of v 18, which is clearly creedal/liturgical, and too little to 1 Kgs 11:48, upon which our passage is dependent.

10.d-d. Note also the similar vocabulary in 16:36 = Ps 106:48, the conclusion of the Fourth Book of the Psalter, as well as in the final psalm of the remaining books (Ps 41:13; 89:52; 72:18–19, and Psalm 150).

11.a. If כי "indeed" be understood as emphatic (BDB, 472), there is no need to emend the text as suggested by *BH³* and *BHS*.

11.b-b. The syntax is obscure, perhaps again because of the profuse use of the prep *lamedh*. A few MSS and Vg omit the *lamedh* on ראש "head."

12.a-a. The two terms are also parallel in v 28, and in 2 Chr 17:15; 18:1; 32:27, pointing to stereotyped language.

12.b-b. Cf. the very similar expressions in Jehoshaphat's speech, 2 Chr 20:6.

13.a-a. Although ידה "give thanks," hiph, and הלל "praise," piel, are often paralleled and the piel ptcp of הלל is frequent, the hiph ptcp of ידה occurs only in Prov 28:13 (sg) and here (pl).

13.b. A frequent epithet of Yahweh; cf. v 11; Ps 71:8; and of his house, Isa 60:7; 63:15; 64:10. Used in Isa 63:14 of Yahweh's name, as here.

14.a. The use of עצר with accus כח in the sense of "to be able" is unique to Chr (29:14; 2 Chr 2:5 [6]; 13:20; 22:9, and, with כח omitted, 2 Chr 14:10; 20:37) and Daniel (10:8, 16; 11:6) in the OT.

14.b. Cf. n. 5.b-b.

15.a. While גר "sojourner" is common throughout the OT, תושב, rendered here "pilgrim," is termed by BDB "only P (H) and late." Note the close parallel in Ps 39:13 [12]. The two nouns also occur in parallelism in Gen 23:4; Num 35:15; Lev 25:35, 47 (2x).

15.b-b. The figure is common in the Psalms and Wisdom Literature; see Ps 90:9–10; 102:12 [11]; 109:23; 144:4; Job 8:9; Eccl 6:12.

15.c. מקוה "hope" is unusual in this context (cf. Rudolph), the Chronicler's language here is liturgical and highly stylized. (Cf. Job 7:6.) Otto Plöger sees this hopelessness of man apart from God as one of the distinctive themes of the Chronicler and compares Ezra 9:6-15 (*Festschrift für Günther Dehn*, 47–48). See also Ezra 10:2.

16.a. In this uncommon sense of "abundance," see also 2 Chr 31:10.

16.b. On this favorite word of the Chronicler, cf. once again Curtis, 30, #54, and Williamson, *Israel*, 53, who notes the word is found some forty times in Chronicles, but only twice in Ezra. See also vv 18, 19.

16.c. K היא "she," Q הוא "he," for the pronoun indicating the linking vb.

17.a. בחן "examine" is found only here in Chronicles. For the combination with "heart," see also Jer 11:20; 12:3; 17:10; Hos 7:10; 11:4–5; Prov 17:3.

17.b. Only here in Chronicles. With "heart" also, in Deut 9:5; 1 Kgs 9:4; Ps 119:7; Job 33:3.

17.c-c. See n. 5.b-b.

17.d-d. See n. 9.a.

18.a. I.e., Jacob; cf. 2 Chr 30:6: 1 Kgs 18:36. See also n. 10.c.

18.b-b. The Heb. is almost impossibly verbose, no doubt due to the quotation of the phrase from Gen 6:5; cf. also 1 Chr 28:9. That one or the other words is a later addition is a possibility.

18.c. See n. 16.b.

19.a-a. See n. 9.a.

19.b. לעשות הכל "doing all" seems impossible in its present position. Its frequent occurrence in other sections with strong Deuteronomic coloring such as 1 Chr 22:13 suggests that לעשות, with or without הכל, may first have been a marginal gl to לשמר "watching," later inserted into the text at the wrong place. The frequent repetition of עשה in parallel with another vb in Chronicles (cf., e.g., the late 1 Chr 22:16) presents yet another possibility.

19.c. See n. 1.c.

19.d. See n. 16.b.

Form/Structure/Setting

Apart from the brief introductory framework of v 10a, this unit consists of a single prayer of David, which may be divided into three subsections.

1. Ascription of praise, vv 10b–12
   a. Formula of blessing, v 10b
   b. The incomparability of Yahweh, vv 11–12
2. The thanksgiving, vv 13–16

a. Statement of thanksgiving, v 13
b. Reason for thanksgiving, vv 14–16
3. The supplication, vv 17–19
a. The basis for the supplication, v 17
b. The supplication, vv 18–19

David's prayer is introduced with the familiar ויאמר דויד "and David said." Structurally each of the three major divisions of the prayer begins with a highly stylized liturgical formula: ברוך אתה יהוה "Blessed are you, Yahweh" (v 10b); מודים אנחנו לך ומהללים לשם תפארתך "we give thanks to you and praise your glorious name (v 13); and יהוה אלהי אברהם יצחק וישראל אבתינו "Yahweh, God of Abraham, Isaac, and Israel, our fathers" (v 18). The transition from the first unit to the second is marked by the ועתה "and now" of v 13, and it may be that the ועתה of v 17b serves a similar function.

In form, this prayer is a blending of three major psalm types, the hymn, the thanksgiving, and the petition, with marks of the lament as well. The introductory ברוך אתה יהוה "Blessed are you, Yahweh" and the extended description of Yahweh's incomparability (vv 10–12) are most clearly related to the hymns of praise. The explicit statement of v 13, however, and the relationship to the prior contributions mentioned in v 14, point to the thanksgiving aspect of the prayer as well. Finally, the prayer concludes with two petitions (vv 18–19) which have no part in hymns of thanksgiving in the narrow sense. It is then apparent that the distinction between the various types of prayers and psalms were largely ignored by the Chronicler, who blended closely praise, thanksgiving, and petition. (Cf. B. Hornig, "Das Prosagebet der nachexilischen Literatur," *TLZ* 83 [1958] col. 645, who states that the post-exilic prayer should be viewed as a living intercourse of the pious with his God which involved not only petition, but praise and thanksgiving as well.)

Particular attention may be given to the fact that each of the three units of the prayer is supplied by the writer with a basis or reason. The blessing of v 10b is supported by the description of vv 11–12; the thanksgiving of v 13 finds a similar ground in vv 14–16; and the supplications for Israel and Solomon in vv 18–19 have their support both in the statement of God's delight in righteousness and in Israel's present righteous state as seen in the generous and joyous contributions.

There is no reason to doubt that this fine prayer of David reflects in considerable measure the usage current in the temple or synagogue of the author's own day (cf. A. S. Herbert, *PCB*, 364; Coggins, 142; Ackroyd, 93–94). In that light the author's use of the various traditions is of a different sort here, involving not a direct use of biblical texts and traditions, but a more direct one of these as they have become embedded in the liturgical use of the congregation and the piety of the individual.

That the piety reflected here is in large part that of the pious Israelite in the author's own day is apparent from a comparison of the vocabulary of this prayer with the Psalms. Almost every item in the opening verses has numerous counterparts in the psalms, in the manner of Hannah's song in 1

Samuel 2 or Mary's song in Luke 1. Most telling in this regard is the introductory phrase, "Blessed are you, Yahweh our father, the God of Israel, from eternity even to eternity." The opening phrase, ברוך אתה יהוה "Blessed are you, Yahweh," with the 2nd person pronoun, occurs only twice in the OT, the more common ברוך יהוה "Blessed be Yahweh" is found in Ps 66:20; 68:36; 135:21, where it serves as a conclusion to the entire Psalm. That this was common liturgical practice, more or less like the recitation of the *Gloria Patri* in Christian tradition, is clear in that four or five "books" of Psalms end with a similar termination (cf. Pss 41:13; 72:18–19; 89:52; 106:48 = 1 Chr 16:36). Examining the remainder of the occurrences in this light, it can be seen that the majority introduce conclusions of psalms of lament where, after describing his previous plight, the individual thanks God for the deliverance promised or bestowed upon him (cf. Pss 28:6; 31:22 [21]; 18:47). Closely related to this is David's prayer here, which, beginning with a thanksgiving, is introduced with ברוך אתה יהוה "Blessed are you, Yahweh," as is the case also in Ps 144:1. See S. Blank, "Some Observations Concerning Biblical Prayer," *HUCA* 32 (1961) 87–90, who believes the phrase originated no earlier than the fourth century.

The phrase "from eternity to eternity," which occurs in several differing but similar forms, is also seen to be a standard liturgical expression apart from the doxologies listed above (cf. Ps 90:2; 103:17; 106:48; Neh 9:5). Other correspondencies exhibit overwhelmingly the provenance of the Chronicler's language.

(1) גדולה "greatness"   Ps 71:21; 145:3, 6 (Q), cf. 2 Sam
                           7:21, 32 = 1 Chr 17:19, 21

(2) גבורה "might"   Ps 89:14 [13]; 90:10; 106:2,8;
                           145:11,12; 150:2, etc.

(3) תפארת "splendor"   Ps 71:8; 78:61; 89:18 [17]; 96:6 (and
                           seven times in Isa 60–66)

(4) הוד "majesty"   Eight times in the Psalms, often in
                           combination with והדר, "and
                           honor" as in 96:6, quoted in 1
                           Chr 16:27

(5) בשמים בארץ "in the heaven   Ps 115:15; 121:2; 123:1; 124:8;
    and on earth"   134:3; 135:6, etc.

Many other parallels might be drawn. The noun נצח "eminence," is common in the Psalms, though with the meaning "permanence." Yahweh is viewed as ruling (משל) in Ps 22:29; 59:14 [13]; 66:7; 89:10 [9]. While the verb ידה "to give thanks" is common in the Psalms, for the plural as here see Ps 44:9 [8]; 79:13. Phraseology such as "your/my/his holy name" is found in Pss 33:21; 103:1; 105:3; 106:47; 145:21, as well as frequently in Ezekiel and Isa 56–66. The phrase "you test the heart" recalls not only Jeremiah (cf. 11:20; 12:3; 17:10) but also Pss 7:10; 11:5; 17:3. The rather rare מישר "righteousness" has seven of its nineteen occurrences in the Psalms. (Five of the remainder are in Proverbs, which, together with the remaining wisdom literature, frequently shows correspondence with Chronicles in vocabulary.) The phrase בישר לבב "in uprightness of heart" is found in Ps 119:7. The list can doubtless be extended.

Other references indicate that while the Chronicler has expressed himself chiefly in cultic language, he has continued to deal eclectically with other biblical materials as well. The idea of placing a blessing into David's mouth probably stems from 1 Kgs 1:48. The designation of Yahweh as the God of Israel, *"our father,"* is found elsewhere only in Isa 63:16; 64:7 [8]. The mention of the God of Abraham, Isaac, *"and Israel"* (v 18) is found only in 1 Kgs 18:36. The combination עשר וכבוד "riches and honor," which occurs some seven times in Chronicles, is probably dependent upon 1 Kgs 3:13, while the "frame of the thoughts of the heart" (v 18) is a clear reference from Gen 6:5 (cf. 1 Chr 28:9).

We have noted above one connection between David's prayer and the lament. The words of v 15, like Psalm 39:13 [12], reflect a common vocabulary with that portion of the lament in which the worshiper recounts his helplessness in the situation at hand. In choosing terminology that refers to Israel as being "sojourners," "pilgrims," and "without hope," the author seems to move quietly from the age of David to a much more troubled one such as the exile. O. Plöger finds here a common theme of the Chronicler, and points to 2 Chr 20:12 and Ezra 9:6–15 (cf. especially the ואין מקוה "there is no hope" of v 15 with the יש־מקוה "there is hope" of Ezra 10:2). Similarly Williamson has found in David's prayer here three themes—those of the sojourning patriarchs, the kingship of Yahweh, and petition—which echoes those found in the anthology collected in 1 Chr 16:8–36. So at both the beginning and end of the preparations for the temple (1 Chr 17–29), there stands a prayer in which the expressed ideas are of primary importance for the writer's understanding of Israel's existence before God.

Comment

10–12 Note that the Chronicler does not refrain from David's blessing the people, v 10 (as will Solomon, 2 Chr 6:4) though that is sometimes considered a priestly prerogative. On ברוך "bless," see also J. Sharbert, "ברך *brk;* ברכה *berahkah," TDOT* 2:279–308. J. Hänel, who completed Rothstein's monumental commentary from 29:10, calls David's prayer *"eine rechte Schule des Gebets"* (523). The terminology, as noted above, is throughout that of Israel's psalmody, and much is retained also in the prayers of the synagogue even today. In vv 11–12, which are unsurpassed in proclaiming Yahweh's praise, is surely to be seen also the source of the doxology appended to the Lord's Prayer in many later manuscripts of Matt 6:13.

13–19 Vv 13–14 combine the theme of thanksgiving with an emphasis upon the fact that it is God alone who is the source of all gifts (cf. Deut 8:18; Jas 1:17), including those which David and his people have offered for the building of the temple. At the same time, the "Who am I, and who are my people" recalls also the words of David's prayer in 17:16. The wording of v 15, referring to Israel as sojourners and pilgrims, would appear to refer to Israel's exilic or post-exilic situation; cf. Ezra 9:6–15. V 17 again raises the points of Yahweh's omniscience and the necessity for a perfect heart (cf. 28:9), and repeats enthusiastically the emphasis upon generosity and joy seen in 29:9. David's supplication is that Yahweh himself would establish such a perfect heart in both Israel and Solomon that God's commandments might be kept and the temple built (vv 17–19).

Explanation

In this beautiful prayer are woven together thoughts and emphases very close to the heart of the Chronicler. In David's prayer is reflected a faith that looks to and gives thanks to God for every good, and expresses itself in praise of God, in generous support of his temple (both monetary and otherwise), and in obedience to his law flowing from a joyful and undivided heart. While an expression of concern for the other peoples of the world is lacking, it would otherwise be difficult to improve upon such an expression of the faith. The fact that Israel sees its own situation as in some sense transitory or in jeopardy does not detract from, but rather contributes to, this faith and confession.

Particularly instructive is the position that the temple occupies even within this prayer. In one sense the temple remains central. God's goodness is understood as the goodness that has enabled his people to prepare to build a temple, and David's final petition is directed toward the keeping of the law in order that the temple might be built.

On the other hand, however, the writer has not permitted the temple to replace or obscure the primary responsibility for praise of and obedience to Yahweh, for whom it is to be erected. Rather he has through this fine prayer given exemplary expression to the relationship that exists between Yahweh and his people, a proper appreciation of which can only result in worshipers who come before him in humility, thankfulness, obedience, generosity, and joy.

The application of this prayer to the faithful of every age, as well as its use, is readily apparent. The note of praise and thanksgiving always remains dominant, even in the midst of an existence that suggests a vocabulary like "pilgrims" and "sojourners." And for our day too, the formalities of religion, be they churches, liturgies, or our own pious traditions, can never interfere with nor abrogate the responsibility of the individual to respond to God personally with his or her praises and petitions.

Solomon's Enthronement   (29:20-30)

Bibliography

See the *Bibliography* at 1 Chr 22:2–19.

Translation

^{20} *Then David commanded all the assembly, "Bless* ^{a} *Yahweh your God," and all the assembly blessed* ^{a} *Yahweh, the God of their fathers, and bowed down and did obeisance* ^{b} *to Yahweh and the king* ^{b} ^{21} *and offered sacrifices to Yahweh.* ^{a} *On the next day (also) they sacrificed burnt offerings,* ^{a} *a thousand oxen, a thousand rams, and a thousand sheep, together with their drink offerings,* ^{b} *sacrifices in abundance* ^{c} *for all Israel.* ^{22} *So they* ^{a} *ate and drank* ^{a} *before Yahweh that day* ^{a} *with great gladness,* ^{a} *and they made Solomon* ^{b} *the son of David king . . .* ^{c} *and anointed him as Yahweh's prince* ^{d} *and Zadok* ^{e} *as priest.* ^{23} *So Solomon sat upon* ^{a} *the throne of Yahweh* ^{a} *as king instead of his father David and prospered, and all Israel was obedient to him.* ^{24} *And all the chiefs and warriors, and even all the sons of King David, vowed their allegiance to Solomon the king.* ^{25} *And Yahweh made Solomon very* ^{a} *great* ^{b} *before all Israel and gave him royal honor such as there had not been upon any king over Israel before him.*

^{26} *David the son of Jesse was king over all Israel.* ^{27} *He was king over Israel forty years; in Hebron he was king for seven years and in Jerusalem he was king for thirty-three years.* ^{28} *He died in a good old age, filled with days, riches, and honor; and Solomon his son became king in his stead.* ^{29} *And the words of David the king, the former and the latter, lo, they are written in the words of* ^{a} *Samuel the seer, and in the words of Nathan the prophet, and in the words of Gad the visionary,* ^{a} ^{30} *together with all his dominion and might and the events which affected him and Israel and all the kingdoms of the nations.* ^{a}

Notes

20.a. See n. 10.a.

20.b-b. Such a direct parallel between Yahweh and the king is astonishing, but see also 2 Chr 20:20 for a similar juxtaposition of Yahweh and his prophets and, less strikingly, of God and his priests in 2 Chr 13:12.

21.a-a. This translation, which separates the זבחים "sacrifices" from the עולות "burnt offerings," agrees with RSV against NEB and JB and most commentators. While the nature of any two-day ceremony is problematic, the unusual position of למחרת היום ההוא "on that next day," together with the repetition of ליהוה "to Yahweh," appears to favor the translation given above.

21.b. See also 2 Chr 29:35. נסך "drink offering" never occurs in Deuteronomy, the Deuteronomic History, Ezra, or Nehemiah; it is found in Exod 29:40, 41; Lev 23:13, and some 27x in Num 15 and 28–29.

21.c. Note the characteristic themes and vocabulary of Chronicles in this and the following verses, found also in 1 Chr 12:39–41 [38–40], including the themes of all Israel, eating and drinking, the perfect heart, and such vocabulary as לרב "in abundance" and כון "prepare," hiph.

22.a-a. See n. 21.c.

22.b. The *lamedh* is the sign of the accus, after the Aramaic manner; cf. Polzin, *Late Biblical Hebrew*, 64–66.

22.c. The word שנית "a second time" appears to be an addition to reconcile the passage with 23:1, adjudged above to be a later insertion. Its deletion is further suggested by its omission in G^B Syr α'. Williamson's argument that 23:1 is to be understood as the title for the subsequent chapters is unconvincing in the light of the materials following it, even in the much briefer portions of chaps. 23–27 which he considers primary. The unusual translation of JB, "Then having made Solomon son of David *their second king*, they anointed him," appears unjustified. Not only would such an expression of coregency be unique, but the fem ordinal שנית "second" also opposes such an understanding.

22.d. The use of נגיד here is probably related to that in 1 Kgs 1:35. Whether it should be translated "tribal chieftain" or "crown prince" cannot be determined with certainty. The Chronicler's use of נגיד elsewhere is very broad; cf. BDB, 617–18, and 1 Chr 28:4, which is late.

22.e. The reference to Zadok appears out of place here, and whether it should be ascribed to a later hand is problematic. Such an anointing was commonplace in post-exilic times and may be said to be demanded by 1 Kgs 1:34, 39; 2:35; cf. Exod 28:41; Lev 8:12; 21:10 (Rudolph). Since Zadok had apparently been functioning as a priest for some time prior to this, some understand this anointing to be to the high priesthood.

23.a-a. Cf. 1 Chr 17:14.

25.a. Curtis, #87; Williamson, *Israel*, 55, #47; Japhet, *VT* 18 (1968) 357–58; Polzin, *Late Biblical Hebrew*, 140–41, #46, who sees this usage as unique to Chronicles.

25.b. גדל "made great," piel, is used in Chronicles only of Solomon; cf. v 12; 2 Chr 1:1.

29.a-a. For extensive discussion of the problem posed by such references, see esp. O. Eissfeldt, *The Old Testament: An Introduction*, 535, and the references cited there, although I do not agree with Eissfeldt's conclusions regarding the nature of the midrash. It seems probable to me that Chronicles has adopted the idea for such closing summaries from the Deuteronomic historian, frequently, as here, referring to the prophets who were known to be active during the reign of the king in question. Cf. Curtis, 307; Rudolph, 194.

30.a. For the pl, see Curtis, #6; Williamson, *Israel*, 43, #10; Polzin, *Late Biblical Hebrew*, 127, #6.

Form/Structure/Setting

The Chronicler concludes his David story with a narrative which may be outlined as follows: (1) events surrounding Solomon's accession, vv 20–22; (2) preview of Solomon's reign, vv 23–25; (3) David's death, vv 26–30.

The first of these units is directly related to 29:10–19 through the blessing theme. David, having completed his own prayer of blessing, continues by exhorting the assembly to do the same (v 20). While the content of the people's blessing is not recorded, it is related that they "blessed" Yahweh and prostrated themselves before both Yahweh and King Solomon. Other festivities mentioned surrounding the accession are sacrifices (v 21), apparently offered on two different days, a joyous meal "before Yahweh" (v 22a), and the anointing itself.

In vv 23–25 attention is shifted to an anticipatory picture of Solomon's reign. While this insertion breaks somewhat the connection between Solomon's accession and David's death, it is easy to see how it was suggested by the statement that Solomon became king (v 22). The final summation of David's reign (vv 26–30) gives the customary information concerning the duration of his reign, with v 27 taken from 1 Kgs 2:11. The concluding unit is completed with the customary citation of other sources concerning David's reign available to the reader; cf. 2 Chr 32:33; 35:26.

Largely on the basis of the anointing of Solomon (1 Kgs 1:38–48; 1 Chr 29:20–25) and Joash (2 Kgs 11:12–17 = 2 Chr 23:11–16), de Vaux has listed the following components of the rite of coronation: (1) investiture with the insignia (not mentioned in the case of Solomon); (2) the anointing; (3) the acclamation; (4) the enthronement; and (5) the homage of the high officials. According to de Vaux, the first part of the ceremony took place in the temple, with the king standing on his daïs (cf. 2 Chr 34:31; 6:13) and the anointing being performed by the priest. After the acclamation all left the sanctuary and entered the palace, where the new king took his seat on the throne, marking his assumption of power (*Ancient Israel,* 102–5).

That the account of Solomon's accession should be dependent upon the last chapters of the Succession Document, 1 Kgs 1–2, is to be expected. Rothstein and Hänel (XVIII, ii, 514) had studied this area in great detail, and concluded that every facet of the Chronicles account is present in Kings. While the evidence may at times be overstated, the following nine correspondents are worthy of mention: (1) The prayer of the assembly (v 20) corresponds to the pious wish of Benaiah (1 Kgs 1:36–37). More specifically, the prostration before Yahweh and the king corresponds to the two parts of Benaiah's wish. See also 1 Kgs 1:16, 31. (2) The anointing (משׁח) of Solomon and the great joy of the people (v 22) correspond to 1 Kgs 1:38–39. (3) The statement "so Solomon sat upon the throne . . . of David his father" (v 23a) recalls 1 Kgs 1:46; 2:12a. (4) Solomon's feast and sacrifices recall Adonijah's (1 Kgs 1:9, 19, 25) and the eating and drinking of 1 Kgs 1:41; 4:20. (5) Solomon's prosperous reign (vv 23b–25) has its counterpart in 1 Kgs 2:12. The root גדל "great" used in this connection is found in 1 Kgs 1:37, 47; and the mention of עשׁר וכבוד "riches and honor" recalls 1 Kgs 3:13. (6) The use of נגיד in the sense of "king" is found in 1 Kgs 1:35 as well as 2 Sam 5:3; 7:8. (7) The account of David's death (vv 26–30) is dependent upon 1 Kgs 2:11. (8) The devotion of the people, offices, and heroes (v 24) may be seen also in 1 Kgs 1:9, 19, 25, 38–40, 49, 53. (9) The background of Zadok's ordination to the priesthood is found in 1 Kgs 1:38–40; 2:35, where Zadok functions as high priest.

Thus while there is little doubt of the dependence of Chronicles upon the Kings account, other items suggest that the Chronicler is here broadly dependent upon a wider range of OT traditions. The fact that the Chronicler specifically names the people's prayer as a "blessing," together with the indication of response to David's exhortation, reflects more the tradition of the Psalms than it does Benaiah's remarks. The note of sacrifice and festal meal are common in the OT, including the Deuteronomic History and Chronicles (for sacrifices see Exodus 29; 40:29; Lev 9:22–24; 2 Sam 6:18; 1 Kgs 8:62–64; and for the eating and drinking see Exod 24:11; Deut 14:26; 2 Sam 6:19; 1 Kgs 4:20; 1 Chr 12:40, etc.). It could be that the Chronicler is indebted to a common tradition concerning the components of such festal services rather than the abortive ceremony of Adonijah.

Other details support the assumption that the Chronicler has drawn freely from a larger body of traditions. While the "great joy" of v 22 is found in 1 Kgs 1:40, it is commonly joined with such festivities in both the Deuteronomic History and Chronicles (cf. 2 Sam 6:5 = 1 Chr 13:8, 1 Kgs

8:66 = 2 Chr 6:10). Although the root גדל "great" is found in 1 Kgs 1:37,
47, the parallel is closer with Josh 3:7; 4:14. Hänel does not mention the
"all Israel" so important in the narrative (vv 21, 23, 25, 26), primarily of
Deuteronomic origin, nor the significance of צלח "prosper," likewise of Deuteronomic origin. Marks of other traditions that show the Chronicler's eclectic
disposition include the mention of drink offerings, an element from P (cf.
BDB, 651a) and the specific vocabulary applied to David upon his death
(בשיבה טובה שבע ימים "he died in a good old age," v 28), otherwise applied only to Abraham (Gen 25:8, P), Isaac (Gen 35:29, P), and Job (Job
42:17) among all OT saints. (The usage in 1 Kgs 1:1 recalls rather Josh
23:2.)

Comment

20–22 *Solomon's accession.* For the assembly of all Israel, see also 11:1;
13:1–2, 5; 15:3; 28:1, 8; 29:1. On the blessing, see 29:10 and the reference
there. On the ceremony itself, see above, *Form/Structure/Setting.* The note
of a common obeisance (השתחוה "to bow down to, prostrate oneself, worship") to Yahweh and Solomon is surely striking. (There is a similar parallel
between Yahweh and his prophets in 2 Chr 20:20.) The number of sacrifices
offered is enormous (at least three thousand animals) and points to the significance of the event (cf. 2 Chr 7:4–5 = 1 Kgs 8:62–63, and also 2 Chr 30:23–
27 for Hezekiah's Passover, where an explicit parallel is drawn with Solomon's
age [v 26]; cf. also Josiah's Passover in 2 Chr 35:7–9, where in v 18 a parallel
is mysteriously drawn with the age of Samuel), as does the extension of the
sacrifices to a second day. (Note the similar device in 2 Chr 7:8–10, where
festivities are lengthened by a week, in contrast with the writer's *Vorlage* in
1 Kgs 8:66, and 2 Chr 30:23.)

The mention of sacrifices for "all Israel" recalls that common motif found
first in 11:1 (repeated here in vv 23, 25, and 26) and points forward to the
significance of sacrifice exemplified in the Chronicler's addition to 1 Kgs
9:3 found in 2 Chr 7:12. The fasting, eating, drinking, and joy attending
Solomon's coronation are yet another mark of the Chronicler's interest: cf.
12:39–41 [38–40]; 16:3; 2 Chr 7:8–10; 30:21–22, 23–27. K. Baltzer finds this
passage with its mention of prince and priest most important for the development of the "two Messiahs" idea at Qumran (cf. also 2 Chr 19:11; Jer 33:14–
26) and relates the hope for a coming prophet to the need for a prophet
to anoint the other two ("Das Ende des Staates Juda und die Messiasfrage,"
Studien zur theologie der alttestamenlichen Überlieferungen [Ed. R. Rendtorff und
K. Koch; Neukirchen: Neukirchener Verlag, 1961] 40–43).

23–25 *Solomon's reign.* The mention of both Solomon and David in both
vv 23 and 24, as in v 22, seems somewhat contrived, and brings together
the two unique kings of the United Monarchy. The note that Solomon prospered (צלח, v 23), is striking in that the reign of Solomon has not yet begun.
That the kingdom is Yahweh's kingdom, however, is affirmed emphatically
(cf. 1 Chr 17:14; 2 Chr 9:8). Such prosperity is for the Chronicler a regular
mark of God's blessing upon the reign (or parts of reigns) of pious kings,
representing the positive side of retribution (cf. 22:11, 13; 2 Chr 7:11; 14:6

[7]; 31:20; 32:30; and, negatively, 2 Chr 13:12; 24:20). The mark that "all Israel obeyed him" (v 23) is even more tendentious, ignoring the strong opposition to Solomon's reign and affirming, in the face of the evidence to the contrary (1 Kgs 1–2), that "also all the sons of David pledged their allegiance to Solomon" (v 24). The concept of Israel's unanimous support of David and Solomon is thus brought to a climax (see on 11:1–3). V 25 continues its heaping of praise upon Solomon. Such glory is ascribed to Yahweh in 16:27; 29:11. On גדל "make great," piel, see 1 Kgs 1:37, 47 (of Solomon); in Chronicles the construction is used only of Solomon (29:12, 25; 2 Chr 1:1). If the words are taken in any literal sense, v 25 ranks Solomon's "royal majesty" above that of any king of Israel before him—i.e., Saul or David. The expression, however, is probably a stereotype.

26–30 *David's death.* David's rule over "all Israel" is affirmed (v 26), as is Solomon's (vv 23–25). That David's seven-year reign at Hebron is mentioned is surprising in view of the treatment of 2 Sam 5:1–5 in 1 Chr 11:1–3 (1 Chr 3:4 belongs to a later strand of the book), but there is even here no indication that the Hebron rule was over only a part of "Israel." A formal evaluation of the quality of David's reign is lacking in Kings as in Chronicles (cf. 1 Kgs 2:10–12); however, the laudatory words of v 28 surely picture David in a more favorable light than do 1 Kgs 1:1; 2:1. For further information on David, the reader is referred to the "words" or acts (דברי) of Samuel the seer, of Nathan the prophet, and Gad the visionary. The designations ראה "seer" and חזה "visionary" applied to Samuel and Gad are of course archaic. (See n. 29.a-a.) Such concluding references are probably conventional, and based loosely upon those of the Deuteronomic historian (see n. 29.a-a.).

Explanation

Into this final section of the Davidic history, which may appear at first reading to be a rather annalistic recitation of stereotyped words and phrases borrowed from here and there, the Chronicler has woven together a comprehensive presentation of numerous ideas of importance for understanding his view of the reigns of David and Solomon and their relationship to both Yahweh and the people.

First, the emphasis upon the "all Israel" theme seems to reach a climax in this section, where it occurs no less than four times. David speaks to all the assembly, and the response of "all the assembly" is duly noted. But it is also noted that the sacrifices were offered for "all Israel" (v 21). It is explicitly mentioned that "all Israel" was obedient to Solomon (v 23) upon his accession (v 23), a picture in sharp contrast to that in 1 Kgs 1–2, and that Yahweh made him (i.e., Solomon) great before all Israel (v 25), a statement perhaps to be read in connection with the closing notice concerning David that he was king over all Israel (v 26). The two areas to which "all Israel" appears to have reference are then: (1) the vast extent of the kingdoms of David and Solomon; and (2) the unanimity of the people's response in participating in Solomon's inauguration and in obedience to his rule.

Second, the cultic nature of the ceremony is evident. As a component of the sacrificial meal accompanying Solomon's accession, the note of joy is again present, recalling Deut 12:7, 12; 14:26; 16:15. The Chronicler never permits the solemnity of such events to detract from their joyful nature. The importance of the ceremony for the Chronicler is seen not only by his extending it to cover a period of two days—a device he will also use for the dedication of the temple (contrast 2 Chr 7:8-9 with 1 Kgs 8:66), but also in the large number of animals sacrificed.

Third, David continues to occupy a central place, as is apparent both from his taking the initiative in leading the people in their worship (v 20) and in the favorable notice concerning his death (v 27). However, the major emphasis here is rather on Solomon, whose coronation forms the backdrop for the narrative. We have noted the emphasis placed upon the involvement of all Israel in that coronation and the unanimous support given by all, including David's other sons, to Solomon's rule. But the prosperity which is to mark Solomon's rule is also given considerable attention. This is remarkable since Solomon's reign has not yet begun, and this account is actually found within the Davidic history. That it was Solomon, and not the insurgent Adonijah, whom Yahweh made great, is the likely meaning of v 25 viewed in connection with David's prayer in 1 Chr 29:12b. That this prosperity is programmatic rather than merely descriptive of a single aspect of his rule is also likely on the basis of 1 Chr 22:11-12, where this prosperity was on the one hand conditional upon Yahweh's presence with Solomon and his gift to him of wisdom and understanding and, on the other, was to result in obedience to the law and the successful completion of the temple. The exalted position that the writer wishes to ascribe to Solomon is nowhere clearer than in his statement that Yahweh bestowed him honor "such as no king over Israel before him had had" (v 25).

Fourth, the Chronicler has used the occasion of the transfer of the rule from David to Solomon to state his view of kingship in Israel. This is most clearly seen in his statement that "Solomon sat upon the throne of Yahweh as king" (v 23), where the kingship of Yahweh over Israel is stated with absolute clarity and King Solomon's subservient role to Yahweh is implicit. The same is true of the description of Solomon as a king/prince of Yahweh (v 22). That this subservient role of the king does not detract from, but rather adds to, his importance, and the necessity for absolute obedience to him is also clear. The Chronicler does not avoid positing the identical obeisance to both Yahweh and the king!

Finally, several items in the text appear to forge the link between David and Solomon very strongly. Throughout chaps. 22, 28, and 29, the focus has been directed toward both David and Solomon. Nowhere else in the OT has the relationship between a father and son, or a king and his successor, been dealt with in such a manner. (The closest parallel is that of Moses to Joshua, which we have seen to lie behind David's speech in 1 Chr 22.) V 22 mentions that "they made Solomon, the son of David, king," a qualification hardly necessary for those who have been following the narrative of the last several chapters. Similarly, the statement that "Solomon sat upon the throne of Yahweh as king instead of David his father" (v 23), while apparently equally superfluous and not at first striking in view of similar statements elsewhere (cf. 2 Chr 9:31; 12:16), deserves more attention. Closer scrutiny reveals that the explicit mention of the deceased king's name in the closing part of the formula is indeed exceptional, the more usual form being that of v 28b; "Solomon *his son* reigned in his stead." That David's other sons supported the new king, thus recognizing the legitimate authority as passing from David to Solomon, might be still another attempt to join these two reigns more closely. Finally, that "David the son of Jesse was king over all Israel" (v 26) is parallel to the obedience of all Israel tendered Solomon in v 23.

We have had occasion throughout the commentary, and more extensively in the *Introduction,* to note the relevance of this message to its original audience. (See pp. xxv–xxix.) Although it is primarily in the application of the final and total message of the book that believers of a later age are addressed, we have pointed out also specific applications of the Chronicler's thought for us as well. The God who furthered his plans through David, Solomon, and the temple, and summoned his people to identify themselves with him in those plans, is still mightily at work, and still summons "all Israel," i.e., all his chosen ones, to accept his lordship and respond with lives of obedient service. In that service, they are assured, they will find perfect freedom and joy.

Index of Authors Cited

Abba, R. 80
Abel, F.-M. 117, 119
Achtemeier, E. R. 139
Ackroyd, P. R. xvii, xxvii, xxix, xli, 11, 145, 188, 192, 275, 283
Aharoni, Y. 3, 8, 25, 26, 41, 42, 44, 47, 56, 59, 63, 65, 67, 75, 125, 126, 255, 262
Ahlstrom, G. xli
Albright, W. F. xviii, xx, xli, 30, 31, 47, 53, 63, 76, 95, 97, 98, 110, 113, 241, 247, 254, 255, 262
Allen, L. C. xxi
Allrik, H. L. xli
Alt, A. 256
Amit, Y. xli
Amsler, S. xxxii
Ap-Thomas, D. R. xxiv
Asmussen, P. xli
Auld, A. C. 95, 97, 98
Avigad, N. 47, 53
Avi-Yonah, M. 126, 141

Bach, R. xxxii
Baltzer, K. xli, 290
Barag, D. xlii
Barnes, W. E. xviii, xxxii, xlii
Bartlett, J. R. xxxi
Batten, L. 129, 133
Baudissin, W. W. 80
Bea, A. xviii
Beck, H. F. 35
Beer, G. 209
Begrich, J. xxxi, 64
Beltz, W. 25
Bennett, W. W. xviii
Benzinger, I. xviii
Bertheau, E. xviii, 107, 159
Bickerman, E. J. xlii
Bin-Nun, S. P. xli
Blank, S. H. xxiv, xlii, 284
Blenkinsopp, J. xxxii
Boecker, H. xxiv
Böhmer, J. 241
Botterweck, G. J. xxi, xxii, xxv, xxxii, 150, 195, 201, 210, 212
Bowman, R. A. 1
Bratsiotis, N. xxiv
Braun, R. L. xviii, xx, xxiv, xxv, xxix, xxxiii, xxxiv, xxxv, xxxvii, xxxix, 115, 145, 195, 198, 219, 223, 275
Bright, J. xlii, 75, 95, 100, 101, 149, 178, 203, 262
Brin, G. 1
Brongers, H. A. xlii
Brown, F., S. R. Driver, and C. A. Briggs xi, 15, 19, 23, 29, 30, 56, 57, 64, 70, 71, 82, 89, 90, 93, 103, 132, 148, 158, 164, 173, 184, 185, 203, 209, 224, 257, 278, 280, 282, 288, 290
Brown, R. E. 1
Brueggemann, W. xxxii, xlii
Brunet, A. M. xix, xxi, xxii, xxiii, xlii, 1, 13, 25, 195, 211
Bückers, H. xviii
Busche, H. van den xlii
Bush, F. W. 34
Butler, T. C. 180, 187, 193

Calderone, P. J. xlii
Caquot, A. xlii
Carlson, R. A. xxxii, 195, 219
Cazelles, H. xviii
Clements, R. E. xxix, xxxii, xlii, 195, 271
Cody, A. 80
Coggins, R. J. xvii, xxv, xxviii, xlii, 11, 55, 64, 65, 75, 77, 119, 283
Cohen, M. A. 25, 37, 42, 69
Cohen, S. 254
Cooke, G. xlii
Corney, R. J. 93, 167, 170
Cross, F. M., Jr., xvii, xviii, xx, xxi, xxii, xxix, xxxi, xlii, 1, 11, 25, 47, 80, 83, 85, 145, 167, 170, 195, 197, 198, 212, 214, 215, 216, 223
Cross, F. M., Jr., and G. E. Wright 25, 256, 262
Curtis, E. L. (and A. A. Madsen) ix, xvii, 10, 11, 16, 25, 29, 37, 38, 43, 45, 56, 57, 65, 66, 67, 70, 71, 78, 81, 85, 89, 90, 92, 93, 98, 99, 103, 104, 106, 111, 115, 119, 123, 125, 136, 137, 138, 139, 140, 142, 149, 151, 157, 160, 165, 166, 168, 170, 173, 177, 185, 189, 215, 216, 220, 226, 232, 234, 240, 246, 252, 262, 263, 267, 275, 277, 278, 280, 282, 288

Dahlberg, B. T. 52, 53, 85
Dalglish, E. 124
Damsky, A. 25, 129
Danielou, J. xxxii
Delcor, M. xlii
Delekat, L. xxxii, 95, 97
Dijkstra, M. 25, 57
Dillard, R. B. xxxii, xxxvii, 212
Dion, P.-E. xlii
Donner, H., and W. Röllig xii, xlii
Driver, S. R. 156, 160, 173, 273, 275

Eissfeldt, O. xxv, 130, 138, 288
Elliger, K. xxxii, 25, 63, 65, 66, 69, 103, 106, 110, 113, 114, 115, 117, 118, 153, 157
Ellison, H. L. xviii
Elmslie, W. A. L. xviii, xlii
Emerton, R. xxxi

Freedman, D. N. xvii, xviii, xx, xxv, xxvii
Fuente, O. G. de la xlii

Galling, K. xviii, xxix, 11, 56, 81, 214, 215
Gaster, T. H. 217
Gehrke, R. D. 156
Gerleman, G. xxi, xlii
Gese, H. xxxi, xxxii, 80, 93, 95, 244
Geus, C. H. J. de 1
Glueck, N. 33, 58
Goettsburger, J. xviii
Gold, V. R. 23, 41, 43, 44
Gooding, D. W. xlii
Gordis, R. xlii
Goslinga, C. J. 201
Gottwald, N. 1
Gray, J. xlii, 67, 80
Greenberg, M. xxi, 80, 95

Grindel, J. M. xlii
Grintz, J. M. xxxii, 156
Grohman, E. D. 75
Gunneweg, A. H. J. 80
Guthrie, H. H. 119, 141

Haldar, A. 78, 111
Hamburg, H. 278
Hanson, P. D. 80
Haran, M. xxix, xxxi, 80, 95
Harvey, D. 35
Harvey-Jellie, W. R. xviii
Haupt, P. 241
Hayes, J. H., and J. M. Miller xlii
Herbert, A. S. xvii, xxix, 278, 283
Hertzberg, H. W. 156, 196
Hick, L. 33
Hill, A. E. 180
Hillers, D. R. xlii
Hodges, Z. C. xlii
Hoonacker, A. van 80
Hornig, B. xxiv, xlii, 283
Huffmon, H. B. xlii, 274
Hurvitz, A. xlii

Janssen, E. xlii
Japhet, S. xvii, xviii, xix, xx, 1, 11, 80, 90, 172, 174, 177, 288
Jellicoe, S. xxi
Johnson, A. R. 241, 245
Johnson, M. D. xliii, 1, 2, 3, 4, 5, 6, 11
Johnson, R. F. 34, 84, 85, 95, 108
Jones, B. W. xliii

Kallai-Kleinmann, Z. 1, 25, 63
Kapelrud, A. S. xxxii, 201
Kautzsch, E., and A. E. Cowley xi, 15, 29, 48, 56, 70, 90, 103, 121, 131, 138, 164, 168, 209
Keil, C. F. xviii, 11, 33, 37, 45, 46, 49, 52, 99, 107, 165, 187, 188, 277
Kennedy, A. R. S. 156
Kennett, R. H. xliii
Kittel, R. 11, 56
Kittel, R., and D. C. Siegfried xviii
Klein, R. W. xliii, 212, 216, 217
Knox, J. 262
Koch, K. xliii
Kohler, L. xliii
Kraft, R. A. xliii
Kraus, H.-J. xliii, 271
Kropat, A. xliii, 90, 147, 149, 226
Kutsch, E. xliii

Lambdin, T. O. 174
Laurentin, A. xliii
Leach, E. xxxii
Lemke, W. xvii, xxi, xxii, 145, 185, 198, 205
Levine, B. 80
Liver, J. xxxii
Lohfink, N. 219, 222
Loretz, O. 195

MacDonald, J. xliii
MacKenzie, J. A. R. xliii
MacLean, H. B. 40
Maisler, B. xliii

Malamat, A. 1
Mangan, C. xviii
Mangenot, E. xix
Margain, J. L. 219
Marsden, E. W. xliii
May, H. G. 47, 51
Mazar, B. xxxii, 95, 97, 98, 99, 100, 101, 106, 115, 153, 247, 254
McCarthy, D. J. xliii, 219, 222, 223
McKenzie, J. L. xliii
Mendelsohn, I. 25, 69, 73, 153
Mendenhall, G. E. xliii, 1, 4, 6, 7, 170, 271
Mettinger, T. xxxv, 256, 261, 263
Meyer, E. 76
Michaeli, F. xviii, 1, 11, 110, 148
Milgrom, J. 80
Miller, P. D. xliii
Mohlenbrink, K. xxxi, 80
Montgomery, J. A. xxi
Moore, C. A. xliii
Moran, W. L. xliii
Morgenstern, J. xliii
Moriarity, F. L. xliii
Morton, W. H. 43, 56, 59, 125. 141
Mosis, R. xvii, xxvii, 147, 149, 150, 151, 155, 172, 173, 175, 178, 179, 189, 214, 218
Mowinckel, S. xliii
Muilenberg, J. xliii
Murtonen, A. xliii
Myers, J. xvii, xxviii, xliii, 11, 17, 33, 40, 43, 44, 45, 47, 54, 56, 58, 59, 60, 73, 75, 81, 109, 111, 116, 126, 129, 133, 147, 165, 169, 170, 187, 209, 239, 245, 251, 266, 277

Newsome, J. xvii, xviii, xx, xxvi
Noordtzij, A. xxvi, xxvii
North, R. xvii, xix, xxix, xliii
Noth, M. xiii, xxvi, xxxi, xliii, 8, 9, 11, 12, 16, 25, 26, 33, 34, 45, 58, 69, 76, 81, 109, 118, 149, 160, 168, 169, 187, 216, 221

O'Ceallaigh, G. C. xxxii
Orlinsky, H. M. xxi
Osborne, W. L. 1, 2, 4, 11, 129

Pavlovsky, V. xliii
Payne, D. F. xxvi, xliii
Pedersen, D. L. xvii, xliv, 166, 241, 242, 243, 244, 245, 246
Phillips, A. xxxii
Plöger, O. xix, xxi, xxiv, xliv, 282, 285
Podechard, E. 13, 24
Pohlmann, K.-F. xliv
Polk, T. 80, 181, 194, 247, 254
Polzin, R. M. xvii, xxviii, 11, 71, 90, 177, 277, 278, 288

Pope, M. 43
Porten, B. xxxii
Porter, J. R. xliv, 219
Pritchard, J. B. xi, 52, 75, 76
Purvis, J. xliv

Rad, G. von xvii, xxiv, xxv, xxvii, xxix, xxxi, xxxii, xxxiii, xliv, 13, 199, 219, 225, 241, 271, 273
Rahlfs, A. xiv
Reed, W. L. 59, 115, 258
Rehm, M. xviii, xxi, 80, 83
Richardson, H. N. xliv
Richter, W. xliv, 64
Rinaldi, G. xliv
Roberts, B. J. xxi
Roehrs, W. 13
Rost, L. xxxii, xliv
Rothstein, J., and J. Hänel xvii, 11, 25, 26, 53, 57, 149, 153, 187, 207, 220, 243, 246, 266, 269, 278, 281, 285, 289, 290
Rowley, H. H. xxix, xliv
Rudolph, W. ix, xvii, xxvii, xxxi, xliv, 10, 11, 12, 15, 16, 17, 19, 25, 26, 29, 31, 33, 37, 38, 41, 43, 44, 45, 46, 50, 51, 53, 56, 57, 58, 59, 60, 64, 67, 71, 73, 78, 81, 87, 97, 99, 103, 104, 107, 109, 111, 112, 114, 115, 116, 117, 121, 123, 124, 129, 130, 131, 133, 147, 149, 150, 155, 158, 165, 168, 169, 170, 173, 184, 187, 189, 197, 199, 203, 211, 215, 218, 221, 238, 242, 243, 244, 245, 250, 253, 257, 261, 263, 266, 269, 277, 278, 281, 282
Rylaarsdam, J. C. xliv, 288

Sasson, J. 1
Scharbert, J. 281, 285
Schnell, R. F. 76
Schofield, J. N. xxxv
Schumacher, F. T. 31, 83, 85
Schumacher, J. H. xliv, 124, 139, 240
Schürer, E. xliv
Seeligman, I. L. xliv
Shenkel, J. D. xxi
Simons, J. 69
Skinner, J. 13, 73
Smith, H. P. 156
Smith, W. R., and A. Bertholet 80
Speiser, E. A. 13, 80
Steck, O. H. xliv
Stern, E. 47
Stinespring, W. F. xvii, xxvi, xxvii, 115, 153, 171, 203
Swete, H. B. xliv

Taber, C. R. 1
Talmon, S. 47, 53, 188

Thackeray, H. St. J. xxii
Thackeray, H. St. J., and R. Marcus xliv
Theile, E. R. 76
Thomas, D. W. xliv
Thornton, T. C. G. xxxiii
Torczyner, H. 241, 245
Torrey, C. C. xvii, xxii, xliv, 45
Trever, J. 177, 258
Tsevat, M. xliv

Vannutelli, P. xxii, xliv
Vaux, R. de xliv, 7, 25, 99, 153, 156, 256, 261, 262, 278, 289
Vink, J. G. xxxi
Vogt, H. C. M. xliv
Vriezen, T. C. xxxvi

Waetjen, H. 1
Wagner, S. 151
Waltke, B. K. xxvi, xxviii
Waterman, I. 1
Weinberg, J. P. 1, 109
Weinfeld, M. xliv
Weiser, A. xxix, xxxiii
Welch, A. xvii, xxvii, xliv, 80, 185, 187, 228, 241, 253, 266, 268
Wellhausen, J. 25, 37, 80, 277
Welten, P. xvii, xxvi, xxviii, xxxix, 155, 188
Wenham, J. xliv, 204
Westermann, C. xliv
Wevers, J. W. xlv
Whitley, C. F. xlv
Whybray, R. N. xlv
Wifall, W. 47
Wilda, G. xxvi
Willi, T. xvii, 147, 149, 218
Williamson, H. G. M. ix, xvii, xx, xxvi, xxviii, xxxi, xxxii, xxxiii, xxxiv, xxxvi, 11, 19, 25, 26, 27, 31, 32, 34, 35, 37, 38, 39, 40, 42, 44, 57, 72, 73, 80, 89, 90, 93, 95, 106, 107, 140, 145, 153, 157, 160, 184, 185, 187, 188, 189, 192, 194, 195, 198, 199, 203, 205, 211, 213, 216, 217, 218, 219, 220, 223, 226, 228, 231, 234, 238, 239, 240, 241, 244, 245, 246, 249, 254, 258, 263, 269, 275, 278, 282, 285, 288
Wilson, R. R. 1, 2, 4, 5, 6, 8, 9
Wolf, C. V. 1
Wright, G. E. xxix, 256

Yadin, Y. 256
Yamauchi, E. xlv

Zachmann, L. 1
Zerafa, P. xlv
Zeron, A. xxxi, xxxiii, 153
Zimmerman, F. xlv

Index of Principal Subjects

Ark 172, 177, 180
Asher 117–19

Benjamin 106–9, 120–28, 132, 139, 165
Bibliographies, xvii, xli–xlv, 1, 80

Caleb 33, 39–45
Census 212–18
Chronicles
  authorship xx
  date xxv
  integrity xx
  literary forms in xxiv
  name xviii
  place in canon xviii
  purpose xxv
  sources xxiii
Cities, Levitical 95–102
Commentaries xvii
Craftsmen 59–60

Dan 100, 106, 107
David xxxii–xxxv, 47–55, 145, 153–71, 172–94, 195–200, 201–11
  Officials of 255–64, 265–76
Dynasty, Davidic 195–200

Ephraim 113–16, 138

Family terms 7

Gad 69, 74, 76, 165
Gatekeepers (see also porters) 132

Genealogy 1–12, 143
Gershom 92, 101, 231, 232
Gibeon 193

Heart, disposition of xl–xli, 275
Hiram 178

Induction, form of 222
Israel
  all xxxv–xxxvii, 138, 153, 154, 160, 171, 174–75, 187, 210, 291
  sons/tribes of 8–12, 29–31
Issachar 103–5

Jeconiah 52
Jerahmeel 33–35, 45–47
Jerusalem, inhabitants of 129–44
Joab 155
Joshua 115, 224
Joy xxviii

Kohath 91

Manasseh 70, 74–75, 77, 110–16, 138, 166
Merari 93, 101, 234
Military 156–62
Music/musicians 30–31, 241–46

Obed-edom 187, 193, 250
Outline xli, 12

Porters 141, 247
Prayer 283–86

Priests xxxi, 82–86, 100, 132, 134–35, 140, 187, 236–41
Prophet/prophecy 164, 192, 245
Psalms 186

Ram 33–37
Repentance xxxix
Rest 210–11, 223–25, 270
Retribution xxvii, xxxvii–xxxix, 208, 275
Reuben 69, 72–74, 75

Saul 124, 127, 132, 147–52, 154, 169
Simeon 63–68
Singers 94, 132, 137, 187
Solomon xxvi, xxxii–xxxv, 145, 225, 226, 271–74, 289–93

Temple xxvi, xxix, 199, 225, 276, 277–93
Tribes (of Israel) 8–12, 169, 260

Unity (of Israel) xxvii

Warfare/warriors 101, 119, 167, 201–2

Zadok 170, 238
Zerubbabel 52–53

Index of Biblical Texts

A. Old Testament

Genesis

1–10	15
1:5	15
2:12	279
4:17–22	24
4:17–24	15
5	16, 21
5:32	16
6:5	266, 275, 282, 285
8:21	275
10	15, 17, 21
10–11	16
10:1	16
10:2	15
10:2–4	15, 17
10:3	15
10:4	15
10:5	17
10:6	67
10:6–7	15
10:6–20	17
10:8	15, 17
10:9	15
10:9–12	17
10:13	15
10:13–18	15
10:18–20	17
10:21	17
10:21–23	15
10:22–29	17
10:23	15
10:24–29	15
10:28	15
10:30–32	17
11	21, 22
11:10–26	20, 21
11:26	16, 21
12:1	7
12:1–3	24
12:3	166
15:20	209, 211
17	22
19:30–38	24
22	218
22:1	218
23:4	282
23:9	215, 217
24:48	281
25	20, 22
25:1–3	20
25:1–4	22
25:3	22
25:4	20
25:5–6	22
25:8	234, 290
25:9	22
25:12–13	22
25:12–16	20
25:13–14	67
25:13–15	22
25:15	19, 77
25:16	22
25:16–18	22
25:19	22

25:19–26	20
25:20–34	23
29	170
29:31–30:24	8, 9
29:32–35	8
30:5–8	8
30:10–13	8
30:17–20	8
30:22–24	8
34:25	66
34:30	66
35	170
35:2	189
35:16	37
35:16–20	8, 9
35:22	73
35:22–26	8, 9, 10
35:23–26	20
35:29	234, 290
36	20, 21
36:1	23
36:1–5	20
36:2–5	23
36:5	23
36:8	23
36:9	23
36:9–14	23
36:10–19	20
36:11	24, 25
36:12	19, 23, 24
36:14	23
36:15	24
36:15–19	23
36:18	23, 24
36:19	23
36:20	23, 42
36:20–28	20, 23
36:22	19
36:23	19, 42
36:24	23
36:25	23
36:26	19
36:27	19
36:28	20
36:29	23, 42
36:30	23
36:31–39	20, 21, 23
36:35	20
36:39	20
36:40–43	20, 23
36:43	20
38	29, 30
38:2	29, 123
38:7–11	31
38:12	29
41:52	114
46	11, 29, 107, 108, 109, 118, 122, 125, 170
46:8–27	8, 9, 10, 20
46:9	33, 44, 73, 75
46:10	45, 63, 64, 65, 66
46:11	82, 83
46:12	29, 30, 33
46:13	103, 104
46:16	74, 118

46:17	117, 118
46:20	77, 112, 114, 115
46:21	106, 107, 108, 109, 121, 123, 125
46:23	106, 107, 109, 125
46:24	107, 109
46:24–25	106, 109
46:25	106, 109
48	73
48–49	73
48:15–16	73
48:20	73
49:4	70, 73
49:5	254
49:8–12	73
49:22–26	73
50:23	111

Exodus

2:23	90
6	81
6:14	73
6:15	63, 64, 65, 66
6:16	82, 249
6:16–25	83, 85
6:17	92, 232
6:17–19	88
6:18	189, 249
6:18–24	141
6:19	87, 93, 233
6:20	82
6:21	249
6:22	189
6:23	34, 87
6:24	87, 251
10:2	148
12:2	209
12:3	269
12:40	34
15:15	23
15:20	30
19:5	278
19:5–6	247
19:10–15	189
24:11	289
25–31	279
25–39	277
25:1–8	280
25:2	272, 280
25:3–7	279
25:7	277, 279
25:9	272, 275
25:10–15	190
25:40	272, 275
28:3	272
28:9	279
28:11	278, 280
28:17	279
28:18	277, 280
28:20	279
28:41	288
29	289
29:2	185
29:40	287

Reference	Pages
29:41	287
30:22–38	142
31:2	27
31:3	272, 275
31:6	272
33:7–11	90
35–40	279
35:1	269
35:4–9	280
35:5	267, 272, 280
35:5–9	279
35:9	277, 279
35:9–10	276
35:10	267, 272
35:20–29	280
35:21	272, 280
35:22	272, 280
35:22–28	279
35:24	272
35:25	272
35:25–26	280
35:26	272
35:27	277, 279
35:29	272, 280
35:30	27
35:30–35	266
35:31	272, 275
35:35	272, 278, 280
36:1	272
36:1–3	272
36:2	272
36:4	272
36:8	272
36:8–9	280
37:1–5	190
38:23	278, 280
39:11	277, 280
39:13	279
39:32	90
39:32–43	275
40:2	90
40:6	90
40:29	90, 289

Leviticus

Reference	Pages
2:2	185
2:5	230
2:9	185
2:16	185
5:12	185
6:8	185
6:14	230
7:9	230
7:12	288
8:4	269
8:12	288
9:22–24	289
19:35	230
21:10	288
23	272
23:13	287
25:35	282
25:47	282

Numbers

Reference	Pages
1	260, 261
1:2	230
1:3	258, 261
1:4	261
1:5–15	9
1:10	114
1:17	64
1:18	230
1:20	230
1:20–42	260
1:20–43	9
1:22	230
1:29	104
1:37	109
1:40	119
1:47–54	252, 261
1:49	214
1:50	184
1:53	261
2	166
2:2	137
2:3	34
2:3–31	9
2:17	137
2:28	119
3:1–4	83
3:2–4	238
3:5–9	235
3:17	82
3:18–20	88
3:19	83
3:20	87
3:21	92, 232
3:21–37	235
3:31	235
3:33	233
3:39	231
4:3	231, 246
4:15	189
4:18	7
4:23	231, 246
4:36	231
4:40	231
4:44	231
5:26	185
7:12–83	9
8:23–26	231
8:24	246
8:25	246
9:14	30
10:1–10	187
10:8	173
10:14–28	10
10:33	270
10:33–35	270
10:38	270
13:4–15	9
13:6	34
13:20	64
15	287
16	136, 251
16:3	175
16:5	271
16:7	271
16:9	90
16:21	165
17:20	271
18:1–7	235
20:4	175
24:20–22	43
25:6–13	137
26	10, 11, 107, 111, 114, 115, 118, 125
26:5–6	24
26:5–51	9
26:9	78
26:12–13	63, 65
26:15–17	74
26:20	57, 119, 131
26:21	33
26:23	103
26:23–25	104
26:25	104, 113
26:29	74, 77, 82, 111
26:29–34	111
26:30	111
26:30–32	111, 112
26:31	110
26:33	111
26:35–36	114
26:37	116
26:38	106, 107, 108, 121, 123, 125
26:39	107, 121, 123
25:39–40	108
26:40	123
26:41	109
26:42	106
26:44	117, 118
26:46	118
26:47	119
26:48–49	109
26:57	82
26:57–60	83
26:62	231
27:1	110
28	272
28–29	287
29	272
32:34	75
32:38	75
32:39–42	40
32:42	40
34:4	33
34:39	34
35:15	182

Deuteronomy

Reference	Pages
1:1	20, 269
1:29	223
2:11	209, 211
3:4	40
3:8–9	78
3:9–10	76
3:14	40, 111
4:29	273
5:33	274
6:1–3	274
7:5	179
8:10	281
8:18	185
9:5	282
9:24	274
10:8	188
12:3	179
12:7	292
12:8–11	224
12:9–11	198
12:11	226
12:12	292
14:26	289, 292
16:15	292
17:8–13	232
17:9	254
17:15	271
17:16–17	xxxiv
18:5	184, 188, 271
20:3	223
20:8	220
21:5	271
21:15–17	73
23:2–9	175
26:19	225
28:29	223
29:1	269
31	223
31:1	269
31:6	223, 273

Reference	Page
31:8	273
31:14–15	223
32:49	75
33	169
33:10	254
33:18–19	103
34:9	223

Joshua

Reference	Page
1	222, 223
1:2–9	223, 273
1:5	273
1:6	222
1:7	273
1:7–8	223
1:8	223
1:9	222, 223
1:13	224
1:15	224
3:7	290
4:14	290
5:2	278
5:9	278
5:13	214
5:13–15	218
6:18–19	64, 65
6:21	64
7	31
7:1	29, 30, 31, 64
7:7–15	64
7:14–18	7
7:18	29, 30, 31
7:24–26	29, 31
10:25	223
11:23	224
12:5	111
12:17	45
13	223
13:5	71
13:8–13	75
13:11	111
13:13	40, 111
14:6	33
14:6–15	33
14:14	33
14:15	41, 97
15	41, 65, 66
15:3	33
15:8	155
15:13	41
15:13–17	57
15:16–17	56
15:16–19	41, 42
15:17	33
15:21	65
15:21–42	65
15:21–62	262
15:23	45
15:25	33
15:26	41, 64
15:27	41
15:28–36	65
15:29	64
15:30	64
15:31	42
15:32	64
15:33	42
15:34	59
15:35	59
15:42	65
15:44	41
15:48	59, 240
15:50	58
15:51	97
15:52–54	33
15:53	41
15:55	41
15:56	38, 41, 44, 59
15:57	42
15:58	41
15:59	44
15:60	42
16–18	116
16:5–10	116
16:6–8	101
16:7	45, 113
16:9	116
17	111
17:1	111
17:1–3	110
17:1–4	111
17:1–6	111
17:2	74, 77, 111
17:2–3	111
17:3	116
17:7	116
17:11	113, 116
18:1	224
18:13–14	115
18:14	42
18:16	155
18:22	116
18:24	125
18:25	126
18:26–27	41
18:28	155
19	65, 66
19:1	68
19:2–8	65
19:3	64
19:4	64
19:5	42
19:6	64, 65
19:7	64, 66, 67
19:8	64, 66, 67
19:13	98
19:21	98
19:26	98
19:35	43
19:40–46	126
19:41	42, 100
19:42	126
20:7	116
20:7–8	97
20:8	98
21	100, 101, 118
21:1–3	100
21:1–42	98
21:2	97
21:4	96, 97, 99, 100
21:4–8	99
21:5	97
21:5–9	99
21:5–20	115
21:6	97
21:8	97
21:9	97, 99, 100
21:9–40	99
21:10	96, 97
21:11	97, 100
21:13	97
21:15	97
21:16	97
21:17	97, 100, 125
21:18	97
21:19	97
21:20	97
21:21	97, 116
21:22	97
21:23	97
21:24	101, 126
21:25	97, 98
21:26	98
21:27	97, 98
21:28	98
21:29	98
21:30	98
21:31	98
21:32	97, 98
21:34	98
21:34–35	98
21:35	98
21:36	97, 98
21:38	97
21:39	97
21:40	97, 98
21:43–45	198
21:44	224
22:9	76
22:12	269
22:33	281
23:2	290
23:14	197
24:1	269
24:29	114

Judges

Reference	Page
1:11–15	41, 42, 58
1:22	116
1:27–30	98
1:35	126
3:3	71, 77
3:9	33
3:11	224
3:12–4:1	125
3:15	121, 123, 165
3:21	148
3:30	224
4:11	43
4:17	43
4:21	148
5:2	278
5:9	278
5:14–18	269
6:34	166
7:1	49
8:28	224
10:1	104, 105
10:1–2	240
10:4	40
10:9	138
16:31	43
20:1–2	269
20:12	7
20:16	165

Ruth

Reference	Page
1:2	37
4:11	37
4:13–17	34
4:18–22	33
4:19	32, 33
4:20	32
4:21	32

1 Samuel

Reference	Page
1:1	87, 88
1:24	188
2	284
2:10	246
2:11	88

Ref	Page
2:18	88
2:22	188
4–7	150
5–6	173
6:8	148
7:1	175
7:5	269
8:2	87, 88
8:4	269
9:1	124, 127
10:24	271
12:1	269
13	151
13:13	151, 152
13:14	151
13:17	123
13:19–20	56
14:37	152
14:48	67
14:49	121, 124
15	151
15:3	67
15:6	43
15:22	151
15:23	151
15:31	152
16	34
16:6	258
16:7	275
16:8–10	271
16:9	32
16:10	33, 34
17	211
17:4	158
17:7	158
17:12	37
17:12–14	34
17:13	32, 258
17:25	33
18:14	180
20–23	83
21–26	166
21:5	189
22:20	238
23:6	238
23:14	165
23:19	165
24:1	165
27:5	258
27:6	67, 165
27:10	33, 45
28	151
28:6	152
28:18–19	149
29	166
30:27	67
30:29	33, 43, 45
31	149, 150, 151
31:1	147, 149
31:2	124, 147
31:4	147
31:5	148
31:6	127, 148
31:7	148
31:9	148, 150
31:10	148, 150
31:12	148

2 Samuel

Ref	Page
1–4	154
1:23	165
2–4	150, 165
2:12–17	126
2:18	34
2:32	35
3:2	32
3:2–5	49, 177, 179
3:3	40, 48
3:4	48
3:5	48
4:3	115
4:4	124
5	154, 177, 178
5:1	xxxvi, 153, 154, 155, 269
5:1–3	154
5:1–5	291
5:1–7:2	188
5:2	153, 155
5:3	153, 289
5:4–5	154, 179
5:5	50, 54, 154
5:6	xxxvi, 154, 155
5:6–10	154, 177
5:8	154, 155
5:9	154, 155
5:10	155, 180
5:11	226
5:11–12	178
5:11–25	173, 174, 177
5:12	177, 180
5:13	32, 177
5:13–14	49
5:13–16	178
5:14	39, 48, 50
5:14–16	49, 50, 179
5:15	48, 177
5:16	177
5:17	177
5:17–25	178
5:18	177
5:19	177
5:20	177
5:21	177, 179
5:22	177
5:23	177
5:24	177
5:25	177
6	174
6:1	174, 188
6:1–2	xxxvi
6:1–11	173, 174
6:2	173
6:3	173, 175
6:4	175
6:5	155, 173, 289
6:6	173
6:8	173
6:11	173
6:12	185
6:12–19	191
6:12–20	186
6:13	185, 191
6:14	185
6:15	155, 185, 188, 191
6:16	185
6:17	185, 188
6:18	191, 289
6:19	173, 185, 289
6:20–23	192
6:21	271
7	xxxix, 152, 196, 198, 199
7:1	180, 196, 198, 224
7:1–7	198
7:1–14	198
7:2	196
7:3	196
7:4	196
7:5	196, 199
7:6	194, 196
7:7	196
7:8	289
7:8–11	198
7:9	197
7:10	196, 197, 235
7:11	197, 198, 224
7:11–16	198
7:12	197, 199
7:13	197, 226
7:14	197, 274
7:15	197
7:16	197
7:18	197
7:19	197
7:20	197, 274
7:21	284
7:22	197
7:23	197
7:24	197
7:25	197
7:26	197
7:27	197
7:28	197
7:29	197, 199
7:32	284
8	201, 204
8–21	201, 202
8:1	203
8:1–8	204
8:2	60, 203, 204, 209
8:3	203
8:4	203
8:5	203
8:6	203
8:8	203
8:9	203
8:9–12	204
8:10	203
8:11	203
8:12	67, 204
8:12–13	204
8:13	204, 205
8:13–14	204
8:14	204
8:15–16	204
8:15–18	261
8:17	83, 204
8:18	204
9	201, 210
9:12	127
10	201, 207
10:1	206
10:1–6	207
10:2	206
10:3	206
10:4	206
10:5	206
10:6	206, 207
10:7–12	207
10:8	207
10:11	207
10:12	207
10:13–19	207
10:14	207
10:15	207
10:16	207
10:17	207
10:18	207
10:19	207, 208
11	201
11–12	201
11:1	201, 209, 210
11:2–27	201, 209
11:3	48
11:21	49

Ref	Page
12	201
12:1–25	201, 209
12:11	201
12:24–25	54
12:26	201, 209, 210
12:27–29	201, 209
12:30	209
12:30–31	201, 210
12:31	209
13	49
13–20	210
13–21	201, 210
13:1–21:14	201, 210
13:37–38	40
14:27	32
15:27	82, 85
15:32–37	263
15:36	82
16:23	263
17:23	263
17:25	35
18:26	137
20:23–26	261
21	201, 216
21:1–4	216
21:1–14	216
21:6	211
21:8	211
21:14	216
21:15–17	201, 210, 211
21:16	109
21:16–17	210
21:18	44, 209
21:18–22	201, 210
21:19	209, 211
21:20	209
21:21	209
21:22	209, 210
22	216
22:1–51	216
23	159, 160, 161, 260
23:1–7	216
23:8	157, 160
23:8–12	160, 161
23:8–14	159
23:8–39	159, 216, 258
23:9–11	157
23:11	257
23:12	157
23:13	157
23:13–17	159
23:14	158
23:17	158
23:18	157, 158
23:18–23	159, 161
23:20	158
23:21	158
23:24 ·	158
23:24–39	159, 161
23:25	158, 161
23:26	158
23:27	44, 158
23:28	158
23:28–29	43, 141
23:29	158
23:30	158
23:31	158
23:32	158, 161
23:33	158
23:34	158, 161
23:35	158
23:36	76, 158, 159
23:37	159, 161
23:38	42
23:39	157, 159, 161

Ref	Page
24	xxiii, 215, 216, 261
24:1	213, 216
24:1–25	216
24:2	213
24:3	213
24:4	213
24:4–7	214, 216
24:8	214
24:8–10	216
24:9	214, 217, 218
24:10	214
24:11	214
24:11–13	216
24:12	214
24:13	214
24:14	214
24:14–17	216
24:15	214
24:16	214, 215
24:17	214, 215
24:18	215
24:18–25	216
24:19	215
24:20	214, 215
24:21	215
24:22	215
24:23	215
24:24	215
24:25	215, 216

1 Kings

Ref	Page
1	xxxiii
1–2	xxxiv, 289, 291
1:1	231, 290, 291
1:9	289
1:16	289
1:19	289
1:25	289
1:31	289
1:34	288
1:35	288, 289
1:36–37	289
1:37	289, 290, 291
1:38–39	289
1:38–40	289
1:38–48	289
1:39	288
1:40	289
1:41	289
1:46	289
1:47	289, 290, 291
1:48	285
1:49	289
1:53	289
2	234
2:1	291
2:1–4	223
2:10–12	291
2:11	288, 289
2:12	289
2:27	83, 238
2:28–29	170
2:35	161, 170, 238, 288, 289
3:2	xxxiii
3:2–3	xxxiv
3:3–5	194
3:5–14	194
3:13	285, 289
4–5	261
4:2	82, 85, 86
4:3	204
4:5	263
4:7–19	99, 260
4:10	45

Ref	Page
4:13	40
4:20	289
5	xxxiii, 179, 226
5:1	60, 180
5:11	29, 30, 31
5:15	226
5:15–32	225
5:17	224
5:17–19	224
5:18	224
5:18–19	226
5:20	226
5:21	281
5:27	225
6–8	xxxiii
6:1	34, 86
6:3	266
6:14–22	225
6:31–34	225
7:14	280
7:14–47	225
7:50	225
7:51	225
8:1	175, 269
8:4	188
8:12	235
8:15	281
8:16	226, 271
8:19	226
8:20	226
8:29	226
8:44	271
8:48	271
8:54–61	224
8:55	xxxvi
8:56	180, 198, 224
8:57–58	224
8:61	275
8:62–63	290
8:62–64	289
8:63	xli
8:65	175
8:65–66	175
8:66	xxxv, xl, 289, 290, 292
9–10	261
9:3	290
9:4	282
9:15	225
9:22	225
9:28	278
10	178
10:1	xxxiv
10:9	281
10:14	226
10:23–29	xxxiv, 180
11	xxxiii, xxxiv, 194
11:4	xxxiii, xxxiv, 275
11:6	xxxiii
11:7	209
11:8	xxxiii
11:9	xxxiv
11:11	266
11:14–25	xxxiv
11:34	271
11:41–43	xxxiv
11:42	xxxiv
11:48	281
12:1	xxxvi
14:19	xix
14:29	xix
15:1–2	40
15:3	275
15:7	xix
15:9–10	40
15:11	xxxvii

15:14	xl, 275
15:16–21	xxxviii
15:20	98
15:22	125
15:23	xxxviii
16:24	119
18	218
18:36	282, 285
18:38	215, 218
22:12	223
22:15	223

2 Kings

7:10–11	137
9:30	277
11	170
11:3	51
11:9	86
11:12–17	289
12:10	137
14:21	91
15:3	xxxviii
15:5	76
15:19	70, 71
15:29	70, 71, 75
15:33	76
16:7	70
16:10	70
16:11	86
17	78
17:6	71
17:7–23	75
18:19–21	77
20:3	275
21:1	xxxviii
21:10–15	xxxviii
22	83
22–23	98
22:3	xxxviii
22:13	xxxvi
23:2	245
23:3	xl
23:4	137
23:26	xxxviii
23:34	51
24:1–7	51
24:6	51
24:6–9	51
24:12	51
24:17	51, 52
24:18	51
25:18	137
25:23	43

1 Chronicles

1	45
1–8	xxiii, 132, 138, 143
1–9	xix, xx, xxix, xxxi, 97, 102, 145, 149, 165
1:1	xix
1:1–4	15
1:1–54	12
1:4–23	16
1:4–27	12
1:5–7	15
1:8	67
1:8–16	15
1:13	226
1:17–23	15
1:24–27	20
1:28	20
1:28–37	12

1:29–30	67
1:29–31	20
1:31	77
1:32–33	20
1:34	20, 29
1:34–37	32
1:35	23, 106
1:35–37	20, 29
1:36	33
1:37	45
1:38	42
1:38–42	12, 20
1:38–54	21, 29
1:40	42, 45, 125
1:41	45
1:42	45
1:43–51	20
1:43–54	12, 21
1:51–54	20, 158
1:53	33
2	38, 58, 260, 261
2–8	9, 10, 169
2–9	2, 11, 30, 61, 107
2:1	1, 3, 28, 32, 105, 107, 138
2:1–2	4, 8, 9, 10, 12, 20, 27, 61, 170, 260
2:1–4	20, 24
2:1–5	25
2:1–8	39
2:1–9	26, 44
2:1–17	44
2:1–23	46
2:1–9:44	12
2:2	114
2:3	28, 32, 48, 54, 57, 59, 61
2:3–8	26, 27
2:3–4:23	12, 32, 80
2:4	61
2:5	60
2:6	7, 61
2:7	31, 38, 44, 65, 138
2:9	4, 7, 25, 27, 28, 34, 35, 37, 38, 41, 45, 57, 58, 60
2:9–10	61
2:9–17	26, 49
2:9–4:23	31
2:10–13	118
2:10–17	25, 26, 27, 39
2:10–3:24	26
2:11	32, 42, 43
2:13	34, 258
2:13–15	165
2:16	161
2:18	28, 32, 33, 38, 39, 41, 57, 60, 61
2:18–19	26, 27, 28, 42, 44
2:18–24	25, 26, 38, 39, 40
2:18–55	39
2:19	4, 37, 39, 41, 45
2:20	27, 30, 39
2:20–23	27, 42
2:21	27, 28, 37, 61
2:21–23	26, 27, 39, 42
2:24	26, 27, 28, 37, 39, 41, 42, 44, 45
2:25	4, 26, 28, 33, 34, 39, 41
2:25–33	25, 26, 27, 28, 39, 40, 41
2:25–41	40
2:27	39
2:28	41
2:32	41
2:33	26, 38, 39
2:34	61
2:34–41	26, 27, 39, 41, 45
2:41	46

2:42	26, 28, 32, 33, 37, 38, 39, 41, 45, 57, 59
2:42–45	41
2:42–49	42
2:42–50	26, 27, 28, 38, 39, 45, 46, 58
2:42–55	26
2:43	165
2:44	118
2:45	59
2:46	39
2:46–47	41
2:47	38, 39
2:47–48	41
2:49	2, 41, 58, 61
2:49–55	26
2:50	3, 8, 26, 28, 38, 39, 44
2:50–52	27
2:50–55	8, 26, 38, 39, 40, 46, 119
2:51–52	28
2:52	27, 38, 39, 44
2:52–54	125
2:52–55	27, 39
2:53	38, 44
2:53–55	26, 27, 28, 38, 39, 44
2:54	28, 32, 38, 44, 141
2:55	56, 58, 61
3	5, 44
3:1	3, 28, 32
3:1–3	165
3:1–4	177, 179
3:1–9	54
3:1–24	25, 26, 27
3:1–4:23	26
3:2	40
3:4	32, 48, 154, 291
3:5	28, 32, 39, 61, 177
3:5–8	179
3:6	242
3:6–9	179
3:8	48, 177
3:9	48, 61
3:10	2
3:10–14	2, 54
3:15	54
3:16	51, 52
3:16–24	54
3:17	51, 52
3:17–19	xxvii
3:18	52
3:19	49, 52
3:19–24	5
3:20	49, 52
3:21	49, 52
3:22	8, 49, 52
3:23	49, 52
3:24	49, 52
4:1	4, 8, 27, 38, 65
4:1–4	27, 39
4:1–7	38, 39, 40, 46
4:1–23	26
4:1–24	28
4:2	27, 38, 43, 44, 118, 240
4:2–4	27
4:2–7	27, 39
4:4	26, 28, 37, 39
4:5	28, 44
4:5–6	38
4:5–7	27, 39
4:7	57
4:8	38, 57, 118
4:8–23	27, 39
4:9	56, 65
4:9–10	43, 57
4:11	38
4:11–12	56, 57

Ref	Page	Ref	Page	Ref	Page
4:11–15	28	5:25–26	72, 79, 130	6:40	97
4:12	28, 60	5:26	70, 72, 77, 138	6:42	97
4:13	61	5:27	81, 87, 94, 231, 232	6:43	44
4:13–15	56, 57	5:27–29	83	6:44–47	88, 233
4:14	8, 28, 43, 56, 60, 278	5:27–30	80	6:45	97, 98
4:15	57, 61	5:27–41	5, 81, 82, 83, 94, 233, 238	6:46	97, 107
4:16	57	5:27–43	90	6:46–48	101
4:17	56, 57, 61	5:27–6:33	189	6:46–51	115
4:17–18	56, 57	5:27–6:66	12	6:47	103, 118
4:17–20	57	5:28	189	6:48	98
4:18	56, 60	5:28–29	87	6:50	97, 98, 100
4:19	57	5:29	82, 87, 237	6:50–53	81
4:20	57	5:29–41	84	6:52	97
4:21	131	5:30	83	6:54	107, 126
4:21–23	8, 26, 28, 31, 57	5:30–41	118	6:56	97, 103
4:22	57	5:31	81	6:59–60	118
4:23	57, 60	5:31–41	80	6:60	125
4:24	64, 65	5:34	204	6:61	97, 98
4:24–27	65	5:35	82, 83	6:62	103
4:24–43	12, 64	5:35–38	81	6:63	97
4:25–27	65, 66	5:36	83	6:65	97
4:26	64	5:37	82	7:1–5	6, 11, 12, 109, 119
4:27	7, 65, 68	5:38	204	7:2	19
4:28–33	65, 67	5:38–40	140	7:4	19, 119
4:31	66	5:40	135	7:5	103
4:32	66	5:41	83, 86, 138	7:6	4, 108, 121, 125
4:33	64, 66, 67, 138	6	189, 231, 246	7:6–11	104, 125
4:34	64, 66	6:1	81, 82	7:6–12	6, 10, 12, 119, 122
4:34–37	66, 67	6:1–4	81	7:6–13	123, 125, 128
4:34–43	65, 66, 67	6:1–9	81	7:7	108, 119, 123, 124
4:35	66	6:1–15	81, 82, 93, 94	7:9	19, 119
4:37	66, 230	6:1–16	93	7:10	106
4:38	66, 67	6:2	82, 92, 231, 232	7:11	119
4:39	68	6:3	87, 289	7:12	10, 11, 12, 110, 121, 124, 125
4:39–40	66, 67	6:4	93, 233	7:12–13	118
4:39–43	64	6:4–5	93	7:13	10, 11, 12
4:40	64, 67	6:5	82	7:14	10, 116
4:41	6, 64, 66, 67, 68	6:5–6	92, 232	7:14–19	12, 77, 113
4:41–42	74	6:7	92, 189	7:18	34
4:42	67	6:7–8	249, 251	7:19	116, 119
4:42–43	66	6:7–9	91	7:20	115
4:43	67, 68	6:7–13	91	7:20–29	2, 4, 12
5	65, 85, 101	6:9	91, 189	7:23	119
5:1	72, 114	6:10–13	91	7:25–27	2
5:1–2	7, 116	6:14	93, 233	7:30–40	11, 12
5:1–26	12	6:14–15	81, 93, 233	7:32	117
5:3	33	6:15	189	7:34	117
5:6	70, 72, 74, 77, 130, 138	6:16–33	81, 82, 88	7:35	117
5:7	19, 70, 71	6:16–38	81	7:37	117
5:7–10	70, 71	6:18	88, 90	7:38	117
5:9	74	6:18–19	141	7:40	6
5:9–10	71	6:18–23	91, 136	8	10, 107, 150
5:10	74, 77	6:18–33	251	8:1–2	4, 108
5:11	71, 72, 74, 77	6:19	87, 189	8:1–5	123
5:11–17	11	6:20	44, 87, 98	8:1–7	122
5:15	71	6:22	251	8:1–40	12
5:16	71	6:23	87, 141	8:2	56
5:16–33	82	6:24–28	92, 232, 249	8:3–4	108
5:17	6	6:25	141	8:6	121, 126, 138
5:18	72, 74, 77, 186	6:26	141	8:6–12	126
5:18–22	6	6:27	232	8:7	138
5:18–23	74	6:28	82	8:8	107, 126
5:18–26	7, 111	6:29	184	8:8–12	122
5:19	19	6:29–32	92	8:10	126
5:19–20	76	6:31–48	xxxi	8:11	107
5:19–22	72, 79	6:32	233	8:12	126
5:20	7	6:33	81, 140	8:13–14	121
5:20–22	75, 78	6:33–38	88	8:13–28	122
5:21	186	6:34	81	8:14	121
5:22	72	6:34–38	81	8:14–28	121
5:23	72	6:35	85, 141	8:18	121
5:23–24	72	6:35–38	81, 82, 84, 85, 86	8:20	121
5:23–26	116	6:39–40	98	8:28	19, 122, 128, 138, 142
5:24	74, 186	6:39–43	88	8:29	132
5:25	151	6:39–66	81, 82, 94, 95	8:29–32	122, 127, 139

8:29–38	122, 142
8:29–40	122, 138
8:30	7, 122, 127, 128, 132
8:31	132
8:32	126, 128, 132
8:33	132, 147
8:34	127, 132
8:35	132
8:36	132
8:37	132
8:38	5, 128, 132
8:39	4, 5
8:39–40	122
8:40	6
9	127, 132, 133, 134, 143, 150, 250, 251
9:1	7, 130, 132, 143, 149
9:1–2	132
9:1–3	143
9:1–18	xxxi
9:1–34	128
9:1–44	12
9:2	90, 133, 134, 138, 139, 143
9:2–3	133
9:2–44	149
9:3	12, 123, 126, 130, 132, 133, 138, 139, 142, 143
9:3–9	132
9:3–23	xxiii
9:4–6	132
9:5	59, 131, 139
9:7–9	128, 132
9:9	19
9:10	239, 250
9:10–13	132, 134
9:11	83, 84, 131, 135
9:12	135
9:14	250, 254
9:14–16	2, 132, 134, 142
9:16	139
9:17	136, 250, 251
9:17–22	136
9:17–27	4, 132, 133
9:17–32	136, 143, 250
9:17–34	132, 136
9:18	136, 137
9:18–19	166
9:18–21	250
9:19	5, 7, 136, 137, 140, 249, 251
9:19–20	249
9:20	136
9:21	136, 137, 251
9:22	119, 137, 251
9:22–32	252
9:23	137
9:26	131, 136, 252
9:26–32	253
9:28	131
9:28–32	132, 235
9:29	131
9:30	131
9:31	5, 131, 136, 251
9:31–33	251
9:32	131
9:33	132, 133, 137, 142, 143, 250
9:34	19, 122, 123, 124, 126, 132, 138, 139, 142
9:35	121, 127
9:35–38	132, 139, 143
9:35–44	122, 133, 138, 142, 148
9:36	7, 121, 124, 127
9:36–37	124
9:37	121, 127
9:38	121, 126, 139
9:39	124, 147
9:39–40	150
9:39–44	2, 3, 127, 132, 137, 143
9:40	121, 124
9:41	3, 121, 122
9:42	122
9:43	122
9:44	3, 5, 122, 149
10	5, 11, 127, 128, 133, 143, 145, 167, 178
10–11	xxiv
10–12	xxix
10–21	145
10–2 Chronicles 36	xxxvi
10:1	148, 149
10:1–7	148
10:2	124, 263
10:3	215
10:6	127, 128, 154, 201
10:8	147
10:8–10	148
10:10	215, 230
10:11–12	148
10:13	29, 154
10:13–14	xxxvii, 143, 148, 160, 173, 179, 184, 253
10:14	148, 152, 169
11	169, 262
11–12	xxiii, xxix, xxxvi, 145, 170
11:1	xxxvi, 154, 159, 160, 169, 188, 274, 290
11:1–3	xxix, 154, 169, 210, 291
11:1–9	165
11:1–10	167
11:3	155, 167, 169
11:4	xxxvi, 154, 155, 159, 160
11:4–9	151, 154
11:6	154, 155
11:7	165
11:8	65, 155
11:9	155, 180
11:10	xxxvi, 159, 162, 167, 169
11:10–31	259
11:10–41	216
11:10–47	xxiii, 169, 258, 259, 260
11:10–12:41	177
11:11	147, 160, 257, 260
11:11–14	159
11:11–41	216
11:12	257, 260
11:13–14	157
11:20	147, 157, 160
11:20–21	260
11:20–25	159
11:21	157
11:21–27	158
11:22	170
11:22–24	263
11:24	157
11:25	157
11:26–41	159
11:27	257, 260
11:29	44, 260
11:30	43, 141, 257
11:31	260
11:33	165, 262
11:38	76
11:40	42
11:41–46	159
11:41–47	157, 159, 160
11:45	108
12	xxiii, 104, 159, 173
12–17	224
12:1–8	164
12:1–23	169
12:2	77, 170
12:8	77, 266
12:9	164, 166
12:9–16	164
12:17	165
12:17–19	164
12:18	275
12:19	166
12:20	165
12:20–23	164
12:23	159
12:24	77, 160, 168, 171, 269
12:24–38	9, 10
12:25	77
12:25–38	168
12:27	231
12:27–29	254
12:29	109, 159
12:30–37	77
12:31–32	115
12:32	186
12:33	77, 103, 104
12:34	77, 107, 168
12:36	118
12:37	77, 119
12:39	77, 168, 173, 188, 269, 275
12:39–41	xxxiii, xxxvi, xl, 210, 278, 280, 287, 290
12:40	289
12:41	103
13	xxix, 151, 177
13–14	xxiv
13–17	145
13:1	188, 269
13:1–2	274, 290
13:1–4	xxxvi, 173, 174
13:2	174, 179, 184, 189
13:3	151, 178, 179, 184
13:4	175
13:4–14	175
13:5	174, 175, 184, 188, 274, 290
13:5–6	xxxvi
13:5–14	174
13:8	190, 246, 289
13:11	173, 179
13:13–20	77
13:14	xxxvii, 188
14	xxix, 172, 180, 186
14:1	226, 278
14:2	180
14:3–7	50, 177, 178
14:4	39, 48, 50, 215
14:4–7	49
14:5	48
14:7	48, 49, 50
14:8–14	77
14:8–16	177, 178
14:11	179
14:16	209
14:17	178
15	193
15–16	xxix, xxxi, 94, 172, 180, 246
15:1	185, 189
15:1–3	186
15:1–24	186
15:2	94, 176, 194
15:3	xxxvi, 184, 290
15:4	187
15:4–10	186, 187, 192
15:6	94
15:8	xxxvi
15:11	184, 187, 193, 238
15:11–13	186
15:11–15	186
15:13	xxxvii, 151, 176
15:13–15	176

15:14 — 184, 187
15:14–15 — 186
15:16 — xl, 93, 171, 246, 278
15:16–21 — xxxi
15:16–23 — 194
15:16–24 — 186, 187, 188, 192, 246
15:17 — 91, 193
15:17–18 — 187, 190, 192
15:17–19 — 81
15:17–24 — 188
15:18 — 175, 184, 185, 187, 246, 250
15:19 — 93, 94, 193
15:19–24 — 187, 190
15:20 — 184
15:21 — 184, 187, 246
15:22 — 185, 245, 253
15:23 — 141
15:24 — 175, 184, 187, 250, 251
15:25–29 — 186
15:25–16:3 — 186
15:27 — 57, 253
15:28 — 173, 188, 245, 246
15:29 — 278
16 — xxiv, 194, 218, 251
16:1 — 90, 141, 185, 188
16:1–3 — 186
16:3 — xxxvi, 290
16:4 — 94, 186
16:4–6 — 186
16:4–7 — 194, 246
16:4–36 — 186
16:5 — 184, 186, 187, 190, 193, 246
16:5–6 — 187, 188, 190, 246
16:5–38 — 187
16:6 — 94, 184, 187, 188
16:7 — 94, 193
16:7–36 — 186
16:8–9 — 194
16:8–22 — 186
16:8–36 — 188, 244, 285
16:13 — 31
16:17 — 31
16:23–33 — 186
16:27 — 284, 291
16:34 — 185
16:34–36 — 186
16:35–36 — 186
16:36 — 194, 281
16:37 — 94, 186, 191
16:37–42 — xxxi, 94, 186, 235
16:38 — 187, 194, 249, 250, 251, 252
16:38–42 — 188
16:39 — 90, 94, 141, 188
16:41 — 64, 65, 119
16:41–42 — 81, 187, 246
16:42 — 187
16:43 — 186
17 — xxix, 172, 223
17–21 — xxiv
17–29 — 285
17:1 — 224
17:1–2 — 198
17:2 — xxxvi
17:3–15 — 198
17:4 — 199
17:5 — 199
17:6 — 198
17:9 — 235
17:10 — 198, 210, 224
17:11 — 198, 199, 200
17:11–12 — 218
17:13 — 200
17:14 — 198, 199, 200, 288, 290
17:16 — 285
17:16–27 — 198

17:18 — 274
17:19 — 284
17:21 — 199, 284
17:27 — 199, 200
18–20 — xxix, 199, 200, 201
18–21 — 145
18:1 — 179
18:1–8 — 204
18:5 — 203
18:6 — 202
18:6–8 — 252
18:8 — xxx, 202, 227, 253
18:9–11 — 204
18:11 — 202
18:12–13 — 204
18:13 — 202
18:14 — 202
18:14–17 — 204, 261
18:15 — 263
18:16 — 238
18:17 — 263
19 — 201
19:1–7 — 207
19:2 — 206
19:6 — 207, 209
19:6–9 — 111
19:8–13 — 207
19:13 — 202
19:14–19 — 207
20 — 54, 201
20:1 — 201, 210
20:1–3 — 210
20:1–30 — 77
20:2–3 — 201, 210
20:3 — 202
20:4 — 44, 56, 179, 202
20:4–8 — 201, 210
20:7 — 262
20:8 — 48, 202
21 — xxiii, xxx, xxxiii, 104, 201, 211, 261
21:1–4 — 216
21:1–27 — 216
21:2 — 214, 261
21:3–4 — 261
21:4–7 — 216
21:6 — 261
21:8–12 — 216
21:9 — 246
21:13–18 — 216
21:16 — 179
21:18–27 — 216
21:28–30 — 215, 216
21:28–22:1 — 216
21:29 — 90, 188, 235
22 — xxiii, xxiv, xxx, xxxv, 267, 268, 269, 272, 274, 292
22–29 — 145
22:1 — xxx, 215, 216
22:2–5 — 221, 267, 268, 279
22:3 — 202
22:3–4 — xxxv
22:5 — 177, 218, 277
22:6 — 267
22:6–13 — 221
22:6–16 — 221
22:7 — xxvii, 266, 267, 268
22:7–9 — 267
22:7–13 — 269, 276
22:7–16 — 221
22:8 — xxxiii, 198, 202, 267
22:9 — 218
22:9–10 — 90, 267, 270
 — xxxiv
22:10 — 267, 274
22:11 — xxxix, 267, 291

22:11–12 — 292
22:11–13 — 267, 268
22:12 — xxxv, 267
22:13 — xxxix, 267, 268, 282, 291
22:14 — 202, 221
22:15 — 278
22:16 — 272, 282
22:17–19 — 221, 226
22:19 — 272
23 — 228, 239, 240, 252, 263
23–27 — xix, xxxi, xxxv, 145, 219, 221, 231, 234, 240, 258, 268, 274, 275, 278, 288
23:1 — 219, 224, 288
23:1–6 — 274
23:2 — 184, 227, 228, 234
23:2–6 — 258
23:4 — 228, 253, 254, 258
23:5 — 252
23:6 — 228, 237, 253
23:6–7 — 82
23:6–23 — 88, 238
23:7 — 87, 253
23:7–9 — 253
23:7–11 — 239
23:7–19 — 239
23:7–23 — 235, 240, 241
23:8 — 87, 189, 253
23:9 — 230, 253
23:10 — 230
23:10–11 — 44
23:11 — 230
23:13–14 — 236
23:16 — 249
23:17 — 177
23:18 — 253
23:19 — 237, 250, 255
23:22 — 239
23:24 — 230, 235
23:24–32 — 236
23:25 — 228, 235
23:26–32 — 253
23:27 — 230, 235
23:28 — 235
24 — 228, 233, 243
24–25 — 252, 255
24:1 — 228
24:3 — 230
24:4 — 237
24:4–6 — 240
24:5 — 237
24:7 — 140, 238
24:7–18 — 170
24:7–19 — 244, 250
24:9 — 140
24:14 — 140
24:17 — 140
24:18 — 232
24:20 — 230, 242, 253
24:20–25 — 233
24:20–26 — 233
24:22 — 44, 253
24:23 — 255
24:26 — 233
24:26–27 — 237
24:27 — 237
24:29–30 — 233
24:30 — 233
24:31 — 247, 252
25 — 228
25:1 — 228, 247
25:1–7 — 243, 244
25:2 — 192
25:3 — 242, 243, 254
25:4 — 243, 245

25:6	242	28:6	xxxiv, 220, 267, 271	2:3	xxvii
25:7	243	28:6–7	267	2:5	282
25:8	240, 247, 252	28:7	xxxiv, 223, 267	2:6	279
25:8–31	243	28:8	175, 266, 290	2:6–13	272
25:9–31	243, 244, 250	28:9	xxv, xxxvii, xl, 171, 223,	2:11	226, 281
25:11	242		226, 266, 267, 275,	2:13	57, 279
25:17	242, 246		279, 280, 282, 285	2:16	220, 225
25:19	254	28:9–10	224, 267	2:17	220
25:20	242	28:10	xxxiv, 227, 267, 271	3	275
25:22	242	28:11–12	267	3–4	275
25:23–31	245	28:11–19	267	3:1	218
25:27	242	28:18	278	3:8	278
25:31	232	28:19	266	3:10	278
26	228, 258	28:20	180, 220, 222, 267	3:14	57
26:1	136, 228, 249	28:20–21	267	3:16	278
26:1–3	252	28:21	280	5:1	225
26:1–11	251	29	xxiii, xxiv, xxx, xxxv,	5:2–5	137
26:1–19	250, 253, 255		xl, 223, 269	5:4–5	90
26:2	136, 142, 249	29:1	175, 220, 271, 279, 290	5:5	188
26:6	179	29:2	221, 279	5:12	xxxi, 57, 190
26:7	249	29:3	177, 202, 222, 268, 278	5:12–13	xxvii
26:8	249, 253	29:4	221	6:1	235
26:9–11	252	29:5	278	6:4	281, 285
26:12	232	29:6	250, 278	6:10	290
26:12–13	240	29:6–9	279	6:13	289
26:13	247	29:7	221	6:14	275
26:14	136, 251	29:8	252, 253	6:20	xxvii
26:15	249	29:9	xl, 171, 275, 278	6:41	xxvii, 225
26:16	240	29:10	175, 281, 282	6:41–42	270
26:17–18	232	29:10–12	282	7:4–5	290
26:20	252, 258	29:10–19	288	7:5	xli
26:20–32	250, 255	29:11	282, 291	7:6	xxvii
26:21	87, 88, 231, 232, 249	29:11–12	282	7:8	xxvi, 175
26:21–22	232	29:12	xxxv, 288, 292	7:8–9	292
26:22–28	275	29:13	283	7:8–10	290
26:24	233	29:13–16	282	7:9	xxx
26:25	233, 249	29:14	278, 282	7:10	xxv, xl, 278
26:25–26	233	29:14–16	283	7:11	xxxix, 291
26:29	232, 258	29:17	xl, 171, 278, 283	7:12	xxvii, 290
26:30	250, 262	29:17–19	283	8:5	115
26:30–32	99	29:18	282, 290	8:14	xxvii, 94
26:31	19, 233	29:18–19	283	8:18	278
26:32	165, 246	29:19	275, 279, 282	9	xxxiv
27	10, 11, 118, 228, 274	29:20	175, 281	9:4	230
27:1	228, 232	29:20–25	289	9:8	281, 290
27:1–15	232, 258	29:21–26	268	9:13	221
27:1–22	266	29:22	xl, 171, 193, 290, 291	9:26	xxxiv
27:2–15	162, 259	29:22–25	xxxiv	9:30	xxxiv
27:5	170, 263	29:22–26	xxxvi	9:31	293
27:11	44, 257	29:22–30	234	10–36	xxx
27:13	43, 257	29:23	xxxiv, xxxix, 223, 290	10:1	xxxvi
27:15	43	29:23–24	210	10:14	266
27:16–22	169	29:23–25	291	11:5–10	44
27:16–24	9, 258	29:24	266, 268	11:10	44, 126
27:17	254	29:25	xxxiv, 177, 180, 290	11:12–17	180
27:18	33, 103, 107	29:26	290	11:16	xxxvi, 151
27:20	115, 258	29:27	50, 154, 255	11:17	xxxv
27:24	xix	29:28	282	11:18–22	40
27:25	258	29:30	192	11:18–23	179
27:25–31	258, 266			12:2	151
27:30	76	*2 Chronicles*		12:5	xxxvii
27:32–34	258			12:5–6	xxxix
28	xxiii, xxiv, xxx, xxxv, xxxvi,	1	54, 127	12:6–12	xxxix
	219, 221, 222, 223, 292	1–9	145	12:12	xxxix
28–29	227	1:1	177, 288, 291	12:14	151
28:1	175, 184, 227, 231, 234, 290	1:2	269	12:16	293
28:1–2	267	1:2–6	94, 141, 193, 235	13	xxiii, xxvi, xxx, xxxvii
28:1–21	267	1:3	90, 137	13:2	40
28:2	xxvii, 24, 225, 235, 267, 278	1:3–6	xxxiv, 188	13:4	xxxvi, 269
28:2–3	267	1:5	27, 90	13:5	xxxvi
28:2–10	267	1:10	xxxv	13:5–11	xxvi
28:3	xxxiii, 198, 202, 224, 267, 279	1:11–12	xxxv	13:7	220
28:4	288	1:18	xxx	13:8–12	xxx
28:4–8	266	2	179, 226, 227	13:12	287, 291
28:5	184, 271	2:1–2	xxxv, 224	13:13–18	166

Reference	Pages
13:15	xxxvi
13:17	147
13:18	xxxvi
13:19	xxxvi
13:20	282
13:23	xxxvii, 225
14:4-5	225
14:4-7	xxxix
14:5	xxxix, 225
14:5-7	xxxvii
14:6	291
14:8-14	xxxviii
14:9-15	166
14:10	282
14:12	166
15-16	79
15:1	166, 266
15:1-7	xxxviii
15:2	xxxvii
15:4	xxxix
15:7	275
15:8-15	xxxviii
15:9	166
15:9-10	xxxvi
15:12	279
15:15	xxxix, xl, 171, 225, 275, 279
15:17	xl
16:6	125
16:9	275
16:10-12	xxxix
16:12	xxxviii, 177
17:3	xxxviii
17:5	180
17:7-9	34
17:10-12	178
17:12	177
17:15	282
17:16	278
18:1	282
19	255
19:1-11	254
19:4-11	232
19:7	222
19:9	131, 171, 275, 279
19:11	85, 222, 272, 290
20:1	64
20:6	282
20:12	285
20:14	166, 245
20:15-17	xxxix
20:19	136, 177, 251
20:20	xxxix, 287, 290
20:23	65
20:26	281
20:27	171
20:30	xxxix, 225
20:34	130
20:37	282
21:11	xxx
21:16	78, 266
22	xl
22:9	275, 279, 282
22:11	86
23	170
23:1	86
23:6	280
23:7	254
23:11-16	289
23:13-18	171
23:18	xl
24:1-10	254
24:2	86
24:6	90
24:9	90
24:10	171
24:24-25	86
24:18	275
24:20	245, 266
24:5-6	xxxvi
24:10	xl
24:12	278
24:14	65
24:20	xxxvii, 166, 291
24:20-22	xix
24:20-27	xxxix
24:27	185
25:2	171, 275, 279
25:7-13	xxxix
25:8	222, 272
25:13	115
25:15-16	xxxix
25:24	xxx
26	xxiii, 51
26:1	91
26:1-15	178
26:4	xxxviii
26:5	xxxix
26:5-15	xxxviii
26:7	64
26:8	177, 178
26:15	xxviii, 71, 178, 180
26:16	xxx
26:16-21	xxxviii
26:18-19	xxxix
26:21	76
27:1	76
27:7	130, 138
28:8-15	xxxvii
28:15	64, 186
28:18	126
28:20	70
28:24	xxx, 86
29:1	37
29:3	xxxviii
29:3-11	xxx
29:4	184
29:6	90
29:12	87, 88
29:12-36	xxx
29:13	139, 189
29:13-14	xxxi
29:15	184
29:16	94
29:20	184
29:20-24	xli
29:25	190, 245
29:26-7	173
29:30	xl, 171, 246, 278
29:31-35	xli
29:35	287
29:36	xl, 171, 278
30:1	138, 166, 175
30:1-13	175
30:2	175
30:4	175
30:5	138, 175
30:5-6	173
30:6	65, 282
30:6-9	xxxvii, xxxix
30:8	xxvi, xxx, 275
30:10	138, 166
30:11	xxxvi, 118, 166
30:12	275
30:21	xxxvi, 103, 118, 166
30:21-22	xxxvi, xl, 171, 279, 290
30:23	xl, 171, 175, 269, 290
30:23-27	175, 290
30:25	xxxvi, xl, 171, 279
30:25-26	xxxvi
30:26	xxx, 171, 279
31:1	xxx, xxxvi, xl, 116, 138, 166, 175, 269
31:2	137, 166, 185
31:2-19	xxx
31:4-10	xli
31:8	281
31:10	140, 257, 282
31:12	131
31:13	252
31:15	131
31:17	231
31:18	131
31:19	64, 186
31:20	291
31:21	xxx, xxix, xl, 275, 279
32:4	xxxviii
32:7	223
32:10	77
32:14	65
32:22	xxxix, 225
32:23	178, 180
32:26	xxxix
32:27	282
32:30	xxxix, 291
32:31	275, 279
32:33	288
33:12-14	xxxviii, xxxix
33:13	71
33:16	275
33:19	71
33:22	xxxviii
34-35	83, 98
34:3	xxxviii
34:6	xxxvi, 166
24:9	xxxvi, 65, 115, 138, 166, 254
34:11	278
34:12	44, 131
34:12-13	232
34:13	232
34:21	xxxvi, 65
34:30	245
34:31	xl, 279, 289
34:33	275
35-36	xx
35:2	94
35:3	235, 275
35:4	xxxv
35:7-9	xli, 290
35:8	140
35:9	254
35:15	xxxi, 245
35:21-23	xxxviii
35:26	288
35:27	130, 138
36:4	51
36:6-7	51
36:8	130, 138
36:9	51
36:10	51, 52
36:15-16	xxxix, xl
36:17	278
36:19	xxxi
36:20	138
36:20-21	5
36:21	xxvii
36:22	78, 166, 266
36:22-23	xix, xxxi, 5
36:23	xx

Ezra

Reference	Pages
1-3	xxi
1-6	xxxi
1:1	78

1:1-3	xxxi, 5	6:2	126
1:2-3	xx	7	133
1:6	278	7:1	83, 132, 133, 137
1:8	53	7:1-5	132
1:11	53	7:4	134
2	133, 134, 231	7:5	130
2-3	53	7:5-72	134
2:1	138	7:6	138
2:2	83	7:7	83
2:6	43, 60	7:11	43
2:21-22	43, 141	7:26	43, 141
2:22	141	7:30	125
2:23	109	7:37	126
2:26	125	7:39	240
2:33	126	7:39-41	240
2:36	240	7:44	xxxi
2:36-39	240	7:45	136, 251
2:41	xxxi	7:52	64
2:42	136, 251	7:57	131
2:50	64	7:73	132, 133, 134, 147
2:59-62	6	8	xxi
2:68	278	8:1	269
3:2	49, 52, 84	8:12	xl, 279
3:5	278	8:17	xl, 279
3:7	49, 52, 231	9	xxi
3:10	173	9:1	269
3:12	279	9:5	284
3:13	xx, xl, 279	9:8	131
4	xxi, 46	9:25	64
4:6-6:18	xx	9:35	64
5:1-6:19	xx	10	xxi
5:2	52, 53	10:3	83
5:15-17	53	10:3-9	238, 239
6	xxi, 5	10:4	85
6:14-18	xxi	10:20	109
6:15-18	xxxi	10:30	90
6:22	xl, 279	10:33	140
7	85	11	68, 132, 133, 134, 135, 137, 139, 140, 141, 142, 143
7-8	xxi	11:1	139
7:1	149	11:1-2	132
7:1-5	84, 85, 86	11:2	134, 139, 278
7:1-15	82	11:3	130, 132, 133, 134, 139
7:2	86	11:3-4	133, 139
7:5	257	11:3-19	xxxi
7:13	278	11:4	131, 132, 133, 134, 139
7:15	278	11:4-6	132
7:16	278	11:4-9	132
8:4	60, 85	11:5	59, 131, 134, 139
8:13	139	11:6	134, 139
8:20	64, 186	11:7	131, 134
8:23	71	11:9	131, 139, 140
8:25	278	11:10	131, 133
8:27	278	11:10-11	84
9	xxi	11:10-14	132, 134
9:6-15	282, 285	11:11	83, 131, 135, 140
9:8	65	11:12	131, 135, 140
9:14	65	11:13	131, 135, 140
9:15	65	11:14	135, 140
10	xxi, 222	11:15	131, 135
10:1	269	11:15-18	132
10:2	282, 285	11:16	135, 254
10:4	272	11:17	131, 135, 136, 141
10:5	269	11:18	135, 139, 141
10:8	65	11:19	131, 132, 134, 136, 143, 251
10:24	251	11:19-24	132
10:30	60	11:20	134, 139
		11:20-21	132
Nehemiah		11:20-24	132
1:1	149	11:21	134, 139
1:2	65	11:22	139
3:1	240	11:24	139
3:7	127	11:25	41
3:14	43	11:25-35	139
5:18	119	11:25-36	132, 139, 143

11:26-29	67
11:29	44
11:31	125
11:31-36	132
11:35	59, 126
11:36	134, 139
12:1	52, 83, 140
12:1-7	170, 239
12:2	85
12:7	139
12:12	140
12:12-21	238
12:13	84, 85
12:15	84
12:19	85
12:22-23	85
12:23	xix, 251
12:24	240
12:25	136, 251
12:25-26	136
12:27	xl, 190
12:27-28	43
12:28	133, 141
12:29	125
12:35	173, 246
12:41	173
12:43	279
12:45	xxxv
12:45-47	133
13	xxi
13:26	xxxv

Esther

1:6	57
2:6	51
2:23	xix
6:1	xix
8:15	57

Job

1-2	216
7:6	282
8:9	282
28:16	278, 279
33:3	282
42:17	234, 290

Psalms

6:1	184
7:10	275, 284
11:5	284
12:1	184
12:7	278
14:4	274
17:3	284
18	216
18:47	284
22:29	284
28:6	284
28:7	71
29:6	76
31:22	284
32	93
33:12	271
33:21	284
38:1	185
39:13	282, 285
41:13	281, 284
42	251
44-49	136, 251
45:10	278
46:1	184

59:14	284	132:13	271	33:9	225
62	93	132:14	270, 273	33:14–26	290
66:7	284	134:3	284	35:4	137
66:20	284	135:4	271	37:1	51
68:36	284	135:6	284	40:8–9	43
71:8	282, 284	135:21	284	48	75
71:21	284	139:1	275		
72:18–19	284	144:1	284	*Ezekiel*	
72:18–19	281	144:4	282		
77	93	145:3	284	1:3	240
78:9	138	145:6	284	4:3	230
78:61	284	145:11	284	4:11	230
78:67–68	70, 138	145:12	284	4:16	230
78:67–70	271	145:21	284	17:3	278
78:68	271	148:14	246	20:5	271
78:70	271	149:3	30	24:24	240
79:13	284	150	281	27:16	57
83:7	76	150:2	284	28:13	279
84–85	251	150:4	30	34:14	64
88–89	30			34:20–24	200
89:10	284	*Proverbs*		44:8	235
89:14	284			46	141
89:18	246, 284	17:3	282		
89:30	273	28:13	282	*Daniel*	
89:52	281, 284				
90:2	284	*Ecclesiastes*		9:11	90
90:9–10	282			10:8	282
90:10	284	2:8	278	10:16	282
96	193	6:12	282	11:6	282
96:1–2	185			11:34	71
96:1–13	186	*Canticles*			
96:6	185, 284			*Hosea*	
96:9	30, 185	4:8	78		
96:10	185, 193			2:19	49
96:12	185	*Isaiah*		7:1	115
96:13	185			7:10	282
102:12	282	11:1–5	200	8:2	274
103:1	284	13:12	278	11:4–5	282
103:17	284	14:1	271	11:8	115, 138
105:1–6	192	22:23	148	13:4–5	274
105:1–15	186, 192	22:25	148		
105:3	284	25:7	278	*Amos*	
105:6	31, 185	28:21	179		
105:7–11	192	38:3	275	1:1	45
105:8	185	44:1	271	3:2	274
105:9	185	45:1	xx	6:14	71
105:12	185	54:11	277	9:11–12	200
105:12–15	192	55:3	xx		
105:14	185	56–66	284	*Micah*	
105:15	185, 192	60–66	284		
105:16–45	192	60:7	282	5:1	37
105:23	31	63:14	282	5:2–4	200
106:1	185, 186	63:15	282		
106:2	284	63:16	285	*Zephaniah*	
106:8	284	64:7	285		
106:10	185	64:7	285	3:19–20	225
106:40–43	193	64:10	282		
106:45–48	186	66:3	185	*Haggai*	
106:46–48	193			1:1	49, 84
106:47	186, 193, 284	*Jeremiah*		1:12	52
106:47–48	186, 193			1:14	52
106:48	186, 193, 281, 284	1:6	220	2	55
109:23	282	4:30	277	2:2	52
115:15	284	11:20	275, 282, 284	2:23	52
119:7	282, 284	12:3	282, 284		
121:2	284	13:11	225	*Zechariah*	
123:1	284	17:10	282, 284		
124:8	284	17:24–27	200	1:17	271
132	270, 271	22:11	51	2:16	271
132:1	221	22:24	51	3:1	216
132:3–5	270	22:28	51	3:2	271
132:6–8	270	24:1	51	9:7	23
132:8	225, 270	27:20	51	12:5–6	23
132:8–9	270	28:4	51	14:14	64
132:10–12	270	29:2	51		
132:12	273	29:13	273	*Malachi*	
		31:34	274	3:3	278

B. Old Testament Apocrypha and Pseudepigrapha

1 Esdras

1–9	xx
2:12	53
2:15	53

5:8	83
5:65	xx
6:18	53
6:20	53

1 Maccabees

2:1	238, 239
2:17	254
5:8	254

C. Ugaritic Manuscripts

3 K 4:6–8; 17–19	23

2 Aq 5:16	23

D. New Testament

Matthew

1	16
1:1	200
1:1–17	14
1:3–4	32
1:6	200
6:13	285
23:35	xix

Luke

1	284
1:5	238
2:10	280
3:23–38	14, 17
3:27	52
3:38	18

John

2:21	264
4:21–26	264
9:3	180

2 Corinthians

9	280
9:6–8	280
9:11	280

Galatians

3:1–14	276

Ephesians

2:8–10	276

James

1:17	285

1 Peter

2:9–10	247

Revelations

7:6	138

Index of Key Hebrew Words

אלהים	164	
אברם	22	
אברהם	22	
אלף (thousand, clan)	170	
אין	226	
אמונה	131	
בחר	188, 271	
בית אבות	7, 109	
בן, בנים	7–8, 17, 19, 49	
ברוך	283–4	
ברך	285	
דרש	148, 151, 173	
דברי הימים	xix	
זכר	185	
חול	30	
חזק	157, 246	
חזק ואמץ	222, 272	
חרם	64, 67	
חרש	280	
ידע	274	

יהי יהוה עמך	222	
יחל	147	
יחש	138	
ילד	22, 38	
כון	173	
כי	131	
כלי	131	
כל	173	
מחול	30	
מטה	7	
נוח see מנוחה		
מעונים	64	
מצא	67, 273	
משכן	90	
נדב	280	
מנוחה, נוח	198, 223–5, 270	
נצח	184	
נשיא	67	
נחינים	133	
עלמות	184	

עם	7	
עצב	58	
עתה	268	
פרץ	173, 179	
קהל	174, 175	
רב	226	
שאר (be left)	65, 173	
שאר (porter)	137	
שבט (tribe)	7	
שכן	235	
שלש	157, 158, 160	
שמינית	184	
שמעוני	274	
שנית	288	
שקט	224	
שרת	192	
תבנית	272, 275	
תולדות	19	

CPSIA information can be obtained
at www.ICGtesting.com
Printed in the USA
JSHW020959240521
14885JS00002BA/2